.

The
Complete
Works
Of
Thomas
Boston

Volume 12

The Complete Works Of Thomas Boston

Volume 12
of
12 Volume Set

Sovereign Grace Publishers, Inc.
P.O. Box 4998
Lafayette, IN 47903

Printed In the United States of America
By Lightning Source, Inc.

THE

WHOLE WORKS

OF THE

LATE REVEREND THOMAS BOSTON
OF ETTRICK;

NOW FIRST COLLECTED, AND REPRINTED WITHOUT
ABRIDGMENT;

INCLUDING

HIS MEMOIRS, WRITTEN BY HIMSELF.

EDITED BY THE
REV. SAMUEL M'MILLAN.

VOL. XII.

ABERDEEN:
GEORGE AND ROBERT KING, ST. NICHOLAS STREET.
M.DCCC.LII.

MEMOIRS

OF THE

LIFE, TIMES, AND WRITINGS,

OF THE

REV. THOMAS BOSTON,

OF ETTRICK.

WRITTEN BY HIMSELF.

TO WHICH ARE ADDED,

ORIGINAL PAPERS AND LETTERS.

"Come and hear, all ye that fear God, and I will declare what he hath done for my soul."—
PSALM lxvi. 16.
"The righteous shall be in everlasting remembrance."—PSALM cxii. 6.
" By it he being dead, yet speaketh."—HEB. xi. 4.

ABERDEEN:
GEORGE AND ROBERT KING, ST. NICHOLAS STREET.

1852.

CONTENTS.

AUTHOR'S ADDRESS TO HIS CHILDREN.

TO JOHN, JANE, ALISON, AND THOMAS BOSTON,—

My Dear Children,

I APPREHEND, that by the time it is designed, under the conduct of all-disposing Providence, this should come into your hands, ye may be desirous to know your father's manner of life, beyond what ye saw with your eyes; and it is very pleasing to me that, as to that point, I am capable, in some measure, to satisfy you, by means of two manuscripts, which I leave unto you, committing them to the Lord my God for preservation, and a blessing on them.

The one is a bound book in quarto, intitled, "Passages of my Life," at writing hereof, consisting of three hundred and sixty-two written pages, beginning from my birth, ending October 19, 1730, and signed.* I was not arrived at twenty years of age when, without a prompter, so far as I know, I began collecting of these passages, for my own soul's benefit; and they being carried on, have often since that time been of use to me. For which cause I recommend the like practice to you; remembering the promise, Psalm cvii. 43, "Whoso is wise, and will observe those things, even they shall understand the loving-kindness of the Lord."

The other is the following general account of my life, at writing hereof, consisting of two hundred and seventy-nine written pages,†

---

* The author, before his death, added some pages more.

† In the years 1730 and 1731 the author added a good many pages more. The first MS. consists in whole of 371 pages, and the latter of 342.

beginning from my birth, ending October 24, 1730, and signed. How I was led thereto, much contrary to my inclination, you will find in the manuscripts themselves. But, now that it is done, I am obliged to say, "The foolishness of God is wiser than men;" and I bless the Lord who gave me counsel. It was in obedience to his call that I did it; "Let the Lord do with it what seemeth him good." Ye will not readily have meaner thoughts of that matter than I myself had.

I presume you will judge that it had been more natural to have made one continued history of both; and I, being of the same mind, would indeed have so done, had I thought it worth my pains, in this decline of my age and strength. But not seeing myself called thereto, I am satisfied as to the design of Providence, which hath modelled that matter as said is.*

You will not therein find yourselves descended, by me at least, from any ancient or honourable family in the sight of the world; which is a matter of some significancy, I own, before men, for a few passing years; but you will find yourselves children of the covenant, devoted unto the God and Father of our Lord Jesus Christ, my God, by me having power over you for that effect; whom therefore I charge to ratify the same with your own consent, and personal acceptance of the covenant; and to cleave to this God as your God, all the days of your lives, as being his only, wholly, and for ever; so shall that be to you a matter of eternal value and significancy, before the Lord, of value to you in this and the other world.

If some things in these manuscripts appear trifling, bear with them. Had I thought it worth time and pains to have written them over a second time, it is likely several things now found in them had been dropped. Meanwhile it may reasonably be allowed that some things now appearing trifling to you, might have been of some weight

---

* In preparing this work for the press, it was judged absolutely necessary, in order to prevent repetitions, and references from the one volume to the other, to reduce both into one continued narrative or history, taking care all along to insert the passages of his life in the general account, in their proper places, according to their respective dates and years, and as the nature of the subjects treated of required.—*Note to First Edition.*

to me, and may be so to you afterwards; and if never to you, yet some one time or other to yours after you.

I hope you will find some things in them worthy of your imitation; the which I was the more willing to record, that I did not think I ever had the art of education of children; but might thereby do somewhat toward the repairing of the loss you by that means sustained. It is my desire and will that, while the Lord is pleased to preserve them, and that in the power of my offspring, any of them whosoever be allowed free access unto them; yet so that the property thereof be vested from time to time, in such an one of them, if any such there shall be, as shall addict himself to the holy ministry. And in case I be allowed by him in whose hand is my life and breath, and all my ways, to make any continuation of the purpose of these manuscripts, the same is to be reckoned as here included.

I hope you will use no indecent freedoms with them; considering that, for ought you or I know, there is a *jus tertii*, a right of a third party in the matter, whom also I have a view to, with an awful regard to the sovereign disposal of holy Providence, to which I desire to submit all. Some few things which I saw meet to delete, I have signified and signed on the margin.

And now, my dear children, your lot is fallen in a sinning time, beyond the days of my fathers; and I am mistaken if it issue not in a time proportionally trying, by " the Lord's coming out of his place to punish the inhabitants of the earth for their iniquity." I obtest and beseech you, as you regard your eternal welfare, " save yourselves from this untoward generation." See the absolute necessity of regeneration, the change of your nature, by union with Jesus Christ the second Adam; as it was corrupted by means of your relation to the first Adam fallen. Labour for the experience of the power of religion in your own souls, that you may have an argument for the reality of it, from your spiritual sense and feeling; and cleave to the Lord, his way of holiness, (" without which ye shall not see the Lord,") his work also, his interests, and people, on all hazards; being assured, that such only will be found wise in the end. If your mother, undoubtedly a daughter of Abraham, shall survive me, let your loss of a father move you to carry the more kindly and affectionately to her, supporting her in her desolate condition. Let the same likewise engage you the more to be peaceful, loving, and helpful, among yourselves.

The Lord bless each one of you, and save you, cause his gracious face shine on you, and give you peace; so as we may have a comfortable meeting in the other world.—Farewell.

T. Boston.

From my Study in Ettrick Manse,
October 28, 1720.

MEMOIRS, &c.

THAT my life may be more fully known unto my posterity, for their humiliation on the one hand, and thankfulness on the other, upon my account; for their caution also in some things, and their imitation in others; and that they may set their hope in God, and not in the empty creation,—I have thought it meet to give the following general account of the days of my vanity, in the several periods thereof.

PERIOD I.

FROM MY BIRTH, TILL I LEFT THE GRAMMAR SCHOOL.

I WAS born of honest parents, of good reputation among their neighbours, in the town of Dunse, on the 17th, and baptized on the 21st, of March, in the year 1676; being the youngest of seven children, four brothers and three sisters, pro-created betwixt John Boston, and Alison Trotter, a woman prudent and virtuous. I was born at a time when my mother was thought to have left bearing; for which cause a certain woman used ordinarily to call me God's send. The youngest of my sisters I saw not; but the rest lived, and had all of them several children; many of whom have now children of their own. Meanwhile my brothers and sisters are all of them gone, several years ago, into the other world, which I have now in view.

Andrew Boston, my grandfather, came from Ayr to Dunse, and possessed the tenement given afterward by my father to my eldest brother, and belonging to his heirs to this day. But before him had come William, his brother, as I suppose; whose name the tenement next on the west side, to that which my father gave me, bears. When I was a boy, I saw a grand-daughter of his from England, by his son Mr. William, a churchman there; a very devout woman in her way, and married to one Mr. Peter Carwain, another churchman; but I suppose childless.

My father was a knowing man, having in his youth, I think, got good of the gospel. Being a nonconformist during the time of

VOL. XI.   B

Prelacy, he suffered upon that head, to imprisonment and spoiling of his goods. When I was a little boy, I lay in the prison of Dunse with him, to keep him company; the which I have often looked on as an earnest of what may be abiding me; but hitherto I have not had that trial. My mother once paying, to one Alexander Martin sheriff-depute, the sum of £50 as the fine of her imprisoned husband, for his nonconformity, desired of him an abatement; whereupon he, taking up a pint stoup standing on the table, therewith broke in pieces a part of a tobacco pipe lying thereon; bidding the devil beat him as small as that pipe stopple, if there should be ought abated of the sum. And once walking through the street, while my father was with the masons that were building his house, he looked up, and said to him, that he would make him sell that house yet. Nevertheless he and his posterity were not long after rooted out of the place; and that house was not sold, until I, not for need of money, but for my own conveniency otherwise, sold it some years ago. May all my offspring be saved from ever embarking with that party; of whom I say from the heart, " O my soul, come not thou into their secret; mine honour, be not thou united with them."

The schoolmistress having her chamber in my father's house, I was early put to school; and having a capacity for learning, and being of a toward disposition, was kindly treated by her; often expressing her hope of seeing me in the pulpit. Nevertheless, for a considerable time, I wept incessantly from the time they began to put on my clothes till I was up stairs in the school. Thus my natural temper of spirit appeared, being timorous and hard to enter on, but eager in the pursuit when once entered.

By the time I was seven years old, I read the Bible, and had delight in reading it; would have read with my schoolmistress in the winter nights, when the rest of the children were not present; yea, and got the Bible sometimes to the bed with me, and read there. Meanwhile I know nothing induced me to it, but the natural vanity of my mind; and curiosity, as about some scripture histories. However, I am thankful, that it was at all made my choice early? and that it hath been the study of my ripest years, with which I would fain close my life, if it were his will.

Sometime in the year 1684, or at farthest, 1685, I was put to the grammar school, under Mr. James Bullerwall, schoolmaster in the town, and continued at it till the harvest, 1689, save that one summer I was kept at home, while the rest of my class were going on in the grammar.

When I was very young, going to a neighbour's house, with a halfpenny, or some such reward of divination, in my hand, to a fortune-teller; after entering the outer door, I was suddenly struck in my mind, stood musing a little between the doors, durst not go forward, but came stealing away again. Thus the unseen Counsellor preserved me from that snare.

I remember some things which I was, by hearing or seeing, in persons come to years, witness to, in these days, leaving an impression on me to their disadvantage. Wherefore care should be taken, that nothing should be done or said, sinful or indecent, before children; for their memory may retain the same, till they are capable to form a right judgment of it, to the staining of the character of the party with them afterward.

By means of my education, and natural disposition, I was of a sober and harmless deportment, and preserved from the common vices of children in towns. I was at no time what they call a vicious or a roguish boy; neither was I so addicted to play as to forget my business; though I was a dexterous player at such games as required art and nimbleness; and towards the latter end of this period, having had frequent occasion to see soldiers exercised, I had a peculiar faculty at mustering and exercising my school-fellows accordingly, by the several words and motions of the exercise of the musket; they being formed into a body, under a captain. The which exercise I have managed, to as much weariness and pain of my breast, as sometimes I have preached.

During the first years of my being at the grammar school, I kept the kirk punctually, where I heard those of the Episcopal way; that being then the national establishment; but I knew nothing of the matter, save to give suit and presence within the walls of the house; living without God in the world, unconcerned about the state of my soul, till the year 1687. Toward the latter end of summer that year, the liberty of conscience being then newly given by King James, my father took me away with him to a Presbyterian meeting in the Newton of Whitsome. There I heard the worthy Mr. Henry Erskine,* minister of Cornhill before the Restoration, mentioned in Calamy's Account of the Ejected Ministers, vol. II. p. 518, and in the continuation of that Account, vol. II. p. 678; *et seq.*; by whose means it pleased the Lord to awaken me and bring me under exercise about my soul's state; being then going in the twelfth year of my age. After that I went back to the kirk no more, till the Episcopalians were turned out; and it was the common observation in these days, That whenever one turned serious about his soul's state

---

* This Mr. Henry Erskine was father to the late Messrs. Ebenezer and Ralph Erskines, whose praise is in all the churches.

and case, he left them. The which experience in my own case, founded my aversion to that way, which hath continued with me all along to this day.

But how blameless and harmless soever my life was before the world during my childhood, and while I was a boy, whether before or after I was enlightened, the corruption of my nature began very early to shew and spread forth itself in me, as the genuine offspring of fallen Adam. And this not only in the vanity and ungodliness of the general course of my life before I was enlightened, living without God; but in particular branches thereof, which I remember to this day with shame and confusion before the Lord. And indeed in this period were some such things as I have ever since looked upon as special blots in my escutcheon; the which, with others of a later date, I have been wont, in my secret fasts all along, still to set before mine own eyes, for my humiliation, and lay before the Lord, that he may not remember them against me; though I hope they are pardoned, being washed away by the blood of Christ my Saviour. I remember my gross and unbecoming thoughts of the glorious, incomprehensible God; keen hatred of my neighbour, upon disobligations received; and divers loathsome sproutings of the sin which all along hath "most easily beset me," as the particular bias of my corrupt nature. Two snares I fell into in that period, which have been in a special manner heavy to me, and have occasioned me many bitter reflections; and, I think, they have been after the Lord had begun to deal with my soul, and enlightened me. The one I was caught in, being enticed by another boy to go to Dunse-law with him on a Lord's day, and, when on the head of the hill, to play pins with him. The other I narrowly escaped, being put into the snare by the indiscretion of one who then had the management of me; all circumstances favouring the temptation, God alone, by his Spirit, working on my conscience, delivered me as a bird out of the snare of the fowler. The particular place I well remember, whither after the escape I went, and wept bitterly, under the defilement I had contracted, in tampering with that temptation. Such is the danger of ill company for young ones, and of indiscreet management of them. However, that they were the genuine fruits of my corrupt nature I do evidently see; in that, however bitter both of these had been to me, I did some years after run, of my own accord, into two snares much of the same kinds, narrowly also escaping one of them, but so as it occasioned to me great bitterness.

Two of Mr. Erskine's first texts were, John i. 29, " Behold the Lamb of God," &c.; and Matth. iii. 7, " O generation of vipers, who hath warned you to flee," &c. I distinctly remember, that from this last he ofttimes forewarned of judgments to come on these nations, which I still apprehend will come. By these, I judge, God spake to me; however, I know I was touched quickly after the first hearing, wherein I was like one amazed with some new and strange thing.

My lost state by nature, and my absolute need of Christ, being thus discovered to me, I was set to pray in earnest; but remember nothing of that kind I did before, save what was done at meals, and in my bed. I also carefully attended for ordinary the preaching of the word at Revelaw, where Mr. Erskine had his meeting-house, near about four miles from Dunse. In the summer time, company could hardly be missed; and with them something to be heard, especially in the returning, that was for edification, to which I listened; but in the winter, sometimes it was my lot to go alone, without so much as the benefit of a horse to carry me through Blackadder water, the wading whereof in sharp frosty weather I very well remember. But such things were then easy, for the benefit of the word, which came with power.

The school-doctor's son having, in his childish folly, put a pipe-stopple in each of his nostrils, I designing to pull them out, happened so to put them up that he bled. Whereupon his father, in great wrath, upbraided me; and particularly said, Is that what you learned at Revelaw? which cut me to the heart, finding religion to suffer by me.

In these days I had a great glowing of affections in religion, even to zeal for suffering in the cause of it, which I am very sure was not according to knowledge; but I was ready to think, as Zebedee's children said; Matth. xx. 22, "We are able." I was raw and inexperienced, had much weakness and ignorance, and much of a legal disposition and way, then, and for a good time after, undiscerned. Howbeit I would fain hope, there was, under a heap of rubbish of that kind, "some good thing toward the God of Israel" wrought in me. Sure I am, I was in good earnest concerned for a saving interest in Jesus Christ; my soul went out after him, and the place of his feet was glorious in mine eyes.

Having read of the sealing of the tribes, Rev. vii., Satan wove a snare for me out of it, viz. That the whole number of the elect, or those who were to be saved, was already made up; and therefore there was no room for me. How that snare was broken, I do not remember; but thereby one may see, what easy work Satan, brooding on ignorance, hath to hatch things which may perplex and keep the party from Christ.

At that time there was another boy at the school, Thomas Trotter of

Catchilraw, whose heart the Lord had also touched; and there came to the school a third one, Patrick Gillies, a serious lad, and elder than either of us ; but the son of a father and mother, ignorant and carnal to a pitch ; which made the grace of God in him the more remarkable. Upon his motion, we three met frequently in a chamber in my father's house, for prayer, reading the scriptures, and spiritual conference; whereby we had some advantage, both in point of knowledge and tenderness. It was remarkable concerning the said Thomas, that being taken to the first Presbyterian meeting that was in the country after the liberty ; where I suppose the worthy and famous Mr. James Webster, afterwards a minister in Edinburgh, preached ; he, upon his return from it, giving an account in the school concerning his being there, ridiculed the Whigs ; the which I, who nevertheless was not there, was very sorry for, on no other account, I reckon, but that my father was one of that sort of people. But going afterwards to the like meetings, he turned a very devout boy.

To bind myself to diligence in seeking the Lord, and to stir me up thereto, I made a vow, to pray so many times a-day ; how many times, I cannot be positive ; but it was at least thrice. It was the goodness of God to me, that it was made only for a certain definite space of time ; but I found it so far from being a help, that it was really a hinderance to my devotion, making me more heartless in, and averse to duty, through the corruption of my nature. I got the time of it driven out accordingly ; but I never durst make another of that nature since, nor so bind up myself, where God had left me at liberty. And it hath been of some good use to me, in the course of my after life.

The school-house being within the churchyard, I was providentially made to see there, within an open coffin, in an unripe grave opened, the consuming body just brought to the consistence of thin mortar, and blackish ; the which made an impression on me, remaining to this day ; whereby I perceive what a loathsome thing my body must at length become before it be reduced to dust; not to be beheld with the eye but with horror.

In the course of years spent at the grammar school, I learned the Latin rudiments, Despauter's grammar, and all the authors, in verse or prose, then usually read in schools; and profited above the rest of my own class, by means of whom my progress was the more slow. And before I left the school, I, generally, saw no Roman author, but what I found myself in some capacity to turn into English; but we were not put to be careful about proper English. Towards the end of that time, I was also taught Vossius's Elements of Rhetoric ;

and May 15, 1689, began the Greek, learned some parts of the New
Testament, to wit, some part of John, of Luke, and of the Acts of
the Apostles.   And helping the above-mentioned Patrick Gillies, in
the Roman authors, in our spare hours, I learned from him, on the
other hand, some of the common rules of arithmetic, being but a
sorry writer.   And this was the education I had at school, which I
left in harvest, 1689, being then aged thirteen years, and above five
months.

PERIOD II.

FROM MY LEAVING THE GRAMMAR SCHOOL, TO MY LAUREATION.

BETWEEN my leaving of the grammar school, and my entering to the
college, two years intervened.   And here began more remarkably
my bearing of the yoke of trial and affliction, the which laid on in
my youth, has, in the wise disposal of holy providence, been from
that time unto this day continued, as my ordinary lot; one scene of
trial opening after another.

Prelacy being abolished by act of parliament, July 22, 1689, and
the Presbyterian government settled, June 7, 1690, and the curate
of Dunse having died about that time, the Presbyterians took possession of the kirk, by the worthy Mr. Henry Erskine's preaching
in it on Wednesday, being the weekly market day; the soldiers
being active in carrying on the project, and protecting against the
Jacobite party.   The purity of the gospel being new to many, it had
much success in these days, comparatively speaking; and in the
harvest that year, my mother fell under exercise about her soul's
case, and much lamented her misspent time; and there was a remarkable change then made upon her.

My father, as well as myself, inclined that I should proceed in
learning; but apprehending the expense unequal to his worldly circumstances, was unwilling to bear the charges of my education at
the college; whereupon he tried several means for effectuating the
design otherwise, particularly in the year 1690; but prevailed
not.   Hereby I was discouraged, and had some thoughts of betaking
myself to a trade; the which being intimated to him, he slighted, as
being resolved not so to give it over; and I entertained them not,
but as the circumstances seemed to force them on me.

In the end of that year he took me to Edinburgh, and essayed to
put me into the service of Dr. Rule, principal of the college, not
without hope of accomplishing it; but one who had promised to recommend me to the Doctor, having forgot his promise, that essay
was made in vain; and I returned home, having got that notable
disappointment on the back of several others.

Meanwhile the difficulties I had to grapple with, in the way of my purpose, put me to cry to the Lord in prayer on that head, that he himself would find means to bring it about. And I well remember the place where I was wont to address the throne of grace for it, having several times thereafter had occasion to mind it, in giving thanks for that he had heard the prayers there put up for that effect.

About, or before this time, was the melancholy event of Mr. J. B——'s falling into adultery. He was born in Dunse, and so an acquaintance of my father's; and he was minister of the meeting-house at Mersington, and not young. This dreadful stumbling-block, laid especially at such a critical juncture as the Revolution, filled the mouths of the ungodly with reproach against the way of religion, and saddened the hearts of the godly to a pitch. I well know, that many a heavy heart it made to me, and remember the place where I was wont heavily to lament it before the Lord in secret prayer.

On the 1st day of February 1691, it pleased the Lord to remove my mother by death, not having lain long sick. To the best of my knowledge, she was not above fifty-six years of age, my father and she having lived together, in the state of marriage, from their youth, about thirty years. While she died in one room, my father was lying in another sick, as was supposed unto death; and heavily received the tidings of her departure. Returning from bidding some friends in the country to her burial, I met on the street one whom I asked concerning my father, that told me, in all probability he would never recover. This so pierced me, that getting home, I went to the foot of the garden, and cast myself down on the ground, where, according to the vehemency of my passion, I lay grovelling and bemoaning my heavy stroke in the loss of my parents, looking on myself as an absolute orphan, and all hopes of obtaining my purpose now gone. Thus I lay, I think, till my eldest brother, a judicious man, came and spoke to me, and raised me up. But it pleased the Lord that I was comforted in the recovery of my father some time after. About this time, I suppose, I myself was sick about eight days.

Some time after, my father, in pursuance of what had passed betwixt him and the town-clerk, sent me, at his desire, to write with him. But whatever way they had concerted their business, he drew back, took no trial of me in the matter, and I returned. And that project was blown up.

But being, it would seem, put in hopes by my father of proceeding in learning, towards the middle of June I betook myself to my books again, which I had almost given over; and I applied myself to the reading of Justin at that time, the malt-loft being my closet; but beginning thus to get up my head, my corruption began to set up its head too; so necessary was it for me to bear the yoke.

Meanwhile I was, that year, frequently employed to write with Mr. Alexander Cockburn, a notary. The favourable design of providence therein, then unknown to me, I now see, since it could not be but of some use to help me to the style of papers; the which, since that time, I have had considerable use for. And thus kind providence early laid in for it.

But here I was led into a snare by Satan and my own corruption. Mr. Cockburn being in debt to me on the foresaid account, I saw Dickson on Matthew lying neglected in his chamber; and finding I could not get the money due to me out of his hand, I presumed to take away the book without his knowledge, thinking I might very well do it on the foresaid account. I kept it for a time; but conscience being better informed, I saw my sin in that matter, and could no more peaceably enjoy it, though he never paid me; so I restored it secretly, none knowing how it was taken away, nor how returned; and hereby the scandal was prevented. This, I think, contributed to impress me with a special care of exact justice, and the necessity of restitution in the case of things unjustly taken away, being like a burnt child dreading fire.

My father being fully resolved to put me to the college on his own charges, I began on the 15th of October, to expound the Greek New Testament: which, I think, I completed betwixt that and December 1; at which time he took me to Edinburgh, where being tried in the Greek New Testament by Mr. Herbert Kennedy, regent, I was entered into his semi class, my father having given him four dollars, as was done yearly thereafter, paying also all other dues.

Thus the Lord, in my setting out in the world, dealt with me, obliging me to have recourse to himself for this thing, to do it for me. He brought it through many difficulties, tried me with various disappointments, at length carried it to the utmost point of hopelessness, seemed to be laying the grave-stone upon it at the time of my mother's death; and yet after all he brought it to pass; and that has been the usual method of providence with me all along in matters of the greatest weight. The wisdom appearing, in leading the blind by a way they knew not, shinned in the putting off that matter to this time, notwithstanding all endeavours to compass it sooner; for I am convinced I was abundantly soon put to the college, being then but in the fifteenth year of my age; and the manner of it was kindly ordered, in that I was thereby beholden to none for that my education; and it made way for some things which providence saw needful for me.

During the whole time I was at the college, I dieted myself, being lodged in a private house, to which I was led by kind providence, as fit for my circumstances.

1692. The first year, being somwhat childish, but knowing with what difficulty I had reached what I had obtained, I lived sparingly, and perhaps more so than was needful or reasonable. Being deject-ed and melancholy, I went but little out of my chamber, save to the class; and thus my improvement was confined in a manner to my lessons.

1693. The second year I attended the college, I had an entire comradeship with Andrew (afterwards Mr. Andrew) Elliot, a minis-ter's son, and now minister of Auchtertool in Fife, which several ways contributed to my advantage, and lasted during the rest of the time we were at the college. Meanwhile I still lived sparingly.

In the spring that year began a breach of my health, whereby I became liable to swoonings, which continued for several years after. It was, I think, in the month of April, when being on my knees at secret prayer, my heart began to fail, and I rose up, and fell on my back on the floor, and lay a while in a swoon. Recovering, I called the landlady; then I went to bed, but fainted a second time, in which she took care of me. Afterwards she unwarily suggested to me, that it might be the falling-sickness, which occasioned me se-veral thoughts of heart. Wherefore as I came home in the middle of May, I consulted it; and was delivered of these fears, which were groundless; but being at home, I was, on the 2d of June, overtaken with another fainting-fit, in which beckoning with my hand I fainted away; and while they were lifting me into bed, I heard my sister say, that I was gone. In a little I recovered, and my father went to prayer at my bed-side.

The first or second winter I was at college, being in company with a dumb man, I was urged by some to ask him a question about my brother William. He answered me in writing, as it is Deut. xxix, *ult.*, "Secret things belong unto the Lord our God," &c.; and, moreover, that there is no such thing communicated to the dumb, but that through importunity he himself had sometimes spoke what he knew not. Thus was I reproved. And I desire that all who may read this or such like my failings, may beware of splitting on the same rocks, so heavy to me.

About December 20, I gladly went to Edinburgh again for the last year, thinking that course of difficulties near an end. I was therefore more cheerful, and in point of diet managed more liberally.

1694. About the latter end of February, I came home with John Cockburn, a comrade, son to John Cockburn in Preston. I could not get him out of the town till a good part of the day was spent; and when we were come out, he expended a little money he had left, without asking questions till it was done. Then finding there was no money with us but what I had, which could scarcely procure us both a night's lodging, we resolved to hold on our way, though our journey was in all twenty-eight miles long. Night drawing on, we were twelve miles from home, and got nothing in the inn but bread and water; there being no ale in it, it seems. Then under night we went on our way, in the moonlight; but on the hills we began to fail, travelling a-foot, and having had but sorry refreshment at the inn. Meanwhile, as we lay on the highway to rest our weary limbs a little, a farmer came up to us, who offered to lodge us with him near by; which was gladly embraced.

That youth and I had been schoolfellows at Dunse, and so much resembled one another in face and stature, as if we had been twins; the which being noticed by our fellows, made a most entire friendship between us at school. It lasted for a while; but was at length, upon some childish controversy, quite blown up, and was never recovered. For at the college, being more liberally furnished, he overlooked me, and gave himself to diversions; so that there was no communication, but what was general, betwixt him and me, as I remember, till the last of the three years. At what time, being once in company with him, I was like to have a plea to rid betwixt him and another; and, to the best of my knowledge, left them at length. And then again I came home with him as aforesaid. He and I both were designed for the study of divinity; but in a little time he gave up with it, went to London, applied himself to book-keeping, and went abroad, I suppose, and died. Wherefore, when I was honoured of God to preach the gospel of Christ, I was often a moving sight to his sorrowful father. Whence I must needs conclude, that "it is good for a man to bear the yoke in his youth;" and surely it was good and necessary for me.

Being allowed only £16 Scots by my father for the laureation, I borrowed 20 merks from one of my brothers, and so went to Edinburgh for that end in the summer. But the day signified to me not being kept, I returned without my errand. This disappointment, with other discouragements I had met with in prosecuting my studies, furnished my evil heart, when going in a second time that season to the laureation, the occasion of that unbelieving thought that I would never believe I could obtain it till I saw it. For this thought I presently smarted, meeting suddenly on the back of it with a dispensation which threatened to lay the grave-stone upon all that I had hitherto attained; for some officers took me up by the way to be a soldier; but the Lord delivered me quickly.

Thus holy wise providence ordered my education at the college; the charges whereof amounted in all but to £128, 15s. 8d. Scots; of the which I had 20 merks as aforesaid to pay afterwards. Out of that sum were paid the regent's fees yearly, and the college-dues, and also my maintenance was furnished out of it. By means thereof, I had a competent understanding of the logics, metaphysics, ethics, and general physics; always taking pains of what was before me, and pleasing the regent; but I learned nothing else, save short-hand writing, which an acquaintance of mine taught me, namely, a well-inclined baker lad. My design in acquiring it was to write sermons; but I made little use of it that way, finding it to mar the frame of my spirit in hearing, which obliged me to quit that use of it. But kind was the design of providence in it notwithstanding; for besides its serving me in recording things I designed to keep secret, and otherwise, it has been exceeding useful to me of late years, in making my first draughts of my writings therein. "Known unto God are all his works from the beginning."

PERIOD III.

FROM MY LAUREATION, TO MY BEING LICENSED TO PREACH THE GOSPEL.

THAT summer the bursary of the Presbytery of Dunse was conferred on me, as a student of theology; as was that of the Presbytery of Churnside on my comrade John Cockburn. And after the laureation, sometime before harvest, I entered on the study of theology; Mr. James Ramsay, minister then at Eymouth, now at Kelso, having put the book in my hand, viz, Pareus on Ursin's Catechism; the which I read over three or four times ere I went to the school of divinity. Among the first books of that kind which I had a particular fondness for, was " Weem's Christian Synagogue."

I went, on invitation, to F——s, and spent some weeks there, after the harvest, with his two sons, and James (after Mr. James) Ridpath, students in philosophy, to whom I was there helpful in their studies. And that I may reckon the only time of my life in which I had a taste for youthful diversions; whereof I soon saw the vanity, and wherein I drove but heavily, the family being altogether carnal. But while I was there, I kept up the worship of God in the family; nevertheless I found that manner of life ensnaring.

1695. About January 20, 1695, I went to Edinburgh to the school of divinity, then taught by the great Mr. George Campbell. There was then a great storm of snow on the ground. By the way, being extremely cold, I alighted off my horse, (I think it was betwixt

Ridpath-edge and Redstone-ridge), and walked. Having walked a
mile, a swoon began to seize me, and I could walk no more. I took
horse, but was scarcely able to sit on it. My brother, who by good
providence was with me, put a bit of bread in my mouth; and I
had scarcely as much strength left as to lift my jaws and chew it. It
would have been desirable to me to have been near the meanest cot-
tage. And I recovered. At that time I took a chamber, and dieted
myself again, about the space of a month; but weary of that way,
Mr. Ridpath aforesaid, and I tabled ourselves as most convenient.
He being a smart youth, and disposed to profit in philosophy, I did
good to myself, by being serviceable to him in the matter of philosophy, which was his only study at that time. Having some taste of
music before, we went to a school one month, and made good proficiency; pressing forward our teacher, and pursuing it in our chamber; so that by that means we had the tenors, trebles, and basses,
of the common tunes, with some other tunes, and several prick-songs.
My voice was good, and I had a delight in music.

A few of us, newly entered to the school of divinity, were taught
for a time Riissenius' compend, in the professor's chamber. Publicly
in the hall he taught Essenius' compend. For exercises that session,
I had a paraphrase on Isa. xxxviii. 1—9; a lecture on Prov. i. and
an exegesis *de certitudine subjectiva electionis ;* and in a private society,
another *de jure divino presbyteratus.* I was also for a while, at that
time, I suppose, with Mr. Alexander Rule, professor of Hebrew; but
remember no remarkable advantage I had thereby.

About the latter end of April, I returned home, clothed with testimonials from Professor Campbell, bearing, that I had diligently
attended the profession, dexterously acquitted myself in several
essays prescribed to me, behaved inoffensively, gravely, and piously.
He was a man of great learning, but excessively modest, undervaluing himself, and much valuing the tolerable performances of his
students.

Mr. James Murray, minister of Penpont, whose schoolfellow I
had been at Dunse a little while, having engaged me to embrace the
grammar school of Penpont, came to the Merse about the harvest,
and invited me to go with him, shewing considerable encouragement.
I could not then go along; but afterwards I made ready for it, and
exhausted what remained of my burse, which was in all, £80 Scots,
in fitting out myself. Upon this view, shewing a minister of the
presbytery, a wise man, that I minded not to desire the burse again,
he bade me fasten one foot before I loosed the other; an advice
which I had frequent occasion of minding thereafter.

In September, Mr. Murray having sent his horse for me, but withal

in a letter signified his fears of the miscarrying of that project, but
that in that case I might have another school; I, not a little
troubled at the sudden change, did notwithstanding go to Penpont,
in company with the worthy Mr. Henry Erskine aforementioned.

There I continued with Mr. Murray about a quarter of a year, in
suspense with reference to that project; in which time, Mr. G. B.,
minister of Glencairn, desired me to take the school of that parish;
which I was unwilling to accept. All hope of the school of Penpont
being at length cut off, and I ashamed to return home, Mr. B——
was wrote to, for what was before refused; and he made return,
that he could not be positive as to the matter. Under this trial,
which I was brought into by precipitant conduct, I was helped in
some measure to trust God.

After this, Mr. Murray being in Edinburgh, Mr. B—— sent for
me, and agreed with me to teach the school there for 100 merks of
salary. Thereafter came to my hand a letter from Mr. Murray, desiring me to come in to Edinburgh for a pedagogy provided for me.
Whereupon I earnestly dealt with Mr. B—— to quit me, while I was
not yet entered; which nevertheless he would by no means agree to.

1696. On the first day of the new year, 1696, being in his house,
his manner was most grievous and loathsome to me; so that I feared
I might there come to be hardened from God's fear. On the 9th,
much against the grain, I took up the school, never having inclined
much to that employment, but being quite averse to it there. I was
kindly and liberally entertained in Mr. B——'s house, and that
freely; but the vanity and untenderness of his carriage, and of his
wife's, I was not able to digest. He was wont, among other pieces
of conduct very unacceptable to me, to go to an alehouse, taking me
along with him, much against my inclination, under pretence of discoursing with an old gentleman. There we were entertained with
warm ale and brandy mixed, and with idle stories; I obtaining by
his character not to be pressed to drink. These things made me
earnestly cry unto the Lord, that he would rid and deliver me, and
dispose of me so as I might be freed from them and their society.
He was a young man, his wife an old woman; they had no children;
and there, I think, was their snare. Being sunk in debt, they left
the country at length.

After I had kept the school a little while, the lady Mersington
wrote a pressing letter to Mr. Murray, that I should take the charge
of her grandchild Aberlady, as his governor. Whereupon Mr.
B—— was again addressed to quit me; but could not be prevailed
with. I committed the cause to God, to be by him determined what
to do. And considering that no time of my continuance there had

been condescended on, that the scholars were but few, and that the presbytery was clear for me going away; and above all, considering that God, according to my earnest prayer, had opened an outgate from the heavy situation I found myself in, as above said, I began to question, if I could, without sin, let such an occasion of riddance from it slip; so being at length fully determined, I gave up the school on the 8th February, much against Mr. B——'s will, having kept it a month. At Candlemas the boys had gifted me about 10s. sterling, which I took from them with the usual civilities, but immediately returned each one his own; so that I had nothing by them.

While I was in that country, I had advantage of converse with Mr. Murray, a learned and holy man; the meeting of which two in a character was not very frequent there; as also of Janet Macleunie, an old exercised godly woman. She obliged me to take from her about half a dollar; which, as a token of that woman's Christian love, I do to this day value more than gold. I remember not but another instance of that nature, which I shall also mention in the due place. I bless the Lord, who gave me counsel then and afterwards, to seek and value conversation with serious Christians, in the places where my lot was cast; being confident, I had much advantage thereby towards my preaching of the gospel. But the small number of hearers I often saw in the kirk of Penpont, and the thronging away to separate meetings, kept, I think, by Mr. Hepburn, with other things respecting ministers and people, made a lasting bad impression of that country on me. Meantime it was my endeavour to live near God, and I was helped, while there, in some measure to live by faith. And there it was, that I first of all began to record passages of my life; the which I did on loose papers.

Having gone to Edinburgh, in pursuance of the proposal above mentioned, I did on February 18, take the charge of my pupil, Andrew Fletcher of Aberlady, a boy of about nine years of age; whose father having died young, his mother was married again to Lieutenant-Colonel Bruce of Kennet, in the parish of Clackmannan. The boy being at the high school, with a servant waiting on him, I waited on the school of divinity; which advantageous occasion proposed, had been a great inducement to me to engage in that business. And there I had a homily on Mark x. 27, which is *in retentis;* but to my great disappointment we were removed from Edinburgh to Kennet, whither we came on the morrow after, viz. March 7, and where we continued all along till I parted with him.

At Kennet, my pupil going to the grammar school at Clackmannan, with the servant attending him, and being of a towardly and tractable disposition, my business with him was no burden; taking notice of him at home, and sometimes visiting him in the school. But my business was increased toward the latter end of the year, teaching two boys of Kennet's to read. My pupil died afterward in his youth, while I was at Simprin.

I gave myself to study, kept a correspondence with the neighbouring ministers, there being an Episcopal incumbent in the parish when I went thither, and conversed much with some serious Christians about the place.

Though I was not properly the chaplain of the family, nor had, that I remember, any particular order from the master of the family, and neither laird nor lady were at home for a considerable time after I went thither; yet finding myself providentially settled there, in the character I bore, I judged myself obliged in conscience to seek the spiritual good of the family, and to watch over them, and see to their manners. Accordingly I kept up family worship, catechised the servants, pressed the careless to secret prayer, reproved and warned against sinful practices, and earnestly endeavoured the reformation of the vicious.

This course not having the desired effect on some, created me a great deal of uneasiness for the most part of the time I was there, the which arose especially from an ill-disposed and incorrigible woman, who was steward, and so did of course sometimes extend itself to my entertainment; which I bore with, that I might not mix quarrels on my private interest with those I was engaged in for the honour of God. And this principle I have all along, in the course of my ministry, aimed to walk by.

Meanwhile the united Presbyteries of Sterling and Dumblane meeting at Tulliallan, a neighbouring parish, June 22, a motion was made to give me a piece of trial, which I refused; but afterward Mr. George Turnbull, a grave learned man, then minister at Alloa, now at Tinninghame, gave me a text; John viii. 32, which I received, declaring it to be without view unto my entering on trials before the presbytery, being convinced I was not ripe for it. On that text I wrote a discourse, and gave it him. Afterward he shewed me, by a letter, what he judged amiss in it; but was pleased to add, that he observed a very promising gift in it. Thereafter Mr. Thomas Buchanan, then minister at Tulliallan, afterward at Dunfermline, gave me another text, viz. Acts xxi. 28, on which also I wrote a discourse, not unsatisfying to him. Both these discourses are *in retentis.*

My circumstances continuing uneasy through the means aforesaid, Mr. Turnbull did, on the 7th of September, by appointment of the presbytery, desire me to wait on them, bringing my testimonials along with me, on design to enter me on trials. He also spoke to Kennet about my removing out of his family; an opportunity of my going into the family of Colonel Erskine, then governor of Stirling castle, offering at that time; but Kennet shewed an unwillingness to part with me; in which I believe he was very ingenuous, being a man that had some good thing rooted in him. Wherefore, though I inclined to, I could not insist for the removal; but the entering on trials I was not clear for, and so could not promise to go to the Presbytery. Howbeit, being afterward persuaded to go to their meeting, I was minded to do it; but was providentially stopped.

But on the 23d I waited on them at Stirling, leaving my testimonials at home, of set purpose. Notwithstanding they appointed me to give in my thoughts on Phil. ii. 12, the following presbytery-day, producing my testimonials. This I could not undertake, having no freedom to enter on trials as yet; and, I think, I saw them no more till I was going out of the country. But these things obliged me to lay that matter to heart, for light from the Lord therein, to know what I was called of him unto.

I had in the summer represented to the lady the careless and ungodly lives, cursing and swearing of the steward and another servant, persisted in after many admonitions; and hinted to her, that it was her duty to reform them; and if they would not be reformed, to dismiss them from her service. The answer was favourable; but the term drawing near, she gave over the only two common servants who had any shew of religion, keeping the rest. This was very grievous to me; I told her the evil, and at large testified my dislike of that manner of management; and it was received civilly, but prevailed nothing. Meanwhile I was still acceptable to Kennet; who, when again I had an occasion of entering into Colonel Erskine's family, still refused to part with me. But by reason of his post in the military he was not much at home.

I held on, as new occasions offered, to discharge my conscience, until I left the family. And though it prevailed not according to my desire; yet, by the good hand of God fencing me, my struggle had an awe with it, and was not openly treated with contempt; though their words of me were like sharp swords, yet to me they were smooth as butter. I remember, that one Saturday's night they had set on a fire in the hall for drying their clothes they had been washing, not to be removed till the Sabbath was over. Grieved with this as a profanation of the Lord's day, I spoke to the gentlewoman; who insinuating, that she had not done without orders what she had done, refused to remove them; whereupon I spoke to the lady, who soon caused remove the clothes, and dispose of them otherwise. In

VOL. XI. c

like manner, on a Lord's day, word being sent me that my pupil was not going to church that day, I went and inquired into the matter, and he was caused to rise out of his bed ; and both the mother and son went to church that day.

On the 6th of June, there was a sacrament at Culross, which I had no mind to go to, upon the account of a carnal reason. On the Saturday night, God reached me a reproof by one of the servant-women; which filled me with confusion, set me to prayer, and to re-examine my reasons, which I found to be but consulting with flesh and blood. I went away therefore on the Lord's day, was deeply humbled, and had very much ado with unbelief, struggling to get my feet fastened. But at the table my soul, I thought, met with him in such measure, that ofttimes I have remembered my God from Culross and Tulliallan, when he has hid his face from me. On the Thursday before I had kept a secret fast.

July 26.—The Lord's day after the sacrament at Tulliallan, where the Lord was very kind to my soul, a godly family that had been at the same sacrament, had forgot it was the Lord's day; so that they told me afterward, they had fallen to their work, had I not come to their house, and asked them if they would go to the church.

On the second of August, I was at a sacrament, where I thought myself sure of great things, from the Lord's former kind dealing with me, I think ; but before I went to the table, I was deserted, tempted, perplexed with doubts whether to partake or not; yet I thought it duty to go forward, I endeavoured to take hold of the Lord; but staggered sore, came away with that it had been better I had not gone. But there I saw how little I could do without Christ, thought the Lord would come back again, and I had a longing to be in heaven. Betwixt sermons I went to a place I will ever mind, and would have been content there to have ventured on eternity as I was; desertion, a body of sin, &c., being very heavy, and recommending heaven to me.

On the 30th of November, having prayed with confidence to the Lord for light and direction concerning my passing trials before the Presbytery of Stirling, which they had been for some time urging, as I have noticed above, I took up my Bible, and going to turn to my ordinary, there cast up to me, Job xxii. 28, " Thou shalt decree a thing, and it shall be established unto thee ; and the light shall shine upon thy ways." This passage was very refreshful, coming so surprisingly, while I was turning to another place.

The space of a year being near expired, without any motion of a new bargain, on January 25, 1697, I wrote to Kennet, signifying, that I desired not to stay, being useless, and in a sort noxious, in his family. This letter I showed to the lady before I sent it off, and she quarrelled nothing in it; we being both, I believe, weary. This done, finding my heart disposed to sing, I sang in secret, Psalm xxxvii., near the latter end; whereby I was much cheered, and prayed cheerfully after. I was then, as it were, in sight of the shore of that troublous sea.

A little after that, I found there was no hope of entering into Colonel Erskine's family; and on Feb. 17, just the day before the year's expiring, I was told that Coulter had no mind to keep a pedagogue for my pupil. And thus providence shuffled me out of business of that kind, being entangled there, when a door was opened elsewhere; which again was shut when I was disentangled; thus working towards the leading me into business of another kind. So on Monday, Feburary 22, I took leave of my pupil, and that family. The day before, I thought it my duty to speak some things to the servants before I left them. I prayed to God for light; but was deserted, and could get nothing. I lay down on my bed in great heaviness, and thought with myself, What folly is it for me to think of passing trials to preach the gospel, seeing I cannot buckle two sentences of good sense together in my own mind? In this perplexity I went out to the field, and prayed earnestly; came in again, had no time longer to think; but was helped of God to speak without confusion, and with great facility, to my own wonder. This was useful to me afterwards, and did drive the bottom out of a grand objection I had against passing my trials, taken from my unreadiness in ordinary discourse.

The time I was at Kennet, continues to be unto me a remarkable time among the days of my life. Once I fainted there, being on my knees at evening secret prayer; and coming to myself again, was eased by vomiting. Another time praying in the Ferrytown, in Thomas Brown's family, I found my heart beginning to fail; which obliged me quickly to break off, and go to the door, where I was eased the same way as before. It was a time of much trouble to me, yet in the main, a thriving time for my soul. My corruption sometimes prevailed over me; but it put me to the using of secret fasting and prayer; whereunto I was also moved by the case of the poor, it being one of the years of dearth and scarcity that the Lord was then contending by year after year. And this I did not without some success. Then it was on such an occasion I drew up a catalogue of sins, which, with many unknown ones, I had to charge on myself; the which hath several times been of use to me since; there I had some Bethels, where I met with God, the remembrance whereof hath many times been useful and refreshful to me, particularly a place

under a tree in Kennet orchard, where, January 21, 1697, I vowed
the vow, and anointed the pillar. That day was a public fast-day;
and the night before, the family being called together, laid before
them the causes of the fast, and thereto added the sins of the family,
which I condescended on particularly, desiring them to search their
own hearts for other particulars, in order to our due humiliation.
After sermons, going to the Garlet to visit a sick woman, I was
moved, as I passed by the orchard, to go to prayer there; and being
helped of the Lord, I did there solemnly covenant with God under a
tree, with two great boughs coming from the root, a little north-
west from a kind of ditch in the eastern part of the orchard.

Though it was heavy to me that I was taken from the school of
divinity, and sent to Kennet; yet I am convinced God sent me to
another school there, in order to prepare me for the work of the
gospel, for which he had designed me; for there I learned in some
measure what it was to have the charge of souls; and being naturally bashful, timorous, and much subject to the fear of man, I
attained, by what I met with there, to some boldness, and not regarding the persons of men when out of God's way. There I learned, that God will countenance one in the faithful discharge of his
duty, though it be not attended with the desired success; and that
plain dealing will impress an awe on the party's conscience, though
their corruption still rages against him that so deals with them. It
was by means of conversation there that I arrived at a degree of
public spirit which I had not before; and there I got a lesson of the
need of prudent and cautious management, and abridging one's self
of one's liberty, that the weak be not stumbled, and access to edify
them be precluded; a lesson I have in my ministry had a very particular and singular occasion for.

On the Friday before I left Kennet, it was proposed to me by
Messrs. Turnbull and Buchanan, that I should now enter on trials;
and withal, that the elders of Clackmanan being unwilling I should
go out of the country, it was desired, that I should take for myself,
or allow to be taken for me, a chamber in the town of Clackmanan;
and they desired me to give my answer on the Tuesday, and go along
to the Presbytery on the Wednesday thereafter. Having taken
these things under consideration, I was that same night almost resolved to comply with the call of that Presbytery for entering on
trials before them. But just next morning I received a letter from
Mr. Murray, desiring me to come with all speed, and pass trials before the Presbytery of Penpont; withal, shewing that if I pleased I
might in the meantime keep the school of Penpont, it being then
vacant. Thus providence opened a door for my entering into an-

other station, and doubled the call thereto. But then I was in doubt, racked betwixt these two, whether to address myself to the Presbytery of Stirling or Penpont; which I endeavoured to table before the great Counsellor for his determination. In this suspense, I went, on Wednesday, February 24, to the Presbytery of Stirling, where I obtained their testimonial, having promised to return to them if my circumstances would permit. Having spent some days more in that country, I came to Edinburgh by sea on the 4th of March, having got an edge put on my spirit for passing my trials, by the dishonour I heard done to God on the shore of Leith, where we landed. The case is as follows. Sailing by the shore, I heard such cursing, swearing, &c., as made me to wonder at the patience of God towards sinners, and to think I would be very willing to do any thing I could for suppressing these horrid sins or the like. This was useful to clear me in that point, which was now, and had been, my exercise for a good time.

About this time twelvemonth there came a young gentlewoman to see my pupil, with her face bespattered with patches; and drawing him to her to salute him, he endeavoured to pull off her patches. She put back his hand, that he could not reach her face; but he pulled a paper out of his pocket, giving an account how the devil murdered a gentlewoman for pride, and gave it her; which did much confound her.

While I was at Kennet it was a time of much trouble to me, but a time wherein the Lord was very kind to me. I was helped of God in some measure to my duty, as has been [observed, and it was that which enraged them against me. The lady was my great enemy; but professed great kindness to me when she spoke to me, or to the ministers of me. One of those profane servants whom I could not induce her to put away, she was afterwards obliged to discharge with disgrace. I have often looked on the Lord's sending me thither, as done in design to fit me for the work of the ministry, to which it contributed many ways, as I have already noticed.

At Edinburgh I received my wages, being 100 merks; wrote a letter of excuse to Mr. Murray, and another letter to the place whence I had come, bearing my design to return thither shortly. And indeed, when I came to Edinburgh, I was not fully resolved to go home at all; and having writ to my father, I signified the same to him, who being, unknown to me, in terms of a second marriage, gave me an answer, advising me to return to Stirling, as I had said. Howbeit I afterwards saw a necessity of going home, to procure money for my maintenance, during the time of passing my trials before the Presbytery of Stirling, being unwilling to accept of the offer of the elders of Clackmannan aforesaid, and the money received not being sufficient for that and other necessary uses. Accordingly, just upon that design, I went home to Dunse, March 13; but he who "leads the blind by a way they knew not," led me hither on two material designs hidden to me; namely, the diverting of the marriage, which was unknown to me, and the passing of my trials there, which I was far from having in view.

The week after I went home, being still bent to return to the Presbytery of Stirling, and there being no small hope of getting the money for which I had come, I received another letter from Mr. Murray, wherein having answered all my excuses, he still insisted on my coming to Penpont to pass trials. Thus I was again put upon the rack between the two; and not knowing whither to go, I earnestly desired counsel of God, both as to the main thing, and the circumstance of place; and shewing my situation to Mr. Alexander Colden, then Minister at Dunse, now at Oxnham, he proposed, and persuaded me, to enter on trials before the united Presbyteries of Dunse and Churnside. Considering the course of Providence, and finding myself by his proposal freed from the former perplexity, which I could no otherwise get over, I yielded. And certainly it was a kind conduct of providence that led me to pass trials in the place of my nativity; though, for that very reason, it would seem, that it was my native country, I had no thoughts of passing there; for it was most for my reputation to pass trials where I was known from my childhood; and, besides, it was the more convenient for me in my then circumstances, having my father's house to remain in.

Accordingly, on the 23d of March, 1697, I being, just the week before, twenty-one years of age complete, Mr. Colden went to the Presbytery, sitting at Churnside; and having proposed their taking me on trials, they appointed me a piece of trial on James i. 5, "If any of you lack wisdom, let him ask of God, that giveth to all men liberally," &c., and that to be delivered at their next meeting in Dunse. The which being reported to me by Mr. Colden, I addressed myself to that work, kind providence having, on the Friday after, prepared me a private chamber in my father's house, which had been occupied by another when I came home.

On the 2d of April I spent some time in fasting and prayer, for the divine assistance in what I was called to, and was going about; and in the time I found myself helped, in prayer, to particular trust and confidence, that God would actually grant what I sought. The Presbytery meeting at Dunse on the 6th, I delivered before them a homily on the foresaid text, and was helped of God therein accordingly; and to this day I have a sense of the divine indulgence, determining them to prescribe me that text which was so much suited for my support in the disposition I was in. They appointed me then a common head, *De viribus liberi arbitrii circa bonum spirituale.*

I delivered an exegesis on that head, after prayer made, both in Latin, May 11, at Churnside. Much time being spent ere they called for that piece of trial, I went out a little to revise it; but by the time I had come the length of what I reckoned myself least master of, I was called to deliver it; but withal, by the kind conduct of providence, when I was coming on to that part of it, they stopped me. I distributed my thesis on that head, and was appointed to exercise and add next presbytery-day on Jude 15.

On the 1st of June they met at Dunse. The day before it was the great fair in that place; but I was earnest with God for his assistance in the work before me; and was helped of him to seek his help. In the morning before I went to the kirk, I renewed covenant with God in my chamber; and I had much encouragement from the help of the prayers of my godly friends in Clackmannan, who, I trusted, were concerned for me. By a peculiar kind disposal of providence, when I went to the pulpit, the precentor, who used to keep an ordinary, was not come; so, according to my own desire, I pitched on Psalm xviii. 25—29, and precented myself; and was greatly strengthened by the singing thereof. I delivered the exercise and addition to the foresaid text, being well helped of the Lord therein. I have still a peculiar remembrance of that part of the Psalm, as occasionally it comes in my way. I admire the indulgence of providence in the matter; for the precentor should have been singing when I went into the pulpit. And withal I have often wondered, how, considering my temper, I got confidence to give out that psalm on that occasion; but the obvious difficulty on that head was then, for any thing I know, hid from mine eyes, which were fixed depending on God alone, according to his word. They appointed me a popular sermon on John i. 16, against their next meeting, with the rest of my trials, if I could get them ready.

At Churnside, June, 15, I delivered my popular sermon on the foresaid text, as also a chronological discourse in Latin; which, with the other discourses aforementioned, are yet *in retentis.* The same day, all the rest of my trials, viz. in the languages, and catechetics, were taken; the which last are now, and have been for many years, taken first, with more reason. Thus all my trials being expeded, I was that day licenced to preach the gospel, as a probationer for the holy ministry, near about three years from my entering on the study of divinity. And looking on myself as a child of providence, and considering the manner of my education, I cannot but observe the

kind conduct of that providence in carrying me through sundry
states of life, and parts of the country, in that short time allotted for
me, in the character of a student.

PERIOD IV.

FROM MY BEING LICENSED, TILL I REMOVED INTO THE BOUNDS OF THE PRES-
BYTERY OF STIRLING.

BEING licensed to preach the gospel, I passed two years and three
months in the character of a probationer; the first part of the same
in my native country, the second in the bounds of the Presbytery of
Stirling, and the third in my native country again, where I was
settled. These years brought in continued scenes of trial to me;
being through the mercy of God, generally acceptable to the people;
but could never fall into the good graces of those who had the stroke
in the settling of parishes.

Having, on the 18th of June, studied, and once mandated, the first
sermon I preached, and having gone to a fellowship meeting, and
upon my return fallen again to work, I was so confused, that I lay
grovelling on the ground for some time in great perplexity, wishing
I had never undertaken that work. But recovering myself, I betook
myself to prayer; and thereafter it came so easily to hand, that I
saw the finger of God in it.

According to the impressions wherewith I was prompted to enter
on trials, I began my preaching of the word in a rousing strain; and
would fain have set fire to the devil's nest. The first text I preached
on, the Sabbath after I was licensed, was Psalm l. 22; the second,
Matth. vii. 21; the third, on a week-day, Hos. xiii. 13; the fourth,
Psalm l. 21; the fifth, Ezek. ix. 4; the sixth, Prov. xxix. 1; and
the seventh, Matth. iii. 7. Thus I went on for the first two months.
But speaking with Mr. John Dysart, minister at Coldinghame, of·
the strain of preaching I had continued in, he said to me to this
purpose: But if you were entered on preaching of Christ, you would
find it very pleasant. This had an effect on me so far, that immediately I did somewhat change my strain; where I had occasion to
enter on a new text; and then I preached, first, on Isa. lxi. 1, and
next, on 1 Pet. ii. 7. I have often, since that time, remembered
that word of Mr. Dysart's, as the first hint given me, by the good
hand of my God, towards the doctrine of the gospel.

The first Sabbath I preached, being timorous, I had not confidence
to look on the people; though I believe I did not close my eyes;
yet, as a pledge of what I was to meet, an heritor of the parish, on
that very sermon, called me afterwards, in contempt, one of Mr.

Henry Erskine's disciples. In which he spoke truth, as Caiaphas did, that worthy minister of Christ being the first instrument of good to my soul; but the thing he meant was, that I was a railer. The second Sabbath I had more confidence; and the next again more, till very soon I had enough; and was censured as too bold, particularly in meddling with the public sins of the land. The truth is, my God so far pitied my natural weakness, indulging me a while after I had first set out to his work, that, whatever fear I was liable to ere I got into the pulpit, yet when once the pulpit-door was closed on me, fear was as it were closed out, and I feared not the face of man when preaching God's word. But indeed that lasted not long, at least after I was a minister.

Soon after I was licensed, I was peremptorily resolved not to continue in the Merse, though there was appearance of encouragement; and I received a letter from the Presbytery of Stirling, inviting me to their bounds, whether it was my own inclination to go. So, on July 27, I craved of the Presbytery an extract of my licence. But they, designing to have me settled in Foulden, would not grant it. By this time I had preached once in that perish, and they were inclined to have me to be their minister; but I was not fond of it. Their Episcopal incumbent had newly removed from them; and when I was to go thither, I foresaw a strait, in allowing his precentor to officiate as such to me, without a judicial acknowledgement, which I, not being a minister, could not take. Consulting it with Mr. Colden, he would not urge me against my light; but told me, he feared the bailie, being Episcopal, would take it ill. I resolved to venture on that. So when the precentor came to me, in the Sabbath morning, I told him, I myself would precent; but shewed him no reason why. This I took to be the most reasonable course in my circumstances, having no authority. Nevertheless the bailie was favourable. Thereafter I preached frequently in the parish while I continued in the country; had many good days in it, the meetings frequent, and people very desirous to hear the word. Meanwhile I still precented there, till about two Sabbaths before I left the country; by which time the Presbytery had confirmed the precentor in his office.

I was still detained in the country by the Presbytery, that I might be settled in that parish aforesaid. But that could not be done without my Lord Ross' concurrence. Wherefore the Presbytery appointed Mr. Colden and Mr. Dysart to speak to him at Edinburgh for that effect. And the former, upon his return from Edinburgh, told me, on September 10, that my Lord Ross did not refuse his concurrence; only he desired me to come to Paisley to see him, that he might go on with the greater clearness; and hereto he withal advised me. But I had no freedom for it. So, October 5, I desired of the Presbytery my liberty to leave the country, which I had in vain desired of them three several times before. In answer to which, Mr. Colden afterwards told me, that the Presbytery would let me go, providing I would go to Paisley to see my Lord Ross. I would have been content to have been providentially led to have preached in my Lord's hearing; but to go to him directly on that purpose, was what I could never digest, though I was dunned with advice for it, and had no body to bear with me in resisting it, but the unhappy Mr. J—— B——, then living a private man in Dunse. I considered, that I had done all that lay in my road in the matter, having preached several times in the parish which in the designed event was to have been my charge; they were satisfied, and should have had their Christian right to choose their minister; I looked on the method proposed, as an interpretative seeking a call for myself; a symbolising with patronages, and below the dignity of the sacred character; and I never durst do any thing in these matters which might predetermine me; but behoved always to leave the matter open and entire, to lay before the Lord for light, till he should please to determine me by the discovery of his mind therein; and I could not look on the matter of my compliance with the call of Foulden as entire, after I should have done as I was advised.

Wherefore, upon the 13th, I insisted as before, and the Presbytery granted my desire; but withal demanded of me, 1. That I should preach a day at Abbay before I went away; 2. That I should go by Paisley, and see my Lord Ross; 3. That my licence should bear, that I should not, without their advice, engage with any parish. To the first and last I readily yielded; but the second I could by no means comply with.

Being resolved to take my journey for the bounds of the Presbytery of Stirling, on the Tuesday after the October synod, now at hand, I sent to the presbytery-clerk for my licence accordingly; the which I received; but so very informal, that it could not well be presented to a Presbytery. Whereupon I was persuaded to go to Kelso to the synod, that I might get it drawn there in due form; resolving to go straight from thence, without returning to Dunse. But providence had more work for me to do at home.

The Presbytery having appointed me nowhere, for the third Sabbath after I was licensed, I was invited to preach that day in the parish of Abbay, one of the four kirks of Lammermoor; the which invitation I accepted, and studied a sermon for that end on Rev. iii. 20, which I believe was never delivered. But Mr. Colden being

on the Saturday called to a communion at Earlston on the morrow,
I was obliged to preach for him at Dunse that Sabbath.   The Presbytery would never send me to the said parish of Abbay till I was
just going out of the country, as said is; they having a design to
transport unto it the laird of Abbay, minister of Aiton, whom they
looked on as unfit for that public post.   But he being both a weak
and untender-man, was unacceptable to the parish of Abbay, as well
as to his brethren.   By their appointment foresaid, I preached there
the Sabbath before the synod, October 17.   There had been before
that an inclination in that parish to me to be their minister; the
which was first moved to me by Abbay himself, and afterward by
an elder with much affection.   After being appointed to preach
there, they shewed themselves very cordial for my settlement among
them, very affectionate to me, and unwilling that I should go out of
the country.

Having come to Kelso as aforesaid, the drawing up of my licence
in due form was shifted and put off.   It was represented, that a
lady had engaged to write to Lord Ross in my favour; I was urged
to fall from my intended departure; and Mr. Colden, whom I particularly regarded, told me, he thought providence lay cross to it.
So I behoved to return home again without my licence, unexpected,
to my friends.

Being thus locked in at home for that season, I preached several
times at Abbay during the winter, lodging ordinarily in Blacker-
stone; where, at family prayer, December 14, I fainted away, not
having got the prayer formally closed, as they afterwards told me.
There was an appearance of my settling there; the people were knit
to me; and that was the only parish, I think, that ever I was fond
of.   But I smarted for the loose I foolishly had given to my heart
upon it.   I proposed to myself to be very happy in such a small
charge, being told that they would be but about four score people;
but then there appeared to be an occasion of diffusive usefulness in
that hill country, the other three kirks thereof being still possessed
by curates.   The stipend was about 700 merks, the place retired
among the hills, the manse pleasantly situate on Whitwater, and
within three or four miles of Dunse.   But the Presbytery was still
against settling me there.

1698. On January 16, 1698, the elders, who twice before that had
desired a minister to moderate in a call there, but were repulsed, applied to them again for the same end, and were repulsed as formerly;
notwithstanding that the same day there was read before them a
leter from Lord Ross, bearing, that since I had not come to him, he
had another in view for Foulden.

About the latter end of that month, Abbay being in Dunse, told me, that sometime he had a mind for that parish himself, but now he had changed his resolution, and would join with the elders, in order to my settlement there. And about the 8th of February, the elders appearing again before the Presbytery, renewed their address for a minister to moderate in a call there; and Abbay himself joining them accordingly, as an heritor, the Presbytery could no longer refuse it; but, in the meantime, they took a long day for it, purposely it would seem, and appointed the 10th of March for that effect. As we came out of the Presbytery, Abbay told me, according to his manner, he would preach my ordination sermon.

Now the poor parish thought themselves secure; and things seem-ing to go according to my heart's wish, I was much comforted in the thoughts thereof. But, behold, in a few days Abbay changed his mind, and all endeavours were used to turn about the call for him; which with the heritors was easily obtained, none of them residing within the parish. The point on which it seemed to turn was, that now or never was the occasion of consulting his interest; which missed, the Presbytery would by some means get him turned out of Aiton. This, I was informed, some ministers did put in the head of his friends, by whose persuasion he changed his mind and courseagain in that matter.

Observing the matter to be going thus, I fell under great dis-couragement, by means of the disappointment, having foolishly judged that place the fittest for me. Then it was my exercise, and a hard one, to get my heart brought to a submission to providence in that point; the which submission I desired, if my heart deceived me not, more than the removal of the stroke. Being sore broken by the disappointment, I took hold of an occasion to preach, for my own ease, a sermon on 1 Sam. iii. 18, on a week-day at Dunse. After sermon, one of the hearers came to me, and thankfully ac-knowledged God's goodness in bringing her to that sermon, so suited to her case. She was a godly woman of Polwarth parish, who shortly before had lost her husband. This sermon was not without advantage to myself in the point I was aiming to reach. Howbeit, that discouragement and the spring season trysting together, there was a notable breach made in my health, which continued for a long time after, the which I dated from the beginning of that month of March. When I had near studied that sermon, I was in hazard of fainting away; but being taken care of, and laid to bed, I re-covered.

March 6.—Preaching in Dunse, such an indisposition of body and faintness was on me, that I thought either to have swooned in the pulpit, or to have been obliged to go out abruptly; but, by good providence, there was opposite to the pulpit an aisle wanting some of the roof, by which came a refreshing gale that supported me, and the Lord carried me through, giving me a taste of his goodness, of which I was preaching. The same day eight days, after preaching in the same place, the indisposition recurred; and as I was going into the kirk very pensive, and thinking of the hazard of swooning in the pulpit, and how it would be matter of reproach, I heard the precentor reading, and found them singing Psalm lvii. 3, "From heaven he shall send down, and me from his reproach defend," &c. which was sweetly seasonable to my soul.

Having been for some time very indisposed, I was under some apprehensions of death, but very unwilling and afraid to die; in which case I had occasion to ride by that spot of ground where I was formerly so content to die, (see p. 26), which let me see a great difference in the frame of my spirit now from what it was then.

March 10.—The call was drawn up for Abbay himself, my lord Mersington, a good-natured, well-inclined man, being the main agent in the affair; at whose door the poor people, among whom there were wet cheeks on that occasion, laid the blood of their souls; but it prevailed not with him. One of the elders, Abbay's own tenant, was brought to subscribe the call. It was brought before the Presbytery on the 15th; and Mersington having a commission from Abbay, had signed it for him in his name as an heritor. Two elders and a parishioner appeared that day before the Presbytery, and reclaimed, earnestly entreating them to consider, that they behoved to answer to God for what they did. But the Presbytery sustained the call. Mr. Colden would say nothing in the matter, but went out in the time. They appointed him to write to lord Ross, and to the minister of Paisley, to deal with my lord on my account with respect to Foulden. This was the ungospel-like way that even then much prevailed in the case of planting of churches; a way which I ever abhorred. I had been named by the commission of the assembly to go to Caithness, a few days before the moderating of that call; but Mr. Colden telling them, that, on the Thursday after, a call was to be moderated for me, it was dropped. So by it providence diverted that mission of me, which would have been very heavy.

On the 29th, the writing of the letters aforesaid having been forgot, a letter from Mr. Wilkie, bailie of Foulden, was read *coram*, bearing, that he would cordially concur for my settlement in Foulden; but thought reason and good-breeding required that I should go to lord Ross. Whereupon they peremptorily enjoined me to go

to him; and Mr. Colden told me, I would be out of my duty if I
went not. Nevertheless, having no clearness for it in my own conscience, I continued unmoved in my resolution; though it troubled
me that they should have appointed me.

At the April synod I was invited to the Presbytery of Kelso;
but being advised to wait till the following presbytery-day, I preached at Foulden; and, May, 1, hearing there that my lord Ross was
was to send them another man, I resolved forthwith to go to the
Presbytery of Stirling, having given over thoughts of Kelso.

Accordingly, having got up the extract of my licence, and testimonials on the 10th, I went away on the 15th; and having come
to my quarters at Edinburgh, I was overtaken with a fainting-fit.
On the 17th I arrived in the bounds of the Presbytery of Stirling.

Providence having thus tried me in my native country, especially
in the affair of Abbay, I was so taught, that no place did ever after
get so much of my fond affection. But, notwithstanding all the
bustle made for the laird's transportation to that place, it did not
at this time take effect: but, after I was gone, Mr. George Home
minister of Selkirk was planted in it, he having been uneasy in that
public post. And afterward, when I was a member of the Presbytery of Churnside, a process of drunkenness was commenced against
Abbay, which yet proved ineffectual for his removal out of Aiton.
But Mr. Home being dead, he was at length, I think, before I came
to Ettrick, transported thither; the people by that time being
taught more tamely to bear the yoke.

PERIOD V.

FROM MY REMOVAL INTO THE BOUNDS OF THE PRESBYTERY OF STIRLING, TO MY RETURN UNTO THE MERSE.

HAVING come into the bounds aforesaid, I took up my lodging with
Thomas Brown of Barhill in Ferritown, with whom I had contracted
a particular friendship when I was at Kennet, he being a good man.
I was once and again invited to Kennet's family to lodge there, but
declined it; a plain evidence of no real inclination to settle in
Clackmannan parish. I continued with Thomas Brown while I remained in that country, which was near about a year; and in these
days that text had weight with me, " Go not from house to house :"
judging that course unworthy of the sacred character.

The parishes which I preached mostly in, while in that country,
were Clackmannan and Airth, and after some time Dollar, all of
them being then vacant. The Lord was with me in my work there,
and did some good by me, especially in Airth and Dollar. The

minister I conversed most with was Mr. Turnbull in Alloa, a steady friend. Mr. Hugh White in Larbert, a man of considerable abilities, great piety and tenderness, was also very friendly and affectionate; but I had little occasion of converse with him, being on the other side of Forth.

Having preached some time in these parts, and before the Presbytery of Stirling on July 13, some of the parish of Carnock, in the Presbytery of Dunfermline, took occasion to hear me at Clackmannan and Airth. Whereupon I had two letters from Mr. John Wylie, then minister of Saline, afterwards of Clackmannan, inviting me to preach at Saline, a parish neighbouring with Carnock; but Mr. Turnbull shewed me, that I behoved not to go; and I went not. William Paton, one of the elders of Clackmannan, was clear for my going, and told me, what others kept secret from me, that they had a design on me for Clackmannan; but withal, that Mr. Inglis, tacksman of the estate of Clackmannan, whose coal grieve he was, and Kennet, would set their foot against it. But on July 26, two of the elders of Carnock came to the Ferritown unto me, trying how I would relish a call to their parish. I left the matter open, saying little, and desiring them to seek a minister from the Lord.

About the beginning of August, Mr. Wylie wrote to the Presbytery of Stirling, in name of the Presbytery of Dunfermline, desiring them to allow me to come a day or two to them; the which they absolutely refused; and that day, or soon after, I perceived the Presbytery had a design on me for Clackmannan. That their refusal I did not take well; but they never asked my inclination, and I had no freedom to urge their letting me go. However, afterward, on a letter from Mr. James Fraser of Brea, minister of Culross, inviting me to assist by preaching at the communion there, on the 21st, I went and preached there accordingly in the churchyard; Mr. Turnbull having allowed, if there was such a necessity as was alleged in the letter, it could not well be refused. At this time began my acquaintance with the worthy Mr. George Mair, Brea's colleague, whose conversation was afterwards of good use to me, in regard to the spirituality of it, and the insight he had into the doctrine of the gospel. I think, that holy and learned man Brea died not very long after.

On the 14th of August I communicated at Larbert, and was not altogether deserted in it; but I think, as I was walking alone to my lodgings, I got my communion indeed. Two or three days before, I did endeavour to examine myself thus: They that have a sincere desire of union and communion with Christ, have true faith, Matth. v. 6; 2 Cor. viii. 12; and such are those who, 1. Choose and desire Christ, without desire to retain sin; that choose Christ whatever may follow; Heb. xi. 25. 2. That are not carried forth after spiritual good things merely as profitable to themselves, but as things in themselves good and desirable; Psalm lxxiii. 25; 3. Who desire a whole Christ, as well for sanctification as justification; 1 Cor. i. 30; 4. Who esteem Christ above all; 1 Pet. ii. 7; 5. Who have a sense of sin pressing the conscience, and serious displeasure with it; Matth. xi. 28. 6. Who make suitable endeavours after Christ; Prov. xxi. 25. But I (I appeal to God's omniscience) have such a desire. For, 1. I desire Christ without exception of any sin, or the cross; I am content to part with all sin, and take Christ to follow him in his strength whithersoever he goes. 2 I desire union and communion with Christ, though there were no hell to punish those who are united to their sins. 3. I desire a whole Christ, and would as fain have sin subdued and mortified, as guilt taken away. 4. I esteem Christ above all; give me Christ, and take from me what thou wilt. 5. Sin is a burden to me, especially my predominant lust. 6. I endeavour, in some measure, to seek after Christ; Lord, thou knowest. Therefore I have true faith.

The week after the communion at Culross, my acquaintance with Katharine Brown, now my wife, was carried on to a direct proposal of marriage made to her. She was fifth daughter to Robert Brown of Barhill, in the parish of Culross; her mother, then a widow, and her eldest sister, who had been married to Thomas Brown above mentioned, being dead more than a year before. I had, while I was at Kennet, heard a very favourable report of her; and from the first time that I saw her, which was March 3, 1697, the day on which I left that country, something stuck with me. A few days after I had returned, as said is, she had occasion to come and tarry some time with her brother-in-law. And my health being broken as above mentioned, I was valetudinary, and particularly subject to faintings; with one of which I was seized, June 3, she being present; but by her advice, whose father had been a practitioner in physic, I used wormwood boiled, and applied it to my stomach in linen bags, that month, and was much relieved of these faintings. Howbeit, when they left me, I was seized with a binding at my breast; and for a long time that year I used Lucatellus' balsam by the same advice. What engaged me to her, was her piety, parts, beauty, cheerful disposition fitted to temper mine, and that I reckoned her very fit to see to my health. I never was in a mind to marry before I should be settled; but I judged both the one and the other requisite for my health. But though I made choice of a most worthy woman, I was afterwards obliged to confess, before God, my sin, in that I had not been more at pains to know his mind in the matter before I had proposed it. And howbeit I did frequently that summer lay it before the Lord, and consider it; yet I can never forgive myself, though I hope my God hath forgiven me, that I did not set some time or times apart for fasting and prayer for that end, before I made the proposal. But God did chastise my rashness, partly by my finding that process very entangling to me in my vagrant circumstances, partly by suffering perplexing scruples to rise in my mind about it : while yet he did, in the issue of them, convincingly shew the matter to be of himself, and bound it on my conscience as duty; which cleared, my difficulty was not to get love to her, but rather to bound it.

In the beginning of September I had a letter from Mr. Wylie, desiring me to preach a Sabbath-day, either at Salin or Carnock, or on a week-day at Carnock. In answer to which, I promised to preach a Sabbath-day at Salin, if they would procure the day from the Presbytery; but declined seeking it for myself.

About the middle of that month, I received a letter from Mr. Murray, inviting me to Nithsdale; and had thoughts of complying with it. On the 11th, being a national fast-day, I had preached at Clackmannan, the Lord helping me; and that night going to bed weakened and wearied, I found myself, notwithstanding, able to lie on my back; a posture which for a long time before I could not place myself in, without being in hazard of fainting. Some were offended at that day's work, others much endeared to me. But about this time the business of my settlement there being still in agitation, and the elders not speaking of it to me, till they might see the matter brought to a bearing, I thought it meet to shew one of them, that it was needless to make a bustle between heritors and elders on my account, in regard, for any thing I knew, I should never accept of a call to Clackmannan.

So, on October 5, I went to the Presbytery, with an intention to crave my testimonials, in order to leave that country; but ere I got it moved, there was produced and read a letter from Kennet, desiring, that in regard, the parish of Clackmannan had a desire for me to be their minister, they would interpose with me not to leave the bounds, and appoint me to preach three Sabbaths at Clackmannan, in regard some of the heritors had not heard me. Whereupon the Presbytery urged me to stay till the next presbytery-day at least, and appointed me two days at Clackmannan; whereto I at length yielded; though it troubled me somewhat after, that I should have consented to preach there on that account.

On the 18th came to me an elder of Carnock, with a line signed

VOL. XI.   D

by five of their number, shewing that they had the Presbytery's allowance for drawing up a call to me; but that Kincairdine and Sir Patrick Murray would not allow it to be done for any young man, till once the parish had a hearing of him; and desiring me to shew, whether they might go on or not. I found by the bearer that they were not unanimous; shewed them I could not have access to preach a day to them; left them to their liberty; and desired they might not on my account deprive themselves of any other whom they pleased.

Having preached the two days at Clackmannan, the elders could not prevail with the heritors to join in a call to me. Mr. Ingles aforesaid set himself against me particularly, alleging for a reason, that I was young, and but a probationer. It was supposed, that my not bowing in the pulpit, and going with none of them on the Sabbath-nights, rendered me unacceptable; and I do believe, that they and I both agreed, that, in respect of my temper and way, I was not fit for the parish of Clackmannan. However, the said Mr. Ingles, who was a friend of Brea's told me some time or other, while in that country, (I apprehend it has been after this, when Brea was deceased), that there was something in my sermons so like Brea's, that one would have thought I had seen his notes, but that he knew I had no access to them; which last was very true.

By this time I had preached twice at Dollar, then lately become vacant through the removal of the Episcopal incumbent; and an inclination towards me there was signified by some of them; and thinking about settling in that country, I could scarcely be able to say in my own heart, where I would desire to settle in it, if it was not in Dollar; and hardly there either. But went to the Presbytery, November 2, fully resolved to have my liberty, thinking to go to Nithsdale. Accordingly I desired their testimonial, shewing that I could stay no longer. Mr. White, being moderator, did long press my stay; which, with all the modesty I could, I declined, representing, that if I continued longer, I behoved to continue all the winter, in respect of the broken state of my health. (I was now using conserve of roses, by the advice aforesaid). After they had urged me till I was ashamed, two ministers, whereof Mr. Turnbull was one, took me out to converse with me privately. In the meantime a man from Dollar, with much concern, addressed himself to me, that I might not go away, shewing the inclination of that parish toward me; and elders of the other vacant parishes urged me. Finding myself perplexed, and not knowing what to say, I left myself to the Presbytery's disposal, and so received their appointments after.

Being thus locked in there again, the tongues of many were let

loose on me; and my railing and reflecting, as they call it, came
often to my ears. Preaching at Clackmannan on the 27th, some
were vexed, and one in a rage went out of the church. When I
came home to my lodging, I was much affected that my preaching
was so stormed· at; and the rather, that I thought 1 had not the inward support requisite in such a case; but I was comforted at family-worship, singing, Psalm lxix. 7, and downwards. That same
week, it was uneasy to me to hear that some concluded I had an inclination for the parish of Clackmannan, for the zeal shown for it
by my most intimate acquaintance, thinking they could not have
done so without encouragement from me. Upon which I find I
made this reflection, setting that matter in a due light, viz. "But,
Lord, thou knowest, that it was not my inclination, though in
my thoughts I would not be too peremptory, not knowing how God
might call me."

In the month of December, some of the elders of Dollar signified
to me their inclination to give me a call, if they could get it done;
but withal I had an account of an appointment on me to go to the
north; and, on the 27th, came to my hand the commission's letter,
requiring me forthwith to go to Angus and Mearns. On the morrow I
went to the Presbytery, where Mr. John Forrester, one of the ministers of Stirling, keenly urged my going to the north; but I told
them I could not go, in respect of the state of my health; and they
did not so much as recommend it to me to go. By this I judged,
that providence did not call me to that removal, and the rather that
the motion had been made about a call to Dollar. Howbeit, the
going to the north was, for a long time after, a sore exercise to me
at times, as will be observed afterwards. That same day, the fast
of January 4, 1699, being appointed, the land still groaning under
dearth and scarcity, year after year, the said Mr. Forrester moved,
that it should be recommended to the brethren that to deal prudently
in their preaching with respect to the cause of the fast, and hinted
at some affecting singularity, which I knew very well to be directed
against me; but since he named me not, I said nothing on the head.
That month also was observed, that one Alard Fithie in Powside of
Clackmannan, who being enraged at my sermons at Clackmannan,
September 11, was wont to go out of the parish after, when I preached in it, was then broken, and obliged to leave the parish, it not
being known whither he had fled.

On the 29th, I found that my friend Katharine Brown, who some
time before had given a favourable answer to my proposal, had afterwards been much troubled about it, that it was not enough deliberate.
Had I taken that way in my own case, which I ought to have done

as aforesaid, it is likely I would have put her on the same method, whereby this might have been prevented. But one error in conduct makes way for another.

For about fourteen months after this I kept a large diary, moved thereto by converse with Mr. Mair. In that time I filled up the book I had then begun, and a whole second book, though I wrote in short-hand characters, till July 7, 1699. Several of the passages of that time are from thence transcribed into this account of my life.

January 1, 1699.—I had more than an ordinary measure of God's presence and help in preaching. In the morning in secret I was earnest with God for it, but had a temptation to think that God would leave me, which did perplex me sore. When I was coming home from the sermons, Satan fell to afresh again, the contrary way, tempting me to pride. It came three times remarkably on me, and was as often repelled by that word, "What hast thou that thou has not received?"

During the remaining time that I continued at Ferrytown, I wrote a "Soliloquy on the Art of Man-fishing," which was never finished, but is *in retentis.** The occasion thereof was this, January 6, 1699, reading in secret, my heart was touched with Matth. iv. 19, "Follow me, and I will make you fishers of men." My soul cried out for accomplishing of that to me, and I was very desirous to know how I might follow Christ, so as to become a fisher of men; and for my own instruction in that point, I addressed myself to the consideration of it in that manner. And indeed it was much on my heart in these days, not to preach the wisdom of mine own heart, or produce of my own gifts; but to depend on the Lord for light, that I might, if I could have reached it, been able to say of every word, "Thus saith the Lord." That scribble† gives an idea of the then temper of my spirit, and the trying circumstances I then found myself in, being every where scared at by some.

January 21.—When I arose this morning, I began to look for something to meditate on, and that word came; Jer. xxxi. 3, "I have loved thee with an everlasting love; therefore with loving-kindness have I drawn thee." My soul grasped at it; I meditated on it with a heart somewhat elevated; yet I saw much unbelief in my heart, which was my burden. I thought I loved Christ; and then that word; 1 John iv. 19, "We love him, because he first

* This "Soliloquy" was published in 1773, being prefixed to a collection of the author's sermons, intitled, "The Distinguishing Characters of True Believers," &c.
† So the author modestly calls his "Soliloquy," though, since its publication, it has been universally admired, and considered as a masterpiece of the kind.

loved us," came. I saw love began on Christ's side; yet I could
not but with doubting assent to the conclusion, that God loved me.
I went to prayer, poured out my soul, lamenting over my unbelief,
which did then eminently appear and shew itself to me. I was
called thereafter to breakfast, but that word, Jer. xxxi. 3, stuck
with me, and yet does; it is sweet as the honey-comb. When I was
at prayer, I thought the Lord explained that word to me; "Therefore with loving-kindness have I drawn thee," that God's drawing
me to himself by the gospel in a loving way, was an evidence and
token of his everlasting love. While I meditated on my sermon,
that word, Psalm cii. 16, "When the Lord shall build up Zion, he shall
appear in his glory," came again to me, (for at this time it was much
on my heart). I thought on it. My soul was deeply affected under
the sense of Christ's withdrawing from ordinances, and my heart
groaned under the sense of his absence. My soul longed for the
day that the house should be built, and the rubbish taken away. It
sent me to prayer. I began to this purpose, Why hast thou forsaken thine own house? and it was presently suggested to me, that
Christ doth as a man that hath his house a-building; he comes now
and then and sees it, but does not stay, and will not come to dwell
in it till it be built up. My heart and soul cried vehemently to the
Lord for his return, and the grief of my heart often made my speech
to fail. I cried to the Lord as the great watchman, "What of the
night?" this sad night, when the sun goes down at noon-day? I was
once going to say, Lord, what need I preach? but I durst not bring
it out; so I was silent for a time. My soul desired, that either he
would come to me in ordinances, or take me to him in heaven, if it
were his will. When I arose from prayer, I could get nothing but still
that word; Psalm cii. 16. Lord, hasten the day then. When I
went to bed this night, that word came into my mind; "Whom
shall I send? Send me." I thought on going to the north, and was
content to go any way, north, south, or wherever. My heart began
to wander (I think, falling asleep); and I said in my heart the
words of a curse against myself used by rude ungodly people, "If,"
&c. They came like a flash of lightening, and immediately made
my very heart to leap for dread. This, I saw, was one of Satan's
fiery darts. To-morrow morning, being the Lord's day, I found my
heart dull; I endeavoured to apply that word; Hos. xiv. 5, "I will
be as dew unto Israel;" and was somewhat revived. But in prayer
thereafter he covered himself with a cloud. I cried, that if there
were any accursed stuff I knew not of, he would discover it to me;
and had a sad prospect of this day's work. I would have been content with a sick bed, rather than to be carried hence without his pre-

sence to the pulpit. Intending to read, I prayed for a word that might revive me; and reading in my ordinary; Matth. xvi., my heart moved and leapt, I thought within me, when I read ver. 8, "O ye of little faith, why reason ye among yourselves, because ye have brought no bread?" I took it to myself; I saw it was my unbelief, and that I behoved to depend on God, laying all the stress on him. Afterward I got that word, "When I sent you out, lacked ye any thing?" I poured out my soul when in the manse, and suffered the bell to toll long; and when I was going out and heard it tolling I thought it was now tolling for me to come to preach, maybe ere the next Sabbath it may toll for me to the grave. This was useful. The Lord was sweetly and powerfully with me through the day. After the lecture we sung part of Psalm li., the last line of it, at which I stood up, was, "With thy free sp'rit me stay;" I stood up with courage, for I thought the Spirit of God was my stay; and in the night when I awoke, I was still with God.

On the 23d, reading in secret, Matth. xix. and coming to ver. 29, "And every one that hath forsaken houses," &c. I found my heart could give no credit to it. I would fain have believed it, but really could not. I meditated a while on it, with ejaculations to the Lord, till in some measure I overcame. I then went to prayer, where the Lord gave me to see much of my own vileness, and particularly that evil and plague of my heart. I blessed the Lord for sealing ordinances, for then I saw the need of them to confirm faith.

On the 24th came to me one of the elders of Carnock, and shewed me a letter they had from the Countess of Kincardine, desiring them to go to the Presbytery of Stirling, to get me to preach two or three days with them; and if they and I should be both pleased, she would concur in a call, and Sir Patrick Murray would join with her. But by means, I think, of a sister of my friend's living in their neighbourhood, I had been strongly impressed with a very hard notion of that parish, as a self-conceited people, among whom I would have no success; and though I durst not forbid them to proceed, yet I told plainly, that I found my heart was not with them, thinking myself obliged, in justice to them, to declare the matter as it really was. Thus I stood in my own way with respect to that parish; but providence had designed far better for them, the worthy Mr. James Hog being thereafter settled there, where he continues to this day, [1730], faithfully declaring the gospel of God. And there fell to my lot, several years after, a people fully as conceited of themselves as those of Carnock could be.

On the 27th, I wanted to be determined what to preach, even after I had prayed to the Lord for his help; prayed again, and was nothing cleared; and so was much cast down. I thought of praying again; but, alas! thought I, what need I go to prayer? for I can get no light. I urged my soul to believe, and hope against hope; but I found I could not believe. Thus was my soul troubled. Sometimes I stood, sometimes sat, and sometimes walked; at length I went to my knees; and so I sat a while, but not speaking one word. At length I broke out with that, "How long, O Lord?"—and panting a while again, I cried to the Lord to shew me why he contended with me. Whereupon conscience spake plain language to me, and told me my fault of self-seeking in speaking to a man yesterday, and writing to my brother; for which I desired to humble myself before the Lord. In the issue I was determined what to preach. I had many ups and downs that day. This sermon was for Airth; and on the morrow, when I was going there, I observed how I was two several times kept back by storm of weather from that place, and how these two last times I have, in my studies for it, been plunged deeply; which made me wonder what might be the matter. But the storm was not yet over; for though the Saturday's night was a good time to my soul, and I think I will scarcely ever forget the relish the 21st chapter of John, especially that word, "Children, have ye any meat?" had on my soul being the ordinary in the family-exercise; yet to-morrow morning I was indisposed both in body and spirit. I thought I lay a-bed too long in the morning, and that gave me the first wound. The sweet word aforesaid I did reflect on; but now the sap was gone out of it, as to poor me. The public work was heavy. I had much ado to drive out the glass with the lecture; and so confounded and deserted was I, that I could not sing the psalm with my very voice. 1 could scarcely pray at all. I had neither light nor life in the first part of the sermon; the little light I had in it went away by degrees, as ever the light of the sun did by a cloud's coming over it, till I thought I should quite have given it over. At that juncture of time, a word was given me to speak, and the gross darkness was dispelled; and this continued till the end. In the afternoon I had some help from the Lord, which I had now learned to prize. As I was going to the afternoon's sermon, I thought the people in that place esteemed me too much, and took that as a part of the cause of this desertion. When I came out to my lodgings, one says to me, You need not shun to come to Airth, you are so well helped to preach there. When, said I, was I so helped? ANSW. In the forenoon, (for the speaker was not present in the afternoon.) The rest said, it was a satisfying day's work to the souls of many. This was astonishing. The same thing I heard of it, next day, from another godly woman. The causes of this deser-

tion I afterwards inquired into; and found, 1. There was something
of that former quarrel, because of self-seeking in the particular above
said; 2. My sleeping too long in the morning; 3. The people of Airth's
esteem of me, as noticed above, or to keep me humble; 4. That the
Lord might let me see, it is not by might nor by power, but by his
own Spirit, that souls are edified; 5. To learn me to be thankful for
a little.   Several years after this, meeting with the minister of Airth
at the assembly, he told me, that by conference with some of his
parish before the administration of the sacrament, he found several
persons there own me as the instrument that the Lord made use of
to do good to their souls.

There was at that time, for the encouragement of probationers
preaching in vacancies in that country, on the north side of Forth,
a legal allowance of 18 merks a-sabbath, as in the north; the which
fell to me in Clackmannan, and I suppose also in Dollar.   I had
been appointed to preach at Clackmannan on the 8th of January, but
was called to go to Airth that day, exchanging my post with another
probationer who could not go thither.   On that occasion I received
a compliment of two dollars at Airth, being the first money I got
in that country.

The affair of Dollar was now in agitation.   And coming up to the
Presbytery, February 1, I found an elder of that parish there, who,
it would seem, had been moving for their proceeding to a call, without having his commission in writing; which was appointed to be
seen to, in the case of any that should come to the next Presbytery
from thence.   In a private conference I had with him at his desire,
he shewed me, that Argyle, their superior, had signified his willingness to concur in a call to any whom the parish and Presbytery
should agree on, and that the call was designed for me; but withal,
that eight or ten of their parish had subscribed and sent to Argyle,
a paper, bearing their dislike of me; that one John Burn was
reckoned an enemy to my settlement there, yet would not sign it, in
regard, he said, I was a servant of God.   I learned afterwards, that
one of the subscribers wished he had quit a joint of his finger, or the
like, rather than he had subscribed that paper; as also, that Mr.
Forrester had given the foresaid elder but a very indifferent character of me, saying, that now they were going to call a new upstart,
one that broke the thetes.   This character from that good man was
affecting to me; considering that going under such a character, I
was so unholy, my corruption prevailed so much over me, and that I
was really weak in comparison of others, who took a more smooth
way than I durst take in my public performances; and so it convinced me of my need to live more near God.

Being to preach, Feburary 5, at Alloa, on Zech. xiii. *ult.*, I was somewhat shaken in my mind about my call to preach it; the doctrine thereon being almost only for exercised souls; but going to family duty, which the landlord performed, he sung Psalm cxi. by which, especially vers. 2, 4, I was cleared in this point, instructed, and comforted; and was also cleared somewhat by the chapter read. But that which did fully confirm me, was a word brought to me by the way, "When thou art converted, strengthen thy brethren." So that I was assured I was called to preach that doctrine there. That word foresaid was very applicable to my case; for on the Thursday before I had a very sharp exercise, and a sad struggle. The matter was this :—

Awakening a long time ere day-light, I found my dream had been sinful. At first I was rather amazed than truly affected with it, being overwhelmed with sleepiness. I thought to lie waking, and think on it sometimes, and sometimes I thought to pray in my bed; but while thus minded, the temptation I had while asleep, set on me when awake; and sleep prevailed so, that I had almost given myself up to it; and while I was thus slumbering, I said twice or thrice within myself, with a terror from God on my soul, What if I be damned before I awake? After this, my soul was under so great terror from the Lord, that my very heart began to fail; and I wanted not thoughts of expiring just there where I was. Yet I cast up ejaculations to the Lord, put on my clothes, and lighted a candle, groaning under the sense of guilt. While I walked up and down, that word, 1 John i. 7, "The blood of Jesus Christ cleanseth from all sin," came into my mind, and did somewhat fasten my sinking soul. I then went to prayer, confessed, and poured out my soul before him, and that with some confidence of mercy. Then I feared that confidence was not well got, and was afraid God would give me up to hardness of heart, which plague I feared as death, and cried that the Lord would not plague me with that, which was terrible as hell to my soul. I made use of that promise; Prov. xxviii. 13, "He that confesseth and forsaketh, shall find mercy," and gripped it as spoke by the God of truth. But my soul began again to sink and despond. I wrestled against it; cried to the Lord, that he would not be terrible to me, &c. till I got up again somewhat. When I arose from my knees, I walked up and down with ejaculations, striving to grip to that foresaid promise, and I thought it was faith whereby I did so. I made much use of that promise, thought it was God's word, and that God would not deny his own word. The causes of the Lord's leaving me I found to be, 1. My coldrife prayers the preceding night; 2. Some guilt the day before not yet mourned over, viz. a blasphemous thought that went through my soul at the blessing before the exercise. 3. I was even thinking last night while a-bed, what victory I had got over, that which so overtook me; so that it seems I was too secure. The effects of this tragedy were, that I saw my own vileness, and felt what it was to be near giving over hope; but thanks be to God that giveth me the victory through the Lord Jesus Christ. I love the Lord, my soul loves him for his wonderful mercy towards me, supporting me, hearing my prayers, and helping me to grip a promise. But how will I get through the world? Happy are they that are in heaven. I made much use, in that sad hour, of the covenant, namely, my engaging with him at Culross, Tulliallan, and under the tree in Kennet orchard. After this the language of my soul was, " My feet had almost slipt, but thy mercy held me up;" while I proposed the question again to my soul, How will I get through the world? and that word came; Cant. viii. 5, " I raised thee up under the apple-tree;" and that, Psalm xxii. 8, " He trusted in the Lord, that he would deliver him;" and I sang, Psalm lxxiii. 21, to the end, but with a weak body. That word was sweet to me, " Go thy way, thy faith hath made thee whole." Satan set again on me with the same; but I cried to the Lord, and he fled. When I went in to the morning-exercise, (which the landlord always performed), he gave out Psalm cxxxviii. 6, which was very confirming to my soul, especially ver. 8; it answered my question foresaid. He read 2 Cor. vii., whereby I was instructed, comforted, and edified, so as I saw a special hand of God in his reading that chapter, and singing that psalm. When I came away, these words were to me sweeter than honey. I could have put the Bible in my heart, and was helped to believe, &c.

On the 13th, arising from prayer in a dead frame, and having endeavoured to descend into myself, I thought I saw my heart like a clear pool. I thought I knew there were many things there to humble me, but I could not at all see them. At last I remembered my miscarriage this day, in not giving testimony against one profaning the name of Christ by a vain obsecration. Whereupon going to prayer, and reading the Lord's word, I recovered my frame. I remember, on this occasion, that being in company with Brea, a gentleman said to him, For God's sake do so and so; and he replied, Nay, I will do it for your sake. The day before I preached in Airth, and reflecting on the last time I was there, that word came, " He will not chide continually," &c., and was sweetly verified in my after experience.

On the 19th I preached at Dollar, where, on the Saturday's night, it was shewn me, that some there had little liking of me, because of my severe preaching; and James Kirk, an elder, told me of Paul's catching men with guile; signifying, that some of the heritors. when desired to subscribe a commission as aforesaid, said they would hear me again before they did it; and therefore he wished they might not be angered any more, for that the elders had enough ado with them already. I told him my resolution to speak what God should give me, without feud or favour; and could not but observe that special providence, which after this conference, ordered our singing at family worship the two last verses of Psalm xxvii., and our reading Matth. where, in this case, I was instructed, forewarned, and comforted. But thereafter I was baited with a temptation to fainting in the matter, and my courage damped. And here lay my snare, that being at this time in fear of a mission to the north, which I had a great aversion to, I was afraid the people of Dollar might be quite scared at my freedom in delivering the word, and so that mission might take place. This was a heavy exercise to me that night. I prayed, read, meditated, struggled, urged my heart with these scriptures; Matth. xx. 39; Prov. xxviii. 21; Acts. xvii. 26, hard put to it, but still in hope the Lord would not leave me to "transgress for a piece of bread." But as I was putting off my clothes for bed, my text I was to preach on came into my mind; John i. 11, "He came unto his own, and his own received him not." This enlivened my heart with zeal and courage to speak without sparing in his cause. But next morning the temptation was renewed; and I never had seen my own weakness in that point so much as I saw it then. Nevertheless I was still in hope, that God would not suffer me to yield, but would help to speak freely the word he should give me. After all this, as I was going down to the kirk, John Blackwood, another good man, and an elder, put me in mind, to be sure to hold off from reflections as far as I could; for the which I reprimanded him. In the issue the Lord gave me freedom to preach his word, whatever was to become of me; and my soul found cause to bless the Lord, that that temptation, had not prevailed to render me unfaithful in his work.

That Sabbath-night I catched cold in my head while I sat at family worship, by an open window, which I apprehend I had not observed. It issued in a suppuration in my left ear, and was for many days a grievous trouble to me. On the Saturday's night after my pain being very violent, I had a weary night of it; but being to preach in Clackmannan, I ventured in the morning to cause ring the bell, the pain being somewhat assuaged, and finding it would be a grievous affliction to me to have a silent Sabbath, the Lord's word being the joy and rejoicing of my heart. In the issue I felt no pain in preaching, but was strengthened both in body and spirit for my work. But I had a weary night of it again.

On the 22d those of the parish of Dollar craved of the Presbytery a minister to moderate in a call; but they delayed it till their next meeting at Alloa, March 1. That day they delayed it again, till they should get an answer of a letter they were to write to Argyle; and Mr. White told me, there was some mention of another young man whom that noble person minded for Dollar. On the 15th, as I was going to the Presbytery, Mr. Turnbull told me, that Argyle had returned an answer to their letter, and therein told them of the young man he designed for the parish, but took no notice of me. By the Presbytery's minutes that day, I understood their letter had been to take off some misrepresentations made of me to him.

The meeting of the commission of the General Assembly was now near; and Argyle's letter aforesaid trysting therewith, seemed to be a providential inclosing of me for the north; which occasioned me great heaviness. On the morrow the Lord comforted me, by giving me light into that word, "That stone is made head corner-stone which builders did despise;" thinking, that if Christ was despised by the builders, no wonder I should be so too; and that however I was despised by them, God might do great things for me, and by me. At this time the trouble in my ear was but going off, so that it kept me near a month. I wonder that I do not find that I took it for a rebuke of my listening so far to that temptation to fainting aforementioned.

March 20.—Being on my way to Edinburgh to the commission, I was by storm stopped at the North-Ferry that night. Then and there were two words brought to me; the one, Zech. iv. 6, "Not by might, nor by power," &c.; the other, Dan. i. 15, "At the end of ten days, their countenances appeared fairer, and fatter in flesh, than all the children which did eat the portion of the king's meat." This also was made sweet and strengthening to my soul; and I enjoyed a great calm and serenity of mind, which, by the mercy of God, lasted all along with me, till on the 23d I was freed from the mission to the north, which for a long time before had occasioned me much perplexity. I had resolved to attend the Presbytery, to get them to speak for me to the commission; but was hindered by the boil in my ear; and minding to make up that with a letter to one of the Presbytery, it was miscarried; and this was the reason of my going to the commission. As I was blessing the Lord with my soul for the serenity arising from the consideration of the aforesaid scriptures, Satan set on me with a fulsome temptation, as if God had dealt so with me for my preaching so yesterday. I presently no-

ticed it, prayed, and protested against it, and disowned it; and took
a look of my black feet, particularly as they appeared that day.
The main stress of the business, as to the mission, was at a committee, where I had no acquaintance but one, who was none of my
best friends. Having been advised before to cut out my hair, for
my health, at that time I got a wig; and thereafter wore one all
along; till after my coming to Ettrick, finding it troublesome when
going abroad, I laid it aside, and betook me again to my own hair;
which to this day I wear.

Upon my return to the Ferrytown, considering that Dollar, the
only place in that country where I could have desired to settle,
was now blocked up; I was in a strait how to dispose of myself
next, knowing of nothing, but to go to Nithsdale, which I had no
great inclination to. In that case was useful to me that word, which
used to come slipping in, as it were, into my mind; Psalm lxxi. 20,
"Thou, Lord, who great adversities, and sore, to me didst show,
Shalt quicken, and bring me again, from depths of earth below;"
and on the 31st, together with it, that text; 2 Cor. iv. 8, "Perplexed, but not in despair;" and Psalm lv. 22, "Cast thy burden
on the Lord, and he will sustain thee."

Robert Kemp, a noted professor of the stricter side, in the parish
of Airth, had, on March 10, asked me, if a certain elder had spoke
to me about their calling me to be their minister; the which I having answered in the negative, he told me there was such a motion;
and that if the elders would not move in it, they would present a
supplication to the Presbytery for that effect. But having, on
April 16, preached the last sermon I had there, on the morrow after,
that elder, William Colvan in Powside, did signify their design to
call me. I told him very seriously, that such an attempt would be
needless; the thoughts of it were indeed terrible to me, being very
sensible of my unfitness for such a post. But there was no probability of that project's taking effect, my friends being, part of
them, not acceptable to the Presbytery; and a certain person of
eminence there, upon hearing sometime that I was to preach there,
had cursed me; at the report whereof coming to me, I thought upon
and saw the use of, that word; Matth. v. 11, "Blessed are ye, when
men shall revile you," &c. That Sabbath at Airth, I found, 1. That
in the morning, especially in prayer before I went to the kirk, I was
tempted to think I had been rash in a certain business, not yet accomplished. I slighted the temptation, knowing it to be a device of
Satan to mar me of what I was about. I thought it no time then to
consider, whether it was really so or not, it being a thing that could
not be quickly cleared. 2. That in the forenoon I had light, but

little life; in the afternoon I had both, and some things useful and seasonable were laid to my hand. 3. That I was helped betwixt sermons and in the afternoon, to live by faith; and I had a serenity of mind, and contentment of heart, flowing from dependence on the Lord.

Being resolved to part with the Presbytery of Stirling in a little time, I had also got over the perplexity by the strait aforesaid, how to dispose of myself next, resigning the matter freely to the Lord; till on April 20, it began to recur. I considered then the two words given me at the North Ferry, viz. Zech. iv. 6, and Dan. i. 11, that the former was accomplished already, in the manner of my deliverance from the northern mission, and hoping the latter would be accomplished too in its time. And that very day, in the afternoon, I received a letter from my father, desiring me, on the account of private affairs, to come home. Hereby the Lord himself did seasonably mark out to me my way, in the which he hath by this time fulfilled that word also unto me.

About this time began a second alteration in the strain of my preaching, which by degrees, though with much difficulty in the way thereof, ripened into a more clear uptaking of the doctrine of the gospel; which by the mercy of God I arrived at, after my settlement in Simprin. Having been at Barhill on the 11th, I heard at Culross a week-day's sermon, on the excellency of Christ, from Phil. iii. 8, by Mr. Mair; and thereafter was entertained by him with edifying discourse suitable thereto. Upon the back of this, I sometimes thought I had preached but too little of Christ, which I would have been content to have reformed. On the 18th I went to God, and begged an answer of some suits I had had long depending before the throne of grace; which were especially two. The one was, That I might see Christ by a spiritual illumination, with more fulness of the evidence requisite to believing on him, according to that word; John vi. 40, "That every one which seeth the Son, and believeth on him;" to a particular notice of which passage, I had sometime or other, been led by Mr. Mair's means also. The other was, that I might be helped to live, by faith, above the world. On the morrow after, as I arose, I thought on these words; Psalm cv. 13—15; and the view of the Lord's concern about his people, in all their removes, was sweet. After which, going to prayer, the Lord was with me in it. My soul went out in love to Christ, followed hard after him, and I saw much content, delight, and sweet in him. The issue hereof was, that I found myself somewhat helped to believe; the which, though it carried me not so far above the world as I would fain have been, yet it rendered the world in some sort contemptible in mine eyes; and I found my heart desirous to preach Christ's fulness, his being " all, and in all."

This issued in my being determined, on the 21st, to that text; Matth. xiii. 45, 46, unto which I addressed myself, after bemoaning, before the Lord, my ignorance of Christ, and begging the revealing of him to me; being convinced I was but a child in that matter, yet seeing it my duty to preach him. Having entered upon it, I saw it a very full text; but going on in it, I found myself dry and barren upon it; which left me much dejected, seeing I could not preach Christ, and beholding much of my ignorance of him. On the morrow I got more light, ease, and insight into the excellency of Christ, from the Lord. And reading in my ordinary thereafter, I fell on that Col. iv. 3, 4, which afforded me this instruction, That whereas I had been discouraged, for that I could not preach Christ: I saw it indeed a mystery; and such a one as the great apostle found a need of the prayers of the saints, that he might be enabled to preach it. I saw the preaching of Christ to be the most difficult thing; for that though the whole world is full of wonders, yet here are depths beyond all. I was to preach in Clackmannan, where most were for for me to be their minister, and some that had the greatest power were against me, as it ordinarily fared with me in the places where I used to preach. On the Saturday's afternoon there comes a letter to my hand, desiring me to give the one half of the day to one Mr. J. G., whom those that were against me had an eye upon. The letter I received contentedly, granted the desire of it, and blessed the Lord for it. In these circumstances, seeing what hazard I was in of an evil eye, I committed my heart to the Lord, that I might be helped to carry evenly. I cried to the Lord for it; and got that word, " My grace shall be sufficient for thee." Sabbath morning I found in myself a great desire to love Christ, and to be concerned solely for his glory; and prayed to that effect, not without some success. He got the forenoon, for so it was desired by them. I was helped to join in prayer, was much edified both by his lecture and sermon, and I sung with a sweet frame after sermon; yet in the time I was thrice assaulted with the temptation I feared; but looking up to the Lord, got it repulsed in some measure; and found my soul desirous that people should get good, soul-good, of what was very seriously, pathetically, and judiciously said to us by the godly young man. Betwixt sermons I got a sight of my own emptiness, and then prayed and preached in the afternoon with very much help from the Lord. Yet, for all that, I wanted not some levity of spirit; which poison my heart sucked out of that sweet flower. When I came home, my heart was in a manner enraged against my heart on

this account, and I confessed it before the Lord, abhorring myself,
appealing to God's omniscience, that I would fain have had it otherwise, and would have been heartily content to have sold my own
credit in the matter for the glory of Christ. As I was complaining
that Satan had winnowed me, and brought forth much filthy stuff
out of my heart, notwithstanding all my prayers, &c. it came into
my mind, how Christ said to Peter, "Simon, Satan hath desired to
have thee, that he may sift you as wheat; but I have prayed for
thee, that thy faith fail not;" and yet Peter denied him, even with
oaths, on a very silly temptation. This was comfortable. There
were four things suggested to me in the morning, as antidotes
againt the temptation; whereof this was one, That I was conscious
to myself of my being unwilling to engage with such a post, in regard of my unfitness for it, though they were all willing. In the
evening, while I sat musing on what I had been preaching, viz. That
the soul that has got a true discovery of Christ will be satisfied
with him alone, I proposed the question to myself, Art thou content
with Christ alone? wouldst thou be satisfied with Christ as thy portion,
though there were no hell to be saved from? and my soul answered,
Yes. I asked myself further, Supposing that, wouldst thou be content with him, though likewise thou shouldst lose credit and reputation, and meet with trouble for his sake? My soul answered, Yes.
Such is my hatred of sin, and my love to Christ. This was the last
sermon I preached in that place, for I was going out of that country;
and neither of us two was the person God designed for the place.

On the 30th I preached at Dollar. The work being closed, thinking with myself, while yet in the pulpit, that might be the last of
my preaching there, as it indeed proved to be, with my eyes lifted
up towards heaven, I looked unto the Lord, comforting myself, that
I had declared to that people the whose counsel of God, as he had
given it me; the which was sweeter to me than their stipend would
have been, got by following some advices given me as above mentioned. I lodged in the house of Simon Drysdale, who regretted the
Presbytery's untenderness in their case; and on the morrow came to
me James Kirk, with other three of the elders, who shewed their concern in the account of my departure, and withal their continued resolution to prosecute the design of my settlement among them, still
regretting the Presbytery's slipping the occasion that was in their
hands, and shewing that their two neighbouring ministers, on the
west and east, were and had been their enemies in the design. The
same week Mr. Turnbull told me, that the Presbytery might, and,
if they would take his advice, should go on, withal complaining
somewhat of them in the matter; so that by him, as well as the

people, the blame of the marring of the settlement, so far, was laid at their door. Perhaps the trouble they had by Mr. Mair, in Airth, on the strict side, made them the more wary as to me, though I never entertained separating principles.

I had the comfort of the testimony of judicious Christians, that my work in that country, and particularly in that parish, was not in vain in the Lord; and found from several persons, that the Lord had made the word in my mouth to reach their own case, and to be a discerner of the thoughts of their hearts. The same which, it seems, fell out in the case of some others, who knew not so well how the word was directed; whereof a judicious Christian gave me this instance, namely, that discoursing with a certain man in Dollar, whom he knew to be of a violent disposition against Presbyterian preachers, and expected accordingly to find ruffled by the sermons on the fast-day; he, on the contrary, found him to shew a liking of me, especially by reason of these sermons, for that they had let him see things to be sin which he never thought before had been so. Moreover, he said, I had great skill, and told things strangely, even some things which he thought no body knew, and that he wondered who could tell me; and that if William (his son I suppose) had been any way abroad, he would have thought he had told me. His wife signified, that some of the parish said, I had more wit than my own. These things were encouraging to me, as they discovered the character of the Lord's word in my preaching, namely, that it is " a discerner of the thoughts and intents of the heart."

May 3.—The Presbytery granted me testimonials, I promising to satisfy them if they should write for me, probable grounds of encouragement appearing; and they appointed a minister to preach at Dollar on the Sabbath was twenty days, and, on the Tuesday following, to moderate in a call there. On the 8th I took my journey, having had an affecting parting with several Christian friends; and some truly it was no small part of my grief, if not the greatest to leave serious souls, whom God had made me an instrument of good to, and to whose prayers I doubt not but I was obliged. I came that day to Barhill, where, upon some event or other I cannot now find, I thought I saw an end of all perfection, and that nothing was satisfying without Christ. I think it has been, that having my friend to part with, added to the weight on me in leaving that country. However it was, the impression lasted with me many days thereafter. On the morrow I went to Edinburgh, and the day following got home to Dunse; which, when I saw it, was terrible unto me, my inclination not being towards that country; but thither the Lord led me unto the bounds of my habitation before appointed.

VOL. XI.   E

PERIOD VI.

BEING thus returned home again, I had no occasion to go out of the town above a mile, until four Sabbaths were past; and during that time, in the end of May and beginning of June, the thoughts of my uselessness were very heavy to me; which put me to beg of God an opportunity to serve him, whatever pains it should cost me to accomplish it. Howbeit I was not altogether idle on Lord's days, being employed mostly in Dunse, and once in Langton.

While this lay upon me as the main weight, I found myself beset with several other difficulties. The unacquaintedness of most of my friends with religion was grievous, and made their conversation but uncomfortable; but my eldest brother Andrew, being a judicious man, and of experience in religion, was often refreshful to me. I had no heart to visit the ministers, knowing none of them I could unbosom myself to, save Mr. Colden at Dunse, and Mr. Dysert at Coldingham. The binding at my breast had returned, and I was seized with pains in my back, and in the hinder part of my head, so that I began to apprehend my time in the world might not be long; and on that occasion I found I had some evidences for the better world, and was somewhat submissive to the divine disposal, in the case as it appeared. Withal the consideration of the case of the land was heavy on me, and I had a sorry prospect of what might be to come, so that I judged them happy, who, having done their work in the vineyard, were called home, and not made to see the dishonour done to God amongst us. Wherefore I was desirous to be out of my native country again, and wished for a providential relief. But by a letter from a friend, shewing that the business of Dollar was like to succeed, I found that I behoved to continue yet a while where I was on the account thereof.

It now lay heavy on my spirit at several times, as above noticed, that I was cast out of a corner, in which the Lord was pleased to make use of me, and own me with some success in his work, into another corner where I had nothing to do. This occasioned variety of perplexing thoughts. I inquired what might be the Lord's end in it, and nothing doubted but that I was called to leave that place, from whence I came. May 25, in prayer it was suggested to me, that God had so dealt with me, for my former levity, and misimproving his help given me in preaching; for which I endeavoured to be humble. On the 26th, I had engaged to lecture next Sabbath for

Mr. Colden. Finding my heart disposed for prayer, light from the Lord in two or three particulars was much in my eye. In prayer I had a frame from the Lord, serious, earnest, depending, bare, and laid open to hearken to the counsel of God. Before I came to pray for what I should lecture on, my heart was raised to an admiration of, and love to Christ, and desire to commend him; and it was laid before me as my duty to lecture on Psalm xlv. and this with life and elevation of my spirit, which continued with me when I prayed for the lecture. Thinking on this after prayer, I began to suspect that light; because it came before I had prayed for it, expressly at least. But considering that I went to God for light in it, and considering that passage, Isa. lxv. 24, and finding my inclination to commend Christ remain, I was satisfied. There was a second point in my eye, which still remained dark; and therefore I went back purposely to God for it. I found my heart in prayer much going out in love to Christ; my heart was knit to him as the dearly beloved of my soul; which made me to express my love to Christ, not in an ordinary way, as I used to do. I was helped to depend, and got strength to my heart to wait for light in it. And the nature of it was such, that it might bear a delay. As for the third point, it was not ripe, and I could but table it before the Lord. The Lord was not wanting to me in the delivery of that lecture.

In the meantime, my settling in Simprin had been first moved to me on May 19, in Mr. Colden's house, by his wife, in his presence; and that, till another occasion should offer. He seemed to me not to have confidence directly to propose it; but told me, the stipend was five chalders of victual, and 80 merks. But as I never durst entertain the thoughts of settling with such a design, I shewed that I had no mind to engage with any but such as I might continue with. Thinking afterwards on these things by myself, I found no great unwillingness to venture on the stipend; the rather, that my father having disponed his interest in Dunse to me, I reckoned I would have about £100 Scots yearly there; but the people being only about ninety in number, and in a quite other situation than the parish of Abbay, I found I could have no heart to them. On the 26th again, Mr. Colden proposed to me, that if I would settle there, he would write for that effect to Langton, to whom the parish entirely belonged. I told him, that for me to say so, would be to cut off all future deliberation, which was what I had no freedom to do; the which he acknowledged to be true, and therefore urged me not. That worthy man was indeed concerned for me, and told me, he was persuaded God had thoughts of good towards me; and that, notwithstanding all the difficulties that had cast up in the way of my settle-

ment, the event would be to the glory of God, and comfortable to
myself. And therein he was not mistaken. In this his concern
for me, he took me to Coldingham, June 8, to see Mr. Dysart, who
formerly had been minister of Langton. There they concerted to
move for that settlement; and in consequence thereof Mr. Dysert
wrote to the elders to Simprin, to that effect. And judging the matter might easily be compassed, they told me that I might be settled
in Simprin, if I would. But having heard them speak of the vacancies in Galloway, and that I was particularly desired by some
there, I thereupon found an inclination to go to that country, if I
should not be called back for Dollar. The letter to the elders of
Simprin, as aforesaid, was unadvisedly put in my hand to dispatch;
which I, not having confidence, it seems, to refuse it, did receive;
but it was never delivered, for afterwards I tore it in pieces. And
this their conduct could hardly have had a different issue, according to the principles by which I steered my course, that justly made
all activity in procuring my own settlement frightful to me.

The bent of my heart to preach Christ continued all along, from
the time above mentioned, as I had opportunity; but for a considerable time I met with many rubs in my way. On the 2d of June,
after prayer for a text, and help to study, I could fix on none,
though I sought it till my body was weary, and my spirit much dejected. Next morning my darkness remained, and nothing could
gain clearness to me. Thus my heart being dejected through desertion, I went to prayer again; but my very heart and flesh were like
to faint. Such was the grief of my heart, that I could not speak a
word to God, after I had begun, but groaned to the Lord; I got
words again, but was interrupted the same way, not being able to
speak. I saw the misimprovement of former help still to be the
cause of the Lord's pleading with me; but having so often confessed
it, being grieved for it, &c. I thought there behoved to be something
else; and some other thing I suspected, but could not fix on it. I
thought I was most unworthy to be a preacher, and that it would be
well done to silence me, as ignorant of the mystery of Christ; for,
from the beginning of this exercise, it was always in my heart to
preach Christ, and denying of ourselves to all things but Christ; and
though it succeeded ill with me, I durst not change my purpose. My
soul being somewhat encouraged by that word, Matth. xi. 28, "Come
unto me, all ye that labour," &c., I was helped to believe in some
measure, and conversed with God in prayer, and that word was
brought to my mind for a text; Psalm lxxiii. 25, "Whom have I in
heaven but thee?" &c. I had much difficulty in my studies on it.
The word read in the ordinary at evening-exercise, came pat to my

case with a check; Heb. xii. 5, "My son, despise not thou the chastening of the Lord," &c. My dejected frame of spirit often recurred, and was with me on the Lord's day morning, June 4; at which time, in prayer, the Lord put in his hand at the hole of the lock, and my bowels moved for him; my heart was touched, and in a mournful mood I cried to him. Some time after I found I could not believe; and how shall I preach? thought I; yet I thought I would venture, and lean on Christ; and this I thought was faith, notwithstanding my former denial. In the forenoon, I thought my heart was very unwieldy. In the afternoon I had several ups and downs in the very time of the work. My soul bear me witness, that I was not satisfied with ordinances without Christ. And after all was over, in my retirement, I was clear, in that, though I many times fear I have never yet got a sufficient discovery of Christ, yet whatever discovery I have had of him, I was satisfied to take Christ alone, and that I could not be satisfied without him, though I had the whole world, yea heaven itself. The Lord gave me such a sight of my own vileness, that when I looked to myself in that pulpit, I loathed myself, as unworthy to have been there with such a whole heart, and without right uptakings of Christ. I examined myself on my desire of Christ, saying, What if it be merely from an enlightened conscience? but my soul said, it would desire him, though there were no fear of wrath; and though (per impossibile) I had a dispensation for my most beloved lusts, I would not desire to make use of it. I thought I loved him for himself. I preached this day in Langton; and after the evening exercise Mr. Dysert said to me, You would have done better to have gone to the west, beside Mr. Murray, for there you would have got a kirk. My proud heart took this ill, and I had a secret dissatisfaction with my own lot, in that I was not settled. Reflecting upon this in secret, I observed, how in three things, since I came to this country, Satan has overcome me, even in those things that I preached against. 1. Preaching at Dunse, I preached against immoderate sleep as a great waster of time; and quickly after I fell in to this. 2. Last Thursday I preached, that unwatchfulness was the cause why it is not with God's people as in times past; and the very same night my heart fell a-roving. 3. At this evening exercise I lectured on Heb. xiii. and particularly that word, "Be content with such things as ye have;" and immediately after this, dissatisfaction seized me, for which my heart abhors my heart. Wherefore being convinced of my danger, I resolved, in the Lord's strength, from henceforth to make my sermons the subject of my Sabbath-night's meditation, and so to improve them for myself. The sermon I found was not lost as to some others.

I was also extremely hard put to it the week following, after my return from Coldingham, insomuch as having attempted to study Cant. i. 3, I was obliged to give it over, and fall on Luke xiii. 24. By this means, preaching became, in a sort, a terror to me; so that on the 14th I quite declined preaching the week-day's sermon for Mr. Colden. The reason of which being asked by Mr. Balfour above mentioned, as he and I were walking alone by the way; I freely told him, that preaching was become another kind of task to me, than sometime it had been; that I was discouraged, through the straitening I found as to the preaching of Christ, arguing my ignorance of Christ; the which ignorance of Christ, in the very time I was speaking this, was most grievous to my soul; to that degree, that my very body was affected, and my legs began to tremble beneath me. He said, it was an eager temptation, to drive me off from preaching Christ. Parting with him, I came home very sorrowful, yet looking upward, seeing the emptiness of all things besides Christ, or without him. The Lord was pleased to lay bands on my unstable heart, till I got my ease shewed before him; and he let me see my need of Christ, and I began to apply the word, Matth. v. 3, "Blessed are the poor in spirit." The Lord shewed me the vanity of health, wealth, &c., and made my soul prefer Christ to them all; and indeed I contemned all things in comparison of him, yea even heaven itself. I sung with my heart, Psalm xl. 11, and downwards, and in prayer pleaded the promise with some confidence; being resolute for Christ, and that no other thing should ever satisfy me. On the morrow, the Lord helped me to apply the promise; Isa. lvii. 15, cited by Mr. Colden in his sermon; the very reading of the words, "to revive the heart of the humble," was reviving to my soul, which saw its own emptiness. That straitening aforesaid sometime seemed to me to say, that for all the motion made for my settlement in my native country, I behoved not to think of settling in it, where I was thus hardly bestead as to the preaching of the word. But the issue of this exercise was, that I was made less concerned, how I might be disposed of as to my settlement; not caring what place I should go to, so that I got Christ; and my soul said to him, "Set me as a seal on thine heart, as a seal on thine arm!" On the 18th, preaching at Berwick, my subject was, a discovery of Christ made to the soul; and in the study of it I was not straitened; but in the delivery of it I was so deserted; that in my retirement after, I had most heavy thoughts of my unworthiness, and unfitness for the great work of preaching Christ. In like manner, after the communion at Coldingham, where I preached on Saturday, and Sabbath afternoon without; I was pressed with a sense of my insufficiency for that work, that heaven was very desirable to me; withal I was but little edified with one of the sermons I heard on the Monday, there appearing too little of Christ in it.

Thus it pleased the Lord to humble me to the dust, and to empty me of myself, with respect to the great mystery of Christ; and to give my heart a particular set and cast towards it, which hath continued with me to this day; and shall, I hope, to the end, that I get within the vail.

I had on the 15th received a letter, shewing, that, on the day appointed, the votes had been gathered at Dollar; and that, about three of the malignant party and three of the elders being excepted, they were all with one voice for me to be their minister; but that, notwithstanding, the Presbytery had still some dependence on Argyle in the matter. This account of the state of that affair, as being yet undetermined, was straitening to me; inasmuch as it obliged me to continue a while longer in the Merse, which I could not well do.

June 22.—Having been for some time in great deadness, this morning I had a kind of impulse to pray, with a willingness in my soul to go to duty; and having found by several sad experiences the danger of delays, with all speed I embraced the motion; and the Lord revived me, in so far that my heart and flesh longed for the living God, and cried out for him as tho dry parched ground for rain. The Lord loosed my bands; and though I studied the sermon I preached this day, being the weekly sermon at Dunse, in very bad case; yet he was with me in preaching it, and the Spirit did blow on my soul, both in public and in secret thereafter; so that my heart loves Christ.

On the morrow my frame lasted; and being to go to the sacrament at Coldingham, I saw my hazard from my malicious enemy, that he would be fair to assault me before such an occasion. I thought I endeavoured to commit my heart to the Lord. But, alas! that which I feared came upon me; which brought me to a sad pass; my confidence in prayer was marred; my guilt stuck close to me, and cost me much struggling by the way as I went to Coldingham, so that I will not forget the pitiful case I was in while going through the whinny moor. I made use of and endeavoured to apply that word, "I, even I am he that blotteth out thy transgressions" &c. which did some what stay my soul. I went halting all the day; but at evening exercise, to which I went with a deep sense of my unworthiness, the Lord loosed all my bands. But another sharp trial followed, a great fear that Satan might as before give me another bruise. I went to God with it, prayed for a word of promise to grip to for security; and when I arose from my knees, that word, Isa. xxvi. 3, " Thou wilt keep him in perfect peace," &c., came to me with some life and support to my soul, and was afterwards sweetly made out to me.

July 2.—Preaching in a certain place, after supper the mistress of the house told me, that I had put not only those that never knew any thing of God in the mist, but even terrified such as had known him. This was by my doctrine of coming out of self-love, self-righteousness, self-ends, privileges, duties, &c. She restrained hypocrites to that sort that do all things to be seen of men; thought it strange for people to think of meriting any thing at the hand of God, or that hypocrites would crush inward evil thoughts; and harped much on that, How can it be that one can be a hypocrite, and yet hate hypocrisy in others; that one could be a hypocrite, and not know himself to be a hypocrite? I have been preaching much this long time to drive people out of themselves to Christ, and this let me see the need of such doctrine.

In the beginning of that month, no word being come from the Presbytery of Stirling, I had laid my plot to remove; and first to go to that country upon business, and then to Galloway. Meanwhile the Presbytery, whe met at Churnside on the 4th, had desired me to preach at Simprin the following Lord's day; to which I consented, being to continue in the country till the Sabbath was over, and no where else engaged.

July 6.—Yesterday and this morning there was in my heart a great averseness to duty. I heard Mr. Colden's weekly sermon, and got several checks and rebukes from it. The psalm we sung held my sin before my eyes. After dinner I began seriously to reflect on my case. I dragged myself to prayer, but it was a strange exercise to me. Many sad halts I made in it. I saw my dreadful departings from the Lord, so that I durst scarcely seek any thing of God, and not but with great difficulty seek a crumb of mercy, or that the Lord would take away this averseness from duty. I remember I was going to seek one drop of Christ's blood for my miserable soul, but with horror of mind, and a shivering of my very body, I durst not ask it. I thought I would have been content to have been revenged on myself, and to have put a penknife into my heart. I laid myself down before the Lord, desiring him to do with me what he pleased, though it were to make me a monument of his indignation. Afterwards I sat and walked like one out of his wits, took up the Bible to read, and that word at the first met me; Jer. viii. 9, " The wise men are ashamed," &c. This put me to a sad pass. I turned to my ordinary; but there was no help. Afterwards I was saying within myself, O what will the Lord do with me? and that word came into my mind; Isa. xlix. 16, "Behold, I have graven thee upon the palms of my hands," &c. I frequently rejected it, yet it still returned; at last, thought I, dare I believe it? and by this time I had more up-takings of mercy, went to prayer, and was somewhat helped to believe.

On the 8th, considering the perplexing circumstances I was in, and finding my heart brought to a better temper with respect to them than some time before, I began at night seriously to deliberate how I might carry under them as a Christian; which was continued next morning, being Friday. There were three things I saw weighty in the complication: 1. The broken state of my health; 2. My being in terms of marriage; 3. No probability of my settlement. To carry Christianity in these perplexing circumstances, I proposed to myself, that I should, 1. Live near God, so as my heart should not have wherewith to reproach me, Job xxvii. 6; Acts xxiii. 1; 2. Beware of anxious thoughts about them; lay them before the Lord in prayer, and leave them on him, trusting him with him, though in a manner blindly, Phil. iv. 6; 3. Believe the promise, that all things should work together for my good, Rom. viii. 28; 4. Remember man's extremity is God's opportunity, with my former experiences of the same, Gen. xxii. 14; 5. Use of the means with dependence on the Lord for success; 6. Be diligent about the work of my station, and ply my studies more closely; and for this end, beware of sleeping too much; Lastly, Not think that, because God doth not presently answer, therefore he will not answer at all, but wait on him; Isa. xxviii. 16; and that if at any time I begin to faint under my difficulties, I should press myself to hang by the promises, remembering the shortness of my time, and that no man knows love or hatred by all that is before him; and should read Heb. xii. And my conscience bare me witness, that to be helped so to live in a course of filial obedience, would be more sweet to me, than to be rid of all these difficulties. These measures thus laid down, I thereafter went to prayer, especially for direction unto a text for Simprin, and help in my studies; and the Lord dealt well with me. I had light and life in prayer, and a contented mind after: and it was but a little ere I fell on that text; John vi. 68, "Lord, to whom shall we go?" &c., being still resolved to preach Christ; and I had very satisfying and sweet thoughts on it in the general; but having put off beginning my study of it till I should consult the commentary, which I had not by me, I read on in my ordinary, with much edification, especially Deut. viii. and the 2d, 3d, 5th, and 16th verses thereof, particularly, were sweet and seasonable to my soul. These things were dispatched before breakfast in the Friday morning.

And here, I think, was the full sea-mark of my perplexing circumstances aforesaid ; at which they did immediately begin to go back, and providence began to open toward my relief, though as yet I perceived it not. But my God had carried them forward to an extremity, and caused them to appear in their full weight, and had moulded my heart into a calm, contented, and depending frame. And meditating on that, How I should know whether this keeping of my heart under my difficulties was Christian or merely rational, I thought I knew it to be Christian, 1. In that in some measure it was from a sense of the command of God; 2. By means of the promises; 3. I desired it for God's glory, as well as my own good. That word, James i. 4, was brought to me, with a commentary on it, q. d. Wait patiently, and that constantly, till God's time come for deliverance, without which patience is but imperfect. This was occasioned by a petition I had put up in my giving of thanks after breakfast.

Towards the evening of that same day, I understood by a letter, that the business of Dollar was still in agitation; and that they desired me not to dispose of myself otherwise, seeing they were like to succeed in their attempts for my settlement among them; as also, that Mr. William Reid, minister of Dunning, in Strathearn, desired that I should come and stay a while with him, He was a worthy man, one of the old sufferers in the persecution; and had a heavy task in that parish. In the time of the rebelion, several years after this, he was lying a-dying, when the news came in the morning, that that town was to be burnt by the rebels. His afflicted wife being greatly moved, on the account of him, who could not be carried off, while every moment the rebels were expected to execute the fatal design; he comforted her, and bid her be easy, for that they should not have power to hurt a hair of her body. Accordingly his master called him home; he expired, and was in the grave too, before the town was set on fire; being buried in haste, while he was yet almost warm, the melancholy circumstances of the place so requiring. This account his widow gave my wife. Before I came south, he had invited me to the Presbytery, on a design for Auchterarder, then vacant; but I could not then answer the invitation. This being now providentially laid before me, I went to God for direction in it, being laid open to his determination, and helped to trust him for light. Thereafter considering of it, there was one scruple in the way of that motion that I could not get over, viz. that it might be constructed a-going to seek and hang on the parish of Dollar.

And on the morrow, before I went off to Simprin, I received a letter from Mr. Robert Stark, minister at Stenton, in East Lothian, proposing to me to go to the north for the Presbytery of Dunbar, and inviting me to the communion in his parish, on the Sabbath was fourteen days after ; and Mr. Colden invited me to preach at Dunse the Sabbath preceding that, though in the event I preached that day at Eccles. This conduct of providence laying work to my hand in the country, considered with my other circumstances, was a plain stop to my design of removing at the time I had determined, and was determining me to stay at least for that time. But for several obvious reasons, I hearkened not to the proposal relative to going to the north.

After some necessary business dispatched, I prayed with confidence for what I asked; and having made myself ready, and devoted myself to the Lord, I went towards Simprin, my heart being heavenly, and tending upward, by the way. I find I have, in the memoirs of that day, called the religious action used before I went away, by the name of *devoting* myself to the Lord; and though I have now no distinct remembrance of the thing, yet I judge, that, had it been no more but committing myself to him as usually, I would not have so expressed it; and that it has indeed been such an action, as the word bears, an action very suitable to the way the Lord was leading me, however unknown to me. That night, being at Simprin, I found once a desire to be very remote, and in an inconsiderable post, and even a kind of content to be posted there; and this, I think, was an effect of my looking on the vanity of the world; but that lasted not. The day before, ere I entered on the study of my text, I had a temptation, not to enter on that great text in such a mean place as Simprin, but to reserve it for some other place; but repelled it as a temptation indeed. I was obliged to enter on the study of it, without seeing any commentary upon it; afterward I saw two; but both were unsatisfying, and mainly served to confirm me in the great purpose thereof. The Lord was gracious to me in the address I made to him, with respect to my study; and I had advantage to my own soul, by getting a view of the emptiness of all things besides Christ, and thereby seeing him more precious. On the Sabbath morning I had a desire after Christ, and his presence in ordinances; but was somewhat discouraged with the prospect of a small congregation. In the forenoon I was solidly in earnest in my discourse, but without the least moving of affections as at other times; but the unbeseeming carriage of the people, few as they were, partly by going out, was very discouraging. I had never preached there before; and after the forenoon sermon, I thought I could not like to preach to so few; but in the afternoon, the Spirit blowing

somewhat on me, I had forgot almost whether they were many or
few. At night the two elders proposed my settling with them, and
desired my consent; which I told them I could give to none before
a call. And that night I found my heart somewhat inclined to embrace that charge; but they seemed not to be very pressing. I note
the circumstances of this affair so very minutely, because the event
shewed, that much depended thereon, and that that was the place
determined of God for the bounds of my habitation; and in this
progress towards that event, there was an emblem and pledge of
what I afterward met with during the time I was minister there.

On the Wednesday morning after, Mr. Colden coming to my
chamber, seemed to approve of my going to Galloway; but did not
once ask me, what I thought of Simprin, or how I stood affected to
it; but being but little moved towards it, that could not much affect
me. A little after, one of the parish came and told me, that he had
spoke with Langton, who shewed a forwardness for my settlement
there; and in the evening, Mr. Colden and Mr. Balfour came and
told me, that Langton and the parish of Simprin minded to give me
a call, but feared they would not get me; to which I answered,
with an air of indifference, Well, let them be doing. But, according
to my manner of too great thoughtfulness on matters of weight once
set before me, I could sleep none at all that night, though I was
to preach the week day's sermon on the morrow. On Saturday's
morning, Mr. Colden told me plainly, that it was not his desire I
should settle in Simprin, because I would have so little opportunity
to do service there; yet concluded the necessity of walking by the
determination of Providence. In the afternoon I went to Eccles.

In the Sabbath morning at Eccles, July 16, I was concerned
rather about how to preach, than what; had a prospect of great
difficulties in a little t6 be encountered; Stenton communion approaching, the business of Simprin now in motion, and the affair of
Dollar in I knew not what state, together with other straitening
circumstances. Fearing lest these should make a deep mire for me,
drove me nearer to God, sensible of my need of a token for good
from him in such a situation. And I had some help from Cant.
viii. 5, " Who is this that cometh up from the wilderness, leaning
upon her beloved?" and Isa. lxi. 8, " I will direct their work in
truth." I had that day much help, light, and life, in delivering the
word; and my heart was wound up in prayer, elevated, and entirely
set on the work. The two Sabbaths immediately preceding, I had
in converse discovered, in professors of religion, much unacquaintedness with Christ, and with their own hearts, particularly as to the
legal bias thereof; which occasioned my preaching the week-day's

sermon aforesaid, on Deut. ix. 6. And this Sabbath, in converse with a professor, I saw the pride of my own heart, the levity of others, with little appearance of the power of religion; which made me sadly to fear settling in the Merse; where I found I could meet with few exercised to godliness, and made partakers of the knowledge of Christ.

July 22.—Being at Stenton, and in good case spiritually, by reason of the Lord's helping me to right uptakings of himself in some measure, and dealing bountifully with me in prayer, I was attacked with discouragement upon the prospect of my difficulties; which sent me to the Lord, and I got some help. I heard the sermons preparatory for the sacrament in some good frame; but near the close of the last prayer, thoughts of my difficulties bore in themselves on me; which, as they came, I rejected again and again; and after these repulses they got, I became more serious. But Satan, who was in earnest, would not let me pass so; but in came other thoughts, which raised my heart into a violent passion, and in a strange manner I rejected them, repelling one sin with another, wishing evil to the person of whom I thought. This wish came in most suddenly upon me as lightning, and did very much confuse me, was heavy to me, and marred my confidence with the Lord. So when I came in from the kirk, I was most ugly and hell-hued in my own eyes, and verily believe there was none so unworthy as I. Then my heart-monsters, pride, worldly-mindedness, discontent, &c., stared me in the face, and my poor heart was overwhelmed with sorrow. In the meantime that word, Isa. xli. 17, 18, "When the poor and needy seek water," &c., came sweetly to me, and was a little supporting; but I found it a great difficulty to believe. Being diverted, much of this wore off my spirit, and a dreadful deadness succeeded. To-morrow morning I got a revival; and through the day, for the most part, it was not very ill. But being to preach without in the afternoon, I got up to Mr. Stark's garret betwixt sermons, and at the south-east corner of it, I conversed with Christ, and it was a Bethel to me. Long-looked for came at last. If ever poor I had communion with God, it was in that place. The remembrance of it melts my heart at the writing hereof. And accordingly my public work was sweet; for God was with me, and, as I learned afterwards, it wanted not some success. God's voice was discerned in it. I shall only remark further, that at the communion-table I mainly sought, not comfort but grace and strength against corruptions. I got both in some measure.

I had determined to go from Stenton to Clackmannan-shire; and coming home on the Monday, I received a letter from thence, ad-

vising, that the elders of Dollar had applied once and again to the
Presbytery; but nothing could prevail with them, till the parish
should get a new consent from Argyle. This confirmed me in my
purpose, as shewing the Presbytery not to be fond of my settling
there, nay, nor in earnest for it. I went to God for help, to carry
right in my difficulties; and was encouraged. After which, providentially falling on " Flavel's Mystery of Providence," I got my
own case seasonably discussed therein, p. 201. And by the means
of resignation there proposed, I endeavoured to bring my heart to
that disposition; and so went to prayer with confidence in the
Lord. I found also spiritual advantage in this case, by reflecting on
former experiences; so that I came to be content to follow the Lord
implicitly, as " Abraham went, not knowing whither he went."

That afternoon, being at Langton, Mr. Balfour told me, that the
laird had not taken the method laid down by Mr. Colden and him;
whereby the call of Simprin might have been before the Presbytery
that day fortnight; and thereby I saw, that I would not know before I went to Lothian, whether that affair would issue in a call or
not. Coming along the way with Mr. N—— H——, then minister
of Preston, a man of great parts, but not proportionable tenderness
and now several years ago deposed, I was much satisfied with his
converse; so that the night was far spent ere we parted. And as
we were about to part, he told me of a design some had for another
to Simprin; with which I was surprised and amazed; but in the progress of our discourse, I found that design to be, only in case I
would not accept. Whereupon he advised me to accept, and was against
going to Galloway. After I came home, reflecting on these two
things, I took both of them to be intended by providence, letting
me see what were my thoughts under both, to clear me towards accepting of the call of Simprin, if offered. That night I lay down,
meditating on that word, " Abraham went out, not knowing whither
he went."

On the morrow after, conferring with Mr. Balfour, we judged the
affair of Simprin could now hardly be expeded before Michaelmas.
And finding the hardship of my being in a fixed charge, for a whole
year, without receiving any stipend, which in that event behoved
to be the case, would render my settling there at all impracticable;
I thought it necessary to intimate the same to Mr. Dysert before
I went out of the country.

Next day, being the 20th, I began to study for Stenton communion,
having the night before gone to God for a text, with confidence and
particular trust; and in a little got one; being to go away the following day. But betwixt ten and eleven, forenoon, I was sent for

to a monthly meeting for prayer, at Polwarth, two miles from Dunse. Being strained with this message, I laid it before the Lord, and was determined to go; considering that the day and way were ordinarily alike long with me, as it has continued to be in my experience to this day; and judging that my spirit might thereby be more fitted for that communion-work; and that going at God's call I might expect necessary furniture for what I had to do after. Accordingly I went away, studied by the way a part of the forenoon's sermon was countenanced by the Lord there, and returned home again about six o'clock. I completed what I minded to deliver, before or in time of the action; and having prayed again, went on and studied the sermon to be delivered after the action, without, having burnt a candle. Thus as much was got done, as I would have done had I been no where abroad that day. I found my spirit bettered by all, my soul somewhat heavenly, and raised towards the Lord; I saw it was good to follow duty, and trust God; and that it is "not by might nor by power," but by the "Spirit" of the Lord, things are got comfortably done.

On the 21st I went to Stenton, where that night, in meditation, I got a view of the transcendent glory and excellency of Christ, with the emptiness of all things besides him; and the desire of my heart was towards him. How it fared with me at that communion, I have related above. Under the deadness there mentioned, which was on the Saturday's night, being to make public exercise in the kirk, I went to secret prayer; but really could not pray, yea, not so much as groan sensibly unto the Lord; only I was sensible of my hardness of heart, and in a sort grieved for the Lord's absence. So entering on the work in this heavy case, the tears broke out with me; but all along I was under desertion. When I came in from that exercise, I went to prayer; but could not pray; and joined but very lifelessly in family prayer. But afterwards reading over my notes, which were on Jer. xxix. 13, "And ye shall seek me, and find me," &c. I got somewhat above that deadness, and reached to some confidence in the Lord in prayer. The Lord lifted me up in that place; but thus low was I laid before it. Sitting down at the Lord's table on the morrow, I took it for a sure sign I should yet sit down at the table above; and among other particular requests there, I had one for light in the call of Simprin, if offered; and came away with hope, but no more. The remaining part of the night, after the happy afternoon's work and entertainment mentioned above, I was kept in a heavenly frame, with love to Christ, and admiration of his goodness, loving the very place where he manifested himself. And on the morrow having insisted on the requests I had at the table, I found afterwards the Lord had made my soul satisfied, as to what way he might dispose of me, especially with respect to Simprin.

Being resolved to go from Stenton as above said, on that Monday's afternoon, Mr. Stark having given me a compliment of two dollars, and the use of his horse for my journey, I went to Edinburgh; and being engaged to return on Saturday, and in the morning sought of the Lord a text for the following Sabbath, I did by the way think on, and get some insight into Psalm cxix. 32, " I will run the way of thy commandments, when thou shalt enlarge my heart." On Tuesday I went to Barhill; and on Wednesday to Clackmannanshire, where I met with one of my correspondents, who told me, that the elders of Dollar, whom he had discharged to come near me, were wrestling as eagerly as ever to accomplish their designs, and were waiting the return of a letter to Argyle. I shewed him my situation, and committed to one to shew the Presbytery of Stirling, that I looked on myself as absolved from my promise to them. On the Tuesday I went back to Barhill, on the morrow after to Edinburgh, and returned to Stenton on Saturday about four o'clock. Mr. Stark had come back from some intended journey, but would take no part of the Sabbath's work; so after prayer, being cleared and satisfied as to the text aforesaid, I studied my sermons with ease in the space of little more than three hours; the Lord laying things to my hand, and that with enlargement of heart. So still day and way were alike long; and I had much of the Lord's help in the whole Sabbath's work.

On the morrow, Mr. Stark invited me to go next day to their Presbytery of Dunbar, on design I might be appointed to preach at Innerwick a day, then vacant. I had some difficulty about it, in respect of my situation; but endeavoured to consult God in it once and again; and was cleared, that my staying another week in Lothian, would be more useful than going home; but referred the full determination of the point aforesaid till the morrow. Which day proved rainy; and Mr. Stark went off, without moving again my going along; this I took in ill part, not knowing the kind design of Providence therein. There Mr. Stark having moved for my preaching at Innerwick, it was opposed, particularly by Mr. John Forrest, an old man, and rejected, on pretence, they had not seen my licence. Some time after, the Lady Presmennan, she took occasion to clear herself of her having taken any offence at my afternoon sermon without on the communion day, injuriously imputed to her; but declared, that at the Monday's dinner she did say to Mr. Forrest, she thought the covenant would be up yet. This seemed to point at the spring of the opposition to the motion foresaid.

I had been much satisfied in converse with some serious Christians in that country; and esteeming the Merse an overgrown piece of the vineyard, there sat down on my spirit a great aversion to settling in it; insomuch that I prayed against it, but with submission.

In the middle of the week, one came from Dunbar inviting me thither, intimating to me the desire of some to see me there. I went along with him, and spent the time in visits; but mostly with Bailie Kellie, who was in distress, and conversed suitably as a good man. At night several coming in to the exercise, I lectured. There was an Episcopal incumbent then in their kirk; and the Presbyserians had a meeting-house. This meeting-house they proposed to me, and urged; but finding that their preacher was to continue in the character of a probationer, while with them, I could not relish the motion; and their Presbytery's coldness to me justified the refusal.

On Saturday August 5, being at Stenton, where I was to preach on the morrow, after I had begun my studies, we were called to family-worship. Being desired, I prayed with composure for a while; but being in the kitchen, where was a great heat, my heart began to fail, so that I was obliged to break off; and going straight to the door for air, fainted away. Lying in which case I lifted up my heart to the Lord, boding kindness on him; recovered and was eased by vomiting, as usual. I had rested little that week, but had been riding hither and thither; which kind of tossing I have seldom been the better of. Being confused through the remains of my indisposition, my studies took all my time. Meantime this new experience of my frailty, made the little charge of Simprin more acceptable to me. Sabbath forenoon I was indisposed both in body and spirit, yet had some help of the Lord. Betwixt sermons I cried for an alteration, and got it, both in body and spirit; and was helped to express matters of some difficulty, with that distinctness, which I was sure I could not have treated of them in private. Hereof I had then had frequent experience, and since too.

On the morrow, August 7, being to return home, I was comforted by a Christian woman, goodwife of Roughlaw, blessing God that ever she saw me, and shewing that never one had read her case, as the Lord had helped me to do, in my sermons first and last. At parting she put in my pocket about 2s. sterling, which I value as a token of Christian affection. That night I came to Dunse.

And thus, after all my perplexity, when the matter was brought to the utmost pinch, kind providence opened an unexpected way for expediting one part of my design; and removed the other, viz. the

going to Galloway, much out of my view. I was, after great straitening, liberally provided for, beyond expectation. And the Lord's making my itinerant labours, not unsuccessful, but useful at least to his
own, and giving me a large room in their affections, afforded me a
satisfaction, which I thought might be an equivalent of the comfort
of a settlement.

Next day, having heard of nothing done in the affair of Simprin,
it was suggested to me by one, that Langton minded to shift it till
Michaelmas were past; so that night, and the morrow morning,
being the 9th, thinking with myself that the Lord minded to grant
my desire of not settling in the Merse, I desired of him he would be
pleased to shew me how to dispose of myself next; and the same
day, some time after that, I was surprised with a visit of Mr.
Murray, who continued to desire me to go to Nithsdale. And
indeed his coming to me at such a nick of time, did seem at first to
be determining; but even while he was with me, came in one from
Simprin, shewing that Langton had moved in the affair, and that it
might yet be done in due time; and a little after I found that he had
writ to the Presbytery to go on towards my settlement there. Now
my inclination was to go to Nithsdale, and I was racked betwixt the
two. That night I thought seriously on them, went to God, particularly for light and direction therein; and after, as I was going
to bed, I found I durst not as yet leave Simprin. On this occasion
I observed the subtilty of self in two cases; 1. I feared my seeking of light proceeded more from self-love than love to Christ;
2. That my seeking the very mortification of my idols, discontent,
worldly-mindedness, &c., did likewise proceed from the same fountain, which might be in regard of the disquiet the want of the one,
and having of the other, occasions me. This selfishness I did manifestly observe; yet I found there was respect to the command of
God in this, and thought it predominated. I thought I should have
light from the Lord, or I durst not do it, though it should be to my
temporal loss.

On the 10th, having occasionally continued my former request, I
found that afternoon my soul content I should settle in Simprin,
if the Lord should give me a clear call to it, that being then my
exercise, of the issue whereof I was much afraid. At night I went
to the meeting for prayer, found my heart much affected with the
sad state of my native country the Merse, in respect of religion, and
cried to God for an alteration therein to the better. I desired James
Minto, a godly man, and a mighty pleader in prayer, though otherwise of very ordinary abilities, to remember in prayer my situation,
and to plead for light to me; and my difficulties pressed me forward unto God.

The day following having gone to prayer for a text, I was, through the blowing of the Spirit on me, brought to a contented frame of heart with respect to the affair of Simprin. And indeed at what times I was most heavenly in the frame of my spirit, it was easiest for me to get over those things that were straitening and discouraging to me in it, and founded my aversion to it. These were, 1. The rarity of the godly there, and in the country; 2. The very smallness of their number; 3. The smallness of the stipend; moreover, 4. The temper and way of the fraternity, though good men, and several of them learned men too, not agreeable to mine; the which fully opened itself in the different way that that Presbytery and I took in the year 1712, and ever since; and, 5, which was the main thing that then stuck with me, The little opportunity to be serviceable there. It indeed bred some scrupling in the matter, that I was not far from thinking I was more useful in my unsettled condition, than I would be if minister of Simprin. But I thought with myself, if the Lord will shut me up there, why not? and I feared that in this there might be something of the pride of my heart, and of ignorance of the weight of the ministerial work; and therefore desired to say, " The will of the Lord be done." At night having gone to my eldest brother's, and joined with him in his family worship, to my great satisfaction, he came along with me, to my chamber, and by our converse I was led to Psalm cxix. 96, " I have seen an end of all perfection," for my text, being to preach in Dunse the following Lord's day.

On the 12th I studied my sermous on it; and in prayer in the time thereof I got some sight of the world's vanity, and in prayer after my studies, the Lord did blow on me, and as I was much concerned for a lasting impression of the vanity of the world, and of the weight of the work of the ministry; the which two things I reckoned would much conduce to the easing, quieting, and clearing of my mind, with respect to the affair of Simprin. I thought then I had never seen so great difficulty to get my heart weaned from the world; but it was my soul's desire the Lord himself would wean me, being content to part with a carnal worldly mind, if he would rend it from me, and convinced, that it would abide a pull of his hand. After some time spent in necessary business, I betook myself to meditate on my sermons that I had studied; and while, in my meditations, I was upon that head of them, the vanities of riches, just then one knocked at my chamber-door, whom opening to, I found to be a man from Simprin, who delivered to me a letter with their call. This did somewhat damp me. The letter was from a committee of the Presbytery, signifying that the call, being presented to them, and sustained legal, they exhorted and invited me

F 2

to accept thereof ; and had appointed me a common head, together
with exercise and addition, to be delivered at Churnside on the 22d.
I read also the call, and returned it to the bearer, shewing him,
that I would consider of it, attend the Presbytery, and also preach at
Simprin on the morrow eight day for my own clearing in the matter ;
charging him to tell the elders, to be serious with God for light and
direction to me therein. After his departure, I went and poured
out my soul before the Lord, for the discovery of his mind concerning it. Afterwards I thought thereon, and found my unwillingness on account of the smallness of their number ; but in opposition
thereto, a fear of my ignorance of the weight of the work of the
ministry, seized me ; and it seemed to me I had not been enough
humbled for my former levity, but that the Lord saw it necessary
to humble me farther for it ; and I got my heart contented, and
found that the Lord " strengthened me with strength in my soul''
to wait on him, and follow the conduct of his providence. Thereafter I meditated on the rest of my sermons.

Having preached at Dunse on the Sabbath, I gave myself on the
Monday to fasting and prayer, to seek of the Lord a right way, in that
matter now laid before me ; breaking over an averseness I found to
that exercise ungrateful to the flesh. Three things were suggested to
me, prompting me to be so at pains for light in that matter; thinking with myself thus : 1. Unless I be sure of my call to it from the
Lord, how will I stand against the discouragements I will meet with
there ? 2. How can I think of profiting them, if he send me not to
them ? 3. How will I stand with them before the tribunal of God,
if I join with them without a call from himself ? Having read Ezra
ix. and x., I went to prayer, to prepare my heart for the work ;
thought a while, and then went to prayer again, and poured out my
soul before the Lord. Thereafter I read the written confession of
sin, which is above mentioned, and then made an additional one, in
writing too. Which done, I thought on my sins and heart-monsters,
till my soul was more humbled in me, then bowing my knees before
the Lord, I read over the two confessions aforesaid ; poured out my
soul before him, making a particular confession of my sins, so far
as I could remember them ; arraigned and condemned myself, and
looked to the Lord, in the promise, for mercy. After that, minding
to renew the covenant with God, and subscribe it with my hand, I
drew it up in writing ; which done, I prayed, the Spirit blowing on
me ; and I was greatly helped to resoluteness for Christ, resolving, if I perished, I should die at his door. Then I examined myself, as to my willingness to adhere unto it, and subscribe it, in all
the parts thereof, severally and distinctly ; and having found my-

self willing, I poured out my soul before him in prayer; in which
prayer, having some such expression as this, " O Lord, art thou
willing!" that word came to me, " All things are ready, come to the
marriage;" to this, " Amen" said my soul. Rising up, I wrote
down these words in the paper I had drawn, and looking up to the
Lord, I subscribed it with my hand. I wrote down there also, Jer.
xxx. 22; Deut. xxxiii. 27; 2 Cor. xii. 9. That paper is *in retentis.**
After this, I meditated a while; then I went to prayer for the benefits of the covenant, particularly for that which was the occasion
of this day's exercise; I cried for light, and was laid down at his
feet; and came away cheerfully and contentedly, my soul saying,
" Where thou wilt, Lord; for he strengthened me with strength in
my soul." Then, thinking on the business, I considered and put
down in writing, that I might the better judge thereof, First, Some
things seeming to clear my call to Simprin, as follows: 1. My being
cast into this country, where I was exposed to it, and God's closing
up all other doors hitherto. 2. On the 10th of June, Mr. Dysert
wrote a letter in my favour to the elders of Simprin, and gave it me
to dispatch to them. I took it, but afterwards tore it in pieces (on
what occasion, I cannot now find out); yet on July 4, being resolved to leave this country next week, being resolved to go over
Forth first, and then to Galloway, I was obliged to go to the Presbytery of Churnside, to meet with Mr. Dysert, to borrow some
money of him necessary for my going out of the country; but when
I saw him, I could not command so much confidence as to ask it of
him. But the Presbytery took occasion to invite me to preach at
Simprin next Lord's day; which I could not but consent to, knowing of no other place I was trysted to; and this was the first time I
ever preached in Simprin. My father went to Mr. Dysert on the
morrow for that purpose; but he could not answer my desires. Thus
was I locked in. 3. I have experienced, that I have been most for
complying with it, when I saw most of the vanity of the world, and
had meanest thoughts of myself. 4. On the 8th of August it was
told me, that Langton minded to shift the business of Simprin till
Michaelmas were over, which would have made the closing with that
call almost impracticable, on account of my particular circumstances; so that it seemed the Lord had a mind I should not settle
in the Merse. So that night and the morrow morning, thinking the
business of Simprin all over, I desired of the Lord he should shew
me how to dispose of myself. And after this, August 9, I was sur-

---

* An exact copy of it is annexed to the author's " Body of Divinity," printed in
1773.

prised with a visit from Mr. James Murray, who entreated me to go
to Nithsdale, giving good hopes of a comfortable settlement there.
His coming to me at that nick of time seemed at first to be determining; but in the very meantime there comes in one from Simprin,
shewing me, that the Laird had written a letter to one of the ministers; and that the business might yet be done in due time. This put
me again to a stand. Thereafter I found the Laird had written to
the Presbytery to go on. My inclination was to go to Nithsdale,
and I was racked betwixt the two. After prayer for light, I
found I durst not yet leave Simprin. 5. I could not but notice my
preaching at Simprin on the emptiness of all things besides Christ,
the only sermon yet preached there by me. On the 12th of August, in
the forenoon, I studied a sermon of the vanity of the world, on
Psalm cxix. 66, being to preach it in Dunse; and just when I was
meditating on that head of it, the vanity of riches, one knocks at
my chamber-door, I opened, and found it was a man from Simprin,
who delivered me a letter from a committee of the Presbytery, with
the call of Simprin; which did somewhat damp and discourage me.
Hereby the Lord seemed to try whether I was really in earnest
with these things or not. When the man went away, I poured out
my soul to the Lord for light, afterwards thought on the business,
got my heart contented, and I thought the Lord strengthened me
with strength in my soul, to wait on and follow the conduct of providence. 6. The light I have attained in this business bridles my
corruptions of worldly-mindedness, &c., and my own inclinations.
And I have attained to a more deep impression of the weight of the
work of the ministry than before; which I find, contributes to my
clearness as to the accepting of that call. The consideration of these
things after prayer, makes it some more than probable to me that
this matter is of God, and fully determines me to go on in my trials,
leaving the more full determination of the main thing till afterwards. Secondly, The grounds of my aversion to it. 1. The rarity
of the godly in this country. This I found to be but a discouragement. 2. The very smallness of the charge. When I was considering the weight of the work of the ministry, I got a silencing answer
to that. 3. The smallness of the stipend. This seems to be a temptation. The light I had from the Lord this day hath downweighed
this. 4. I suspect I am more useful for God in my vagrant state,
than I would be if minister of Simprin. It may be otherwise. The
Lord is to make use of me as he pleaseth. I truly fear it is the
pride of my heart that is the source of this. This however I found
could be no just ground of scrupling, though a discouragement; and
I further considered, that I knew not what honourable use the Lord

might have for me there.   I had formerly taken some thoughts of my call to the preaching of the gospel in general, which are noted in the above mentioned soliloquy, pp. 29, 30, [of the printed copy.] And there remained no doubt thereof with me; and my clearness in that point had been a good support to me, under the discouragements I met with.   Having thus considered these things, I went to God again, poured out my soul, and laid all out before him; and had that word, Matth. vi. 33, "Seek ye first the kingdom of God, and his righteousness; and all these things shall be added unto you."   Afterward I wrote a line for some books necessary for me on my trials; and in the meantime came in to me the above-mentioned Patrick Gillis, one of my two praying school-fellows.   Him sovereign providence had entirely laid aside from his design of pursuing learning; and with him I conversed a while, and prayed.   After he went away, I went to prayer again, with confidence in the Lord, having such clearness as said is.   By this time the sun was down; then having given thanks to the Lord, for his assistance through the day, and for what light I had attained unto, and sought strength for carrying me on in the work immediately before me, viz. my trials, I went forth.

It hath cost no small struggling to put the knife to the throat of my inclinations in this affair, and to sacrifice them to the good pleasure of God.   In the remaining part of that week, I prepared my exegesis *de idololatria*, exercise and addition on Eph. i. 5; and on the 18th, thinking on a text for Simprin, found none, till in bed in my meditations, that word; 1 Pet. v. 5, "For God resisteth the proud," &c., came to my mind; which I thought I would take, and that in regard I find the pride of my heart creating me much trouble. while I think on the business of Simprin; for I reckon always, that if I were more humble, I would go on more cheerfully in that affair.   I was waiting for further light therein, to break up to me from my trials; thinking with myself, that if the Lord should please to help me in them, it would much contribute to clear me.   But after my entering on the study of the exercise, with a pretty good run, the wind fell; and I was left to tug and row in it, and in the addition, even to the end.   But behold! this very thing, shewing me my own emptiness, contributed not a little to the clearing of me, that if I was at all to be admitted to the holy ministry, it should be at Simprin, as unfit for a more considerable post.   Thus the Lord brought about what I was waiting for, in a way quite contrary to that wherein I was looking for it.

On the Tuesday after, being the 22d, I went to Churnside to the Presbytery, by that time disjoined from the Presbytery of Dunse.

Before I went to the pulpit, my case, with respect to myself and others, lying heavy on me, did, with other needs, send me often to God by prayer. But after one prayer in public, wherein I had something of his presence, my frame much decayed, and the Lord left me much to the weight of my natural disposition; fear of man so prevailing, that the glass being run twice, I thought it had run but once, and so held on; inasmuch that the exercise lasted above an hour and a quarter; and they stopped me after delivering a part of the addition. This made me wonder how I had passed my first trials; but God fits the back for the burden. I overheard their censures. The manner of management could not miss to fret them; but I was approved in that piece of trial, as afterward in the exegesis. The moderator presented me the call of Simprin, which I received of his hand; but returned it to the clerk, shewing I would further consider of it. At the dinner I was much discouraged, and was inclined to wish in my heart I might not be settled in that country.

In the latter end of the week, the frame of my spirit being bad, and even unfit for study, it was grievous to me in respect of my circumstances, which called for another temper of spirit. But preaching at Lennel on the Lord's day, I got some relief; and on the Monday after, that word, Numb. xxiii. 19, "God is not a man, that he should lie, neither the son of man, that he should repent," was exceedingly useful to me, for quieting my heart, with respect to all baseness concerning me; having some confidence, that his purpose would be found for good to me, what way soever things should go. And on the morrow, after reading for my chronologic trials, I was inclined to pray, and did so, rolling all over on God.

On Wednesday the 30th, Mr. Colden shewed me, he was sorry I had so far accepted the call of Simprin, in regard to a call to Hownam might have been procured. I told him, I durst not do otherwise than I had done; and shewed him a providential step pointing that way; the weight whereof he owned. On the morrow, having perfected my popular sermon, I was edified and satisfied therewith. At night I began to think of the near approach of the Presbytery. when I might be required to give an answer to the call. The prospect of this was very heavy to me. I considered it a while with a sad heart; Dollar was desirable to me; Simprin was not so. When I thought how God owned me elsewhere, and what converse I had with the godly in that country, my heart was much cast down, being to be closed up in such a part of the country as is most dead and lifeless. I have little myself of life or heat, and I fear I may lose what I have or have had. I saw then my sin in itching after a

settlement, when the Lord did countenance me so much in my vagrant state. So I poured out my soul before the Lord, mainly with
respect to the present exigence. That word, Psalm xxv. 9, came
into my mind. Wherefore my soul desires to lay down itself at his
feet. Let him do with me as he will; I am his own.

Sept. 1.—Being conscious to myself of my desire to follow God's
call, the above-mentioned word; Psalm xxv. 9, "The meek will
he guide in judgment, and the meek will he teach his way," was
sweet. I began to think about closing with the call to Simprin. I
think providence seems to determine to it; but I cannot yet think
of giving a positive answer against Tuesday next, but would fain have
some days after to think on it, when I am free of other business : not
that I think to get free of it, but that in the use of means I would
wait for such light as may make me go on more cheerfully in it,
and deliberately, for a foundation for the time to come. So I went
to prayer; and thereafter began to think on it; but could not attain such serious thoughts of it as I would have had; so that I have
nothing to mark as the product of it, save the deceitfulness of my
own heart, which is more ready to close with any thing than what is
present duty. On this day, I resolved to crave of the Presbytery the
following week further to advise, proposing to give my answer to
him who should be ordered to serve the edict, and might act according to my answer; for I found not myself in case to do otherwise. After this, in the afternoon of the same day, Mr. Colden told
me, it was still against his will I should settle in Simprin; and that
he understood, that Mr. Gabriel Semple, minister at Jedburgh, one
of the old sufferers, who in the time of the persecution was eminently
countenanced of God, with success in the work of the gospel, especially in the borders of England, had taken it amiss that I was
not sent to him; the design whereof was to be his colleague, though
there was no legal fund for it in the place. This oftener than once
had been moved; but I could by no means listen to it; but Mr.
Colden desired me not to consent to the call of Simprin till he
should speak with Mr. Semple on the affair of Hownam; the report
of which conference I should have that day eight days. I being,
before this proposal was made to me, resolved as aforesaid, had no
scruple in it; but told him, that whatever might be the issue of
that conference, I would not dare to determine the rejecting of the
call of Simprin by myself; and I was resolved still to follow on, in
what appeared present duty, let the Lord do with me as should seem
good in his eyes.

On the morrow, September 2, I received letters, but no word
of the affair of Dollar. In the twilight, weary with study, I went

to prayer, and, with confidence in the Lord, unbosomed myself to him. And, O but a heavenly frame was sweet in my eyes! and I saw how pleasant a life a habit thereof, if I could reach it, would make. On the morrow after I preached at Simprin.

On Tuesday the 5th, I did with more freedom than the former presbytery-day, deliver my popular sermon, and undergo all the rest of my trials, and was approved. At the Presbytery's desire I gave answer to the call, and that in the terms I had before resolved upon; but with submission. They appointed the edict to be served the following Lord's day, and my ordination to be on Thursday the 21st.

Sept. 7.—I set some time apart for prayer, in order to get direction in this affair. I found no small averseness in my heart to that duty. After prayer, my thoughts being hard to be gathered, that word came; Exod. xxxiii. 15, "If thy presence go not with me, carry us not up hence." I went to God and poured out my soul, wrestling against the bad frame of spirit, blessed the Lord for what he had done for me since I was a preacher, and cried for his countenance in this, meditated on the matter, but with little success. I went to God again; and afterwards some things came to me, clearing me further to accept. And as for my inward thoughts, they were such, that I saw I durst not but go on with it, finding that the more serious I am about light in it, it is the clearer. Afterwards I went to God again, and with much more life and earnestness, the Lord helping, I made my requests, and in prayer I found that word; Psalm xviii. 28, "Thou wilt light my candle; the Lord my God will enlighten my darkness;" which I sung the first time I was in a pulpit; and that; Job xxii. 28, "Thou shalt also decree a thing," &c., given me before I entered on my first trials; and that, Psalm xxv. 9, [above quoted], very strengthening to my soul, and most useful to me. Lest I should have provoked God to withdraw the light I have, which I began to fear upon my crying still for light, I saw myself called to bless God for what he had given me. And now my confidence in the Lord was raised, and my soul blessed the Lord; I am his; let him do what seemeth him good with me. Catching my heart at the season when it was willing, I went to God again, and poured out my soul? but really had not freedom to harp longer on light as to the main thing, the accepting of Simprin, (but rather to seek God's presence to go with me); for this seemed to me now almost, if not altogether, a tempting of God, who hath already made my way clear. Further, I observed,

1. In the Lord's way of dealing with me, that the Lord has brought about for me what I was most against. A notable instance

parallel to this I had at the passing my first trials; in that I was
brought to pass them in my own country, which of all other places
was least in my eye. This way of providence with me I have so
often observed, that I have thought indeed such or such a thing
would come to pass, just because I was averse to it. And as to
this business, besides my aversion to the whole country, Simprin,
by any place of it, I never dreamed of, and was very much against
it since it was talked of.

2. The Lord hath hitherto prevented such remorse in this business as I expected, other three irons in the fire with this, having all
got leave to cool, viz, 1. Mr. Mair had resolved to endeavour, that I
should be invited to their Presbytery of Dunfermline; but there
was no word from him. 2. Mr. Murray had told me, he would
hasten home to prevent my settling in the Merse; but I had not
heard from him. 3. The affair of Dollar was dead as to me, though
when I was in that country they were moving in it.

3. Sometime I thought I would wait to see how the Lord would
help me in my trials for Simprin; and I thought I would take it as
clearing my call thereto, if I were helped and enlarged in them;
and contrariways. But in studying my exercise and addition,
August 17, I was straitened, and was very much discouraged through
that straitening; and behold, this very straitening (reflecting on it
afterwards) seemed to me to clear my call to Simprin; if I were at
all to be a minister, that I should be minister of Simprin, for thereby I saw much of my own emptiness. This had a convincing impression on my heart; wherefore I thought I was called of God to
join with that people; and the sense of the command of God urged
me, otherwise unwilling, to it.

Nota. As to that aversion I had to settle in Simprin, I have ofttimes since thought it was no disadvantage to me; in regard it was
far more easy to me to discern the light of the Lord, and what
moved me to accept that charge, when it crossed my inclinations,
than it would have been, had they gone both one way. In that case
it had been more difficult for me to have known which of them I followed. It has been ofttimes supporting to me.

On the 9th I received a letter from my friend, such as became a
Christian, bearing that her heart did indeed rise at my last, showing I had received the call of Simprin, but withal desiring me to
follow my light, and to be single in my accepting or refusing it, that
the world might not cast the balance: the same Christian disin-
terested course she steered all along in these matters being my wife.

Mr. Colden being returned from Teviotdale on the 11th, spake
nothing of the affair of Hownam, whereof I was to have the report

upon his return. He calling me aside that day, I was afraid he might
have something to propose in opposition to this current business of
Simprin; it was my heart's desire to the Lord, that it might not be
so; and it was not. Thus did the sovereign Manager, by a train
of providential dispensations, mark out my way to Simprin. Meanwhile the man whom he had designed for Hownam, was at that time
in the seat appointed next for me, viz., Mr. James Macmichan, minister of Ettrick, afterward transported to Hownam.

Being under some discouragements at home, September 13, I began to be somewhat uneasy and discontent with my settling in Simprin. I was now hampered in my chamber; I had lent out my
money and could not get it back, to procure myself necessaries.
These, with my future circumstances, were grievous to me. Finding
myself hereby carried off my feet as a Christian, I resolved to spend
some time on the morrow in fasting and prayer, for these causes:
1. To get habitual nearness to God; 2. For a due impression of the
weight of the work I am called to; 3. His presence with me in it;
4. For content with my lot. Addressing myself to the intended
exercise of that day, I added to these aforesaid causes, 5. That I
might get victory over a particular corruption wherewith I had been
often foiled; Lastly, That I might be kept from cooling in my zeal
in that country. After prayer and meditation with respect to the
aforementioned causes, I went to prayer with the same requests.
Meditating how to reach the things above mentioned, I found, that
as to the first, viz., habitual nearness to God, I might attain it, by
observing what I had written in my sermons, lib. 3. p, 104, and 277.
As to the second, a due impression of the weight of the work I was
called to, that helps were laid down in the Soliloquy, p. 22, [of the
printed copy], and that I should consider the worth of souls, of
which ibid. p. 34. As to the third, viz., God's presence with me in
my work, the 1st, The Lord hath been with me, and done good by
me to souls heretofore, and thereby had sealed my call to the preaching of his word; and, 2dly, That I had his promise annexed to his
call, " Go, and lo I am ;with you." Now, thought I, I am called by
himself to undertake that charge, and from a sense of his command
I do undertake it, therefore he will be with me. As to the fourth,
viz., contentment with my lot, I found that there were helps to it,
Soliloquy, p. 51, and downwards. I knew I had reached it, hoped
yet to reach it, and my soul cheerfully desired it. Thinking further on this of my lot at Simprin, I found that it did run almost
parallel with assurance of my interest in Christ, which at this time
was much shaken with the last dream. This sent me to God again,
where again I appealed to the omniscience of God as to my sincerity.

And afterwards I began to examine myself. My trial by the dream
was, that I was but a hypocrite, and would continue so. Being left
alone, I went to prayer; and was helped to plead and claim an interest in Christ, come of me what will, resolving to do it; though
devils should combine to tear me from it, I should through his
strength hold the gripe. That word, Isa. 1. 10, "Who is among
you that feareth the Lord," &c., was comfortable in prayer; and I
forced myself as it were to believe, that I should yet praise him,
pleading that promise; John xiv. 18, "I will not leave you comfortless; I will come to you." So examining myself, I can say,
1. I am poor in spirit, I have no righteousness of my own; and if I
get not a borrowed righteousness, I see I will perish; and I count
all my own righteousness as filthy rags, loss and dung; 2. I hunger
and thirst after an imputed righteousness and the righteousness of
a holy life, Lord thou knowest; 3. Christ is precious to me; I have
none in heaven but thee, and there is none on earth that I desire besides thee; and I would willingly quit all for Christ; 4. That was
supporting to me in prayer, "He will give the Spirit to them that
ask him;" I have done it, and do it; and the Spirit of sanctification is the delight of my soul; 5. My heart approves of and loves
the law of God, even when it strikes against those corruptions I
am naturally most inclined to; 6. I have received him, and am willing to receive him, in all his offices. Lord, thou knowest I speak as
I think, and my conscience bears me witness; therefore I am a
child of God in despite of Satan; and I will not quit my former
experiences, nor say that all were delusions; and whatever come of
me, I will venture myself on Christ. Afterwards in prayer I was
resolute; I would not quit my claim to him, which made me speak
boldly, and that so as is not ordinary with me. Let the Lord do
with me as he will. It was he that said to me on the 21st of January last, "I have loved thee with an everlasting love," and had
"therefore with loving-kindness drawn me;" and I will abide by
it. He may give his comforts when he pleaseth; no wonder I want
them. And now I am content with my lot, and believe I will get
the things that I sought this day; for he shall be my God while I
live; and he has said, "All things whatsoever ye shall ask in
prayer, believing, ye shall receive, Matth. xxi. 22. For the fifth,
Mic. vii. 19, "He will subdue our iniquities;" and for the last,
Mal. iv. 2, "Unto you that fear my name, shall the Sun of righteousness arise with healing in his wings; and ye shall go forth and
grow up as calves in the stall." Hos. xiv. 7, "They that dwell
under his shadow shall return, they shall revive as the corn," &c.
And I resolved to hold by his word, which he neither would nor

could deny. And now I must say from my experience, that "there failed not ought of those good things which the Lord had spoken: all came to pass." I am glad to find, that I had marked in the memoirs of that day, as above inserted, that I really believe I would get the things I sought that day. Toward the evening, being somewhat faint, I closed the work with singing Psalm xlii. 5, "O why art thou cast down, my soul," &c., to the end, and prayer; and my heart was strengthened and encouraged in the Lord. And so I took a refreshment. Thereafter I found an inclination to preach on the foresaid words; Psalm xlii. 5, the following Lord's day, mostly on my own account.

Nota. 1. I think God sent all this to shake me out of myself, to strike at the root of my corruption with respect to my settlement, and to make me glad to creep into Simprin. 2. I am sure God gave me in Simprin the most of the things above recorded, and though I am now, at the writing hereof, removed from it, I will ever remember it as a field which the Lord blessed.

On the morrow, going to God for a text, laid open to the divine determination, I was determined to the text aforesaid, even as I was determined to, and confirmed in that of Feb. 5, narrated above, p. 51; and as after my studies thereon, in which the Lord helped me, I was concerned for a blessing on it, not only for the people, but for myself; so on my meditating thereon next day, I found advantage to my own soul; as also in the delivering of it on Sabbath, September 17, and singing that after sermons; Psalm xiii. 6, "Thee therefore mind I will," &c., my soul was raised in hopes of the Lord's return to me as at some other times of sensible manifestations, and the unchangeableness of God was sweet to me. But after sermons, in converse, speaking of the godly people in Clackmannan, and the paucity of such there, a fit of discouragement seized me, where I saw how, after I had been preaching against it, I was overtaken with it. But that word is helpful, "When I sent you, lacked ye any thing?" and that, John xiv. 18, "I will not leave you comfortless; I will come to you." O I find it a difficult thing to be really religious. I preached it in Langton, having procured the minister of that place to preach in Simprin that day, being the Sabbath immediately preceding my ordination; and upon that day's work, I find I had the following reflection: "What good this preaching hath done to others, I know not; yet I think myself am not the worse of it; O! that it were written in my heart, as it is in my book?"

On the Monday I went to Simprin, and found, that Langton had ordered a decent entertainment for the ministers at the ordination, which I was almost hopeless of. On the morrow I went to an ordination, where I saw the candidate answer the questions by a nod or bowing of the head, which I wished not to imitate. From thence I went to Berwick; and having nighted at Churnside, returned to Dunse on the Wednesday, where I got some impression of the weight of the work of the ministry fixed on my spirit, which continued with me, while at my chamber, and while abroad about necessary business, and received some comfortable account of the preceding Sabbath's work.

Sept. 20, After prayer, meditating on what is before me, I saw much of the weight of the work; wherefore I went to God mourning, and poured out my soul to him. I saw it a great matter to have the charge of souls, and to be faithful. Two things were mainly before me; the difficulty to carry right in the ministry in general; which was heightened from the consideration of the present state of affairs, and an impression I had of matters turning worse; and then the difficulty of carrying right to the poor parish to which I am called. These made my heart almost to sink; and indeed my heart and flesh did faint and fail; but that word; John xiv. 18, above cited, and especially that, Isa. xl. 11, " He shall feed his flock," did bear me up. When I went to prayer again, I had more confidence and courage; and when I came away, that word came; Heb. x. 35, " Cast not away your confidence," &c. And while I was meditating, J. F. came in to me; and told me, that last Lord's day at Langton was, in her opinion, an extraordinary day, particularly to her case and feeling; and that her case was read in the sermons. This is the second time that sermons preached for my own case had so reached that woman's. Having spent the time in prayer, meditation, and reading, till the night was well far on, and remembering how Satan is sure to lay wait for me in a special manner before some great work that I have to do, I committed soul, body, and spirit, to the Lord, and so went on with spiritual thoughts.

Sept. 21. But that which I feared came upon me; Satan got advantage of me indeed, and his hand appeared eminent in it. This did sadly cast me down; so I poured out my soul before the Lord, hoping against hope while I walked up and down; for in so far as it came from the devil, it dashed my confidence the less. Afterwards I grew more dull in my frame; but going to God again, I got a little more of God. I spent the rest of my time in my chamber in prayer and meditation. After I had been a while in company in Mr. Colden's I retired to his garden and meditated, my heart being in a tender frame. And when I came away, and through the day that word was given me for support; Deut. xxxiii. 27, " The eter-

nal God is my refuge, and underneath are the everlasting arms."
And I came to Simprin in a solid composed frame of spirit, leaning
on the foresaid word. This was the doing of the Lord, and wondrous in our eyes. I heard sermon with some good frame; but my
heart was very much moved when I came in to the kirk. Mr. John
Pow, minister of Lennel preached from Acts xx. 24, "But none of
these things move me, neither count I my life dear unto myself, so
that I might finish my course with joy, and the ministry which I
have received of the Lord Jesus, to testify the gospel of the grace
of God." After sermon I was ordained and set apart to the holy
ministry, by prayer made over me, with the laying on of the hands
of the Presbytery. I thought the text was ordained of God for me,
and my heart desired to go along with the doctrine, that ministers
should prefer the faithful discharge of their ministry to all their
other concerns in the world. While I answered the questions,
which I did at some length, being sensible in some measure of my
weakness and unworthiness to be a door-keeper in the house of my
God, my heart being great, I had much ado to contain myself; and
in that time there were many wet cheeks among the people. So I
was ordained; and while the words of ordination were said, I freely
resigned myself wholly to the Lord, my soul in effect saying, Even
so, Lord. After the ordination, I received the right hand of fellowship from the brethren; but had no heritor, nor representative of
an heritor, to take me by the hand; and I think there were but two
elders in the place at that time. Then I received some exhortations
from the minister aforesaid, actor in the work; and the work was
closed as ordinary.

In this period of my life the dispensations of God towards me
have been very wonderful, as in the former. I must say, upon the
whole, "The Lord's ways are not our ways, &c. His paths are in
the deep waters." My soul is well satisfied with the determination.
He hath inured me to hardness by the opposition I met with while
a preacher. He frustrated all designs for my settlement, till the
time before appointed, and the bounds of my habitation determined
by him were come to; Acts xvii. 26. This was an useful word to
me in my vagrant state, supported my heart often, and kept me
from transgressing for a piece of bread. My itching desires he
would not grant; but by this he hath tried me how I would deny
myself, and what I would make of my own inclinations. Blessed be
my God that has helped me to trample on them, and made me content with my lot. It is the Lord's way with me, to shake me out of
myself, and to make me renounce my wisdom, or rather folly.
When I came home from Kennet, I little thought of passing trials

here, yet I behoved to do it. When I had done it, I had no will to stay; yet the Lord would. Afterwards, when I left the country, I had ill will to leave it, but God had said it. When I was in Stirling Presbytery, I would have gladly staid there; but the Lord would not. When I came home, I had no good will to do this business: but God had said it, and it behoved to be done. When my head was away, he put his bridle in my mouth, and turned me again. " How unsearchable are his judgments, and his ways past finding out!" And now I have undertaken this work, in confidence of support by the everlasting arms. My itching desires after a settlement have been, and are grievous to me now: but the Lord is my God, who blotteth out mine iniquities as a thick cloud. To his name be glory in the highest for ever. Amen, yea and Amen.

And thus I have followed the course of this affair, in order narrating the several steps thereof, however minute some of them may appear; and that because it issued in what was to me one of the weightiest matters of my life; namely, my ordination to the ministry, and first sitting down in the world. And the reflecting on the clear divine conduct, in pointing out unto me, and carrying me to, these appointed bounds of my habitation, is like a rock of comfort to me unto this day; as it obliged me to look well about me for the like discovery of the Lord's mind before I moved my foot again.

PERIOD VII.

FROM MY ORDINATION, TO MY MARRIAGE.

I RETURNED to Dunse that night. In prayer I had much confidence in God. I found my heart well content with my lot; and the sense of God's calling me to that work, with the promise of his presence; O it satisfies my soul, and my very heart blesseth him for it; for really it is the doing of the Lord, and wondrous in my eyes. I have a prospect of comfort and success in my labours among that people, and my soul rejoiceth in the Lord. He hath enlarged my heart, I will run the way of his commandments. O! my heart is almost fond on God's good dealing with me. By the mercy of my God, I was not disappointed in my prospect. I closed that night with singing Psalm xvi. 5, " God is of mine inheritance and cup the portion," &c., to the end, and prayer.

From this time more than two months passed ere I took up my settled abode at Simprin; during which time, my ordinary residence being at Dunse, as before, I applied myself to my work, as I had opportunity.

Sept. 22.—It was long ere I got a text for the Sabbath. When I got it, my studies went slowly on. On the morrow also my thoughts were very confused, and it went very ill with me. I comforted myself with the example of Jacob's going at God's command, on his return to his own country, and yet the Lord met him as an enemy; so it went some better with me. Yet while I studied that sermon, my soul was solidly affected with the weight of the work of the ministry. I meditated on the forenoon sermon with more satisfaction than I studied it. I had desired the people of Simprin to send a horse for me; but it was so long a-coming, that I despaired of its coming at all. This was a piece of exercise to me; for I thought it strange to be thus treated at the very first; so I began to lay my account with trouble, and to be concerned for the salvation of the people, though I should meet with discouragements from them. The horse came, and it was not their fault that it came not sooner. I was bettered by the dispensation. After studying the preliminary sermons, as above, on Heb. xiii. 17, "For they watch for your souls, as they that must give account," I went to God by prayer for his countenance, and for direction toward such things as might be most profitable for that people; and found my soul much strengthened in confidence of the Lord's owning me, by means of that word, "Go—and lo I am with you alway, even to the end of the world." And I was then determined to begin with the book of Psalms for lecture; and for the exercise on the Sabbath evenings, to explain a question of the catechism.

Sept. 24.—Having allotted the morning entirely for prayer and meditation, some worldly thoughts crept in; yea, on a sudden my heart made a contrivance for staying in Simprin, which perhaps it would not easily have fallen on, if I had thought on the business seasonably. But I thought I bought it at the rate of the loss of that liveliness I expected. In the afternoon I somewhat recovered my forenoon's loss. At night, I had an exercise on the first question of the catechism, with some good frame of spirit; and on the morrow after I visited the people, exhorted to secret prayer, and family-worship; and found in all eighty-eight examinable persons. On the Tuesday, returning to Dunse, I received a letter from Mr. Murray, inviting me to the west, and shewing great encouragement, but God had now shewed me the appointed bounds of my habitation.

Sept. 28.—I never found that word, "Go—and lo I am with you alway," &c., so strengthening to my soul, as since I was a minister.

Having that week, upon weighing my circumstances, laid down a resolution to delay my marriage till the spring, 1701, I was brought into a grievous strait on the Friday's night; finding, that I behoved either to hasten it sooner, or not at all. This sent me to

God once and again, laying down the whole at his feet; and the sovereign will of God, tempered with good-will to his people, was my stay. But being to preach at Dunse on the Lord's day, and having sought a text for that end once and again, but in vain, I was hereby led unto one; viz. Col. iii. 2, " Set your affections on things above, not on things on the earth;" and I gained some advantage in my own case, by the study thereof. That Sabbath, having the first occasion of my administering the sacrament of baptism, I had endeavoured to frame some discourse for it aforehand, but altogether unsuccessfully; howbeit, when the time came, I was sufficiently furnished for that part of my work, though I could not before so much as order the duty of the parent in my own mind, to my own satisfaction. Thereafter, coming home to my chamber, I spent some time in meditation, and much in prayer, which at that time I could not well leave off, which was far from my ordinary. I laid out my case to the Lord, and he turned not away his ear. But that night it was a concerning question to me, How it came to pass, that I could not get above the world, notwithstanding all my endeavours, by meditating, praying, and preaching for that effect, being earnest to have my preaching effectual on my own heart? I thought with myself, how, in the time of such holy exercises, I was somewhat hoised up above it; but afterward, when the trial comes on, I am again just where I was. And I feared it was too much by myself that I wrestled against the world; that I was too legal in my endeavours, and knew not the way of making use of Christ for that great purpose; but I found I was content to learn.

Toward the end of that week, I had a secret check for forgetting my charge, and was desirous to be with them fixedly, praying the Lord would find out means for that end. I found also my heart much quieted, as to the divine disposal of the affair of my marriage; settling it in my mind not to proceed before a proper time. And with respect to my work in my charge, I was determined to begin with preaching to them the doctrine of man's natural state; judging the sight and sense thereof to be the foundation of all real religion. And minding to take it in parcels, for the more clear discovery thereof, both in the sinfulness and misery of it, I began my study of it, for that Sabbath, on the guilt of Adam's first sin, or original sin imputed. On the Saturday, the precentor professing his sorrow for his offence, was re-admitted sessionally. On the Sabbath, being October 8, entering accordingly on the subject aforesaid, I found things palpably laid to my hand; and together with the exercise on another question of the catechism, I required of some au

G 2

account of what they had heard, in which I had but little satisfaction.

On the morrow, having visited the sick, and desired some to meet in my chamber on Tuesday's night for prayer and Christian conference, I went to Kersefield, the house of the Lady Moriston, within a mile of Simprin, whither at that time I sometimes resorted. There my soul was made to bless God! for that when I reflected on the frame and disposition of my soul as to my marriage, I found myself freed of many things which before disturbed me, and my mind resting in the Lord. This was the doing of the Lord, and an answer of prayer. On Tuesday's night, returning to Simprin, the meeting aforesaid was held accordingly; in which, after singing of a psalm, I shewed them from the word the warrantableness of such exercise, and withal the seasonableness of it for the time; prayed with them; and then two of them prayed. And the Lord giving them some measure of his countenance, I was encouraged. The day following I went home.

Oct. 13.—I had much difficulty as to the getting of a text. I prayed, and thought again and again, but could get none, and so on a long time. In the meantime I was much discouraged, saw and confessed my distance from God, the cause of it, and pleaded on the tenor of my commission. At last, thinking on my own unworthiness, I was made to say within myself, " It is of the Lord's mercy I am not consumed." This was the text I was thus led to, and determined after prayer to take. But so few things presented themselves to me, that I feared I would not get two sermons on it. Thus being in the same difficulty, September 29, the Lord in his providence sent me a piece of trouble, which led me to a text. An eminent parallel to this I had, when I was led to that text, Psalm cxxvi. 5. On the morrow I received a letter, and by it expected trouble on trouble. I opened it not till after prayer. Opening it, I was freed from that fear; and going on in my feared studies, things were laid to my hands; and my heart blessed the Lord, who takes such care of me. And considering how these things put me to prayer, I saw them sweet mercies that come as these did, as answers of prayer; and it is much my advantage that the Lord deals thus with me. Thereafter I did some business, and found that another business was frustrated; but I was ashamed to distrust God. On the 15th, being the Lord's day, I preached at Edrom on Lam. iii. 22, " It is of the Lord's mercies that we are not consumed;" unto which also I was led by my own case, as is above noticed; and I had much of the Lord's assistance therein all the day, and in my prayers more than ordinary.

I went to the synod on the Tuesday. Returning to Simprin on the Thursday, I visited the school on the morrow, and went to Dunse. And having spoke with Langton on the affair of the stipend, I found no great encouragement; but these things moved me not being under apprehensions of public troubles, which were then very likely to ensue; there being a general ferment then in the spirits of men through the nation, by means of the disaster of Caledonia. At night, upon occasion of discourse concerning the access allowed some unto God in duty, I found myself much excited to seek him. On the morrow, before I went off to Simprin, being somewhat moved with the shortness of the time I had to study my sermons, I got confidence in God for that effect, by reflecting on former experiences; and in the meantime was quieted in another case which I had been in fear of. Coming to Simprin about two o'clock, I got my studies dispatched accordingly; and on the Sabbath was much helped in the lecture and afternoon sermon. I had ordered the visiting the town that day in the time of the public worship, and found afterwards there was some need for it. The evening exercise was in all respects as before.

Having come on Friday to Kersefield, on the morrow I studied for the Sabbath, having the help of former notes on the subject. But I then observed, that I had frequently found I had hastened my studies, in as short time when I wanted, as when I had help of that kind; and that when I wanted, my studies were more sweet, and I saw best into my subject. And that observation hath, in my experience, held to this day. At night, being returned to Simprin, towards the time of going to bed, I heard an unsavoury noise of men drinking in a neighbouring house, on the occasion of a wedding in view. After waiting a while, and finding they were not dismissed, I went out; and meeting with the master of the family, shewed him the evil of that unseasonable practice. Coming in again, I poured out my soul to God; and their case considered with my own was heavy; my heart was humbled within me, seeing them an unworthy people, and myself an unworthy minister, making an unworthy couple in my eyes. As I went to bed, I had a motion to pass my ordinary I had studied, and to preach on James iv. 7, "Resist the devil, and he will flee from you," being to go abroad from them for a time. And having, on the Sabbath morning, consulted God once and again as to that motion, I was reasonably determined to embrace it. So I reviewed my former notes on that text; and having no time to study new sermons, had no scruple to preach them over again. The which also I did; but with less assistance in the forenoon's exercise than the afternoon, excepting in the preface. The

custom of prefacing in the entry of the forenoon's work, I did then
use; and I reckon had used from the time I was licensed, if it was
not the first day or so I preached; and having retained it all along
to this time. Only in planted congregations, where the minister of
the place used it not, I think I forebore it. I noted that day, that
I still thought, I rarely, if ever, had such freedom of spirit and assistance in preaching, in that country, as I had had in the bounds
of the Presbytery of Stirling; but, by the mercy of God, that observation did not long hold. In the evening exercise I went on as
before, but got a more satisfying account of the sermons.

On the 30th I set out for Barhill; but was in hazard of my life
in Musselburgh water, having ignorantly adventured to ride it when
the sea was in. The horse, I think, was quite off his feet, and
swam. And there being a piece of brae on the far side, he leaped
up, and I held. In the meantime, with serenity of mind, I lifted
up my soul to the Lord, not knowing but it might cost my life. On
the morrow, coming to the ferry, the sea was very rough; but having secretly poured out my soul to the Lord, my heart was calmed,
and I took boat, and was safe. I have formerly taken notice, above,
p. 19, of another hazard I was in. I was in Clackmannanshire the
two first Sabbaths of November. I had determined in my own mind
to preach at Clackmannan the first of these two; but on the Saturday morning early, Mr. Mair entreated me by a line, to preach at
Culross, in regard he was obliged to go to Edinburgh on a certain
emergency; which in these circumstances, though contrary to my
inclination, I could not refuse. After dinner I went down to the
manse, supposing him to have taken his journey; but he had put it
off. Wherefore I endeavoured to make away for Clackmannan;
but he would by no means allow me to go, urging the determination
of providence for my stay, by the violence of the weather through
wind and rain in the time; withal hinting, that he and others desired my preaching there, on a design to endeavour a call for me to
be his colleague, if they could effectuate it. I declared myself as I
always thought, unfit for such a post; but it was not likely that he
would get a colleague of his own choosing, who some years after left
the place himself, and died minister of Tulliallan. When thus detained contrary to my inclination, I retired to my chamber, and
spent some time in prayer, and meditation on my sermon; but was
seized with a severe fainting-fit, and had almost fainted away, but
that I was eased by vomiting, as usual. On the morrow, Nov. 5,
he preached in the forenoon, and I was helped to hear, but somewhat indisposed; which indisposition it pleased the Lord timely to
remove. Howbeit, my legs trembled underneath me as I went into

the pulpit in the afternoon; but when I went to prayer, the trembling went off, and I had much freedom of spirit in preaching the word. Most of the remaining time that night I spent alone, and with Mr. Mair, of whose conversation I ever reaped advantage.

On the Monday, some time was spent in his family in prayer, with fasting? of which I had no notice, till about nine or ten o'clock, when I was thinking of returning to Barhill. Being desired, I stayed, and joined with him in that exercise. The family being gathered together, he began the work, shewing the causes of it; which were 1. The afflicting hand of God on his family, particularly on a child of his at Edinburgh; 2. To prepare for a congregational fast at Carnock; 3. To pray God in behalf of his parish. Then I prayed; after which, he, having spoke a little again, prayed also. These prayers continued long; but we had ended about half an hour after twelve o'clock. After which, retiring to our several apartments, we dined about two, having had no breakfast. This was the first example of a family fast I had ever seen, neither do I remember to have been witness to another without my own family. But I bless God, I saw that, which was the happy occasion of bringing in that part of family devotion into my family afterward at times.

Some time after this a blustering student informed me, that Mr. Mair taught, that all members of the visible church have a general right to Christ, and the benefits of the covenant; and that baptism seals absolutely, that is, as I afterwards understood, that baptism seals that right to them all. Both these things were, at that time, as strange to me as they were to my informer. But now I believe, that sinners of mankind indefinitely, within and without the visible church, have a real right to Christ, and the benefits of the covenant, so as they may warrantably take possession thereof by faith; the which right is contained in the holy scriptures as the original charter, and is legally intimated to all that hear the gospel; all which I have elsewhere more fully declared. But as to what concerns baptism, having conversed Mr. Mair on the head, I could not be of his opinion, which I remember he built on that right, at that time not appearing to me neither. And though afterwards, in process of time, the said right did convincingly appear to me; yet I could never be satisfied as to baptism's sealing of it, so as that ordinance might therefore be lawfully administered to all who with us are called members of the visible church; forasmuch as I look on that sacrament as a seal of the benefits of the covenant in possession, and which the party has a special saving interest in. However, I reckon that worthy man one of the happy instruments of the breaking forth of a more clear discovery of the doctrine of the gospel, in this church, in these latter days thereof.

Returning on the Saturday to Ferrytown, my spirit through grace being in good condition, I preached at Clackmannan on the Lord's day. At Ferrytown I was called to visit a sick man, whom I knew to have been a very profligate person, but found stored with a great deal of ill-grounded confidence. I applied myself to bring him to a sense of his sin and danger; but saw no success thereof. That week I returned from that country to my charge.

From thence, on the Tuesday after, being November 22, I went to Langton, and on the morrow to Dunse; found worldly business very uneasy to me, and ensnaring to my mind; and so it hath been with me all along, having neither heart nor hand for it. On the Thursday I went to Lennet, and married a couple of persons; in which action, relying on the Lord, I found I was helped accordingly. Thereafter, meeting with Abbay above mentioned, his foolish talking afforded me heavy reflections, on the unedifying converse of ministers, and my own among others, as one great cause of the unsuccessfulness of the gospel. From thence I came to Kersefield, where on the morrow I found a dissatisfaction with myself, for that I was not more strong in the Lord, but easily brought, on the least temptation, to distrust God. I continued there till the Sabbath morning that I came to Simprin, where the Lord was with me in my work. On the 25th I had gone to prayer, in which I found palpably on my heart the blowings of the Spirit, loosing my bands, and enlarging my heart with ardent desires after Christ; and these two days my mind has been habitually disposed to spiritual discourse, not finding other discourse pleasing to me. But on the morrow, being the Lord's day, I found matters were not right, which was occasioned by my unwatchfulness, having ventured too far on ground slippery to me, wherein though I kept my feet a while, yet I slipt at length. My heart not being lively before, became more dead, with unseasonable thoughts, or rather fancies. The consideration of which did empty me of myself, and made me see it would not be poor I that would work the Lord's work. Yet it pleased the Lord to help me well all this day, from the lecture forwards; for I lectured with a good frame, having light, life, sense, and heart satisfaction; and had more than ordinary help in the prayer after it. In both sermons I was helped to be serious for the good of the people's souls, somewhat pithy, peremptory, and particular, in the strength of the Lord. Betwixt sermons, walking a little at the end of the kirk, reflecting on the unsuccessfulness of the gospel, and withal on the prayer after the lecture, I thought all that was left us now was some greedy looks and desires after a hidden Christ. After sermons I went to God, and poured out my soul before him for a blessing on what he had helped me to deliver; was owned of him in all the parts of the evening exercise, and got a more satisfying account of the sermons than sometimes before.

On the Thursday after was a national thanksgiving to be observed. But being now on the point of taking up house, I went on the Monday to Dunse, where I continued till Wednesday, finding the great disadvantage of an unsettled abode, and more disadvantage of being employed in worldly business. That night I returned to Simprin, where, with no great difficulty, I studied my sermons before I slept, having on the day before, in which I had no opportunity of studying, sought light and furniture from the Lord for his work, and been determined to a text. I was helped through the day. After the public work was over, I had great fear of evil days; and I am almost persuaded that I will see evil days, if God spare me any considerable time; and how to carry rightly through them, is my exercise. But that word; Psalm xxxvi. 9, "With thee is the fountain of life;" in thy light shall "we see light," was sweet and seasonable to my soul. On Tuesday last I met with some printed scruples concerning this thanksgiving. I sought light from the Lord, and they proved no scruples to me; only one of them had some weight with me, which was too scrimp dealing with the Lord, in that we were ordered to pour out prayers that day likewise, because of the great sickness now raging, and the disaster of Caledonia, and that there was not a particular day of fasting for them. This I resolved to testify against; yet when the time came, it was still kept out of my mind, and I was borne off it. It may be it was of God; for it is thought that such a fast at this time would greatly weaken the king's interest in Scotland. *N. B.*—Thus political views have influenced our church management all along. The evening exercise was made that day as on Sabbaths.

Next day, December 1, I was obliged to go to Churnside fair. Having come to my sister's house, it was against the grain with me to go to the market-place. Seeing the multitude, I thought I could have entered in among them more boldly, if I had been to preach the gospel to them; and I went out forward into the market place, but immediately retired into a house, and my father did my business. Returning that night to Dunse, I was on Saturday taken up with business, having only so much time left as to go to Simprin, wearied of an unsettled abode, both in respect of its taking me off from the work of my calling, and the trouble thereof otherwise. After prayer I had very much of the divine assistance in studying my sermons, with much satisfaction; and thereafter was helped to pour out my soul before the Lord, feeling the blowings of his Spirit;

wherefore I took that occasion to mind the affair of my marriage.
On the Sabbath I had the same assistance in delivering the word.
And here I find I made the following comfortable reflection, viz.
The Lord is indeed good to me; blessed be the name of the Lord:
for I have now the same freedom every way, in preaching, as when
in the Presbytery of Stirling. The evening exercise, on the question
concerning the providence of God, was sweet to me; and in converse after it, it was a pleasure to think and speak of the saints'
grounds of encouragement from that head, under trouble, particularly, how it is their God that guides the world; and nothing do
they meet with but what comes through their Lord's fingers; how
he weighs their troubles to the least grain, that no more falls to
their share than they need; and how they have a covenant right to
chastisements, to the Lord's dealing with them as with sons, to be
rightly educated, not as servants, whom the master will not strike,
but put away at the term.

On the Monday, being now resolved to remove, I went to Dunse
to make ready for it. Thence on the morrow I went to Churnside
to the Presbytery, where one Mr. Watson, a north-country man,
rejected before by the Presbytery, was again brought on the field,
sore against my heart, perceiving him to be a man of no manner of
modesty, nor sense of the weight of the work; but a brother from
his own private motion, had given him a text. He was appointed
to deliver his discourse on it that day eight days, at Hutton, before
three brethren, whereof 1 was one. At night I returned to Dunse,
where, on the morrow, the pressure I had in the presbyterial affair
foresaid, made me look to the Lord for his own helping in the case,
and for my direction therein. And such matters have all along,
generally, been of great weight with me; judging it always to be a
most momentous part of the ministerial charge, the admitting of
men to the preaching of the gospel. That night, being December
6, I went to Simprin for good and all.

On Thursday the 7th, came the wains with the household furniture from Dunse, my father coming along with them on my horse;
so that day I took up house with him, and Alison Trotter my cousin-
german, a servant. The manse being in ruins, I settled in an old
house in the west end of the town, formerly belonging to Andrew
Home, sometime portioner there; and there I dwelt till towards the
latter end of the year 1702. Things being put in some order that
night and the morrow, as I walked through the floor, seeing myself
in my own house, I was but little affected with it, and thought that
now I had it anew confirmed, That worldly things are greater in expectation than in fruition. When we were quiet, that word; Psalm

lxviii. 6, "God setteth the solitary in families," which was once very sweet to me when at Kennet, came into my mind. On Saturday, after the morning family worship, viz. singing, reading, and prayer, and having determined to read in the Old Testament in the morning, and in the New at night, I addressed myself to my work for the Sabbath; and, after prayer, did with some difficulty fall on a text, viz. Rom. i. 23; but I had much of the divine assistance in my studies, and meditating thereon; so that my false heart, taking occasion therefrom to be lifted up, sent me groaning to the Lord, for help against it.

On the Lord's day, being the 10th, I had signal assistance in every part of the public work; howbeit I had seen no commentary on what I lectured; and I preached with light, life, and zeal, man's heart's fulness of all sin by nature; and some strangers seemed to be affected. Coming home, I saw cause to bless the Lord, for his return to me in public ordinances; and went immediately unto my closet, to secret prayer; the which, since that time all along unto this day, hath been my ordinary practice. After supper, I spent the time till the evening exercise, in meditation and prayer, with special respect to my not finding on my own heart such impressions of my own vileness as I ought to have had; yet so much of it I did see, as obliged me to say, "It is of the Lord's mercies that I am not consumed." Moreover I found cause of thankfulness, that I was in some concern that the devil might not pick up the seed sown. In the evening exercise I again found the deceitfulness of my heart, so as it immediately after sent me unto God, groaning under my mismanagements. I have frequently observed, that as soon as I have begun to complain to the Lord of my spending my strength in vain, I have been led to lay my hands on my mouth, considering how Christ himself spends more invitations, &c., for nought; and what am vile I, that I should be discouraged on that account? Many times I have feared, that the pride of my heart, too high thoughts of my own pains, weariness, &c., have had a hand in these complaints; and that I have not, as I ought, been purely concerned for the glory of God; and that the command to preach has not sufficiently satisfied me. I have been helped to speak to the people by similitudes; but exacting an account of the sermon from the people, several of them told me the earthly part, but quite forgot the heavenly part; which was very wounding to me; so that I know not how to preach so as they may be profited. I have been made sometimes this night to think, what the Lord means by this signal help he gives me, especially these two last Sabbaths, (in respect of which I have been made to notice the return of the Lord's presence to me in his work, as at Clackmannan, or in the Presbytery of Stirling, which I feared had been quite gone); sometimes I think, it may be God has some lost sheep to find here, and sometimes I fear, it is only for a testimony. Only I desire to bless the Lord who so helps me, both in studying and preaching; and it makes my soul say, as Job xxiii. 3, " O that I knew where I might find him !" for, notwithstanding all God's goodness to me, I cannot attain to such lively exercise of faith, love, and heavenly mindedness, as some time before.

On the morrow I went to Dunse, to a monthly meeting for prayer, from several parishes; the which had been set up by the worthy Mr. Colden. Here a heaviness and indisposition of body and spirit fell on me, so that I both wandered and wearied in the time of it. Sometimes I faintly got above it, but fell into it again. I thought in the time that I would get on the finger ends for this; and so it fell out very quickly; for coming from that exercise, I met with a piece of trouble that perplexed and confused me, so that what to do or say I knew not; only I resolved to lay it down before the Lord, being ready to comply with what the Lord would shew to be duty. This was occasioned by a letter from my friend, and I was troubled about putting an end to my marriage with her. It was my unbelief that occasioned my perplexity. In it, my eldest brother was useful to me, encouraging me to trust in God, before whom I laid the case. While I was imparting my uneasiness to him, that word came to me checking me, " When I sent you out, lacked ye any thing ?" And on the morrow I was much enlarged in prayer, for light to know my duty therein; and was hopeful that the Lord, who had given light in other things relative thereto, would give light in that point too. Thereafter I went towards Hutton to hear Mr. Watson's discourse, which affair had made me oftener than once to implore the divine conduct. Coming near the place, I was informed, that the business was done by others on the day before; that the discourse was much of a piece with his former, and they had given him a new text. Coming home, I was in perplexity about my own affair aforesaid, went to God with it, thought on it, but could not bring the matter to a point; but, by the good hand of God, one of the members of the meeting for prayer, began the exercise that night with singing, Psalm lxi. from the beginning, " O God—What time my heart is overwhelmed, and in perplexity," &c. Afterwards conversing with my father on my business, I was somewhat eased, perceiving it might be accomplished about August following. And afterward having occasion to write about it, I went to God for guidance and direction therein, and things seemed to be cleared to me.

Dec. 12.—I have had, for a long time, a desire to set up week-day sermons. And since the synod (at which time I had great apprehensions of evil days, which pressed me to be busy in my time) I resolved to try what encouragement I might meet with in prosecuting it. This night I proposed it to two of the members of the meeting for Christian fellowship; who received the motion with all gladness; and I was desired to begin it next Thursday's night. Upon which immediately I found a great averseness in my own mind to it; thinking withal, that I should have tabled it particularly before the Lord ere I had proposed it. Thus I saw the dreadful deceit of my heart. I pressed my heart with that word; 2 Tim. iv. 2, " Preach the word, be instant in season, out of season;" but it would not do. And as I was going out of doors, it was suggested to me, that the Lord had thus punished me for not seeking light expressly as to that particular. While I wrote this, I thought it indeed a temptation of Satan to divert me from this work. (*Nota*, It seems both were true.) I was helped earnestly to seek light from the Lord in it. On the morrow I went to God again with this business; yet could I not be satisfied to undertake that work, so long and so much before desired by me; neither had I any thing material to object against it. Wherefore I renewed my suit; and thinking about it, got my heart more satisfied and inclined thereto, urging myself with the Lord's kindness to me in his work, and the necessity of the people's souls. I went to God again with it; and, in fine, the assiduity of the faithful ministers, the apostles, and others, preaching both by day and by night, and no doubt sometimes to a small handful, did overcome me; so that I determined to go on, desiring heartily to comply with it. On Thursday the 14th, at night, I began this exercise; having spent the afternoon in catechising. I went about the examination under a sense of my own emptiness and insufficiency; and was well helped while my heart kept right; but it turning to some one or other of its biasses, my help decayed. In the evening exercise the Lord's presence was such, that I was made to say, " It is good for us to be here." When alone, the mismanaging of the examination, yea, and the sermon too, lay heavy on me; and therefore I went to God for pardon of my weakness. And that exercise I kept up all along after, during my continuance in Simprin; and had many a sweet refreshing hour of it. In the winter season, our meetings were in my house, and in the night; in the summer, they were in the kirk, at the time of the day wherein the men rested from their labour; for the people were servants to Langton. And I believe that, for the same reason, it was only the women whom I catechised at any other time of the day;

being solicitous that the master's business might not suffer by me, nor my good be evil spoken of on that account. On the morrow after, having visited the sick, and found how the Lord had laid his rod on my handful, I was thereby convinced, that, had I slighted the motion for the Thursday's sermon, I would have had no peace in so doing. Having come home from this visitation, I reflected on it, and saw what secret averseness was in my heart to it, and how poorly I had managed it. I got a clear sight of the freedom and riches of grace, went by myself, and lamented my emptiness and unworthiness; which when I saw, it gave me a check for an inward itching after more work, whereby I might have a little more stipend. That work was, I think, to have been a catechist in Dunse, the encouragement £100 Scots. I had such an offer, and refused it; yet since that time I had such an itch after it. Last night in reading the latter part of John vi. the Lord held his candle before me, helping me to understand it. This night having consulted some books, and my own heart, on the sinfulness of man's natural state, to see what further of that subject remained to be handled; there occurred only man's death in sin, to which I was determined accordingly. On the Saturday I studied it, but not with my former assistance; but, after having prayed, and found it to be owing to that I was not so much emptied of myself as before, reckoning the subject more easy, I recovered the divine aid, in meditating afterward on what I had prepared.

Dec. 17.—Being the Lord's day, in the morning I was somewhat heavenly, and had some desire after, and delight in the Lord. As I went to the kirk, seeing a student going thither, it was a temptation to me not having studied my lecture with commentaries, for at that time I had few, or none at all. My frame decayed. Singing after the lecture, an unseasonable thought a little entertained, did me inexpressible prejudice. In prayer I knew my distemper, had some kind of grief for it; but my heart, I thought, was not softened; and the preaching going away with little pith, I cut it short. Betwixt sermons I went into a barn near by the kirk, much dissatisfied with myself; saw how I had brought on myself that heavy alteration, went to God taking shame to myself, wrestled with him for pity, laying all oars in the water, especially pleading the covenant, and cried that he would remember it according to his promise; Lev. xxvi. 40—42. Then going away again with the promise of his presence, we sang the 6th psalm from the beginning, being my case. Having prayed with a deep sense of my own vileness, and the falseness of my heart putting me wrong after God had set me right, I preached at first with some life, till, through the

Spirit's blowing more upon me, all my bands were loosed; then I went on with light, life, satisfaction, and concern for their souls; and especially found my heart enlarged to preach the freedom and riches of grace, with a hearty abhorrence of the doctrine detracting from the praise thereof. All went right in some measure that afternoon; and I had rather more than less of my former aid; withal there was some appearance of the word's making impression on some of the hearers. The time being far gone, no psalm was sung after; in which I think, I did amiss, if it was in my power to have commanded four lines. With the student above referred to, I had sometimes had some scuffles on the Arminian points; he coming in a little after sermons, expressed his satisfaction in opposition to these. After supper, having read something for the question to be handled, the people came to the evening exercise; and with a sense of my own emptiness and insufficiency for the least duty, I went to God for his aid, seeing how I could not go but as led, nor stand but as holden up; and I was helped. A while after, desiring to note the progress of that day, such was the temper of my evil heart, in consideration whereof the states of innocence and of glory were that night big in my eyes, that I was averse to go to prayer beforehand; but I, finding this, peremptorily resolved, that go I should; and durst not delay it, fearing, from former experience, the growing of that distemper; the which I also did accordingly. Ah for the power and prevalency of unbelief! I think if there were no more in heaven but freedom from this master-devil, it were most desirable. That night I began the catechising of the servant; the which part of family duty I continued in my family on the Sabbath nights, till of late years my strength decaying, I almost confine it to the time of the year wherein we have but one sermon.

On the morrow I visited the sick, and spent the afternoon in catechising, and found great ignorance prevailing. On the Tuesday, visiting a sick woman grossly ignorant, after I had laid out before her, her wretched state by nature, she told me she had believed all her days. I thereupon sat as astonished for a while, lifted up my eyes to the Lord, and addressed myself to her again for her conviction; howbeit nothing but stupidity appeared. Therefore I saw I had enough ado among my handful. I had another diet of catechising on Wednesday afternoon; and looking to the Lord for help, I got it; and I had some more comfort in them than before. Having inculcated almost on each of them their wretched state by nature, and they frequently attending the means of instruction, there were but few examined that day who did not shew some knowledge of that point. But the discovery I had made of their ignorance of God and of themselves, made me the more satisfied with the smallness of the charge.

On the Thursday, thinking to preach the weekly sermon on 2 Cor. xiii. 5, "Examine yourselves," &c., after prayer for light and direction, I was surprised with that word slipping into my mind; Hos. iv. 6, "My people are destroyed for lack of knowledge." And hereto I was, after prayer, rationally determined; and that was the first particular subject I entered on in that exercise. At night the Lord was with me, and I had a pretty frequent auditory. That opportunity of serving the Lord was big in my eyes, and my soul blessed him for that he had put it in my heart. After this, with joy I saw myself in Simprin, as in my nest, under the covert of Christ's wings. Reading divinity that night, I was caused to lift mine eyes to the Lord, for light into his truths, seeing the emptiness of book-learning without the Spirit.

Next day I visited one of my neighbouring brethren, with whom I found not the affection I wished for. My preaching twice on the Lord's day in the winter was reckoned unneighbourly, notwithstanding the singular circumstances of my charge, all in one little town, within a few paces from one end to the other; the which, shewing no necessity of making a difference betwixt summer and winter in that point, did put me upon the quarrelling method, and kept me at it while in that place. Returning home, I read a while; and at that time I was reading "Witsii Œconomia fœderum," which I had borrowed. To that excellent book I was seasonably led by kind providence at that time. Having left off reading, and made a review of the day's progress, I saw an end of all perfection, no satisfaction in the creature, all treasured up in Christ alone. I found the hardship of having almost none in the country to tell my mind to, but Mr. Colden, who was then about to leave it, going to Oxnam, where he continues to this day. I had a very heavy heart that night on the account foresaid. I would fain have writ to Mr. Mair, but his speaking of my transportation barred that. But my soul blessed the Lord, that I had Christ to run to; it was the very support of my soul, that God governed the world, and that I might pour out my complaint in his bosom. Accordingly I lay down a-bed with that word; John v. 22, "The Father hath committed all judgment to the Son;" which many a time had been sweet to me.

Saturday the 23d, the day was far spent ere I fell on a text; which having got at length, being Rom. vii. 9, "I was alive without the law," I went upon with some help from the Lord. At even I was ruffled with some household furniture procured for, and brought to me, but not agreeable to my mind.. Withal I received

information, by a letter, of a piece of the blustering student above
mentioned his management with respect to me, which touched me in
the quick. I went and unbosomed myself to the Lord; but my discouragement remained, by means of that galling trial. I observed
the Lord's kindness in that, in our ordinary, that first met me;
John xiv. 1, "Let not your heart be troubled; ye believe in God,
believe also in me;" and the latter part of the 13th Psalm in singing.
After the unbosoming aforesaid, I found myself faint, not having
dined at my ordinary time; therefore I immediately supped; and
my body being strengthened, but my mind still troubled, I went to
family worship, and thereafter to my studies, endeavouring to
strengthen myself in the Lord. On the morrow, being the Lord's
day, after prayer in the morning I had given way to some worldly
thoughts, which were indeed occasioned by something that concerned my conscience; yet my heart soon went without bounds; so
that though a desire to be near Christ remained in me, yet I found
an averseness to duty even in the very time of duty. Entering on
the public work, my prayer was according to my frame, complaining of a body of death, and an ugly heart, and admiring heaven as
a place of rest from sin. I preached that day man's ignorance of
his wretched state by nature; and was sure that God called me to
preach it, by the voice of the people's necessity, two of whom had
told me expressly that week, they had believed all their days. That
night I altered the evening exercise, from explaining a question
sermon-wise, to catechising, as more fit to profit the people; and to
this I had been determined after seeking a discovery of the Lord's
mind therein. The public work being over, my heart was discouraged; some impressions of yesternight's trouble remained. I was
grieved at this; said, Why art thou cast down, O my soul? It
was answered, Because I have not assurance of God's love. I thought
I had the testimony of conscience, but can never get the testimony
of the Spirit to put me quite out of doubt. I went to prayer, conversed with God; it was wondrous in mine eyes; my morning
averseness was overcome. I was humbled before the Lord, and
would fain have been quit of an unbelieving heart. I pleaded the
promise, "He that loveth me, I will manifest myself to him." But
I feared my love was not of the right sort, upon that very ground
that I suspected Christ manifests himself to his own otherwise than
he has done to me. I put the question to myself, How shall I know
whether Christ has manifested himself to me as to his own or not?
Answ. to this purpose, All have not alike manifestations of him;
he takes three only of the disciples up into the mount. Philip says,
Lord, shew us the Father; yet Christ tells him, "He that hath

VOL. XI. H

seen the Son, (whom Philip had indeed seen), hath seen the Father
also." What effects has the manifestation of Christ had on them
that got it? The Psalmist, that saw him fairer than the children
of men; Psalm xlv. 2, his heart speaks good of him. It has been
the desire of my heart to commend Christ to others, and I have
found my heart bubbling up his commendation. 2. It made him
think and say, "Whom have I in heaven but thee? and there is
none upon the earth that I desire besides thee." My soul can be
satisfied with nothing in heaven or earth, no not with heaven itself,
without him; and I think I could be satisfied with him alone. 3.
It made him say, "Thou didst hide thy face, and I was troubled."
So is it with me. My heart was somewhat lighter, though I was not
raised up much from my trouble. At family exercise my heart was
somewhat raised with respect to that trouble, by some passages,
John xv. Afterwards we sung the latter part of the 14th Psalm;
and I very well remember, I thought I could get nothing there for
me; yet that word, "You shame the counsel of the poor, because
God is his trust," was laid open to me as with a strong hand, it striking at the very root of my particular trouble; and then I saw I had
something to answer them that troubled me. My soul blessed God
for his word, and for that word in particular, that ever it was put
in the Bible. It has loosed my bands, set me to my feet again, and
put courage in my heart. My heart rejoiceth in his salvation, and
in himself. One thing is observable in this, that being this day
persuaded, that my untender walking was the cause of God's hiding
himself, and that a certain foul step was the cause of this particular
trouble, after I was made sensible of it, and lamented it more before
the Lord, then, and not till then, the deliverance came. After the
above happy outgate, I spent some time in thinking of the Lord's
kindness to me, and closed the night, far spent, with singing Psalm
xxxiv. 1—11, and reading the scriptures; observing, meanwhile,
that wanting written commentaries, a heavenly frame of spirit, and
soul-exercise, whether about temporal or spiritual things, were two
excellent commentators; and then praying to my God, who doth all
things for me, went to bed.

On the Monday my heart was borne up with the word which the
night before had set me to my feet again. And for some days, till
I fell by my iniquity, that word was sweet and refreshing to
me; and to this day I look on it as having a particular interest
therein. Having gone to Dunse on business, I had much satisfaction in converse with Mr. Colden; my heart being heavenly, spiritual discourse was pleasant; and on Tuesday morning that scrip-
ture-text; Jer. xvii. 6—8, was sweet to me. Mr. Colden was then

pressing to get away out of Dunse, as a charge too heavy for him; and I was in a particular concern for his continuance. At night I went to Langton, where, while Mrs. Dawson and I were talking, the child in her arms suddenly was seized with a violent convulsion-fit, wherewith we were both struck with surprise, and thinking the child likely to expire, we went to prayer sometimes as occasion served; for it continued long. I observed in my heart, how vain the world was, and the troubles attending the married state; but little knew I then, that the same woman was to be employed to strike me with a heavy surprise in my own case in that state; which came to pass after. The child's fits continuing, I was obliged to tarry all the next day; and there being a project for a catechist in Dunse, for Mr. Colden's case, I went to Dunse on the Thursday to forward it. After conversing with him in the first place, I addressed myself without his knowledge to the main agents for the parish, whom, with some difficulty, I got to condescend to an overture for effectuating that project. Thereafter I discoursed Mr. Colden on the main thing, and thought that by what passed our hearts were more glued together.

Thereafter coming home, I thought on my sermon by the way, and soon studied it, after I was come home; but being seized with a weariness, I left off my proper business, though the time was approaching; and even when the people began to convene, I was sitting discoursing with my father about worldly business. Thus, through the just displeasure of a holy jealous God, I fell into a heavy case, wherein for several days I lay. I was that night deprived of his countenance in his work; on the morrow I was averse to duty; religion was to me as a strange thing; and my mind was darkened as to my uptakings of Christ. I dragged myself to my studies on Prov. viii. 11, for Kelso, then vacant. I studied, but with great deadness and darkness, being most unfit to manage the subject of the commendation of Christ, which yet I was led to. On the Saturday I could do no more but *look up* under the plague of a hard heart, and was sadly checked for my carriage on Thursday night before sermon, which I took to be the procuring cause of all this. In the afternoon I went to Kelso, where, on the Lord's day, I was under apprehensions of the Lord's anger; yet could not my heart be kindly broken, nor could I wrestle with him for his pity. In the forenoon I had the mercy to speak clearly and distinctly; but it was not right with me. I endeavoured between sermons to confess my sin, and cry for the Lord's help; yet faintly; howbeit it went some better in the afternoon; and to some it appeared a

good day; but my guilty conscience kept me from the confidence in
the Lord that sometimes I had reached. Late in the night I got a
a little healing, which I found continuing with me on the Monday
morning.

Jan. 1, 1700.—Which day having come home, I went on the morrow to the Presbytery; where Mr. Watson aforesaid delivered his
homily before them. My heart, troubled by occasion of him, was,
by means of his prayer, somewhat calmed. But his homily was a
mere bawble, therefore rejected by the Presbytery, and he dismissed; and herein the brethren were of one accord, excepting Mr.
Alexander Lauder, author of the book, intitled "The Ancient
Bishops Considered," who in that matter was in the extreme of
modesty. I have oftener than once, in such cases, with concern observed the more learned men easiest to please. Whether it be an
effect of generosity, arising from their superior genius, and their
more thorough conviction of the weakness of human understanding;
or of their not applying themselves to notice strictly, and observe;
or that the warmest heart is not always joined with the clearest
head; however that is, I was much affected with the goodness of
God in that matter I had so much had at heart.

Meanwhile I still walking halted, until Friday, January 5, when,
studying a sermon on John v. 40, things were clearly laid to my
hand; whereupon my false heart began to be lifted up; but the
Lord turned the chase, and I was made to see my own emptiness
and nothingness, and my heart was enlarged in thankfulness, my
mind more than ordinarily cleared as to the uptaking of the Lord's
word, and my heart heavenly; so that I got the revival I had
waited for these several days. But, oh! my joy is mixed with
mourning; for I fear I will not get his smiles kept, and his frowns
are bitter as death. Reading and singing at the exercise were a
little heaven to me; God was a commentator to me. In prayer my
heart was melted for my sins, and that as they separated me from
God, who was now come again to me. I was afraid to live longer,
because of my base heart. Fain would I have been with Christ out
of the reach of it, being content to leave all the world. Afterwards God continued to be gracious; but oh! oh! my heart is
afraid of a back-cast from Satan, and an evil heart, and my soul is
really almost overwhelmed with fears, that matters will not be long
thus with me. In the greatest blink of his countenance, I durst not
say, it is good for me to be here, viz. in the world. Had I but one
wish, it should be, that he would wrap me up in his love, light, and
life, while I am here, and take me away to eternity when he pleased,
though I would fain do something for Christ here; but my own dis-

honouring of him by my unbelief, worldly-mindedness, &c., puts me
on the rack. But ere I fell asleep, that which I feared came upon
me in some measure. I lost much of my frame. The decay, I
thought, began with a wandering thought in prayer. I should conclude it was but a flash, if, upon a review of my heart, I found it not
in love with him, and hatred of myself for my own vileness. In the
time of the best frame, I had a clear view of the freedom and riches
of grace, as now also in some measure I fear I did not guide right
in these fears of losing my frame, which overwhelmed my soul; for
I had strange thoughts of the condition of the godly on earth, in
respect of the certainty of their sinning still. I know not what to
say of myself in this, only I am sure something was wrong. This
was the occasion of writing the discourse on the 5th question in my
Miscellanies.* I fear had I been in Mary's case, I had not guided
as she, when Christ said, " Touch me not, Mary, for I am not yet
ascended." My cup settled below the brim that same night; and
so it was on the morrow : but I had learned to be thankful for what
was left me, On the Lord's day I preached at Kelso again, going
thither for Mr. Dawson in his family distress; and I was somewhat
assisted to my feeling, especially in the afternoon.

From Kelso I went to Dunse, to see what was become of the affair
of the catechist; and I found it quite marred; and more than that,
that I was suspected of double-dealing in the matter, the which was
expressed by Mrs. Colden. Hereon, I find, I made the following reflection, viz. But the Lord knows that I was innocent. Whether
Mr. Colden was willing to have Mr. J—— B—— above mentioned
to be the catechist, or not, I cannot be positive; but the main agent
for the parish was not willing to undertake for the money, viz. £100
Scots to be advanced for that end, unless Mr. B—— was the person;
so that I reckon the suspicion was, that the project was, on the
parish's part and mine too, a contrivance rather in favour of Mr.
B—— than Mr. Colden; agreeable enough to the suspicious temper
of that good man. However my heart was really concerned for his
continuance in the country, and therefore was most earnest for his
case ; but to my great grief, removing to Oxnam, he left it a little
after.

Coming home on the Tuesday, I visited the sick; and much of
that night I spent in my studies; on which also I was intent the
day following; and on the Thursday's night had advantage by the
sermon.

---

* These Miscellanies were published by the author's son in 1753, being prefixed
to a collection of his sermons, in two volumes, octavo.

On Friday the 12th, at night, the wind was so boisterous, and my house in so ill case, that I was obliged to rise out of my bed for help in the case. Lying down again, I observed how that many seek not a shelter for their souls till the storm of wrath is come, and they cannot have it. After all I was obliged to quit my bed, and go to my father's, lest the house should have fallen on me. On the morrow I studied my sermons with some distinctness and clearness; but launching forth into thoughts of some difficulties as yet not removed, my heart was so entangled therewith, that the edge of my spirit was much blunted. On the Lord's day, the 14th, I was in heavy case, being very dead in the forenoon. Betwixt sermons I began to pity the people I was set over, and thought I would never stand in an evil day. Then began I bitterly to reflect on the causes of the Lord's withdrawing, and saw my being too much taken up with the world the cause of it, and my carriage in the interval of Sabbaths; mourned over these things, and cried for his presence; and I found in the afternoon a concern for their souls' good, and my own soul encouraged and strengthened by the sermon. At the family exercise, reading Acts xvi. how cruelly Paul and Silas were treated, my false heart began to stand at that, that it should be one of the articles of the covenant,* finding a secret unwillingness to undergo such things for Christ, which was sad to me. Then turning to our ordinary in singing, (for then I read ordinarily before we sung), and that was Psalm xxii. 27, *ad finem*, which was sweet and seasonable to my soul. The Lord helped me to look on these promises as promises to Christ in the covenant of redemption, whereby the elect's salvation, and their being brought up to the terms of the covenant, are secured. The several "shalls" there, "shall remember, shall worship," &c., O how sweet were they! I was content God should exercise that sovereign power in me, and make me willing; and my soul rejoiced in the promise.

I endeavoured on the Monday, not without some success, to keep my heart in a heavenly disposition; spent the morning in my chamber, the forenoon in catechising, the afternoon in business, and visiting a sick man at night, with help from the Lord. Thereafter earnestly plying my books, I found my heart much bettered, my confidence in the Lord more strengthened, the world less valuable in my eyes, and my soul free of the temptations that otherwise I was liable to. And on the Tuesday morning, when I arose, my soul began to soar aloft in thoughts of the morning of the resurrection.

* N. B. For many years after this, my knowledge of the covenant was very indistinct.

And after earnest prayer, I betook myself to my studies again, as soon as I could. Experience of this kind hath been one thing, which all along, and especially in latter years, hath recommended close study to me, and in a manner bound it upon me, as being that on which much of my peace and comfort depended. The victual being then dear, the payment of my stipend had been shifted, and was like to have been withheld for a season from me. But when thus I was least anxious about the matter, I understood that orders were given for doing me justice. And here I cannot but observe, that matters of the world go best with me when I am least anxious about them. I examined my heart how it stood affected with this, and found it was not lifted up; but I was grieved I could not be more thankful for it; for I was persuaded that it was the doing of the Lord. I went to give God thanks for it, and to beg a thankful heart; and it was not without some success. Visiting a sick man, the Lord bare in on my heart what I spoke to him, and made me see the reality of it. Having gone to G———, while I was there, my eyes were somewhat dazzled with the world's vanity. So poor and foolish am I, and in thy sight a beast, O Lord!

That afternoon I went to Kersefield, having sought of God strength to carry right in all companies; and by the help I had to season converse there, I was more encouraged to venture on company. And there also I spent some time in reading. On Thursday, having studied my sermon, my heart longed to be at the work; and it fared with me accordingly in prayer; but, by a temptation laid to me in the very time of that exercise, I lost all, and the sermon went heavily on. That same night, the factor visiting me, paid the little money payable by Langton, and shewed me I was to have all the victual due as soon as it could be got ready for me. The stipend of Simprin was paid partly in grain, and partly in money; and there was likewise a proportionable allowance for communion-elements. This was the half-year's stipend, crop 1699, which afterwards I received accordingly. And it was near as much worth as any, and more worth than some whole year's stipend after, on account of the advanced price upon grain at that time. The which put me, I believe, in better circumstances than I was expecting, or could foresee; kind and watchful providence then, as always, balancing my affairs, according to the design thereof.

I read not only on the Friday, but some part of Saturday forenoon; which I am surprised to find; but it seems I smarted for that keenness, such indisposition of body and mind seizing me after, that I was quite unfit for my study for the Sabbath. At length I came to myself; saw and lamented before the Lord, my sin; and

he turned my heart back again. So, after dinner, I began and completed my sermons, in a good frame. But in the morning of the
Lord's day, being the 21st, I found it much abated ; and I could not
recover it, till near the time of going to church. That day, I perceived, that, through the corruption of my own heart, the smallness
of my auditory was to my disadvantage ; knowing by experience,
while a probationer, the sight of a multitude was of use to drive me
out of myself. Therefore I endeavoured to be impressed with a sense of
the weight of the Lord's work in itself, to compensate that loss ; and I
had the divine assistance that day accordingly. Even in the lecture,
I endeavoured to level the word to their consciences, and had advantage by that method, Betwixt sermons, considering how I was
helped to plainness and faithfulness in some measure, I saw, in the
meanwhile, clearly, my inability to stand before a holy God, to give
an account thereof ; and the need of Christ's imputed righteousness
to cover the sins of my public capacity as a preacher. Thus it
was also in my coming home from the afternoon sermon, in which
my assistance had been augmented, acknowledging the justice of
God, if he should eternally exclude me from his presence. But it
was heavy to me, that there was no appearance of success.

On the morrow I went to Robert Fairbairn's in Woodside, and
visited a sick person ; who told me of two things he took for the causes
of the Lord's controversy. 1. His being very cold and overly in his
duties before his sickness seized him. 2. His unthankfulness to
God for what measure of bounty towards his soul he had received,
his being so much in complaints of God's hiding his face, though
since he would have been glad of that which he was then unthank-
ful for. There I was refreshed with a heavenly society, the excellent ones of that part of the earth, though they lived then on borrowed meals, an Episcopal incumbent possessing their kirk of
Polwarth. Returning on Tuesday, I spent the time in reading, till
the meeting for prayer ; where, from what I discerned among them,
I pressed the study of the power of godliness, and concern for the
public. But at that time the appearance of the unsuccessfulness
of my preaching and private conference was such, that I was ready
to conclude, I had ate my white bread in my youth ; that the Lord did
more good by me as a probationer, than, as yet, as a minister. Next
morning I spent closely in my chamber, till eleven o'clock, that I
went to Lennel, where I had some edifying converse with Mr. Pow,
a grave, peaceable, and judicious man. At night returning home, I
applied myself again to reading.

Lying abed after my ordinary time, Thursday morning, January
25, I found it, as always almost, prejudicial to me. When I went to

duty, O what a weariness was it to me! Howbeit I found thereafter great dissatisfaction with myself in my own mind, and a nail
in my conscience, by that means. But in the afternoon, by prayer,
and studying my sermon, I recovered, and was that night much
helped to preach with life, strength, zeal, and solidity. But as I
was going to begin, a temptation of the nature of that wherewith
I had been foiled the preceding Thursday's night, was laid to
me; which nevertheless I, like a burnt child dreading fire, did
escape, being unable to answer it, and satisfy myself, resolving
through the Lord's strength to be in my duty, and grip the promises.
Reading Witsius' "De Œconomia Fœderum," concerning the love
of God and that of ourselves, differencing acts of obedience, and
putting these things home to my own conscience, I found I desired to
be like God, come of me what will. Retiring after sermon to my
closet, the Lord was with me in prayer. And now his kindness
made sin appear to me exceeding sinful, and myself hateful to myself. Reading next day the evangelical Witsius, on glorification, I
found my soul raised to an admiration of the free grace and love of
God to man, I thought even to man though he had continued in in-
nocency, there being such a vast disproportion betwixt the highest
pitch of obedience and the glory that is to be revealed, withal,
wondering how man should be *par tanto honori (oneri) ferendo*, seeing a necessity of supernatural strength for earthen vessels their
being kept from bursting, while so filled to the brim; "No man can
see my face and live." On the morrow, being Saturday, at prayer,
my soul (even Christ the soul of my soul) made me as the chariots
of Amminadab; he touched my heart with a live coal, and set it in a
flame of love and desires towards him; so I wrestled for himself.
Christ with any thing would have satisfied me; nothing without
Christ could do it. This kept me above the world, led me to a text;
Job xxiii. 3, and helped me to understand my lecture; John xx. 11,
et seq., for I had no commentary. The temptation above mentioned,
concerning the eventual necessity or certainty of saints sinning, setting on me again, I still got it shifted, resolving to grip the promise. This I think was well done, in these circumstances; Matth.
xv. 24, 25. However, sometime after, I set myself to consider that
point, for my own satisfaction; and, according to a laudable and
profitable custom I then had, in cases of particular difficulty to me,
committed my thoughts thereon to writing; and they are to be
found among the Miscellanies, Quest. 5, "Why the Lord suffers sin
to remain in the regenerate?"*

* See above, the note, p. 109.

The following part of that week, I plied my studies, and my frame continued. Only, the Saturday's night, upon a certain occasion, falling under an uneasy apprehension, it sent me several times to prayer; but I endeavoured, not without some success, that it should not mar me in my public work, nor in my own soul's ease; and to give up the matter to the Lord, seeing and confessing a certain piece of mismanagement to be the just cause of that distress whether there was ground for it or not. Afterwards, in the event, I found there was none; but often hath God chastised my real faults, by such means, laid aside when the design was obtained. The next day I preached at Lennel the one half of the day, on the aforementioned text. I thought I would be shut; but when I found the wind blow, I thought I would not draw down my sails hastily; for he made me say, " It is good to be here." On the afternoon I preached at home, finding my body wearied; but being posted on to more work, I went to God in a few words, with more than ordinary confidence and stayedness of mind, earnestly pleading the promises of his covenant. I had written but the heads of my sermon, began with a preface, knowing of little to say? but God wrapped me up in it; I had no more to do but speak. O it was sweet, sweet! Far more sweet is the Lord himself. It continued with me in the sermon. O he is good, he is good to a vile nothing, yea, worse than nothing! O to trust him! I found by both these sermons solid love to Christ in my heart. He was not wanting to me in the evening exercise; he was a commentator to me; while I was singing his praises, he shewed me the sweetness of his name while I discoursed on it, " the Lord Jesus Christ." Every letter of it was written in gold. But before that exercise I had a temptation, which had almost mastered me, till I went to God with it.

On Monday the 29th, one came and offered me £50 Scots in loan; which I yielded to take, on conditions I might keep it two years. On the morrow I found myself, by too much sleep, unfitted for work and service; and withal was inwardly checked for not having visited the families again, before that time. At night, at the meeting for prayer, I got a little revival again, which I think I slept away on the Wednesday morning, whereof I have had several sad experiences. Howbeit, that day I visited some families. My method in visitation was this; I made a particular application of my doctrines in the pulpit to the family, exhorted them to lay these things to heart, viz. their natural state, and their need of Christ; exhorted them to secret prayer, supposing they kept family worship; urged their relative duties, &c.; prayed with them, and made the master of the family to pray. (Note, I think this last might have been

as well forborn.) Though there was little religion among them,
there was more than I expected; and perhaps my labour was not
altogether in vain in the Lord. But my frame not being good, I
left that work the sooner, and betook myself to my studies.

Feb. 1.—Having gone wrong again, I was a while stupid and unconcerned, till I thought more deeply on the guilt, and then I found
my confidence with God much marred, and rather a going away
from him under the stings of conscience, than drawing nigh to him.
At last I went to prayer, and laid out my case before the Lord;
yet was I very little quieted. I went and saw a sick man, and, by
converse with him, I attained some advantage, and got my heart
calmed and bettered, by speaking to the commendation of Christ as
the best portion. I am amazed at the baseness of my heart, that
can keep so short while right, and am many time afraid my religion
is of the wrong stamp. But that which supports me is, that in a
calm mood I find myself somewhat emptied of myself, admiring the
riches of free grace if ever the Lord shew me mercy, and justifying
him if I perish; flowing from the hatred I bear to myself for these
things. And how gladly I would be conformed to the image of
Christ, Lord thou knowest. I observed this day myself much the
worse, 1. Of not observing fixed meditation when I lie down, and
when I rise, so duly as some time before; 2. Not preparing my
heart more conscientiously for family exercise; 3. Sleeping too much
sometimes; 4. Beginning so soon on the Monday morning to meddle
with any secular business. And I find I am the better, 1. Of spiritual converse with my people; 2. Of plying my studies closely.
Going home, I went to prayer; and my averseness to come into the
presence of God, wherewith I had been seized under conscience of
guilt, was taken away; and the Lord loosed some of my bands. On the
morrow, having visited some families, I found I had not that power and
life in going about that duty that was to be desired. And although I
have endeavoured to amend the first three of the aforementioned things,
which I noted myself to be worsted by, resolving in the Lord's
strength to go on, and endeavoured all that day to watch my heart;
yet it is no wonder 1 go halting, to teach me to know what a bitter
thing it is to be so ungrateful to the Lord. Besides, I am sure I
have been too legal in these things, and have not, as I ought, believed. The following time I spent in preparing the weekly sermon,
and recording the heads of discourse at the two immediately preceding meetings for prayer, in a book. Taking some time to prepare my heart, by prayer and meditation, for preaching, there was
somewhat of a breathing on my dry bones; and then did my distance from God, ingratitude to him, and wearying of duties, espe-

cially secret and private, like darts strike through my liver; yet
found I much hypocrisy in my heart. I set myself to guard against
the rock I had split on before. However, my confidence in God was
very small; and according thereto was the measure of countenance I
had in the sermon. But it was good he did not leave me altogether
to my own weight. A conviction I then had of my loss, by beginning so soon on the Monday mornings to write letters, or meddle
with any secular affairs, prompted me to desire to spend that morning in prayer and meditation, with respect to the Sabbath's work.
And by that time also I had thoughts of preaching one of the diets
of the Lord's day, on a text different from my ordinary.

On the morrow, February 2, I was fastened to my studies till the
evening, mixing them with prayer. At which time, having been at
some pains to prepare my heart, and beg the divine presence, I went
and visited some families; but with little satisfaction. So returning
with a sorrowful heart, I poured out my complaint before the Lord.
But still it lay heavy on my spirit, having withal a sense of my
utter insufficiency for that piece of my work. I found it hard, yea,
without a supernatural power, impossible, to bring people to a sense
of their need of Christ. Meanwhile I was convinced of the justice
of the divine procedure with me in that matter, and of my legal way
of managing duty. I saw then also a secret averseness of heart to
that work, which, when I was probationer, I thought I would have
gladly embraced an occasion of. Considering that night the state of
the public, I thought all ranks of persons, ministers as well as
others, were out of the way. And that same night I learned, that the
Lord had directed to hit the sores of some at the preceding weekly
sermon, so that they thought some had told me; in the which I perceived the divine conduct.

On Saturday, the 3d, it was long ere I could fall on a text for
Churnside, where I was to preach. And when I was fixed in that
point, my studies thereon went on heavily, insomuch that having made
but little progress therein, I behoved to go away towards that place.
At night, being there, my studies succeeded better with me; and I
was enlarged in my meditations thereon. On the Lord's day, I was
more helped in preaching than in prayer; wherein I found myself
under a great restraint. When alone, I was not so confused in my
uptakings of Christ and religion, as in some other times of desertion.
Yea, according to my doctrine that day, no less than Christ could
satisfy me; I saw his supereminent excellency, and the emptiness of
all things besides him; and my soul was in some sort lifted up in the
ways of the Lord. But how to reconcile that with the restraint upon
me in prayer, I knew not. But certainly there may be an enlarge-

ment in affection, where there is a straitening in words; Psalm vi.
3, and lxxvii. 4; Rom. viii. 26. On the Tuesday I visited at Lint-
laws a godly friend, then a widow, who shewed me how helpful the
sermon at Edrom, October 15, 1699, on Lam. iii. 22, had been to her
in her afflicted state; which called to my mind that word, "Who
will hearken and hear for the time to come?" Isa. xlii. 23. After
this I returned to the Presbytery at Churnside, where at the preceding diet, upon occasion of requiring a probationer's subscription,
I had observed, that the formula we of that Presbytery had to subscribe, was a very unfit one, being that which was calculated by the
assembly for those of the Episcopal way who were to be received into
ministerial communion. This was then seconded by Mr. James Ramsay, who further proposed that there should be a new formula made.
And indeed, in presbyterial management of matters of the greatest
weight, Mr. Ramsay and I seldom differed in those days; but at this
diet, the motion was so opposed by some, that nothing was concluded. However, I declared, how I thought the formula above said,
which we had signed, might be prejudicial to the interest of the
church in after times.

Having returned home that night, I spent the next day mostly in
reading, frequently looking upward to heaven; but still thought I
was made to go halting, for my ingratitude for the divine kindness
on the Sabbath was eight days before. But at night, going to bed,
I was helped to pour out my complaint into his bosom. On Thursday morning, the 8th, my frame continued; but I unhappily betook
myself to reading, putting off my studies till the afternoon; at
which time company coming in, I had very little time for study. I
preached and prayed that night in bands, and so was justly chastised for my unseasonable reading. The Saturday I spent entirely
in my studies, which went not ill with me; and I found there was
no ground for the uneasy apprehension above mentioned. Upon that
occasion I observed, what I have in several instances since that time
observed also, viz. That it was easier for me not to be lifted up with
worldly things going according to my wish, than to keep right under
cross dispensations. But upon weighing of that matter, I judge the
observation must respect the first brush or commencement of prosperity or adversity, not the continued train or course of the same;
and that my natural temper hangs is biased that way.

Feb. 11.—This morning, being the Lord's day, I got my heart in
some measure to self-emptiness, and greedy looks to Christ. I had
much of the Lord's help. The lecture on Psalm xvi. was sweet
to me. Betwixt sermons I feared I had not got my heart deeply
satisfied in Christ alone, and contempt of the world; and there-

fore it was my desire to get such grace in the afternoon. O! that 147th Psalm from the beginning, which we sung before the afternoon sermon, was sweet. I got a commentary especially on that, "Who the dispersed of Israel doth gather into one." I thought I saw how believers were like poor straggling sheep in a wilderness; but the great Shepherd would come, and gather them all to himself into heaven, ere long. It is good for all, especially ministers, to be emptied of themselves, and to have Christ and the good of souls before their eyes. Simprin! O blessed be he for his kindness at Simpprin. If I could believe, there would be no fear of me here. When I came home, upon reflection I found much to mourn for in myself and the people. The people came to the exercise; and whatever part I have in Christ, I am sure I took much delight to speak to his commendation, and my heart loved him. I have been pressing self-examination; and I think I will see what I can say to that; Psalm xvi. My heart being in love with him for himself, and desiring him above all, my heart says, "Preserve me, O Lord, for in thee do I put my trust." I know I am surrounded with evils on every hand. I cannot save myself; and though I know no other Saviour but Christ, I find it still somewhat difficult to fasten my feet on the promise. (Here, just here, I was put to a stand). I cannot believe thought I; and so descending to myself, I could not think Christ loved me, and found a secret desire in my heart to leave this work; but, thought I, what am I doing? that is not the first question, (O the deceit of Satan!) I will try whether I have these evidences of faith or not that are set down there. I thought, when I began this, I had faith. 1. "O my soul,—thou art my Lord." Now I have taken Christ for my Lord, and that without any known reserve, Lord, thou knowest. And now again, with my whole heart, O Lord, I am content to take thee still, and that for thyself as well as thy benefits. 2. "My goodness," &c. Though under a temptation (and such temptations have come on me sometimes like lightning, as this very night, at which my heart started) I begin to think something of my silly essays at duty; yet otherwise I find I renounce all my own righteousness, and acknowledge God would be no debtor to me, but justly might damn me, though I should burn quick for him. But what if that be merely from an enlightened conscience? I doubt if that will make men renounce their own righteousness; Matth. v. 3. Though an enlightened conscience may let men see the equity of God's judgments against sinners, even themselves; yet I am sure it cannot make men approve of the law of God; Rom. viii. 7, and vii. 23; Psalm i. 2. But so it is, my soul approves the whole law of God in all its parts, threatenings as well as promises; Psalm cxix. 128, 172. 3. "To the saints"—. I have little experience of this; I have little to give; yet I can willingly, upon the command of God, give what I may to any, and far more would I to poor saints; but I am sure, I would if I could help any of them nearer Christ, and I rejoice in their spiritual and temporal welfare. They are the "excellent" in my esteem, "I delight" in their society (at least I desire to do it) when they are most heavenly; and the Lord knows grace commends any, more to me, than any thing else whatsoever. 4. "Their sorrows," &c. I believe and approve it, though it should be exemplified in myself. Of all "portions" I desire none other but him; I am content to take Christ for all, and think him a goodly, complete, and satisfactory "heritage." And many times my soul blesseth God, that hath "given me counsel" to make that choice. Be "moved" as I will, I resolve to grip to him, and cleave to him for ever. And the Lord knows it is the desire of my heart to keep my eye always on him, and in my preaching this day he was "before me," to bring myself and others near him. I cannot find much heart-joy, but only my heart rejoiceth to use "my glory" to speak his commendation. And I think I could venture "my flesh" and spirit both on his mercy. And God knows, Christ is the "soul," the life, the sap, and marrow of any thing I have or expect. I would fain hope he will "shew me the path of life." I believe that at his face is "fulness of joy," for I have sometimes had great joy in some blinks of it; and that "at his right hand are pleasures for ever more." And O that my soul would be content to be there, to be satisfied with his likeness, Lord, thou knowest. After this I went to prayer, wherein I was helped to cleave to Christ; and protested, that I would resolutely adhere to him, as my Lord, howsoever he might be pleased to dispose of his joy and comforts; it being enough to me to be brought unto himself, though by the brink of hell.

Agreeable to the desire above-mentioned, I spent the Monday's morning in prayer and meditation, not without some countenance from the Lord. And that day I had the following reflection on it, viz., Would to God I may be helped to hold on, for I have found the benefit of it this whole day; if my poor flock should be the better of it too, how sweet would it be to me! And now, by the mercy of God, from that time all along to this day, it has been my ordinary course to spend some time in the Monday morning, in secret extraordinary prayer, according to the apostle's example; 2 Cor. xii. 8, "For this thing I besought the Lord thrice." In which one needs not question, but there has been a great variety both as to management and success; but it is long since become in a manner natural to me now, being hardly interrupted at any time when at home, but on some unordinary emergent. On the morrow, after my secret devotions, a friend coming to me, wearied me with discourse of worldly business, which was a pain to me; the which he perceiving, did desist from it. After reading "Cartes's Meditations" I saw much of book vanity, and found myself more disposed to seek and long for Christ's teaching by his Spirit. Withal I saw myself reproved, for my slackness in pursuing after the knowledge of Christ. At the meeting for prayer, I observed how Providence ordered the reading of Mal. iv. and singing of Psalm cii. 16, giving light into what was to be the subject of discourse that night.

Wednesday the 14th I spent mostly at Kersefield, and was helped to edifying converse with delight. Coming home at night, I spent the remaining time mostly in reading. Upon my calling to mind, and finding out a letter from an exercised Christian gentlewoman, concerning her spiritual condition, (it was one Mrs. Janet Bruce, whom I had been acquainted with at Airth), I was checked for not having answered it before this time; the which had been occasioned through my not knowing where the answer might find her; and was resolved to amend that fault. On Thursday, what spare time I had was spent in preparing my sermon. And it was well ordered; for towards the evening I was necessarily engaged in company; so that I got only a little space for prayer, before the sermon. And at the beginning of the work I was like to have been worsted by means of the worldy business I had been engaged in; but the Lord appearing for my help, the work became easy and sweet to my soul. Thereafter, having retired a little for prayer, as ordinary, I spent some time in profitable converse with two of the people. Then, after seeking the Lord's mind once and again, I wrote to the person aforementioned, according to the impression I had of her case; hoping that, though I knew not certainly how it was, he also directed me to speak, would also direct to write.

Friday forenoon was, after prayer for direction, spent in writing another letter of that nature, to Helen Hamilton, now Mrs. Johnston, in Alloa; and there are few letters of any kind to this day, unto the writing whereof I do not address in that manner. I was helped to take up and speak to her case, with some measure of light, she having imparted it to me in writing. And I rejoiced to be thus employed by strangers in work of which kind I had little at home. At parting with a student that night, I recommended to him the study of the knowledge of Christ, the gospel, and the power of godliness; as I had done more generally in our converse. Upon which occasion I had the following reflection, viz. O what pity is it to see men quick and curious in the intrigues of nature, yet ignorant of Christ! Upon occasion of enlargement of secret prayer that night, I saw the unreasonableness of the conceit of merit, as if a beggar should think he should therefore have an alms, because he can cry for it, or hath a hand to put forth to receive it. I have observed this day, and yesterday especially, that I was more remiss in family duties than in secret; and I think it is occasioned by remissness in preparation for them. It was a sweet reflection to consider, that I am not now so much under the molestations of a particular corruption as sometimes before. I think, that my being taken up more with the proper work of my calling has been helpful in this. But quickly after Satan fell to his old trade, and snarled like a dog at my heels, and it did me good. I was grieved to see myself fall so far short of likeness to the purity of the divine image, which my soul loved. So that afterward my soul went out in love flames to the Advocate with the Father.

Feb. 17.—Having been for some time seeking light from the Lord as to preaching on different subjects in one day, I was cleared this day; and my ordinary being man's natural state, it was for the other subject still in my eye to exalt Christ, and preach his love, and desire of communion with his people, and that from that text; Cant. vii. 11, " Come, my beloved, let us go forth into the field," &c. But after I had studied with ease my forenoon sermon on my ordinary, being to enter on the other, when I read the text, and saw the connection, I found I had mistaken the spouse's words to Christ for his to her. This gave me a sore dash, fearing that my light that I sometimes get be but delusion; yet my heart remained fixed on the subject; but still I had great hankering after these words, though I durst not willingly wrest the Lord's word. In the meantime was that word, " Arise, my love," &c. Cant. ii. 10, brought to me; but the hankering after the other remained. I went to God with it, laying myself open to his beck, and thereafter was cleared to that, " Rise up, my love," &c., and my heart weaned from the other. I wanted not objections within myself against it, saying, To whom shall I preach it? whom have I that understands it! I had these answers: 1. I knew not but there might be some others that would; 2. May be hearing these things might melt some heart; 3. Understand or not who will, it is my duty to exalt Christ, and the riches of his grace. The passage recorded, February 5, 1699, above, p. 49, was useful here. That which more cleared me to that word was, that, after prayer, I found a deal of power and life with it on my own heart, raising my love to Christ. But at my studies I found it hard to believe what I was meditating on, concerning the

love of Christ; so that it sent me to God against it, and I find still
I have but a struggling with unbelief. I have this day found my
heart bettered by a more conscientious preparing my heart for family worship.

Sabbath, Feb. 18.—This morning I spent in prayer and meditation, found my heart much concerned for success, and a firm belief of
the word in my own heart; yet my vigour was in decay ere I went out.
It is strange there is scarcely one Sabbath morning wherein I have
not deadness to wrestle with, either when I arise, or ere I go out.
In the preaching the Lord loosed all my bands. Betwixt sermons
I was helped to see, that I had believed my doctrine, and I did believe it; and I thought it a token the Lord would help me to believe
my afternoon doctrine; and my soul longed to be in the church
again to preach Christ; and I was helped to speak. But O! still I
found it difficult firmly to believe. In time of sermon I sent up
some ejaculations for it. When I came home, I found indeed my
soul receiving Christ heartily, leaning on him, laying all the stress
of my salvation on Christ crucified. As to the particular things in
his sufferings mentioned in the sermon, I had a kind of assent to
them; but it had little power with it. I could get no further than to
lean on a crucified Christ. I found also I could not believe (i. e.,
seeingly be persuaded of) the greatness of Christ's love to believers.
It is a most difficult task. But who can comprehend it? O that
my soul could apprehend it. When I look on Christ's love particularly terminated on Abraham, Paul, &c., it was more easy to
observe it. [Note, here is a poring on some worth in the creature
to commend it to Christ.] At the exercise I got so little satisfaction of my people, that I scarcely got a word of the law-sermon, and
very little of the gospel-sermon. This gave me a deep wound;
and the unsuccessfulness of the gospel has been and is very heavy to
me. Some think me happy because I have so few people, and these
not unruly; some think otherwise, because of the meanness of the
post and stipend; but none of these move me, but that I am like to
spend my strength in vain. Lord thou knowest it was my duty to
preach what I preached this day. I was confirmed in it at the morning exercise from Psalm xl. 10. It was not the least weight that
lay on me this morning, that I have none (if I may say it—I fear
it is so—but G. G.) to give me help by their prayers. [N. B.
Ere they and I parted, glory to the power of grace, I durst neither
say nor think this.] Being to go to family exercise, I went to
prayer, and came away with my soul knit to Christ, all made up of
desires and wants. My father went about the exercise, and he mistaking our ordinary, sung Psalm xli., from the beginning. O it

was sweet to me, it answered my case, being conscious to myself of my concern for others, which I feared might cut my days, exhausting my spirits. That word, ver. 2, especially had life and power with it, in answer to that case. I saw God could preserve me, and would, if it should be for his glory and my good; and if my body should be at a loss, I should get it compensated another way. Now I bless the Lord, this day, March 4, 1730, that I have not been beguiled. The scriptures are really God's word.

Monday, Feb. 19.—I wanted not the blowings of the Spirit in my secret exercise this morning, which I began this day se'ennight. I have already found the benefit of spending the Monday morning in prayer and meditation. While R. N. was at prayer this day, I had an unseasonable good thought, for which the Lord might condemn me; but I will see if I can outshoot the devil in his own bows. Two worldly businesses had prospered beyond expectation. My soul blessed God for the same, with a holy contempt of them, looking up to Christ, and observing, that still the world goes best with me when I am least anxious about it. Soon after I received a gift, which, though no great one, did greatly confirm me in that observe. Having spent the forenoon mostly in reading, towards the evening, after prayer, I went and visited some families; and the Lord was not wanting to me therein. On the Tuesday I betook myself to my studies till dinner; then till near night I was in converse, and my frame continued in some measure. But being, that night, one way or other diverted, that I entered into the meeting for prayer without seeking the Lord beforehand, which I afterward was sure was my sin, I lost my frame. Thereafter I found my heart more earthly disposed than before. Next day going abroad about business, I got one discouragement after another, which I was scarce able to stand under. O to be out of the world, thought I, as I have been sometimes. But I had no pith to overcome them. I found another business had gone right, which I was sometime troubled about; but wo is me that it overtook me in this frame. So do spiritual decays suck the sap out of mercies. On Thursday the 22d, I sought of God a text; and got one clearly, both for myself and the people. viz. Hos. vi. 4, "Your goodness is as a morning cloud," &c. I got also a heavy heart from the doleful laxness I perceived in a minister, who had come to my house from a wedding-house in the town, where he had been waiting on his mistress. The indecency of this in a minister gave me great offence, which I took the freedom gravely to represent to him, And though I was much inferior to him in age, he took it well; but otherwise I had little satisfaction in his way. Comparing my present frame with the frame

of others, I saw God had got little service of any of us. When he
was gone, I sobbed out my case to the Lord; but was sadly clogged
with corruption, and great darkness, being filled with dampish sad-
ness and unbelieving heaviness, seeing no satisfaction in any thing
of the world, and yet could not get my heart poised up to Christ,
for the dead weight that was at it. In this frame I went to the sermon, and was affected with my own case, and that of the people;
with whom I was in earnest, yet still under great darkness. Wherefore I looked to the Lord, and I had some help of that word; Isa.
1. 10. And while I was thus taken up, the world turned again with
me, and I met with a favourable providence in temporals, that came
very seasonably. By the above word and providence, I got my
heart somewhat elevated again. And by what I had seen and observed that day, I perceived, that God had well ordered my lot, in
the place where I was, as most meet for me. The following day,
being the 23d, was spent mostly in writing letters; and what was
most of a secular nature therein, was the most wearisome, and went
on slowly; and what was spiritual was more pleasant, and proceeded in with more enlargement of heart. A business had misgiven,
after several attempts. I set myself to a holy indifferency, tried it
again, and it succeeded. So does the Lord train me to live above
the world. After this my mind went a-wavering after a thousand
vanities, and spurned all calling back. Next morning, being Saturday, my body and spirit were both in ill case; nevertheless after
prayer I fell to my studies, and recovered both ways; and by meditation on the love of Christ, I got love to him, confidence in him,
and contempt of the world, with a soul-satisfaction in him. And so
frequent has that way of the Lord's carrying on my worldly business according to my frame, been with me, that as soon as I begin
to be anxious about a business, I conclude it will go wrong; and
when I am helped to a holy carelessness about it, I am apt to expect
success. I had then, of a considerable time, found my body exceedingly weakened with studying my sermons; and that day I
stressed myself less; and inclined to think, it would be every way
better for me, if I could study less, and pray and prepare my
heart more; the which course I did then purpose to try. The
Lord's day was a heavy day to me. I spent the morning in prayer
and meditation; but I had not so much as a lively desire after
Christ, and this I could not overcome by all my faint lifeless
prayers. I found, it had been better to have been occupied in thinking of what I was to deliver; for the earthly thoughts that mixed
with my other meditations, helped to mar my frame; and I was
also under bodily indisposition. Yet in singing Psalm lxxxix. 25,

and downwards, I thought my heart was led solidly to see my own
case, and God's unchangeableness as a sure anchor of faith, and so
was helped to believe. But it lasted not. I became melancholy;
so that I see, if there were no more but interest obliging me to live
near God, I am a great fool to let my heart aside; for never can
I have any content, but when helped to walk with God.

On Monday the 26th, I essayed my ordinary exercise; but both
body and mind were under heaviness and indisposition; which on
the morrow continued; and in that time I found a great aversion to
duty, yea even to reading of divinity, the gust being lost. Wednesday afternoon, the bodily indisposition increased; and therewith
the prospect of my difficulties created me some uneasiness. Thereafter I was in such disorder, that I forced on a vomit, begun of itself.
The bodily indisposition continued; but by that little twinge my
spirit was somewhat bettered, having got a little revival; and I
was comforted in reading the marks of faith in Craighead's sermons.
Thus it continued on the Thursday, in which I did nothing but prepare my sermon; in delivering whereof I had some light, and a
little life; and durst not but bless the Lord for what I had, however little. I received a letter from Mr. Murray, shewing the untender carriage of some ministers in Nithsdale; which was very
wounding to me, and seemed, with other things, to write death to
the generation.

. Sabbath, March 3.—Two days before I had a twilight frame; it
being neither day nor night with me. I had not so much ado to
strive with the world as before sometimes; nor did my soul go forth
habitually after Christ with any tolerable vigour. But this morning I was quite lifeless when I arose: became afterwards sensible
of my case, but could get no recovery. I was so bound up in one
prayer, that I could not say one word, but either mentally or vo-
cally groan out that, "Lord, have mercy on me." Afterwards
came in some worldly thoughts, that gave me the other backset.
When I went to the church, we sung Psalm lxix. 13—16. My own
case gave me light into it. Then I went to prayer; and my body
and spirit were both like to faint, so that I had not ability to speak
out; and thus continued a while. At last the Lord cast a live-
coal into my dead heart, and quite changed me both in body and
mind; and with light and life I lectured and preached also. This
continued in the afternoon, and at the evening exercise too, where
Psalm xci. 14, and downwards was very sweet and strengthening,
and as a sconce against mine enemies. Yet afterwards I had a
violent temptation to unbelief in a particular point, which I had
designedly for myself, touched in my sermon. This was so strong,

that I could not master it, for all my preaching about it. I laid it
out before the Lord before I went to bed, and while there wrestled
against it, though with little success. In my retirement after sermons that day, blessing God for what I had met with, I had a petition, that God would either keep me from the case I was in before,
or else would take me home to himself. Upon which I find I made
the following reflection, viz. "It may be it will not come into Christ's
censer; but I am sure, it was my love to Christ, and hatred of sin,
that was at the root of it."

On the morrow, having too soon entertained thoughts of a business, though indeed charitable, I was unfitted for my proper work.
I visited a minister that day; when I came away my spirit sunk.
I saw how others, whom yet I dare not in some things imitate, knew
more of religion, were more lifted up in the ways of the Lord, than
I; yea, while I am quite in the dark, I preach, and must preach,
what many others (beside whom I would think myself unworthy to
open my mouth) do pass. This racked my spirit, considering how
little of Christ I knew; how I am habitually cast down, and cannot win to get my heart lifted up in the ways of the Lord. I saw
Simprin, and thought it was the fittest place for me; fearing I may
be, even in it, a cumberer of the ground. When I came home, I
poured out my soul to the Lord, seeing myself of all men most miserable, and not fit to be seen in this world. But the Lord still hid
his face. I was a wonder to myself, and thought I may be a wonder to the world, and that religion suffers by me, while people may
think I am a melancholy fool, with some singular fancies, closed up
in this place. Next day my heaviness continued and increased,
though in the morning I was helped to cry with some earnestness
for a blink of his countenance, but I found it not. I went unto,
and returned from the Presbytery, in heaviness; but, that day,
our owning, by subscription, the divine right of the government of
the church, was carried. When I came home, I became downright
melancholy, insomuch that, at the meeting for prayer, my head was
so confused, that it was in some measure vertiginous, and my imagination troubled; whence it came to pass, that some intermissions
were caused in my singing the Lord's praises. However, conscience
of duty urging, I adventured to speak on the question proposed
to be discoursed; and thereafter I became more serene. Many a
heavy and melancholy day have I had, through various causes and
occasions, which holy providence hath laid before me; but I do not
remember that I had ever before that time been so afflicted, except
once, when I was a boy; at which time I know of no rational
ground it proceeded upon; nor can I remember one instance since,

wherein it acted so mechanically, to such a pitch; if it is not the passage at Kelso, April 23, 1712, to be related of that date. On Wednesday it was not so severe; but there remained a great heaviness, together with a pain in my back, from the riding the day before, though I was distant from the presbytery-seat but five miles. For this cause I lay much on my bed that day, sometimes walking out, to help myself by means of conversation, which I found useful. No religion was left me now, but a sorrowful looking up to the Lord, whom I had provoked to withdraw. On the Thursday my exercises were very uncertain; I was still faint and languishing in religious duties, found my body unfit for much study; yet had solid hopes of the divine assistance in my sermon; the which also I got, with a good deal of serenity of mind. But indeed it was best with me, when in that exercise. On the morrow, the whole day being spent at Kersefield, when I came home, I could nevertheless find no vigour in my spirit. On Saturday morning I got a rousing stroke, by an apprehension of my father's death, who was indisposed; thereafter my bands were all loosed in prayer; and then I studied my sermon; and my love to Christ, and concern for the good of the people, were raised somewhat. But the heavy disposition of my body was still a clog to me. Writing my case to Mr. Murray, I discerned some ground of comfort in it, especially from my deliberate desire of the glory of Christ, come of me what will. My prayers for my father were heard. In the morning of the Lord's day, I took some thoughts of my notes, the rather to keep my heart steadfast, lest by loose meditations altogether it should not so well be held fixed, but beguile me, as sometimes before. And this, I reckon, was the occasion of bringing me off from that way of spending the Sabbath morning in such meditations; and in coming over from it, to the other method, of thinking on my notes, I designed the impressing of my heart with what I was to deliver, and to get it kept in a frame for preaching; thus still pursuing the former design, but in another method, whereby I judged I was more likely to reach it. When I went away to the kirk, I endeavoured to propose to myself the good of the people, and encouraged myself in the Lord. In the preface my vigour was small, the relics of my old frame still hanging about me; but thereafter I was helped in all. I preached mostly from experience, in the afternoon; and it was sweet. When I came home, I was grieved at the heart for my mismanagement of duty, especially some motions to be lifted up on the account of my assistance, though, when I consider things, being sensible of my own weakness, I would be ashamed to open my mouth before many preachers. I had been for some time solicitous how to manage the visiting of families; the masters of families being workmen, and so can scarcely be found in the day-time in their houses, but at prayer, the day before, as I suppose, it slipt into my mind, that I should take the Sabbath afternoons for it, and this when I was not praying about this particular. Afterwards, though the motion, as so timed, was unseasonable; yet on reasonable grounds I thought I would embrace it. But such was the deceit of my heart, and so forward was I, that, without ever once laying it before the Lord in prayer, I made intimation, there would be no public exercise that night; so, when I was to go out for that effect at night, and was praying for the Lord's help, I was severely checked for this my rash determination, and confessed it before the Lord. But seeing all other doors now closed up, I thought it my duty for this time, and the Lord was pleased to be with me in the work. But ere long, viz., Monday, March 11, Satan cast me down. I confessed and mourned, but afterwards guilt lay so heavy on me, that I could have no confidence to pray for the people. After that my heart hardened, and I had no freedom in spirit for prayer. Then did my soul sink, and I found no place of standing, as one forgotten, yea and cast off of God, whose spot is not the spot of God's people. And thus I continued very long, sinking and going down. I went to the family duties, and desired my father to perform them; and I, as a poor malefactor, sung my own doom; Psalm lii. 6, and downwards, approving the justice of God. Retiring, I got leave to pour out my soul before the Lord, and was somewhat eased; and so thereafter endeavoured to hope against hope, sometimes sinking, sometimes swimming. That day I went to Dunse, in great distress of spirit, to see Mr. Colden, with whom I could use some freedom with respect to my case. Being there, in Mr. Colden's house, and there meeting with some of the godly people of Polwarth, my mouth, according to my then heavy case, was filled with complaints in converse with them. This Mr. Colden did wisely signify to me to be unsafe, in respect of the discouragement it might occasion to them, considering my station and character. Howbeit the particular cause of my heaviness I discovered not to them, nor to him neither; but from that distress I was not recovered till the 25th of the foresaid month of March; at which time I was mercifully set to my feet again; though in a little time the clouds returned after the rain.

March 26.—Having had a good day yesterday, I was like to lose all again this day, and had a struggle that way. I retired, and pleaded with the Lord as my covenanted God in such manner, as pinching want makes men resolute; and was kept up.

March 28.—This day being a fast day, the Lord was very gracious.

to me. It was sweet to consider what measure of solidity and firmness in believing the Lord had given me as to what I had been
preaching, and how he had given me several of those suits I had before him on Monday last the 25th. I had a great deal of confidence
in prayer this night; for God is my covenanted God. O! my soul
was filled with joy and peace in believing; and I thought I had a
feast. Afterwards great fears of temptation seized me, lest Satan
should steal a dint of me; wherefore I communed with myself out
of the scriptures, and got answers to all the reasons of my fears,
till my heart was calmed, and strengthened in the Lord. When I
had passed the difficult step safely, my mouth was filled with praises;
and I saw myself infinitely indebted to free grace, that should
thus give answers of prayer, for I had earnestly prayed against it.
O that was a sweet word to me on Monday's night, " I will give her
the valley of Achor for a door of hope," and yet is so.

April 3.—Being in great distress, I wrote a letter to Mr. Colden,
the only minister in the country to whom I could unbosom myself;
but the letter was brought back, he not being at home; and so I
was disappointed. The said letter is as follows:—" It is like you
will be desirous to know how it stands with me now, considering
the case I was in when I saw you last. I can indeed give you but
a very sorry account of matters. I am a man who, I think, have
few, if any marrows in the world. I am often at that with it, that
I know not what to think of myself, or of my state ;(—it is only to
yourself that I unbosom my poor self, and verily my need presseth
me.) All that week when I saw you, my sad case continued, till
the next,—being estranged from the life of God. So this day fourteen days it pleased the Lord to send—a sharp rod,—and I behoved
to lay my hand on my mouth, and take with the punishment of
mine iniquity; yet remained I like a man half asleep, still going to
rise up, but falling down again ;—which was dreadful to me, considering what pains the Lord had taken on me. So on Monday was
eight days I used some means more than barely ordinary, for casting
out the devil, which that affliction could not cast out ;—and it
pleased the Lord (as I thought) to blow upon me ;—and such speedy
and surprising answer of prayer I got, and such outmaking of
(especially) one particular promise, that I was fully confirmed in the
matter of the Lord's accepting me, and taking me within the bond
of the covenant. And this lasted sweetly the three following days.
But going abroad on Friday, rejoicing in the Lord, (it was to make
a visit), I so mismanaged matters, that I came home drooping ;—
and the Lord so left me, as that my strength against corruption was
gone, and distrust of God trampled me under foot. After some

time I thought I got up resolutely again, and endeavoured to encourage myself in the Lord; but Satan soon after got in upon my weak side;—which I think will ruin me, that spurns all means.—And thus was I cast down again; and now my vigour and life, if ever I had any, is gone; and I am fit for nothing, though I must be doing. It is strangely racking to me to observe, how that before some solemn approach to God, or immediately after I have attained (as I think) to some nearness to God, Satan gets victory over me. I many times fear my spot is not the spot of God's people; and though I would fain make use of some former experiences, yet I am dreadfully afraid that the Lord suffers me to fall at such times, to undeceive me as to these things. I shall not trouble you more, though I have many things that are not easy to me. I entreat, if you can have any liberty with the Lord on my account, remember me." Some time ago I could not easily have closed a verbal discourse, or a letter, without something to the commedation of Christ; but, alas! it is not so now! But my heart desires that others may enjoy much of him, though he be still holden back; and that he may be glorified, come of me what will.

How far I followed my above-mentioned purpose, of retrenching my painfulness in study, I cannot determine; but I well remember, that, that season, still finding my strength exhausted on the Saturday nights, I resolved to study my sermons on the Friday. The which course being begun, and the advantage thereof soon perceived, I have since that time kept all along to this day; bating occasional interruptions; which, when they happened, were painful, in respect of my being so habituated to study that day. So I spent the Saturday in other studies, as I found convenient; till night, that I mandated my sermons, and prepared my lecture, leaving the review thereof only to the Sabbath morning. This was all along my ordinary course as to my sermons; but of late years I have been wont to leave the preparing of the lecture to the Sabbath morning; and since I became unfit for study after dinner, through increase of my weakness, I mandated my sermons in the forenoon of the Saturday.

On the 4th of April we began to meet in the kirk, at or about the ordinary time of the day for sermon, for the weekly sermon, which hitherto had been kept in the house, and that in the night.

On the Lord's day after, and Monday morning, I got a revival. I cannot but specially notice, that while it was well with me, Satan was very active; but afterward he let me alone as to a particular temptation. It seems he has not thought it worth his pains to toss the empty traveller.

April 11.—The Thursday before Lennel communion. I had been admonishing one of my parish some days before, and shewing a difficulty of admitting him to the Lord's table; he turned very angry, and wished he had broken his neck.—Stepping a dike, he hurt his back so as this day he was not able to go to the fast, nay, not to turn himself on his bed.

April 15.—Having been at Edrom yesterday, I came to Dunse this day, minding to go from thence to Kelso to the synod to-morrow with Mr. Colden. But when I came, he was going away, and I could not go with him so soon. So I went home that night; for which I knew little reason till I came home, being blindly led to it. But when I came home, my father was very sick, and that dangerously, as was supposed; but I had no apprehensions of his death. So I went not to the synod. On Wednesday he grew better, and I grew secure, and corruption began to work; and leaving him pretty well, I went out a little, but was called for to him in haste. When I came in, he could scarcely speak to me, he was so ill. My heart was like to fail, seeing the son had ate the sour grapes, and the father's teeth were set on edge. After discoursing to him as a dying man, I went to prayer; and at length won to get some hold of the covenant for my support. I sent for my brothers and sisters, look-on him as a dying man, endeavouring submission in the meantime; which I attained to in some measure this day and the morrow after, at which time he began to grow better; but I endeavoured to be on my guard. Had he been removed at this time, I had been involved in great difficulties; but I got above them in some measure, trusting in the Lord; but earnesttly prayed for his recovery, and had much quiet of heart in the Lord. It pleased the Lord to hear me. And still I see the advantage of submission to the will of God. While I spoke to him about his evidences for heaven, my heart was somewhat satisfied in what he told me. By the good hand of God it fell in our ordinary to sing Psalm lxxi., in time of his sickness; particularly, on Wednesday night, it was from ver. 16 to 20.

April, 24.—This day I saw more of my own nothingness, and that Christ must be all for me, or there is no hope; and I feel his covenant my only support. Blessed be the day I renewed it last, for it has been very seasonable to me many times since.

May 5.—Being the Lord's day. Having been at Barhill, after I came to Edinburgh there were great rains, so that I was afraid the waters would not let me see Simprin on the Lord's day; but I thought it my duty to adventure, if by any means I could reach home. So I came from Edinburgh yesterday after nine of the clock, and came home that night. And this day I was very much owned of God in my work, and nothing more wearied by my journey. O but I saw the way of duty crossing people's ease, a safe way.

The week following I grew secure. I wanted not many checks for my spiritual sloth, so as horror hath taken hold on me, under apprehensions of some stroke to come for this; yet was I as a drunken man, incapable to put himself out of the way of the cart wheels. I also had some flashes of a frame, but passing. On the Lord's day morning, worldly thoughts were as bird's lime to my feet; but preaching about the general judgment, I saw the Lord in his glory, and got a sight of my own vileness; and after sermons, under that impression, secret sins, sins of the heart, were very heavy. And I may say I had no power to bring the subscribed covenant out of my trunk, though sometimes I had resolutions that way.

May 26.—Sabbath, being to preach at Greenlaw, my heart in the morning was in frame; which decayed again; but I was revived by hearing some things, that filled my heart with zeal. (N. B. I think it has been some things ill.) O then I thought preaching would have come ready by hand to me. Yet when I went to the pulpit, I was to seek. But in prayer I got my heart lively and composed again; and had light and life there.

June 2.—I found this day I had much more liberty in prayer than preaching. After the work was over, while in my closet, it pleased the Lord palpably to put in his hand at the hole of the door, and move my heart towards him; and a strange melting there was on my heart, while a neighbour family was singing the Lord's praises. So I found this night another relish in God's word than ordinary, particularly, Psalm lxxxix. 9—13. Being to spend some time in prayer to-morrow, I entreated the Lord would keep me for what he had given me, and I was free of tormenting fears of losing it.

June 5.—Studying a sermon for the fast before the communion at Fogo, I had exceeding much of God's countenance in it; I had much light from the Lord, and the matter had weight on my own spirit. On the morrow I preached it; and though I had some tenderness in the morning, it was not so savoury to me in preaching as in studying. I found myself the worse of being hastened in the delivery.

June 9.—Lord's day. When I was yesterday studying the sermons I preached this day, I could have no satisfaction in them; but could not make them better. I reviewed them this morning, but with as little; and thought they would not do. I went to the church with such thoughts as my present circumstances brought to hand, endeavouring to plead the covenant. I prefaced with some liberty on Psalm lxv. 1, but afterwards I had such liberty in prayer, such clear conceptions of things in the lecture, with such a facility of expressing myself plainly in it, and this in the preaching too, that I was indeed a wonder to myself. It was most papably the doing of the Lord, and is wondrous in my eyes. This continued in the afternoon. Only I thought I had more soul-advantage by the gospel-sermon than the law sermon. I was never more convinced of the influences of the Spirit on men's gifts, and of the necessity of the same. It is so palpable to me, that it was the Spirit of the Lord, that I cannot doubt it; for I see it is he that makes one differ in gifts from another, and makes a man differ from himself. And so do I find my soul convinced of it, that I am helped to give the glory entirely (I think) unto him, seeing still my own emptiness; for all which my soul blesseth the Lord.

June 15.—This day, or yesternight, my frame being somewhat above the world, and wearied of a body of sin and death, I thought I would get a feast to-morrow in preaching, being to shew what comfort a child of God had from the doctrine of Christ's coming. But this night my proud heart was so raised upon a business, that I was put all wrong; and so finding what temptations I behoved to have, and how foully I come off, I would again have been content to have left all, to have been out of the reach of these things. On the Sabbath morning the temptation was renewed, and came from the same hand; which so prevailed to discompose me, that it made me go halting all the day. But all these things do still more commend to me being with Christ, which I see is best of all. I ordained three elders this day; and when ordaining them I was on a sudden, in the very act, turned out of my ordinary frame, my soul melted, and possessed with the dread of that holy God, by a new light shining into my mind.

June 23.—I preached at Eyemouth. I had extreme difficulty to get a text. When I got it, I had much darkness and straitening; but got a sermon wrestled out at length. In delivering it, the Lord withdrew still; and in the forenoon I was straitened even in respect of words. Mr. Colden has often told me, that he could never get help to preach in that place. And I have often felt it straitening there. But the Lord had good ground of controversy with me, for I had not got my heart kept with God through that week as sometimes. (N. B. But I had sometimes after that, especially one time, in that place, help from the Lord). I have observed, that sometimes, when it has been ill with me, and particularly at this time, I have observed it, that I have been best when in company, grieving to see others wrong as well as myself, and would fain have had service done to God by others, though I could do none. As also within these two months, I have found I have been more free from temptation when in company than when alone.

June 28.—I observed, that for some days I had more freedom still in secret than in family prayer. Sometimes I have observed the quite contrary.

July 7.—I preached at Edrom. I had something of God in studying these sermons. I was much helped in the first prayer; but in other parts of the forenoon's exercise, though I got what to say, yet I had not such clear uptakings of things, nor that weight on my spirit that I would have had. This made me to cry betwixt sermons; and in time of singing my heart was much affected, and cried for God, the living God, and was helped to pray; but in the preaching I had much struggling for the power of God on my own spirit; yet much darkness and confusion remained, till I came to the application, at which I found myself raised above myself, my soul affected and concerned, and as it were wrapped up in preaching, as it was also in prayer.

July 13.—I have been now for some days habitually kept right; and while it has been so, I have still had a deal of satisfaction in reading and singing in our ordinary for family duties. So I shall once more set my seal to it, that a heavenly frame is the best commentator on scripture; and being to preach at Kelso to-morrow, I had great light into my lecture, on which I had no commentary. My soul has been made frequently, this and the last week, to bless the Lord for something of good that seems to follow my ministry; in that I see some are, at least outwardly, bettered, and all the families, for any thing the elders or I can see, have God's worship in them, and I would fain hope some of them are in the way to Christ.

On Wednesday the 17th of July, I, going on twenty-five years of my age, married Katharine Brown, formerly mentioned, going on twenty-seven, as born, February 3, 1674, and baptized the 22d; providence having seen it meet for me to order the odds to be on her side.—I shall here relate some things concerning that business. The first time I saw my wife was on March 3, 1697, that very day that I left that country. Whenever I saw her, a thought struck through my heart, about her being my wife; and that time, both she and I were in great distress. We had no converse about any thing; only I asked her how her sister was; and that was all. May 23, 1698, she had occasion to come to a place where I was. Whenever I heard she was come, I had a great desire to see her; which I curbed for a while, and afterwards went and saw her; and this was the second time; and at this time our acquaintance was made. August 24, that year, after the matter had been laid before the Lord, and often considered, I proposed it. Her piety discerned

by myself, and attested amply by others, her parts, humour, &c.,
engaged me to her. After which proposal, reflecting, I found myself as solid and composed, my mind as calm and serene as ever,
and looked on it as a token for good. On the morrow, I proposed
what trouble I might look for as a preacher of the gospel; what
she might lay her account therewith, if minded to comply with my
proposal. Thereafter, by converse with her, I was more and more
confirmed in the thoughts of her piety, &c. On the 9th of January, 1699, while I was praying about that business of my marriage, that word was brought to me, "Delight thyself in the Lord,
and he shall give thee the desires of thine heart;" Psalm xxxvii.
3; as was that word; Rom. viii. 28, "All things shall work together for good to them that love the Lord," while praying about
my going to the north, which was an exercise to me at that time;
and I was helped to grip the promise. January 30, being to write
to her, I went to God, and was helped with life and some confidence to implore his guidance as to the main thing, and as to the
letter in particular. When I arose up, remembering what crosses
some wives have proved to ministers, this sent me back to God
again. Afterward I fain would have had something to have confirmed me in the Lord's hearing of me; but I thought I would take
God's helping to cry to him as a sign of that.

On the 1st of February, I observed, that when I am most heavenly in the frame of my heart, my love to her is least shaken, and
I am most satisfied in my choice; and that when I am most carnal
and earthly, it is otherwise. And, on the 8th, that temptation from
the world was very severe, and I found it no easy matter to get
over it, though it is my grief. Wherefore in deep seriousness I proposed that question to myself, Darest thou give over that business?
I thought on it, and that word, Prov. xxxi. 30, "Favour is deceitful, and beauty is vain; but a woman that feareth the Lord, she
shall be praised." I went to the Lord with it, earnestly desiring
light from him; and that word came to me in prayer, and I turned
it into a prayer; Matth. vi. 33, "Seek ye first the kingdom of God,
and his righteousness, and all other things shall be added unto you."
And the Lord gave me a clear commentary on that place, with respect to that business, which I can better think than express. The
Lord made me clearly see, that I had first sought the kingdom of
heaven; for, as I appealed to the Lord's omniscience, unless I had
discerned the sparkles of grace in her, and had thought her acquainted with religion, I durst not have proposed such a thing to
her. So I concluded I durst not; but would follow it as my duty,
hoping other things should be added. Next day, finding my heart

lifted up above the world, I took that nick of time to examine myself on the head foresaid, and my heart said, Now I am well content.

On the 16th of April, this morning, especially in prayer, before I went to church, I was tempted to think I had been rash in my choice; which temptation I slighted, knowing it to be a deceit of Satan, to wear me off what I was about. I thought it no time then for me to consider whether or not, and so rejected it; but it cost me struggling. However, its unseasonable importunity discovered the cloven foot.

April 26.—I was about this time going to leave that country; and having been out in a garden with her, and conveyed her into the house thereafter, I went back to the same place; it was in Barhill in the orchard; and there I had a sweet while of converse with God in prayer, in a sweet hungering frame. My soul was much satisfied in the Lord; and in that place, I will say, I met with God, and there he spoke with me. We were together about three or four days at this time; and the upshot of all was, that I was made often to bless God that ever I was acquainted with her. I understood several things at this and other times, that in this matter she had acted as a Christian, and as under influence of light from the Lord.

May 26.—I was now tossed with scruples and doubts as to my marriage. I thought on it, but found no outgate. I went to God, particularly for light in that matter, which was now overclouded, and earnestly begged it. I found in prayer my heart going out in love to Christ, &c., as I have noted before, p. 63.

June 5.—After I had been writing to her, that word, Psalm cxxxviii. *ult.* "The Lord will perfect that which concerneth me," came with such power as dispelled these doubts; and I was helped to believe that God would order things for my good in that matter. On the 12th, I examined the light I had got in that point, and had help of Durham on conscience. And I found my light in that matter, 1. Was from the word, and pressed me to the thing, as agreeable to the word, and carried me on to it as a duty towards God; 2. It had another kind of authority and stateliness with it than light affection, or passions; it overpowered my worldly-mindedness, discontent, &c., and this very remarkably. And my heart bears me witness, that it had influence on me to humble and abase me in the sight of God. Whence it appears, that it was my duty before; and if then, now too, seeing no new thing has occurred. Whatever affection I have to her, if my heart deceive me not, I would sacrifice my inclinations to the command of God.

Feb. 22, 1700.—There was a considerable time I had not heard from my friend, which bred me much perplexity; but the Lord took that way to rebuke me for my mismanagements. He drew me by it nearer himself, and put me to a holy submission. And the effect of it was, I was more confirmed in the business; and when I was weaned, and brought to stoop to providence, he showed me that the fears were groundless.

March 25.—I had been for some time before this, and was still, under a very dead and drowsy frame of spirit. I was sore racked with various thoughts, and had a sharp exercise of it that night, and next day especially. I therefore resolved, against Monday, to set some time apart for fasting and prayer, that I might get that devil cast out of my heart. So the Sabbath passed, and I walked halting; my case being so after sermon, that if my head had been to have been struck off, I could not have given it a name. The removal then of that spiritual indisposition was the chief cause of that exercise; 2. Victory over sin; 3. Preparation for the then ensuing public fast, and particularly that I might get clear uptakings of what I was to preach; 4. Success in my ministry; lastly, That I might attain to habitual cheerfulness in the Lord. So I spent some time this day in prayer for these things. The Lord in the morning began to blow upon my soul, and continued so to do through the rest of the day I was at that work; and with all willingness of soul I renewed and subscribed a personal covenant with God. And as of myself, so of my friend, I made a solemn resignation to the Lord. And towards the close of that exercise, I earnestly prayed, that if it were his will, I might have a token of his reception of both. My heart was calmed and strengthened in the Lord, and my mind made heavenly. I closed the whole with singing Psalm cxvi. 7, and downwards, and then went down and took a refreshment. The tenor of the personal covenant I then renewed and subscribed is as follows:—

" I, Mr. Thomas Boston, minister of God's word at Simprin; forasmuch as I am in some measure sensible of my grievous, horrid, and frequent backslidings from the Lord, since the last time I covenanted with God; and in particular, having been for some time habitually in a dead and sleepy frame, for which cause (among others mentioned elsewhere) I set this day apart for fasting and prayer; and finding myself called to renew my covenant with God, the rather to obtain the ends of this day's exercise, and to get my soul more confirmed in the Lord, for wading through the difficulties 'twixt me and heaven, in prayer I did, and now (giving it under my hand) I do, adhere to all my former covenants with, and engagements to be the Lord Jesus Christ's, particularly that written and

subscribed covenant of the date, August 14, 1699;* and do now
with all my heart and soul, solemnly resign and give up myself, and
all my bodily and spiritual concerns, unto Christ; taking him with
heart and soul upon those very terms, and no other, upon which he
is offered in the gospel; resolving and hereby engaging, in his
strength, to cleave to him and his truths, so long as I live, whatever
be the hazard. Likeas I have, and hereby do, solemnly give up and
resign K. B. to the same Lord Christ, that I have given myself to
be his for ever. And this before the Lord, the searcher of hearts,
I do with all willingness subscribe, the 25th day of March, 1700
years. T. B."

March 26.—I think I had never more persuasion of God's accepting my renewing of covenant than that yesterday. I rejoice I
have done it, when I think on it; and I am persuaded God has accepted it; for I have had covenanted strength since, as well as the
token aforesaid. That word was sweet to me in my ordinary last
night; Isa. liv. 6, "The Lord hath called thee as a woman forsaken
and grieved in spirit, and a wife of youth, when thou wast refused,
saith thy God."

April 23.—My father, in the time of his sickness, had (as he had
also before) urged me to put an end to that business; and then I
found I was inclined not to delay it long. And another thing came
immediately after, which obliged me to be at a point in that matter.
This day I set myself to spend some time in seeking light from the
Lord in that point. I prayed twice, but was in no good case, and
so could not fall on what I aimed at. I tried it again, and after a
while I got my feet fastened; the Spirit did blow on me, and the
matter was laid out before the Lord; and my conscience told me,
that I did sincerely desire God's determination in the case; which
desire I saw as the sun at noon-day. The upshot of all was, to
follow the conduct of providence. On the morrow, having gone to
God with it again in particular, and after considering the business,
I found reasons weighty for not delaying it much longer. I also
found I was in better case for expediting it than I had thought,
being then made sensible of a mistake. Providence, even in the
review at this distance, I plainly see to have been, at that time,
clearly pointing and conducting me, by several steps thereof, unto it.
Accordingly, on Monday the 29th, I went away to visit my friend;
and, following the conduct of providence, we determined the business to the middle of July; and so I returned cheerfully, and ever
after was well satisfied as to the determination of the time.

* This form is annexed to the author's Body of Divinity, vol, III.

May 24.—At night, before family exercise, I was somewhat cast down and troubled by reason of some remaining difficulties in the accomplishing of my business. At prayer I took occasion to bewail this; and so it was, that my soul seeing more of the vanity of the world, and longing for heaven, I found my soul blessing God for troubles in the world; for I well saw, that otherwise I would have been saying, "It is good for me to be here." Blessed be the Lord for that word which we sung; Psalm lxxxv. *ult.*, "What is good the Lord will give." I think I can believe it, though I see it not. Lord help my unbelief. May 28 and 29, I was taken up in business relative thereto, and was helped to manage matters with an eye to God, and my heart was lifted up in admiration of divine conduct, making mountains molehills.

June 3.—Having purposed to spend some time this day in prayer, with fasting, with respect especially to my marriage, I rose early this morning; and though I found much of yesterday's frame continuing, yet wanted I not some secret heart-averseness to that work. After prayer, I considered what I was to plead for. And, *First,* As to my marriage, 1. That the Lord would clear up duty more and more, that we may go on under a sense of God's command; 2. That he would pardon mismanagements in the oncarrying of it; 3. That he would give us a suitable frame for such a weighty business, and particularly in the time of it; 4. Conjugal love and concord; 5. Contentment as to our choice, and with our lot in the world; 6. That we may be spiritually useful to one another, and particularly with respect to a time of trouble for the gospel; 7. That we may live loose to one another, ready to part on a call; and that God would provide things necessary for our through-bearing; Lastly, That I may be spared with her a while; and if I be taken away, she may not be left destitute, but God may be her tutor. *Secondly,* Victory over corruption. *Thirdly,* Success in my ministry. Lastly, Preparation for the fast at Fogo. These things I earnestly sought of the Lord; and as I went on, I won very near God, attaining to familiarity and confidence with the Lord; so that I was made to bless the day I set about this work. My heart and flesh were all aloft towards Christ. After I had come from that exercise, in the afternoon I received a letter from her, wherein she showed me some piece of exercise she was under, and the prevalency of unbelief with her, with something importing fears of approaching death. This did somewhat amuse me, and made me wonder what might be the language of it to me. I had prayed for a token of the Lord's accepting this service, and this seemed not to be such. But, on further consideration, I found I had no great reason to complain, but rather to bless the Lord, who made her careful of her salvation, and exercised with her own heart at such a juncture. And I had liberty with the Lord on her account. As for the fears of approaching death, it is like God has sent it to ballast me, and keep me watchful; and I am the Lord's, let him do what seemeth him good. I found my heart last week, and at this time, more clear in the sight of the world's vanity, and going more after being with Christ, which I see is best of all, than a good while before. Her case and my own sent me sometimes to God. But at night I grew so very apprehensive of her death, that my ballast was like to sink me. I strove to encourage myself, but nothing could effectually do. But I saw the cause of it. And on the morrow morning so was it with me, still I sunk, when I thought on it; so easily was I overcome after such kind dealing. It sent me again and again to the Lord. (N. B. See how Providence filled up what I had most unaccountably forgot in the causes above mentioned; for what reason can be given, that when I had made it one of my errands to God, that I might be spared with her, that I should not also with that have been concerned that she might be spared with me?) I behoved to go to the Presbytery; and I won but so far above it, as to let it be only ballast to my heart, and to make me watchful, and prepare for whatever should come. And so it proved very useful to me this day both abroad and at home. And so was it the next day while studying the sermon for Fogo.

June 8.—I minded to declare my purpose to two of the elders, and went to God on that head; but was very dull in my frame; but one of them could not be got. So I delayed to this day, at which time it was better with me. So that I came to them with confidence in God, leaning on and getting use made of that word which God said to me before I came to Simprin, "The eternal God shall be thy refuge," &c. And I could not but observe the Lord's putting a stop to it till I was in this case.

June 13.—Thursday, I met with a severe stroke. On the Monday afternoon and Tuesday I had fallen secure again; had only some awakening gliffs, and sad experience of the instability of my heart; which lay so heavy on me on Tuesday's night, that I would have been content to have quitted all, to have been out of the reach of a woful heart, and to have had a dying-day instead of a marriage-day. On Wednesday, it was once better; but ere that day was gone, my vigour spiritual was gone. This morning I had little freedom in prayer. I preached the weekly sermon with an overly superficial moving of the affections. After the sermon a while, I went out to the garden, and there was a spit sticking in the wall of the house, with the small end of it outmost. I rushed inadvertently my face on it, and the wound that I got was about a straw-breadth beneath the eye. I was stupified with it, and knew not but it had gone into the eye-ball. It swelled to a great bigness, and covered a great part of my eye. I was afraid of losing my eye. It sent me to the Lord, confessing my sin, and taking with the punishment of mine iniquity; and I got a patient, quiet, submissive, and contented frame under the rod, endeavouring to trust God come what would. Great mercy it was that it was not a straw-breadth higher; for then it would have digged out my eye. I endeavoured to sit loose to my friend, and all created enjoyments, which I thought God called for by that rod. On the morrow the thoughts of my falling off so frequently to provoke the Lord, and so bringing one rod after another on myself, made heaven very desirable to me. And noticing the way of providence with me, I kissed this rod, for there was a deal of kindness in it.

June 23.—I preached at Eymouth, under great withdrawings of the Spirit, as before narrated. This business has been a snare to me since it came so near a period. If I had not guided better before, I could have had little comfort in it. God is my witness, that it has been and is my grief, that in my thoughts of it I cannot be more heavenly; and that I cannot more vigorously look to God with respect to it. If this day eight days, when I am to be proclaimed, be such a day as this, I think I will be wounded with the arrows of the Almighty; for that it should be so at this juncture is a double misery.

June 28.—Wherefore I spent some time this day in prayer, with respect to my marriage mainly; was solidly affected with it, and helped to believe; and have hitherto felt my spirit bettered thereby, keeping somewhat more closely with God than before. Yesterday I had a view of my need of Christ, and the supplies of his grace; and had much inward satisfaction flowing from the sense of my soul's nearness to God, and my heart's being kept in some measure with God. And this day the thoughts of that business was a spur to duty.

June 30.—This day was a good day. I got my heart earnest for God's presence, and I wanted neither light nor life in my work. And finishing a particular subject that day, my soul was affected and melted with the people's case.

July 9.—This day I found myself under a great decay again; but discoursing with a good lad, he had occasion to speak of these two scriptures, "Truly God is good to Israel," upon which I seemed to have a sight of the Lord's goodness; and that, "If thy presence go not with me, carry us not up hence;" which had such an impression

on me, that upon it I had some revival. But by my carelessness it
slipped away, and great darkness and hardness of heart succeded.
A while after these seemed to be going away; but neither was that
right guided; and then I was carried quite off my feet. On the morrow
especially, I saw my confidence with God was quite marred, and sin
lay heavy on soul and conscience. And though I spent a good part
of the day, the weary day, in fasting and prayer, the Lord would
not hear me, neither could I win to any meltedness of heart; only
I had tormenting light without life. Afterwards Mr. G—— R——
came; but I was indisposed both in body and mind, heavy and melancholy, unfit for any thing whatsoever. Yet at length, while I
lifted up my dejected eyes to the Lord, and we conversed about the
measure of humiliation requisite in a sinner before he come to Christ,
concerning self-condemnation, &c., I found I spoke only what I felt.
So in the very time while we thus walked up and down, and discoursed, the Lord loosed the poor prisoner; my heart loosed, and
my bands were taken off. And I observed my body grew better,
when the cure was begun in my soul. Afterwards I went to God,
poured out my soul before him like water, with grief for sin, and
confidence of his mercy. And then I was helped to wrestle in
earnest with God for his presence to be with me with respect to my
business. By the Lord's dealing thus severely with me, I had a
sight of the excellency of Christ; and when I won near God, O but
my soul prized Christ as the Mediator, and way to the Father; and
my heart was in love with the doctrine of the gospel, even free
grace. I spent some time thereafter in the fields meditating, with
a deep sense of my own vileness. On the morrow I had real struggling ere I could get my heart right, but not without success. I saw
nothing desirable in the world but Christ and ordinances. And I
had much of the felt presence of God in preaching my sermon, (it
being Thursday.) Thereafter, in secret, I found my confidence in
the Lord was enlarged, as to what is before me, and otherwise; and
my soul was affected with a sense of my misery and nothingness;
but blessed be the Lord for his kindness to vile me.

July 11.—Towards night I met with a sweet seasonable providence, which enlarged my heart in thankfulness to God, encouraging me in the business before me, and making me set up another
Ebenezer. Thereafter meditating in the fields, I was filled with joy
in the Lord, and my heart was glad, while I had discoveries of
Christ made to my soul, and was helped to see his sufficiency, and
to believe. So that my soul was filled with praises and admiration
of the Lord's kindness to poor me at this juncture, notwithstanding
my woeful backslidings from him before. O the doctrine of the

gospel, and revelation of Christ, is sweet to my soul. I have had felt strength against corruption this day.

July 13.—Saturday. This day I was to go to Kelso, from whence I was to go straight to Culross. And I found the Lord was with me, and helped me to wrestle with him for his presence to my marriage, and to-morrow's work. The testimony of my conscience witnessing to me, that I had acknowledged God in this my way, was a sweet help to me, to believe my steps should be directed by him. I found a more than ordinary concern on my heart for my charge, and their case touched my heart very nearly. I came away in the strength of the Lord; and the serenity of my mind that I enjoyed at this time was sweet to me.

July 14.—This morning when I awoke, I was with God, and my soul had confidence in the Lord; yet ere I went to the church, some wandering thoughts rushed in and marred my case; so that in the first prayer I was much deserted, and very faint both in body and mind. But being thus emptied of myself, the Lord filled my sails in all the other parts of the day's work. And betwixt sermons I had such felt strength from the Lord, that I admired and rejoiced in his love; for he really set me on my high places; and his love at this juncture was wondrous in my eyes. So in his strength I went away again, and we sung Psalm cxxxviii. 5, and downwards. I sung it with an uplifted heart, and light from the Lord; and for the 5th verse, " Yea in the righteous ways of God," &c., though I saw little in it when I gave out the psalm, yet when sung, O how sweet, confirming, and soul-strengthening was it to me, even with respect to my business; for I saw it was the way of commanded duty. For the whole of it, I thought, if I had been at the penning of that part of that psalm which we sung, for my present case, I would not have altered one word of it. I preached and prayed with great light and life from the Lord. At night my heart was glad, and my glory rejoiced to speak of Christ. And thus was it with me when honest J. E. came in to me, with whom I conversed with an uplifted heart. When we were going to part, I told him of what was before me; but he was an instrument of discouragement to me, by means of my own corruption. The good man said particularly, If you acknowledge God in your ways, &c. This seemed to me said with such an air of jealousy, that my proud heart murmured at it; which was after matter of mourning to me. Thereafter I found my strength abated; but I gave myself to prayer, and wrestling with God for his presence to go with me. As I was filling a pipe, and my heart was discouraged in that, I found not God with me as before, I gave a glance to the Bible lying open on the table before me, and met with that word; Isa. xl. 27, "Why sayest thou, O Jacob, and speakest, O Israel, My way is hid from the Lord, and my judgment is passed over from my God?" and finding it so speaking, I read on to the end of the chapter, where all was most seasonable, and suited to my case. So I went away immediately to the Lord with it, cried to him, and got strength to believe, that seeing I waited on God, my strength should be renewed.

July 17.—I came yesterday to Barhill in the strength of the Lord, leaning on that promise; Isa. xl. *ult.*, "They that wait upon the Lord shall renew their strength; they shall mount up with wings as eagles, they shall run and not be weary; and they shall walk and not be faint;" and that was all I had. This day in the afternoon I withdrew from company, and sought the Lord in secret; and afterwards, before the minister came, I went to prayer with the family and relations present, particularly for the Lord's blessing with respect to the marriage; and was much helped of the Lord. Mr. Mair having come, went alone into a room, and staid some time; and I went into another alone, and spent the time in prayer; and then the Lord was kind to my soul; he drew near to me, and said to me, Fear not; and I came forth in the strength of the Lord. The action was gone about most sweetly by Mr. Mair. The Lord directed him to most seasonable and pertinent exhortations, and they came with power and life. Of a truth God owned it, and it was sweet both to him and us. As for my part, my heart being touched with the finger of God, was sensibly going forth in love to Christ, and admiration of him, to my great comfort and satisfaction. So we were married betwixt eight and nine o'clock at night. Immediately after I withdrew into the room where I was before, and went to God, (it was the upper western room), and there the Lord filled my heart with joy in himself unspeakable, and loaded me with loving-kindness, truth, and faithfulness. Verily he made me renew my strength, and gave it me with palpable increase. Verily the Lord did great things for me at that juncture as ever; and my soul was made to rejoice in him.

Thus was I by all-wise providence yoked with my wife, with whom I have now, [1730], by the mercy of God, lived thirty years complete; a woman of great worth, whom I therefore passionately loved, and inwardly honoured; a stately, beautiful, and comely personage, truly pious, and fearing the Lord; of an evenly temper, patient in our common tribulations, and under her personal distresses; a woman of bright natural parts, an uncommon stock of prudence; of a quick and lively apprehension, in things she applied herself to; great presence of mind in surprising incidents; sagacious and acute in discerning the qualities of persons, and there-

fore not easily imposed upon ; modest and grave in her deportment, but naturally cheerful ; wise and affable in conversation,
having a good faculty at speaking, and expressing herself with
assurance ; endowed with a singular dexterity in dictating of letters ; being a pattern of frugality, and wise management of household affairs, therefore entirely committed to her ; well fitted for,
and careful of, the virtuous education of her children ; remarkably
useful to the country-side, both in the Merse and in the Forest,
through her skill in physic and surgery, which in many instances, a
peculiar blessing appeared to be commanded upon from heaven ; and,
finally, a crown to me in my public station and appearances. During the time we have lived together hitherto, we have passed though
a sea of trouble, as yet not seeing the shore but afar off. I have
sometimes been likely to be removed from her ; she having had
little continued health, except the first six weeks, her death hath
sometimes stared us in the face, and hundreds of arrows have pierced
my heart on that score ; and sometimes I have gone with a trembling heart to the pulpit, laying my account with being called out of
it, to see her expire. And now for the third part of the time we
have lived together, namely, ten years complete, she has been under
a particular racking distress ; and for several of these years, fixed
to her bed ; in the which furnace, the grace of God in her hath
been brightened, her parts continued to a wonder, and her beauty,
which formerly was wont, upon her recoveries, to leave no vestige of
the illness she had been under, doth as yet now and then shew some
vestiges of itself.

PERIOD VIII.

FROM MY MARRIAGE, TILL MY REMOVAL TO ETTERICK.

At and about the time of my marriage, it pleased the Lord to deal
bountifully with my soul. And the Lord's day immediately following I preached at Dunning in Strathern. I was habitually kept
right these days, and the Lord was kind to me. I met with a
sharp trial after so fair a blink as I had ; and while I was musing
on the causes of the same, I found myself called to go to secret
prayer at a time unexpected ; and within a little after, the Lord
was graciously pleased to let me find he had heard me, and the dispensation was sweet, coming as an answer of prayer. But when I
came to Dunning on the Saturday's night, I found myself wrong, having neither heart nor hand for my work. On the Sabbath morning
my indisposition continued, save that at family prayer my affections
were loosed, and I had a deep sense of my own vileness on my

spirit. In the forenoon it was neither very ill nor very well; but in the afternoon my bands were freely loosed, and I had light and life from the Lord. I preached on Psalm xviii. 46, "The Lord liveth, and blessed be my rock;" the which text I was led to, as my anchor-ground, in my new circumstances through the change of my lot. And that week we came home to Simprin.

Until the 15th of August, the weekly sermon was continued in the kirk; at which time, being intermitted because of the harvest, it was begun again on the 7th of November in the house, and that in the night. And after that manner that exercise was managed during the remaining time of my ministry in that place.

Nov. 14.—This has been a time of many troubles to me, so that I have sometimes wondered what the Lord minded to do with me. Now, I had a very sharp one, but was quickly delivered; so on the morrow I spent some time in fasting and prayer, and renewed my covenant with the Lord; and it pleased the Lord to let out something of himself to me, so that, reflecting on my troubles, I clearly saw my need of them, with a deal of convincing power, and my soul was made to see God's love in them all, and from my heart I was made to say, he had done all things well. The fruit of them is, that I have thereby seen the vanity of all things besides Christ, and that there is no rest but in him alone, and to desire to be with him, which is best of all.

In April 1701, my dear father sickened again; and death appearing on its way, the rest of his children were sent for. They being come, he, on Sabbath the 13th of that month, after a sore toss of sickness, especially after sermons, died that night, in the 70th year of his age, having been born in December, 1631. This sharp rod the Lord had shaken over my head that time twelve months before, for my warning. However, being laid on, it went to the quick with me. It was a heavy death to me, the shock of which I had much ado to stand. He was a man of a low stature, of a fresh and lively complexion; nimble, strong, and vigorous: active, and given to application in business; one who, in the worst of times, retained his integrity, beyond many; and, in view of death, gave comfortable evidences of eternal life to be obtained through the Lord Jesus Christ. His body lies interred in the church-yard of Simprin, in the burial-place of the ministers there, whereof I thereby took possession, and soon had more occasion for.

On the 24th of May, about two or three o'clock in the morning, my wife, after long and sore labour, brought forth her first child, a daughter, called Katharine; having, at the holy and just pleasure of the sovereign Former of all things, a double harelip, whereby she was rendered incapable of sucking. My wife having a great terror of the pains of child-bearing, had before-hand laid her account with death; as she always I think, did on that occasion thereafter; having, at the same sovereign pleasure, an uncommon share of these pains, the remembrance whereof to this day makes my heart to shrink. When I, understanding her to be delivered, and preserved, was coming towards the chamber to see her; Mrs. Dawson abovementioned meeting me, intimated to me the case of the child; with which my heart was struck, like a bird shot and falling from a tree. Howbeit I bore it gravely; and my afflicted wife carried the trial very christianly and wisely, after her manner. Thus it pleased my God, to correct me for my sins; to balance my enjoyment; and to teach to acknowledge him, in the formation of children in the womb. The child being weak, was baptized by Mr. Dawson the same day; and was for a long time watched in the night, through the summer. In that dear child's case, I had a singular experience of tender love melted down in pity; as considering her teeth set on edge through the parent's eating of the sour grape.

After my father's death, his tenement in the Newton of Dunse falling to me, by his disposition thereof in my favour, I thereby became liable to a burden of 1000 merks; whereof 100 had been borrowed money, the rest allotted by him for the portions of two brothers and two sisters; my eldest brother having long before received another tenement for his portion, and discharged my father and his heirs. They having also charged me with an account of his moveables, which I then possessed, or claimed, I took advice about it; and being convinced in my conscience, that their design was quite beside the intention of the dead; and that, in law and justice, I had a charge upon them, more than sufficient to balance the same; I resolved to assay to satisfy these my brothers and sisters, by advancing their money as soon as might be.

In pursuance of which project, I went to Barhill about the harvest; and the child having appeared to grow better at the quarter's end, took my wife along with me. There I received a part of her portion; for which I paid interest to my mother-in-law till the year 1709, at which time she was removed by death; the remains thereof, some time after that, I received being in Etterick. But that journey proved a very heavy one, for our trial. By the way thither, my wife swooned at Danskin; which seemed to be occasioned by ram's mutton afforded us there to dinner. She recovering, we accomplished our journey. And being in Inzevair [in the parish of Torryburn, Fifeshire], in her sister's house, on a morning she lying abed after I was risen, dreamed that she saw the child perfect, the

natural defect being made up, and extraordinary beautiful. This
making impression, as it could hardly miss to do, we returned homeward as soon as conveniently we could. Arriving at Black's-mill,
about eight or nine miles from home, in a little our hearts were
pierced with an account, that our dear child was dead and buried.
After which, we came home in great heaviness; and found, that
very day, and hour of the day, as near as could be judged, wherein
my wife had the dream aforesaid, the child had died. Thus it
pleased the Lord, to exercise us with one affliction on the neck of
another; and, as I have often experienced, the world's laying their
over-load above the burden from the holy sovereign hand ; so it
was afterwards found, that one of our acquaintance had very unjustly spoke to the grief of us whom the Lord had wounded.

Being through the interest of Mr. James Ramsay aforesaid, and
other friends, chosen by the synod to be their clerk, I entered on
that office, at their meeting in October this year; and continued
therein till the close of their meeting in April, 1711, at which time
I did demit. That work was a matter of great weight on several
accounts. When I first took the seat among them, and stood up
for to read, being in great confusion, through my natural diffidence
and timorousness, I blundered; but recovering myself, with much
ado made it out. Upon which occasion, Mr. Ramsay did seasonably
express his confidence of me notwithstanding. The oath *de fideli
administratione* I declined ; and they were pleased to accept of my
promise, to serve them faithfully, and keep their secrets; which I
strictly observed. It was a work of great labour and painfulness;
even the reading of papers was a business of great toil. In time of
their sederunts, I took short minutes of the substance of their actings,
which in the interval of diets I extended; the which occasioned my
sitting up great part of the night. And their meetings falling in
the times of the year wherein I was weakest, I could not have endured, but that they did not last long. After the two first synods,
being always desirous to do the business to the best advantage I
could reach, I did of my own proper motion ordinarily make a third
copy of the minutes; but this at home, at my leisure. Then the
synod-book was once a-year to be filled up, for the general assembly
to visit it. I often sat in my seat among them, as one wandering in
a wilderness, while I observed the sway of their opinions and reasonings, in order to take up the mind of the court; but through the
divine assistance, I ordinarily took up, and expressed, their affairs,
so as to please, and to facilitate their work. And I had a very
honourable testimony, in that point, of my Lord Minto, who had been
clerk to the council of Scotland, expressed on occasion of his being pre-

sent at the synod; the which testimony raised in my heart, admiration of the divine condescension, and thankfulness to my God. When I entered on that office, the fees were 14d. a-synod by each minister; afterward they were advanced to five groats; but, in the year 1703, they raised the same to half a dollar, being 29d. And during the time I continued in Simprin, these fees were paid very well. By an account of the gain, by that office, kept for the first five years, I find it was better than £100 Scots *communibus annis.*

The synod meeting at Jedburgh, on Tuesday, April 21, 1702, I was obliged, upon that occasion, to leave my wife, having, I think, passed her reckoning. And by the disposal of holy Providence, for our farther trial, the synod continued sitting even on the Thursday afternoon. They being at length risen, I took horse that evening; and riding all night, got home about the morning-light; where, by the mercy of God, I found my wife still well, though in perplexity. On the Wednesday after, April 29, about the going down of the sun, she brought forth her first son, John, who was baptized on the 1st day of May, by Mr. John Pow, minister at Lennel. In his appearance our hearts were comforted, after the heavy trial in the case of his sister; finding that our God would " not chide continually, nor keep his anger for ever." And as he was always a proper child, so he is this day a very stately and pretty man; the which I deem just to remark, to the praise of our merciful and compassionate God, who formerly had afflicted us.

Being invited, I assisted at the communion in Morbattle, in the month of June this year. And here began a particular friendship between the worthy Mr. John Simson, minister there, and me; which lasted till he was removed by death in or about the year 1722. He was a serious good man; a most pathetic, zealous, and popular preacher, and withal substantial in his sermons; having a most ready gift; always concerned to gain souls to Jesus Christ; blessed with a great measure of his Master's countenance; and most acceptable to the people. He had a singular easiness and sweetness of temper, which continued with him to the last. He was, in the end of his days, confined for a long time to his bed; in which time, visiting him, in company with my two friends Messrs Wilson and Davidson, we found him still lovely and pleasant as before.

The first time I administered the sacrament of the Lord's supper in Simprin, was on the 2d of August that year; and it was done yearly thereafter, while I continued in that place. At that time it was administered in the kirk, there being sermon also without; but I think that was the only time, except in the winter, that it was not celebrated without doors. The Lord was very gracious to me in that work; and I have a savoury remembrance of my delivering of that my first action-sermon on Psalm xl. 7, " Then said I, Lo, I come." Going out in time of serving the tables, and finding the meeting without wanting a minister, I, under the impressions of the Lord's goodness then upon me, stepped into the tent, and preached a while to them extempore, on Deut. xxxiii. 29, " Happy art thou, O Israel; who is like unto thee, O people saved by the Lord, the shield of thy help, and who is the sword of thy excellency !" &c. Mr. Simson aforesaid was one of my assistants at that time; and we continued our mutual assistance thereafter for ordinary; only it was once interrupted a little, after the year 1709, as will be noticed in the proper place. And many a good day of that nature we had together, especially at Morbattle.

This was the first year of the reign of Queen Anne, the oath of allegiance to whom I took; but did thereafter often desiderate a due impression thereof on my spirit. I endeavoured, while she lived, to keep the sense of it on my heart; but unto this day I never took another, whether of a public or private nature.

Hitherto we lived in the house where I settled when I came to the place; and while there, though I remember not the particular time, I began the evening lecture in my family, on the chapter read in our ordinary, nightly. And that custom I have continued to this day; save in the Sabbath-nights, of late years at least. When at any time there seemed to be some occasion of intermitting it, I chose rather to say a very little, than quite to let it alone; fearing that one intermission thereof, at our ordinary times, might make way for dropping it altogether.

In the end of the year, the winter being begun, we removed into the new manse, built for me from the foundation, and by that time covered; but little of the wright's work within it was then done; but was a-doing through the winter. The ground whereon it was built, being quite new, we were obliged at first to straw the floor of our bed-chamber with shavings, which was afterwards laid with deals. This hardship of entering the new house, we preferred to suffering the inconveniencies of the old. Langton's estate going then from hand to hand, it was not without considerable difficulty, and expense too, that I got that house carried on. Afterward I formed a large garden, and built the dyke; the which was a work of some time, trouble, and expense too. And herein also was the saying verified, " One soweth, and another reapeth."

In the month of March following, met the first general assembly in the reign of Queen Anne; of the which assemby I was a member. Seafield being the Queen's Commissioner, Mr. George Meldrum was chosen moderator, as the man who to him would be most acceptable. The asserting of the intrinsic power of the church, was then the great point that some laboured for; but in vain; it was told them by their brethren, They had it, and what then needed the waste of an act asserting it? The assembly having sat several days, were upon an overture for preventing Protestants marrying with Papists; in the time whereof, a whisper beginning about the throne, and a motion being, I think, made for recommitting the overture; the commissioner, rising from his seat, instantly dissolved the assembly in her Majesty's name. This having come like a thunder-clap, there were, from all corners of the house, protestations offered against it, and for the intrinsic power of the church; with which I joined. But the moderator, otherwise a most grave and composed man, being in as much confusion as a school boy when beaten, closed with prayer; and got away, together with the clerk, so that nothing was then got marked. This was one of the heaviest days that ever I saw, beholding a vain man trampling on the privileges of Christ's house, and others couching under the burden. And I could not but observe, how Providence rebuked their shifting the act to assert as above said, and baffled their design in the choice of the moderator; never a moderator since the Revolution to this day, so far as I can guess, having been so ill treated by a commissioner. The learned and pious Mr. James Brisbane, late minister of Stirling, a young man at that time as well as I, pulled me down, when offering to join the protesters; and the same very worthy man, many years after, joined not with the representers in the affair of the Marrow; though he had no freedom to go along with the assembly, but was obliged to declare himself in favour of truth, before they should close that affair. And I remember, that with respect to this last case, he, in private conversation, said in his pleasant manner, thereafter, he had so done, but knew not if he would have full satisfaction in it, when he got home, and reflecting thereon in his closet. Meanwhile the dissolving of that assembly by Seafield, was the occasion of adjusting that matter betwixt the church and state, and settling it in the manner wherein, I suppose, it hath all along since continued, the assembly being first dissolved in the name of Jesus Christ, by the moderator as their mouth, and in the name of the magistrate by the commissioner.

In April following, the Synod meeting at Dunse, entered on making an act, asserting their principles with respect to the established government of the church. Against which, Mr. Alexander Orrock, minister at Hawick, a man of vast parts, and the greatest assurance I ever knew, protested, and left the synod; pretending the same to be a raising of groundless jealousies against the magistrate; though in the meantime the grounds of jealousy were looked on as not small. With him joined Mr. Robert Bell, minister at Cavers, now at Crailling, Mr. Robert Cuningham at Wilton, afterward at Hawick, and Mr. Robert Scot at Roberton. Upon the other hand, I was dissatisfied with the act, for that it touched not the particular point, in which the church was at that time especially aggrieved; namely her intrinsic power of meeting, and treating, in her judicatories, of her affairs, as necessity might require, for the honour of her Head, and the spiritual welfare of her members. And since, for the said cause, I could not approve of it, and had not so clear access as ordinary to give my vote, I declared this my mind before the synod ere it was put to the vote. Whereupon Mr. Charles Gordon, minister of Ashkirk, a learned and holy man, of uncommon integrity, sometime chosen to be professor of divinity in Aberdeen, though he accepted it not, spoke something in answer thereto, and for the act, which thereafter was voted, and approved by the rest. But that same night, I think, he sent for me to his quarters, where he lodging together with Mr. William Macghie, minister of Selkirk, we supped together, and were brought acquainted. And this, I believe, was the occasion of the Presbytery of Selkirk their setting their eye on me for the parish of Etterick. And I had the comfort of his declaring to me, on his deathbed, some time after my coming to Etterick, the satisfaction he had in having seen Mr. Gabriel Wilson, my friend, and me, settled in their Presbytery.

I being only a singular successor, and not heir to my father, was liable to Drummelzier, the superior, in a year's rent of my tenement, for entry, which otherwise would have been but the double of the feu-duty; so, on the 15th of April, I compounded with him for £60 Scots; for which the town-clerk having drawn a bond in the jog-trot style of bonds for borrowed money, I refused to sign it; but drew a bond with my own hand, with the which Drummelzier was satisfied. This I signed accordingly; and relieved, by paying the money, on May 14, thereafter. Having upon that affair had occasions of conversing with Drummelzier, who was a sober sensible man, I afterward found, he had upon occasions shewn himself disposed, in his own way, towards me; particularly, that it being told him, speaking of planting me in Dunse, then vacant, that I was too hot; he thereupon mentioned another place for me, as one as hot as I, viz. Etterick. So early providence was at work for bringing about my settlement in that place, where I was to spend the most of my strength and days.

Invited by Mr. Gabriel Semple retaining of his former disposition

towards me, I preached at Jedburgh, Feb. 27, forenoon and afternoon. The congregation being convened again, about a quarter of
an hour after, he, from the reader's desk, made a short discourse on
the fifth command, particularly the duties of husbands and wives.
The things he insisted on were indeed common and ordinary; but
they were delivered in such a manner, and such power accompanied
them, that I was in a manner amazed; and they went out through
me, and in through me, so that I said in my heart, " Happy are
those that hear thy wisdom." Mr. Gabriel Wilson being then his
assistant, but preaching that day at Oxnam, there began at that
time an acquaintance betwixt him and me, which by some inter-
views afterward, and particularly by a meeting at Simprin, advanced to a particular friendship. And after I was settled in
Etterick, and he in Maxton, the same grew up into a noted and uncommon strictness, continuing, through the mercy of God, inviolate
unto this day.

On March 21, about two o'clock in the morning, my son Robert
was born; and he was baptized on the 26th, by Mr. John Lithgow,
minister at Swinton.

This year was remarkable to me, with respect to my ordinary in
preaching, and my studies; of both which I shall here give an account.

As to my ordinary in preaching, occasionally mixed with other
subjects; having begun, as said is, the second Sabbath in Simprin
after my ordination, I continued preaching man's natural state,
until August 10, 1700. At which time I entered on preaching
Christ the remedy for man's misery. From which I proceeded, Oct.
19, 1701, to the doctrine of the application of the remedy; in the
which, entering February 18, 1702, on the particulars of the ordinary method of the Spirit with sinners in conversion; being sensible
of the delicacy of the subject, and desiring to say nothing thereon
but what I had digested beforehand, I began writing my sermons at
large, and to venture very little on extemporary expression. And
this was the occasion of my falling into a habit of writing my sermons at large, which I have since for ordinary continued, as I had
access, and could reach it; a yoke which often since that time I
would have been glad to have shaken off, but could not get it done.
Nevertheless I have been convinced, it was a kind and honourable
dispensation of providence that kept it on me. Howbeit, whereas
in my notes at that time, as also before and after unto this day, may
be sometimes found Latin, Greek, and perhaps Hebrew, it was not
my manner to express them in the pulpit to the people; but in
their mother tongue to express the thing the best way I could. In

sermons indeed *coram clero*, as presbyterial exercises, I used all freedom in that point; but so doing in sermons before the people, in
country or town, I ever despised, and had a contempt of, as pe-
dantic, and unbecoming the weight of the sacred mysteries. Meanwhile, having dispatched that subject, I proceeded, November 15,
1702, to the privileges of believers in Christ. And finally, on
February 14, 1703, I entered on the believer's duty; wherein, after
the general doctrine, coming to particulars, I went through all the
ten commands; which done, I shewed the use of the law to those
that are out of Christ; the believers' deliverance and freedom from
the law as a covenant; and pressed the regarding thereof, as a rule
of life; with which I closed that ordinary of subjects, in the month
of April this year 1704.

Withal on the 4th of May following, I began an ordinary of
week-day's sermons on the Song of Solomon; in which, I think, I
continued till my removal to Etterick; where I had no more access
to service of that kind. In that time I went through the 2d and
3d chapters of that book, and had entered on the 4th; and these
afforded us many a sweet hour together. These sermons are *in
retentis*. But I judge I had before that gone through the first chapter in some exercises, without writing any notes.

As to my studies, when I was settled in Simprin, I had very few
books; which occasioned my borrowing, as I had access; and moreover, where I wanted to be satisfied in some particular points, obliged me to think of the same, if so I could find out what to rest
satisfied in, not having access to consult many authors. And thus my
scarcity of books proved a kind disposal of providence towards me;
I, in that method, arriving at a greater distinctness and certainty
in these points, than otherwise I could readily have obtained. The
chief of these points I wanted to be satisfied in, were two; namely,
the doctrine of the grace of God in Christ, and the subject of
baptism.

As for the doctrine of grace, how the Lord was pleased to give
my heart a set toward the preaching of Christ, and how I had several convictions of legality in my own practice, is already narrated.
I had heard Mr. Mair often speak of being divorced from the law,
dead to it, and the like; but I understood very little of the matter.
Howbeit, my thoughts being, after my settlement at Simprin, turned
that way, that I might understand somewhat of these things; some
light, new to me, seemed to break up from the doctrine of Christ;
but then I could not see how to reconcile the same with other things
which seemed to be truth too. And I think, that among these first
rays of light, was a notion, that the sins of believers in Christ, even

while yet not actually repented of, did not make them, being in a state of grace, liable to eternal punishment. And on this head I did, by a letter, consult Mr. Murray in Penpont; but was not thoroughly satisfied with what he advanced upon it. Meanwhile, being still on the scent, as I was sitting one day in a house of Simprin, I espied above the window-head two little old books; which when I had taken down, I found entitled, the one "The Marrow of Modern Divinity," the other, "Christ's Blood Flowing Freely to Sinners." These I reckon had been brought home from England by the master of the house, a soldier in the time of the civil wars. Finding them to point to the subject I was in particular concern about, I brought them both away. The latter, a book of Saltmarsh's, I relished not; and I think I returned it without reading it quite through. The other, being the first part only of the Marrow, I relished greatly; and having purchased it at length from the owner, kept it from that time to this day; and it is still to be found among my books. I found it to come close to the points I was in quest of; and to shew the consistency of these, which I could not reconcile before; so that I rejoiced in it, as a light which the Lord had seasonably struck up to me in my darkness.

What time, precisely, this happened, I cannot tell; but I am very sure, that, by the latter end of the year 1700, I had not only seen that book, but digested the doctrine thereof in a tolerable measure; since by that time I was begun to preach it, as I had occasion abroad. Such opportunities I took, to give way to the then bent of my heart, which I could not so directly satisfy at home, being on the ordinary aforesaid.

The first parcel of books I got added to my small library, was in the year 1702. The which year, in August, Mr. Simson aforesaid being in my closet, and looking at my book-press, smiled; the which, from whatever principle he did it, touched me to the quick, being conscious of my want of a tolerable quantity. Among these were Zanchy's works, and Luther on the Galatians, which I was much taken with; and providence also laid to my hand, about that time, Beza's Confession of Faith. Most of the books mentioned in the 2d, 3d, and 4th pages of my catalogue yet *in retentis*, whose prices are set down with them, were purchased in that year, and the following 1703. And from the year 1704, the catalogue aforesaid goes on orderly, according to the years, generally, wherein the books came to my hand.

Being thus provided, I was in better case to pursue my search, to my farther instruction and confirmation. In this manner, I reached, through grace, a distinctness and certainty, as to several points of the doctrine of grace, that I had not before. And what contributed thereto was, that I purposely studied some points of that nature, for my own satisfaction; and set down my thoughts in writing; particularly these three points, viz:—1. Whether or not the sins of believers, while unrepented of, make them liable to eternal punishment? 2. Whether or not all sins, past, present, and to come, are pardoned together and at once? 3. Whether or not repentance be necessary, in order to the obtaining of the pardon of sin?

Meanwhile, after I was let into the knowledge of the doctrine of grace, as to the state and case of believers in Christ, I was still confused, indistinct, and hampered in it, as to the free, open, and unhampered access of sinners unto him. And thus, I am sure, it was with me, till the year 1702. How long I continued so thereafter, I know not. But, through the mercy of God, I was by the year 1704, let into that point also; and so far confirmed therein, that, on the 9th of July that year, at a communion in Coldinghame, I preached on Matth. xi. 18, "Come unto me, all ye that labour and are heavy laden," &c., then and there giving the true sense of that text, since published in the notes on the Marrow, and prosecuting it accordingly. And by the same time also, I reckon I had the true sense of the parallel texts; Isa. lv. 1; Matth. ix. 12, 13, since that time also published in the notes aforesaid. How I was led thereto, I cannot distinctly tell; but I apprehend I had taken the hint from the Marrow; and I had no great fondness for the doctrine of the conditionality of the covenant of grace.

With relation to the point last named, I remember, that upon a young man's mentioning, in a piece of trial before the Presbytery, the conditions of the covenant of grace; I quarrelled it, having no great gust for faith's being called the condition thereof, but abhorring the joining of other conditions with it. Thereupon he was appointed to deliver an exegesis on the question, "An fœdus gratiæ sit conditionatum?" This the young man, in his exegesis, resolved in the affirmative; though, I think, he held by faith only as the condition. I impugned this thesis, using this argument, viz., "I will be their God, and they shall be my people," is not conditional, but absolute; but this is the covenant; ergo, the covenant is not conditional. To which Mr. Ramsay aforesaid answered for the young man, That the covenant of grace was indeed a testament, and not, properly speaking, conditional. Herewith I was satisfied, and declared I would not insist, since I had been in earnest; but withal that I thought it was pity, that such an improper way of speaking of faith should be used; since it was not scriptural, was liable to be abused, and ready to lead people into mistakes.

These things, in these days, while I was in the Merse, gave my sermons a certain tincture, which was discerned; though the Marrow, from whence it sprang, continued in utter obscurity; but they were acceptable to the saints; neither did brethren shew disgust of them. I conversed occasionally on some of these points with brethren, particularly with Mr. Ramsay, then in Eymouth; and indeed he was still on the other side of the question. We had then some of the same arguments, that, afterwards in the year 1723, were cast up before the synod, in Mr. Wilson's affair; but these disputes marred not our friendship, he being still pleased to call me to assist at the communion with him in Eymouth, though he used not to be with me at Simprin on that occasion. The worthy Mr. Colden also had a difficulty to admit what I advanced on the first question aforesaid; but after some reasoning, he owned there was some weight in that argument, If believers were liable to eternal wrath in the case mentioned, they behoved to be so, either by the law and covenant of works, or by the gospel, and covenant of grace; not the first, for believers are dead to it; not the second, for that it condemns no man.

As for the subject of baptism; after I was settled among the people of Simprin, and had entered closely on my work, finding some of them grossly ignorant, and hardly teachable in the ordinary way, and casting in my mind what course to take with such, I drew up in writing a little form of catechising in the fundamentals, in short questions and answers, on design to teach it them privately in my my house. I do not well remember the progress of that affair; nor do I well know where these questions are; but afterward I used the same, in the case of my little children, in the first place, when they became capable of instruction. Among other such grossly ignorant, there was one, who desiring his child to be baptised, I could not have freedom to grant his desire for some time; neither am I clear, whether, when the child was baptised, it was baptized on a satisfying account of the fundamental principles from him or his wife. Whatever had laid the foundation of such scrupling, I was, by means of such straitening in practice, brought closely to consider that point. And having purposely studied the question, Who have a right to baptism, and are to be baptised? I wrote my thoughts thereon also. And being one day in conversation on that head with Mr. William Bird, dissenting minister in Barmoor in England, he presented to me Fulwood's discourse of the visible church, for clearing me. Bringing home the said book with me, I considered it, and wrote also some animadversions on a part of it. From that time I had little fondness for national churches strictly properly so called, as of equal latitude with the nations ; and wished for an amendment of the constitution of our own church, as to the membership thereof.

There were, besides these, other two questions I bestowed some thoughts on, in like manner. The one, Where had sin its lodging place in the regenerate ? the occasion whereof was a discourse with Mr. Mair on that head; but I doubt if I have well understood him in that point. The other, Why the Lord suffers sin to remain in the regenerate ? which had its rise from a particular straitening on that head in my own private case, as before narrated.

My thoughts on these several subjects, written for my own satis- faction, I had, by the 4th of August this year 1704, all fairly trans- cribed for conservation, in a book purchased for the purpose, and which I have called "The Miscellany Manuscript;" and thereby it was filled up to p. 325.* But whereas I had, in May 1703, begun exercises on the Confession of Faith, written at large for my own instruction, and the edification of the people, to whom I delivered them, for the evening exercise on Sabbaths for ordinary, that work was continued only to the end of that year 1703. And in the said space of time I went through the first two chapters only. I judge its proving sometimes too strong meat for the people ; and its re- quiring more time and study than my other affairs could well allow, contributed to the breaking me off from that design, that otherwise would have been very profitable to myself for my instruction in the whole system.

I had, on the 3d of September, in my course of lecturing, pro- ceeded unto the epistle to the Romans. And whereas it was not my ordinary practice to write my lectures; yet having considered that epistle, as the proper fountain from whence the doctrine of justifica- tion was to be drawn, I had an earnest desire of insight into it, so far as I could reach; for which cause, having gathered together some commentaries upon it, I studied the doctrinal part thereof, viz., to chap. xii. with that design, and wrote some thoughts thereon, which are in retentis. But sticking too precisely unto the lecturing of a chapter every Lord's day, this did, of course, make them the more superficial ; and withal the work was interrupted in the 5th and 7th chapters.

As in the former part of this year, I had got a new parcel of books, so toward the latter end thereof, in October, I got another. This parcel I had bought in England. Ere I got them home, they

---

* All these questions were printed in 1753, except the animadversions on Ful- wood ; the manuscript of which is now imperfect.

had stolen away my heart, and I was extremely fond of them. This raised me in a great fear while the lad was gone to fetch them; and it sent me to God; but I had no confidence. The books were taken, and then I saw well that my sin had found me out. This was a piece of trouble to me for two or three days. At length I resolved to lay myself down at God's feet, and to leave caring for the books; which that I might the better do, I applied myself to the work of ministerial visitation of families. Having spent but a forenoon in that way, when I came in, it was told me, that the books were in Ladykirk, and I might send for them when I would. Among these books were some of Lightfoot's pieces, the which did especially take with me, in respect of the Jewish learning therein; to which a particular bias seems always to have been hung on me, plainly perceiving the singular usefulness thereof for understanding of the holy scriptures. While I proceeded in acquainting myself with these, as I had access, I studied his description of the temple, so as I made a draught of the temple and the altar accordingly, which to this day hang in my closet. And though, being an utter stranger to mathematics, I could not represent things in their proper figures; yet that draught such as it is, so fixed the idea of the temple with me in some measure of distinctness, that it soon became familiar to me, and hath since that time been of very great use to me on several occasions.

That winter I visited a woman in Homtoun, who alleged the devil was in her. After I had spoke and prayed with her, I went out, and in the meantime she got out of the bed, and cried with a most horrid cry, without intermission, near a quarter of an hour. Coming in, and finding her in this case, I often desired her but to say, God help me; and she still said, she could not, and cried again. A weaver-lad had prayed with her; she told him the devil had said to her, she could be nothing the better of that good prayer, because it was not her own prayer, but his. To which the young man answered, The devil is a liar; for the prayer was not mine, but the Spirit's. I admired the answer.

Being with E. P. the night before she died, I had no satisfaction in converse with her; which affected me exceedingly. Thereupon I came in to my closet, and set myself to wrestle with God on her account; and then went to her again, and was much comforted in her; so that my spirit was more than ordinarily elevated. She said she fixed on that word, "Thou hast played the harlot with many lovers; yet return again to me, saith the Lord."

In the latter part of the month of December, it pleased the Lord to threaten to remove my wife by death, being violently sick. I was anxious exceedingly, and above measure grieved on that account. She recovered ; but God met me in such a manner, that I was most convincingly made to smart for that excess.

After having closed the ordinary of subjects for the Sabbath, as before narrated, I handled some texts for exciting unto exercise to godliness ; and, upon a particular occasion from the parish, I treated of divine desertion ; a subject which, together with that of communion with God, was, in the early days of my hearing the gospel, much in the mouths of the old experienced ministers, though now much worn out of our practical divinity, through the decay, I doubt, of soul-exercise and experience among ministers and people. Afterwards I did, on the 10th of December, enter on the epistle to the church of the Laodiceans ; Rev. iii. 14—22, on which I dwelt till May 6, 1706.

Having administered the sacrament of the Lord's supper in the summer season, yearly, hitherto from the time I began that course, I did, on January 28, 1705, administer it again ; and this course of administering it in the winter season also, was continued from that time yearly, till I was removed from that place. And thus we had that soul-strengthening ordinance twice a-year from this time. My son Robert was sick before ; and I was laying my account with his death, even in the fore-end of that month. It was the first sacrament I gave in the winter-time. I was engaged to that way, for the benefit of the good people in the corner, who through the winter have no occasion of partaking of that solemn ordinance ; and I found it was what I could get done. It pleased the Lord to meet me as an enemy in the way. My child died on the Friday, and was buried on Saturday, the preparation-day, after sermon. I was reproached through the country ; for, by the instigation of the devil, it was spread through the country, that I would allow none but those of our own parish to communicate, which (as it was said) kept away several persons. These things were very heavy to me and my afflicted wife, who yet was helped to carry the burden very christianly. They were the more affecting, in that I knew some ministers had no good eye upon the project, whereof one particularly helped to spread the report above said. However, all my losses were made up, the work went pleasantly on, the Lord sealed it in the consciences of many godly, with most evident tokens of his good pleasure, there being very much of God's presence with us at that work. And I observed the impression of it lasted longer on the parish, and the fruits of it were more visible, and in greater measure, than any other I remember we had before. While I had been laying my account with the death of the child in the fore-end of the month,

I had wished in my heart, that seeing there was nothing but death for him, it might so fall out, that he might be buried on a Lord's day after sermons, by which means a competent number of people might be gathered together with little trouble and expense. This sin was lively painted out to me in this stroke. We had but one sermon on the Saturday, and another on the Monday, preached by Mr. Colden, the only minister assisting to me ; and I think Mr. David Brown, then probationer, now minister of Selkirk, preached on the Sabbath afternoon. I added some exhortations on the Saturday, and also on the Monday after the sermon ; the which are *in retentis*, in the folio note-book. As the former was ordinary, so the latter, viz., the exhortation on the Monday, I have used for many years, and, I hope, with advantage ; having learned it from the example of Mr. Bird, the English minister aforesaid, whom I was wont to be assistant to on such occasions. I never had a gust for gathering together many ministers at communions ; though, in the meantime, I continued to call two or three in the summer, and had two sermons on the Saturdays and Mondays. Soon after my ordination, I got a great disgust of the Monday's dinners, perceiving what snares they were, not only to the families of the respective ministers, but to the guests also. And by this course I was free of both these, providing a moderate entertainment for my few assistants. And now in Etterick, our Monday's dinners are turned to the entertaining especially of strangers, who coming from afar, have real need of a dinner to fit them for their journey homeward again. By occasion of these communions in the winter-season, many of the godly throughout the country were gathered about us ; which made these latter years of my ministry in Simprin more especially comfortable ; but these halcyon-days of my ministry lasted not long, but were soon at an end.

On Thursday, November 1, about the evening-twilight, my daughter Jane was born, and she was baptized on the 8th, by Mr. John Dysert, minister at Coldinghame. I had gone away that morning unto Preston, to join in a congregational fast there, where Mr. Colden, and Mr. Laurence Johnston, minister of Dunse, preached ; and coming home at night, I found the child was brought forth ; the only one, in bringing forth of whom I shared not of the pangs, according to my capacity. By that child's birth at that time, providence was laying in for the heavy days we have seen of late years, in my wife's case.

Proceeding in my course of lecturing, December 23, unto the epistle to the Galatians, I considered it also as a fountain of the great doctrine of justification ; and therefore was in particular con-

cern for understanding thereof. Wherefore, addressing myself to
the study of it, I wrote a paraphrase thereon, from the beginning to
the end thereof : the which is to be found in the folio note-book
aforesaid.* And this was all, I think, of that kind, which I did at
Simprin.

There it was, that, by the kind conduct of providence, I was led
to, and acquired, the French tongue. What time I began it, I do
not remember; only I am sure I had not seen the grammar till after
I was removed unto the new manse. But by this year 1705, I had
read French books, and made some things therein read my own in
English. From Mr. Charles Murthland, governor to Moriston, I had
got a paper of rules for reading that language ; the which I trans-
scribed into a note-book. And from thence it was that I learned the
pronunciation. The grammar, and all the books of that kind which
I read, except an old one, being borrowed, I was the more careful
to transcribe things out of them into my own *Adversaria*, or common-
place book ; the which also was my manner with other books too,
especially borrowed ones. About that time I framed a part of the
folio note-book aforesaid, for recording therein any remarkable ex-
position of scripture-texts, which should occur to me in reading.
My hands, having, of later years, been otherwise providentially filled
up, I made but small progress therein ; but I judge the pursuing of
the design, to the filling up of the blanks, might be of very good
use.

Jan. 9, 1706.—This night I was under great discouragement, and
temptation, to give over the weekly sermon, or at least not to be at
such pains about it. The temptation arose from the badness of the
night, (for in the winter it was kept in the night in my own house,
and in the summer in the kirk in the day-time); whereupon I concluded, that few would wait upon it. The temptation spread to several other things, as that none of my neighbours did so, &c. Nevertheless the people came very frequent to it; and the Lord struck
the bottom out of my discouragement, by giving me more than ordinary of his presence in the sermon ; so that I would not for any
thing have given it over. This has often been my temptation ; and
thus ordinarily the Lord delivered me out of it.

On the 27th of January, the sacrament was administered again.
Before I proposed it to the eldership, I spent some time in secret
prayer with fasting, and saw it my duty to insist in that way,
though the entry to it had been very hard. The day being condes-

* This paraphrase was published in 1753, being annexed to the miscellany questions.

cended on by the session, and Mr. Colden written to, for assistance, but the day not being publicly intimated, my daughter fell very ill of that disease her brother died of last year. This was a heavy exercise to me; what to do, I knew not. Should I go on, and the child die at this time, then said my heart, " What wilt thou do to thy great name ?" My good will be evil spoken of, which the Lord knows I intended for his glory, and the refreshment of his people in the country-side. It will be thought testified against by the Lord himself; and it will be said, that what man could not hinder me to do, God would; and so my design will be broken, and I broken by it. On the other hand, thought I, will the neglect of duty preserve my child, or fit me for bearing the loss of her? Again therefore I went to God, by prayer with fasting; and still my cry was, " What wilt thou do to thy great name?" At length I was led to think, Why am I thus continually crying, " What wilt thou do to thy great name ?" cannot God provide for his glory, though I cannot see how, even though my former tragical affliction be reacted? It is my duty, I will venture; let the Lord do what seemeth him good. So I intimated the diet fourteen days before. And it pleased the Lord, that my child began to recover quickly after, my fears were dispelled, and the Lord did more for me that way than I could have expected in so short a time. I do not remember that ever I gave the sacrament, but I had some trying affliction in my way, either from the congregation or otherwise, Satan being on my top before or after. I had readily always something to thurst through violently ere I could get at it.

Since December, 1704, I have preached on the epistle to the church of the Laodiceans; and at the two last sacraments I changed not my ordinary. At the sacrament in June, 1705, the 18th verse, Rev. iii., fell to be the ordinary, and the action-sermon closed my discourse on that verse. One way and another I was held on the 19th verse, so that the preparation-sermons for the sacrament in January, 1706, fell in the ordinary on these words, ver. 20, " If any man open to me, I will come in to him," and the action-sermon on these, " And will sup with him, and he with me." I and others of the congregation could not but mark, how those large offers came, in the providence of God, to be so sealed. I remember, when I had been preaching against the delaying of repentance from ver. 19, God preached that over in bulk, and in some particulars, by his providence immediately after. And the sacrament, that fell to be the ordinary, ver. 21, " To him that overcometh," &c, on which verse particularly we had several sweet days. The second Lord's day after the sacrament, one of the best of the parish fell under such a trial as I had been warning them of, about two hours after she went home from the church that day. That day I resolved to preach short, but could not get it done; those particular heads which came last behoved to be delivered that day; the design whereof I quickly saw by that dispensation, being called that night to see that person.

On the Sabbath night, after the public work was over, Mr. Colden, my assistant, gave me the news of a call to the parish of Etterick for me. The same was shortly after brought before our Presbytery; who, finding it to be a mere presbyterial call *tanquam jure devoluto*, without concurrence of the parish, referred the affair of the transmitting thereof unto the synod, which was to meet in March.

March 4.—My health being broken, and thinking to go to Dunse to speak with Dr. Trotter about it; after I had once and again gone to God by prayer, to see what was my duty, I did see it was my duty to go that day. And being just ready to go away, my wife, out of tenderness to me, dealt with me to stay at home for that day, and I yielded. Then I fell on writing up the synod-book, to be ready for the general assembly. Having written some of it, I fell into two blunders, such as I never fell into while I had written that book. Beginning the third page, I fell into a worse error; so that I was forced to lay it aside. At first I thought my indisposition was the cause of this; but at length I saw as clearly as the light, that it was the punishment of my mocking God, in that I had sought to know my duty, God had discovered it, and after all I laid it aside. But after all I was made to bless God for these errors. And when I was helped to see my sin, and take with the punishment of my iniquity, then, though not till then, saw I how to get them amended. It was the Lord's goodness that they fell to be where they were.

My health being broken as aforesaid, I took advice about it. And this was not the first time that it had been so with me, even since my marriage. Some former year I had gone to Berwick, to consult upon that account Dr. Alexander Home, who, in the former part of the time I was at Simprin, was our ordinary; and shewing him, that I feared a consumption, he freely told me, that I had reason for it; and gave his advice. He was a plain man, good-natured, religiously disposed, ready to do good, and sparing no pains for for that end; easy to all, and would never take a farthing from me. My wife having, by his advice, cut out her hair, and washed her head every morning with cold water, got pretty clear of the pain of her head, for about the space of a year; but at length spurning the remedy, it recurred, and went on periodically as formerly. By this time Dr. John Trotter at Dunse was our ordinary. From him I got a receipt for a diet drink, dated March 7, 1706, consisting of anti-scorbutics; the which I used for many years, though now the disease hath much overcome me, maugre all opposition made to it, by that and the like means.

Some time before this, there had been an acquaintance begun between the said Dr. Trotter and me, which arrived at a particular friendship; and towards the latter end of the time I was in Simprin, became most strict and intimate; and so it continued until his death, about the year 1717.

He was second son to Alexander Trotter of Cattlesheil, and married Mrs. Julian Home, sister to the laird of Kimmerghame, a grave, virtuous, and pious gentlewoman. By her he had several children, but all dead by that time, except his daughter Elisabeth, a pleasant and promising girl. She also died of a lingering disease, some little time after his own death; by which means his substance went to his elder brother. He was a grave man, truly religious, acting from a principle of conscience towards God, temperate to a pitch, concerned for the spiritual good of others, particularly his relations; useful by his advice and converse, not only to the bodies, but to the souls of his patients; skilful in his business; and more ready, than ever I knew another, to shew to such as he judged capable, the *rationale* of his practice in physic; withal he was ready to do good to all, but especially to those of the household of faith. He had something severe in his temper, but was nevertheless a most affectionate and useful friend, whose memory is exceeding dear to me. He not only laid out himself, and that always freely, for my health, and that of my family, both at Simprin, and in Etterick; but upon my removal from the former, to the latter, proposed my looking out a piece of land in Etterick for him to buy, that we might still live together; the which, though it did not take effect, was a sign of singular friendship. To him it was owing, that I ever thought of writing the Fourfold State. I have a piece of gold of his, which I received after his death as a token, and keep wrapt up in a letter of his to me. Besides, there were about 50 merks received for a token to my two eldest children, and about £3 sterling for the two youngest. But by this time I have had occasion to give all of them, except my youngest son, their parts thereof, and much more.

The synod meeting at Dunse, March 19, there was no motion about the affair of Etterick, the whole Presbytery of Selkirk being absent, through mistake of the diet; but there was laid before them a competition of calls for the parish of Kelso; the one to Mr. Andrew Mitchell, minister at Manner, given by the Earl of Roxburgh, other heritors, and several inhabitants of the parish of Kelso;

the other to me, by some other of the heritors, the elders, and other inhabitants of the parish aforesaid. That was a business which I think I neither hoped nor feared. The synod waved determining in the competition, but recommended to the parties to agree to one of the ministers called; and if that could not be obtained, to some third person. Meanwhile my health was so broken, that I looked rather like one to be transported into the other world, than into another parish.

At the first meeting of our Presbytry after the synod, none of the Presbytery of Selkirk appearing, at our instance the call to Etterick was declared fallen from. At the following meeting one did appear to pursue it; but his commission was so informal, that it was not sustained. Only our Presbytery declared, that, if they would ask the synod's advice at their meeting in October, they would not reclaim. Thus Providence staved off the commencing of that process, while it stood upon a footing on which it could never have been rendered effectual.

About the beginning of May, I was vehemently importuned to assist at Ednam sacrament. I could get no clearness to yield, in regard of the stumbling I thought it might give to those of the Earl of Roxburgh's party in Kelso; fearing it might be looked on as a fomenting of the division in that parish. However, I yielded to go thither on the Thursday, and preach that day, if no better might be. There I was, by their importunity, put on a most violent rack. However, providence diverted them from urging me to preach that day, on a design to engage me to assist the following days. And after I came, I was more averse from preaching that day than before I came. The more I heard the sermons, the greater were my inclinations to be at that sacrament; the more I prayed, the less I saw it to be my duty; wherefore being fully cleared, I was peremptory for going home. And by the Lord's unexpected providing instruments there, and his dealing with me at home, I saw more and more it was of the Lord. I never yet lost (so far as I remember) by that which some account niceness, in not going to sacraments when I thought I was called to stay at home. And this has oftener than once been my trial, and ground of reflection on me to others, who looked on it with an evil eye.

June 23.—This day being very warm, I was helped to pray to the Lord to keep the hearers from sleeping. I was heard, so as I could not but observe it. In the prayer before the afternoon's sermon I was helped more than ordinary, and in the sermon there appeared a more than ordinary frame on the people; which when I perceived to abide with them, and that my frame was like to go away from me, I left off. The subject was, That no unworthiness, sinfulness, &c., could be a just hindrance of the soul's coming to Christ. When the Lord minds a mercy to a people, he helps them before hand to pray for it.

At the meeting of the synod in October, the Presbytery of Selkirk, having got a more firm footing for the affair of Etterick than their presbyterial call, appeared and gave in a petition to the synod about it. And together with them appeared, and concurred, the laird of Elliston, an heritor of that parish; Walter Bryden, an elder, tenant in Crosslee; and William Linton, tenant in Cossarshill; and these two latter, by commission from several inhabitants of the said parish. Likewise a petition for the said parish to the Presbytery, signed by five elders, and several masters of families, craving the presbytery would prosecute their call to me, testifying their concurrence, and promising all subjection to me in the Lord, was given in, and read. Hereupon the synod ordered our Presbytery to deliver the call to me, and to transmit the reasons of transportation to me and the parish of Simprin; and appointed some of their own number to meet with our Presbytery, as assistants in the affair, on the second Tuesday of December.

Last spring I was desired in Drummelzier's name to preach at Whittinghame, then vacant; but smelling the design, I was averse to it, and got it shifted. On the 23d of September there was an express sent me, by his order, to preach there next Lord's day, being the Lord's day immediately before the sacrament here. This I was exceeding averse to; but having Mr. Brown to preach for me, that made his agent the more pressing. I went to Dunse to meet Drummelzier, to see if possible I might be excused for that day; but he was not there, as was expected; so I returned, and went back on the Friday, not knowing whither I was going; but observed that morning I was taught to pray that God might divert it. When I came to Dunse, I was presently told, that Drummelzier had sent word, that I needed not come that day. This I gladly received; for I was straitened on the one hand, that I was to give the sacrament the day after, and, on the other, that Drummelzier had said, he would see that no other preached there that day. When, at the last synod the day was fixed for the determination of the business of Etterick, I thought it necessary to go and see the people beforehand, having never yet been in that place. The next week I am to go there. And being again invited to preach at Whittinghame, I had promised to preach there to-morrow, and was resolved to go to Dunse yesternight, but the badness of the weather hindered. This morning I attempted to go away, but found by one that I sent to Leek, that it

was utterly impassable. Thus Providence has twice stopt my
preaching in that place. I think the Lord means something by it,
which afterwards I may see. The first time I could not get a sermon for that place; but after many fruitless endeavours, I saw I
would be obliged to take one preached before. The meaning of that
was soon opened, as above said. But this time I got my sermons for
that place with a great deal of ease and satisfaction; and after
studying them, I thought that I would not have a free day from my
coming from Whittinghame to my going to Etterick; therefore I
began to study for Etterick; but by no endeavours could I get a
text, so that I was forced to give it over, till I should have preached
at Whittinghame, which I will not now see.

The matter being thus brought close home on me, I, considering
myself to be an utter stranger to that place and people having never
seen them, judged it altogether necessary to visit them, as is said
above, before the said diet of the Presbytery, with the assistant.
Accordingly I went to Etterick, accompanied by my dear friend
Dr. Trotter. I preached there on a Lord's day, November 3, but
in bonds, though the Doctor said he observed no such thing. Even
in secret prayer, from the time I left the Merse, I was sadly dried
up, at least till the work was over on the Lord's day, except a little on
the Lord's day morning. In fine, I judged I met with no such entertainment from the people, as could signify any earnest desire in
them to have me to be their minister. So we left them on Monday
morning. On Tuesday about ten o'clock we came to Charterhall,
where I was surprised with the news of a fast through the two Presbyteries. Not knowing well what to do, Providence led me straight
home, having some thoughts of taking another day for our congregation. As I was coming by the end of Swinton loch, that word,
Ezra viii. 21, " Then I proclaimed a fast there, at the river Ahava,"
&c., came into my mind; and I had some thoughts on it, as a text
for the fast, which was about the Union, the parliament being then
sitting upon it. When I came home, contrary to my expectation,
the people were in the church, Mr. Mair preaching. So I went immediately into the church, and preached on the aforementioned text
in the afternoon, wondering how the Lord had led me in the way I
knew not. I was never so willing to be transported to any place as
to Etterick; particularly I apprehended it might be better with me
as to my own soul's case there than at Simprin. But men's thoughts
are vanity. I am now afraid of that transportation. My soul
trembles to think of it, and my freedom in prayer about it is, to
protest against it before the Lord, unless he *command* me to go;
which does not yet appear.

Our Presbytery forgot to transmit the call and reasons, and to summon us, in due time, to the diet appointed by the synod; but recovering themselves, they appointed a new diet, viz. December 12. On the 10th and 11th of that month, came on such a violent storm of snow, that I concluded there would no pursuers be present. And comparing this occurrence with the course of Providence all along in the affair, I began to think (but too hastily making a judgment therein), that God had thereby sealed his design, that I was not to be minister of Etterick. Wherefore, before I went to the Presbytery that day, looking on the affair as in a sort already determined, I could not be very serious for light therein; but coming up to the place, I found myself disappointed; two ministers, and two elders of the parish, pursuers, being there. Sir William Cockburn appeared for Simprin. And the affair was issued that day in a reference to the synod in March.

Dec. 31.—The affair of Etterick having occasioned various thoughts of heart to me at several times, I set myself to view the several steps of Providence in it on both sides. Upon the one hand I observe, 1. That Mr. H. having come with the call to our Presbytery, in Feburary or March last, he staid all night in my house; but I was from home. And the call was found to be a bare presbyterial call, without concurrence of heritors, elders, or parish. 2. But the Presbytery having referred the affair of the transmitting of the call and reasons to the synod in March, the whole Presbytery of Selkirk, through a mistake of the diet, was absent from the synod, so there was nothing done in it; and at our next Presbytery after, none of the Presbytery of Selkirk appearing, at our instance the call was declared to be deserted and fallen from. 3. The next Presbytery after, Mr. B. appears; but his commission was so informal that it was not sustained; only our Presbytery declared, that if the Presbytery of Selkirk would ask the synod's advice in this affair, against October next, they would not reclaim. 4. The Presbytery of Selkirk having so managed their business at the October synod, that the synod ordered the call and reasons to be transmitted, and appointed a committee of their number to meet with our Presbytery the first Tuesday of this instant, to determine in that affair; our Presbytery forgot to transmit the call, and reasons of transportation, and to summon us in due time. 5. Being an utter stranger to that people but by report, I thought it duty to go there and preach, before I would hazard the determination; but the letter I sent to Mr. M. to warn the people of my coming, came not to his hand till the Saturday that I was in Etterick. 6. My entertainment there was not promising, and I was straitened, as above narrated. 7. Our Pres-

bytery having appointed a new diet, viz. December 12, I got the
reasons of transportation, which seemed to me so weak, as that it
looked like a particular design of Providence, and an infatuation.
8. I went out of Simprin pulpit towards Etterick ; for that day I
went away, I lectured and baptized, and presently took my horse ;
and (so to call it) I returned from Etterick to the pulpit of Simprin as above related. 9. Thursday, December 12, the day anew
appointed for the meeting of the Presbytery and assistants for determining that affair, was a bad day; a violent storm of snow having come on, on the Tuesday and Wednesday before, (whereas the
diet appointed by the synod was excellent weather), so that it could
scarcely be thought that either pursuers or assistants would come ;
and on the Wednesday's night, finding none of them come, I began
to conclude, that none of them would appear ; and so that, by such
a train of providences, the Lord had sealed his design of my not
going to Etterick to be minister there. Wherefore, on the morrow,
before I went away to the Presbytery, I could scarcely pray seriously about it for light in it, seeing the affair as it were already determined.

But when I went to the Presbytery, within a little of the town, I
was surprised with the news of the pursuers being there ; and there
I found two ministers of the Presbytery, and two elders of the
parish. Two papers were shewn me, when I alighted, importing the
heritors falling from their opposition. The business was by that
meeting referred to the synod in March. When I came home, I had
several reflections seeming to favour the design of Etterick ; and as
to some of them, I was made to wonder how my eyes had been held
that I could not see them before. They are as follows :—1. That
was a surprising turn of Providence, when I went to the Presbytery,
expecting none of the pursuers there, that came so quickly after I
had thought God had sealed his pleasure in it, and put the top-stone
on the providences crossing. I remember, while I was making that
conclusion, I was withheld from making it peremptory, by that
word; James v. 11, " —have seen the end of the Lord." 2. It was
told me, that the unanimity of the Presbytery in that call was very
remarkable ; some of them that had other views and engagements
to act for others, laying them by for this. 3. Thus far it has been
carried over difficulties, particularly the people, refusing their concurrence, who have now with the elders (last summer) given in a petition to the Presbytery, bearing their calling me to be their minister,
and promising to submit to my ministry ; and the heritors none of
them appearing to oppose ; only one appeared to pursue it, and
that only at the synod. 4. The Lord did signally bind me up from

going to Whittinghame, whereas I am informed there was a design of a call for me; and I was led to preach the sermon at Etterick that was designed for Whittinghame; the suitableness whereof I was fully convinced. 5. Some time before the presbytery-day I grew uneasy in my mind, for that I had never preached designedly some particular duties to my people; which things I thought I might dispatch in the space of two or three months; so I resolved, without delay, to fall about them, and have begun already. 6. The desolation of that parish, ever since I saw it, hath had great weight on me; and I am convinced I should have more opportunity to do service for God there than here; but success is the Lord's. 7. Concerning those providences that seemed to cross the design of Etterick, it was a strange thing, that the whole Presbytery should have mistaken the diet of the synod, and that when they had such business before it. But had they been present, the business doubtless would have been tabled; if in that case the synod had refused to transmit the call, the business would have been crushed in the bud; had they ordered the transmitting of it, no doubt the Presbytery had continued me in Simprin, it being contrary both to their light and mine, to transport on a mere presbyterial call. The same is to be said of Mr. B's informal commission; for at that time the business stood only on that weak foot; whereas by these lets the business never came under a judicial cognisance tending to a determination, till it got the people's call as a firmer foot to stand upon. As to our Presbytery's forgetting the synod's diet, I can only remark one thing, that the coming to prosecute the call at that time when they came, was a greater evidence of their affection to me than had they come then, when, according to the synod's appointment, the business should have been discussed. The miscarrying of the letter to Mr. M. seems to have been subservient to the cold entertainment I thought I met with there. As to which in particular I have remarked, 1. That it was very necessary for me to take off that disposition of spirit, whereby I was too easy in my own mind as to that business; and it set me where I had often desired to be, even afraid of that transportation. 2. I find I have made the very same remark as to the inclinations of the people of Simprin, the first time I preached in it, the business being then set on foot. As to my straitening, I find also I have remarked concerning my first preaching in Simprin, that what account to give of that day's work, I knew not very well.

Jan. 4, 1707.—Monday. This day I went towards Oxnam, to take Mr. Colden's advice about the business of Etterick. As I was going away from home, I began to be very perplexed about that business, and, by the way to Stitchill, the dispensations crossing that affair, seemed so big in my eyes, that I thought it was not the Lord's mind that I should be transported thither. And that night I could not pray about it, any other way than that God would avert it. On the morrow Mr. G., Mr. K., and I went to Oxnam, and found that Mr. Colden was at Edinburgh. Thus was I disappointed. I minded also to have taken his advice, whether to give the winter sacrament at the ordinary time, or delay it. This disappointment determined me to do it at the ordinary time. As to Etterick, I looked on that disappointment as a dispensation confirming the conclusion, that God designed me not for that place. When I came home, I found, that, seeing I had missed my mark at Oxnam, it was necessary to set some time apart for seeking the mind of the Lord himself in it; for now again the cross providences had not such a determining aspect as before.

This I did on Saturday, January 9, having studied my sermons the day before. The upshot of it, with respect to that particular, (for I had also the public affairs and the sacrament in view also), was, that in some measure I could say, that " my countenance was no more sad," the Lord calmed my spirit, which before was perplexed, and helped me to believe, that he would clear me in that matter in due time, and to depend on him for the same; and that word, " He that believeth, shall not make haste," was helpful to me. The Lord helped me to lay it before and upon him, especially towards the close of that exercise; so that it was a blessed disappointment at Oxnam; for by that means I was driven to the fountain of light.

Jan. 19.—This day being to seek something with respect to the public, I prayed particularly, that God would guide tongue and heart. On reflection, I must say, he is the hearer of prayer; for my heart and tongue were guided in that particular, far better than my pen in my notes.

Three things make me hope, that the Lord will clear me in the business of Etterick, and bring it to a happy conclusion; 1. The calming of my spirit after prayer, 1 Sam. i. 18. 2. Several that have interest with God, are concerned to cry for light to me at the throne of grace; Jam. v. 16. 3. I am willing to go or stay, as the Lord shall give the word; Psalm xxxii. 8, 9, and xxi. 9. And, as often before, upon this matter, so this night I was helped with some boldness to protest before the Lord, that I must be caused to walk in his way; Psalm xxv. 8; Ezek. xxxvi. The occasion of these thoughts was, that about two or three days ago I received a letter from Mr. M——, touching that affair, another from Mr. B——, in name of the Presbytery of Selkirk, desiring me to go to Etterick again. This I could not yield to; because, 1. The main thing they desired it for was, that I might be satisfied as to the inclinations of the people; but unless other things did it, I could not have it that way, in regard I had signified my dissatisfaction with their carriage towards me; 2. I thought it would make my own people and them also mistake me.

Jan. 25.—My servant yesterday went to D——, with beer. We waited long for his coming home, but he came not, and we were afraid he had filled himself drunk. When we were going to bed, and he not come, we were afraid he had either perished, or was lying by the way unable to help himself. I minded to set some time apart for fasting and prayer in my family, as was ordinary before sacraments; and this determined me to this day. So it was observed for these three causes especially : 1. The sacrament; 2. The state of public affairs; 3. The business of Etterick. This day when we arose, and found he was not come, we resolved to wait till eight o'clock, and then send one to seek him, if he came not ere then. I went to my closet in great distress, as all my family was; and while I was begging a blessing on the scripture I was to read, I earnestly prayed the Lord would calm my spirit, and help me to depend on him. The Lord answered me presently, and so I fell on to read. And when I had read about ten or eleven verses, my son came to the door, and told me the lad was come. This helped me to pray, wondering at the Lord's goodness. Our fears in one part had good ground; for so it was with him. The family met, and the Lord was with us, and filled us with goodness and thankfulness. I observed here, 1. That the devil was driving on the old trade of raging about the time of a sacrament, as he uses to do. But he was outshot in his own bow; for, 2. This affliction was a vast help to me and my family, to the work we were going about; it put us in another frame than readily we would otherwise have been in; 3. I learned the necessity of taking more care about the unhappy lad's soul than I had done. 4. That a depending frame is a pledge of the mercy desired. And this lesson came seasonably to me at this time, with respect to the business of Etterick, for light wherein I am helped to depend. 5. My wife expected workmen to have come yesterday, and the family fast was to have been next week; but God hindered them, and the disappointment determined us to this week, as the other dispensation to this day, which we could not have got done if they had come.

Feb. 2.—The sacrament was celebrated. I had great difficulty to get a text. On Wednesday I began to study the text I preached on, but was obliged to give it over. On the Friday I began it anew,

and hammered out my sermon on it that day. The confluence of
people was extraordinary; so that I behoved to send for more wine,
and set up another table on Saturday's night. It was thought my present circumstances contributed to it. When I began the work on the
Lord's day, I was much discouraged by reason of the confusion and
disturbance, occasioned by the unusual throng, and by reason I could
observe few of my own handful among them. I had no straitening in
my preaching, nor any other part of the work. Something of a more
than ordinary frame was upon myself and the people, in the first prayer.
The work at the tables was signally owned of God. Some professed,
they were in hazard of disturbing the work, by crying out at the
first and second tables. I understand by many, that there was
something of an unordinary frame among the people in the byre.
While I was communicating, one that was near me seemed to me
not to have taken the bread; I gave her a sign while she seemed to
be meditating, and found she had taken it. This discomposed me;
I saw it had been a temptation, and that my business then was to
have been taken up about my own case. Being brought to the
pinch, I wrestled to get to my feet again, fleeing to the blood exhibited, and set myself to present duty. Let this be a lesson to me.
At night in my closet, partly desiderating the impressions of communicating on my spirit, as was due; partly reflecting on that disorder at first by the throng, having never seen any here before, I
was discouraged, and poured out my complaint before the Lord, was
sore weighted and bowed down; my eyes, meanwhile, being withheld from seeing what glorious power of God appeared at that
work. Blessed be the Lord, it was good ballast. And I have received something of what I then desiderated. On the Monday, Mr.
Colden preached a sweet sermon, with much tenderness. I knew not
whether to speak after him or not; but found at length, though I
desire not to speak after him, that yet I durst not forbear. And
so, with the Lord's help, I spoke a word to all, to strangers, and,
with more than ordinary vigour and concern on my soul, a word to
my own people. All the three days I found two of my neighbour ministers offended at me, which was but a new thing as to one of them;
and considering that with Mr. B——'s persecuting me in many companies with his tongue, upon the occasion of a proposal I made to
him in Mr. B——n's favour, before one other minister only, which
he received very calmly in the time, though he yielded not to it, but
we parted good friends, till Mr. B——n had seemed to balk his carnal project, that he had interwoven with the calling of him to be his
colleague, and afterwards to be sole minister of G——w. Thus was
I grieved, and my spirit affected, seeing some of my friends now

turned my enemies; which made me say in my heart, "O that I
had in the wilderness a lodging-place of wayfaring men," &c.

Feb. 9.—This morning the Lord was pleased to blow on me more
than ordinary; and with thankfulness my soul acknowledged the
goodness of God, in that ever he sent me to Simprin, gave me a less
charge than others, provided for me here, gave me the blessed occasions of sacraments, and hath made unworthy me some way useful
to several of the people. This day was a good day, and I hope a
day of power. (*Nota,* If ever I preached in my life, it was that
day). I preached on 2 Cor. xi. 2, "I have espoused you to one husband." Towards the latter end of the afternoon's sermon, I desired
them to remember, that I had espoused them to Christ, shewed them
in some particulars what had been done that way, and then called
the heavens and the earth, the angels, the stones and timber of the
church and byre, and the people themselves, to witness that they
were espoused. These things were delivered with a change of my
voice, speaking mostly lower than before, but with more than ordinary weight and gravity. Having made that solemn attestation,
my spirit just slipt off into prayer, that the Lord would preserve
them till the day of the Lord, &c, in which I continued a little
while. The like I never did. In that prayer, my voice, that
before was low, and when extended uneasy, turned very high; and I
prayed with as much easiness of my voice as ever in my life. I was
a wonder to myself, and a strange moving was upon the people. It
was observable, as that easiness began with the prayer, it continued
while, in a few words, I exhorted them to endeavour to keep chaste;
and then it left me, which was ere I had altogether done with the
sermon. Afterward I had a temptation to be lifted up. It was
quickly crushed in the bud, but not by me. I had a secret dissatisfaction that arose in my heart as to the managing of that work. In
the fervour of my affections I had expressed a word wrong. This,
whatever be of it, had weight enough then to hold me down, if not
to press me too far. (*Nota,* All this passed, as I remember, betwixt
the pulpit and the garden-door next to the house.) But immediately after I came in, going to my closet as ordinary, at prayer
there, it pleased the Lord to shoot an arrow of wrath suddenly into
my soul, which pierced my soul and body both; so that a great
weakness, and an exceeding great heat, went through my body in a
moment. It lasted not long; but I think, if it had lasted a while
longer, I had been a most miserable spectacle. When it came on,
at first I was tempted to rise from prayer, and flee from the presence of the Lord, and had much ado to resist; but God in mercy
determined me to another way, even to flee under the covert of the

blood of Christ, that only shelter from the terror of God, and that
even to those that had crucified him; and so I held by these scriptures; 1 John i. 7; Heb. ix. 14.   These drops of wrath came in on
me, with a conviction of guilt darted into my spirit, viz. that, in
that prayer aforesaid, I had not suitable affections to that petition,
" Even so come, Lord Jesus, come quickly," which was the last petition in it.   And in a most composed temper of mind, reflecting on
it, I see clearly, that God left me in that, and that that petition
was the product of my own spirit.   This let me see, that my best
duties behove to be washed in the blood of the Lamb, else they,
even they will damn me.   After dinner, singing with my family a
part of Isa. xxxv. that word, ver. 8, "And an high way shall be
there,—though fools shall not err therein," was very sweet to me,
with respect to the business of Etterick.   I went up immediately to
my closet, and meditating, I again got a broad sight of the filthiness of my best duties, and the absolute need of their being washed
in the blood of Christ; saw myself most unworthy to touch the vessels of the Lord; and that I might roll myself in the dust, when
the glorious gospel was to be preached.   This helped me to pray.   I
have sometimes wished for some drops of wrath, to awaken me out
of a secure frame; but I found one drop, one arrow, intolerable.
Who knows the power of his wrath?   Tongue cannot express it.
O precious Christ!   O precious blood!   Horror and despair had
swallowed me up, had it not been that blood, the blood of God.   I
observe now, that, according to my design formerly laid down, I
was to have preached on watching this day; but the Lord withheld
me, and led me to this text; as also that the Lord gave a spirit of
prayer in the private fast before the sacrament, and this morning
also.   These were tokens of good.   But the Lord has been at pains
to hide pride from my eyes.   O that I never saw it more!

  Feb. 10.—This morning coming, in prayer, to the business of Etterick, I thought I saw myself beset with promises; Isa. xxxv. 8;
Prov. iii. 6; Psalm xxv. 9, and xxxii. 8, 9, and cvii. *ult.*, and my soul
was raised to a dependence on the Lord.   At night, fear and darkness
seized on me again, being in company; but by prayer I was raised
up again to dependence.   There is no keeping foot without new
supplies from the Lord.

  Feb. 12.—Concerning that business, which lies very near my
heart, and so much the more as the time of its determination draws
near, I have further remarked, 1. That Providence has been at
pains to keep me out of the way of the parties, that I might
not consult with them; Mr. H. missed me, Mr. M. and those with
him were diverted from coming to my house the night before

the Presbytery. I was invited to Yarrow sacrament last summer, but had no freedom to go. At Melrose sacrament, Elliston's lady desired to speak with me; I declined to speak with her in the church yard, lest people should have misconstrued me, and promised to wait on her any where in the town; but I heard no more of it. About Whitsunday 1703, Drummelzier declared, though not to me, his respect towards me, (having been with him about business), and that he would favour me in any transportation I had an eye to, (so he was pleased to express it, at least so it was told to me.) I said to the person that told me, I thanked Drummelzier for his kindness, but that was not the way I minded to take, but was content to stay where I am. Nevertheless afterward, that same year, I think, I heard he had recommended me to Etterick; but Providence so ordered it, that since that time I never saw his face; wherein I have often admired the good providence of God; for if I had, it would have been hard to have come away with a good conscience and good manners too. (N. B. I have heard since I came to Etterick, that thus I was among the first that were recommended to them after Mr. Macmichen's departure. However, he joined not with the callers, being pleased with the thing itself, but not with the method of procedure.) 2. When the call came first to our Presbytery, my health was sore broken; I looked rather like a man to be transported to eternity, than to another parish. 3. While I was at Etterick, my wife had so little liberty in prayer about that business, that when she saw me first, which was in the church presently after I came home, she was able to guess my entertainment. [N. B. I must do this justice to my wife, once for all, to say, that as to my leaving her country, and not settling there, and as to my settling in Simprin, which was before she was my wife, but not before we were engaged, she interposed not; and as to this transportation, she meddled as little; but in all the three was silent to the Lord, and laid open to follow what God would point out to be my duty.] And C. Wood told me, that the business at first seemed very clear to her, but afterwards grew dark. 4. There was a most remarkable difference betwixt the secret and family fast before the Presbytery, and the secret and family fast last observed. In the former two there was nothing but tugging and heartlessness; in both the latter, there was something of the spirit of prayer. 5. After that exercise on the 9th of January was over, having prayed that the Lord would help me to take up his mind in his dispensations, I thought on the things recorded above, December 31, p. 169, *et seq.* And that day, viz. January 9, the balance was, in my apprehension, cast on the side of Etterick. 6. I thought Mr. Colden should have staid the

Monday night after the sacrament, that I might consult him in that affair; but he went away. Only he told me, that he thought it God's goodness that I was sent to Simprin; but that he was now clearer than ever that I should go away; but he spoke not of Etterick to me, but Ayton and Jedburgh. Many a time has God inhibited that man to help me; but if he had not been more useful to me than others, I had not been so ready to idolize and make an oracle of him, whom my heart will ever love. The last Lord's day another went away, and spoke not with me; but I reverenced the providence of God drying up the streams, to lead me to the fountain. 7. What aspect the Lord's countenance at the sacrament, the exhortation on the Monday, and the last Lord's day's work, have on this affair, the event will make certain. As to the last of these, it was said by Christian Wood, who was with us that day, that it seemed to her from that work, that either I was near an end of preaching for altogether, or near the end of my preaching at Simprin. 8. I think it a strange conjecture, that at this time so great offence is taken at me by my two nearest neighbours, and other two in whom I trusted, without any just ground that I know of. One of them, Mr. P. I used to boast of; that whatever different sentiments we were sometimes of, we still kept from taking offence at one another; but I was surprised, a day or two ago, to hear that it is not so now. 9. About two years ago, when there was no word of any transportation for me, so far as I remember, I had a dream, that I was transported somewhere; and in my dream I was under great remorse of conscience; for that I thought the love of the world had prevailed with me in it. When I awoke, I thought myself thrice happy, that it was but a dream, and that I was still at Simprin. The use I made of it then was, that it might be a warning to me, to take heed to myself, if ever a transportation should offer. 10. That day I went to Etterick I lectured here on Psalm cxxii., insisting mostly on the latter part, ver. 6—9. That day I came home, that word came into my mind; Ezra viii. 21, and I preached on it, though I little thought to have preached any that day. 11. What may be the event I know not; but it has sent me oftener to God than otherwise I would have gone, and my own case has been thereby bettered. C. Wood told me, that when the business was first set on foot, being very much concerned about it, she was brought at length to lay her hand on her mouth, and thought she had this answer, that if I went there, it should be for the good of a young generation. But she said the business grew darker to her afterwards, yet she still thought I behoved to go there. These things she told me after I came home from Etterick.

Feb. 16.—Last night lying down to rest on my bed, I posed my conscience with that question, Whether or not, after all I have thought and seen, I durst peremptorily refuse to go to Etterick? And I thought I durst not. This did much quiet my heart, knowing that the determination is to be made by the synod. The dream I had long ago, had occasioned fears to me very often; and therefore have I asked my own soul, whether the world sways me in this business? And I dare not say it does. And in this inquiry, it was clearing to me, that I am conscious to myself, that if never so great worldly advantages had been proposed to me at the Presbytery, December 12, I durst not have yielded to it, seeing no more of God in it than I saw at that time. But because my heart is a depth of secret wickedness, I have several times this last week prayed with respect to that particular point, that God would search me and try me. And I think, I dare say before the Lord, I was sincere in it, really desirous to know if that wicked way was in me in that matter. I am sometimes helped to depend on, and trust God, for guidance in this matter; but I am often assaulted with fears of being left. And what then should I think of that dependence so often brangled? This has been my case often within this short time. But this morning, at family-exercise, when it was not in my mind, I met with a passage in our ordinary; Jer. xxxix. which was cleared to me, so as I saw an answer to my case. The passage was that, ver. 17, " Thou shalt not be given into the hand of the men of whom thou art AFRAID. 18, For thy life shall be for a prey unto thee, BECAUSE thou hast PUT THY TRUST IN ME." *Afraid* (I thought), and yet *delivered*, BECAUSE he put his trust in the Lord! Wonderful, that God will overlook his people's weakness, and deliver them, even because of that trust mixed with so much fear! That *because* was wonderful in my eyes. This answered my case so patly, that I was much cleared by it. C. Wood was here this day, being the Lord's day, minded to go home; but the Lord hindered her by bodily indisposition. She told me the business was plain to her, that to Etterick I must go. I was anxious the last time she was here, that I might have understood how that matter seemed to go with her; but she was going away, I laid by that anxiety, and God brought this notice unexpectedly to my hand.

Feb. 18.—This morning I arose early, and retired to spend some time in prayer, especially about the business of Etterick. Last night in prayer, once and again, for help to that work, my soul was elevated; but the third time I was sore dried up. This morning I had some tugging with my heart a while; at length I got earnest and solid desires after the Lord. And I remember, I pleaded much on the

Lord's having given me these desires, that seeing he had *made* them, he would *fill* them. Afterwards that frame was lost, and I could say little, but cry, that the Lord would loose the prisoner. While I was at that work, a letter comes which I behoved immediately to answer; and then Mr. M—— came. This was about ten o'clock. So I was taken off. Howbeit, in company, the sad thoughts of this heavy turn in my frame, and the Lord's deserting me, stood before me. I stole away a while to my closet, and thought and prayed. And as to the causes of it, I had before found out one, viz. a woful desire I had of vain-glory last night. This I confessed before the Lord, when the darkness came on; but no alteration of my frame could I get. But now at prayer I was let into another cause. The last year, so far as I remember, my health broke on the 11th of February. On Saturday last, the 15th of this instant, I had re- solved to spend some time in prayer. But finding my body sore weakened after my studies on Friday, I altered my resolution of having that exercise on the Saturday, and delayed it till this week, fearing this weakness might be the beginning of the feared breach of my health. On Saturday my indisposition continued, and on the Lord's day my strength was small. Now I began to fear the Lord had thus left me, because of shifting that duty on Saturday last; but I repelled this, seeing, thought I, my being so very feeble on Friday's night was a just ground to delay it, till my body were fit for that work. But when I came to prayer, in the progress of that duty, a conviction of guilt in that point, and that I had not trusted God for bodily strength, for his service, was so born in and fastened on my soul, that I behoved to let go my carnal reasonings as fig- leaf covers, and take with it. Then I confessed it before the Lord, and fled for refuge to the blood of Christ. And thereupon followed an alteration upon my frame, and my perplexed and confused soul was eased, though I walked halting under the sense of that guilt. So, as I had opportunity, I pursued my design through the rest of that day. At night the society for Christian fellowship met. And I observed, that this business, which has fallen out of their prayers for some time, came in again this night. R. Aitchison prayed first, a man in whom I think is the spirit of prayer. I took notice, that his prayer about it was just as his prayers were this time twelve- month, when that business was set on foot first by the call. He prayed for light to me, that God would prosper my work if I be to stay with them; and that if I go, God may be with me, and loose their affections from me. So prayed he at first. But before the Presbytery on December 12, there was an astonishing boldness and freedom with the Lord among them in that matter, in him especially,

which seemed to me prophetic. Wonderful, wonderful, is the conduct of Providence ! This desertion with the outgate seemed to me
to clear me in another case about this business. On the Lord's day
morning, as said is, I was set on my feet by that word ; Jer. xxxix.
17, 18; but at night I began to stagger again, upon the consideration of my bodily indisposition. It seemed to be coming on as last
year ; and I thought, that if it should be thus with me at the synod,
whatever other things might point out to me, I feared this would
leave me in the lurch ; for if matters, on the one hand, look so as to
bid me yield ; this indisposition, on the other hand, speaks strongly
against it; seeing it would appear unfair towards that parish for
me to yield to take the charge of them under such bodily indisposition. [*Nota*, That which was feared was a consumption.] But hereby, in sad experience, I learned not to shift that which otherwise
appears duty, upon the account of bodily weakness and indisposi-.
tion, but to be at the Lord's disposal, and hold even on the way,
trusting him for strength for his own service. After family worship,
I came to my closet again, and fell to work. And at that time,
after prayer, I read over the above account of the dispensations of
Providence in that business, and in the sight of the Lord, as I could,
communed with my own heart concerning the two foresaid questions
and was answered as above said.

Feb. 24.—Monday. On Saturday last I gave myself for a while
to prayer, especially with respect to the business of Etterick, and I
found my heart ready for prayer, and desirous of it, having laid no
restraint on myself as to time or continuance in that exercise. This
I did, because the last day I found my heart impatient sometimes
under the view of continuing closely for such a time. This day also
I spent some time in prayer, and thinking on that business, in order
to come to a fixed resolution and determination as to what is my
duty. The time of the synod's meeting being now very near,
obliged me to set this time apart for the end foresaid. Wherefore,
after serious applications to the throne of grace, for light, and determination of duty from the Lord, I took a view of those things
noted, December 31, and as to the presbyterial call. And as to the
latter, I see not how it could have been commenced in a more
cleanly way for me ; and it agrees very well with the chain of the
after dispensations. As to our Presbytery's forgetting the day, I
further remark, that it was necessary to bring the business to so
low an ebb as it came to at length. As to my straitening while in
Etterick, it was a time of straitening to others concerned for me,
and so the whole was of a piece. And when I was under an invitation to go back to Etterick again, I was convinced, that no stress

could be laid on my enlargement in preaching; so that though I had been, when there again, enlarged, it would not have taken away my scruple, or determined me. And this in the meantime answered the case of my straitening. As to the weakness of the Presbytery's reasons, I could nowise account for it. As for my going out of and returning to the pulpit of Simprin, and the scriptures I was led to both times, these seem to leave it in *equilibrio*. [*Nota*, I think, if I had said, these seem to call me to make haste in my work there, as having but little time more, it had been no unreasonable construction of Providence. And the other part, to wit, those scriptures I was led to, seem not to have been without design this way, though the union was the occasion of my pitching on both of them.] The last was the seal of dispensations cross to it, which was soon removed. Whatever come of my health after this, my indisposition has not been so violent this season as it was last year. The aspect of the last sacrament, and the Lord's day after it, on this business, has for some time appeared to me, and not to me only, determining.

I remember how yesterday I had a lamentable account; how the devil had set up his trophies against the sacrament in Dunse market on Wednesday last, one of this parish (W. T.) and he a communicant, being so drunk, that he could not hold his feet, but fell, and broke his face in the open street. This created me thoughts of heart, even with respect to this business, and made me stagger not a little; but examining, whether it might be consistent with the Lord's design of removing me, and my submitting to this transportation, I was cleared by that passage, Acts xx. 29, 30.

At length I came to this conclusion, That seeing all the dispensations seeming to cross the design of Etterick (excepting one) may be in some measure accounted for, and appear not inconsistent with the Lord's design of sending me there, and that the most remarkable of these made plainly for it; seeing that by a train of cross providences, Providence made it grow darker and darker, and then suddenly and unexpectedly made such a turn in it; seeing it hath been brought this length through several difficulties, and the Lord seemed to open two doors for my removal at one time, and then shut one of them again, and with that I designed for the one sent me to the other; seeing the dispensations of providence, and the frame of my own, and that of the hearts of others with respect to that matter before the Presbytery, December 12, did in some sort keep pace with the event of that day, and both being now altered, go in another course; seeing the Lord chased me away to himself to seek counsel, kept me from consulting with men, and has so graciously condescended to give me seasonable clearing of particular cases in that affair; and the way

I have been directed to in my preaching here since the prebytery-day, for ordinary changing a text every day or two, which was not my usual way, and the work at the sacrament, and particularly that on the Lord's day thereafter, seem to have such a determining aspect; seeing the Lord hath removed the hinderance arising from the consideration of the state of my health, partly by making it better, and partly, yea chiefly, by shewing me that I ought not to lay so much stress on it, as is above narrated; and seeing, upon the whole, I am convinced, that if I had no charge, I would by these things be determined to embrace that call; therefore I am resolved (*rebus stantibus ut nunc*) to submit to the synod, and leave it to their determination.

And forasmuch as these dispensations of Providence, as observed and applied, look scripture-like, and this resolution hath not been easily obtained by me, having had many ups and downs in this business; seeing the Lord shewed me on the 9th of January, that he that believeth maketh no haste, and I was content to wait, and was quieted in prayer, and helped to depend on the Lord, while as yet I knew not what hand to turn me to; and I have found, for ordinary, when I sought light in this affair, my first care was still for Christ himself, esteeming himself far above light, &c., and now at last I have won at this resolution, in the use of means for clearness, so that I was afraid this day to harp any more on that string, lest I should with Balaam tempt God; and seeing, upon the attaining of that clearness as to my duty, my soul has been made thankful to the Lord for his goodness and condescendence to me in this matter, I must and will conclude, that this resolution is of God; and having examined myself again as to the world's influence, I dare say, and said it, before the Lord, that (in his strength) ten thousand worlds should never have engaged me.

After all, I saw my case in Psalm xl. 1—5, and I behoved to sing it; and so I did with a thankful heart, from ver. 1 to 9. And blessed be God for Christ; thanks to the Lord for his unspeakable gift. I bless him, that the effect of all this is to make me prize Christ; and therefore when I thought I had done, I was obliged to go back again, and, as I was able, to bless God for Christ; and O that I may have the advantage of an eternity to praise him in!

As to the sacrament of Melrose (p. 176,) which was last summer, the letter inviting me to it was given to me only on the Thursday before, when I was preaching at Eccles, being the fast-day before the communion there. This straitened me for time to think on it, and prepare for it, if I should go. Mr. L. had desired me to come thither against the Lord's day, after I had preached at home, to help there. I endea-

voured to see my duty, and studied for Melrose on the Friday, in
case I should go there. But on Friday's night I went to bed, still
in the dark as to my duty. Wherefore I rose early on Saturday
morning, wrestled for light till between seven and eight o'clock;
but could not know what to do. That which helped to difficult me
was, that it was in Selkirk Presbytery, and that some of the people
of Etterick might be there. This darkness distressed me exceedingly, both in body and mind; wherefore giving it over, I went to
bed again to refresh my body. A little after I rose again; and,
seeking the Lord, resolved to take my horse; so I went away, not
knowing whither I was going, whether I would come home again, or
stay at Eccles, or go forward to Melrose. But by the way the light
began to break, to send me to Melrose; and withal I had hopes,
that, at Eccles, I would meet with that which would fully clear me
what to do. And so indeed it came to pass, and I was determined
fully ere the sermons began. So I staid there, and heard sermons;
but after sermons, with all speed, waiting on no person, being resolved not to entangle myself, or cast myself into a new snare, I
took horse, and came to Melrose betwixt seven and eight at night.
I preached on the Lord's day and Monday; and the Lord was with
me, especially on the Lord's day. There were none there from
Etterick. It was my good friend C. Wood that, by keeping up of
Mr. Wilson's letter, occasioned this distress to me.

Feb. 27.—A violent fit as of the gravel beginning with my wife, I
designed to go to prayer on that account; but immediately she was
better; and therefore I prayed, and with her gave thanks for the
receipt of what we were thinking to seek. My heart was enlarged
under a sense of the Lord's goodness. And this new mercy revived
the grateful sense of the Lord's kindness that I have of late met with
in the hearing of prayers. This night the two societies met together
for prayer, concerning the business of my transportation. One of
the western society going to read, asked me where he should read;
I said he might read where he pleased, thinking he would choose
some place suitable to the occasion. And so one tells him, our ordinary in the eastern society (which met weekly at my house) was
Gen. xii. So he begins, and reads, " Now the Lord had said unto
Abram, Get thee out of thy country, and from thy kindred, and
from thy father's house, unto a land," &c. This was very surprising to me, being so pat to my case. Thus was that work begun. As
for their prayers, they were as I noted before, p. 181.

March 2.—I preached on the observing of providences, from Psalm
cvii. ult.; and I observe how the Lord led me to it, through several
difficulties, drying up to me another subject I thought to have been
on. 1 was afraid to venture on this subject, not knowing how to

manage it; but the Lord was pleased to lay to my hand liberally, for all the scrimpness I feared.

March 3.—Latter end of the last week, I began to have some passing fears, that the business of Etterick might misgive at the synod; but last night they became exceeding great and pressing, so that I lay down with such a weight of them, that I had much ado to bear up against them. The precise point on which they rolled, was this, viz. That in case it should misgive, it would brangle me terribly as to my own soul's case, raze foundations, turn all I had got in quest of light in the matter, into delusion; and so, in that event, I would not know any more how to discover the mind of God in a particular case. No wonder that this was most heavy, and perplexing, and racking, as indeed it was, threatening a stroke at the very root of my soul. Only I thought, if I was wrong, I would be content to be undeceived; seeing I was yet in the land of the living, and might yet be set right. This day I had a grateful sense of the Lord's goodness to me, and of his gracious condescension, in that he had been pleased to let me see my duty clearly now eight days ago; and that he did not keep up his light from me till the very nick of time of the determination of the business. O! the wisdom and foreknowledge of God, in letting in these fears, like a flood on my soul! I do with profoundest humility, and thankfulness, admire and adore that wisdom and foreknowledge, when I look back on the heavy task I then was to have, and now have had, in that place; under the which, nothing could have borne me up, but the clearness of my call, from the Lord himself, unto it; and that flood of fears hath since made that clearness, like a wall of adamant, in the face of many a storm and tempest I have met with in that place.

The synod having met, and the affair come before them, I was, on the 6th of March, by their silence, transported from Simprin to Etterick. On the 4th I went to Kelso to the synod; and was scarcely well set down in the church, when Mr. H. C. a member of the Presbytery of Selkirk, told me, that Sir Francis Scot did not take it well, that the Presbytery would needs use their *jus devolutum;* but that he would consent to the calling of me, if they would fall from their call. He asked me what I thought of it. I told him, that, for my part, they might do in that business as they pleased. The way I received it at first was, that I found myself content to stay still in Simprin; but afterwards it was not so easy to me, while it seemed to pluck down all I had been building, as above related. Thus was I by this dispensation sore brangled. The first ease I got was on Wednesday morning; when, after some time spent in prayer, the Lord opened my eyes, and let me see how he had in his providence been pointing out to me my way to Etterick; and I found I durst not shift my duty for the difficulty in the way. After dinner that day, having procured to myself a little time alone, I set myself to prayer; the rather that I thought my business might come in that afternoon; and being yet somewhat uneasy and troubled as before, after prayer I resolved to read the scripture; but that I might not make a fortune-book of the Bible, I expressly resolved I would read in my ordinary; and though my case should not be touched there, I would wait on God. It fell to be 1 Peter i. where I met with that passage, vers. 6, 7, " Though now for a season (if need be) ye are in heaviness through manifold temptations, that the trial of your faith being," &c. This was seasonable and refreshful to my poor soul. But I was called away (by reason of my ordinary office, being synod-clerk) before I got the whole chapter read. It pleased the Lord to bear it off for that diet; only I was almost no sooner set down at the table in the church, but Mr. A. D. told me, he had Sir Francis Scot's letter, that he would make no noise about my settlement in Etterick. On the morrow, by which time I was fully cleared to hold by my former resolution, laid down Monday was eight days, having in secret laid my all down at Christ's feet, I went away and was transported. It was a melancholy time, while parties were removed, and some of the honest men of Simprin were weeping near by me, being hopeless, which was a heavy sight to me, who dearly loved them. Immediately after the sentence, " Transport," I was confounded, and troubled with many fears; and the ease I got, was by reflecting on those fears that I was oppressed with last Lord's day at night, and considering what a dreadful case my soul would have been in, if, after such indications of the mind of God, it had misgiven. When I came out of the church I met with Mr. Colden, who told me he was sorry I was to go out of the Merse. And I remember it was against his will that I settled in Simprin; he would have had me to Teviotdale. Then J. E. met with me, and discouraged me, and told me, I would not come to Kelso, but go to Etterick. I remember he did just so to me at Kelso, that night before I went away to my marriage. But I had no cause to repent either of the two, my settlement at Simprin, or my marriage. The use I made of these things, was to look for trouble, and expect throughbearing. I came home that day. As I was by the way, I had a great calmness and serenity of mind from the Lord; all was well; and when I came home, the Lord was very gracious to me in prayer; and in that prayer I had great liberty to plead with God for my wife's safety, and had a sort of impression that the child in her belly was a boy and the name to be Ebenezer, which, for a memorial of the Lord's kindness to me, I promised, in case it should be so that it was a boy. Hitherto I have had kept up on my spirit, a plain sense of the Lord's calling me to Etterick. Fears of great difficulties are upon me, but the sense of duty keeps me up, and these former fears, p. 183, 184, are a bulwark against my present fears. And my soul has been much enlarged in thankfulness for the Lord's kindness, in guiding me with his eye set upon me.

The synod, in their act of transportation, out of kindness to me, recommended it to the Presbytery of Selkirk to use all tenderness to me ; and in case I should meet with such grievances at Etterick as I might be unable to bear, that they should give and grant to me what might ease me of the same ; and the moderator, in name of the synod, promised the same unto me. In that act, the synod like- wise provided, that I should not (on account of the ruinous state of the manse at Etterick) be obliged to remove my family, till such time as there was a sufficient manse provided for me there.

I judged it expedient and favourable, to have such provisions for my ease, in the act foresaid. But having once taken the charge of that parish, I had no freedom to make use of that touching the manse, but behoved to transport my family to the place, and to bear the inconveniency of our lodging there for the time. And though my grievances there soon came to be exceeding great, and hardly supportable to me ; yet such was the sense of the command and call of God upon me to that place, that I durst never presume to seek ease and relief, by the provision made about it ; so that, under all my sinking burdens there, I never moved any such thing to the Presbytery or synod, but resolved to wait till he who set me there should call me also away from it.

March 9.—Sabbath. This morning I found there was a sad change upon me ; my frame was gone, my spirit straitened, every way unfit for the work of the day ; and therewith came on a great darkness as to my call to Etterick ; and an uneasiness has been on my spirit most of this day, with respect to my going to that place to be minister to that people, the sense of my call thereto being withheld and hid from me mostly till night. The reason of this sad alteration I found to be my miscarriage yesternight ; for A. M. coming up to me at night, I gave too much way to carnal mirth and laughter, till I forgot my work, and out of woful self-confidence would not withdraw from him to go to my studies. It was no time for me to be so merry, when my poor people were so sad. And had I taken time last night for study, I had had more time for prayer this day. So all

went wrong with me together this morning; my frame was gone,
darkness as to my call from God seized me, my son fell sick, and
Mr. Miln too; so that whereas he should have lectured for me, he
told me, when we were at breakfast, he could not do it; so I behoved to fall on studying a lecture then. Thus did the Lord point
out my sin, sending me to study at that time, who would not study
when I should have done it. This I never saw till just now that I
was writing this day's progress. But just when I was going out to
the kirk, Mr. M. arose, and told me he would lecture; and so the
Lord justly put me to needless pains, because I would not be at needful pains. This remark also did but just now occur to me at the
writing of this; which is indeed a fulfilling of scripture.

This day's sermons were as suitable to our case as if I had sought
a text just for our present circumstances. There were three mysteries of Providence; 1. People's walking contrary to God, and yet
Providence shining warmly on them; 2. Astonishing strokes light-
ing on those that are most dear to God; 3. Astonishing afflictions
meeting the Lord's people in the way of duty. (See sermon on
Psalm cvii. ult.*) All which I thought to have delivered the last
Lord's day; but God reserved them for this day, to begin it with as
to me. What may be the design, I know not.

At night, after a fruitless attempt or two, I recovered somewhat;
and at the family exercise, singing that word; Psalm cxix. 143,
"Trouble and anguish have me found,"—"Yet in my trouble my
delight Thy just commandments be," I found it was very suitable to
my case, and helpful to me. From that trouble, besides what is
obvious, I have learned, 1. That if I will keep up the sense of my
call from God, I must live near him; 2. That my transportation is
of God; seeing it looks up in the light, and these fears and doubts
only in the dark; and consequently, 3. That God works by contrary means, making darkness the means of further light, as I have
now found it. From that word meeting me at the exercise in the family, observe, 1. An exercised case is a good help to the judgment, for
understanding the scripture; 2. It is a noble help to the memory; no
doubt I have often read that word, but I think I will not so easily forget it again. [Nota, The narration in this paragraph has been too su-
perficially set down, and I find such impressions may much wear off
through time. I think the case has been this: That after prayer I
somewhat recovered the sense of my call to Etterick; which increasing did comfort me, though I walked halting under a sense of the mis-
carriages the night before; and thus meeting with that scripture, I

---

* The sermons on this text are yet preserved; but the author afterwards preached
more fully from it, which discourses are inserted in the author's body of divinity, vol.
I. p. 260, et seq., and are justly esteemed.

understood it thus (so far as I can remember), That trouble had taken hold on him, and also anguish of spirit, because of mismanagements in his way; but even under both outward trouble and anguish of spirit,—it was the delight and comfort of his soul, that he was, in the main, found in the way of commanded duty. And this seems no improbable interpretation, being confirmed by ver. 144, where he says, "Give me understanding," viz. a practical understanding of them, that I may both know duty, and get the way of duty kept, "and I shall live," to wit, comfortably, though he knew he could manage no duty so, but some blots would be on his conduct, Jan. 26, 1710.]

March 13.—As I was walking through the town, that word was comforting and supporting to me, "He that believeth, shall not make haste," compared with that, "He that believeth, shall not be ashamed." I know I was helped to believe, and not to make haste; and therefore I concluded, I shall not be ashamed. At night I met with a trial. R. A. talking with me of what had happened at the synod, told me, that Mr. Ker said, with the tear in his eye, to him, Sir, ye are unaccountably robbed of your minister. This did sting me to the very heart. So walking up and down, with the dart in my liver, that word; Acts xxi. 13, "What mean ye to weep, and to break my heart?" &c., came into my mind; and at first it appeared very clear to me, and gave me ease; but the life and light of it afterwards wore away. On the morrow I gave myself to prayer, 1. For the more lively revival of the sense of my call to Etterick; 2. To know whether I should go to see Sir Francis Scot, who was patron of that parish, till patronages were abolished by law; 3. Concerning the time of my admission; and, 4. My wife's case. As to the first, the Lord was pleased to clear that passage; Acts xxi. again to me with additions, ver. 4.—"Disciples,—who said to Paul through the Spirit, that he should not go up to Jerusalem." Ver. 12, "—We and they—besought him not to go up to Jerusalem. Then Paul answered, What mean ye to weep, and to break mine heart? for I am ready not to be bound only, but also to die at Jerusalem for the name of the Lord Jesus." And it was seasonably suggested to me, that when I was going to settle at Simprin, it was very perplexing to me, to think, that I had been, and might be more useful as a probationer, than as minister of Simprin; and yet I have seen cause to bless God for what use he has made of me there. This was very useful to me in this matter, in respect of the strait some were in, by reason of my being some way useful in this country. These things struck at the bottom of my present uneasiness. Yesterday I received advice of two brethren, concerning the management of the visit to Sir Francis Scot. I remarked this day, how the Lord had helped me to pray, that they might be directed to advise me right; and they advised me in a point which I did not foresee, but was very necessary, and the missing whereof might have done harm. And now my uneasiness is gone, and I can plead, that the Lord hath sent me thither. And, even in the time of this uneasiness, I could freely pray, notwithstanding, that the Lord would be with me there.

March 17.—This day having an occasion to see an extract out of the presbytery-book of Selkirk, bearing, That Mr. Hugh Craig having delivered the presbytery's letters to Sir Francis Scot, he seemed not averse to Mr. Boston's being settled minister at Etterick, with which Mr. William Scot and Drummelzier complied: That the said Sir Francis told him, that he had written to Tushilaw to object against the serving of Mr. Boston's edict; but now, after second thoughts, would write contrary orders; and promised to cause repair the kirk, and build the manse and office-houses, as good and convenient to dwell in, as any country manse in the bounds. I noticed the date of this, and found it to be of the 5th of December. Now the diet appointed by the synod, and forgot by our presbytery, was on the 3d of December; so that this mistake of our presbytery gave them that material advantage to their cause, which I could not but notice as a particular design of providence.

March 20, or 21.—I went to see Janet Currie, who for some time has been sick; and this day she told me, but not before, though I saw her before on a sick bed, that it was trouble of mind that made her so. Yet she kept up the particular from me, till I guessed it to be blasphemous thoughts. I spoke to her case as the Lord was pleased to help, and particularly desired that she might not be idle, but work with her hands. She came to my house on the morrow, and was abroad last Lord's day, being better.

March 30.—Now it appears what was the Lord's design by this March 9, parag. 2. Troubles have come very thick on me. Isabel Ridpath, the best of my servants, is like to be taken from me, when I am to go to a strange place. On Tuesday last, there came an officer of the army, and another man with a sheriff's warrant, to take my servant lad for a thief, to carry him to Flanders. Sometime before, I durst not send the lad abroad, lest he should have been pressed; and almost every night since, we have been afraid of attempts on our house by these men. My wife and my son were the worse of the fright that this occasioned, while searching the house for the lad. Two lads I had an eye on for servants, I am disappointed of, one after another. I have been distressed sore in my body with the hæmorrhoids; so that yesterday I was forced to give over my studies, and take my bed; and this day to study in my bed.

Yet in wrath God has remembered mercy. The lad being at Nisbet mill on the Monday, they watched to catch him by the way as he was coming home. But he was providentially carried off the eastern, which is the ordinary road, and came the western way. The pursuers, by a mistake, were sent first to Langton; so that ere they came hither, he was gone out of the house; and one of them spoke to him, but knew him not. As for my bodily trouble, it hindered me not from my public work, though it recurred after. [*Nota,* I have preached the gospel now about twelve years and a half, and have had but a tender body; yet the Lord has been so gracious to me, that (so far as I can remember) my indisposition never kept me from my public work of preaching on the Lord's day, but, one way or another, I have got it done; as once, when under a flux at Simprin, I preached in the house wrapped up in a blanket under my gown, and several Lord's days, while scarce able to speak above my breath. Only about a year before I came out of Simprin, I was obliged to give over the Sabbath-night's lecture, by reason of bodily weakness, which would not allow me to undertake it.] Since I began the epistle to the Hebrews, I was never so unprepared to lecture, and never lectured on it with so much satisfaction to myself. That trouble on Tuesday came upon me in that very moment when my heart was excessively carried away from God towards the creature. The instrument of that trouble I saw on Wednesday, and he was ashamed of it. I found it was a pique founded on an imprudent action of the lad. That very same day he was (as I was informed) fined in £50 Scots for striking of a man till he fell down as dead.

April 1.—Having been at prayers in my closet, and helped to pray that God would turn the hearts of the heritors of Etterick to me, I came down, and presently received a letter, which gave an account of Sir Francis Scot's disposition towards me, wherein was nothing discouraging.

April 19.—Having been at Edinburgh, Sir Francis Scot told me, that he was resolved to protest against my call. This day I spent some time in prayer with fasting, for my wife's safe delivery, and concerning the business of Etterick. I found I was for either of these two, to wit, that either God would divert the heritors from opposing, or give me grace to bear up under it, and countenance me in my work; so I laid hold on these promises; Prov. xvi. 7; 2 Cor. xii. 19; Psalm xxxvii. 5. I found I was very unfit to manage matters there, and under the disadvantage of being far from neighbours with whom I might advise. But it has always been my support in that case, that I had God to go to as a counsellor; and this was the only ground of my confidence; wherefore I got hold of that, Psalm cxlvii. 11, and xci. 11. While I was at Edinburgh, there was another attempt to take my servant by the foresaid person, assisted with some dragoons; they had him; but he was rescued by some of the people of the town. The fright was troublesome to my wife. But upon the sight of her trouble, Isabel Redpath, a pious and active servant, who was about to give her over, resolved that day to give her no more trouble, but gave over her marriage that night; and so by one trouble she was freed from another.

April 20.—Sabbath. I was resolved on a family fast on Monday. Christian Wood was with us this day, but could not stay. At parting I told her my design, and desired her help, though at a distance. The causes were the same as of the secret exercises before. She went away; but God sent her back; for her brother had gone away with the horse, and would not wait on her. So on the morrow we spent some time in prayer for the causes foresaid. It was a good time, the Lord gave us his countenance, and we were helped to seek. After the work was over, and we were come to dinner, we had not sat down at the table, when word came, that the foresaid officer was seen at Swintonhill, and that armed men were lying in the western loan for the lad. We blessed the Lord that had restrained them, and prayed for more restraint to them; but saw none of them.

Wednesday, April 23. Last night I was helped to lay the Monday's prayers before the Lord, and to be concerned for them; and this morning, about seven o'clock, my wife was delivered. There was a surprising cluster of mercies here. 1. I awaked about five o'clock, and found she had her pains; and ere I got to prayer, that word sweetly rolled in my mind; Judges xiii. 23, "If the Lord were pleased to kill us, he would not have received a burnt-offering at our hand;" and it filled me with hopes. 2. Her reckoning was to April 27; the presbytery of Selkirk had appointed my admission to be at Etterick the 29th of April; which, when I got notice of it, was very astonishing to me, considering that I had told them by a letter, that I could not be from home at or about that time. Seeing it was so, we resolved to attend the conduct of providence. 3. From what I wrote to the presbytery, I designed they should gather from it, that it would be most convenient for me to be admitted this week; they mistook my meaning; but it was a happy mistake. 4. My wife was more quickly delivered than ever before; and the midwife had been sick, which made us afraid; but she was better; and had it not been so, we had got none at all. 5. My heart leaped for joy, hearing it was a boy, and so Ebenezer. He was baptized by Mr. Pow on the Lord's day after, being the 27th. 6. And all this came about as a quick answer of prayer. O! we saw our Lord loading us with mercies. I had been desired to be at Selkirk to-morrow; was desirous to know my duty; had not freedom for it; but hoped God would clear my way in that, and this did it; and so I went not.

April 28.—One came from Edrom, while I was studying my sermons for my own parish, and told me I was appointed by the presbytery to preach there Lord's day next. I was very averse to it, and humorously refused it. I went to God with it, but got no light. At length I laid by my humour, and laid myself at the Lord's feet, resolving to go over the belly of my inclinations, if God should appear to call me; and thus went to God again with it. And thereupon I found an unclearness to leave my own congregation; which was something extraordinary; for though I did not use lightly to leave our own congregation, yet the disproportion of it to all others in the bounds, when I had otherwise a fair call, used to determine me to leave it. Rising from prayer with this unclearness on my spirit, Mr. B. came and told me, that one was just arrived from Churnside, and said, that Mr. Wilson was to preach there, so that Mr. M. might preach at Edrom. But this man had no certainty for it. However, I sent the man to Mr. M. Immediately there came another, and confirmed what the other had said; and the man from Edrom was within a cry; so he was called back, and confirmed in this. Mr. M. preached at Edrom, and I at home; and our kirk was very throng. This was wonderful in my eyes, and came seasonably as a pledge of further mercies.

On the first day of May I was admitted minister of Etterick; a day remarkable to after ages, as the day in which the union of Scotland and England commenced, according to the articles thereof agreed upon by the two parliaments. And on that very account I had frequent occasion to remember it; the spirits of the people of that place being embittered on that event against the ministers of the church; which was an occasion of much heaviness to me, though I never was for the Union, but always against it from the beginning unto this day. When the edict was returned, Whitslead and another heritor, with John Caldwell, and William Nicol, gave in a protestation to the presbytery against my call. So the Lord guided me well, keeping me at home that day. When I came to Crosslee, it was told me, there was one in Thirlestane from Sir Francis Scot,

to protest against my admission. I was thereupon the rather inclined to go forward to Thirlestane; where I found him, one that
had been in the class with me at the college. When I went to
my chamber, Mr. Paterson told me his errand; and I was very pensive. When I was going to bed, I overheard him say to Mr. Paterson, "Have you told him, that he will neither get meat nor lodging
here? I will get up early, and close the church doors." Though I
was uneasy before, yet then, even by that, I grew easy; from thence
concluding, that the business would be stopped at least for that day.
On the morrow morning I dealt so with two of the brethren that came
thither before the rest, that I had almost gained them to consent to
the delaying of the admission; the rather that Sir Francis Scot had
promised to give me a new call with the rest of the heritors; only
I wanted not thoughts, that if once my neck were out of the yoke,
it should never come under it again; which was the effect of my
weakness and indeliberation. So we went to the church; I scarcely
doubting, but I would come home as I went away. I struggled
against the admission, before the presbytery being convened in mass;
but they would by no means yield to the delay. Being sadly racked,
I went into a room, and sought the Lord; but my trouble remained,
and what to do I knew not. At length the Lord put it in my heart,
to be content, and resolved to meet with difficulties and opposition;
and upon this, presently my heart was calmed, and I was clear to
be admitted. So Mr. B. protested before the presbytery in the
manse in Sir Francis Scot's name. And I was admitted that day.

This struggle that I made against the admission was of good use
to me; for thereby I found favour with Sir Francis, as I did immediately after my admission with Mr. B. who promised faithfully to
relate the matter as it stood to his constituent, promising all favour
he could do me in that matter. Sir Francis Scot's protestation was
to have come out to the presbytery at Selkirk some time before, and
was sent by an express; but the express came not till the day after
the presbytery. On the Sabbath after, I preached to the people of
Etterick on 1 Sam. vii. 12, "Then Samuel took a stone, and set it
between Mizpeh and Shen, and called the name of it Eben-ezer, saying, Hitherto hath the Lord helped us." And thereafter I returned
home to Simprin.

This month (I think) we had a family thanksgiving, wherein the
Lord was very gracious to us, and our hearts were enlarged with
the remembrance of the Lord's hearing our prayers at the last family fast, and with his present goodness. And it being better than
ordinary with me, this exercise was sweetly concluded with solemn
blessing of my family.

May 26.—I had found much favour with some of the best note in
the country, who undertook to speak to those that were my enemies, to induce them to favour me. I was thankful to the Lord;
but my heart protested I would not trust in princes.}

June 15.—Having got back to Etterick about the latter end of
May, not thinking quickly to transport my family, I was while
there, determined to hasten it, and had fixed the time. When I
came home, I was surprised to hear, that the presbytery had declared my church vacant, though the act transporting me, obliged
me not to dwell at Etterick till the Manse was repaired. My heart
was thankful to the Lord, who had led me in the way I knew not,
though it was hard measure from them. From the time that I ended my sermons on the epistle to the church of the Laodiceans, I had
gone through several miscellaneous subjects; particularly a cluster of
them, in the last half-year of my ministry there. These I had just
ended, on the last Sabbath save one before my removal. And this
day I preached, out of one of the barn-doors, to a great multitude
of people, my farewell sermon, on John vii. 37, "In the last day,
that great day of the feast, Jesus stood and cried, If any man thirst,
let him come unto me, and drink." And as the Lord was with me
in that place during my ministry there, so he left me not then, but
was with me at that close of it, and much of God's power appeared
in it. On the Tuesday we came away, and arrived at Etterick on
the Thursday thereafter. Thus ⬤ parted with a people whose hearts
were knit to me, and mine to them; nothing but the sense of God's
command that took me there, making me to part with them. The
three or four last years of my ministry there were much blessed,
and very comfortable to me; not in respect of my own handful only,
who were ordinarily but about ninety examinable persons, but
others of the country-side.

During the time of my ministry at Simprin, I had frequently occasions of assisting at sacraments; inasmuch as I observed, for
some years I was still abroad three Sabbaths together, on such occasions, which allowed some intermission. Meanwhile I never liked
to be even so employed, but where there was need; and if I found
none, I would either not have gone, or else returned home on my
own charge; and that upon this principle, That though it was a
small charge, yet it was my charge; and that I was not to look to
be useful, according to the number of those I spoke to, but according to the call of God to speak unto them, whether many or few.
And I never, that I know, had occasion to rue that part of my conduct. I remember, I once came home, and left the communion at
Fogo, on that principle; and I got a feast in the pulpit of Simprin,

in the evening exercise, on the 23d Psalm, as I think. And upon
occasion of my being urged on that head, that it would be more for
my own edification to be present at such a solemnity, I was brought
to take notice, that according to the scripture, 1 Cor. xiv. 4, 5, one
is to prefer the edification of the church to his own private edification.

Now by means of my going so much abroad to sacraments, and
having that ordinance twice a-year at home, I had frequent occasion
of converse with persons exercised about their own spiritual case;
the which was a great help to me in preaching. It was to such a
conversation with a gentlewoman as the means, that I owed the sermon preached at Swinton, Sabbath afternoon, July 28, 1706, being
the day of the communion there. The text being Lam. iii. 49, 50,
" Mine eye trickleth down, and ceaseth not, without any intermission; till the Lord look down, and behold from heaven;" the ser--
mon not only had more than ordinary weight on the people, but two
ministers present made feeling acknowledgments of it. But the
sweet scene of these days was quickly after turned into a gloomy
one.

As I behoved to have some Hebrew for my trials, both former
and latter, so in Simprin I made some progress in the study thereof,
Having always an inclination towards it, I believe I did several
times, while there, attempt it; but with this little success, having
only an old Psalter and Pagnin's Lexicon, that had been gifted to
me by Andrew Elliot, my comrade at the college, till in the year 1704
I got " Buxtorf's Epitome grammat." and his Lexicon. After which
time, I reckon, I did with much difficulty make my way through the
Psalter. And, by some notes I have on the Psalms, I find I began
it again, having " Bethner's Lyra" in loan. But still my study of
it was confined to the Psalter.

Upon whatever occasion I understood there was any motion for,
or eye to, the removing me out of that place to another, I was helped of God to be scrupulously wary, that I might do nothing towards
the advancing of the same; being always persuaded, that my safety,
welfare, and comfort, depended on my being found in the way,
which the Lord himself should call me to go. The stipend was indeed small; and towards the latter end, the victual was cheap to a
degree; but then my house-rents in Dunse, and the emoluments of
the synod-clerk's office, were considerable towards the maintenance
of the family. And in these days several came about us, and particularly some students continued with us at times; so that we ate
not our morsel alone. But whatever was our manner, when we were
alone, or only with those we counted not strangers, I observed, that

when occasionally we had company otherwise, things honest in the sight of men were readily, by the kind disposal of providence, laid to hand. And during the time of my continuance in that place, I knew little of anxiety for the provision of my family after me. And I am very sure, it was not a more liberal maintenance, but a sense of the divine call, that moved me to leave Simprin, and come to Etterick.

Thus passed the first and most comfortable years of my ministry in Simprin, as in a field which the Lord had blessed. Removing from thence with my family, as I have related above, on Tuesday June 17, we came, on Thursday the 19th, unto Etterick; where, through the mercy of God, I have continued until this day. On the first Lord's day after the transportation of my family, being June 22, I preached on Acts v. 33, " Now—are we here present before God, to hear all things commanded thee of God.*

PERIOD IX.

FROM MY REMOVAL TO ETTERICK, TO THE OATH OF ABJURATION REFUSED.

BEING settled here, I soon found I was come from home, and that I was but beginning to be a minister of a parish. As for the people, the natives, generally speaking, were naturally smart, but of an uncommon assurance; self-conceit, and censorious to a pitch, using an indecent freedom both with church and state. There were three parties in the place. One of dissenters, followers of Mr. John Macmillan, a considerable number; who have been all along to this day a dead weight on my ministry in the place; though not so great now, by far, as in former years. Another was an heritor in the parish, with two elders dependents of his. He himself deserted the ordinances, for about the space of the first ten years, viz. till the affair of Closeburn. One of the elders having heard a little while, went off for altogether to the dissenters. The other, for ought I know, never heard me after I was settled among them. The third was the congregation of my hearers, after the disadvantage of what influence these two parties could have upon them. Their appetite for the ordinances I did not find to be sharpened by the long fast they had got, for about the space of four years. Wherefore, soon perceiving the little value they had for occasions of hearing the gospel, and having called a meeting for business, on a week-day, August 19, I preached to them, that day, the sense I had of their

---

* This sermon is inserted in the author's Body of Divinity, vol. III. published in 1773.

case, from Isa. xliii. 22, " Thou hast been weary of me, O Israel."
I plainly saw, that a brother, who, at the synod which transported
me, was overheard to bid let me go, I would get preaching my fill
there, was outwitted. On the contrary, I behoved to bid farewell to a
pleasant part of my exercise of that nature before ; and to have it
miserably slighted and despised, where occasionally I was called to
it. And for the Sabbath's sermons, they were but coldly enough
received; but remarkable was the pricking up of ears, when any
thing relative to the public fell in ; which was a wondering observe
to me.

To the breeding and cherishing of this disposition among them,
several things concurred. There being little knowledge of religion
among them, till the time of confusion and persecution ; so that John
Andison in Gamescleugh told me of a time, when there was not a Bible
in the church, but the minister's, his father's, and another's ; they
drank in the principles of presbytery in the greatest height, with
the principles of Christianity. The dissenters were in great reputation among them, and continually buzzing in their ears something
to the disparagement of the church and the ministry. Moreover,
the union with England, which they were violently set against,
trysted with my settling among them, and brought in an unacceptable change of the state of affairs. And finally, they lived alone.

A profession of religion generally obtained among them, through
the preaching of the persecuted ministers in and about the place.
Before the Revolution, they were generally made Presbyterians,
praying persons, and several of them, I believe, good Christians.
Often I observed, that I had never seen in a country kirk more
Bibles than appeared in ours ; nor more persons giving in to the
Sabbath's collection for the poor. And indeed they were, and are,
very liberal to the poor, both their own, and strangers passing
through them ; but very unkind to strangers settling among them,
and not very benevolent in neighbourhood among themselves. But
one thing I was particularly surprised with, viz., the prevalency of
the sin of profane swearing ; and was amazed to find blessing and
cursing proceeding out of the same mouth ; praying persons, and
praying in their families too, horrid swearers at times ; so that by
the month of November I behoved to set myself to preach directly
against that sin.*

* The text of these sermons was Matth. v. 34—37. He afterwards preached on
the same subject in 1714, from the third commandment, the explication of which is in
the Body of Divinity, vol. II ; and a third time in 1724, from James v. 12, published
in his " Distinguishing Characters of True Believers," printed in 1773.

The very next day after my preaching from Acts x. 33, as above related, Mr. Macmillan came to Eskdale, and some of my hearers went to him. This was what I got to begin with. On the morrow after I went up to S. to see J. L.'s family and others; my design was to endeavour to prevent their perverting others. When I came there, I went first into the house of one of my hearers; and there I was surprised with the news of Mr. Macmillan's being in J. L.'s, and others with him. The old man came in to me. Is. L. came into that house, but never noticed me; but I carried courteously to her, and told her I had a mind to have come and seen them. She told me, I should be welcome. When I went in, J. L. shewed not common civility. I was set down among three men, strangers, none of whom I knew. They were S. H. of H., Mr. St. and Mr. Sm. The last I took for Mr. Macmillan, having never seen the man. Being set down, I was resolved to divert disputes, at least a while, with some discourse of practical godliness. Wherefore being asked, "What news?" I said, that news were hard to be got here, the place being so far remote from towns; that it was like Jerusalem; Psalm cxxv. 2; which brought us at length to the discourse of communion with God; concerning which S. H. gave his opinion, that it consisted in doing the will of God, keeping his commandments. I told him, that all communion was mutual, and therefore it could not consist in that; and shewed, that actual communion with God, which we ordinarily call *communion with God*, consists in the Lord's letting down the influences of his grace on the soul, and the soul's reacting the same in the exercise of grace. O, says he, that is extraordinary; wherewith I was stunned. I told him, it was that without which neither he nor I would be saved. How will you prove that? said he. So I was put to prove it to him. Thereafter he brought in the matter of the separation; told, that he understood I was an enemy to them, and preached against them. I acknowledged, that I judged their way was not of God; and therefore, when it fell in my way, I did preach against it. And understanding that he meant of a note I had at Morbattle sacrament, I desired him to tell me what he heard I had said. He shifted this; and I told him, viz. that I exhorted those that had met with God at this occasion, to tell them that it was so; and that they thereupon, according to the spirit of the gospel, should say, "We will go with you, for we hear the Lord is with you."* J. L. said, if that were

---

*Mr. Boston preached on this occasion from Psalm iv. 6, both on Monday and Saturday, in June 1707. The sermons are preserved; and there is an exhortation in the close of the last, much the same with what is here related.

true, that the Lord were with you, we would join with you. Mr.
St. having no will to make that the determining point, told me, that
he knew not but the Lord was with the church of the Jews in time
of great corruption.   To which I answered, And neither did Christ
himself separate from them in that time; and urged them with that,
Luke iv. 16.   After other shifts, they were at length brought to
that desperate answer, That Christ was the lawmaker, and therefore not imitable by us. The person whom I took for Mr. Macmillan
was not like to speak, and therefore I asked for Mr. Macmillan.   I
staid there with them an hour and a half at least; but saw not Mr.
Macmillan. When I was coming away, I desired Mr. St. to tell
him, that seeing I had not seen him, he would come to my house and
see me; which he undertook to tell him. Above six weeks after
this rencounter, and my not meeting Mr. Macmillan having made a
noise in the country, I heard that John Scot in Langshawburn had
said of me, that I was a liar, and he would prove me a liar, for I
had never asked for Mr. Macmillan, nor desired him to come to my
house. This was at first very troublesome to me. Afterwards I
found real joy in my heart, in that I was made partaker of the
sufferings of Christ, while I saw a spirit of bitterness possessing
some of that party. However, the truth was brought to light after,
by the confession of some of that party. Mr. Macmillan was in that
house in the time, in an outer chamber; and Adam Linton told me,
that he was certainly informed, that he caused the lass lock the
door, and give him in the key at the door head or foot, whatever
was his design in it.

It pleased the Lord, for my further trial, to remove by death, on
the 8th September, my son Ebenezer. Before that event, I was
much helped of the Lord; I had never more confidence with God in
any such case, than in that child's being the Lord's. I had indeed
more than ordinary, in giving him away to the Lord, to be saved by
the blood of Jesus Christ. But his death was exceeding afflicting
to me, and matter of sharp exercise. To bury his name, was indeed harder than to bury his body; and so much the heavier was
it, that I could fall upon no scripture example parallel to it; but I
saw a necessity of allowing a latitude to sovereignty. I could not
charge myself with rashness in giving him that name. But one
thing was plain as the sun to me, that day eight days before, my
heart was excessively led away from God towards the creature; and
I had not visited my pillar so often and seriously as I ought to
have done.

Nov. 1.—I have been much refreshed and encouraged under my
discouragements, understanding by some, what others of the parish

have told them, of my sermons riping up their case, and discovering the secrets of their hearts, though, alas! with little visible fruit.

Nov. 12.—I saw M. D. a dissenter, whom I could never see before. I was in the next village, and she was coming thither; but seeing my horse at the door, she went home again. I went to her house, and she came to the door, having, as appeared, no will that I should come in. I asked her what were her scruples. She did not readily answer, but at length abruptly said, "The oath sealed with his blood. QUEST. What mean you by that, the covenant, the solemn league and covenant? ANSW. They say there was such a thing. Q. And was the covenant sealed with Christ's blood? A. Yes. I shewed her her mistake. Q. How many covenants has God made with man? A. Two; the covenant of grace, and the covenant of works. Q. Which of the two covenants was first made? A. The covenant of grace. Q. Who were the parties in the covenant of works? A. The Lord. Q. But with whom did the Lord make it? A. With the body and blood of Christ. Q. How many gods are there? A. Three. Q. How many persons are there in the Godhead? A. Three; the Father, Son, and Holy Ghost. Q. Which of these was our Redeemer? A. The Father. Q. What or who is Christ? No answer. Q. What state are you in by nature? No answer. Q. How think you to be saved? A. By serving God as well as we can.—I dealt with her as with a petted bairn; but by no means could I obtain so much of her as to be willing to admit converse with her for her instruction.

In January 1708, the fire in the congregation was blown up into a violent flame, upon occasion of my observing a fast, on the 14th of that month, appointed by the civil magistrate. Upon this many of my hearers broke off, and left me; several of whom never returned. There was such a headiness among the people, and the day was so bad, that few came to it. I had no scruple as to the observing of it; though I thought it a grievance and disadvantage that we were come under by the union, and the taking away of the privy council, whereby there was no correspondence betwixt the church and state as to fasts. But considering the temper of the people, I thought, if I should have yielded to them in this, I would teach them to dictate ever after unto me. There came two of a fellowship meeting unto me the night before; I shewed them the proclamation. They professed they had nothing to say against it, but that it came from an ill airth. They were not disposed to receive light, but most unreasonably, amongst reasons of their dissatisfaction, insisted, that (as they said) the ministers were going to get the abjuration-oath, I was led to that scripture for my text, 1 Sam. iv. 13, "Eli's heart

trembled for the ark of God;" which came suitably to my circumstances; as I had been led another time, on a week-day in August,
to that, " Thou hast been weary of me, O Israel," when the unexpected practice of the people undervaluing the opportunity, was a
confirmation of the doctrine. The Lord's day was eight days thereafter, preaching on Isa. lxiv. 7, the reproof for this practice natively
fell in.* But the Lord's day immediately thereafter, it was so
stormy, that I had only a few to preach to, in the house. Then I
found myself like a bird shaken out of its nest, and was as an owl
in the desert. Instead of the converse I, sometime a-day, had with
exercised Christians about their own spiritual case, I was engaged
in disputes about the public, and about separation, and how to defend the lawfulness and duty of hearing me preach the gospel; and
for the most part to no effect. So that many a time it was a terror
to me to go out among them; and coming to particular places, I
often looked very blunt, finding myself beset with contemners of me
and my ministry; who often kept not within the bounds of common civility.

This humour of deserting my ministry, and breaking off from
under it, continued from time to time, without any notable stop,
till the affair of Closeburn brought it about nine years after. Since
that time there has been a remarkable settling among them, in that
point; howbeit, even since that time I have had as much of that
treatment as will not suffer me to forget where I am. This deserting
of my ministry was the more heavy to me, that ordinarily I knew
nothing about it from any hand, till after a while, that the parties
were gone off, and confirmed in their way; and that few had any
consideration of me, in hiring such into their service. This last
continues in some measure to this day; though the occasion is not

---

* The reproof here referred to is as follows :—

" If Christ depart from us, then the blame lies at our own doors; for he may be
holden still. The case of this land is very dangerous, yet it is not hopeless. Our
Lord is yet within a cry, within the reach of prayers; and if he go for want of serious invitation from us to stay still, we are inexcusable. Alas, that there are so few
stirring up themselves to take hold of him! I must needs say, that the empty room
in this church on the fast-day, is no good sign either for the land or for the parish.
If sitting at home, or going about your work that day, was a way to hold Christ still
in the land, I am much mistaken. Sure the people of Judah did not so despise the
fast proclaimed by King Jehoshaphat; 2 Chron. xx. 3. But if these people did, with
Esther, chap. iv. 16, keep private fasts at home, when others were gathered together
for that work in the congregation, it will say much to clear them of contempt of the
ecclesiastical and civil authority calling them to fast and pray that day, and say, that
they were indeed concerned to hold Christ still amongst us. And sure there was
never more need to fast than at this day," &c.

so much now, as before; insomuch that among the first servants my own elder son had, and that by advice or approbation of an elder or elders, was one who would have gone out of the house if I had come into it to visit the family.

Meanwhile Satan raged in stirring up the sin of uncleanness; so that, by the spring 1709, besides several fornications, there were two adulteries in the parish discovered; and I had heavy work with both. These things often made me look, with a sorrowful heart, on the congregation, as in the case of the church of Corinth, burnt up with the fire of division, and drenched in fleshly abominations.

Feb. 15.—My discouragements increase daily among this people, by reason of the divisive temper inflamed by the late fast, so that there are several of them whose faces I have not seen since that time. My circumstances are extremely heavy; they seem to have little desire for the gospel; the most weighty truths look as nauseous to them; though if any thing relating to the public fall in, they use to prick up their ears. Some have never come to the ordinances since I came, being led by mere laziness and profane neglect; besides those that were always dissenters from the established church. Those that come, many of them think nothing of staying away several Sabbaths; and when they come, they are generally very uncomfortable. My wonted exercise of conversing with exercised souls is gone; there is no converse but about the division; the practice of godliness is thereby stifled, and burnt up with the fire. The crown is fallen from my head, and I am brought very low! The approaching Sabbath, that sometimes was my delight, is now a terror to me; so that it is my business now, to get my forehead steeled against brass and iron. On Sabbath was fourteen days, I felt the sad effects of giving way to discouragement, and this has put me on my guard. I have sometimes asked myself, Whether, if I had known all that has befallen me here, I would have accepted the call, or not? and I cannot say, I durst have refused. Two things are supporting to me; 1. My clearness as to my call from the Lord, which has not been perplexed by all that I have met with, but still remained as a ground of comfort. 2. An amazing conduct of providence in preaching the word, whereby I am guided in my ordinary to speak to their case. As, particularly, these two last Sabbaths it fell in my ordinary to lecture the 7th and 8th chapters of the Revelation, where I had occasion to speak largely of schism and division, with the effects thereof. And in this very time Mr. Macmillan was preaching in the bounds. And in my ordinary sermons I find the same conduct of providence.

On the 22d of February this year 1708, the first of the aforementioned adulteries was delated ; but the parties were not got convicted, till May 14. During which time, I was with some elders
four times on the spot, at Buccleugh-shiels ; the adulteress alleging
a rape by an unknown person. One of these times I preached in
the house ; on Rev. xx. 12, " And the books were opened," having
occasion to baptize a child, but in vain as to her. Her brother, who
had deserted on account of the fast aforesaid, left the house in time of
the sermon ; but returning after, caused set down meat to me, and the
elders with me, and urged me to eat, the which also the elders urged ;
but though we did need it, I peremptorily refused to eat ; so the elders
ate not either, and the meat was set up again untasted. As I was
about to go away, being alone with him, I told him, it was religion to me, not to eat there, where I had come with my master's
message, and he had turned his back on it; and that I caused his
meat to be set up again, without being tasted, for a testimony ; and
so I left him. The man returned afterwards, to wait on the ordinances ; and some time after, occasionally told me, that that had
stuck with him. This is the only instance I remember, of a conviction in that point of deserting the ordinances, made by means of
any thing said or done by me for that end, where the party was not
some way inclining, before, to return.

After the woman was brought to a confession, the adulterer stifly
denied. Dealing with his conscience, I took one of the twins she
had brought forth, and holding it before his face, posed him with
his being the father of it. Nevertheless he persisted in the denial
though evidently under consternation, his moisture being visibly
dried up in the struggle with his conscience. He being removed, I
went out, and dealt with him privately ; and having observed, that
two of his children he had by his wife, had been removed by death,
soon after, or about the time, in which, as was alleged, he begot
those two adulterous ones, I told him, that it seemed to me, God had
written his sin in that his punishment. To which he answered,
That indeed he himself thought so ; and so confessed. Being called
in again, he judicially confessed his guilt of adultery with that woman, and that he was the father of her twins.

That spring, being the first I had in the place, the change of the air,
appeared, on my body's breaking out in sore boils. For great was
the cold and moistness of the air in Etterick, in comparison of that
at Simprin.

In April I was a member of the General Assembly. And the
oath of abjuration being then imposed by law on those in office in
the civil government, there were applications made to ministers, by

several persons whom it reached, for their judgment in the point of
the lawfulness or unlawfulness thereof; and ministers on that occasion coming in to Edinburgh to the assembly, it was earnestly desired, that the assembly might consider that matter, and give their
resolution of the case. But it was waved, and men were left to
their own light. This was heavy to me; and thereupon I could not
but observe the justice of the dispensation, whereby about four years
after, it was brought to ministers' own doors. While I was yet
at Simprin, I had conversed with a minister from Ireland, who had
left that country upon his scrupling to take it; and whereas a neighbouring minister in the English border, having missed the time of
taking that oath, and therefore shifting to preach in his own congregation till another occasion of it should offer, wrote to me to
preach a day for him, I had no freedom to exchange pulpits for a
day with him on that occasion, and so declined it. Now it was
brought into Scotland by means of the Union, as several other
snares have been.

Having hitherto had a sorry habitation in the old manse, it was
this summer razed, and a new one built; I and my family, in the
meantime, living in the stable and barn; in the former of which
were made a chimney and partition. And there, on Wednesday
August 4, about eleven o'clock in the forenoon, was born to me a
son, whom, baptized on the 9th day by Mr. John Rutherford minister of Yarrow, I did, after no small struggle with myself, adventure to call Ebenezer. But it pleased the Lord, that he also was
removed from me, dying on the 1st of October. It fell seasonably
in our ordinary, that morning he was born, at family duties, to sing
Psalm lxxii. 11—14. How to call him, was no small exercise to
me. I went to God, and was laid open to his determination in that
point. I say it was no small exercise; for when I considered, how
that, after the death of Ebenezer, my soul had often said to the
Lord, How will this loss be made up? and my prayer had still been,
that God would give me another pillar to set up, and if he would do
so, he would determine me thereto by his call; for I always thought
I durst not do it without a particular call thereto; and now that
God had so far heard my prayer, in giving me another boy, this
seemed to call me to set up my pillar again. On the other hand it
racked me to think, What if he die too? to this the experience
I had at the second winter sacrament, gave a hopeful answer. Then
I remembered how this had been reasoned in my own mind after the
death of Ebenezer, and was this same way answered. His mother
fell very ill after she was delivered; and my perplexity in this
point continued; besides my trouble about her case, which being so

very bad, I could not yet send for one to baptize the child. On
Friday night, I earnestly entreated of the Lord a token, whereby I
might know my duty; and I thought I would take it as a token if
his mother recovered; and she did recover on the morrow; and the
same day I sent to Yarrow to Mr. Rutherford to come and baptize
the child. This recovery, so seasonable, seemed to be speaking, as to
the point I was concerned about; yet did my perplexity not remove
thereby. Wherefore I asked my own conscience, as before the
Lord, whether I durst call him otherwise or not? And I found I
durst not, seeing God had so answered my prayers, lest it should be
found a mocking of God. Wherefore Ebenezer I called him; and
when I was-holding him up, I thought I saw my action was a
struggle of faith, against sense, and the stream of providence, that
had run so cross to me and impetuously here. But the clouds did
so return after the rain for a long time after that, that I endeavoured to keep loose gripes of him.

Oct. 1.—Friday. About two hours before day he died. On the
Monday after he fell sick, I thought to spend some time in prayer for
his case; but it went not well with me at all. Sitting down, I heavily
thought with myself, This would not do. Presently I was called
on, and he was very ill. I found at that time his case altered just
according to my frame. My wife being scarce of milk, I endeavoured to get a nurse in the Merse, when I was at the sacrament of Simprin the latter end of August; but got none; but had hopes of one
of two there. That week we should have sent back for that end, was
very stormy; so we were diverted, and got one near hand, about
seven days before he died. On the Monday before he died, I resolved to spend some time in prayer about his case, which I did
in the barn. At first I was very dull, and it was like to go ill with
me; but I protested in my heart, that I would not quit it so; and
this resoluteness was ,not without success; for the Lord did indeed
loose my bands; and there I renewed my covenant with God, and
did solemnly and explicitly covenant for Ebenezer, and in his
name accept of the covenant, and of Christ offered in the gospel;
and gave him away to the Lord, before angels, and the stones of
that house, as witnesses. I cried also for his life, that Ebenezer might
live before him, if it were his will. But when, after that exercise,
I came into the house, I found, that instead of being better, he was
worse. The last two days of his life, the Lord struck him with
sore sickness, which at length made me less peremptory for his life.
But in the day of distress the solemn covenant was sweet, and my
heart was thankful to the Lord that helped me to it. At length the
Lord called him away; and while he was drawing his last breaths,

he so smiled that the sight of it made my heart to loup. I have read of other instances of this, but never saw another. On Tuesday or Wednesday before, his sister fell sick of the measles whereof he died, but she escaped. I believe the Lord sent that, as for further trial, so to moderate our sorrow in his case. That the nurse came was good providence; for by her he was supported in his sickness; and that she was got so near hand, and not from the Merse, seemed a design of mercy. When the child was laid in the coffin, his mother kissed his dust. I only lifted the cloth off his face, looked on it, and covered it again, in confidence of seeing that body rise a glorious body. When the nails were driving, I was moved for that I had not kissed that precious dust, which I believed was united to Jesus Christ, as if I had despised it; and I would fain have caused draw the nail again, but because of one that was present, I restrained, and violented myself. So far as I remember, I was never so much straitened to know why the Lord contended with me, as in this. I could not say, that I was secure as to his life since he was born. I know many things in my heart and life offensive to the Lord; but to pitch on any one thing, so as to say of it, this is the cause, was what I could not get done. Often in that distress, my soul has said to the Lord, "Thou knowest that I am not wicked." I remember I had a more than ordinary freedom with God, to refuse process according to the covenant of works, but that it should be according to the covenant of grace. But I see most plainly, that sovereignty challenges a latitude, to which I must stoop, and be content to follow the Lord in an untrodden path; and this made me with more ease to bury my second Ebenezer than I could do the first. That scripture was very useful to me, " It was in my heart to build a house to the Lord." I learned not to cry, How will the loss be made up? but being now in that matter as a weaned child, desired the loss to be made up by the presence of the Lord. I had ground to think, that I had been too peremptory as to his life in seeking it.

Upon public reading of the act of the commission of the General Assembly, against Mr. John Macmillan and Mr. John Macneill, the two preachers of the separation, on the Lord's day, December 12, I preached a sermon from 1 Cor. i. 10, "Now, I beseech you brethren,—that there be no divisions among you," &c. Copies of this sermon, which was directed precisely against the separation, being desired, I having transcribed it, allowed to be given out; and it was of some use for a time. The original notes, and transcript, are both of them *in retentis* among my notes.*

* This sermon was originally printed in 1738, and has been several times printed since, particularly with a preface by the author's son.

The year 1709 was to me a year remarkable among many. In the latter end of March, the second adultery was delated, and confessed by the adulteress; but the adulterer was not convicted till September following. Meanwhile my circumstances in the parish were brought to a pitch of hopelessness, by the Lord's withdrawing supporters from me; that " I might trust in the living God, who raiseth the dead, and calleth things that are not to be as if they were."

Having, in the preceeding August, ordained three elders, the eldership was now seven in number; one of the five above mentioned, as signers of the petition, having soon after my settlement removed out of the parish. The families, in whom was the greatest encouragement I had in the place, from the time of my settling among them, were those of James Bryden, tenant in Coffarshill, Walter Bryden in Crosslie, Robert Paterson in Thirlestone, Adam Linton in Midgehop, and James Biggar in Upper Dalgleish. James Bryden aforesaid was a very friendly man; but he soon broke, his substance failing. Walter was a plain, pious, friendly man, and an elder; but he removed out of the parish with his family this year at the Whitsunday. In July I met with the piercing trial of the death of William Biggar, brother to the said James; who having gone along with me to the communion at Penpont, died there. Of which I shall give an account afterwards. He was a most kindly, pious, good man, unlike the country, an elder also, and most useful in his office. Moreover, Mr. Paterson aforesaid, a third of my elders, a very friendly man, who by that time, I think, had got good of the gospel, and did much balance the influence of an heritor in the parish at first, and friendly to me, having bought the estate of Drygrange, removed to it with his family about the Martinmas the same year. Thus three of the most valuable of my seven elders were taken from me. Adam Linton foresaid was also an elder, and a good man, and he and his family from the beginning really friendly; and those of them who remain, continue so still; but they had about them a great measure of the hardness of the temper of the country. But James Biggar, an elder, with his family, were the family which was the most comfortable to me as a minister of the gospel. So it was all along, and so it continues to this day. May the blessing of God, " whose I am, and whom I serve," rest on them, from generation to generation ! May the glorious gospel of his Son catch them early, and maintain its ground to them to the end; of the which I have seen some comfortable instances already ! Several of them have, of late years, been carried off by death; but they have been comfortable to me in their life, and in their death too.

By the means aforesaid, and otherwise too, the current of holy providence was so strong against me, that I had much ado, to bear up before it; but still God's calling to the place remained clear, plain, and unperplexed. Howbeit the Lord pitied. In the end of the year, James, son to Walter Bryden aforesaid, came in his father's room, an elder, and very well filled up his father's room every way. And I lived in a peculiar friendship with both father and son while they lived.

From the time of my settling here, the great thing I aimed at in my preaching, was to impress the people with a sense of their need of Christ, and to bring them to consider the foundations of practical religion. For the which ends, after some time spent in direct preaching the need of Christ, and handling the parable of the wise and foolish builders, some of which sermons are written in short-hand characters, I did on May 9, 1709, begin an ordinary, the same, for substance, as in the first years of my ministry in Simprin, but prosecuted after another manner. That part of it which contained the doctrine of man's fourfold state, then begun, was ended this year on the 16th of October. The conduct of providence in leading to a second attempt on that subject, was the more remarkable, considering what the same providence had designed it for, unknown to and unlooked for by me, till the event discovered itself years after. And the preaching of these sermons of the Fourfold State, through the mercy of God, was not in vain. Thereafter I proceeded in the remaining part of that ordinary, viz. the nature and necessity of holiness.

Meanwhile, on October 30, I began to preach catechetical doctrine; and I went through the whole catechism, from the beginning to the end; but at several distant times.* At that time I proceeded straight forward, till I came to the application of the redemption purchased by Christ; where I stopt.

Twice a-year I catechised the parish, having no diet but one at the church; and once a-year I visited their families. The former was usually begun about the end of October, the latter about the end of April, or beginning of May. This was my ordinary course all along, save that of some few late years, through my wife's extraordinary sickness in the spring, and the decay of my own strength, I have not got the visiting of families performed as before; neither have I hope of it any more, though I still aim at something of that kind yearly. But I bless God, that when I had ability, I was helped to lay it out that way. Thus the winter season was the time wherein I did most of my work in the parish. Meanwhile that also

---

* This whole work, with several additional sermons on parallel subjects, was published in 1773, in three large volumes octavo; and is justly esteemed a work of great merit, though posthumous.

was the reason wherein I did most in my closet. Being twelve miles distant from the presbytery-seat, I attended it not in the winter ; but when I attended it, I ordinarily went away and returned the same day, being loath to lose two or three days on it.

These things, with other incidents, occasioned me much riding ; in which I must acknowledge the goodness of God, that brought me out of Simprin, where I had but little occasion of riding, and my health was sore broken. But here I had more exercise of that kind, which no doubt was to my advantage in that point, though now at length my strength is much wasted away. The which has necessarily made an alteration in the course of my management ; but the diets of catechising are still in the winter, only I begin now sooner than I was wont ; and the winter nights, that were my best employed times in my closet, I cannot now spend so any more, as before.

July 10.—This year I was at the sacrament in Penpont. When the express came with the letter inviting me, I was indisposed ; but retiring and seeking counsel of the Lord, two things seemed to promise that I should go to that place ; 1. That being invited to the sacrament at G. July 3, Providence hindered me, though very pressing instances were made, partly by bodily indisposition and otherwise ; and Penpont being just the Lord's day after, I could not have left the parish two days at once ; besides there being thirty-seven miles betwixt the places ; 2. The letters not having come the two weeks before, while I was in the Merse, at which time they should have come, if not sooner. On the Wednesday I began to study, and with some difficulty fell on that text ; Gen. xxviii. 17 ; but it went very ill with me ; neither could I alter, though I had frequent thoughts of laying it aside. The vein of it was never opened to me till Thursday betwixt three and four o'clock, and then I studied it that night. But I had no time to study another to preach after the sacrament. On Friday morning, while I was at breakfast, my horse standing saddled for the journey, W. D. came in and told me, that my horse was all swelled in the counter and side, (and my other horse was at Boswell's fair.) This surprising dispensation stung me to the heart, being so timed. I knew not what to do. To get forward appeared a great difficulty ; and to stay at home upon this, seemed to be to make a Bible of providence. So I went away, thinking to hire a horse by the way ; but two that we had a mind for, both misgave. William Biggar, one of my elders, went alongst with me, the rather that I had been indisposed. My horse served me, so that we came to Penpont that night safely. When I came there, I found there were other two appointed to preach on the Saturday ; but Mr. Murray would have me to be a third. I peremptorily refused, and so laid aside thoughts of preaching that day; but withal I was displeased, that I should have been called to come so far, to a place where there was no need, and left my own congregation desolate. On the morrow Mr. Murray pressed me again to preach with the other two; and I yielded; and so went to my chamber to prepare for preaching that day with the other two, Mr. D. and Mr. P. While I was there, I heard some with Mr. Murray in the other room, speaking not very favourably of three preachings. Within a very little I went into that room, upon that occasion, and found Mr. P. there alone, who very freely gave me to understand his mind, and then went away to the tent to begin. Then Mr. Murray and Mr. D. came thither; and I said to Mr. Murray, It is time now we were at a point; pray determine what we are to do. To which he answered, Well, I am content. Very well, said I; and so I went, and cast off my band, and put on my cravat again. This made me very uneasy. I heard sermons, and they were but short; and had I been desired again, I had certainly preached. When we came home, I found this a great temptation; and was sorry I should have come, and left my parish desolate. But it was too far off to help it then. Then they urged me to make the exercise in the kirk, which I very peremptorily refused; and the rather that I had been put to pains before to no purpose; and having had so much vexation, and having been before indisposed ere I came from home, I found my body very weak. However that exercise was as peremptorily laid upon me, Mr. Murray saying to me, You must do it. Well, then, said I, I shall do it. So I retired a little, and then went to the exercise, where, I think, would have been three hundred people in the church. It pleased the Lord to blow upon us, and it was very well with me; and there was indeed an uncommon moving among the people. One told me afterwards, that he never saw the like in that place since he knew it; and told me of some particular persons whose hearts the Lord had touched. After I came out, turning homeward speedily, I saw several people gathered together in the church-yard with some of the ministers, amongst whom there was a man crying under convictions. Mr. Murray's boy came home weeping. When I came home, within a while I heard that William Biggar was sick. To-morrow he continued so, which was afflicting to me. I communicated in a tender melted frame, especially at the first. On the Lord's day night, we began to apprehend that William Biggar was in a dangerous case. He continued ill on Monday, and we were resolved to seek some help for him, and before sermons got one B. to see him. Monday after sermons, as I was going out to see for B. that I might bring

him in to W. Biggar, the smith called me to see my horse more
swelled than before ; and told me, if the smelling in its progress
was as quick downwards as it had been hitherto, he was gone. On
Tuesday morning W. Biggar grew better; the means being so far
blessed, that he got out to and lay down in the garden; but my
fears were not removed. In the afternoon he grew worse, and took
his bed again; whereupon I resolved to send an express home,
though he was not free for it. Accordingly we sent away one on
Wednesday. On Thursday death approached fast, and he died that
day. His brother saw him alive but unable to speak. And he was
buried on the Friday afternoon. He died in hopes of eternal life
through Jesus Christ. Among his last words were, " Farewell, sun,
(to the best of my remembrance), moon, and stars; farewell, dear
minister ;—and *farewell the Bible ;*" which last words especially
made great impression on me. He blessed God, that ever he had
seen my face; which was no small comfort to me, especially in these
heavy circumstances. Thus the Lord pulled from me a good man,
a comfortable fellow-labourer, and a supporter, or rather the supporter of me in my troubles in this place. He was always a friend
to ministers, a fast friend to my predecessor, which helped to complete the ruin of his means. Though he was a poor man, yet he had
always a brow for a good cause, and was a faithful, useful elder;
and as he was very ready to reprove sin, so he had a singular dexterity in the matter of admonition and reproof, to speak a word
upon the wheels, so as to convince with a certain sweetness, that it
was hard to take his reproofs ill. Much of that time I had a very
ill habit of body, and wondered how I was kept up under the burden. It was a complication of griefs; 1. To his poor widow and
children; 2. To Mr. Murray and his family, who spared neither
trouble nor expense; 3. To me and my family. My part of it was,
1. That he died abroad in my company at a sacrament; 2. the great
loss of him as to the Lord's work in the parish, and particularly in
his quarter, the most unruly of the parish; 3. He had been one of
two witnesses to an instrument I had taken in the case of some teinds
due to me, which instrument had not come to my hand extended before we went away. That night I went to Penpont, I said in a jest,
It is like we would be more troublesome ere we go. Alas! little
thought I that I was to see it turned to so sad earnest.

July, 19.—This day I spent some time in prayer, and thinking on
this business. As for the causes of it in general I could be in no
strait; but to condescend on particulars, has not been easy. So
far as I can discern the Lord's mind in it, the great ground of the
quarrel was my refusing to preach on the Saturday, though often

and earnestly called thereto; in which there was much of my own spirit. Three things do bear me in hand, that this was the true cause of it. 1. Though while I was in Penpont Mr. Murray alleged this was the cause; yet I would not admit it, but rather suspected that I had followed my own inclination in going thither, rather than the Lord's mind; which, upon reflection, I see now how I can charge myself with; but the first time I was convinced of this, was on Saturday after I was come home, out of my own mouth. Telling my wife how matters had gone with me, I happened to say, the text I should have preached on was, "How dreadful is this place!" I would not preach it, but God in his providence preached it over to me. These words left a conviction behind them. 2. Last night in prayer, I was carried out in the view of God's jealousy, and particularly the zeal he hath for his worship, and saw how he takes special notice of a fault in or about it. And this is now the third time that I have fallen into this error of late. For

In August or September last, being desired to assist at the Sacrament in Simprin, and to preach there on the Saturday and after the action, I went thither accordingly; where I met with such harsh entertainment from some, as if I had come uncalled. And when I went there on the Saturday, I found two were appointed to preach that day, whereof I was none. Only I got liberty to be a third preacher if I would. This made me very uneasy; and so my exercise was, to endeavour to be as a weaned child, while I saw my corrupt self amidst the sparks of temptation. And then I got time bitterly to reflect on my rashness, in that I had not as I ought consulted God, whether I should go to that occasion or not; the thing seeming at first view so clear to my dark mind. I preached the Lord's day at night a little while, for it was both late and rainy, the work before being drawn out so, that it was told them, it seemed they had no mind that I should open my mouth. I had served one table, and the Lord was with me; which Mrs. L. perceiving said in the meantime to another person, There was devilry there; yet at night invited me again and again to her house; but the person she said it to, who had before engaged me, peremptorily refused to let me go with her. I was invited to preach on the Monday with other two, but peremptorily refused. On the Monday morning I was again desired, but refused; the rather that I had nothing to preach but the Saturday's sermon. But a minister who had no hand in that work, easily dealt with a modest person who was to have preached, so as that he would not preach; and being broke with the intreaties of some with whom I had formerly had good days, I yielded, and preached the sermon I designed for Saturday on the Monday. The

text was Psalm ciii. 5. The last clause of it I preached on the
Lord's day at night, and the first on Monday; and the Lord was
with me. The Lord so transposed these sermons in his providence;
and it was afterwards told me, that if I had not delivered it after
the other, many would not have known where to have fastened their
feet.

Likewise at Morbattle, June 19, 1709, being invited to preach
on Saturday and Sabbath afternoon, I went thither on Friday's
night, and on the Saturday was preparing to preach, till about a
quarter or half an hour before the sermons began; at which time
Mr. D. having come, I overheard him saying to Mr. Simson, that he
would not preach twice unless he preached that day. Finding they
were in confusion, I offered to quit my diet; and it was accepted.
On the Sabbath afternoon I went home before all the tables were
served, and prepared my sermon; but Mr. H. would needs have that
diet. It was grievous to me; but having no confidence to look for
the Lord's assistance if I should be peremptory that I would preach,
I yielded; and so all I did for my riding two and twenty or four
and twenty miles, was to preach on the Sabbath morning, a diet
that in my opinion might be spared, and which I myself use not. So
Mr. H. who preached on Saturday, preached on the Sabbath afternoon, and Mr. D. and C. on the Monday. Mr. Simson urged me to
be a third, but by no means would I yield. This was very heavy,
while comparing it with what I met with at Simprin; it seemed to
me that the Lord was refusing my service there, where sometimes I
had been by his grace useful; and I was unwilling to come much
abroad that way thereafter, finding what temptations I met with.
However, I found the little I was called to do was not altogether
useless.

So this at Penpont was the third time; and though I had escaped
twice, God would not let me go a third time with it. 3. I have
found since the conviction was set in on me on Saturday, that if I
were in such circumstances again, I would yield my service to the
Lord, that he might do with it what he pleased. And although
this may be thought a small thing by such as look on it at a distance; yet considering it was a fault about God's worship, and that
the third of that nature within a short time, the conclusion must be
made as said is. It is true, I was ready to have preached on Saturday
afternoon, yet the old prophet set me off it, that I might be justly
punished, because I would not when God would. As for that more
than ordinary countenance from the Lord, though I dare not, before
a holy God, purge myself altogether of lifting up, yet I can remember no notable uplifting that I had on the back of it. It may be I

had had it if I had not got that ballast, especially when I found others had greater thoughts of it than I. There are two difficulties in the way of this conclusion : First, The straitening I had in study-ing that sermon; but my experience leaves no weight in this : Se-cond, My trouble as to the horse beginning ere I went away. From what I have met with, 1. I have learned, that if the Lord has a mind, he will carry on his work, and no thanks to the instruments; for I took that exercise in hand through a sort of mere force. 2. To be de-nied to my credit in the Lord's matters. One of the ministers that preached that Saturday, never desired me to do it; the other of them did as good as forbid me, and I had no will to have it said, that I loved to hear myself speak, or that the people would be weary, &c. But now I see that these things are but thin fig-leaves. Lord, my soul is as a weaned child. 3. I think I have thereby ob-tained some soul-advantage; more heavenliness in the frame of my heart, more contempt of the world, as the widow that is desolate trust-eth in God. I have more confidence in God, to which I am helped (with respect to my work in the parish) particularly by that word; Isa. xxxiii. 10, " Now will I rise, saith the Lord, now will I be exalt-ed, now will I lift up myself ;" which was a sweet word to me, on the last Lord's day, in my lecture, which fell to be in that chapter that day, in which I had more than ordinary of the Lord's light and life, though I had very little time to study it or the sermons. I have thereby obtained more carefulness to walk with God, and to get evidences for heaven; more resolution of spirit for the Lord's work, over the belly of difficulties. For there was more yet in that affliction. I have been much discouraged with respect to my parish a long time, and have had little hand or heart for my work. I take God's dealing thus with me to be designed as a mean to make me better content. Now the Lord has driven the business to a great height of hopelessness, by the removal of two of the most comfort-able of my elders, I may say three; Walter Bryden went out of the parish at Whitsunday last; now this stroke, in the removal by death of William Biggar ; and Mr. Paterson, a wise, sweet-tempered young man, who by his authority was a ballast in this place to my enemies, is going away against Martinmas next. And I have but four elders behind. And, which is most sad, so rare is an inoffen-sive walk among us, that it is extremely hard to get others in their room, who would not be a reproach to the office. I know not how much further the Lord may carry it; but I desire to take spirits, and when all is gone to look to the Lord.

Last Lord's day night I had some thoughts as to evidences for heaven, which I resumed this day. 1. I am content to take Christ

for my prophet, to be taught by him what is my duty, that I may
comply with it; I am content to know what is my sin, that I may
turn from it; and by grace I know something of what it is to make
use of Christ as a prophet in this case; and I desire to learn of him,
as the only Master, what is the will of God, and the mystery of renouncing my own wisdom, which I reckon but weakness and folly.
2. I know and am persuaded, that I am a lost creature; that justice must be satisfied; that I am not able to satisfy it, nor no creature for me; that Christ is able, and his death and sufferings are
sufficient satisfaction. On this I throw my soul with all its full
weight; here is my hope and only confidence. My duties, I believe
the best of them, would damn me, sink me to the lowest pit, and
must needs be washed in that precious blood, and can have no acceptance with God but through his intercession. I desire to have
nothing to do with an absolute God, nor to converse with God but
only through Christ. I am sensible that I have nothing to commend me to God, nor to Christ, that he may take my cause in hand.
If he should damn me, he should do me no wrong. But the cord of
love is let out, even the covenant in his blood; I accept of it, and
at his command lay hold on it, and venture. This is faith in spite
of devils. And my heart is pleased with the glorious device of
man's salvation through Christ, carrying all the praise to free grace,
and leaving nothing of it to the creature. 3. My soul is content of
him for my king; and though I cannot be free of sin, God himself
knows he would be welcome to make havock of my lusts, and to
make me holy. I know no lust that I would not be content to
part with. My will bound hand and foot I desire to lay at his
feet; and though it will strive, whether I will or not, I believe
whatever God does to me is best done. 4. Though afflictions of
themselves can be no evidence of the Lord's love; yet forasmuch as
the native product of afflictions and strokes from the hand of the
Lord, is to drive the guilty away from the Lord; when I find it is
not so with me, but that I am drawn to God by them, made to kiss
the rod, and accept of the punishment of my iniquity, to love God
more, and to have more confidence in him, and kindly thoughts of
his way, and find my heart more closely cleaving to him, I cannot
but think such an affliction an evidence of his love. I have met with
many troubles, and the afflictions I have met with have been very
remarkable in their circumstances. Often have I seen it, and now
once more, verified in my lot; 1 Cor. iv. 9, "For we are made a
spectacle to the world, and to angels, and to men," &c. Now I am
as a weaned child, through grace, in the matter. Let the Lord do
what seemeth him good. [*Nota*, I was obliged to leave my horse
behind me at Penpont under care, and he died.]

In the latter end of August, I was at the sacrament in Ashkirk. There I preached the sermon, on Saturday, which should have been preached at Penpont. I was helped to deliver it, and I believe it was not without fruit to some. But after sermons I was bowed down under convictions of the want of that fear of God in my spirit, when I delivered it, and was vile in mine own eyes. The Lord's day was a good day to me. Hearing Mr. Gordon speak to his people as under apprehensions of death, and reflecting on how many years, especially since I was a minister, I have spent in preaching the gospel, it was most bitter to me, to see how much time was gone, and how little I had done for God. From the Saturday after sermons I had been in earnest for awful impressions of God on my spirit, and I got them; particularly on the Monday, while Mr. Gabriel Wilson preached, my soul, under impressions of the majesty and greatness of God, was melted within me. While he preached on Psalm cxvi. 9, "I will walk before the Lord in the land of the living," every step of duty he named, gave me a new conviction. So that when I began to speak after him, my soul was so filled with the sense of the majesty of God, and of my own vileness, whereof my heart was so swollen, that I had much ado in prayer to speak plain, and not to break the words. But in the sermon, I had much tugging and drawing with my heart to keep it right, and wanted not ups and downs in it, sometimes out of case, and sometimes helped, but for the most part unsatisfying to myself. After the work was over, I had a sinking afternoon and night of it, often wishing I had gone away when Mr. Wilson ended, seeing myself a vile minister, good for nothing; and the sense of the difficulties of that work, and of my own mismanagements, lay heavy on me. And on the morrow, as I was by the way, I was indeed like to faint under these impressions. As I was coming through W. moor, I mistook the way, and bogued my horse in the moss beyond R. After much toiling with him in vain, I sat down and cried to the Lord; tried it again, but it would not do; so that I had thoughts of losing him. I cast off my boots and cloak, and went to the town to seek help. The person to whom I spoke knew me not, and so sent me to the field to the mowers. I came to one company, who sent me to another, who were more compassionate. So two or three went away with me to the moss; and those in the town having known me after I was gone, had gone to the horse, who had got up to his feet ere they came. So he was got out of the moss, and I was conducted to the right way. When I came home, I met with another temptation, ere ever I sat down, which was another nail to my heart; the rather sharp, that it was driven by a hand from whence I expected it not; which

VOL. XI.   P

brought me in mind of a note to that purpose in the latter end of
my sermon at Ashkirk, fulfilled in myself, whatever it might be in
others. I would fain have had Mr. Wilson staying with me on the
Monday's night, for my support; but the Lord would not. With
these things, and the wonderful conduct of providence towards me, I
was much broken, and made to go with a bowed down back, and my
health impaired. Some others had no mean thoughts of the work
there. Mr. Wilson said, that for the Saturday, had he been to have
preached after me, he would not have opened his mouth, but dismissed the people as they were. I bless the Lord, that lets me see
my own vileness and nothingness; and that seeing my heart is ready
to be vain of little things, he takes such measures to press me
down.

Sept. 11.—This day Mr. Macmillan preached at Hopecross, in the
confines of this parish. On the 12th of December last, I had preached a sermon precisely against the separation, upon occasion of
reading the aforementioned act of the commission from the pulpit.
It was by a mistake I was led to read these papers, I mean that
act of the commission, at least at that time; for I had a letter from
the presbytery clerk, importing, as I thought, their order; but they
had given none about it. However, it was my opinion, that the act
should have been read through the presbytery; but I had no mind
to have made myself singular. But it was a happy mistake, ordered
by the good providence of God. My lecture fell that day to be on
Isa. v.; but I handled only the parable of the vineyard, which was
to me another piece of surprising conduct of providence. It fell to
be an exceeding good day, so that our kirk was thronged with our
own people and strangers. God helped me to deliver it. Copies of
it were desired, and I allowed them to be given out; so copies were
handed abroad, not only in the parish, but several other places;
and this galled that party, and I am confident served to confirm
others. Mr. Macmillan preached within a mile of this parish in
February thereafter, and my people did not shew their wonted instability. At length this day Mr. Macmillan preached a sermon, on
design to confute that sermon of mine, producing the copy of my
sermon, and reading parcels of it before the people. Seldom or
never before came that man to these bounds, but something was laid
to my hand in my ordinary, whereof there is an instance above expressed. But this day there was nothing of that nature; but not
without reason, for our kirk that day was so throng, that I really
thought some had the rather come out that day, that I might see
they were not gone to his meeting.

I understood after, that several who were there were disgusted, and that it had done their cause little service. He left this country, leaving no copy of his sermon behind him; which has been taken notice of by judicious persons. I waited a while, till I should see whether any copy of it appeared or not; at length none appearing, I spoke a little of it in the pulpit, desiring the people to believe what I had taught them, till they should see it confuted by scripture, &c.

In November I met with a surprising mercy. A person that had long been in the wrong to me, in a certain particular, with tears confessed the fault; which did exceedingly raise me in thankfulness to God. This was on the Friday. On the Lord's day night thereafter, musing on it, I found I had met with that mercy before I was prepared for it. It is true, I had often prayed for it; but the sap was squeezed out, by considering that I had not got my heart in that point brought to a submission to the will of God. Upon this account the mercy proved a burden to my spirit, and a great and heavy grief. When I lay down in my bed, my grief increased; my wilful will was a spectacle of horror to me. And, under this conviction, I was so filled with the terror of God, that both flesh and spirit were like to fail and faint away. I endeavoured to flee to, and make use of the blood of Christ for pardon; and though I would have bought that mercy at a very dear rate, yet I was conscious to myself, and protested, that I was not, and would not, be content with that mercy, but with the favour of God and his good-will with it, and desired to give up my will to the will of God. [*Nota*, It was not long ere my patience in this point was put to the trial again; so short-lived are mercies that fall off the tree of providence ere they be ripe.]

Friday, Dec. 30. I received a letter from Mrs. M. Home, wherein she says, she is wearying of "this life of a beast;" which made impression on me. The next day, it pleased the Lord to give me a more than ordinary outletting of his Spirit, which I was somewhat helped to improve; the rather that there was at that time in my mind, a dissatisfaction about my public work, both as to my preaching and the people's hearing, which I fain would have seen changed to the better. And indeed it was better with me on the Lord's day. And now the Lord was a commentator on the scripture to me, at family duties. I spent a part of Monday morning in prayer; and by that exercise, and making conscience of preparing for family duties, I found myself bettered. On the Tuesday I spent some time in fasting and prayer, and renewed my covenant with God; and that week I was kept heavenly for the most part; and till this day.

Jan. 22, 1710.—Though I have had several ups and downs, yet I have at least been kept struggling. And as to this time, I may say, 1. I had never more deep impressions of the life of a beast, being in some sort weary of the necessity of eating, sleeping, &c., with a holy contempt of them, longing to be beyond all these things, and content to part with all my created comforts. I have also felt my soul most sensibly going out in love to God, and seen my soul most plainly taking Christ for my portion, and accepting of the blessed Bridegroom. It hath been my exercise how to direct these things in the life of the beast, to the Lord, to refer them to God, so as that they may be a part of the Christian life. But I have made small progress in the practice of it, but have found slips that way bitter. As particularly on Friday morning, I spent so much time in sleep, when I should have been otherwise employed, that it made me go halting all the day; and so much the more, that I had been attacked in prayer with carnality before, which was not duly resisted; and from thence I dated that carnal frame. Thus I found my conscience defiled, and on the morrow after it lay heavy on me. I came from family prayer that day (viz. Saturday), where I could not get all my mind told before the Lord, unto my closet; whether when I came, the sense of my carnality pressed me so sore, that I could scarcely get out a word for some time. When I got liberty to speak, my soul protested before God and angels, that though I could not shake myself loose of my lusts, Christ should be most welcome to make havock of them. The latter foresaid trysted with a sermon I had been preaching before, of making God our end, as a necessary requisite in holiness; and so it came seasonably to quicken my thoughts and practice in that point. And I design to preach particularly on referring natural actions to God, for my own and the people's case, as God shall clear my way. I have learned two things by experience in that point. The one is, When the will, on a corrupt principle, that may feed spiritual lusts, is averse to what the body requires, to yield to the body the rather to cross the will, and so to seek to please God, and not ourselves, in or about these things. The other, To ascend from and by them, to that infinite satisfaction that must needs be in the enjoyment of God, leaving these ashes upon the earth, and mounting up from them in a flame of love to the Lord, as pillars of smoke ascending towards heaven. Seeing all perfection in the creature is originally from God, whatever is in the creature must be eminently and infinitely in him; therefore, if a bit of bread be so sweet, how sweet must God be, that ocean, whereof that in the bread is but a drop!

Jan. 26.—The last week I spent some time in prayer with fasting, with my family, especially for my wife's safe delivery; but with me it went not well; my frame was not fixedly lively. This upon reflection was terrible to me, as a sign for evil; which was the mean of quickening in secret; where I got what I got not with others. And I have observed, that the thing I have been still led to for her, was a life for God. And it was most clear to me this night in particular, that it was not so much her life, as life for God, that I desired; grace to her (as to myself) to live well, more than life. I have been this day also, from the life of the beast, helped to prize the enjoyment of God; and was led into a sweet view of the purity and refinedness of the pleasures in the fountain, and the dregs mixed with those of the streams, that make them humbling and contemptible.

Jan. 29.—Sabbath. On Friday studying my catechetic sermon,* some surprising thoughts were laid to my hand. My heart swelled with thankfulness, and loathed myself for that there should be so much as a principle of taking any praise to myself in me, though it came not forth into an act. And my soul cried to be emptied of self, that I might be nothing, and the Lord might work all in me. I thought these things were from the Lord, seeing they had that effect on me. On Saturday night I made all ready, that I might employ my time to the best advantage on the Sabbath morning; and I requested, particularly, 1. That I might have whom to preach to; for it was a very bad day; 2. An opportunity to preach without distraction; for my wife had some pains; 3. That the Lord would be with me; for the pulpit without him was a terror. This day was an exceeding pleasant day, and the people came well out. I had no trouble from my wife's case. These things in the morning were a valley of Achor for a door of hope. I gave myself to prayer, and entered to the work in a tender melted frame. I dare not say, that the Lord was not with me; but I had not what I would fain have had. I had several ups and downs in the sermons. I would fain have been at the mark, but the legs would not serve. I found I loved the Lord, and would fain have been there where the executive power would fully answer the will. I know not what the Lord has a mind to do with me, but this good while I have had no ill time of it. 1. I have found frequent flutterings of my soul after the Lord very sensibly. 2. I have found duty very pleasant, and sometimes a pain to give it over. 3. I have found more freedom with God in secret than in family duties, for there I

---

* Viz. that on the first sin in particular.

got leave to tell all I thought. 4. I have sometimes a confusion in
my head in preaching; I prayed against it particularly this day. I
had something of it but it lasted not, though I was about four hours
in constant exercise. But seldom does my body fail in preaching,
when my frame is right. 5. I have found the Lord easy to be entreated, and a recovery to be got without long onwaiting. As yesterday I was somewhat carnal, I sought the Lord, but found him
not; I went back again to God, and was set right again. And seldom has it continued ill with me, for some time, from the beginning
to the end of duty. 6. On Wednesday last a storm that threatened
this parish, already sore distressed, did break. I found myself concerned to get this mercy, both in public and private, and thankful
to the Lord when it was come; and why may not I look on it, as
the Lord's hearing of my prayers, amongst those of others?

Feb. 3.—I had met with a temptation that put me out of frame.
Afterwards I met with another of the same kind, but sharper; with
which I went to God, and it issued in quickening me again. I was
turned off the thing that raised my corruptions, and turned in
against myself, that I could not get my will to comply with the will
of God in this, without fretting, and cheerfully to submit to providence in that particular. It was stinging to think, that whereas I
have several evidences for heaven, this one thing is like to blot them
all out. I have found a satisfaction in seeing the Lord, by his providence, set me on my trials for my humiliation in other cases; but
I think I can never get over this. I wrestled with the Lord to get
my will melted down, that at length in this I might be as a weaned
child. This cured me in another case, and made me fear the being
taken off my trials before some good metal should appear. Last
night, while this case lay heavy on me, it fell in our ordinary to
sing Psalm xxxviii. 10—13. And this day it met me again very
seasonably.

" Adoro plenitudinum scripturæ."

Feb. 4.—My heart had scarce conceived ere my tongue began to
express some regret in the foresaid particular; but through grace
my tongue was silenced, ere it had got sense made of what it had
begun to say. And it was no small joy to me to see my corrupt self
deprived of that satisfaction, and the wilful will balked of its
will.

Feb. 7.—Tuesday. This night I had one of the most doleful times
I ever had in my life, by reason of the same trial aforesaid. The
struggle with my own will was most dreadful, so that I was like to
sink under it, and say, There is no hope, while it lay on me as a giant

bearing down a little child. I laid down my resolution however always to go to God with it again, as it renewed its desperate attacks on me; and so I did, and found some ease that way; though sometimes both heart and hand were taken from me in this combat, and I was almost swallowed up in despair. I felt the power of the bands of wickedness. The first ease I got was, that it was suggested to me in prayer, that it might be God was letting me fall so low before the victory, that I might see it, when it came, entirely due to his grace. In our ordinary that night we sung Psalm xl. where that word, ver. 16, "who seeking thee abide," &c., was most seasonable and comfortable. At this time I was preaching on Gal. v. 24, and I had a trial of the difficulty of the work.

Feb 9.—Thursday. This day, betwixt ten and eleven at night, my wife, after long and sore labour, was delivered of a son, called Thomas, who was baptized on the 15th by Mr. Gabriel Wilson, minister at Maxton. She never recovered with so much difficulty; which seemed to answer to our frame in prayer for that mercy. On the Sabbath after she was very ill: and just when I was going in to the afternoon's sermon she told me, she thought she was in a fever. Whereupon I looked to the Lord, and presently found my spirit calmed, in hopes all would be well; and went to my work; and so it was. While I wrote the letter to Mr. Wilson to come and baptize the child, my soul fluttered away to Christ with my child, and I wept for joy of the covenant, that it was for my seed, as well as for myself.

Feb. 15.—This night I had four particular suits before the throne of grace. And within a few days after, as to one of them, some persons, who, being stirred up by an enemy to me, had created me very much trouble in a particular business, came and agreed with me; so the Lord made my enemies stumble and fall in their measures against me; and O but that mercy was sweet! An only child of a dear friend having been sick, I heard of her recovery. As to a nurse for my child, the Lord answered by that which was better, giving milk to my wife. As to the fourth, I thought it had been answered too; but it failed, and I was set to wait on again.

By this time the friendship betwixt the aforementioned Mr. Wilson and me had arrived at an uncommon height and strictness. That friendship hath indeed been one of the greatest comforts of my life; he being a man of great piety, tenderness, and learning, with a vast compass of reading; a painful minister; a plain preacher, but deep in his thought, especially of latter years, and growing remarkably unto this day in insight into the holy scriptures; zealous and faithful to a pitch; having more of the spirit of the old Presbyterians

than any other minister I know; for the which cause he has been,
and is in the eyes of many, like a speckled bird; but withal a most
affectionate, constant, and useful friend; a seasonable and wise ad-
viser in a pinch; often employed of God signally and seasonably, to
comfort and bear me up, when I needed it extremely; insomuch
that I have often been convinced, he could not have gone the length
that way that he went, if it had not been through a particular disposal of providence indulging my weakness, particularly in this and
the following period, wherein I was in a special manner, from within
and from without, at once sore bowed down.   Whatever odds there
was in some respects betwixt him and me, there was still a certain
cast of temper by which I found him to be my other self; [and
though we have passed, especially since the year 1712, through
several steps, at which many chief friends have been separated;
yet, through the divine mercy, we still stuck close, speaking the
same thing; the sense whereof has often obliged us to give thanks
unto God expressly on that account.]   He was extremely modest;
but, once touched with the weight of a matter, very forward and
keen, fearing the face of no man; on the other hand, I was slow and
timorous.   In the which mixture, whereby he served as a spur to
me, and I as a bridle to him, I have often admired the wise conduct
of providence that matched us together.   But now, alas; he is left
alone for me, in public struggles, I being through frailty laid aside
from appearing at synods; with which I was indeed disgusted ere
I left them; and very seldom now appearing in the presbytery.   Mr.
Davidson, minister of Galashiels, who afterwards came to be a third
in this friendship, is now also through his frailty laid aside from
much of his helpfulness to him in these cases.   However, the friendship remains inviolate, and will, I hope, till death; Psalm xciv. 11,
"The Lord knoweth the thoughts of man, that they are vanity."

April 9.—The last week I was at the synod; and seeing all things
like to go wrong with the church, I had great desire to be kept
straight in God's way.   I was not so well provided for my work
this day as ordinary, but it went rather better than ordinary with
me.   I was much affected to think how I would get silent Sabbaths
spent, and what reflections such a case might produce.

I think I can say now, that the thing which was once so hard for
me to submit unto, the Lord hath been pleased to make more easy
and give me some victory over it now, more than these two months,
"Blessed be the Lord, who teacheth my hands to war, and my
fingers to fight."

I proceeded on the subject of the nature and necessity of holiness,
from the time aforesaid, and therewith ended the ordinary above

mentioned, on May 28th, this year. After which I addressed myself to preach sermons preparatory for the sacrament of the supper,
[from 1 Cor. xi. 23, and Jer. l. 4, 5.]

And on July 16, I administered that ordinance. This was the
first time I administered it in Etterick; but from that time it has
been done yearly, for ordinary, all along, the few interruptions
thereof hitherto made [viz. 1717, 1726, and 1729], being occasioned
by the affliction of my family of late years, and other incidents. I
thought myself obliged to deal with every communicant personally,
but had little encouragement to the work from the parish; but I
behoved to try all means. I was very much discouraged while I
set to that work; but the nearer it came, I was the more carried
above discouragement. While I visited the parish, I found I had
not been altogether useless here, and particularly that the sermon
on the fourfold state of man had done some good. Seldom do delays
prove advantageous. God had more of his own, so far as I could
discern, to feed here, the last year, than this, three of the most comfortable families in it having removed at Whitsunday last. The
sermons on the Lord's day before, seemed to have weight, and I
found my soul pressed particularly to follow that day's work with
prayer. As for the work itself, it was much more comfortable than
I expected, and there seemed to be some blowings of the Spirit with
it. I never saw a congregation more remarkably fixed and grave
than they were on the Lord's day. On the Thursday was eight days
before, in the family fast, the Lord helped us to pray, and seek his
presence. I had palpable assistance in studying the action-sermon
on Luke xiv. 23, "Compel them to come in;" and though being
much hurried on the Saturday, I found myself quite out of case, and
had little hope of it when going to the work, yet verily the Lord was
with me in that sermon. It was once my regret, that the national
fast and our congregational one should have fallen both on one day;
and I had expectations of two ministers' help that day, but got
none at all. God ordered both well to my conviction. However it
was, some communicated with us, who had either never or not these
twenty years communicated; and I had some ground to think that
by that sermon the bands of some were loosed. In all there were
about fifty-seven persons of our own parish communicants; few indeed, but yet more than I expected amongst them. The Saturday was
very rainy, which put us in confusion for the following day; but God
disappointed my fears, and gave a pleasant day till towards the end
of the afternoon's sermon. The rain returned on Monday. That
was wondrous in my eyes. I afterwards revised the action-sermon,
with a view to publish it in the Fourfold State; but gave over that

purpose.* Meanwhile the divisions made the number of communicants but small. See Appendix No. I.

Thereafter I insisted for some time on a subject suitable to the
communion-work we had been employed in, [viz. Jer. 1. 5.] And
this was all along my manner before and after communions. That
being done, I did, on September 3, enter, for an ordinary, on Mark
x. 21, 22, " One thing thou lackest," &c. And hereto I was led for
the ease of my own soul, and spent thereon what remained of the
year.

On the Friday after the sacrament, I received a letter, desiring
me to come and visit one who had been a dissenter, but had come in
at the sacrament, and communicated with us, now very sick, and desirous to see me. From the letter, I imagined that she was under
remorse for her complying so far with us; which seemed to me to
be a dreadful attempt of the devil against the ordinances in this
parish; however, I went away with boldness to see her; and by the
good hand of God found it was quite contrariwise; for she told me,
that she was under the Lord's chastisement for her deserting the
ordinances so long; that it began with her in the church on the fast-
day, which was her first return to the ordinances; and that she was
then so pressed, that she had much ado to keep herself from either
running out, or crying out, in time of sermon. This was no small
comfort to me, that God had so far vindicated his own cause. This
brings me in mind of the passage narrated above, p. 204.

Sept. 29.—Having been under a great trial from that particular,
of which before, I was so broke with the sin and misery flowing
from it, that I loathed life, and would have been content to have
been away, and left all, to have been freed from the sin and misery
of the case. This sat down on my spirit on the Lord's day, the 13th
of August. The next Sabbath I was at the sacrament at Selkirk.
That was to me a sweet ordinance beyond many. But, behold, there
arose again quickly after a dreadful storm of temptation from the
same quarter. So I preached my experience next Lord's day on
that text; "Job vii. 16, "I loath it, I would not live alway." I
gave myself to secret fasting and prayer on the Wednesday thereafter, being the 30th of August. My case still continuing heavy,
it led me to that portion of scripture; Mark x. 21, as above mentioned. After much sad tossing, I did this day spend some time in
secret prayer with fasting, to seek of the Lord a right way. On the
Lord's day before, I had been preaching directions how to get over

* It was published in 1753, in the same volume with the Miscellaneous Questions
above mentioned.

the one thing lacking; and this day I set myself solemnly to prac-
tise them for my particular case. After a while I laboured to take
up my real case as nicely as I could; for I considered, that unto the
trials God lays in men's way, they often add much of their own,
which makes them far more bulky and weighty than otherwise they
are in very deed; and here I was convinced, that I had laid too much
of my own, suffering some things to sink into my spirit, which were
not so much to be regarded. Thus having as it were removed the
rubbish I had laid upon the stone which was to be lifted up, I went
through these directions; First, Labouring to see the evil of it;
Secondly, Setting myself in a way of believing against it; 1. Endeavouring to be emptied of myself in point of confidence in myself,
with respect to the victory over it; 2. Taking Christ for it; and,
1st, Taking himself instead of it; 2dly, Taking him in all his offices
for it; as a Prophet; a Priest, in his merit and intercession; and
as a King, with particular respect to that one thing; 3dly, Believing the promises suited to that case. The third direction was my
present work, fasting and prayer. And, lastly, I resolved through
grace to watch. In a special manner I did that day solemnly renounce, and give over into the hands of the Lord, that thing, and
take Christ in the stead of it; so making the exchange, resolving
to take what he should please to give me of my desire, but to quarrel no more with the Lord upon the head, but to be as a weaned
child.

Oct. 2.—Immediately on the back of that exercise my temptation
was renewed, which gave me much ado; but yesterday, being the
Lord's day, I found that out of the eater meat was brought to me.
The honour of all the saints; Psalm cxlix. with respect to the desired
victory over my lusts, was sweet to me; and that of the afflictions
and consolations of ministers being for people's sake; 2 Cor. i. 6,
(both falling in our ordinary in the family), was sweet and seasonable. My soul longed to be free of sin, and was really in love with
Christ; he was the desire of my soul, which longed for him; and
when I considered my one thing lacking, I was well content to part
with it for him, and to seek my soul's rest in himself. Much had I
laboured to get the crook in my lot made straight; but it would not
do; yea I was often made worse by seeking to even it. This I took
up as the wrong way, but saw the necessity of bowing my heart to
it. This day I had much satisfaction in the resignation and exchange made in this matter, and found my heart so loosed from the
bonds of my corruption, that the hand of the Lord appeared eminently in it.

Oct. 6.—I have seen that under temptation I have magnified my

trial, so that now it appears much less than sometimes it did. The
Lord has driven the mists from about it, that made it look bigger
than it was. And this I take to be the effect of Christ's executing
his prophetical office in me, as I gave myself to him as a Prophet in
that matter particularly. And this day reflecting on the Lord's
dealing with me, I found my soul purged from guilt, and helped to
serve the Lord; whereas I could not serve him before, while my
conscience was defiled in that matter. I found my corruption laid
low, in comparison of what it had been before. And thus Christ
exercised his priestly and kingly offices over me. Upon this occasion I have been much inclined to cry to the Lord for the light of
his Spirit wherewith to read the scriptures; and I have found that
I am heard.

Oct. 8.—My heart has been looking back toward its old bias,
which was heavy to me; but I observed my heart said, that the full
enjoyment of it without Christ would not satisfy, but Christ without
it would satisfy. I found sensible strength this day, from considering that fulness of satisfaction that is to be had in God himself, for
which I have made the resignation. I had an answer of prayer also
brought to my hand just before I went out to the church, the lack
of which was like to have been a temptation to me. The Lord continues to make me read the scriptures with more than ordinary insight into them. [N. B. I think I never had so much of a continued
insight into the word as I had this winter, which made it no ill time
to me.] " He that overcometh shall inherit all things," was a sweet
word to me.

Oct. 22.—Last week at the synod, I was surprised with an unusual temptation, which meeting me, struck me with terror, and
filled me with confusion, having a native tendency to heighten my
great trial. Wherefore seeing how I was beset, and what danger I
was in, I set myself the more kindly to bear my trial, and in that
respect was bettered by that temptation. Being very apprehensive
of the evil that might ensue upon this, I did, after much fluctuating
in my mind, not knowing what to do, resolve to go to a certain
place to prevent the ill I feared; and accordingly went to a friend
at the time indisposed. When I came thither, in the simplicity of
my heart I was going to tell him my design to go elsewhere, but delayed it a while; and then I fell very sick, and was obliged to go
to bed, where, through indisposition of body and thoughtfulness of
heart, I had a weary night. I saw I could not go whither I had designed. About four o'clock in the morning, while I lay and could
not sleep, I could not see how the evil I feared could be prevented,
seeing my design was broken; nor wherefore providence had brought

me to where I was. But at length I really believed that God had
done both for the best ; and where sense failed, faith helped me out:
and this gave me great ease. On the morrow, being still indisposed,
I came homeward. The next day, while on my way home, matters
were made so clear to me as to the conduct of providence, that my
soul blessed him for that seasonable sicknesss, and keeping my design entirely secret. This I desire to mark as one of the most signal marks of the Lord's tender care over me. At that time there
was a reproof given me, on account of a boy that kept a school
here, that sometimes he was not called in to the family exercise out
of the school. I judged the matter was such, seeing the school was
public, kept in the kirk, and the reproof given with such an ill air,
that I could not take it well off the hand that reached it; but it let
me in to more than that, that that boy appeared to me the messenger of the Lord sent to tell me my faults, so as I could have under
that notion hugged him in my bosom. And that I got for going so
far. So I came home rejoicing in the Lord's kindness to me in these
dispensations.

Oct. 23.—This night was a sweet night to me, being let into the
view of the 6th chapter of the epistle to the Galatians, and loving
the Lord and holiness. It hath been my wonder, that the faith of
heaven should not more wean my heart from the world.

Nov. 4.—A woman who had fallen into fornication told me, that
the Lord began to deal with her soul, while she was young, and that
for several years she continued serious; but for five years before her
fall, she was under a plain decay; that she never awaked till the
child was one night overlaid, and found dead in the morning. She
said, that in the time of her travail she was no more concerned than
that, pointing to a form or seat.

Dec. 9.—This night I was in bad case. I find it is not easy to
me to carry right, either with or without the cross. While I was
walking up and down my closet in heaviness, my little daughter
Jane, whom I had laid in the bed, suddenly raising up herself, said,
she would tell me a note ; and thus delivered herself.—Mary Magdalen went to the sepulchre.—She went back again with them to the
sepulchre; but they would not believe that Christ was risen, till
Mary Magdalen met him; and he said to her, "Tell my brethren,
they are my brethren yet," This she pronounced with a certain air
of sweetness. It took me by the heart; "His brethren yet,"
(thought I); and may I think that Christ will own me as one of his
brethren yet ? It was to me as life from the dead.

As for my studies; from my settling in Etterick, I gave myself
to reading, as I was disposed and had access ; making some ex-

cerpts out of the books I read. I began the book of the passages of
my life, which before had been kept in the two manuscripts above
mentioned, and some other papers. My son John was begun to
learn the Latin tongue, February 16, 1708, and had domestic teaching till the year 1712; for which cause I had several young men in
that time for teachers; but often the burden lay on myself. And
there was no legal school in the parish, till of late, when none of my
children needed it. I read some of the books of Antonia Bourignon,
for understanding her principles, which made a considerable noise at
that time; and making some excerpts out of them I left a column
blank for animadversions thereon; which I, finding no occasion for
after, did never make. I began lecturing in Etterick where I left
off in Simprin; and proceeding to the book of the Revelation, I
wrote some lectures thereon, from the 4th chapter, but in short hand
characters. The same I did on some chapters of Isaiah afterwards.

This was the happy year wherein I was first master of a Hebrew
Bible, and began the study of it. About the time of my coming out
of the Merse to Etterick, I borrowed a piece of the Hebrew Bible,
containing the books of Samuel and Kings; and having got that, I
went on accordingly in the study of the holy tongue. For which
cause I did this year purchase Athias's Hebrew Bible, of the second
edition, having been long time lured and put off with the hopes of a
gift of Arrius Montanus from an acquaintance in the Merse; the
which were not like to be accomplished, and in end were frustrated.
Thus provided, I plied the Hebrew original close, with great delight; and all along since, it hath continued to be my darling study.
But I knew nothing then of the accentuation. Howbeit, I took some
notes of the import of the Hebrew words with much pleasure. I had
got another parcel of books in the year 1706, the chief of which was
Turrettine's works, in four volumes 4to, wherewith I was not altogether unacquainted before; and, in 1707, before I went to Etterick,
I purchased Pool's Annotations, having had no entire commentary
on the whole Bible before that, except the English Annotations,
edit. 1, purchased in 1704. But from the time I left Simprin, I set
myself no more to purchase parcels of books as before; but got
some particular books now and then, as I found myself disposed for
them.

About the end of this year, my friend Mr. Wilson and I began
epistolary conmmunication, whereby we might have the benefit, each
of the other's reading and study, for our mutual improvement. And
then I wrote the meditation on the day of expiation and feast of
tabernacles, to be found in the miscellany manuscript, p. 325—

332.* About this time also I did, for my diversion, compose a kind of a poem on friendship, in an enigmatical or allegorical strain, consisting of some sheets ; a part of which, it seems, I had sent him by that time. [But last winter, 1729, I committed it to the flames, with any thing else of that kind done by myself.]

Feb. 8, 1711.—There was a great storm of snow on the ground ; and our parish, with many others, about two years before, having been almost broke with such a storm, it lay near my heart ; and therefore I moved for a congregational fast on that occasion ; which the elders fell in with, being called together betwixt sermons ; and in the afternoon it was intimated, to be observed on the Wednesday thereafter. I was helped in my secret prayers on this occasion, which made me to hope. On the morrow, the weather began to be so easy, that I thought our fast was like to be turned into a thanksgiving. But that lasted not ; so that I think it was never more violent than on the fast day. And the Lord was with us in praying, and in preaching too on Joel i. 18, " How do the beasts groan," &c. The Lord graciously heard our prayers. The morrow after was no ill day ; but on the Friday the thaw freely came by a west wind, without rain. So the Lord's day was a thanksgiving day to us. I preached on Psalm cxlvii. 12, 18, " Praise the Lord.—He sendeth out his word, and melteth them." This day, with the day of the first communion, were the most joyful days I ever saw in Etterick. The hand of the Lord appeared in it to me, and to others likewise ; though our congregation made but very little bulk this day, after the Lord had done so great things for them. Lord, lay it not to their charge. Some afterward told me, that they had but one day's meat for their flocks when the storm brake. They were generally designed, on the Monday after, to have gone to seek pasture in other places ; but in time of the storm they professed they knew not well whither to go ; those places where they were wont to go to in a strait, having enough ado to serve themselves. About this time as I was lecturing on Proverbs, I took some notes of the import of the Hebrew words, to chap. xv. to be found in a 4to notebook.

On Friday June 8, about three in the morning, my daughter, Alison, was born ; and was baptized on Wednesday the 13th, by Mr. John Laurie, minister of Eskdalemoor.

The epistolary communication aforesaid betwixt Mr. Wilson and me, was carried on till towards the end of this year, at which time

---

* These were published in 1753, in the same volume with the Miscellanies, and have been greatly esteemed.

providence began to lay other work to hand. His letters to me of that kind are *in retentis ;* but I have no copy of mine to him. Only, what is preserved in the Miscellany manuscript from p. 333, to p. 349, on Eccl. x. 15, on Conversation, and on Garments, was written on that occasion.*

For my ordinary, I dwelt on the solemn call to faith, and gospel obedience; Matth. xi. 28—30, from Jan. 14, this year, till Aug. 26. And then to commend Christ to the souls of the people, I did, on Sept. 2, enter upon Phil. iii. and went through the first twelve verses thereof in order, which continued, I think, till May 1713.

Aug. 11.—After a long time of freedom from a temptation that had often worsted me, it began again about a month ago, and made fearful havock on my case. It was no little time ere I began so much as to think, that this was a taking up what I had before so solemnly renounced ; but still I found myself fettered, and could not shake off my bonds. On the 7th instant I set apart some time for fasting and prayer, eating only a little bear bread; but matters went not well with me. It burst out on me as a breach in a high wall, whose breaking cometh suddenly in an instant, when one is labouring to keep and prop it up. This day I fell to that work again, but considering that my head was the worse of fasting before, I ate as ordinary. In the very time I met with a new temptation akin to the grand trial, which was like to baffle me; but I was helped to struggle against it. I meditated, and read over that of September 29, last year; and there saw I had taken Christ instead of that which I had renounced. The renunciation indeed was still in my view ; but though within this short while I had often read over that, my taking of Christ instead of it was never in my eyes. My eyes were held that I could not see it. But then I took up the case, and was like Hagar having the well that was near her shewn her, when the child was laid by for death. I saw it was in vain to attempt to empty the heart of what is its carnal choice, unless I got it filled with something better than what I was to take from it. And thus my bonds were loosed, and I made the exchange over again in a solemn manner. And then my soul in some measure rested in the Lord, and I came away rejoicing in him. Joshua's laying an ambush against Ai, that small city, whereas the walls of great Jericho fell down at the sound of rams' horns, let me see how holy guile must be used in the spiritual combat. And I found by experience, the import of selling all for Christ, whereby the scripture expresseth the great transaction between the Lord and a soul. For he that

* These were also published, in the same volume with the Miscellanies, in 1753.

selleth, though he part with what is his, yet he gets that in its room which to him is better than what he gives away; and so lives on the thing he receives, instead of what he parts with.

On the last Lord's day of October, I was assisting Mr. James Ramsay in the celebration of the Lord's supper at Kelso; and the synod being to meet there ten days after, having demitted my office of clerkship at the April synod before, I could not go home, but went to the Merse, to Dunse. There Dr. Trotter taking me out to the fields, surprised me with a motion to print some of my sermons, shewing that I should not want encouragement. I had spent two days seeking something wherewith to go to Kelso, but could command nothing; so upon that account, and not knowing what otherwise I might be called to, I took old notes with me, and among others those on man's fourfold state. Upon the Doctor's urging his proposal, I made mention of these, as what seemed most suitable, if any thing of that nature were to be done. On his desire, I left them with him. On the morrow, ere I came off, Mr. Willis pursued the Doctor's motion. At the synod, speaking of it to Mr. Wilson, he declared, that he minded to have proposed it to me himself, and was sorry he was prevented. When I came home, there was a letter for me from Mr. B. for a loan of some of my sermons. A while after, the Doctor and Mr. Willis having read the papers, sent pressing letters to put me on to that work. All which obliged me to serious thoughts on the matter.

Nov. 30.—Some things this night observed and considered (after prayer) with respect to the publishing of the sermons. 1. With respect to our parish. 1st, I have many that will not hear me preach, and so have no access to be useful to them that way, they being dissenters; yet I have ground to think that they would read my sermons. 2dly, There are several that make no conscience of ordinary attendance on the public ordinances, and so have heard but few of these sermons. 3dly, There are some who cannot get attended punctually, and to whom silent Sabbaths are a grief; and it is hoped they might be welcome to those, especially at such times. 2. With respect to my friends in the Merse. As the Lord was pleased to own me while there, making me serviceable, not only to my own parish, but to many of the godly in the country; so copies of my sermons, since I came from them, have been desired and got by several there; which shews the interest I have in their affections, and promises a kindly reception. 3. With respect to myself. 1st, I am very little serviceable with reference to public management, being exceedingly defective in ecclesiastical prudence; and very little useful in converse, being naturally silent; but the Lord has

given me a pulpit-gift, not unacceptable; and who knows what he
may do by me that way? 2dly, Though sometimes I wrote as little
of my sermons as many others, yet these nine years at least last
bypast, I have been led into a way of close study, and writing
largely. I have ofttimes wished to have that yoke off my neck, but
still providence held it on me; and though I have several times
been designed for public places, yet I have still been shut up where
I had time for study. 3dly, The Lord has often made me a wonder to myself, and to say from my heart, What am I? and whence
is this? while he has helped me to preach, blessed my sermons, and
given me from thence such an interest in the affections of the godly.
And I will never forget, through grace, the surprising goodness of
God to me, in clerking to the synod; which was so done to satisfaction, that, the Lord knows, it was such a surprise to me, that to
this day (having now given it over) I do but believe it on the testimony of others. That work was taken off my hand at the last
synod, while this was proposed to be put into it. 4thly, I have a
weary task of my work in this parish, the Lord's message in my
mouth meeting with such bad entertainment; what if the Lord
should make up this another way? 4. With respect the sermons
themselves. 1st, The universal usefulness of the subjects, not treated of in that method by any that I know. 2dly, As I had an uneasiness till I got through them, to my parish, in regard of the
great weight of the subjects; so it would be no small comfort to me,
to have them still speaking to them. 3dly, Providence has ordered
that I have been now twice on these subjects, though in a different
method; once at Simprin, and once here. 4thly, These very sermons, I know, were useful to some when preached: I have had express acknowledgements of their efficacy, particularly that of the
corruption of nature, the mystical union, and the eternal state.
Lastly, The steps of Providence in that business; the providential
carrying of these sermons to Dunse, at that time; at the synod
Mr. Wilson's declaring to me, that he minded to have proposed it,
and my being freed of the clerk's office; and Mr. B's letter meeting
me when I came home. Further,

Nov 20.—Though these steps of Providence seemed to have something in them, yet I could never get the matter closely laid to heart;
nor did it go beyond far-off thoughts of it till Saturday last; though
I had a pressing letter to pursue the motion, from him who first made
it. That day I had done studying my sermons for the Lord's day,
and had been well helped of the Lord therein; and then that business came close home on my spirit, so as the matter was laid before
the Lord with weight and deep concern. At night I got three very

pressing letters, in pursuance of the proposal; and the Doctor's particularly did nail my heart; so that, considering the weight of the enterprise, his way of pressing it, my own unfitness for it, and my unholiness in a special manner, it made my heart to quake, and my legs to tremble.—Nov. 23. When most carnal, I have found myself most averse to that work; when most serious and spiritual, most pliable to it.

The sermons in which I have said I had been well helped, were on Phil. iii. 3. I had begun that chapter some time before; and when I viewed the importance of that verse in particular, I was minded not lightly to pass it over; for that cause I purchased a book of Manton's sermons, where he had some on that text. Thus provided, I set to work on the first clause, " Worshiping God in spirit;" but I was miserably straitened and confused in it. I therefore sent the book away, glad to be quit of it; and it came well to hand with me after that; as will appear by inspecting of the papers, and comparing inference 2, from the doctrine from that clause, and downwards, with what goes before. And that help continued through the whole of the sermons on that verse from that time forward, though sometimes less than at other times; so that I judge them to be the best body of sermons I ever studied before or since. September 18, 1714.* The help I had in them had an encouraging influence on me to that work, they being trysted with it, and begun October 21, 1711, and ended March 23, 1712.

Jan. 13, 1712,—Having a month or five weeks ago spent some time in prayer for light in this matter, I considered those things before noted which seemed to me to look favourably towards the design; but the only step I was cleared to take at that time, was, to send the papers to Mr. Colden and Mr. Wilson, for their advice, and help of their prayers; and this day they were returned to me, with letters. In the meantime I received a letter, December 15, from one concerned, wherein he seemed to me to remit somewhat of his zeal for that work; whereby the weight seemed to be wholly devolved on myself. This created thoughts of heart; but the upshot of it was to go on, if otherwise the Lord should clear the matter. And whereas I had been desired to cause call for the papers about ten days after they were sent away, they came not week after week; which seemed to me to presage their burial; so that my thoughts of that work where much laid aside. The issue of this was, that, with submission to providence, I was resolved to lay it by; yet with sorrow

* The date of transcribing this passage into the book of the passages of his life. These sermons were published in 1756, and justly answer the character the author gives of them.

of heart that I should not have the opportunity to be useful, which
sometime seemed promising. The letters that came with the papers
advised me to proceed, and with earnestness sufficient; and the
night before they came to my hand, I heard my eldest brother was
a-dying; which served to tell me, what need there was to do with
all my might whatsoever my hand found to do.

Jan. 16.—I spent most of this day in prayer and meditation, for
light in this matter; and after all I found, that I had rational
grounds to oblige me to make an essay; but could not find such a
lively sense of the call of God thereto as I desired. I observed,
that the papers being kept up so long after I was made to wait for
their return, was of a piece with the Lord's ordinary way with me,
to bring matters first very low before they rise. One told me, she observed that these sermons had more influence on the people of their
neighbourhood, than any before or since. I found myself this night
convinced, that they might be useful to many, in regard of the room
the Lord has given me in people's affections; and this went nearest
to the raising in my heart such a lively sense of the command or
call of God, as might help me to believe, that he would be with me
in the work; which is the thing I want; for with respect thereto,
I believe that the way of the Lord is strength to the upright. I
have read Durham on that head over and over, for light as to the
Lord's call, not without some advantage. But I resolve to wait on
God for his mind, having protested before him this day, (while I
spread these letters and papers before him), that if he go not with
me, I be not carried hence.

Jan. 19.—Yesterday and this day fourteen days, being both these
days utterly indisposed for study, there was as much left of what
was studied for the Sabbaths preceding *respectivè* as served; unto
which I could make no addition. So that although the Lord was
pleased to continue his help all along from the time I parted with
that book, as before said, yet thus was I made to see, that he had
lock and key of my gifts still. This night I was convinced, that
God will have me more holy, before I get through this business;
and therefore I see, that it is my business to labour in the first place
to get my own case bettered, by renewing my repentance.

Jan. 22.—Last night this was fixed on my heart, as the only way
how to get clearly through; and it answers to a confounding sense of
my own unholiness, as well as weakness for writing, which I was struck
with at the reading of the Doctor's letters: therefore this day I
gave myself to prayer and meditation. I found last night that it
was no easy thing to part with sin; and this morning the first impression on my spirit was that of my utter inability to put away

sin. And I think I never had a more solid and serious sense of the absolute need of Christ for sanctification this day. I saw it was as easy for a rock to raise itself, as for me to raise my heart from sin to holiness. I endeavoured to search myself, renew my repentance, and make confession; and solemnly laid over on the Lord Jesus Christ all my sins which I knew, and all that I knew not, that by his obedience, death, and sufferings, he might bear them all away. And having further examined myself, I renewed my covenant with God, taking God in Christ for my God, the Father of the Lord Jesus Christ for my Father, the Son for my Redeemer, and the Holy Ghost for my sanctifier; even that one God in three persons, who is in Christ reconciling the world to himself; taking Christ himself for my head and Husband; renouncing my own wisdom, and taking him for my Prophet to learn of him, and receive from him, the light of life; renouncing my own righteousness, and laying the whole stress of my soul on his merits and righteousness, and taking him for my Intercessor and Advocate; renouncing all my idols, and taking him for my King, and Head of influence for sanctification to my soul; resolving, in his strength, henceforth to hang on him for sanctifica- tion, to watch and more narrowly observe providences, and the way of his dealing with me. Personal holiness was the great thing in my view. After I set myself to cry to the Lord, in respect of the public, the case of the congregation, and my family. Towards the close of the day, I began to take thought particularly of the matter in hand, and set myself to examine myself as to the singleness of my intentions. I considered, that if I were led by base ends, it be- hoved to be either worldly profit, or a name. As for profit, my con- science bare me witness, that I would be content to be a loser, so that they might be serviceable; and as to a name, though at the bar of the law I dare not plead Not guilty, yet at the bar of the gospel I can appeal to God, that it is not a name to myself, but the honour of God that sways with me; and that on these grounds; 1. I do not, nor can I, expect a name amongst the men of name. 2. The Lord knows that I could be content to lose name and credit amongst them, so that the sermons were useful to some poor souls. 3. I am conscious to myself, that I durst not engage in such a business with- out an eye to the Lord for help; which I could not have for getting myself a name, either amongst the learned or unlearned. And upon the ground of my respect to God's honour, I find in myself a disposi- tion, to look to himself for his help. Thus I seemed insensibly to slip into what I was in quest of, viz. A sense of the command of God, such as might be a foundation of confidence in the Lord for help in the matter. That sense of my aiming at God's honour, and there-

upon the disposition to look to him for help, was followed with that
word, " Him that honoureth me I will honour ;" but I saw little to
my purpose in that word. So it cost thoughts of heart, seeking
some word of God that I might found upon in this point, viz. That
having such rational grounds for the thing itself, and being conscious of the singleness of my heart therein, I might look for God's
help in it. I turned to my ordinary, and there met with Psalm
xliv. 5, 6; which though it was of use to me, yet did not seem to
answer the point. Afterward that word, 1 Sam. ii. 30, returned
with a new light about it, appearing pat to my case. I saw that
promise particularly directed to priests in the exercise of their
office; and my soul desired no more, but what is in the compass of
that word. It melted my heart, and I said I would believe it. If
I had had the word a-framing for my case, I would have desired no
more in the matter secured to me, than walking before the Lord, as
a child before his father. After this, minding to read over what I
had marked from the beginning about this business, together with
the letters relative thereto, I went to God by prayer, for help to
make a clear judgment upon the whole. Thereafter I read, first my
own remarks, and then the letters, so far as they related to that
affair. Mr. Colden's letter was the last; and among the last words
of that part of it, were these following, viz, " Let respect to duty,
and the salvation of perishing souls, sway you." That word, " perishing souls," nailed my heart; and it burst out and answered, " Then
let me be a fool for perishing souls." And now for perishing souls
I dare not but try that work, come of me what will. Sense of duty
has now the heels of my inclination. Let the Lord do what seemeth
him good as to the use of them, whether they be published or not.
Blessed be the Lord, that has thus heard my prayer, and cleared
me to put pen to paper.

Jan. 24.—This day I minded to have put pen to paper in that
work; but last night a temptation was laid in to me, and increased
this day, so that I could not pursue my resolution. I saw the necessity of praying, "Lead us not into temptation;" was convinced
that I had let down my watch, and one evil still made way for another.

Jan. 27.—This night the consideration of the temptation wherewith I have been baffled, was most stinging, being so very quickly
after my solemn covenanting with God. I was made to groan out
my case by reason of a body of sin and death. One thing has still
been my temptation, and my heart said, "Any way let me be delivered, (only in mercy), though by cold death." I had been preaching, that the gracious soul could be content with Christ alone. And

it was some stay to my heart, that I knew the time when I had been content without such a thing; and when I seemed to have it, was not content with it, nor would be; it could not fill up his room.

Jan. 29.—Last night I was concerned to get my soul's case bettered; for I saw Satan was busy with me now, having this work in hand. I found great difficulty in believing my welcome to the blood of Christ, after I had been so baffled by temptation, and that so quickly after covenanting with God, and making use of that blood. Verily the way of the covenant of grace is not the way of nature. But by the tenor of the covenant; Heb. viii. 10, 12, my faith of this was raised. And this morning I found my soul sweetly composed, believing that the covenant of Tuesday last yet stands; and was inclined to put pen to paper without delay, the rather that it might be a mean of personal holiness to myself.

Feb. 3.—Accordingly that day, Tuesday the 29th of January, after prayer, and getting my heart composed to a dependence on the Lord, I began to write these sermons, and did something therein; but the temptation recurred, and was laid to me violently, till Thursday's night very late. On the Wednesday I was quite laid aside with it, deeply melancholy, and unfit for every thing. In which case, in the afternoon, I went up the brook to a solitary place, prayed, and sung Psalm cvii. 8, and downwards; and came home pretty well recovered, violently and resolutely plucking up my spirit; and though the temptation lasted, it no more got me down to that degree. On the Thursday I proceeded in writing; and in the very time I got a new assault, but resisted it and went on. At length, going on in the work, there was a new assault; which so discomposed me, that I was obliged to lay it aside, and betake myself to a study requiring less thought. Thus Satan has made a strange bustle against this work; and though my misbehaviour under it is a matter of mourning, yet considering the issue of it, in its effect on my heart, I cannot think on the dispensation, but my soul blesses God therein. The effect was very necessary to fit me for the work in hand; and indeed, so far as I remember, I never felt it so easy to keep up.

This morning my heart began to swell with vanity; but God corrected it, by his leaving me in confusion there where I thought I was best buckled. O the deceit of my heart! O the goodness of God that has so quickly checked my folly! Praises to him for it.

This day eight days before day, I was sent for to see a certain young man thought to be a-dying. He confidently gave out, that he was just a-dying; that when he was in Edinburgh last, he thought he would never see it more, and so had been preparing for death. He was confident of his eternal welfare; and spoke so much, that I could scarcely get a sentence spoken to an end; and he disturbed me mightily in prayer with his speaking. I thought it looked not very like the work of the Spirit, and therefore set myself to try his evidences; and though he was not ready to produce them, yet when he did, I could not but acknowledge what he said to be good evidence; for indeed he is a knowing and religious young man. In all that flood of words, there was not one word to the commendation of the ordinances, though it would have been most seasonable from a dying man, especially in regard of the deserters that were there. When I spoke something of the Lord's feeding his people in ordinances, he spoke nothing to the commendation of the word, (though he was wont most diligently to attend); but said only, It was only the Spirit that could make it do good either to the preachers or hearers. And I durst not put the question to him, concerning his own entertainment in the ordinances, because of the deserters that were about. This was very heavy to me. I judge there was something of vapours in the case. From that time he recovered, being quickly better after I saw him. Another case I had of the same nature in a young woman a little after I came to this parish, who was very confident of her state, and that with a sort of rejoicing; though upon further acquaintance after, I could not discern any thing that might be a foundation for such great things. I desire not to be peremptory in particular cases; but I see the need ministers have not to be too credulous, but to try.

Feb. 5.—This day I plainly saw the temptation aforesaid confirming my call to this work, when I considered how quickly Satan flew in the face of it, and how by the same means God had been fitting me for it, clearing, as it were, the ground to lay the foundation.

Feb. 26.—This day I found I had unfitted myself for my work; and it pleased the Lord to withdraw from me in it until I was humbled, and then his help returned. And my soul blesseth him that thus corrects me while about that work.

March 9.—I find my work very difficult, being hitherto little else but a new study; only the Lord liberally recompenseth my toils, so that I am well satisfied with the product of the blessing of God on my pains. I am appointed to go to the general assembly, and that against my will, in regard of the work that is on my hand; but am satisfied in the providence of God, which has a secret design, which, I hope, I will see.

March 12.—On the 10th instant I was very much discouraged as to that work, finding the authentic copy so bare and empty, that I could not but attribute it to a special providence, that the ministers who read them could ever have advised to revise them. I spent this morning in prayer, especially for direction and assistance in that work, and was helped to lay it over on the Lord.

Yesterday being in distress about the weaning of the child, I went to God with that matter ; and coming down stairs presently after, I found the difficulty by the good providence of God removed, by the recovery of the nurse's husband, whose sickness had formed that difficulty.

April 23.—Last week our synod met. I have been busy about these sermons since I began that work, and before the synod had eleven sheets prepared. My health has to my wonder been preserved ; save that in March, by bleeding and purging, (which continued near ten days after I took the physic), I was much weakened, which obliged me for some little time to lay it aside. Having been moderator of the October synod, and being to preach before them in April, I was minded, from the sweetness I had found in the study of the holy scripture in the Hebrew original, to have taken for my text, Ezra vii. 10, " For Ezra had prepared his heart to seek the law of the Lord, and to do it, and to teach in Israel statutes and judgments;" and this in order to stir up my brethren to a due value for the study of the holy scriptures, especially in the originals, and to holiness and tenderness of life, &c. But the lamentable alteration in the state of public affairs and state of the church, brought in about this time by the act imposing the oath of abjuration on ministers, by which I saw the ruin of this church contrived, obliged me to lay aside that design, and suit my synod-sermon to what I judged such a critical juncture required. And so I was determined to Matth. xxviii. ult. " Lo, I am with you to the end of the world." The sermon is *in retentis.* I spent some time in secret for preparation ere I entered upon it. It came to my hand pretty well. On the Saturday before I went to the synod, being to preach at Galashiels, then vacant, my family was in great distress; my wife miscarried, Thomas was very sick, John was to go to Selkirk with me, none of the other two were well ; so that I was in a great strait to leave them that day : but the Lord helped, and melted my soul in confidence in himself ere I went off. But being indisposed in body and spirit too on the morrow, I had scarcely ever a more heavy Sabbath. On Monday night, after I came to Kelso, I had about two hours of easiness; but when I went to bed, I was so oppressed with melancholy, and fears of preaching before the synod, that I slept none at all the whole night ; but still as I closed my eyes, my heart was as it were struck through with a dart; so that it was a most miserable uneasy night. I arose about half six in the morning, and was busy till eight. Then I thought to lie down for an hour's sleep; but instead of sleeping, I grew worse ; soul, body, and spirit, all disordered: so that I thought I could preach none that day. In my distress I would needs have a certain minister sent for, that he might preach in my stead; but he absolutely refused. Wherefore I behoved to adventure; and though in delivering of the sermon I had some fear, yet, through the goodness of God, it had no bad effects on me in it; for I was solidly serious in the whole. I am ashamed of the whole of this; my natural bashfulness and diffidence have often done me much harm. Melancholy is an enemy to gifts and grace, a great friend to unbelief, as I have often found in my experience; but nothing in it touches me more than my folly and imprudence in sending for that minister; for it was too much to the dishonour of God, who has often been good to me, that some bosom-friends saw me in that case; but the other could not but be a disadvantage to the cause of God, in the weighty point of the oath, in which that person and I quickly appeared of different judgments. This day I set myself to pray and think about the oath; and it remains to be a heavy trial to me. The state of public affairs makes me afraid, that the business of the sermons be marred; which puts me now to beg of God, that he would carry on that work over the belly of the difficulties. This day also one who came to my house last summer in deep distress and melancholy, having by the blessing of God recovered, went away but somewhat dissatisfied. Since her recovery, she has been somewhat uneasy to us, and seemed very unconcerned in the distress of our family. Another certain person did not carry right. I had a very sorry account of a third. All the three were much esteemed by me for their piety. These things together made me think that I had seen an end of all perfection. And though I think they were all gracious persons, and dare not think, far less speak, harshly as to the state of any of them, considering my corrupt self; yet I think I will never admire women's religion so very much as I have done. I do judge their passions are apt to make their religion look greater than indeed it is, being naturally easy to be impressed.

May 27.—When I came home from the synod, my son Thomas was still sick; on the last of April he died; was buried May 1; and on the morrow I went to Edinburgh to the general assembly. Never was the death of a child so useless to me, being put out of order by a temptation. The prospect of evil times alleviated the case of his death; but the disorder of my own spirit wofully marred the kindly good effect it might have had. Satan watches to prevent the good of afflictions; much need is there to watch against him.

In the assembly, the lawfulness of the oath of abjuration was de-

bated *pro* and *con*, in a committe of the whole house, betwixt the
scruplers and the clear brethren. All I had thereby was, that the
principles on which the answers to the objections were founded,
seemed to me of such latitude, that by them almost any oath might
pass. The parties were (at that time, as I think) at the very point
of splitting; till Mr. William Carstairs, principal of the college of
Edinburgh, and clear for the oath, interposed and prevented the
rupture; for the which cause I did always thereafter honour him in
my heart. For all that I heard advanced to clear the difficulties
about it, I still continued a scrupler ; and therefore, a little before
I came away home, the act imposing the oath being printed, and
offered to me at the door of the assembly house, I bought it, on purpose to know exactly the penalty I was like to underlie.

Being come home, I did this day spend some time in prayer for
light from the Lord about that oath. And thereafter entering on to
read the prints I had on it, in order to form a judgment about it, I
immediately fell on the act, whereby it was first of all framed and
imposed ; and finding thereby the declared intent of the oath to be,
to preserve the act inviolable on which the security of the church of
England depends, I was surprised and astonished; and, upon that
shocking discovery, my heart was turned to loath that oath which I
had before scrupled.

From thence, what spare time I had from visiting of the parish, I
spent in considering the oath, until June 17, that our synod met
pro re nata ; I having, by advice of brethren-members of the assembly for our synod, called them together. And by the foresaid
time of their meeting, I had written my thoughts on the oath, being
reasons against it, on about two sheets of paper; the which are *in
retentis.*

There the oath was disputed throughout ; the unclear impugning,
and the clear brethren defending it. But as the declared intent of
the oath above mentioned, did not at all cast up in the reasonings of
the general assembly, which could not have missed, if it had been
then known to the scruplers ; so, as far as I could understand, it
was known to no brother of the synod, clear or unclear, before I
took the act aforesaid along with me to that their meeting. They
seemed to be struck with it, when it was cast up in the synod ; but
Mr. James Ramsay aforesaid, made an answer to it, distinguishing
between the church of England as a protestant church, and as a
church having such a government and worship ; and admitting the
intent of the oath in the first sense, but not in the second. This was
truly stumbling to me, but served to confirm me against the oath.
The conduct of providence determining me to procure the act above

said, was wondrous in my eyes. The Lord was pleased to hear my
prayers, in helping me, with some measure of freedom, to debate the
business at the synod, together with others. I was silenced, though
not satisfied, by an answer to the first argument, (namely the swearing of principles), taken from the national covenant; for on that
occasion it was much improved by those that used not before to
meddle much with it. It seemed plain to me, that the clear brethren were at a loss in the rest, and truly foundered in that of the declared intent of the oath, which a certain person proposed, having
before desired the act from me; from whence he understood I had
it. Though they seemed to be struck with it yet they gave answers
to it; which much confirmed me, when I plainly saw that some
were resolute to answer, when (it seemed to me) they hardly knew
what to answer. I had from that time a particular regard for Mr.
John Gowdie, minister at Earlston, a grave and learned man, upon
the account of his candour and ingenuity, though joined with
principles very contrary to mine; he owned, that the ministers, in
the year 1648, would not have taken that oath, according to their
principles. [And in this regard to that brother, I had been, since
that time, all along confirmed; and even in the assembly 1729, in
professor Simson's affair; the man dealing plainly and candidly,
according to his light; though in such matters, of a more public
nature, he and I were still on opposite sides of the question. He is
this year, 1730, transported to Edinburgh.] I was much comforted
and encouraged in the kind conduct of Providence about me at that
meeting. I desired still to hang about the Lord's hand for further
light in that matter; and I durst not say to any, what I would do
in the matter.

In the visiting of the parish, I was extremely discouraged. The
ministry of this church is like to die unlamented. I have no sympathy from any of my people, or next to none. All were clear against
the oath, and they were in no care that way, but that I kept honest,
and others. That was all their doubt in the matter. Nay, I found some
scrupling to take the sacrament; saying, How could they, when
against Lammas the ministers would, may be, take the oath? [N.B.
In the house of one of these scruplers, there was stolen flesh found
sometime thereafter; and her husband being disgraced, they left the
parish,]

I found myself in great danger by melancholy, and was more broken that way than ever; and unless God would help, there was no
help from any other quarter. On Saturday we spent some time in
prayer, with an eye to the state of public affairs, and the sacrament.

I had a weary morning of it, till the Lord refreshed me in some measure towards the latter end of my secret prayers.

June 29.—This day the sacrament was celebrated here. On the Friday before, being my day for study, I had as great a pressure by my cross as ever before. I was thereby confounded, and unfitted for any thing. However, I got through my studies, such as they were, on Isa. xliv. 5. On the Lord's day I obliged one to preach before me, (which is not my ordinary), that the people might get something; I being confounded and broken. Upon the whole of that work, as to myself, I thought the Lord had cast a cloud over me; and I was well satisfied, judging that God had honoured me very much before; and if he should now bury me, ere I were dead, and continue that vail over me, I was content, hoping I might creep into heaven at some back door. And the reflection on this ease of my heart, while I lay among the dust of the Lord's feet, was my feast, for that time.

Some time before the sacrament, being under conviction of guilt, I found my soul bound up, and my heart hardened; till I looked to the blood of Jesus Christ, and turned to see God in Christ; and thereupon my heart was loosed and melted.

Oct. 21—Our synod met. Being resolved not to take the oath, I took advice at Edinburgh, when I was at the commission, (to which when I was going, I was in hazard of being drowned in a hole by the highway-side, for great rains had fallen; I was pulled out by one that was with me), how to dispose of my effects, if by any means I might keep them from becoming a prey to the government; rigid execution of the law being expected by both parties, clear and un-clear. But the executing of the project was delayed till the synod. At this meeting, the brethren clear for the oath, had concerted measures for bringing such as should refuse it under an engagement not to speak against the takers of it. I was resolved to be very tender that way, and so have been all along to this day; looking on the exposing of them as a hindrance to the success of the gospel; for which cause I have suffered heavily at the hands of the people. But withal I was absolutely against binding up myself in the matter, by consenting to any act for that end; and therefore declared against it accordingly. And, on purpose to break it, I proposed, that since the clear brethren demanded that engagement of us unclear, on the one hand, they should, on the other hand, engage, that they would not join with the magistrate against us. And this broke the con-trivance to all intents and purposes; for they could neither think meet to come under such an engagement to us, nor could they have confidence to insist in their project upon their shifting it. Thus the

Lord honoured me to mar this insnaring contrivance; which gave
me ground to hope, that, notwithstanding my personal guilt and unholiness, the Lord would help me to be faithful, and some way useful in the time of trial. As I came home, I was made sweetly to
observe, what pains the Lord had been pleased then to take to reconcile me to the cross, and to sweeten it to me, in a pleasant mixture of disappointments, straits, and outgates, in the management of
my affairs; for when I came to Kelso, I found the measures before
laid down for that effect, all broken; which much perplexed me;
but on that occasion I was set on other measures thought to be more
sure. I saw myself there a friendless creature; which made me
solemnly take God for my friend, and lay my business over upon
him; and it succeeded. I had business with several persons, as I
came homeward; and they were all made favourable to me; yet still
in a vicissitude of disappointments or temptations; so that it was
all the way, as it were, one step down and another up. Having been
disappointed of meeting with a person I had business with, and that
twice successively, I was thinking, (as I rode on my way), that although such disappointments were but small things, yet being ruled
by providence, they certainly had a design; namely, to try men's
patience, and waiting on the Lord; which my soul desired to do.
In the very time these thoughts were going through my heart, the
boy that was with me asked a woman, where such a one dwelt, a
friend of that person's whom I wanted. She told him; but withal
added, that if he were seeking such a man, he was in that house, to
which she belonged. So we met. This small thing thus timed, was
big in my eyes. I came home with a heart reconciled, in some measure, to the cross of Christ.

By all parties nothing was expected, but a rigid execution of a very
severe law, laying non-compliers with it, besides other incapacities,
under an exorbitant fine of £500 sterling; which was more than all
the stipend that had ever since I was a minister come into my hand,
by that time did amount to. However, I found myself obliged to
go on in preaching the gospel at my peril, to fulfil the ministry I
had received of the Lord. Herein I was confirmed and encouraged,
by a declared resolution to that purpose, of a meeting of several
brethren at Edinburgh, in the time, I think, of the commission in
August. These straitening circumstances obliged me to denude myself of all my worldly goods; that they might not fall into the
hands of the government, when I should fall under the lash of the
law. For this cause I disponed my tenement in Dunse in favour of
my eldest son, and expeded that matter; so that it being sold several years after, he was obliged, being major, to sign the papers.

I also made an assignation of my other goods and gear to John Currie, who came with me my servant to this country, and was then, I think, my precentor. [This paper I destroyed, only the last winter, 1729.] In these things the due forms of law were observed, not without trouble and expense.

Meanwhile, during all this reeling and confusion, I had no encouragement or sympathy, or next to none, as formerly observed, from the parish; which was a great load above my burden. They seemed only to wait to see what proof of honesty would be given, or contrariwise. And their woful jealousy, and their looking so lightly on the matter, was a mighty discouragement to me. However, had they been as much for, as they were against, the oath, I durst never have, whatever had been the hazard, taken it, according to any light in which it did ever appear to me unto this day. But the truth is, the extreme hardship I was under from them, did much alleviate the prospect of the goverment's forcing me away from them, even to confinement and banishment, and this for several years after, wherein there was some appearance of these things. But now, for several years, expectation of relief that way hath been blocked up; and the Lord has seen meet to take trial of me in another, more private way.

On Oct. 26, I preachèd my last sermon, which, as matters then stood in law, I could preach under the protection of the government. My text fell, in my ordinary, to be Phil. iii. 8, " My Lord, for whom I have suffered the loss of all things." And in my notes on that text, are to be found a few things, which, in the close of that day's work, I said on that trying occasion.

Tuesday the 28th, being the last day, according to the law, for taking of the oath, I spent some part of it in secret with the Lord, endeavouring to renew my repentance, and my covenant with the Lord. I had now, since the synod or assembly, lost all heart and hand as to proceeding in the sermons designed for the press; and having finished the subjects of the states of innocence and nature, had laid the project aside. But this day the inclination to go on with that work returned with that, that now I saw I behoved to be a fool for Christ in the matter of the oath, and so I might be in the matter of these sermons too. And withal, whereas I had foreseen a peculiar difficulty as to the managing of the sermons on the state of grace, it was given me to see how to get over that difficulty, and that by casting my thoughts into a shorter and more natural method than before; which never came into my head before that day.

PERIOD X.

ON the following Sabbath, being November 2, I did, under a great
pressure, from the consideration of the severity of the law upon the
one hand, and the temper of the parish upon the other, enter again
on my work, at my peril. What I said by way of preface that day,
is also to be found in the notes aforesaid :* after which I went on
as before, proceeding on the same text in my ordinary, Phil. iii.
And I bless the Lord, who gave me counsel, not to intermit the exercise of my ministry for ever so short a time, on that trying occasion.

According to what befel me on the 28th of October, with respect
to proceeding in writing of the Fourfold State, I applied myself
closely thereunto again ; I had perfected the following part thereof, viz. the state of grace, by the 23d of December.

Proceeding in writing of the Fourfold State, I finished it on the
9th of March. On the 25th of January, gave myself unto prayer,

---

* The preface here referred to is as follows :—

"The Lord God of gods, the Lord God of gods, he knoweth, and Israel he shall
know, if it be in rebellion against the government that I appear here this day, to
preach unto you the gospel of Christ. Contempt of magistrates, and of their laws, is
no part of my religion ; but it lies upon my conscience to cleave to the laws of my
Lord and Master Jesus Christ, the only king and head of his church ; from whom I
have received the office of the ministry, by the hands of church-officers, and not by
the hand of the magistrate ; even when these laws of his are crossed and contradicted
by the laws of men ; 2 Tim. iv. 1, 2. The magistrate has the same power over ministers' persons and goods, as over other men's ; and if he abuse it, it is his sin. But
he has no power over our office ; he has no power to deprive the ministers of the
gospel of their ministerial office, nor yet of the exercise of it formally and directly.
For the kingdom of Christ is a kingdom within a kingdom ; a spiritual kingdom, distinct from and independent on the magistrate. I have now served the Lord in this
work of the ministry thirteen years ; and though he needs none of my service, and his
work might be well done without me ; yet seeing he has not discharged me, I must
say, as the servant under the law, " I love my master," and my children whom I have
begotten in the gospel, or nourished up ; and I desire not to go out, and would be
content my ear were bored through with an awl to serve him for ever. Our Lord has
given us a plain and positive allowance, " When they persecute you in one city, flee
unto another." I cannot reckon this persecution to be begun yet ; therefore I must
work the work of him that sent me while it is called to-day, not knowing how soon
the violence of our enemies may bring on the night. What I desire of you is, that
as the Israelites of old were to eat the passover, you will eat your spiritual food, in
haste, not knowing how soon your table may be drawn. Let us then go on as formerly."

with new endeavours after personal holiness. Then I went on; and, according to my natural disposition when once engaged in a work, was too eager. Rising to it long before day, on the Saturday morning thereafter, that day my body was sore weakened, my spirits exhausted, very little was done, and that little very unsatisfying. At length I was obliged to leave it, with that check, "It is vain for you to rise up early," &c., Psalm cxxvii. 2; and I resolved through grace to do so no more. And now do I bless God, for that that eagerness is removed, and it goes better with me. However, on the 9th of March the work was finished; and for the help of the Lord I had therein, I desire to be thankful. Whatever the Lord minds to do with them, I had worth my pains in the work, with respect to my own private case; for they made me many errrands to the throne of grace, and helped me to keep up a sense of religion on my spirit. Writing of heaven, I found it no easy thing to believe the greatness of that glory which is to be revealed. The copy then written in octavo, which is *in retentis,* was not the copy from which it was afterwards printed.

On Friday, April 3, about eight minutes after one in the morning, my youngest son Thomas was born; and was baptized on the 14th, by Mr. William Macghie, minister of Selkirk.

Coming in view of the sacrament this year, the impression I had of the low state of practical religion in the place, led me to a new ordinary, viz. Hos. xiv. which chapter I began May 17, and proceeding therein to the last clause of ver. 6, dwelt long on it.

I find, that about this time, having seen Cross's Taghmical Art, I was begun to have some notion of the accentuation of the Hebrew Bible, according to the principles of that author. Having been with Mr. Macghie foresaid in his closet at a time, he happened to speak of his acquaintance with Mr. Cross at London, and of his giving him a copy of his book above mentioned, which I believe I had never heard of before. I desired thereupon to see the book; and, finding it relate to the sacred Hebrew, I borrowed it from him. This behoved to be, either in the spring this year, or else in October, 1712, what time I was assisting at the sacrament there. Had I known then what was in the womb of that step of providence, I had surely marked the day of my borrowing that book, as one of the happiest days of my life.

Great was the stumbling among the people through the south and west, on the account of the abjuration-oath, taken, in the preceding year, by about two parts of three of the ministry in Scotland; and I gained but little in our parish, by my refusing it; because I would not separate from, but still kept communion with, the jurors; meet-

ing with them in presbyteries and synods. And now was beginning
the schism made by Mr. John Taylor, ministry of Wamphray, on
that account. I had been assisting to the said Mr. Taylor at the
sacrament in the year 1711; and he to me in the year 1712; as he
was also this year, June 7,* on the same occasion. On that night,
after the public work was over, finding him inclined to separation
upon the account of the oath, I earnestly argued against it from the
holy scripture; and he seemed not to be very peremptory, nor much
to set himself to answer my arguings. But immediately after this
conference on that subject; going to family worship, whereat a
great many were present, but perhaps all strangers, except my own
family; he surprised me with his discourse on Psalm xxiii. delivered
in a very homely manner, and just feeding the reeling, separating
humour among the people; the which I looked upon as a sorry piece
of service at best, and unbecoming a man of sense and consideration,
in these circumstances.

On the 12th of July, I was assisting to him again. And the
work being begun before I got thither, on the Saturday, I sat down
on the brae-side among the people; where, after sermons, I was surprised to hear him shew their resolution to declare their adherence
to the covenants, national and solemn league, for which they had
made some preparation on the fast-day; but withal leaving others to
their liberty. The people, having got the call from him for that
effect, rose up on every side of me; and by holding up their hands,
as had been agreed on, testified their adherence. I was not ap-
prised beforehand of this design; and judging it a matter requiring
due preparation, and not to be rashly entered upon, sat still, and
joined not. By all the accounts I had of it, I judged the management thereof not suitable nor proportionable to the weight of the
matter. Through the mercy of God, I found no ill effect of this
piece of my conduct, at home, which I feared.

Some time after, being called to answer for himself, before the
presbytery, in matters unquestionably scandalous, whether right or
wrong alleged against him, he did most unwisely decline them, and
separate. But I think, that, even though his separation had been
warrantable, he ought, for the honour of God, and the cause of religion, to have appeared, and purged himself of these things to their
face, in the first place. Hearing how matters were like to go betwixt him and the presbytery, I wrote to him, whom I always took
for a good man; offering my best offices and advice, if he would give
me a view of the state of his matters. The letter he received, but

---

* The action-sermon on Heb, xi. 28, was published in a volume in 1753.

made me no return; and I never saw him since that time. A great many of the parish of Eskdale-moor joined him; the which, by reason of the neighbourhood, was another fountain of trouble and uneasiness to me, giving me another class of dissenters, servants coming in from thence to our parish; though I remember none of our congregation that went off to him, but one inconstant woman, who joined with his way for a time.

At first Mr. John Hepburn, head of an old and considerable party, Mr. John Gilchrist, minister of Dunscore, and he, joining together, formed a presbytery; which lasted very short while. At length his own party broke among themselves, and many of them left him; so that this day, though he still continues his schism, his affairs and reputation are in a sorry situation.

Amongst us who assisted in those days, as aforesaid, at Wamphray, was Mr. Thomas Hoy, minister at Annan. Him also, some time after, lodging a night in my house, I was at pains to convince of the unwarrantableness of the separation on account of the oath; but prevailed not. Howbeit, some time after, I heard with indignation, his taking of the oath itself; such a propensity there is in human nature to run to extremes, and such a need of walking by a fixed principle of church-communion, established from the holy scriptures.

On August 30, continuing my ordinary; Hos. xiv. I did withal return to explain the catechism; but began at the duty which God requireth of man. And judging the discovery of the exceeding breadth of the command to be of great importance, I did insist on the ten commands very largely; so that the sermons on them ended not till August 28, 1715, two years after this. Which brings to mind an occasional encounter, before our presbytery, with Mr. John Gowdie above mentioned; who happening to tell us of his preaching catechetical doctrine, shewed, that he had cursorily gone over the ten commands, as judging that best for the case of the people; I found myself obliged to declare before them all, that I was quite of another mind; the fullest unfolding of the holy commandment being necessary to discover the need of Christ, both to saints and sinners. But I have always observed narrow thoughts of the doctrine of free grace, to be accompanied with narrow thoughts of the extent of the holy law.

About this time I set myself to consider the mass-book, and the English service-book; between which I found a surprising agreement, several particulars of which I marked on the service-book, which remains as yet among my other books. For the course of public affairs had taken such a turn, that from the year 1710 they had run straight towards the interest of the pretender; and continued so to do, till, being brought to the point of full ripeness, it pleased the Lord, suddenly and surprisingly to break the measures of the party, through the removal of Queen Anne by death, August 1, 1714; so that king George had a peaceable accession to the throne, as much unexpected, as the Queen's death at the time foresaid. Meanwhile, at this time, matters had a formidable appearance, and a terrible cloud seemed to hang over the head of the nations, hastening to break. Papists and Jesuits were flocking hither from beyond seas; and things great and small were set a-going, to prepare people for receiving what was a-hatching. Sitting at meat in time of the synod at Kelso, in the house of a presbyterian silly woman, I was surprised with, and filled with indignation at, the sight of the picture of Christ on the cross, hanging on the wall over against me. Lodging, in time of a communion, in a certain house of some distinction, I got a loam bason to wash my hands in, with the Jesuits' motto in the bottom thereof, J. H. S. And many other such arts were then used to catch the people, while the great artifices for compassing the design were going on successfully. Withal, there were mighty fears of an intended massacre.

But national fasts were very rare, as they have been all along since the Union unto this day. Wherefore on February 17, 1714, we kept a congregational fast, upon the account of the aspect of affairs at that time, more particularly declared in our session's act thereanent, of the date Feb. 14, 1714. I preached that day on Psalm lxxiv. 19, " O deliver not the soul of thy turtle dove unto the multitude of the wicked." Which sermon agreeable to the state of that time, being *in retentis*, may be consulted.*

On the Sabbath immediately following, I entered, in my catechetical ordinary, on the second command; upon which I did for some time set myself to discover the evil of Popery, and of the English service. With respect to the former, I explained to the people the national covenant at large, judging the case of the time a sufficient call thereto. The latter I insisted on as particularly, and as much as I thought to be for edification, from the pulpit; yet not so much as I fain would have done; which was the occasion of the blank left in that part of my notes on the commands; the which, it seems, I had some thoughts of filling up afterwards, for my own satisfaction; which yet was never done.†

* This sermon was published in the author's Body of Divinity, vol. II. by way of a note on the second command; and was also printed separately, with an addition of part of another sermon, on account of the great increase of Popery in Scotland.

† See the author's Body of Divinity, vol. II. p. 512, 3, 4, notes.

The aforesaid copy of the Fourfold State having been revised by several ministers, I went in the summer to Edinburgh, with my dear friend Dr. Trotter, on purpose to speak with a printer on that head. And while I was there, I was free, willing, and resolved to venture it into the world. But a friend there, at that time a student, now a minister, advised to delay it upon the ground of the fear of the pretender's coming in. This being so feasible, I could not in modesty refuse the advice; but after that, my courage in the case abated and sunk.

Aug. 24.—This day the sacrament was administered. There were 103 tokens given out to parishioners, whereof 23 to new communicants; and there were never so many communicants of this parish before. The work was begun on Thursday with a sermon on Amos vi. 1, which I believe drew the stool from under most of us; surely it did so to me. On the Saturday and Sabbath morning, the weather looked gloomy; but I had a most quiet resigned frame of spirit, with respect to it, leaving it on the Lord without anxiety. And it was a grey day, with some pleasant blinks. A little ere I went out, I was stung with the conscience of my neglect of self-examination, though I had solemnly done it on the Monday before, being our family fast-day for this occasion. I had attempted it on Saturday's night, but was carried off. Let this be a lesson to me. In this case I took a short review of myself, as the time would allow; but that neglect stuck with me. I preached on Hos. ii. 19, which I had entered on July 11. The rest of the ministers were well helped. I was not straitened for words in that sermon, and had some solid seriousness as to the success of it; yet I thought the Lord cast a cloud over me, and that the people seemed unconcerned. So, in the midst of it I knew not what to do, fearing the people's weariness. I looked about, wishing in my heart that some body would tell me whether to leave it or not; yet I went on to the second general head, being loath to leave it altogether, and passed only a twelfth part of the sermon; which was delivered after the action with more satisfaction to myself. Having consecrated the elements, and said, that they were no more to be looked on as common bread and wine, but as symbols of the body and blood of Christ; immediately I felt a great change on my spirit to the better, which made me speak with an unusual concern on my soul; and my natural spirits, that were low before, were raised, so that I had a new vigour for speaking. I blundered however in delivering the bread, saying " This cup ;" but I recovered myself, though not without difficulty, having much ado to fall upon the very words of institution, " Take eat," &c. This was stinging and humbling, lest it might be an occasion of triumph to the wicked. I communicated at the fourth table, and thought I

had faith, love, &c. in exercise; and there, with myself, gave up my
wife, my children, one by one, by name, my servants, parish, &c. to
the Lord.   When I came in that day, the work being over, and began to look through what had passed, my soul was humbled in me,
and much broken; for upon the whole I thought there was never
less of God's presence with a communion-work here than that, except that recorded, p. 277.   But God seasonably opened the mouths
of some to speak, for his own praise and for my comfort; particularly Mr. O. desired me that night to thank God for the great things
he had met with; adding, (to my wife, who told me), that he was
scarcely able to contain himself, and came into the house.   And she
telling this to a gentlewoman, that person replied, There were
more so than he; and that she heard an old professor say, What's
this we meet with! that he had not seen such a thing for many years.
This is not the first time God has done great things, and hid them
from me in the time; for he is infinitely wise.   The sermon I preached on this occasion, was afterwards published, under the title of
"The Everlasting Espousals;" Providence thus quickly beginning
to move, towards bringing forth of that work foresaid, in its due
time.

On the morrow, a goodly minister and I conversing about the
work, he told me there were two expressions used by me at serving of
the table that were offensive to some.   The one was misrepresented and mistaken, being that of signing the wrong paper, which
see in the authentic MS. sermons on Hos. ii. 19, p. 26, which
some had turned to signing a compact with the devil.   But I had
not expressed it so fully as in the notes; which I should have done,
there being some there that had not heard it from me before.   The
other was misapplied, having no ground at all, but the jealousy of
the person offended.   However, these, especially the last, cast me
down very sore, who before was lying very low.   From these, and
the blunder, I got a plain lesson, to beware of mixing my own spirit
with the Lord's Spirit.   In these damps I unbosomed myself to my
friend Mr. Wilson, (for whom I bless the Lord), and he was useful
to me.   Let me learn to be humble, watchful, and dependent, while
I think it goes well with me.   I am persuaded they have great
need to take heed to their feet that are let in within the vail; for
he is a jealous God.

On the Tuesday having convoyed the minister some miles, Mr.
Colden, at parting (as before also) had so expressed what he had
felt in that (to me) overclouded sermon, that I was made to believe
the Lord had owned it.   And then my heart was opened to give him
the due thanks.   And the effects of my believing it I found to be,

1. That I was thankful; 2. It humbled me, seeing it as a great
debt upon me; 3. It kindled in my heart more desire after holiness.
So retiring, by the way I poured out my soul before God, according
to these impressions.

Wednesday. But this day the glory of that work was quite out
of my eyes again, and I could not be thankful; but was confounded
and sunk, when I looked back on it. I wondered at Mr. Colden's
speaking as he did, on Monday's night, before all the company, concerning that work and me. I thought that whatever had been my
mind of another, I could not have spoken so, before the person himself; and I have often wondered on such occasions. But now I see
how needful these things are for me, and how by them the Lord in-
dulgeth weak me, when I cannot see the thing, to be thankful for it
notwithstanding all these helps and props. One thing comforts me,
that the Saturday's work had such influence on me, that it occasioned my uttering these words to the congregation, " I would fain hope
God will do great things here to-morrow; he can do wonders with
little noise," &c.

Dec. 16.—One having a while ago desired a copy of my action-
sermon on Hos. ii. 19, that he might publish it, and he having taken
advice about it at Edinburgh, I set some time apart this day for
light from the Lord in that matter. I laboured some time in confessing of sin before the Lord, in renewing my covenant and renunciation. And two things were wondrous in my eyes. 1. The
unalterableness of the covenant. I had a sweet view of it as a covenant which after many slips might be renewed. There is no renewing of the covenant of works, once broken; but this covenant will
not break; one is welcome to renew it after backslidings. 2. That
I had this opportunity without disturbance; whereas I had attempted it twice before, and on my unwatchfulness had marred it; whereby, though something was done, as on Tuesday last, yet the business
was not carried through. Then I set myself to seek light from the
Lord in prayer, and thought on the business; and considering that
I was urged by a repeated call from that person, and that this is a
fair way to try what acceptance the book may meet with if published, I resolved to attempt it. I had a discouragement in this matter
from the same quarter from whence I had the temptation at my entering on writing the sermons aforesaid. It was comfortable to me
to think, that whatever have been the transgressions of my private
walk, God has been very gracious to me in the public steps of my
life. And so I stepped over that discouragement, which I could
not get removed.

Jan. 3, 1715.—Having finished the sermon, I took up Dempster's

Antiquities, to refresh myself, where I read something *de expositione infantum*, that seemed to give light into Ezek. xvi.; and pursuing the thing, several thoughts offered themselves, which I cast into a paper with much satisfaction, and some design to insert them into a sermon. [N.B. They are inserted in the printed sermon]. So this morning I was very easy as to the publishing of the sermon. But at night there came one whom I respect and value, and would have employed in the business; but in the holy providence of God he carried so strongly, with respect to the book, and this sermon too, that I was confounded, and quite discouraged in the design. However, I sent it to Mr. Wilson, seeing I had written it. He approved the motion of printing it; but withal told me, that the printers would hardly take such an interlined copy. Whereupon, though, by the foresaid discouragement still remaining with me, had no heart for publishing it; yet I resolved, come what will, that I would transcribe it over again.

Jan. 13.—I began to transcribe it; but on the 15th at night, while I was busy with it there came an express to me, calling me to go to Dunse, to my brother a-dying. So I laid it aside, wondering at this next dash. I took it with me, and shewed it to Mr. Brown; who did encourage me to publish it; and I think, if I had not met with him, I had not recovered that damp to the design given by the person aforesaid. So providence made use of that my being called away from the work, to forward it, which it is likely had lain if that had not come.

I went off Sabbath afternoon, Jan. 16, after sermon, and returned next Saturday's night. My sermon was studied before, and so it was (except a very little) the last time I had occasion to be so abroad. So does the Lord encourage me to study. My brother grew better, while I was there; and, for my own use, I received an instruction and warning, and a check, from the dispensation.

Jan. 26.—This day, observed to determine me to the publishing of the sermon, 1. That as I was cleared to put pen to paper, so the publishing of it encouraged by the two ministers that saw it. 2. That dispensation of providence whereby the damp was taken off, though it seemed itself to concur to the laying the design aside when I first met with it. 3. It is desired by many, and I hope it may be useful. 4. The Lord helped me in it, particularly with that on Ezek. xvi. to my own surprise. 5. There seems to be a necessity laid on me, to make this essay, that so I may at length come to a point, whether to venture the publishing of the book or not.

After the Queen's death, King George safely arriving, had a peaceable accession to the throne; for which cause there was a

thanksgiving appointed to be observed, January 22, 1715. But at
that time, I having been called to Dunse, as is above related, we
could not observe it on the day appointed. Howbeit we kept it on
the 3d of February; which day I preached on Esther ix. 1, "Now
when the king's commandment and his decree drew near to be put
in execution, in the day that the enemies of the Jews hoped to have
power over them, (though it was turned to the contrary, that the
Jews had rule over them that hated them)." This sermon is to be
found next to that of the fast-day above mentioned.

Feb. 6.—This day being the Lord's day, in the time of the first
prayer, in the pulpit, one drew my sleeve; which put me into some
disorder; quickly after, I heard a muttering about me; which
struck me with terror; so, recommending the case to God, whatever
it was, I closed the prayer. (N.B. I think, upon reflection, I should
have immediately stopped upon the first sign given, and known what
the matter was, ere I had gone further; for I could have no composure till I had done that, and that sign was a providental call,
under which I knew not what might be.) Then I was told that one
was a-dying at the park-foot, betwixt that and the water, little
more than a stone-cast from the church. The congregation being set
to sing a psalm I went out; but he was dead ere I got to him. He
was a strong old man about seventy-six years old, who having come
over the hills from Upper Dalgleish four miles a-foot, and having
taken a drink of the water, and said he had left the rest about a
quarter of a mile behind him, never spoke more, but fell down, gave
two shivers, and died between the water and the western park of
the glebe. Thus coming to the church, he came to the church-yard;
he came heartily and cleverly to his grave, instead of being borne.
Lord teach me so to count my days, as I may apply my heart to
wisdom. Reflecting on my being so lately alarmed, and obliged to
ride on the Lord's day, and this day again brought out of the pulpit,
on the occasion of death, I thought it had a language to me, fearing
the next might be a more home stroke.

Feb 10.—Having received letters desiring me to come to the presbytery, I went, contrary to my inclination; but out of conscience
towards God, lest his cause by my absence should suffer any detri-
ment, upon which account I durst not sit at home. The Lord made
it a comfortable and happy journey; for not only was the business
(the affair of Mr. J. D.) kept from going farther wrong; but the
Lord honoured me to be the instrument of peace in the presbytery,
(which had been split the day before my protestations and counter-
protestations), and brought that business to the desired issue, with
respect to the presbytery's management of it. I have often found
it good, to follow duty over the belly of inclination.

The aforementioned alarming dispensation led me, on the following Lord's day, to a new ordinary; 2 Cor. v. 1, "For we know, that
if our earthly house of this tabernacle were dissolved," &c. on which
I dwelt till May 22, that, for the sacrament, I entered on Heb. x. 22,
" Let us draw near with a true heart, in full assurance of faith," &c.
pressing the confidence of faith. On the same text was the action-
sermon, as were also some sermons after the sacrament. A godly
minister, then a nonjuror, and one of my assistants at the sacrament,
(Mr. Colden), as I was convoying him and the rest away, on the
Tuesday after; upon occasion of discourse about the action-sermon,
particularly that a pious gentleman had said it was above his capacity; moved me to write practically on the doctrine of justification;
the which I had, some years after, frequent occasion of calling to
mind; when he having taken the abjuration-oath in the year 1719,
proved thereafter a too keen party man against the doctrine of the
Marrow, and the defenders thereof. So doth one false step make
way for another.

Feb. 15.—In answer to the former calls of Providence, I spent
this day in fasting, prayer, and meditation, with respect to my leaving the world. I endeavoured to antedate my reckoning with
my judge, acknowledging my sins and applying to the Lord through
Christ's blood, for pardon. I made a comfortable review of my evidences for heaven. I neither could nor durst name what sort of
death I would desire to die; but renewed my covenant with the
Lord, with a view to eternity, leaning on that bed (my closet bed)
which perhaps may be my death-bed, taking the several quarters of
it witnesses, that I had gone in under the covert of blood, the covert
of the covenant, for death. I laid over my wife and children on the
Lord. There was one little circumstance (the recording of which
may be of some use), namely, that at night, about the latter end of
this exercise, while I was at prayer, a dead-bell tinkled down stairs,
the hearing of which surprising sound made some impression on me.
It was gifted by Sir William Scott to the parish, and at that time it
was, though not expected so soon, brought home by John Currie, who
had been at Edinburgh, about the printing of the sermon, and brought
home a specimen of it. In the remaining part of that week, I set
in order my worldly affairs, by a will written with my own
hand. And this, I think, was the first time I made my testament;
the which I always after kept by me, but several times renewed,
destroying the preceding one. And I reckon it was about this time
that my contract with my wife was destroyed, with consent; the
settlement being made more to her advantage.

On the 10th of March, John Currie being at Edinburgh to bring

out the copies of the sermon, I met at Selkirk with him who had
the oversight of the press; who surprised me with the news that
the press was stopped, one of this parish having brought word to
him for that effect, as from me or the publisher; which was a groundless mistake. This occasioned me thoughts of heart; the rather that
the sacrament being to be celebrated at Edinburgh at that time,
many there were desirous, on that occasion, to have had it; and it
was thought this had marred the going off of many upon that occasion, some hundreds, as he expressed it. But on second thoughts
I was satisfied in the favourable conduct of providence; for had
they come forth at such a nick for sale, I could not have judged of
the acceptance of the book by that means. On the 26th I received
a copy; but withal saw another fair occasion for the sale of them
lost, though I had endeavoured to secure it. I could perceive no
reason for it, but that so providence saw it meet, and I believe for
the same reason foresaid. And one delay of bringing the copies
out, came one week after another, till John Currie going in at length
to bring them, there were few left to be brought out. It is the
usual way of providence with me, that matters of moment come
through several iron gates. I could not but observe, that, by holy
providence unknown to me, at what time the press was stopped, I
had no freedom in prayer about it, but several times forgot it, and
wondered how I had forgot it. But when the work went on it was
not so. The publication of that sermon was my first-fruits in that
kind. I had a comfortable account of its acceptance.

April 15.—I received a letter from Mr. Wilson, shewing me, that
two persons had written to him from Edinburgh about the sermon,
(though he had written to none there about it); the one desiring
to deal with me for more, which it is heard are ready by me, and
assuring of the esteem of the godly and judicious. The other's
letter he sent to me, bearing that it had there a very welcome reception from all having any sense of religion.—" Seasonably," says
the author of the letter, " it came to my hand,—at a time when I
was under much deadness and hiding of the Lord's face; I was walking in darkness, and saw no light; yet by a secret power was kept
from drawing rash conclusions while I was reading it. I can com-
pare it to nothing more fitly than a cordial to a fainting spirit
or a ray of light shining in a dungeon. The surprising turn which
it gave to my sunk spirit, is beyond what I can express. The
heavenly eloquence and divine rhetoric which was in it, brought
some transactions to my remembrance, which had been for some
time out of sight, and I made a new Amen to the marriage-covenant."—This melted my soul in thankfulness and admiration

of the goodness of God to vile me, and sent me to my knees immediately with these impressions. It also filled me with courage; and
now I was well content to lie down and receive my lashes from
other hands; for now I had a pleasant view, how God would be
beforehand with me, laying in that timely to prepare me for other
sort of entertainment. And indeed I am well hired to abide all.

May 14.—Saturday. I spent a part of this day in humiliation,
renewing my covenant with God, and prayer for the Lord's presence
in the work of the sacrament of the supper to be celebrated here, last
Sabbath of this month. The Lord was pleased to help me to confidence, believing in God as my God.

May 19.—Since Saturday last, I have had most sensible experience of the solid joy and peace, in believing God to be my God in
Christ. I find it is a blessed means of sanctification. It strengthens
to duty; for I have been helped in my work of visiting since
that time. It nourishes love to the Lord; and consequently love
to and desire of the thriving of this work in people's souls. It
creates a sweet calm, and quiet of mind, in doubtful events; for I
have been tried, and yet am with a prospect of the Lord's keeping
back the one half of my helpers in the work before me; but I have
no anxiety that way. It sweetens other enjoyments, and carries
above things which at other times are irritating, and create disgust.
I have compared flashes of affection, with a calm sedate tender love
to the Lord; and I prefer the latter to the former, and have been,
and am, happy in it.

May 27, Friday. In the time foresaid, I thought I would meet
with a trial. It came just on the morrow, being my study day. The
text I had in view for the Sabbath was that, "This cup is the new
testament in my blood." And I had a great desire to be at it, that
my soul might dip into the sweetness of it. But though in this case
I set about it, God bound me up, it would not do with me. I could
neither go forward in it, nor come off from it. Thus I spent that
weary day, praying, thinking, striving to keep up my confidence
that the Lord would help. My confidence in the Lord was tried
now; and though I got it kept up better than ordinary in
such a case, for some time; yet at length it was brought to a
low ebb, and almost exhausted. In this weary time I got a seasonable letter from my friend, shewing my helpers were secured
for me. So the Lord lightened my burden, while my strength
was less, and also gave some new discovery that it is not in vain
to trust him. About eight o'clock at night, another text was
given me, namely, Heb. x. 22, "Let us draw near with a true
heart, in full assurance of faith," &c. And then my heart was taken off the former. I was well guided to this, as pursuant to what

I had been upon, since the man's sudden death at the park-foot; 2 Cor. v. 1, "We know that," &c.; and agreeable to what the Lord had been secretly teaching me, by experience, before. I studied the sermon on it to-morrow, which I preached on the Lord's day. On the Monday we kept the family-fast. I had not recovered my former frame; but, in reference to our prayers, was helped to believe that word; Matth. vii. 7, "Ask, and it shall be given you," &c. I drove heavily in studying the communion sermon. This day I had a sweet while in confidence on the Lord as my God, grasping the promise over the belly of felt foolishness.

Wednesday, June 1.—On the 29th of May the sacrament was celebrated here. All the three days there was some rain; but on the Lord's day it was exceeding great, and greatest of all in the time of the tables; only it was fair weather in the time of the first two. Yet the Lord made it a great day of the gospel; assisted his ministers, and the people generally, to very much composure, though several went away for fear of the rising of the waters. It was somewhat discouraging to me, in respect of the disturbance it might create to the people; but I was helped to submit to it as a trial to them and me. I cried to the Lord in the morning prayer, to preserve the people from bodily hurt; for there was a great wind with the rain; and I have not yet heard of any that was the worse of it; but some whom we suspected might be the worse, particularly a woman that had lately been ill of the flux, were well carried through safe. Being warned by experience formerly, I was helped to hold off from two rocks I split upon at the last sacrament. One was concerning self-examination; whatever was done in it on the Monday, being the family fast-day, I set about it on the Saturday's night, got a humbling view of sin, and a satisfying view of the grace of God in me. The other was the mixing of my own spirit with influences from heaven. The danger from this quarter had been frightful to me, and in secret I had been remarkably carried out in prayer against it, and for a solid frame of spirit, and a feeling of what I was to speak. And indeed the Lord heard me, preserving me from that unhallowed mixture in the sermon, in some measure, and giving an unusual measure of solid, serious feeling, in the rest of the work, especially the invitation, (where influences begin to rise higher), the prayer for consecration of the elements, and the discourse at the table. In the sermon I had not the desired feeling. The elements after consecration being declared to be no more common bread and wine, but sacred symbols of the body and blood of Christ, I felt in my spirit a sensible change accordingly; I discerned the sacramental union of the signs and the thing signified, and was thereby

let into a view of the mystical union. I saw it, I believed it, and I
do believe it this day. I do not remember myself ever to have been
so distinct in the view and faith of this glorious mystery; and that
with application, for I do believe that Christ dwells in me by his
Spirit, and I in him by faith. And the objection, How can this be?
is silenced. I feel the sacrament of the supper to be a divine ordinance; I see it, and believe it. This is the second time I have
most remarkably felt that change on my spirit, upon the declaring
as above said. May I never miss to declare, as said is, in the administration of that ordinance. In partaking I was helped to the
exercise of faith, took God for my God in Christ, claimed him as
my God, and laboured to improve the claimed interest, by believing
the promises of the covenant, which was the scope of the action-
sermon. My wife with the child in her belly, and the other children by name, I gave away to the Lord with myself. And having
been in fear about my wife's death in the bringing forth of that
child, I had there, in that solemn approach, a concern on my spirit
about that case; but could not see it dangerous, whatever it may
turn to after. This made me to hope, that a stolen dint (with profoundest reverence be it spoken) would not be taken of me. But
yesterday, praying in these terms, in that case, that the Lord would
not take a stolen dint, I durst not abide by that petition; thinking
with myself, what if God keep the tormenting impressions of her
death from off my spirit, is that unkind? So I knew not what to
make of that petition, but left it to the Lord, to do as he saw best.
My wife parted with the ministers the same day as never to see
them more. At parting with Mr. Colden, he desired there might be
no discouragement in her case. I told him I could not see the danger; and he told me, it was so with him too, with respect to that
case. The sermon was more than two hours' long, which I think
was too much. A certain gentleman said, it was above his capacity; upon which a minister (Mr. Colden) observing the need professors have to be better informed in the doctrine of the gospel,
moved, that I should write practically on the doctrine of justification;
which inclined me somewhat to publish the sermons on Phil. iii. 3.
A godly countryman told me, that he had not so much of that sermon to carry away as ordinary. I resolved to be shorter; and
learned from these things, that however my gift seems to be plain, I
have need of dependence on the Lord, even for plainness in treating
of gospel-mysteries. Satan was at my heels ere that work was over.
Being surprised to hear singing of psalms in the kirk, and stunned
to see the people running away into it, leaving the solemn work we
were at; so that the rump of the meeting seemed only to remain,

being in the south-west side of the church-yard; having sent one, and after that another, to stop that disorder; and it continuing still; I went and put a stop to it, with a sharpness, which no doubt irritated the brother who was the cause of it. So we became snares to one another. And so quickly did my spirit go without bounds. I knew God was not the author of this confusion; but the way of my spirit in removing it was, and is, humbling upon reflection. It hung about me most heavily, till the whole day's work being over, I had occasion to shew him the sorrow of my heart, that Satan should so soon have got advantage against us, and to entreat him to join with me in withstanding the progress of this flame that the tempter had kindled; and hereunto the good man shewed all readiness. I have sometimes observed the Lord's being very gracious to me in matters of public management; but the keenness of my spirit, at the last synod, in the case of Mr. J. D. aforesaid, (though I dare not overlook the sensible help I had of the Lord in the management of that matter there; a matter nearly touching my conscience, and the welfare of many souls, which I know was the cause of God; in pleading of which, I was carried over all the impediments ordinarily arising from my weakness and natural temper; but when I saw a combination to run down the cause, my zeal, mixed with some fire from my own hearth, in the further management of it; my keenness of spirit, I say, in that matter,) and in this, shews me, that my natural modesty and diffidence is not a sufficient guard to my spirit, in public appearances, though they be very few. To thee, then, O Lord, I will look for it. That day's work was concluded with a most savoury sermon, by that brother, though he was out of humour when called to it. So the Lord can outshoot the devil in his own bow. When I was about to make this review, I found my spirit out of order; and finding the disorder of my natural spirits contribute thereto, I went out, and walked, to refresh myself; then returned, and set to the work. It is heard to play, when the instrument is not in tune.

The week before the sacrament Satan stirred up the spirits of some neighbours against the work and me, apprehending there would be a great gathering, whereby their corn would suffer. And one of my few elders (from whom I have little help,) was at least a silent witness to the rage and spite. But the cloven foot was too visible, to discourage much. In a little time after the sacrament, the same person acted with the same spirit of spite against me in another case. However, there was no complaint of the corn; whence I may know there was no ground, though indeed the company was great. At this time there were ten tables, though we used to have but about seven ; and the tables were longer than ordinary, and people came from a far distance.

Having been taken with the design of Cross's Taghmical Art aforementioned, I would fain have understood it ; but could never reach it to my satisfaction. The nature of the subject treated of, the indistinct way of the author's writing, and the false printing of the book, which was to a pitch, made the difficulty insuperable to me. What pains I was at before and about this time, to understand that book, and to gather the author's meaning, by comparing passages, may be seen in an octavo paper-book, whereof forty-four pages were written for that end, consisting mostly of excerpts, and partly of my own reasonings and conjectures thereon. but all to very little purpose ; so that at length I laid the matter aside.

But the kind reception the "Everlasting Espousals" met with, whereof 1200 copies being printed, were mostly dispatched by the end of May, recovered my courage for publishing the "Fourfold State," which had sunk as aforesaid, And after some time spent in prayer about it and my wife's case, on June 16, I began on that view to transcribe it over again. The acceptance of the sermon appeared in the gathering aforesaid ; and that very thing apprehended was the rise of all that rage above mentioned. I had encouraging testimonies about it, from the feeling of some godly ministers.

June 7.—This day the affair of Mr. J. D. aforesaid, which lay weighty on my spirit, had a happy issue, in a committee of the synod. And I having laid it over on the Lord before I went into the church, my heart was filled with thankfulness in the issue. My spirit also in the management of the matter, so far as I was concerned, was kept from what I was afraid of. It was good to keep the way of duty ; for though we were generally ill looked on by others in that matter, the Lord brought forth our righteousness as the noon-day ; and there was not a man had a mouth to open in the cause that we were set against, ere all was done. I desire from this to learn to act faith in such matters, and with confidence in the promises to recommend them to the great Master of the vineyard.

July 8.—This day Mrs. Martin, spouse to Bailie Martin in Hawick, tenant in Crosslee, was buried. She came to this parish at Whitsunday, was present at the fast before the sacrament, but that night was seized with indisposition, which so increased that she had no access to be witness to more of that work. I saw her on the Tuesday after, much broken with that dispensation ; for she was a godly woman, and minded to have partaken. Her case grew worse till she sickened unto death, having a bloody flux ; in the time of which she miscarried; and the flux continuing on the tenth day from the birth of the child in the seventh month, she died. In the time of her sickness, on many accounts, her case lay very near my heart, and I was full of hopes that the Lord had not sent the good woman to die here. Her coming hither was by several in this parish looked on with an evil eye, according to their uncharitable, selfish disposition, &c. So that foolish I thought the honour of God was almost engaged for her life. And her death was an astonishing dispensation to me, calling to eye sovereignty, which challengeth a latitude. Besides, my hopes in her case miscarrying, quite perplexed my hopes as to the case of my own wife. I had been preaching on contentment for some Sabbaths; and Sabbath the 17th of this month, being our marriage-day, and her reckoning out on the 15th, that 17th day was of a terrible prospect to me. Wherefore yesterday I gave myself unto prayer, to entreat the Lord for her, and to provide for the worst; and came away with that, namely, That God will do the best.

On Saturday, July 9, my wife had some pains, and also on the Sabbath morning; at which time I had thoughts of sending for the midwife. I went to prayer, which produced some reluctancy to it; and thereafter my wife shewing her unwillingness, I easily yielded, being the Lord's day. Afterwards in prayer my heart was fully calmed in that matter, that all would be well for that time. And so it was. But next morning betwixt twelve and one I sent off the lad for the midwife, who was at the distance of about eighteen miles.

July 27.—On Friday the 15th of that month, my wife was delivered of a daughter, about one after noon, our last child, called Katharine; who, on the the 20th, was baptized by my friend Mr. Wilson. The day before, I studied my sermons for the Lord's day, and giving some directions against discontent, some things came so pat to my feared case, that I was astonished somewhat with it. I was brought in that matter to a resignation unto the will of God; and having been helped, by the sermons on contentment, to believe that all that God does is best done, (which I bless God has now, for a considerable time, been much on my spirit,) I often left it on the Lord in these terms, that he would do the best, without determining one way or other. And behold he has heard my prayer, and hitherto wrought the deliverance very graciously. I see the way of trusting in God at all times, with positive resolutions, not to distrust him, whatever he will do with us, (which was much the language of my heart, and lips too, at that time), is the true way to rest, in the time of doubtful events, and also to get one's will. I myself have been several times, on this occasion, taking a view of death; and I have found, that faith in God through Christ makes another world not quite strange. I have seen so much of late, how God baffles hopes and fears that my spirit seems disposed to leave all to the Lord; *et nec sperare nec extimescere, sic exarmaveris;* —neither to fear nor hope, but according to God's promises and threatenings.

Being invited to assist at the sacrament in Morbattle and Maxton, the one immediately after the other, which appeared inconvenient for me; the which Mr. Wilson considered; but I wrote to him, that I was content the Lord should lead, and I follow; and therefore that he should not incommode the work for me. And I saw in end that he guided better than I could, if I had had my will. So I went from home, August 5, and returned not till August 18. When I was going away, and to leave my wife lately delivered, and my family, I was helped to apply the promise made to the Israelites going up to the solemn feasts, with respect to the safety of their families left behind; and it stuck with me while I was abroad. And indeed it was accomplished to me far beyond my expectation: being, upon my return, quite surprised with the case of my wife's health, which had advanced to the degree I could not have looked for; there being something preternatural in her case when I left her, which I judged could not miss to weaken her exceedingly; but the event was quite otherwise. That day I rode to Morbattle, I met with a man providentially, and the water being great beyond expectation, I got a fright by it, as it was; but had I been alone, the event might have been dangerous. I preached at Morbattle on Saturday the 6th, and Sabbath the 7th of August, from Rev. xxi. 22, "And I saw no temple there." On the Monday two of the elders there desired a copy of the sermons transcribed, insinuating their design to print them; which I took to consideration. On Wednesday thereafter I preached in Oxnam parish; on the Thursday, Saturday, and Lord's day afternoon, at Maxton; on the two last days from the text just mentioned; Rev. xxi. 22; and for some time had thoughts of preparing the whole for the press.* I hope the Lord owned all these sermons, but that on the Saturday at Maxton seemed to me most countenanced of God. For my private case, I had not guided well at Morbattle. So on the Thursday thereafter, in Mr. Wilson's prayer and confession, I got a broad view of the corruption of my nature; which afterwards in secret proceeded to that, that I thought

* These four sermons were transcribed from the author's original copy, he not having transcribed them himself, and were published in a pamphlet, with two others, in 1772.

it needless (so to speak) to confess particulars, being ready to cry, Guilty, to whatsoever the broad law of God forbiddeth. But after that, my running issue (as Mr. Wilson termed it in his action-sermon) broke out, so that on Lord's day morning at Muirhouselaw I was in a dreadful case, in the fields there. At which time, in the great bitterness of my spirit, that word came; 1 Cor. vi. 9—11, "Know ye not that the unrighteous shall not inherit the kingdom of God? Be not deceived; neither fornicators, nor idolaters, nor adulterers, nor effeminate, nor abusers of themselves with mankind, nor thieves, nor covetous, nor drunkards, nor revilers, nor extortioners, shall inherit the kingdom of God. And such were some of you; but ye are washed, but ye are sanctified, but ye are justified in the name of the Lord Jesus, and by the Spirit of our God." I walked up and down with the Bible in my hand opened at that place, holding it towards heaven, as God's own word, pleading and improving it, for the cleansing of my vilest soul. O how seasonable a support was it to my fainting soul! Mr. Wilson's great sermon of the good news brought in the gospel, from Luke ii. 10, was as balm to a wounded soul, and good news from a far country. And there I put all in Christ's hand.

While I was abroad, the news of the invasion came, and a bond of association contrived by some honest people at Edinburgh, to resist with armed force, came to my hand for our parish, and the whole country was astir that way. But on the Monday morning, August 15, an express came to me, calling me to Dunse, to my brother's burial; and on the morrow there I found, that the proceeding in that association was stopped from court, the invasion being found to be laid aside for the time. Here I saw the favourable conduct of Providence, in carrying and keeping me so long abroad; for I had good ground to think, that our parish would have given the association but very cold entertainment; not from any other cause but their selfish principle and disposition. As to the invasion, I was afraid of myself, for that I could not be afraid of it.

At these two communions I preached, as I have already said, on Rev. xxi. 22, a text that for many years I had in view. When I began it, I expected little of it but a sermon for Sabbath afternoon. But all that about the preciousness of the ordinances came forth to me in the breaking.

Now the oath of abjuration was in hand again, being to be imposed with some alterations, which I saw. Being much hurried with business after I came home, but getting one free day, I set myself to seek the Lord in that matter, and took it again under consideration. The result of all which was, that it seemed to me like the

s 2

house with the leprosy in the walls, under the law, that nothing could cleanse but the pulling down of the walls. So a meeting of nonjurors being appointed at M. August 30, I went thither, purely out of conscience towards God, to discharge my conscience in that matter. And Providence opened my way to it through iron gates; for when I took my horse, I knew not what I was to do, to go, or come back; but the Lord cleared my way.

About the latter end of August, the rebellion having broke out, the King's army began to draw towards Stirling. On the 28th I closed my sermons on the ten commandments in the forenoon, which were begun about two years before, and which I often feared, through the difficulty of the times, I should not have had occasion to finish. I bless God who led me to that subject, where I met with things, which otherwise, through the course of many years' preaching, would hardly have come in the way. It gives great ease to my heart upon reflection. In the afternoon, for the case of the times, I entered on that text; Isa. xxxii. 2, "And a man shall be—as the shadow of a great rock in a weary land." Next Sabbath, being September 4, in my sermon, I took occasion, not only to shew the people their danger, but to excite them to a due concern for religion and liberty, and to be ready to act in defence thereof. But not very long after, I found that all was but as the sounding again of the mountains, the lying stories of enemies so prevailing, that the reflection of some that seemed to be somewhat was, that I was more afraid than I needed. Finding the heart-staying doctrine of that text was unseasonable, because not needed, (I mean not to make no exception at all, I believe it was seasonable to some, though very very few), I was obliged to cut it short; and on Sabbath, September 25, entered on Amos iv. 12, "Therefore thus will I do unto thee, O Israel; and because I will do this unto thee, prepare to meet thy God, O Israel." And upon this I dwelt for several months of the public confusions. Sabbath, October 2, in the morning, I received a a letter from one of the lieutenant-deputes for our shire, with an intimation for all betwixt sixteen and sixty to rendezvous at Selkirk on the 6th, and desiring me to send the roll of these to the review. I called for one reckoned the most judicious of our elders, and proposed to him a meeting of the parish at the kirk on the 4th; which he quickly agreed to. I desired him to speak with some others, and give me notice ere I went into the pulpit, if it was their mind that the parish should meet, that I might warn them from the pulpit. The intimation being read by the precentor, I exhorted accordingly; and having received notice as above said, I intimated the meeting. When they met on the 4th, I told them, I would not take it on me to make a roll of the fencible men, but proposed to them to make it themselves. Accordingly it was done, and I gave them my roll; out of which they made another, casting out and putting in as the meeting thought fit; but I wrote it. When this work began, I foreboded my ease in this place (which never was great) to be at an end; they usually wreaking themselves on the ministers as the cause of all public evils. I was not out in my conjectures; for accordingly they gave themselves the loose, and that very night I heard of burning my house, &c., upon the account of that day's work. However, on the morrow I drew up an address for them, and went towards Selkirk, the place of the review, to help them all I could. Next day, within two miles of the place, several of the parish being in company the elder aforesaid, who also was present at the making of the roll, fell on me bitterly in that matter. And there was not a man that had a mouth to open in my behalf, in all the company, except one servant, who (as he told me) spoke to him secretly; but another told me, he heard me reflected on upon that score. I saw myself hardly bestead, and evil rewarded for good; and therefore desired them to meet me in the town, further to consider of the matter. There while I was sitting with them, in great distress, not knowing what to do, and not having as yet entered on the business, I was called to speak with one in another room; with whom conversing, being a brother of the presbytery, I found the review of his parish had been made without a roll. Thus Providence most seasonably discovered a way to extricate me out of this perplexity; and calling for the roll from the clerk, I secretly burnt it, shewing them I would rather undergo censure from others, than fill their hearts with prejudice against me, to whom I must preach next Lord's day: and giving them the address, I left them, and went to the presbytery, which (unknown to me before) met that day; for I had no other design in the town that day, but to see their business managed equitably. The issue was, all the rest of the parishes called thither that day were reviewed, and the rolls produced; ours was called; but none were in the town when called, except a few, none of whom answered.

The southern army of rebels being a-forming, several went through our parish in their way to the appointed place. On Saturday, Oct. 8, their general, with seven or eight with him, lodged at C——m and C——e, and the standard with them, which fell as they were riding by T. barn-yard. On the Monday's night lodged the Earl of Winton at M——p, and about as many with him. On the Tuesday, while I was at T. I saw seventeen pass by. The water being exceeding great, I was in fear they would lodge about the kirk all night.

So being in concern for my family, I made after them ; but being
come to R. I saw them on the other side, and was thankful.   On the
Thursday we were alarmed with their new army's being at Moffat ;
and at night a brother whom they had taken prisoner by the way,
but dismissed again, came to my house, and told us, they were on
their way to Dumfries. Which made us fear blood there that night,
the country about having gone into the town to resist them.   The
rebels not daring to attack them, turned eastward.   But all this did
not awaken us.

The highlanders having landed at North Berwick the latter end of
this week, an intimation was made on Sabbath, the 16th, by the
lieutenant-depute's orders, intreating all to meet at Kelso, with
their best arms, on the morrow, to receive orders, so as the country
might be defended.   And I had a letter from one of them, to come
on the head of our parish, to the place where our shire was to meet,
that they might go together to Kelso, being I was to go to the
synod, which met on Tuesday the 18th.   I exhorted the people, and
read to them Prov. xxiv. 11, 12. "If thou forbear to deliver them
that are drawn unto death, and those that are ready to be slain ; if
thou sayest, Behold, we knew it not ; doth not he that pondereth
the heart consider it ? and he that keepeth thy soul, doth not he
know it ? and shall not he render to every man according to his
works ?" Judges v. 14—23, "Out of Ephraim was there a root of
them against Amalek ; after thee, Benjamin, among thy people : out
of Machir came down governors, and out of Zebulun they that
handle the pen of the writer.   And the princes of Issachar were
with Deborah ; even Issachar, and also Barak, he was sent on foot
into the valley ; for the divisions of Reuben there were great thoughts
of heart.   Why abodest thou among the sheep-folds, to hear the
bleatings of the flocks ? for the divisions of Reuben there were
great searchings of heart.   Gilead abode beyond Jordan ; and why
did Dan remain in ships ? Asher continued on the sea-shore, and
abode in his breaches.   Zebulun and Naphtali were a people that
jeoparded their lives unto death, in the high places of the field.   The
kings came and fought, then fought the kings of Canaan in Tanaach
by the waters of Megiddo, they took no gain of money.   They fought
from heaven, the stars in their courses fought against Sisera.   The
river of Kishon swept them away, that ancient river, the river
Kishon ; O my soul, thou hast trodden down strength.   Then were
the horse-hoofs broken by the means of the prancings, the prancings
of their mighty ones."   I went off on Monday, but not one person
more out of the parish ; nay, I could not have so much as an elder
to go to the synod.   The rebels who were at Hawick, on the Lord's

day, were expected on the Monday at Selkirk; so I knew not
whether I could get to Kelso or not. However, I resolved, if possible, to be there. And from that time the Lord graciously gave
me an unusual courage, which continued with me always till the danger was over, and I came home; and then my spirit returned to its
ordinary. I met with no trouble that day, nor did the rebels come
to Selkirk at that time.

On Tuesday the 18th, when I went into Kelso, the horse were out
to observe the enemy, and the town was looking for their approach
to attack them, for they were at Jedburgh the night before. People from all corners, and from our neighbouring parish of Yarrow
particularly, had come in to the help of the Lord against the mighty;
which made me ashamed, considering that there was none of ours
there. The thoughts of the synod's meeting, and the sermon, were
given over for that day at least, in respect of these circumstances; and
it cost Mr. Wilson and me no little struggle ere we could obtain
them; which at length, with much difficulty, we did, about three in
the afternoon, being desirous to be found in the way of duty, whatever should happen. The synod appointed a committee to draw up a
warning against the present rebellion; who meeting that night, and
discoursing a little on it, left it on me to prepare a draught thereof;
but I refused it, not daring to undertake it, from a real persuasion
of my unfitness for it. So when the synod met next day, there was
nothing done in that affair. Whereupon the synod appointed Mr.
Ramsay and me forthwith to withdraw, and bring in one; which,
with much reluctancy, for my own part, I obeyed. So we brought
in a paper; in the framing of which, it was acknowledged, with the
no small joy of several brethren, that the Lord had honoured me to
do good service to the church. It passed with little difficulty, in respect of the present circumstances. O that I could learn from this,
not to shift occasions of doing service, when I am called thereto,
though it may appear a burden too heavy for my shoulders? The
synod rising that day, I came off in the afternoon; but immediately
my horse failed; and with much difficulty getting to Mackerston, I
was obliged to hire another there to carry me to Maxton. It was
as plain to me, as if written with a sunbeam, that God was, by that,
contending with me for a heart-sin hid from all the world, namely,
the misgiving of my treacherous heart, upon those pieces of service
the Lord honoured me with at the synod; for though Mr. Wilson's
zeal did excite me much to the former, and the cowardly weakness
of my heart frightened me from the latter, till I was in some sort
compelled to it; yet when they have done, such was the base weakness of my spirit, that I could not carry even under the same, but

wofully miscarried through vanity, as if poor I had been somewhat.
But thanks be to a good God, that quickly pursued me, till I was
laid low again. This is not the first time, that, on such occasions, I
have fallen into this shameful sin, and quickly have been rebuked
for it. I desire, in time coming, to watch on such occasions, if ever
I have more, which God may justly deny me. The enemies passed
on Tuesday toward Northumberland, not coming near Kelso. So
the people dropped away. When I came home, I found, that a report having come that day I went away, that the rebels were coming down Tima, several were in no small consternation and confusion; but by kind providence, it was kept from my wife's knowledge till the fright was over; wherein I could not but observe the
Lord's hand eminent. The army aforesaid having joined the Northumberland rebels, and the highlanders having come from Lothian,
and all joined together, they came to Kelso on Saturday the 22d.

Sabbath, October 23.—I read the paper aforesaid, according to
appointment, before the congregation; enlarged on the particulars,
and laid before them the singularity of their carriage, in the present conjuncture; which was the more heavy to me, in respect of my
circumstances concerning the oath. This week one came running,
and another riding full speed to me, telling me the highlanders were
at Thirlestane; whereupon presently I went up the brook, and then
towards the head of the hill, my family being in great distress, expecting to be plundered. A little after, one came and told me, it
was a false alarm; but in my eyes it was a kind providence that I
was tried with a false alarm, before I should get a true one. Next
Sabbath, being the 30th, upon a report that the rebels were coming
our way toward the west, I was advised to set watches in time of
sermon. Accordingly one was set on E. hill, another on R. hill.
The Lord gave a calm within, and there was no disturbance from
without. Sabbath, November 6, an order from the general, inviting
men to the king's service, was read. I sat till it was done; but
knowing it would be in vain as to us, as it was, I said nothing. The
issue of it was, that I found I had the concern of religion in the war
to teach again; which gave occasion to these notes in the sermons,
p. 72, app. No. 2.

Sabbath, November 13.—The which day the battle of Dumblane
was fought; and that day also they fought at Preston, beginning on
the Saturday; but it was the Monday at noon ere all was over.
The said day an order was read for our parish to set out four militia-
men. The letter about it came not to me, till I was in the pulpit;
but the sermons were so pat to the emergent, that not having the
desired effect, they proved irritating; which shortly after I felt.

Now they could shift no longer; so they went about it, not owning me in the least in it, nor I them. Only notes of the sermon were invidiously used against me. The four men they hired all out of the parish, except one, who had been a while in it. Masters and servants, and old men, all paid alike 5s. 6d. sterling, which occasioned great clamour. And being singular in this, beyond all their neighbours, the managers were ashamed of it. My servant being called among the rest, I found means to shew them, that I thought he was not obliged to pay. But about the 22d or 23d of November, a constable, with three militia-men, came to my house, and, by orders, they said, from a principal heritor of the parish, demanded the militia money for my servant, and my son, (not fourteen years of age); and, failing him, for myself. And they shewed me the roll, wherein I saw my son and servant's name. I told them, that I regarded no such orders. Thus my shewing them their duty, was resented with sufficient contempt. The servant paid. That day I left them at Selkirk, I made an overture to the Presbytery, that ministers should contribute to the raising of men for the support of the government; which being fallen in with by them, was ordered to be laid before the synod; and I spoke to a man with that view. But the synod, at that time, saw it not needful to go into it. That morning I went off to the synod, I did secretly advise Tushi-law to call the heads of the parish, (seeing I was so unacceptable to them in these matters), and counsel them to look to themselves, and offer some men to the government voluntarily. But this advice was rejected by him. So I would heartily have given of my money in a suitable way; but to be compelled thereto, and that by them, was what I could not comply with.

Being wrestled out of breath with the parish, in this time it began to sit down on my spirit very much, beyond what it had done formerly, that I was very unfit for them, and that they would require a man of another temper. And the first day of December being the last day for the oath, after which I could not preach more with the countenance of authority according to law, I began to be very apprehensive, that my work in this place was near an end. And several things concurred to the strengthening of it. On the last Sabbath of November, being the 27th, I fell on that part of the text, namely, preparation for trials, which, though the main thing I had in view when I chose that text, yet providence kept me off till then, several things coming forth in the breaking, very seasonable. When I was about to study that sermon, consulting former notes, I was somewhat moved to find, that that was the last subject I handled at Simprin before the farewell sermon. November 8, was the first

diet for examination, which day proved so stormy, that I could not
get out. On the 10th, in another place I had a diet, when I was
attended but with one man, and a few women and children. In
other three places after, it was not very much better. My wife was
much of the same apprehension as I, and observed that I preached
as when I was to leave Simprin. My getting through the ten commands looked like my getting through those subjects I was on in the
last months I was in that place. And my present circumstances
answered to the uneasiness I had from neighbours, ere I left that
place. What the Lord's design in these things is, I know not yet;
but in my circumstances they could hardly miss to make some impression.

Dec. 1.—Being the last day for taking the oath, I spent some time
in fasting and prayer, I found my courage for suffering was not such
as on the former occasion of this oath. Though I could not ward
off the thoughts of that foresaid, yet I desiderated such an impression
of the thing as might make me speak to them as about to leave
them; therefore I begged to be led of God, whether I saw or not,
as he had led me to my amazement, for some time past, and so left
it on him. At night my natural spirits being sunk, I was sore broken and discouraged, seeing the law so hard upon the one hand, and
the parish on the other. This held me under for three days following. That same night, I think, the Lord made my wife, being sick,
and unable to converse, to speak two words in season to me. I told
her, that I found I had not courage for suffering, &c. Her answer
was, You need it not yet. My heart, said I, is alienated from this
place. She answered, It seems there is need for it. This matter
of the oath I altogether kept up from the people, looking for no
sympathy, by the discovery of it, but affliction upon my affliction,
if they should know of it, as I got the last time I had this trial.
Some time before the last sacrament, being asked news, I told the
elder aforesaid, it was said the abjuration-oath would be imposed
again. His answer was, "I think we must even let you all do as
ye like, and strive to know Christ and him crucified;" as if we had
been seeking it, or had no conscience, but as guided by them.

Sabbath Dec. 4.—Thus shattered and broken in body and spirit,
I preached my first sermon in my new circumstances; but recovered
somewhat ere I came out of the pulpit. That very same day, Mr.
Taylor, who has made a new schism, preached in Eskdalemoor, got
several of this parish to hear him, and those such as were not wont to
wander, whatever number he had of others formerly of another temper. At night I heard of two new deserters said to be broke off
from me, one whereof I was told broke off on account of my med-

dling in the rolls aforesaid. The burden of the parish lies on me alone, having no tolerable support of my interest in it, from any. And the word not having efficacy on people's consciences, and those of the schism being in every corner of it, it is little wonder poor I am unable to stem the tide. I have for some time been much afraid of being cast over the hedge; but otherwise an honourable discharge from him who sent me hither, has often been beautiful in my eyes. But when I think on leaving them, the case they will apparently run into in these circumstances, is terrible to me. So I am tossed as from one sharp rock upon another every way.

The conduct of Providence in leading me in my preaching, in this place, has often been remarkable; but never more so than of late amidst these discouragements. Since the 4th of September that I preached first to stir up the people as above said, what day the lecture fell, Jer. iv. where we had a most lively description of the calamities of war, &c. I have often been amazed to see the Lord leading me in lectures and sermons, in my ordinary, so pat to the dispensations of the day, as they fell out one after another, and to my own case with the parish, that I could not but say, This is the finger of God. The Sabbath after the rendezvous at Selkirk, the lecture fell Jer. ix.; the Sabbath after the victories; Jer. xv.; the Sabbath after the oath; Jer. xvii; and few days there were, wherein was not something most seasonable in them, as may appear by comparing what is noted above with the order of the chapters, allowing one to each Sabbath. As for the sermons, I have dated, that before the battles, November 6, and that on the very day of the battles, November 13. This has been no small stay and support to my heart.

As to the Fourfold State, though, the rebellion breaking out, I saw there was no access to publish it; yet I went on, (as the time would allow), and by the 21st of November had the three first states transcribed, minding to do no more till I see what comes of that. I have often and again committed it to the Lord, and for preservation particularly that day foresaid, if he has any use for it. For now it has been, and often is heavy to me, that the season of publishing it is slipt; and the confusion of the times has made me afraid of the losing of the copy; and, to my apprehension, the fittest season for publishing it is gone. Only I know the Lord has before this served his own holy wise ends, by my folly, cowardice, and bastard modesty, in his cause. I have formerly related how the design was stopped when I went in to Edinburgh, to get it put to the press. It was indeed an ungrateful service given to me in the time; but the thing being so feasible, I thought I could not in modesty resist it. The kind re-

ception the printed sermon got, recovered my courage and resolution
for the book; though some professors of this parish, my constant
hearers, thought it not enough to slight that sermon when printed,
but not obscurely shewed their grudge and indignation against it,
on no other reason I can divine, but that they grudge any thing
tending to my reputation. In the transcribing, several things are
left out, with a design to shorten it, some few things put in, scripture-texts filled up that were only cited before, a great many expressions altered, and the copy divided into chapters or sections, or
what else may be thought meet to call them. And for these causes
I undertook the transcribing of it. It was a remark of Mr. Flint's
on the state of grace, that the texts cited were often not filled up.
And an observe of Mr. Halyburton's, in the Memoirs of his life,
namely, That when he found the word had done good, it was usually
God's own word in the scripture, brought in in his sermons, carried
that remark home on my conscience which Mr. Flint had made.
And by this means I suppose it will be found little shorter, if any
thing at all, than formerly. I heard no more of the sermons at Morbattle, the rebellion breaking out soon after.

In the first week of January, 1716, I was, by the good hand of
God upon me, moved yet again, to attempt inquiring into what Mr.
Cross calls the Taghmical Art, viz. the sacred stigmatology, or accentuation of the Hebrew Bible. And having by prayer addressed
the Father of lights expressly on that particular, he was graciously
pleased to help me afterwards therein, to my great satisfaction.
And I came to be persuaded of its being of so great use for under-
derstanding the holy scriptures, that, it being a time of great confusions, I was satisfied I might have full peace within myself, to be
found by public troubles in the study thereof.

And here began the most busy time of my life, which continued
while my strength lasted.

Jan. 16.—Being on my way to Edinburgh, on the account of a
project on foot for clearing the nonjurors to the government, day-
light failed us between the Craig and Blackhouse, there was a drift
in our face, and we were in fear of wandering; yet came safe to
Blackhouse, almost senseless with the stress. While I went up
that burn, walking, not daring to ride, that word, " Lord, thou pre-
servest man and beast, how precious is thy grace! Therefore in
shadow," &c., was sweet and encouraging. There was no proceeding
in the journey for the storm; so coming back again on the morrow,
I wondered how we had got through in the night in that case, having so much ado with it in the day-light.

After I had ended my ordinary on Amos iv. 12, " Prepare to

meet thy God," &c., before I had access so much as to enter on another, there began a distress in our parish, by a storm, such as they had not felt for forty-two years before. And this led me to a new ordinary, viz. Rom. viii. 22, "For the whole creation groaneth and travaileth in pain together until now." I entered on it, Jan. 22, and continued till March 4. The Lord's day was such, that but few could come out. I had once thoughts of taking another subject; but the discourse being so seasonable, that he who had given me that, could give me more, I resolved to preach it, however few should hear it. So to a few in the house I delivered it with much satisfaction.

Since, by reason of the woful unconcernedness of the people in the public cause, I could not appoint a congregational fast for the King's army, for the Lord's help to them, I had no confidence to move for one upon the account of the storm, which was our private cause in a special manner, and heavy to the parish, and by which I saw the Lord was pleading against us on account of our unconcernedness about the public cause. Therefore, on the morrow after, being the 23d, I kept a family fast for both, and, as to myself in particular, for the divine assistance in the study of the Hebrew accentuation. And being helped to confidence in the Lord as my God, I was made the more freely to lay out my requests before him. As to the study of the Hebrew accentuation, no body considering what pains I had been at to understand Mr. Cross's book, and that the Hebrew Bible was my delight, will doubt but by this time I had some notion of that accentuation, however lame, dark, and confused; and I resolved to put in writing what I thought I had reached of it, to the end I might not forget it.

At this time, lecturing on Jeremiah's prophecy, I wrote the specimen of the Taghmical Art on chap. xxiv. to be found in the miscellany MS. p. 350—356; a performance of little value, done on Mr. Cross's principles, so far as I understood them; and therefore to be very little regarded.

Feb. 2.—We kept a fast by order of the presbytery. The Lord heard the prayers of his people; and on the Saturday thereafter, the thaw began. The storm aforesaid was followed with an extraordinary mortality in our parish, such as none, I could hear of, pretended to remember of the like therein; and I heard of no such thing neither, in the places about. My dear child Katharine died among the rest. In April the mortality ceased.

Feb. 22.—Last Lord's day being quite out of case ere I went into the pulpit, I prayed to the Lord; and remarkably he heard me, and made all right beyond expectation. I have been most comfortably surprised with discoveries of the Lord's mind in his word of the

Hebrew text, which he has been pleased to make to me by means of is accentuation. Particularly, the discovery of the true sense of that passage; Gen. xlix. 10, by that means, did so affect, strike, and transport me, that it did most sensibly affect my very body, and that from head to foot.* And by the light into the Lord's word so given me, I have found my soul sanctified, and made to love the Lord. This makes me to account the better of these titles of the law, as divine. By this means, what I designed in the writing afore-said, as introductory to what 1 was to note of that which I had learned on the thing itself, has been spun out quite beyond any thing I could have in view when I began it; so that I cannot yet get my collections on the art itself begun; and by the same means I am persuaded, that these accents are the key to the true version and sense of the Hebrew text.

March 21.—This day we spent some time in family humiliation and prayer, on the account of the death of our youngest child Ka-tharine, who departed on the 12th instant : and the hand of the Lord still on Thomas and Alison by the chincough; also for the state of the public; and as to myself, for the study of the accentuation. That child was very comfortable to me; but I bless him I was helped to part with her; and saw and believed much of the Lord's good-ness in that dispensation. Coming home from Selkirk on the 2d instant, and thinking on the time of the land's trial, I had two main questions as to my family. The one was the case of that dear child, the other, the then case of my wife. I dare not say I was faithless as to either, but believed God could see to them very well in the worst of my circumstances. As soon as I came home, I found the Lord was in his way to answer the last; and shortly after the other was hid. I never had such a clear and comfortable view of the Lord's having other use for children than our comfort; for which ends he removes them in infancy; so that they are not brought to the world in vain. I saw reason to bless the Lord, that I had been made father of six children, now in the grave, and that were with me but a very short time; but none of them lost; I will see them all at the resurrection. That clause in the covenant, " And the God

---

* The author, in a manuscript, containing a new translation of the last fourteen chapters of Genesis, thus translates this passage : " The sceptre shall not depart, from Judah ; and-a-lawgiver, from-between his-feet ; until, that-Shiloh-come ; and to him *be,* the-gathering of the-people." And in his " Tractatus Stigmologicus Hebræo-Bib-licus," he thus renders it : " Nonrecedet sceptrum, a-Juda ; et legislator, ab-inter pedes-ejus ; adusque, quumadvenerit Shilo ; atque-ei [fuerit], aggregatio populorum." And then he adds, " Neutiquam dicitur, *nec* sceptrum, *neque* legislatorem recessurum, adusque tempus illud præfinitum ; verum non *utrumque.* See more in that Essay, p. 76.

of thy seed," was sweet and full of sap. The mortality in our parish is not over yet, though I hoped my child had closed it; but just while I was writing this, I heard of the death of a mother of four small children, who I am told, has not been well these twenty days, but never lay; was better yesterday, but carried off at night by a sickness, so far as I could understand, not above two hours' long. Alas! we have provoked our God.

By the awful voice of Providence continuing, I was led to Zech. xii. 12, "And the land shall mourn, every family apart," &c. on which I dwelt from March 11, till May 20; and for some time after, on Psalm cxxvi. 5, "They that sow in tears, shall reap in joy."* Upon the former of these I pressed the duty of personal and family fasting, among other things. And this was not without fruit. I knew that some were engaged in these duties; particularly James Biggar's family, on which the hand of the Lord lay long and heavy, and carried off several of them; in their death, as in their life, comfortable to me as above said.

Immediately after the family-fast of Jan. 23, I pursued my resolution of putting in writ what I thought I had reached of the accentuation; the which I reckoned, when I began it, I might comprise in two or three leaves; but even what I designed for introduction thereto, swelled to about six sheets; and was not finished till March 23; the bread by the divine blessing, increasing in the breaking. Reading the Hebrew Bible, I was most pleasurably, beyond what one can readily without feeling imagine, surprised with discoveries of the Lord's mind in his word; by means of that intrinsic light I perceived it to be illuminated with, by its own accentuation. Thus I came to be fully persuaded, as of what I saw with my eyes, that the accents are the true key to the genuine version and sense of the Hebrew text; and that they are divine. As from time to time, in that happy study, I met with new discoveries of that nature; I often thought with myself, What a trifle my digging up gold in some mine I might have fallen upon in Peru or elsewhere, would have been, in comparison of this, which I found in my accentuated Hebrew Bible!

Just on the morrow after my finishing of what I designed for introduction, and have now so intitled, came to my hand "Wasmuth's Institutio Accentuationis Hebrææ; the which I took for a

---

* The author afterwards transcribed his notes on Zech. xii. 12, and they were published in 1734, under the title of "A Memorial concerning Personal and Family Fasting," annexed to his "View of the Covenant of Grace;" and the sermons on Psalm cxxvi. 5, were published in 1772, in a small collection, with some other of his sermons.

token for good. Having glanced it the week following, I found it
miring, and perceived that it wanted the tables often therein mentioned. So I was set anew to turn my eyes towards the Lord, from
whom my help behoved to come; and to depend on him for that
effect. And here I cannot but admire and adore the conduct of sovereign wisdom towards me in that matter. I had no character of
Wasmuth aforehand, to prepossess me; and before his book came
to my hand, I was set a seeking the knowledge of the accentuation,
by the study of the sacred Hebrew text itself, considering the same
as it stood accentuated. And I found so many turnings and windings, and heaps of irregulars, in that learned man's account of the
accentuation, that I saw nothing therein to remove me from the method of inquiry I had been led unto, to the study thereof instead of
it. Upon the account of the defect above mentioned, that copy of
Wasmuth's book was returned; and some time after, I got another
copy thereof having the tables, the which is yet among my books.

About this time I received letters from Edinburgh, moving the
reprinting of the " Everlasting Espousals," because of the continued
demand for the same; the which, after being laid before the Lord,
and considered, was ordered to be done. So in a short time after,
there was a second edition of that sermon.

March 26.—An old temptation recurred; but I bless God the
edge of it is now much blunted, in comparison of what it has been.
But my heart bleeds afresh for my dear child Katharine.

On March 29, I began to make collections on the accents themselves; encouraged, and more fitted thereto, by what had fallen out,
in the case of the aforesaid introduction which is *in retentis.* Reading the sacred text, I studiously gathered what I could observe.
And, what was of great use to me, as my pole-star in this study,
was a notion, which by the discoveries aforesaid I was confirmed in;
namely, The true construction of the words of the text, was to be
determined by their accentuation, as the rule thereof to us; and not
the power or value of the accents, by what seemed to us the construction of the words. This natural and most rational point was,
I think, originally owing to my reading somewhere in Cross's Taghmical Art, that the verbs of the first hemistich; Psalm ii. 2, were to
be repeated in the following one. I very well remember, that that
had a particular light with it to me. And accordingly, considering
other texts at this rate, and thereby obtaining convincing discoveries of their true sense, I was fixed in that point; so Wasmuth's
notion of the ambulatory value of the accents, could not take with
me.

April 25.—This day I kept a secret fast, 1. To seek light in the matter of a transportation to Ligertwood, proposed to me when at the synod, in the matter of adding to the eldership here, my wife's journey to Fife, the determining about the celebration of the sacrament, and the disposing of the MS. on the Fourfold State of Man. 2. To seek the Lord's presence and help in my study of the accentuation, and his blessing on the second edition of the sermon, now, I suppose, in the press. 3. On the account of the affliction of my wife and children, and of James Biggar's family, Mr. Borthwick, Lev-Muir. 4. The case of the church, the parish, and the vacancy of Simprin. These things I laid before the Lord, with some confidence in himself, minding to hang on for them. The mortality is ceased.

May 4.—But alas! I found, three or four days ago, that I had not hung on; and therefore God has pursued me with darkness in the point of the sacrament, being extremely perplexed and embarrassed in that matter, which should have been determined on Wednesday last, but I am not clear in it as yet. I have seen my mismanagement, in that I have not prayed ·and thought about it more; and have got a dear-bought lesson, to pursue by thinking, for light, in what I consult God by prayer.

Meanwhile, since that time, some things have looked better in the parish. On the day after, the examination was frequented unordinarily. On the Lord's day two contumacious persons submitted. On Tuesday, one that has been of the new separation by Mr. Taylor near a year bygone, and whom I parted with last summer as no more one of my flock, came to me, and acknowledged her sin; declaring, that from the Sabbath night after I had spoke with her, she had no rest in her mind; but that that wore off in some measure, yet a great while ago returned more vigorously; that it had worsted her private case, wishing never any might do as she had done, and bring such bitterness to their own souls, These things had weight against the business of Ligertwood.

May 11 —Friday I was almost on the 9th resolved to celebrate the sacrament on the first Sabbath of June, and to venture over difficulties standing in the way, minding to seek the Lord on Saturday morning for a full determination. But this night arrived an express from Mr. Murray, obtesting me, as I would not have a hand in strengthening a most sinful schism, to come and assist him on the last Sabbath of this month at the communion there. This carried my perplexity to the height. I went to the Lord with this, took with my sin in not insisting as aforesaid after the fast, endeavoured and was helped to believe over the belly of that provocation. Thereafter I found the light clearing, to my answering of that call to Penpont; and having sent for two elders, they advised to it. Thus I

was both punished for that sin, and matters were kept open for sending me thither. I have but four elders at this time, but design an
additional number. While assisting at that sacrament, was conceived a project of transporting me to Closeburn, a parish in that neighbourhood; of which I shall take more notice afterwards.

. *July* 19.—On the 15th the sacrament was celebrated here. The
fast-day was extraordinary stormy with wind and rain; but the three
days fair; and for some time before, and since, there has not been
one fair day to an end. On Wednesday, in studying my action-sermon, I was sore bound up; and little better on the Tuesday afternoon, when I began it. But on the Thursday, being the fast-day,
the Lord sent us two sermons with much of his countenance; hence
my heart was loosed, and I resolved to try the study of the sermon
again. Accordingly on the morrow I studied the last half of it anew,
to more satisfaction to myself. It was delivered with some measure
of solid seriousness. But in the invitation I was straitened, and yet
more in the prayer for consecration of the elements; I laboured to
improve the declaring of them no more common bread and wine, yet
not with desired effect. But my spirit opened a little ere the table
was ended. I communicated as I preached. The work from the beginning to the end, had a favour of God upon it; felt, I am persuaded, in the spirits of many; and his servants were remarkably helped
in their work.

. Having been at the communion at Maxton Aug. 12, and at the
presbytery for Mr. B.'s business on the 14th, I have to remark, 1.
The Lord's hearing of the joint prayers of his people, and that in
two instances. One was, I had been led in the Saturday's sermon,
which was on Exod. xxiv. 11; to beseech for and require the prayers
of serious Christians, for the private cases of ministers, which I
doubt not had influence on several of that sort in the meeting; and
it went well with me at that communion. I think I saw the lights
spoke of in that sermon, and believed. The other was, my wife,
who minded to have been there, but was taken ill just the night before I went away; her case was remembered not only in private, but
in the public prayers, as one kept from that occasion by the afflicting hand of God. And the Lord made it a good time to her soul.
2. The hearing of prayer, and the good fruit of dependence on
the Lord in presbyterial management, being sensibly assisted to a
clear uptaking of matters in that difficult business. 3. The Lord's
leading the blind by the way they knew not, being sweetly surprised
with a providential management of matters, in two particulars, to a
better account than otherwise they could have been brought.

. As I came by Closeburn house, in my return home from the com-

munion at Penpont in the end of May, the chaplain met me, and told
me, that at supper on the Sabbath night they were speaking of transporting me to that parish. He had no orders that I know of to
speak of it to me; so I gave a suitable return, without any shadow
of encouragement. When Mr. Murray was at the sacrament here
in July, he proposed it to me in earnest; and I, with all the earnestness I was capable of, discouraged the motion; so that I thought it
might be laid aside. But some time in harvest I received a letter
from him, shewing that the parish of Closeburn were to apply to
their presbytery for that effect. This letter I judged meet neither
to make public, nor yet to keep altogether secret; so I imparted the
purpose of it to one of our elders. And about the 11th of September I wrote a most pathetic return, to stop that procedure of that
parish.

At the which time I was writing my collections on *Silluk,* in a
folio book I had prepared for putting down my materials in. And
herein I so prospered, by the good hand of my God upon me, that,
as I reckon, I began from that time to apprehend, that this business
I had engaged in, for my own private benefit only, might possibly
in end turn to a book for public use. And all along thereafter,
until it was done, I looked upon that study as the business of my
life.

About the end of this month of September, came an account to
our parish, that a call to Closeburn was drawn up for me. Herewith they were much alarmed; and, in their own rough way, shewed
a mighty concern for my continuance among them. And thus the
trouble of the parish about *me* began just about the time wherein the
year preceding, my trouble with them was going to the highest pitch.

What influence the awful steps of Providence that followed upon
this last, as above narrated, had upon them, I cannot say. But as
the spring of comfort, from the study aforesaid, was most seasonably struck up to me in my closet, when without I was so much oppressed; so, about the latter end of April, some things in the parish began to look with a better face towards my encouragement, as
I have related above, p. 281, in so much that they had weight with
me against a transportation to Ligertwood, which at the April
synod had been proposed to me; so as I had been obliged seriously
to seek the Lord's mind in it, and was one of the causes of the
secret fast above mentioned. Moreover, whereas the session had
been reduced to a very small number, by death and otherwise, I prevailed this summer to get their number increased; so that, on July
12, being the fast-day before the sacrament, there were seven added
to the eldership. Among these seven was Thomas Linton in

Chapelhop, a man of weight and activity; who, together with another elder, and Michael Anderson younger of Tushilaw, went in December to Closeburn, by conference and reasoning to divert the storm
of the designed transportation thither; but it prevailed not. But
this was perhaps the last journey that Thomas Linton made; being
seized with a sore and vehement trouble in his mouth and head,
which kept him till he died about the end of the year 1718. He
had been a notable sufferer in the time of persecution, and spoiled of
all his goods; but was become very wealthy; and moreover he had
a heart given him to do good with his wealth, and was very useful
in the country that way. On him I bestowed this epitaph, which I
suppose is to be found on his tombstone in Mary church-yard in
Yarrow :—

> All lost for Christ, an hundred-fold
> Produc'd, and he became
> A father, eyes, and feet unto
> The poor, the blind, the lame.

Tushilaw younger died also not very long after. He was a man
of a gentle disposition, and likewise was endued with a principle of
beneficence to mankind; so that, dying before his father, he was
much lamented, as a father of the country.

Nov. 14.—Being at Edinburgh to put my son to the college, and
all comfortable views I had had, as to the disposing of him for his
quarters, having failed, I was directed to a stranger; but there were
some things in that case that disgusted me. I had laid the matter
over on the Lord; and behold, at the nick of time, when I was come
to the last point, just going out at the chamber-door, to agree with
that person for his quarters, because I could do no better, one came
to me, and told me of a religious private family, which I knew nothing of, desirous of my acquaintance, and therefore of entertaining
my son. This appeared to me the finger of God, and I lodged him
there. This step of kind Providence was big in my eyes. After I
came home, I was perplexed as to his learning, fearing his rust in
that point should expose him; but within three weeks after, by a
letter from the boy himself, I was delivered from that fear.

Jan. 1. 1717.—I spent some time in prayer, and humiliation, concerning the affair of Closeburn, my study of the accentuation, the
case of some afflicted in the parish, and some other particulars in my
own case, and that of my family, and renewing my covenant with
God, not without some soul-advantage in the time. By this time I
had seen the Lord's jealousy against me, for sinking so far under
my pressures; and against the people, for their having been such a
burden to me.

I had on the 19th of the preceding August, begun an ordinary of
subjects, for pressing into the life and power of religion; and, in
pursuance thereof, preached on walking with God*, the study of the
holy Scriptures, and the observing of providences.† But while I
was on the sweet subject last mentioned, I was, by scandals abounding
at that time, obliged to cut short, and forced away from it, (the which
hath oftener than once been my lot), unto the doctrine of repentance,
which I began on Jan. 27, and, pursuing it from several texts, ended
it not till the 21st of October following. But I had no sooner
ended the sermons on observing of providences, but, by the commencement of the process of transportation aforesaid, Providence
did, in their sight and mine, begin a web which filled both our hearts
and hands, till in August following it was wrought out. So the very
first of these sermons on repentance, delivered Jan. 27, as aforesaid,
was heard by one or more of the commissioners from Closeburn, who
had obtained the calling of the Presbytery to hear them, on the
Tuesday after.

Feb. 7. This forenoon I spent in secret prayer. My ordinary affliction and temptation so set upon me at first, and embittered my
spirit, that I was like to have given over the work. But reading
the 59th of Isaiah for my humiliation, that word, ver. 19, " When
the enemy shall come in like a flood, the Spirit of the Lord shall lift
up a standard against him," met me most seasonably when I was as
one like to be carried away with a flood. I went to God with it,
and pleaded it. And though it was not presently accomplished; yet
after about two hours and a half heartless work for the most part,
it was made out; the temptation was banished away, and my heart
was touched with his hand put in by the hole of the lock. Among
many other ills of my life, I was particularly convinced, 1. Of my
sin of superficial reading of the Scripture, not subjecting my soul,
in reading it, unto it, as the divine word; whereby it has come to
pass that I have not had the feeling of the power of it that otherwise
I might have had; 2. The remissness of my spirit, and heartlessness
in family worship; 3. Not depending more on the Lord, in the work
on Ezekiel that I am now upon; 4. Not wrestling with God more
in secret for the congregation, and some particular persons. Two
things I had a comfortable view of; 1. An unfeigned desire of universal and perfect holiness, however vile I am; 2. That though my

---

* The sermons on this subject are printed in the volume entitled " The Christian
Life delineated.

† These are also inserted in the Body of Divinity. . All three are justly esteemed
most excellent discourses.

departures are many, thou knowest, O Lord, that I am not wicked, nor have I wickedly departed from thee ; not daring to do deliberately what I think to be an ill thing, and being in some measure tender as to endeavouring to know the mind of God with respect to the way I should go.   I was concerned in the affair of Closeburn, Dr. Trotter's indisposition, the affliction of those of Midgehop, &c. Concerning the affair of Closeburn,

REMARK 1. About the time of my great trouble by this parish last year, the trouble of this parish by that business began this year. 2. The Lord has punished them and me both, as above noted, by the terror of the prospect of that affair.   3. Just as I was writing this, a stranger came in and gave me a most discouraging account of that parish.   4. I was led this day to pray for a blessing on that parish, and some particular persons in it.   5. On Jan. 29, the commisioners for Closeburn produced their commissions before our presbytery.   I saw what I judged a flaw in that from the parish, urged it, and the commission was rejected thereupon.   What moved me to this was, that I thought strict justice did not require the sustaining of that commission, and I durst not make a compliment of it, lest I should seem to lead, and not wait to be led by, Providence ; and I knew not what might be in that minute circumstance.   6. But the rejecting of a commission was also the first step in the business of the transportation to Etterick.   7. The commissioners being in our house on the Wednesday's night before the presbytery, the ordinary sung in the family was Psalm xvii. 41—45.   After we had done with family worship, Mr. Murray bid me to take notice of ver. 43, if I right remember.   I took little notice of it on that ; but on Monday night immediately before the presbytery, we sung at their family worship the same part of the 18th psalm, and then I could not but notice it.   8. While in our house those of that place spoke of the benefice there, for that I cared not ; neither was moved by it in the least.   I bless the Lord, my weak side lies not there ; but the Lord let me see that I was not to be secure on that quarter ; for hearing what I yet apprehend may be a lying story, but of that kind, my heart was catched ; which I quickly perceived to my shame and sorrow ; but through grace I soon got over it.   9. On the morrow after the presbytery, riding with the men commissioners from Closeburn, some women came forth and wept ; which moved me as an emblem of what would likely follow in the event of a transportation.   So I gave over talking with Mr. Murray, with whom I could prevail nothing ; and spoke with the other two men, till we parted in a hurry, and they appearing more hopeless than ever.   This I pursued, and this I had satisfaction in, that I had discharged my conscience ; and if they do return, it is on all grounds of hope from me (which I never designedly gave them) razed by me ; so that if there be any further procedure in the matter, there is clear ground for holy providence to work on. That word, Psalm lvi. ult., " Thou hast delivered my soul from death, wilt thou not deliver my feet from falling ?" has been big in my eyes and often in my mouth, on this occasion. And that word this day was staying to my heart in some measure; Prov. iv. 12, " When thou goest, thy steps shall not be straitened ; and when thou runnest, thou shalt not stumble."

Feb. 27. On Monday last came Sir Thomas Kirkpatrick, with two ministers of the presbytery, and W. G. from the parish, in their way to Selkirk, to prosecute their call. Their coming was stunning ; they staid about three quarters of an hour. When they were gone, I went and poured out my soul to the Lord, and was very remark-ably carried out, to be very particular, that God would frustrate the errand they were going on. Their commission was again rejected, and they appealed to the Synod. This day returning with the two ministers and W. G., their management and converse was such, that my heart was extremely set against that place.

On the 27th of March, a congregational fast was kept, at the de-sire of the session, on the account of the threatened desolating of the parish by the transportation foresaid. Three brethren of the Pres-bytery, being invited, preached ; and that day, an heritor of the parish, who all along to that time had deserted my ministry, came to the kirk, being zealous for my continuance in the place. He gave due attendance all along thereafter while he lived ; but in a few years he died.

Meanwhile, though that heritor had thus laid aside his opposition to me, Satan had beforehand stirred up another adversary to fill up his room ; and who was far heavier to me than ever he had been. This was ——— ———.

He had been educated under my ministry, profited in knowledge, and gave hopeful signs of his seriousness ; so that he was admitted to the Lord's table ; but he was snared with youthful lusts, and first convicted of fornication on Dec. 14, 1716. But not being duly humbled on that oc-casion, but making great difficulty in satisfying the discipline, he fell into one mire of filthiness after another, some being legally discovered, some spurning all means of legal discovery ; so that I had almost a con-tinual fight with him for many years after. And to this day he con-tinues an adversary, only he never deserted the ordinances ; and I still think he hath some good thing about him, that may at length prevail against this profaneness, pride, and vanity.

Lecturing on Ezekiel, and by means of accentuation making such

discoveries as I was loath to lose, I translated a part thereof, and
wrote some notes on the translation ; the which retarded me in my
main work. This performance, which is *in retentis*, goes from the
beginning of that prophecy to chap. xxi. 23, consisting of about
seventeen sheets. It bears the marks of the lame notion of the accentuation I was then arrived at ; and must be judged according to
the more perfect account of the accents, now long ago written in
Latin ; but it may be useful. The affair of Closeburn not leaving
time necessary for it, obliged me to lay it aside.

April 27. In the end of March, my wife and I spent some time in
prayer on the affair of Closeburn. Last week the Synod sustained
the commission rejected by the Presbytery, appointed the Presbytery
to meet on this affair on the first Tuesday of June, allowing the pursuers to appeal to the Synod, to meet on the third Wednesday of
June ; and this, that there might be no ground of complaining of
them to the General Assembly. Howbeit, the pursuers appealed to
the General Assembly. Yesterday, I spent some time in prayer,
laying the call of Closeburn before the Lord ; having received it at
the Synod, but never opened it till before the Lord in that exercise.
I observe, 1. Whereas three ministers preached at the fast in the
the congregation, the first was remarkably carried out in prayer for
averting of this stroke ; the second touched it but little ; the third,
least. Both the times aforesaid, in secret, I was remarkably carried
out for my own private case, but less when I came to that business.
The first of these times, the stream of influences ran, in wrestling
with God for grace towards personal holiness ; yesterday, in embracing personally the covenant, or covenanting with God ; in the
which the Lord was pleased so to blow upon me, that I think, in all
my life, I never had more, if ever so much, clear and distinct uptakings of the gospel offer, solid, distinct, and hearty acceptance of it,
and confidence in managing it. I had an unusual view, and in some
measure yet have, of God as creator loving his creatures, and giving
his own Son for sinners to bring them to be happy in the enjoyment
of himself ; producing in me confidence in, and love to, this bountiful and gracious God. 2. Having spread the call of Closeburn before the Lord yesterday, though the subscriptions, being 118,
did touch me, yet I could have no view of the matter, but as leaving
behind me a broken parish, and one I must be rent from, to go to
another broken parish, where I must expect but cold entertainment ;
so that nothing of a call from God appears to me in it. Otherwise
I was helped to be easy about the matter, having laid it over on the
Lord ; and being somewhat apprehensive, from the Lord's way of
dispensing his influences to me, that my trial must be of another

sort, whereby possibly I may be laid aside from both. [*Nota,* This apprehension has been so far verified in the event, that I was delivered from the strivings of the people; by the issue of the process, from the strivings I was to have with the parish of Closeburn in the event of a transportation; and by the whole business from the strivings with my own parish; which, from that time, has never been so unmanageable as before, though I have not wanted trials from particular persons heavy enough. But I have been engaged in strivings of a more public nature since, and in a long and heavy family affliction, whereof the eighth year is now running, Aug. 28, 1727.] 3. I remember not, that ever I had, on an occasion of weight, at the Synod, so much ado to fix my feet, in point of confidence in the Lord, when praying about the particular, as I had at the Synod last week in this affair. Some untenderness in my conversation at home, found me out, and hung about me there; so that it cost sore struggling. 4. The minute circumstance of the commission, p. 286, has now brought forth a great matter, viz., the carrying the matter of the transportation, so as it cannot come before the next General Assembly for decision, though it do otherwise. And though it go to the commission, and I should be laid under their sentence, without light in my own breast; I would look on that as a light matter, in comparison of a sentence of the General Assembly in such circumstances. I am fully satisfied in my following the conduct of Providence nicely on that little head; *In minimis Deus maximus.* 5. Sir Tho. Kirkpatrick owned to me at the Synod, that my letters to Mr. Murray put him to a stand, but that he came the second time upon hearing that I would be submissive; though, much I think to the confounding of us all three, it was owned that the most I said was these words, "No less will make me to go to Closeburn, than what would make me to take a mountain on my shoulders." 6. The heritor aforesaid, who would never come to the kirk since my settlement in this parish, by the prospect of this transportation, was brought to come on the fast day, and continues so to do, being zealous for my staying among them. Meanwhile scandalous outbreakings in the parish, have abounded more since this business commenced, than for a good while before. And this affair has obliged me some time ago to lay aside the work on Ezekiel, having no time for it.

May 1. I went to Edinburgh to the General Assembly, and returned on the 17th. On the last of April, I designed to have taken journey, my wife being indisposed. I was ready to take my horse; but going to prayer with my wife, to commit the family to the Lord, I could not get my family committed to him as usual. So rising up from prayer. I presently concluded I could not, and should not go.

It was well ordered; for afterwards my wife was better, and I found there was no need of the haste which I then apprehended there was.

In Edinburgh I found some were impressed with my inclination to go to Closeburn, which I endeavoured to carry off. On the 8th of May I had a toss with Mr. Murray before Sir Thomas, he affirming, and I denying, that I had given them ground by word or deed; and Sir Thomas declaring, that if he had not been informed so, he would not have insisted. When the business came before the committee of bills, Mr. P. opened up the case of the parish of Closeburn. This obliged me, otherwise unwilling to speak, to open up the case of Etterick too; which, with much difficulty I obtained leave to do, a plain sway to the other side appearing in that committee; which much oppressed my spirit. When it came before the assembly, our synod was mostly absent, those of them present little to be trusted, (and the truth is, I saw none of our synod there, but those of our own presbytery, I could have confidence in), and the same sway appeared there. This made me break silence there, which I had kept for seventeen years in that judicatory; and being touched, the Lord helped me to speak without fear. I cannot but observe kind Providence that suffered Mr. P. to make that unseasonable discourse on the merits of the cause, and that our synod was mostly absent when it came before the assembly; for these things obliged me, otherwise unwilling, to speak; whereby the respective judicatories could not but perceive how I stood affected to the thing.

The issue of the conference with Mr. Murray and Sir Thomas, and of the sway I perceived in the committee and assembly, ready to make a compliment of the business, was, that still there appeared to me less of God in the matter; and so it tended to my farther clearing, as to my not being called to go to that place.

The synod of Dumfries seemed at first (according to my information), while they thought I was willing, not to be disposed to be active in it; afterwards they seemed to be keen. Wherefore meeting with one of their leading men, I represented some things concerning myself, that I thought might cause them to remit of that keeness, as my not employing jurors, &c. (though by the by what I have done that way is merely on the ground of offence, not that I am straitened in my own conscience as to such joining); and it seemed to have something of the desired effect. So in the end I became very easy.

At that assembly, the affair of Mr. John Simson, professor of theology in the college of Glasgow, pursued by that great man, Mr. James Webster, one of the ministers of Edinburgh, and which had been in dependence for several years, was ended, with great softness

to the professor; who, from the attempts he had then made against
the doctrine of the grace of Christ, hath since advanced to attack
the doctrine of the person of Christ, and to overthrow the foundations of Christianity. The said affair being ended at one of the
diets, in the following diet was taken in a proposition, calculated by
the presbytery of Auchterarder, for opposing the erroneous doctrine
of Professor Simson, on the occasion of a suspected young man on'
trials before them. This proposition, called in derision " the Auchterarder Creed," was all at once at that diet judged and condemned;
though some small struggle was made in defence thereof. And poor
I was not able to open a mouth before them in that cause; although
I believed the proposition to be truth, howbeit not well worded. It
was as follows :—" It is not sound and orthodox to teach, that we
must forsake sin, in order to our coming to Christ, and instating us
in covenant with God." For this, when I came to my chamber, my
conscience smote me grievously; for that I could speak in my own
cause, as said is, but could not speak in the public cause of truth.
And I was obliged yet to speak upon it, and exoner my conscience,
when it was out of season; that is, upon the reading over of the
minute about it, in the following diet. But this was made an useful
lesson to me afterward; and gave me something to balance my natural diffidence and bashfulness, and to incite me to speak when I
saw the cause of truth call for it.

And here, namely, in the condemnation of that proposition, was
the beginning of the torrent, that for several years after ran, in the
public actings of this church, against the doctrine of grace, under
the name of Antinomianism; and is unto this day overflowing.
Meanwhile, at the same time sitting in the assembly house, and conversing with Mr. John Drummond, minister of Crief, one of the
brethren of that presbytery above mentioned, I happened to give
him my sense of the gospel-offer; Isa. lv. 1; Matth. xi. 28, with
the reason thereof; and withal to tell him of the Marrow of Modern Divinity. Hereupon he, having inquired in the shops for
the said book, at length got it; and from him Mr. James Webster
getting it, was taken therewith; and afterward, Mr. Drummond
himself being hardly allowed time to read it through, it came into
the hands of Mr. James Hog, minister of Carnock; and in end
was reprinted in the year 1718, with a preface by the said Mr. Hog,
dated at Carnock, Dec. 3, 1717. The mentioning of that book in
the said conversation, I had quite forgot; and that these things following thereupon, I did not at all know, till about half a score years
after this, that Mr. Wilson my friend, having got the account from
Mr. Drummond occasionally, did relate it to me. But the publish-

ing of that then obscure book, at that time, having been so remarkable in its consequences, and this to the signal advantage of the truth of the gospel in this church, I could not but rejoice from my heart in that relation, reckoning it a great honour the Lord had put upon me, that by such a beautiful step of providence I had been made the remote occasion thereof.

At this time my daughter Alison, having a trouble in her nose, got by a fall when a child, for which, of a considerable time that season, we had, by advice of a surgeon, washed it by the help of a syringe; I, in the time of the assembly, having been advised by my wife that the trouble had grown worse, consulted two surgeons about it. And they, apprehending danger, moved that she should be brought in to Edinburgh to them, for cure. So coming away, I left my son John in the town indisposed, and returned home, looking on myself as a candle burning at both ends, considering my son's case behind me, and my daughter's before me, but labouring to encourage myself in the Lord. On the 26th of May, I had advice that my son was sick of the measles. The 29th was prefixed for carrying in Alison, for the end foresaid; but the Lord mercifully broke that appointment, by my wife's becoming unfit for travel, the night before; and on the day appointed there was an extraordinary fall of rain. Then that day eight days was prefixed for the effect foresaid; but on the intervening Saturday, after some time spent in prayer that morning, my wife and I sitting together in the garden, were surprised to hear by the servant, that something had fallen out of the child's nose. The same being taken up, and brought to us, was found to be a piece of the cartilage, and to smell very rank; but there was no rank smell in the nose any more, nor yet any wound; but as the deliverance came in an instant, it was perfect too, and most seasonable. My son, having been sent for, came home in health on the Wednesday after; which was the day that had been determined for carrying in my daughter. This was a surprising deliverance in a case appearing very hopeless, and was wonderful in our eyes. O the wisdom and goodness that appeared in it, and in timing it and my wife's indisposition, and in making the rain to come on that day, whereby our purpose was broken! This was a most signal piece of the conduct of Providence towards me, of a most diffusive usefulness in point of practice, however it has been improved.

Being called to exercise the last Sabbath night I was in Edinburgh, I had prepared to speak on Gen. v. 24, "And Enoch walked with God, and he was not; for God took him." Betwixt sermons I got notice, that I behoved to have that exercise in another house than had been designed, the family of that other house having received that morning the news of a son dead abroad. The suitableness of the text to that unexpected occasion, was worth observing; he leads the blind in a way they knew not.

The affair of Closeburn coming again before the presbytery, they refused the transportation. The pursuers appealed to the synod, which met at Kelso on the 18th of June, and sat but one day. I went thither, secure that the synod would refer it to the commission, and that I would not need to speak much on the business. When I came there, my measures were quite altered by means of my best friends, who judged it necessary that the synod should come to a sentence, and that I should speak very fully. The pursuers were most vigorous in their management, which obliged me to produce what I thought to have kept up till the commission. So I told the synod plainly, that it was not only contrary to my inclination, but to my light; and that unless my conscience were convinced, I could not comply, and mere human authority would not do it. The synod refused it also, and so the pursuers appealed to the commission. I found myself at a great loss, in point of confidence in prayer for light and furniture for speaking before the synod; having thought there would be little need of speaking there, I had been very little concerned to prepare for it, and now there remained no competent time for it. But in the very little time I had, I endeavoured to fix my confidence in the Lord, notwithstanding my former security, making free grace my refuge, labouring to believe his grace should be sufficient for my throughbearing, as if I had been at all pains before. Here I saw the advantage of my heart's being impressed with the doctrine of free grace; whereas had I been in fetters that way, I would here have had no way to have settled my heart in the faith of the promise. After the synod was over, some of the members seemed to intimate to me, that I would be transported by the commission. This damped me exceedingly, judging them to be such as might know the minds of the leading men there; and this damp continued long with me at home.

July 13.—This day having spent some time in prayer about the affair of Closeburn, I found my heart was much quieted, in that I was conscious to myself, that, whatever my aversion thereto is, I would be ready to put the knife to the throat of my inclinations, if the Lord should discover his mind in favour thereof, though no such thing as yet appears. I found also a serious concern in my spirit to be guided of the Lord in it; even of him who leads the blind in the way they know not, and to whom all his works are known from the beginning; seeing myself in hazard of falling into some piece of mis-

mangement that afterwards may prove a snare. And for this in
in particular I put myself in the Lord's hand.

On Thursday, August 15, the affair of Closeburn came before the
commission for final decision. Much dealing there was with the
members, by both parties. The speat ran high for the transportation, when we came to town; but by dealing with members it was
somewhat abated. Advocates were employed on both sides; but
after reading of papers, and hearing of parties and their counsel on
both sides, when we were to be removed, I did with great affection,
being in deep concern, deliver before them, from a paper I had prepared, besides my answers to the reasons of transportation, a
speech, the tenor whereof, as setting my case and circumstances in
due light, here follows:

"MODERATOR, It is with the utmost concern I see myself sisted before the Rev. Commission of the General Assembly, in a process for transporting me to the parish of Closeburn; having sometimes hoped, that such an obscure person as I might have finished
his course and ministry, without being heard, in such a judicatory, at least on such an occasion. But since, by an excess of
charity towards me, in the honourable persons and Rev. ministers
concerned in the call of Closeburn, whose undeserved respect I shall
always be sensible of, this appearance is forced upon me; my hearty
concern for the good of the parish of Etterick, which is very dear to
me, for the true interest of the parish of Closeburn, and for my own
welfare, obliges me, freely to speak, before you, the thoughts of my
heart, in this affair; resolving rather to run the risk of being accounted imprudent, than to mince the matter so as the cause may
suffer, wherein I judge the interest of the gospel, and my comfort,
lie so much at stake. And if anything shall, in my discourse, be set
in the light which otherwise should have been veiled with silence, I
humbly beg the rev. Commission, those of mine own parish, and the
pursuers, will only impute it, as it ought to be, to the extreme necessity I am reduced to, for my own defence, in which I am not indifferent, but in earnest.

"Moderator, When I consider how hard my work has been, in the
parish of Etterick, by reason of the divisive temper which has prevailed in that place, it fills me with confusion and terror, to think I
am in hazard of being thrown into a far hotter flame. I own God is
just in it; but I hope for compassion from him, to whom the quarrel
is open and manifest; and I expect it also from his servants, to
whom the cause of this is not certainly known. I enjoyed the fruits
of peace, for some years, elsewhere; otherwise perhaps the want of

it had not been so bitter to me; but since that time, my eyes have
seen but little of it. I have stood as in a pass, for the space of ten
years; and possibly if I had had less trouble, others had got more.
Had I been so happy as to have seen the breach of the parish of Etterick healed, there had been some appearance of reason, in putting
me on new work of that kind; for then would I have had hope of
success. But it is not so. I have said in my answers, that the
breaches in the parish of Etterick are still as wide as they were that
day I came first among them; but, what is truth, now necessary to
be discovered, they are indeed far wider. The Old Dissenters whom
I found there at my coming, continue as they were, having lost none
of their number, but one, who, being educated in that way, left it
about a year ago. But I have lost many, who, breaking off from
under my ministry, have separated themselves from the communion
of this church. This deserting of my ministry began, not long after
I was settled in that place; and while I was grappling with these
difficulties, it pleased the Lord, in his holy, wise providence, for my
further trial, to remove by death, and otherwise, several of the eldership. And though, for several years, I made attempts again and
again, to get the session supplied; yet could I not prevail to get a
competent number of elders, till about a year ago. And I am persuaded I had not obtained it at that time neither, but that, no end of
the deserting humour appearing, and finding the misled persons, time
after time, confirmed in their prejudices, by absenting from the ordinances, a considerable space before I knew that they were led
aside, I was like to sink under my burden; which I discovered to
some; whose hearts were at length moved with compassion, and
otherwise, to take part with me and the rest, in the Lord's work in
the congregation; whereby my heart has been encouraged, and my
hands strengthened. And now that I have obtained this, must I see
I have obtained it, only to the end I might leave them? that I have
tasted of the comfortable fruits thereof, only that by the plucking them
from my mouth, my being condemned unto my former uncomfortable
work might be made more bitter? Must I be obliged to leave that
congregation, just when, by the good hand of God upon me, I am
put in a capacity to be more serviceable among them than ever I
was all the nine years preceding.

 "Although I cannot own this change in the state of the parish of
Etterick to be owing to the struggle made for this transportation,
since it was begun ere the least motion was made in that affair; yet
it is evident, the congregation of Etterick in the communion of this
church, have all along, in the progress of that business, cordially adhered to me, and exerted their utmost endeavours for my continu-

ance among them; and that there is no removing of me out of that
parish, but by rending me from them; which I hope may be admitted as an evidence, that my labours have not been altogether in vain
there. I beg the Very Reverend Commission to consider, what will
be the consequences of rending me, by this transportation, from that
congregation. The desolating of that parish, which lies at such a
distance from neighbour-kirks, as has been represented; and that
in a mountainous country, which it is hard to travel to or from in the
winter-season, as appears from their not having one sermon in their
church for eight or nine Sabbaths successively, in time of their last
vacancy; the desolating, I say, of that parish in such circumstances,
would challenge the serious regard of our Rev. judges, though both
they and I were indifferent in the matter of this transportation. But
since it is far otherwise, on their part, as well as on mine, how can I
think on their case, as left irritated, both heritors and people.

" Moderator, I was planted in that parish under a great disadvantage, with respect to most of the Honourable persons, heritors of it;
yet now it is quite against their mind that I be removed. And I
doubt they think themselves but harshly treated by the judicatories
of this church, if my removal from, and my settlement in, that parish, be so much of a piece as this transportation will make them. And
as there is very little hope, that they and the people will agree in
the choice of another minister, so it is hardly to be expected, but
that the manner of my settlement in that parish will be remembered
on another such occasion, to the prejudice of the interest of the
gospel there, and I fear (not without ground) to a more public prejudice. What shall become of the irritated people, bereaved of their
pastor, to whose ministry, by the good hand of God, they have adhered, notwithstanding of their manifold temptations to desert it,
and the communion of this church? How will the scorn of their deserting neighbours work on their passions? Can any who know the
circumstances of that country, obtain it of themselves to think, that
such a fair occasion for promoting the schism there will be neglected? Will not those who have kept their meetings several times
within the bounds of the parish since I was settled there, return
again to the church-yard, where they have met in the time of the
last vacancy? The parish of Etterick is almost quite surrounded
with neighbouring parishes, notably broken, as well as they are
themselves; in one of which, Eskdalemoor, separatists of different
factions have their distinct parties, and their meetings one after
another; and some of my congregation are almost as near to a
church, which the presbytery has seldom, if ever, access to, viz.,
Wamphray, as they are to their own church. I am loth to be more

particular on this head; I with the Reverend Commission may in due time inquire further into the state of that country. But from what is said it appears, that the parish of Etterick, lying in the centre, is, by this transportation, threatened to be made the very seat of separation in that country.

"Moderator, The parish of Closeburn is so considerable, numerous, and divided, that it is a burden quite too heavy for me, and requires a minister endued with qualifications I cannot pretend to, and withal of another spirit than I am; being very unfit, on many accounts, to appear in the world in any such post, even though it were an unanimous parish. But as it is a parish notably divided, I am still the more unfit for it. I have had too much acquaintance with myself, in the management of the parish of Etterick, to think I am fit to undertake the charge of the parish of Closeburn, wherein (I am persuaded) the work of the gospel would egregiously suffer in my hands. I know, that little stress is sometimes put upon proffessions of this nature; but I do ingenuously declare, that, in my most retired thoughts of this transportation, the disadvantages I find I labour under from myself, in managing my work in the congregation I am set over, do so stare me in the face, that I cannot encourage this design, without a witness against me in my own bosom, testifying I should be injurious to the parish of Closeburn, in accepting their call, which I plainly perceive has proceeded on a mistake concerning me. For though it has pleased the Lord sometimes to make my preaching-gift acceptable to his people; yet it is well known to those of my acquaintance, I labour under some uncommon disadvantages, which render me unfit for such a post.

"Besides, Moderator, I have seriously considered the matter of this transportation again and again, and I can have no other apprehension of it, but that it will be a rending of me from a congregation whose hearts are pierced with the thoughts of my removal from them, and a throwing me undesired into another. I am convinced, that upon whatever views that parish made choice of me to be their minister, when they signed their call to me, matters are now so far altered, that had some things, with relation to the parish of Etterick and to myself, which in the progress of this affair have manifestly appeared, to the conviction of all unbiassed persons, been believed before this process was commenced, they had not proceeded therein. And whatever reason the pursuers may have to go on, since they have begun, I hope our Very Reverend Judges will find themselves obliged to determine as the present state of affairs requires. Several persons, commissioners from the parish of Closeburn, at different times, have had the trouble of several long journeys in this

affair, which I am heartily sorry for. And I freely own, that Sir
Thomas Kirkpatrick, and another of that parish, have all along appeared cordial and serious in that matter; but I must have been
unaccountably blinded, if, by repeated evidences otherwise, I had
not perceived the parish of Closeburn not inclined to be hard on the
parish of Etterick in this affair. And however this might perhaps
be deemed to be of small importance in the case of one inclined to
embrace their call; yet it cannot but have weight with our Reverend and compassionate judges, in the case of a fixed minister,
whose congregation and himself must both suffer violence, in order to
the casting him in upon another that desires him not.

"Moderator, I need not put the Reverend Commission in mind of
the great end of this project, namely, the healing of the breaches
there; but I heartily wish it may be duly weighed, whether this
transportation be a means proper for attaining that end? And one
would think, some more than ordinary certainty was necessary in
this point, especially considering that the widening of the breaches
in Etterick, and the adjacent parts, will surely follow upon the
event of this transportation; and that a mistake, or false step, in
an affair relating to such a broken country as Nithsdale is, may be
of dangerous consequence. I am, persuaded with the Reverend
synod of Merse and Teviotdale, that this transportation will not
answer the end; and think it strange, if any who know all circumstances be otherwise minded. Whatever measures the wisdom of
some other person, who shall be called to that parish, may suggest
unto him for compassing the desired end, I find myself so straitened
in that respect, that I cannot forbear to say, with all deference to
my Reverend Judges, that the transporting me to Closeburn, will in
effect be a driving me into a snare, where, to which hand soever I
turn, I must be broken.

"Now, Moderator, will the justice of the Reverend Commission
allow them, to lay a congregation desolate, which was planted with
so much difficulty, has been managed with so much uneasiness, and,
upon the event of this transportation, must become the very seat of
separation in the country, and which there is so very little hope of
the comfortable supply of, they in the meantime so vigorously re-
claiming; and all this, in a time wherein there is so very little need
of transportations, but the parish pursuing may be otherwise settled,
to far greater advantage? Will their respect to the peace of this
church, suffer them to give such ground of irritation to a congregation
in these circumstances I have narrated? Will their compassion
allow them, to take one whose spirit is already shattered with the
effects of the divisive temper, and cast him into another place, where

it must be far more so? or to lead out one, and set him upon the ice, where he knows no way (in the course of ordinary Providence) how to keep his feet; and when he falls, must fall for nought, I mean, no advantage to the church gained thereby? Nay, Moderator, I cannot believe these things.

"I have the greatest aversion to this transportation; and whoso considers what I have represented, will not think it strange. I hope the Reverend Commission will not violate me ; which they will do, if they transport me to Closeburn. The case of the Reverend Mr. Warden's transportation to Falkirk, and of the Rev. Mr. Wodrow's to Stirling, which were refused by the Commission, though each of these parishes is more considerable than the parish here pursuing, are such instances of the lenity of this Very Reverend Judicatory, that it will be thought exceeding strange, if it shall be my lot only to be violated.

"Moderator, I have been twice settled already; and I bless the Lord, who was pleased, in both, convincingly to shew me his own call coming along with the call of his church. And I have felt so much need of the former, its accompanying the latter, that I would be most inexcusable to venture on removing to another parish without it. I was persuaded in my conscience of the Lord's calling me to Etterick ; and my clearness as to my call to that place, was never overclouded, no not in my darkest hours; and had I not had that to support me there, I had sunk under my burden. Now I have endeavoured, according to the measure of the grace bestowed on me, to set aside my own inclinations, and the consideration of the ease and satisfaction of my own heart, and to lay this matter before the Lord, for light to discover his mind about it, labouring to wait upon him in the way of his word and works. But I sincerely declare, after all, I have no clearness to accept the call of Closeburn, nor a foundation for my conscience, in this transportation, which ought not to rest on human authority. I have all deference for the authority of this church, and my ministry is very dear to me ; so I cast myself down at your feet, begging that you will not grant this transportation, which has been refused by the presbytery and synod whereof I am a member; and who are best acquainted with the state of the parish of Etterick, and what concerns me ; whereas both that parish and I are known but to very few of our now Reverend Judges. But if it shall please the holy wise God, to suffer me now, for my trial and correction, to fall under your sentence, transporting me from the parish of Etterick to the parish of Closeburn ; since it is a charge I have no clearness to undertake, I resolve, through grace, rather to suffer, than to enter upon it blindfolded. Though,

in the meantime, I cannot help thinking, it will be hard measure to
punish me, because I cannot see with other men's eyes; especially
considering that the presbytery of Selkirk, and the Reverend Synod
of Merse and Teviotdale, have, by their respective sentences, continued me in Etterick, upon very weighty grounds, contained in the
sentence of the latter in this affair."

The deep concern I was in, naturally formed the delivery of the
speech. Parties being removed, I went into a seat in the church
alone, and gave myself to prayer, it being in the night season; I
cast myself over on the Lord, to follow still as he should go before,
but no otherwise ; and in case of the sentence going against me, was
resolved to protest for liberty to complain to the assembly, and
never to undertake that charge, unless light broke up to me, which
had not yet appeared. But by a vast majority, the sentence, passed
in our favour; and others, as well as I, were convinced, that the
speech I delivered, was that which influenced the Commission, and
moved their compassion.

Thus ended that weighty affair, for which several of the godly
through the country, particularly those of the meetings for Christian
fellowship in Galashiels, had been concerned before the Lord. About
fourteen days before, at the sacrament of Maxton, laying hold on the
covenant which is a covenant of promises, I was helped to some distinctness in applying the several sorts of promises, as those for pardon, for
sanctification, for direction, &c., and this with a particular view to that
business then before me. And I must say, the Lord was with me in the
management, giving me in that hour, both what to speak, and courage
to speak it; and even when I ran, he left me not to stumble. One
of our heritors that I had confidence in, quite failed me; but Sir
William Scot, the principal one, surprised me with his personal appearance, and standing by me in judgment, which he had all along
refused. My inclinations in that matter having been most injuriously misrepresented by some ministers and others, by the issue they
were silenced. That which was the real ground of my aversion to
Closeburn, was, that I had a most uncomfortable life in Etterick, and
my work among them had all along been exceeding heavy ; through
the disposition of the people, selfish, conceited, and bending towards
the schism, which has most deep rooting in this place ; hence proceeded contempt of ordinances, ministers, &c., to the great breaking
of my spirit. To have gone to Closeburn, a parish of the same character, I reckoned would have been just to begin my weary task
anew ; in one word, to have cast me out of the frying pan into the
fire. Otherwise, to have been transported from Etterick, and gone

any whither, where the gospel would have been heard and received at my hands, would have been most gladly embraced by me, if the Lord himself had but said it. Besides, I had been advised, that the air did not agree with my wife's constitution, and tended to impair her health; and that it would overcome me at length. Of these my heavy circumstances in this place, I had been speaking to Mr. Murray, and he took occasion to provide this remedy of the transportation to Closeburn, which I looked on as ill as the disease, in respect of the uncomfortableness of my work, which the more wholesome air could not counterbalance to me. As for my wife's conduct in the matter, it was as became a Christian, spoke forth much self-denial, and resignation to the will of the Lord; making not the least uneasiness to me in point of my conscience. The design of Providence in the whole affair, I take to have been, as at first, to rebuke the parish and myself; and, I would fain hope, to cement and knit us more closely for the time to come. And they seem to have a sense of the mercy.

This toss hindered the administering of the sacrament this year; which was the only interruption it had met with, from the year 1710, that the course of it was begun.

PERIOD XI.

FROM THE TRANSPORTATION TO CLOSEBURN REFUSED, TO THE NOTABLE BREACH IN MY HEALTH, AND ALTERATION IN MY CONSTITUTION.

AFTER this affair was over, my wife went from Edinburgh to her own country, to breathe her native air a while for her health, as had been advised in her case. That the air of Etterick did not agree with her, was declared to us; and that was an argument used by the pursuers for transportation. It was also declared to me, by my dear friend Dr. Trotter, that it would overcome me too at length. But what could we do for relief in the case, in the circumstances above narrated?

But as the effects of the rebellion cured our people of their unnatural fondness for public confusions, so that that disposition never appeared among them since, as before; so the attempt to transport me to Closeburn, did bring them to themselves with respect to me; and made my life among them tolerable. Howbeit, since that time I have not wanted enough to keep me from forgetting where I am.

On Sept. 18, there was, by appointment of our session, a congregational thanksgiving observed, upon the account of the favourable issue of the process aforesaid; which was ground of thankfulness to me, as well as to the parish. But to balance the victory I had obtained, I came home from that struggle, with a sore rheumatic pain in my arm, which kept me a considerable time after. On the thanksgiving day, Mr. Henry Davidson, minister of Galashiels, Mr. Gabriel Wilson, and I myself, preached.

Mr. Davidson aforesaid was, by that time, become a third with Mr. Wilson and me, in our bond of strict friendship; a man of great gravity, piety, and tenderness; learned and judicious; well acquainted with books; a great preacher, delivering in a taking manner, masterly thoughts, in an unaffected elevated style; endowed with a gift of prayer, in heavenly oratory, beyond any man that ever I knew; extremely modest, and reserved in his temper; but a kind and affectionate friend. This friendship, most comfortable, and useful as a threefold cord, does by the mercy of God continue inviolated to this day. We have always been so happy as to speak the same thing in public differences.

I had sent in unto Mr. John Flint, one of the ministers of Edinburgh, who had revised the Fourfold State, and was noted for his skill in the Hebrew tongue, two sheets of the performance on Ezekiel, above mentioned. And, being in Edinburgh about the middle of November, he was pleased to tell me, that he judged no great thing could be done by the accents; and advised me to make no bustle about them, as he termed it. On the account of this discouraging event, and other things, I did, on the 23d of this month, spend some time in prayer. And thinking on that study, the conviction I had made upon me by the light into some passages of the holy text, by means of the accentuation, remained to be such, as that I could not see how I could give over the study thereof. And having begged of God a token for good, I was that same night surprised with a light into Jacob's vow; Gen. xxviii. 20—22, " If God will be with me, and will keep me in this way that I go, and will give me bread to eat, and raiment to put on; so that I come again to my Father's house in peace; then shall the Lord be my God. And this stone, which I have set for a pillar, shall be God's house; and of all that thou shalt give me, I will surely give the tenth unto thee;" new to me, and that arising from the accentuation.

By reason of the many avocations I had now for a good time had, there was little done by me in that study, being of such a nature as it could not be managed by parts. But a week or two after the October Synod, I made some collections on the subject. And the winter being come on, which in these days was the time I spent to my greatest satisfaction, I began, Nov. 27, to proceed in my book of materials mentioned above.

Plying it eagerly thereafter, I was, on Dec. 22, being the Lord's day, at night laid under a deep conviction of the woeful disposition of my heart, pursuing like fire the study of the accents, so that I could hardly ever get my heart from off them. I went to God, and bewailed my case, cried to get my heart under command, with respect to that matter; and I got, from my prayer-hearing God, my heart filled with love to Jesus Christ, and set for him as the one thing needful. I had by that time, through the good hand of God upon me, made a comfortable progress in that study; but towards the latter end of that week, beginning to make the observations on the majors, I stuck, day after day. At length I resolved, for that cause, to set some time apart for prayer, which necessarily fell to be Jan. 1, 1718. But the said resolution being laid down, I was helped to make some progress ere the appointed day came.

Jan. 1. I accordingly spent some time in prayer, 1. On the account of my study aforesaid; 2. For the distress of the parish by the storm lying on the ground, &c.; and the Lord was with me. That day, reading 1 Sam. ii. in the original, new light broke out unto me, particularly as to two things; 1st, The abusing of the text by interrogations, where it really bears none, particularly 2 Kings v. 26; Job ii. 10. 2d, Some inkling of quite new light into the repetition of the same majors; with some other things, and my soul was filled with joy in the Lord, and I was made to cry out again and again, " What am I!" As to the storm, the Lord seems to refuse to be intreated therein by congregational fasting with prayer; for it was in my mind to have had it done last week; but on the Lord's day, when it might have been appointed, there was a fair thaw; and when the occasion of appointing it for that week was over, the thaw misgave, I designed it again on Tuesday the 7th, and offered to have kept it on the 6th; but I was told the people could not be present, being to flee with their sheep that day and the next.

In February, having been for some time diverted from my beloved study, and, whereas I was then to enter on the minors, being in much confusion, not knowing where to begin my work, I did on the 13th spend some time in prayer, for light, both as to matter and method: which last I was obliged very particularly to seek of the Father of lights. And having essayed it the same day, I found myself in a hopeful way as to both; and that the confidence I had, through grace, had in the Lord, was not in vain.

At that time I was lecturing on Genesis, and being allured by what I met with in the original, studying my lectures, I began that week to translate as I went on. Afterwards I wrote notes too on the translation. This performance, begun at Gen. xxxvii., is carried on to Exod. xxxv., and to be found among my papers. But this way of doing retarded me in my main study; wherefore finding I had not time for it and other things too, I broke off; and, to the best of my remembrance, left off lecturing on the Old Testament.

March 25. The interjections and interrogations being then before me, I spent some time in prayer for the divine assistance in my studies, and some distress relating to some in my family; and the Lord was found of me, and quickly gave me help and relief, in all the cases that then lay upon me.

A part of my stipend coming in about that time, I did, on the 30th lay by fifty merks thereof for pious uses; and all along since that time I have kept a private box, making up into it yearly the said sum of fifty merks, laying it in mostly by parcels, and giving out of it as occasion requires; and I always keep of it in my left-side pocket. The dealing to poor at the house for their food, continues as formerly, without respect to this; only what wool is given them in the summer, since I have none of my own, is bought out of this fund; out of which, also, our Sabbath's contributions are taken. This course I have found to be profitable to the poor, and affording much ease to myself, for I have thereby been in case to give considerably on special occasions, and that with more ease to myself than otherwise I could have had; always looking on that part of my yearly income as not my own but the Lord's.

After shutting up the doctrine of repentance, in my ordinary, I did, on October 27, 1717, return to the catechism; beginning at the doctrine of the application of the redemption purchased by Christ. And handling these subjects practically, as well as catechetically, at considerable length, I proceeded therein until the sacrament this year, June 8, at which time I closed my sermons on adoption; only, being just entered on justification, I was by some incident or incidents led off to Numb. xxxii. 23, "Be sure your sin will find you out;" upon which I dwelt a considerable time. A third adultery, was about that time, after much pains and toil, discovered; the adulterer being the same man who first filled my hands in that kind, viz. the unhappy J. N. now in the parish of Moffat, as he also was in the time of this last of his adulteries in this parish. Moreover a bastard of —— above alluded to, being at nurse in R. fiery peats were found lodged in the thatch of the nurse's house, two nights, but still discovered before any hurt was done. There was a great stir about this, and search made; but it remains to this day a hidden work of darkness. I and others vehemently suspected it to be purely a trick to screen the nurse and her husband from the displeasure of the father; she having become scarce of milk, and the child begun to go back. Meanwhile, it was weighty to me, that the truth of the matter could not be got discovered. In this case, on the fast day before the sacrament, I read to the congregation the passage relating to the expiation of uncertain murder; Deut. xxi. 1—9; and praying, made confession in that matter accordingly. And on fencing the table on the Lord's day, I did particularly declare to be debarred, the author or authors, and accomplices in that vile action; but when the table came to be filled, the suspected person immediately sat down at it. My case through the whole communion-day, did very much answer my case in the family-fast before it. I had now and then some remarkable tenderness, but that for the most part wanting. But a solid concern for the good of souls, with a deliberate choice of God in Christ for my God, being left me, I was not discouraged. In self-examination I had some comfortable views of the grace of God in me, particularly of faith and love. At the table, the Lord let me in into a glorious view of the fulness of the Godhead dwelling bodily in our blessed Redeemer, and so into a view of the fulness of the body broken for me, and exhibited to me in the sacrament; so that my soul feeding on Christ, fed on the glorious attributes and perfections of God.

On the Tuesday after, my helpers, Messrs Simpson, Wilson, and Davidson, revived the project of publishing the sermons on Man's Fourfold State, and offered to advance money for that effect. That matter had been laid aside through the removal of my dear friend Dr. Trotter, the first mover, by death; and Providence seemed about this time to be laying the grave-stone upon it, by carrying off also Thomas Linton in Chapelhop above mentioned, who, having some time appeared like to fill up Dr. Trotter's room in the matter, was now a-dying. This motion was surprising. I thought, that, should the Lord prosper the work of the accentuation now in hand, that book might prosper after the acceptance thereof. But Mr. Wilson represented this, as carving out by one's own wisdom, when we were near to part, impressed me more than any thing that had been said. For the way of carnal wisdom, for many years, has been always frightful to me; and that disposition of spirit, which I was conscious to in myself, afforded me a comfortable reflection with respect to my state.

On Monday the 7th of July I had taken a vomit, on the morrow after, physic, and likewise on the Thursday again; and that Thursday's night I was sent for to see Thomas Linton, supposed to be a-dying; which at first view was stunning and confounding, in respect of my bodily hazard. I had thankfully observed, and offered my praises, for that, during the time I was under that course, I had got liberty to keep the house; but this trial came ere all was done. On the Monday afternoon one came to me desiring me to go and

baptize his child, supposed to be a-dying; I, never having administered baptism in a private house, without previous intimation to the
congregation, refused; and the parent seemed to be much affected at
the refusal. This set me to beg the life of that child. Going to
God to seek direction upon the express from Chapelhop, I found I
durst not sit the call. So I went away that same night, owing my
all to be at the Master's disposal, in prosecuting the ministry I had
received from him; and withal, with a certain satisfaction in the
Lord's laying trials to my hand. I returned on the morrow, without
the least discernible harm to myself; and the parent came again,
shewing the child to be better, and to be baptised orderly next
Lord's day in the church. And here I must remark, that, through
the whole course of my ministry, then eighteen years, never a child
died without baptism through my sticking to that principle. Glory
to a good God for it.

On Monday, July 14, the saddest trial of all came. I was awak-
ened that morning, to hear the doleful account of a woman's having
murdered herself in Etterick-house; and while I was making ready
to go thither, word came that I behoved to go quickly over to
Chapelhop, to see Thomas Linton a-dying; and on the Sabbath I
had been desired to come down on the Monday to see the goodwife
of Andleshop, who also seemed to be going off. So I went off extremely confounded with the dispensation; beheld the woman lying
dead by her own hands, so far as is known; then I went to Chapelhop, and came about by Andleshop.

On the Tuesday after, I attempted to spend some time in prayer;
but through confusion and heaviness, that work was marred. On
Tuesday the 22d, I spent some time in that exercise, embraced the
covenant anew, and addressed the throne of grace, with an eye to
the sacrament at Maxton, what to preach on to my own people, the
case of another poor woman under trouble of the same nature, and
for the Lord's determination as to the point of publishing of the
book on Man's Fourfold State, or not. The Lord was with me in
some measure. I have had much ado to stand under the thoughts
of publishing that book; being tossed betwixt two, namely, the ven-
turing such a mean piece into the world, while many whose books I
am not worthy to carry, are silent; and the fear of sitting the call
of Providence to it. Thus it has lain so heavy on me, that I have
been as tossed on a sea; and sometimes it has almost quite sunk my
spirits. And as yet I know not what to do; but desire to wait on
the Lord, if he will give me a token of his mind; being conscious
to myself of desiring to sacrifice my credit to his call fairly laid before me.

Being at the communion in Maxton, August 3, two particular providences were remarkable. 1. Mr. Wilson told me, that in his visiting of the parish before that communion, he had ordinarily that word, "Lay your hand to your heart, and halt no more;" and the Lord led me to that text for that occasion, "How long halt ye between two opinions?" which was countenanced with some influence especially on the Saturday. 2. Having been quite at a loss what to do as to compliance with the motion for publishing the book aforesaid, and being just waiting for Providence moving; Mr. Wilson's sister told him in my hearing, that Mr. Robert Wightman, treasurer of the city of Edinburgh, who unknown to me had been addressed for encouraging it, by Mrs. Schiell his sister, through Mr. Wilson's means as I think, had said, he would do nothing in it till such time as he should see the MS. So I, being just waiting for the moving of Providence in the matter, was natively brought to resolve on sending the copy to him.

By the melancholy event of July 14, I was led to preach on Psal. cxlvii. 11, "The Lord taketh pleasure in them that fear him, in those that hope in his mercy." The which, being begun July 27, was ended August 31. After which I entered on the Saviour's commission; Isa. lxi. 1, "The Spirit of the Lord God is upon me, because the Lord hath anointed me to preach good tidings unto the meek, he hath sent me to bind up the broken-hearted, to proclaim liberty to the captives, and the opening of the prison to them that are bound;" and insisted thereon till Feb. 22, in the year following.

Being again engaged, this winter, in the study of the accentuation, and occupied in writing in my book of materials, I stuck. Upon which event, and for other causes, I resolved to spend some time in prayer. A thanksgiving for the good harvest preposed at the synod, did not take. It was proposed to me to observe it however here. But my heart had a secret aversion to it, and I delayed it, to see whether the commission would appoint one or not. These two last Sabbaths I waited for word about it; but none came, nor could I hear what they had done. I saw God was angry with me, and hereby testified his displeasure against my former subtle aversion to it; I therefore on the 3d of December, spent some time in prayer on these accounts. And the Lord was with me. Examining myself for evidences of grace, I found, 1. I was carried out of all confidence in myself to Jesus Christ, on whom my soul relied with confidence, finding I have no other plea before the Lord. I was sensibly brought to this by confession; setting God's mercies to me, and my sins, from my birth, through the several periods of my life, child-

hood, youth, &c. the one over against the other, in confession before
the Lord. 2. My conscience bearing me witness, of hating and despising all things in comparison of Christ ; being desirous to cleave
to him and the way of duty, over the belly of all smiles and frowns
that would carry me away. 3. A desire of universal and perfect
holiness, being conscious my hopes are as earnest for sanctification,
as for justification, from Jesus Christ my Lord. What I had most
at heart in this exercise, was my study of the accents, the thanksgiving, the case of my absent children, the afflicted in the parish,
&c. My daughter Jane about two months ago having gone to
Dunse, I had a special concern on my spirit for her. And by her
letter I was refreshed, both in that it was well with her soul, and my
prayers for her have been heard. I saw myself much indebted to the
divine goodness, in that all my children now appear to have a capacity for learning. I had a special concern on my spirit this day,
for being helped to die to the glory of God, that, when it comes, I
may be full of days, ripe, and content cheerfully to go away. Between the laying down of the resolution for this exercise, and the
performance, I saw what way to get over the particular difficulty
whereat I stuck in my study of the accents. This is the second
time I have found that promise fulfilled in this matter, " Before they
call I will answer ;" Isa. lxv. 24

Dec. 21.—My wife brought me in mind of a story of one of my
daughters which I had forgot, that happened in the beginning of the
1712, or some time before that. A poor boy came into the house
begging, having such a defect in his speech, that he pronounced
the words " father" and " mother," " fea" and " moa ;" at which my
wife and others smiling, desired him to speak over again what he
had said. In the meantime the child stood looking on, with the
tear in her eye, in great distress; and at length came to her mother,
and said, " Mother, did God make that laddie ?" She answered,
" Yes, my dear." Then she replied, " Will he not then be angry at
you for laughing at him ? for my book says, ' He that mocketh the
poor reproacheth his Maker.'" And the boy being very naked, she
was in mighty concern to get old clothes for him.

Dec. 22.—Having had a particular concern this morning on my
heart for grace to the young ones, I spoke affectionately to my
little child Thomas, about the state of his soul, and prayed with him.
Being risen from prayer, and his mother come in, he burst out
a-weeping. Taking him aside, and asking what was the matter, he
said, He knew not how to get an interest in Christ. I said, he was
to seek it, and believe the gospel. He said, he knew not how to
seek it. He went into the western room thereafter, I being abroad,

and being asked, said, He went in to seek an interest in Christ, and to tell Christ he would be his. I note this for an encouragement to hold on to teach and stir them up. I am sorry I have not kept an account of the early movings that were in the rest.

Jan. 1, 1719.—I had resolved to keep my time for prayer, the week following, and not to separate myself any manner of way this day. But Providence laid a necessity on me to do it this day. Treasurer Wightman, having glanced the MS. on the Fourfold State, wrote to me, that he found a vein of true Christianity in it, and therefore would contribute to the publication of it; and this requiring an answer, gave me an unlooked-for errand to the throne of grace at this time. He intimated withal, that the style would be nauseous to the polite world, and that no book had yet been written on the depraved state of man, with true spirit and elegancy of expression. This did not much move me; for I do not think, that way of writing he is so fond of, is the way the Lord has used much to countenance for the advancing of true Christianity. Meanwhile it left me much undetermined what to do with the MS. Three things especially I had in view in this exercise: 1. My management as to that MS; 2. The study of the accents; 3. Divine assistance in revising the larger overtures for discipline in this church, laid on me by the synod, and on some other brethren. In the beginning of this secret exercise, the Lord was pleased to countenance me; but after that I drove very heavily, till towards the end wherein he was pleased to help to freedom and confidence in himself.

The aforesaid overtures having been long in print, the General Assembly had committed them to Synods and Presbyteries, to be considered by them, in order, that being ripely advised, they might be turned into standing rules. The Synod had appointed some few of their number to consider them accordingly, of whom I was one. And, having been almost ever since my entering into the ministry, dissatisfied with several things in our constitution, especially the manner of admitting to the Lord's table and planting of churches, I embraced that opportunity to endeavour to get such things rectified; and accordingly I did, some time after, apply myself closely to consider of these overtures, and wrote several remarks on them, together with new overtures for admission to the Lord's table, and debarring from it; the which are to be found among my papers, App. No, 3. Howbeit, the Synod did not call for them. Nevertheless, by order of our Presbytery, they were laid before the commission, or their committee appointed to receive such remarks. But the matter was dropped; and, for anything I know, no more insisted on since that time. And I apprehend the malady will be incurable, till the present constitution be violently thrown down.

On the 15th of March I returned to the catechism, entering on the question of sanctification. And from that time I went through the whole that remained of it, till I came to the end thereof, in the spring in the following year. Meanwhile, with these catechetic sermons, were joined others directed against formality, from Rom. ii. 28, 29; and profaneness, from 2 Tim. ii. 19; and Rom. i. 18, ended Nov. 8 in this year.

This was another year remarkable on the account of the abjuration oath, as the 1712. Towards the latter end of the preceding year, the non-jurors at Edinburgh thought meet, that one should be sent to court, to represent the loyalty and good affection of that party to his Majesty, notwithstanding that they could not take the oath of abjuration imposed by law. And a form of an oath which they could take, was condescended on, with an address for that effect. The said address was handed about to be signed by nonjurors; and withal, money desired of them to bear the charges of this mission. I refused to sign the address, having no clearness for it; and so did also my two friends Mr. Wilson and Mr. Davidson. However, being clear and willing, that our loyalty and good affection to King George should be represented, I gave my money, a guinea as I remember, towards the bearing of the charges for that effect. Mr. William Gusthart, then minister of Crailing, afterwards transported to Edinburgh, was the man whom they sent to court. And upon his return, what money was left, was restored. Their project so far took at court, that the addressers got the oath so as they embraced and took it. And the first day of June was the term appointed by the act for the taking thereof; and that act did withal bar all young men from being licensed or ordained without taking it. So the body of those who formerly had been non-jurors, were carried off into it at that time; and there remained but a few recusants; among whom, by the divine favour, were my two friends and I still. From the year 1712 to this year, the nonjurors made near a third part of our Synod; and so we were regarded by our brethren jurors, and were in case to be useful among them; but from this time, the few that remained were quite borne down, and could do little in the Synod.

Whatever answer I had given to the above-mentioned letter from Mr. Wightman, about the Fourfold State, I had afterwards again laid aside thoughts of the project, and required back that part of the copy which was at Edinburgh. But it was refused; and the week before the sacrament, which was administered June 7, I had another letter from Mr. Wightman aforesaid, bearing, that he had agreed with Mr. James Macewan to print it on his own expenses, and to give me a hundred copies; and for encouragement of the undertaker foresaid, he generously advanced to him a considerable sum of money for a time. After the sacrament was over, I laid the matter before the Lord, as it had been in the letter aforesaid proposed to me; and having considered it, could not see how I could with safety of my conscience refuse compliance with this fair offer, and to let it go out into the world. Accordingly I signified my compliance therewith. My being threatened with silencing on the account of the oath again, as anew exposed now to the lash of the law, had great weight herein with me; as also the providential bringing about the matter in a manner I expected not, when the apparent instruments of it were carried off one after another; and that this point it was brought to when I had again given over thoughts of it.

Meanwhile I had by this time for some years found my strength decaying, and the preceding winter's study had much weakened me, having in March 1718 completed my sixth septenary, being then forty-two years of age.

Now being thus again called to lay my account with suffering on the account of the oath aforesaid, I wrote a paper, entitled, "Reasons for refusing the abjuration oath in its latest form," 1719; the which is *in retentis*, together with a printed copy thereof incorrectly done. This, a considerable time after, came surprisingly to my hand, not knowing how it came to be published.

As to the sacrament in June, I have little to remark for comfort in my own case. My furnace was hot, partly by reason of the business of the abjuration oath again, which came on like a thunder-clap; and partly, by the affliction of one of mine. The Lord was pleased to withdraw from me in my studies, so that for the two days, Tuesday and Wednesday, I could do nothing therein satisfyingly; but I behoved to go forward as I could in the explication of the text, on Wednesday's night; and on Friday hammered out a sermon on it, with no gust at all. Howbeit I got some gust of it in meditating on it afterwards, and that was increased in the delivery of it. A madman was so unruly that I was much confounded in fencing of the tables; I recovered somewhat at the table, but when I had done, I was much disturbed and cast down. This, however, the Lord was pleased to make use of, to the further discovery of my sinfulness and emptiness, issuing in a melting of heart under a sense of my own naughtiness, and the goodness of God, which was the frame of my spirit in communicating. It was a melancholy time at the sacrament, 1712, the first year of the oath; and this in some measure kept pace with it, though not so ill. The reflecting on that made me wonder the less at this. Surely it is to keep me humble and depending.

Great was the stumbling and offence of the people in the Forest and Teviotdale, on the account of the oath, in its new as well as in its old shape; but the combination among the ministers was now become strong, and the few recusants were treated as aliens by their brethren. The people being in a ferment, there was desired a meet-ing of our Presbytery, with the Presbytery of Jedburgh at Hawick, to confer with the people in order to bring them to peace, and to hear the word from those with whom they were offended. To this meeting I went, with a sincere desire to contribute my endeavours towards the desired peace. But appearing among them, they, to my great surprise, did by their vote force me into the chair, contrary to all right and reason, the moderator of the Presbytery of Jedburgh being *ex officio* moderator of that meeting, since it was a meeting of that Presbytery within their own bounds, to which our Presbytery had been invited. But the design, proceeding from their jealousy, was that I might not have access to speak much in the affair; and indeed they made the seat most uneasy to me; and carrying things with a high hand, nothing was done for healing of the breach betwixt them and the people. But they appointed a committee of their number, to meet at Lilliesleaf in our bounds, for a new conference with the people. When they met there, they tacked about, and without any ceremony set another in the chair, though I, as modera-tor of their constituent judicatory, was their moderator *ex officio*. But I made not the least hint to reclaim. They minded then that I should have access to speak, and out of conscience towards God, I did all I could towards accommodating the matter betwixt them and the people, and the best was made of it that circumstances would allow, a peace being patched up. After all was over, I told their leading men the sense I had of their manner of treating me at both meetings; but that I had resolved to be what they pleased, for reaching the end; upon which they owned I had acted as a good man and a Chris-tian. Meanwhile, in the harvest season, orders came from court to prosecute the non-jurors, but the execution was put off.

When I think on my refusing to sign the address for the oath, which the addressers got granted them, accompanied with barring all young men from being licensed or ordained without taking it, I am thankful from the heart, I was kept from putting my hand to that unhallowed business.

About the beginning of August, I began and transcribed what re-mained of the Eternal State, and ended all October 24. This was the second time I had wrote over that book. And about the middle of November, thirteen of the printed sheets came to my hand, the press having advanced to the head of regeneration. I spent there-

fore the 25th of November in prayer, for a blessing to be entailed on
that book, not only in the time of my life, but after my death ; so
also for the divine assistance in my study of the accentuation, which
I was then to fall upon again ; for the case of the church, my family,
and particularly the children at Edinburgh, and the congregation.
And I came away with confidence in a prayer-hearing God.

It was but a little after this, that having closed that exercise, and
sat down to dinner, an express from Edinburgh, arrived, calling me
thither ; for that my daughter Jane, was dangerously sick of a high
fever, and roving. This surprising alarm touched me to the quick.
Presently the cause was manifest. I had taken her and her brother
John to Edinburgh, and left her uneasy with the cold, as he also
was ; and just on my coming home on the 14th, being attacked with
a certain temptation, which often has been ruining to me, I was
thereby carried quite off my feet ; my heart in the meantime fearing my
dear children, whom I had left, might smart for this. It was ground
of comfort, that the Lord had begun early to deal with her soul ;
and, by good providence, about an hour ere the express came, I had
cast my eye on the passage of Dec. 21, 1718. At five o'clock I took
my horse, and journeyed all the night. Many thoughts about her
went through my heart like arrows, while I was by the way ; but
still I held firm by this, that whatever the Lord should do in her
case, it would be well done, it would be best done, and my soul would
approve it as such. And the faith of this was my anchor. I considered all my children ; and, if any of them was to be removed by
death, I was satisfied it should be her, though she has had a very
particular room in my affection ; for I looked on her as the fittest
for that change. At Peebles, the passage concerning Peter's wife's
mother coming before me in prayer, I was helped to pray that God
would rebuke the fever. Betwixt eight and nine next morning I arrived in Edinburgh ; and having asked if she was alive, my trembl-
ling heart was eased, with the answer, that she was better ; and I
found it was so when I saw her. I continued in Edinburgh from
that Wednesday till the Friday was eight days after, December 4. ;
and she was still better. During that time, I was willingly employed in private houses, in the Lord's work, since the melancholy work
of burying my daughter, which I had feared, was taken out of my
hand. She had got out of the bed six days before I left her. This was
a great mercy in my eyes ; and I was often made to thank my God,
for the kind rebuke he had given me ; for while he smote with the
one hand, he embraced with the other. It was kindness, that the
alarm found me as I had been employed that day. John Currie was
to have gone to the Merse that day, and I thought he had been gone,

but Providence had stopped him, that he might go with me. There
being a sick man in the Crosslie, I thought it best to visit him as I
passed, notwithstanding my haste, and the occasion of it; and God
moved the heart of one of the servants there to guide us over the
hills; the night being so dark, that, going up the hill, I could not
discern the horse that rode before me, I caused one put on his
shoulder a white linen cloth for that end; but to no purpose. The
waters were up; but we got another guide through Yarrow; and
thereafter the two procured us another, who guided us to the Pad-
doch Slacks. We got on our way without mistaking it, but that we
were somewhat puzzled to find the road through two brooks.

On Tuesday, Dec. 8, I spent some time in prayer, singing of mercy
and judgment, and for my daughter, the book, the accentuation, &c.
One thing more occurred to me, thinking on the trial, that I had not
made a more solemn business of the children's going away, by setting
some time apart for prayer on that account, either in the family, or
by himself; and that I had not put the children themselves to it;
and on Jane's going to Dunse, I came home, I had been wrestling
with the temptation aforesaid renewed; so that that day I saw myself standing on the ice, and my flesh trembling for fear of God, and
I was afraid of his judgments.

On Friday, Dec. 11, what I feared came on me, receiving a letter
that Jane was taken ill of the small pox, and that they had broken
out on Tuesday the 8th. The account not being very bad, I stayed,
and preached on the Lord's day, and went off after sermon. On that
morning, such a damp took me in prayer, that I could neither pray
for her recovery nor salvation; which made me ready to conclude
she was dead. It continued in the public prayers, till the last one
after the sermon, wherein my bonds were loosed to pray for her;
which sent me away with hope. I got to Edinburgh on Monday by
four o'clock. Her pox, were many, and of a dangerous kind. On the
Thursday, the pox being about their height, she fell feverish. Fears
of her death came then to an extremity; and while I was thus
hardly bestead, awful impressions of the sovereign God sitting on his
throne in the heavens, having the matter in his hand wholly, to turn
it what way he pleased, were seasonably, by his grace, fixed on my
spirit, commanding me silently to wait the issue. And that word,
Psalm lxxxv. 12; "The Lord shall give that which is good," was
the word I was led to for resting in, during the long time of her illness. When the worst was past on the Monday after, new straits
arose, and I was plunged in difficulties, but deliverances came,
which were sweet as the answers of particular petitions to the
Lord. I was employed there in private houses, not without countenance from the Lord. I left my daughter in a hopeful way of recov-

ery, but weak, Dec. 31, and came home on the morrow, the first day of the new year. And the 5th, being Tuesday, I spent some time in secret prayer for my daughter's case, and several other causes, particularly the accentuation and the book ; renewed the covenant as usual at such times ; and was let in to the application of the Redeemer's blood. I would fain hope this quarrel is not to be pursued farther.

The first week of my being in Edinburgh this second time, new orders came down for prosecuting the nonjurors. And Mr. John Flint, and Mr. William Miller, two of the ministers of the town, formerly nonjurors, but now takers of the oath, having visited us in our distress, told me at parting, that they were just going to the President of the court of Session, to endeavour to divert the storm ready to break out.

Mrs. Bladerstone, to whose prayers I recommended my study of the accentuation, with the rest of my case, was a daughter of Mr. Henry Erskine's, formerly mentioned, whom I account my father in Christ, and a person eminent for piety, Christian experience, and communion with God.

Jan. 9, 1720.—My son Thomas, going in seven, having discovered something of his case to his mother, I did, at her motion, converse with him thereon, and found him sensible of the stirring of corruption in his heart. He told me he was troubled with ill thoughts ; that he would not tell them, for that he could not do it, but with a grieved heart ; that he resisted them, by saying over questions of the catechism, and reading, (adding, sometimes I read whether I will or no ; meaning, his going over the belly of his averseness to it,) and sometimes by saying to them, Go away. He told me further, that God did not hear his prayers ; and that for that sometimes he forgot his prayers at night ; that he wondered why God made the devil, for he tempted men ; but that he thought it was to destroy liars ; that he found his heart fain in some things, when he got them first ; but he prayed to God to take away that fainness. I informed, instructed, and directed him, in the whole case, the best I could.

Jan. 20.—On the 9th, I received letters, shewing, that orders for prosecuting the nonjurors, were again come from court. This was the third time since June preceding. The first orders for that effect came in harvest ; the second, that week I went last to Edinburgh ; and now the news of this last came with the account of my daughter's recovery. They were now put in the hands of sheriffs, magistrates of burghs, &c., and I waited the issue. And for that cause I spent some time in prayer this day, (with other particulars, and particularly the accentuation) ; and embracing the covenant

anew, laid myself for time and eternity on God in Christ, with an eye
to the trials before me; and, with the same view, laid over my wife,
children, and servants, that may be with me in my trial, on the same
God; and also the poor parish.   And now let let the Lord do what
seemeth him good.   Howbeit, this storm, which so often appeared
on the point of breaking forth, has been, through the mercy of God,
averted unto this day.

What time I had in January and the first week of February, I
spent in writing on the accents.   And that first week of February,
I had a very particular accomplishment of the above recorded; Jer.
xxxiii. 3, in several instances, but especially in the light I got into
the true sense of Mal. ii. 15, "And did not he make one? yet had he
the residue of the spirit; and wherefore one? that he might seek a
godly seed; therefore take heed to your spirit and let none deal
treacherously against the wife of his youth." This text had been
for many months in my view, but could never reach the sense of it;
and that week it fell in my way to be directly considered.   It cost
me many thoughts, and particular petitions to the Father of lights
for the meaning of it; but then I was helped to believe, that I would
get it in due time.   And accordingly I at length reached it.   But going to write it, I looked to the following verse, which I presently
saw did not agree, but unhinged all again.   This gave me a new
damp.   But, through the same divine assistance, I quickly perceived
that verse mistaken too, and fell on the true reading of it; whereby
it beautifully agreed, and set it all right again.   The kind conduct
of Providence in these matters, that week particularly, is great in
my eyes; and the passage from Jurieu's Critical History, which I
had never before observed, was sent me most seasonably.

By the disposal of that holy Providence which all along hath
kindly and wisely balanced my worldly affairs, though my tenement
in Dunse had been profitable to me while I was at Simprin, yet
after my removal to Etterick, it afforded me little profit and much
trouble.   For which cause, I had sold it to my brother John; but
he dying, that bargain flew up.   But, about this time, it was sold
for good and all to John Dunse there; my eldest son, when major,
ratifying the sale, on the occasion above mentioned.

In the spring season this year, I was greatly indisposed and weakened, sometimes fearing when I lay down at night, I should not rise
in the morning.   Great also was the distress of the parish, and my
toil by that means.   Having ended my sermons on the catechism,
April 3; on the 10th I entered, by the call of providence, on Psalm
xc. 12, "So teach us to number our days," &c.   And on the 27th

we kept a congregational fast for the great sickness and mortality.*
There was not one of my family, save myself only, that had not been
one way or other laid by, for a time, during that period of general
sickness.

But the 10th day of May this year, was a day remarkable above
many to me and my family; being that wherein my wife was seized
with that heavy trouble, which hath kept her all along since that
time unto this day, in extreme distress; her imagination being vitiated in a particular point: and that improved and wrought upon,
by the grand adversary, to her great disquietment; the which has
been still accompanied with bodily infirmities and maladies, exceeding great and numerous.   Nevertheless, in that complication of
trials, the Lord hath been pleased, not only to make his mighty
power appear in preserving her life as a spark of fire in an ocean,
but to make his grace in her shine forth more bright than before.

Now, the " Marrow of Modern Divinity," part I. being as aforesaid reprinted at Edinburgh, anno. 1718, with a preface by Mr.
James Hog, minister of Carnock, a man of great learning and
singular piety and tenderness, there had been a mighty stir made
about it, especially in Fife, where, for several years before, a con-
test had been agitated, touching the covenant of grace, whether it
is absolute or conditional. So that Mr. Hog found himself obliged
to publish an explication of passages excepted against in the " Marrow ;" the which was printed early in the year 1719. Thereafter
several pamphlets went abroad on that subject, the same year ; as
for some years after also.   And Mr. James Haddow principal of the
college of St. Andrew's, did, in his sermon before the synod of Fife,
April 7, 1719, attack the book foresaid ; the which sermon was
printed at the desire of that synod, under the title of " The Record
of God, and Duty of Faith therein Required." This humour going
on, the " Marrow" was complained of to the general assembly that
year.   And thereupon they appointed their commission to take care,
that the purity of doctrine might be preserved, and to call before
them any authors or recommenders of books or pamphlets containing
any doctrine not agreeable to the Confession of Faith.   At the same
time complaint was also made to them, on Professor Simson's printed answers to Mr. Webster's libel against him, to which the Professor continued to refer in his teaching ; but that matter was drop-
ed, and the motion for inquiring thereinto repelled. The commission of that assemby accordingly appointed a committee of their

* The sermons preached on this occasion are annexed to the author's Body of
Divinity, and may be usefully read on such occasions, which are not infrequent.

number for the effect foresaid; who sufficiently shewed their zeal, but all upon one side, namely, to preserve the doctrine from the mixture of Antinomianism, which the hue and cry was now raised about. That committee divided themselves into two; whereof the one sat at St. Andrew's, and prepared excerpts out of the challenged books and prints, and sent their remarks to the other, who met at Edinburgh. Before these last, about the beginning of April this year, were called to answer for themselves, Mr. James Hog foresaid, Mr. Alexander Hamilton, minister at Airth, afterward transported to Stirling, Mr. James Brisbane at Stirling, and Mr. John Warden at Gargunnock; all of them noted preachers of the doctrine of free grace, and withal nonjurors too. These brethren were examined severally and apart, by the committee. Mr. Hog being called, the first query proposed to him was, Whether he owned himself author of the preface to the last edition of the " Marrow of Modern Divinity ?" To which he answered affirmatively; and, moreover, told them, that that book, whereof he knew nothing before, came most unexpectedly to his hand, and he read it over as soon as he could; that he had no thoughts of the reprinting of it, but complied with the motion thereto, after the project had been laid by others; that at the earnest desire of some who managed the business, he wrote the preface; that the Lord had blessed the reading of the book to many excellent persons of diverse ranks; and that he knew an eminent divine, then in glory, (whom I judge to have been Mr. Fraser of Brae, minister at Culross), who left it in record, that the reading an old edition thereof, was the first notable means blessed of the Lord, for giving him some clearness of impression concerning the gospel; and that for his own part he owned, that he had received more light about some important concerns of the glorious gospel, by perusing that book, than by other human writings which Providence had brought into his hands. This account of that matter I have taken out of a MS. narrative of what passed in that committee, done by Mr. Hog himself.

This run of affairs quickly issued, in the general assembly's condemning the " Marrow of Modern Divinity," by their act of the date May 20, 1720. And three days before, viz. May 17, it pleased the Lord to call home to himself, by death, the great Mr. James Webster before mentioned; a man eminent in maintaining the purity of the doctrine of the gospel, a nonjurant to the last breath; and in or about the last time he was in the judicatory, where the matter of the " Marrow" was considered, expressed his concern that they would beware of condemning it. My friend Mr. Wilson was a member of that assembly, but abhorred that their act, which he and others nevertheless could not stop. Upon which occasion he sometime after wrote the letter, intitled, "A letter to a gentleman at Edinburgh, a ruling elder of the Church of Scotland, concerning the proceedings of the last general assembly, with reference unto doctrine chiefly;" the which was published the year following, and was wont to be called "The London Letter."

June 12.—The sacrament being administered here, I was in great fear as to my holding out, by reason of bodily weakness; yet I was not only strengthened to preach an hour and a half, but to go through the rest of the work with competent ability, with a solid seriousness all along; and, to my wonder, found myself after all less weary than I formerly used to be. My wife was under great weakness, and in a hazardous condition; but was also carried through beyond expectation. It was a refreshing time to many of the people of God here gathered together, and a savoury work all along. While my son John was at the table, I had such a concern for him, as ever a travailing woman for the bringing forth of her child. At the table I had several particular suits, namely, about my wife's weakness, Jane's going again to Edinburgh, the book in the press, my study of the accents, Mrs. Bladerstone's son abroad, and how to be carried through in defence of that truth of the gospel, the doctrine of free grace, which had got a stroke by the aforementioned act of assembly; judging, that, as matters were now going, I might be called also to an account for some things in the "Fourfold State," if once published.

After handling of occasional subjects relative to the sacrament, before and after, I entered, July 10, on the communion of saints as one bread, from 1 Cor. x. 17, "For we being many are one bread, and one body; for we are all partakers of that one bread." The which subject I studied with particular care and considerable earnestness, as a very important point; and dwelt thereon till October 30.

B. S. told me, that the first sermon she got any good of, was that on the Sabbath afternoon at Morbattle, on these words, "Where is the God of Elijah?" and that before that time, having no knowledge of me so much as by face, but hearing her sister speak of me, she could not endure my name, but had a particular aversion to me beyond any minister. This is a pretty odd phenomenon.

Aug. 30.—I went to Edinburgh on account of the book. Having read the sheets once and again, which the printer had sent out to me, I was greatly confounded to see the book pitifully mangled, being full of typographical errors; and, besides, Mr. Wightman had so altered it in many places, that he had quite marred it. I had

now put the most material *errata* in order for the press, and resolved
to reprint several leaves; for in July the book was nearly printed
off, and they had sent to me for the title-page and preface. Thus I
was on this pitiful occasion necessitated to go in to Edinburgh, leaving
my wife in great distress, her trouble being come to an extremity;
and my two dear friends, Mr. Wilson and Mr. Davidson went along
with me. When we came in, one new difficulty came on the back of
another: Mr. Macewan the printer, was at Glasgow; the correcter
could not be found for some time; Mr. Wightman had set the
press a-going to reprint the first three sheets, with his corrections; in the meantime the authentic copy could not be got, most of
it being destroyed by the printers after they had done with it. I
stopt the press quickly, till they should get new orders from me. I
saw a part of Mr. Wightman's preface, wherein I found him recommending the modish style; though some time before I had expressly
wrote to him, not to do it, for that it was fast coming in, while what
is a thousand times better is going out proportionably, as is usual in
a declining time of the church. He had also again altered the title-
page. But in midst of wrath the Lord remembered mercy. I was
by kind Providence directed to Mr. William Hog, merchant, to de-
volve the management of this perplexed affair on, with the printers;
and few men could have bestowed so much time and pains on it as
he did. Ever since that time I have had his friendship most bene-
ficial to me, he all along since sparing neither pains nor expense,
to manage for me the affairs which have in my late years lain
nearest my heart. May the Lord reward to him and his, that his
labour of love, in those things wherein the honour of God, and
my comfort, were so much concerned. With him, dipping into
the business, a long time was spent, in preparing eleven leaves to be
reprinted, nine of which, I think, Mr. Wightman's meddling had
occasioned; and on considering the *errata* to be printed. Resolving
not to be imposed upon more, I went to Mr. Wightman, and modestly dealt with him, to forbear the reprinting of the three first
sheets; to let alone recommending the modish style; and recovered
my own title-page. I recovered also of the authentic copy from
p. 315, thereof, which is to be found among my papers. I dropped
one of his unhappy corrections to him, speaking a little on it, with
which he seemed to be stunned. His preface new modelled he promised to send me ere it should be printed. We soon saw the beautiful conduct of Providence, in carrying Mr. Macewan to Glasgow at
that time, and directing to Mr. Hogg; for that matter could not
have been managed betwixt the former and us to the advantage it
may be betwixt them two now. And the time of our coming in ap-

peared to have been directed by the wisdom of him who leads the blind in the way they knew not; the printers having, just the day before, begun to set for reprinting the foresaid three sheets, which if done had been a most unhappy step.

Sept. 7.—This day I spent some time in prayer, about my wife's case, the case of the book, and the assembly's act condemning the " Marrow." As to the first, I had recommended it to the concern of Mrs. Bladerstone, before the Lord. But as to the last, I am afraid the Lord honour me not to bear testimony for him in the cause of his truth. [*Nota*, But blessed be Jehovah, I have been disappointed in these fears.] The case of the book is an amazing and awful dispensation. Mr. Wightman had desired liberty to smooth some expressions in it, as for " horribly," to read " too much ;"I gave it him freely, and withal that he might delete whole sentences. This was all that passed betwixt him and me on that head ; and indeed it was too much. But I never once dreamed, that he would have extended that liberty at the rate he has done. It was well he had not gone through the whole, but that a good deal in the former and latter part of the book had escaped; but he had used so much freedom with it, from the head, " Of Man's utter Inability," to that " Of the Resurrection" inclusive, as created me a deal of vexation, and new labour. And, so far as I yet understand, the cause of the Lord's punishing me in this manner, was, my base cowardice, and having men's persons in admiration ; so as, after I had brought it by study and prayer to the case it was in, I let it fall into another hand, with so little caution, as to allow any alterations to be made therein, without first seeing them, and being convinced of the necessity or expediency of them. These things were particularly engraven to me, on that, whereas I had put on the title-page of the book, as the very language of my heart; 1 Cor. iv. 10, " We are fools for Christ's sake," he without any ceremony had blotted it out ; and I being urged to set my name to the book, which really from the beginning I designed not to do, could not then do it, for a new reason, namely, That they had so mangled it; and from my own conviction I dropped that scripture, forasmuch as I saw I had declined to be a fool for Christ's sake, in that point; and therefore the Lord had made me a greater fool than I needed to have been. [*Nota*, But O the wisdom and the foreknowledge of God ! This has been of good use to me since that time, to cure me of these weaknesses, and to resolve to see with my own eyes in such matters, whatever be other men's character for piety, or learning, or both. And I hope through grace it shall be useful to me, in these matters, while I live. I have seen more into men, and how much they are to be ceased from, since that time, than ever I was able to see all my life before. And considering what a scene of life the Lord has led me out to, since that time, and is continuing with me to this day, September 5, 1727, I do with profound reverence adore that infinite wisdom and goodness which laid on me that heavy trial, and on the bended knees of my soul return him thanks for every step or part of it, even the blackest. Amen.] Continuing in this exercise only, from six to about eleven, my spirits were exhausted.

The act of Assembly condemning the Marrow was, by concert, brought before our presbytery, Mr. George Byres, minister of Lessudden, a judicious, plain, good man, being, as I remember, employed to move it. And it was by our Presbytery laid before the October Synod, that they might consider of it. It was put on me to show what was offensive therein, to which was joined also what was offensive in their act for preaching catechetical doctrine. I felt the consideration of the Assembly's authority a great weight on me, and I had almost no help at all but by Mr. Wilson. So, instead of getting the Synod to seek redress of these things from the Assembly, we were borne down. And the truth is, the cause was but weakly managed; I fear the Lord has not yet given a spirit for contending with this declining generation. My uneasiness on the account of the management of that affair, deprived me of much of that night's rest. Wherefore, on the morrow, catching the occasion of bringing in that affair again, I exonered my conscience with less ceremony and more freedom than had been used the day before. I cannot but notice the dispensation of Providence in that I was called to make this invidious appearance, at the very time my book was coming forth; but I rested on that holy providence, which, doubtless, on a becoming design, had kept in that book, till that time of darkening the doctrine of free grace, and would not allow it to appear before.

As my two friends and I were on our way returning from that Synod, Mr. Wilson moved that a letter should be written to Mr. James Hog, above-mentioned; showing what had passed in that judicatory on the affair foresaid, and our readiness to concur with others to seek redress therein of the Assembly itself immediately. And at their desire I afterwards wrote a letter accordingly.

Meanwhile I understood that the book would be published the week after the Synod's meeting, if not before. And considering that I have made several steps in the study of the accentuation of the Hebrew text, and that my health was much impaired last spring, and I know not what may be the issue, I have resolved to begin to write an essay on that subject, though my materials are not so fully gathered as were necessary, because the former part of my collection of materials is such as no body but myself can rectify, range into order, and fill up to my mind, being what first occurred when I entered that thicket, though the latter part, and still the nearer to the end, is more distinct and perfect. For which causes I spent some time in prayer, Oct. 26, viz., for the Lord's blessing to go out with the Fourfold State, and for his presence with me, and blessing in the essay now to be made. The Lord helped to cry to him in both these; and for some time I spread the Hebrew Bible, and my written materials before the Lord in prayer, crying to the Father of lights, my Father, over them, for light, life, strength, time, and conduct into all truth; the which practice I found useful to my upstirring. And upon that word, Matth. xxi. 22, "And all things whatsoever ye shall ask in prayer, believing, ye shall receive;" I was helped to confidence of being heard in both these things. At night I attempted to begin to write, wrote the title of chapter 1, but could do no more. On the morrow's night I essayed it again, wrote the first paragraph, but was diverted.

It has pleased the Lord to recover my wife from that extremity she was brought to. She was taken violently ill of her head-ache four days, which, being superadded to her other troubles, seemed to threaten death; but from thence was and began her recovery, and no other way that I could perceive. Thus in the evening time it was light, and not by might nor by power, &c. But I would fain hope these have yet a further look.

Nov 8. This was the first free day I had to bestow on the essay upon the accentuation; and there was a third beginning of it, the former being laid aside. But whether it was precisely on that day, or not, it was begun, has already escaped me. However, I may reckon it so, the first chapter being entirely new. So hard was it for me once to get entered on it, withal other temptations were hanging about me in that time. And a bound copy of the Fourfold State having on the 6th come to my hand, I did, on the morrow after, spread it before the Lord in prayer, for his blessing to go out with it, and to be entailed on it, while I live, and when I am gone, and that it might be accepted. And indeed I think God hath heard these prayers, and oft-times when I have considered the acceptance that book met with, notwithstanding the disadvantages wherewith it was attended, I could not but impute it to an overruling hand of kind Providence that would needs have it so. On the Tuesday I sent my son to Edinburgh to wind up that whole business. He returned on Monday the 14th with the good account of the business comfortably brought to an end, and that the book was going off well, which sent me to God with thanksgiving for his holy conduct of that affair, and his wise and merciful dealing in it.

Now after some time I received from Mr. Ralph Erskine, minister of Dunfermline, and son to the worthy Henry Erskine above-mentioned, an answer to the letter aforesaid sent to Mr. James Hog, and then a return from Mr. Hog himself, bearing their readiness to concur in seeking redress of the injury done to truth by the act of Assembly foresaid. And I did, on Jan. 2, 1721, spend some time in prayer for my own private case, perceiving the danger of my health and life in the ensuing spring; for divine direction with respect to these motions about the said act of Assembly 1720, and for the divine assistance in the essay on the accentuation, which I was now engaged in. Thereafter, on the 8th, I entered, for my ordinary, on preaching of Christ directly, from Prov. viii. 35, 36, " For whoso findeth me, findeth life, and shall obtain favour of the Lord. But he that sinneth against me wrongeth his own soul, all they that hate me love death." Upon which I insisted for a considerable time.*

In pursuance of the motions foresaid relating to the Assembly's act, there was sent from the brethren above mentioned, a draught of a representation to the Assembly, with which draught my two friends and I not being satisfied, I at their desire, made another. This was conveyed to the brethren aforesaid, and a meeting was appointed to be at Edinburgh, in the latter end of February, to consider of that important matter. Both these draughts are to be found among my papers, the one indorsed, " Copy of a representation to be given in to the Assembly, 1721; the other, "The original draught of the representation given in to the Assembly, 1721.

On Feb. 1, I spent some time in prayer, for the same causes as before, and the divine guidance to my son at Edinburgh, in which I had much ado to fix my feet, for at this time there is such a current carrying the young generation to folly, as, I think, I never observed before, and seems to be ominous. As also with respect to my daughter's going to Edinburgh, remembering the dispensation of Providence last year in her case.

Feb. 14, Tuesday. Last Lord's day there was a roll of seven sick persons in the parish prayed for, whereof there was one in Crosslie, another in Falhop, another in Dalgleish. Considering it would take me a day for each of these, I designed Monday for Crosslie, Tuesday for Falhop, and Wednesday for Dalgleish; in the mean time it was a storm of lying snow. The consideration of this toil, and of so much time to be cut off from my beloved work in the closet, raised in my corrupt heart a secret grudge. I had dispatched the Monday's work as said is, and this day going towards Falhop, I under-

* The sermons on this text are to be found in the volume entitled, " The Christian Life delineated."

stood at Cossarhill the person was removed by death. Returning by Ettcrick house, I visited the sick there, and then went towards Dalgleish; but by the way I was told that the sick person
there was removed also that morning. This struck me to the heart,
as shewing the anger of a holy jealous God against me for the secret
grudge aforesaid, and that, as he needed none of my service, so he
would have none of it that way, for which I flee to the redeemer's
blood, desiring grace to take this lesson, and hereafter cheerfully to
be ready at my master's call. I visited one at Craigyford, another
at Deephopgreen, and so returned home. The person at Falhop I
had visited oftener than once ; but knew nothing of the person at
Dalgleish his being sick, till he was prayed for on the Lord's day.

About the latter end of February I went in to Edinburgh, to the
meeting above mentioned. And here began a plunge into public affairs, which so filled my head and hands, that now the proceeding in
the essay on the accentuation was laid aside ; and insomuch that,
excepting a little done in it in the April following, I made no progress therein for a long time.

There met then in the house of Mr. William Wardrobe, apothecary in Edinburgh, Mr. James Kid, minister at Queensferry, Mr.
Ebenezer Erskine at Portmoak, his brother Mr. Ralph, aforesaid,
Mr. James Wardlaw at Dunfermline, Mr. William Wilson at Perth
Mr. James Bathgate at Orwell, my two friends, and I. The first
meeting was spent mostly in prayer, and the Lord was with us at
that and other following ones. We went through the act of Assembly in order, shewing what was in it stumbling to us, and conferring
thereon. In these meetings two things were observable. One was,
that no debate was kept upon selfish motives, but each one was ready
to yield to scripture and reason by whomsoever advanced. Another,
that when we stuck, and could not get forward, but were in hazard
of falling asunder, Providence still interposed seasonably, causing
something to be cast up, which cleared our way and joined us. And
it was agreed that there should be a representation to the Assembly
about it, the forming whereof was committed to Mr. Ebenezer Erskine, with whom our draught was lodged for that effect, and the revising of it when formed was committed to the brethren in that
country. And another meeting was appointed to be in the latter end
of March, in the same place.

From this meeting, Mr. Wilson of Perth, and Mr. Ebenezer Erskine were absent. Mr. Sethrum, minister at Gladsmuir, was with
us at one or two diets, but staid not. Mr. Hog's absence was thought
expedient by some of ourselves, because of his particular interest,
he having writ the preface to the Marrow. Messrs. Hamilton at

Airth, Brisbane and Muir at Stirling, and Warden at Gargunnock,
though invited, came not, to our great discouragement. Then the
draught of the representation sent from us in the south, after several
alterations and additions made thereon, was signed by all there present. And the next meeting was appointed to be the first night of
the Assembly's meeting in May, and it was designed for prayer; but
in regard to my circumstances, I was allowed not to come in till
the Monday after the Assembly's sitting down.

The first night of the Assembly the meeting was in the same
house again, accordingly, and Providence so ordering that I was
chosen a member of that Assembly, I met with them. Mr. James
Hog, whose absence hitherto had been judged expedient, in regard
of his prefacing the Marrow, did join us. Moreover, there came into
us a goodly company of brethren, with whose appearance I was
much encouraged. But, behold, they turned our meeting, designed
for prayer, into a meeting for disputing, jangling, and breaking our
measures; in the which, the main agent was Mr. John Warden,
above mentioned, and next, Mr. Moncrieff of Culfargie. Two things
they mainly insisted on, besides picking quarrels with the representation. One was, a conference with the leading men before any thing
should be done; the other, that all should not subscribe, but only
some few, the rest being reserved for managing, judging, and voting
in the Assembly. This last none of us who had already subscribed
could go into. I was brought to yield to the first, together with
Mr. Bathgate, on condition that the time of giving in our representation should not be cut off. But when it came about to my two
friends, they, smelling the unfair design that I had no dread of, that
was stopped, as not to be yielded to. It was good Providence that
their unfair dealing could not blind us all, else we had in all appearance been ensnared and mired. Thus the whole weary night was
spent till day-light, that they left us in much worse case than they
found us. Thus left of our new friends, it was proposed by Mr.
Kid to drop the things quarrelled by them in the representation;
among which was an entire head, viz., that of the fear of hell; and
this, that our brethren might be obliged to stand by us in the Assembly. In this step unhappily gone into, we took the way of carnal
policy; and I liked it not, but could not oppose it because I had
drawn the paper. However, our politics in the just judgment of
God, failed us. The representation being transcribed accordingly,
was signed by the twelve brethren, as in the printed copy, and was
that same day, in the afternoon, given in by us to the committee of
bills, Mr. Kid presenting it, being a man of singular boldness. This
haste was made to prevent our being teased anew, as the night be-

fore. Mr. John Bonnar, who lodged in Mr. Wardrobe's, where we had our meetings, after signing it with us, went away home ; and I do not remember his appearing with us afterwards, if it was not once, at which time he was called home by an express. Mr. John Williamson of Inveresk made his first appearance amongst us at signing of this last draught; but was very useful after, being a man of a clear head, a ready wit, and very forward. Mr. William Hunter at Lilliesleaf signed it in the church, just before it was presented. It was not then read, but promised to be read at their next meeting. We understood afterward, that Principal Haddow, the spring of that black act of Assembly, was in his way to the committee of bills to bring in some motion about the act, it would seem, for explaining it, &c., but that hearing the tabling of the representation had prevented him, he was disappointed and forbore. Next diet it was read, and at another diet we were to receive their deliverance thereon. The committee for overtures had it under their consideration, and it was resolved, that unless we desired a conference, it should be transmitted to the Assembly *quam primum*. They came in great numbers from the committee of overtures to the bills, and made a terrible company against us. They who would have appeared our friends, fell upon us, urged us to desire a conference, told us that otherwise it was resolved to transmit it to the Assembly *quam primum*, and what the consequences would then be. The matter was so managed to put us in fear, but they prevailed not to fright us from what we had, not rashly, but after much serious inquiry and deliberation, resolved upon. On Monday the Assembly met, and determined in the matter of a call ; as also on Tuesday, but did no business, only appointed the choosing of the commission, the king's commissioner being indisposed. On Wednesday we expected, as we had done the day before, that our representation would have come before them ; but behold, that day the assembly, in regard of the commissioner's indisposition was dissolved, after they had referred our representation, without reading it, to the commission. Howbeit, the commissioner was present in the Assembly both that day and the preceding, and without his presence they did no business. No man spoke a word against the dissolution; but all was carried on in profound peace. Thus our brethren who reserved their appearing for truth to their management in the Assembly, and would not join us in the representation, had all occasion of saying one word in the Assembly about it cut off.

On the Thursday we were called before the commission ; and Mr. Hog not being ready at the call, and Mr. Bonnar gone away home, it was my lot to appear first in that cause. The eleven brethren be-

ing sisted before them, our representation was read; after which Mr.
Hog spoke a little. Then followed a flood of speeches, about the
number of thirteen, by which we were run down, no man standing by
us. And among these speeches was John Warden, aforesaid, a man
well seen in the doctrine of free grace, but of some vanity of temper. Mr. Hog offered to answer in the time, but a hearing was refused; so they went on without interruption. Thus the cause and
we were run down, and the audience impressed, which seemed to be
the design of this management. After this we were allowed to speak,
before we should remove; and the Moderator desired me to speak;
which, lifting up my heart to the Lord, I did for a little; but was
quickly answered. Other brethren spoke also; and particularly
Mr. Williamson was happily guided to tell them, that we had heard
such a multitude of speeches against us, that it was not possible to
remember them, so as to answer them; but that we would recollect,
and afterwards answer. We being removed, they appointed a numerous committee to consider of that affair, to meet on Friday. That
day we were called before them; and at that time, to the best of my
remembrance, a motion being made to purge the house, it was said
to have proceeded from us; which being denied by us, after some
jangling, they agreed to have the doors thrown open; which was effected by my friend Mr. Wilson's means chiefly. And kind providence so ordered it, that the career they were on the day before, was,
through the divine mercy, stopped to conviction, at that and the following meetings. Particularly Mr. Williamson did, in a point in
debate, fairly lay Mr. Allan Logan, minister of Culross; and I was
encouraged by the success of an encounter with Principal Haddow.
We were warned to attend them again on the Monday at ten o'clock,
but nobody came then to call us, till about twelve, a minister came
to call us, we were to attend against two. We waited on till between
six and seven afternoon, that some of us went away; and afterwards
we heard we were to wait on upon the morrow. Thus we spent that
day; they had difficulty in agreeing as to their own management.
On the Tuesday we were again before them, and on the Wednesday
before the commission; at which time we were warned to attend the
commission in August, and the sub-committee the day before the
meeting of the commission, and betwixt and that time, if called.

  The beauty of providence, in this matter, shines in my eyes. The
Lord laid us very low at our first appearance, on the Thursday, before the commission, that we might see, that it was not to be done
by might nor by power, but by the Spirit of the Lord; but afterwards he raised us up, that our adversaries could no more triumph
over us. Many times the appearance before the Assembly had been

a terror to me, and broke my sleep ere it came; but the Lord was with me in the appearance we made, and that terror evanished at length; so that, to my own wonder, I was helped to speak without fear; " It shall be given you in that hour what ye shall speak," Matth. x. 19. *Expertus credo.* I have learned to beware of men, and that all men are liars; but God is a promise-keeping God.

At the April synod, Mr. Wilson being in the chair, I was left alone to bear the shock, and was run down at an unusual rate about a fast; which being appointed by the church, I had observed; but in a few weeks was appointed to be observed again by the King's proclamation, for the very same cause, without the least notice of what the church had already done in it. This I and others observed not. Returning home, I then said in my heart, " O that I had a place in the wilderness !" &c. Jer. ix. 2.

June 11.—The sacrament was administered here. I and some others in this church were now becoming a wonder to many; and God tried me at that occasion, but was very gracious to me, and saved me from the reproach of men. On Thursday, Mr. Wilson came, but not Mr. Davidson, of whom I had made no doubt; so that I preached that day with Mr. Wilson, with much help from the Lord, having been seasonably led the day before, by foreseeing Providence, to have my thoughts that way. Mr. Simpson, one of my three helpers, being under sickness, I had invited Mr. Kid; but on the Saturday I received a letter, shewing him also to be kept back by the Lord's afflicting hand. So the work lay on my two friends, who preached that day, and myself. The communicants appearing, by the tokens, to be near a third part more than usually before, double tables were set, whereas we had used only a single one. Saturday night and Sabbath morning were great rains; so that awaking early on the Sabbath, and beholding the waters swollen, and the rain falling, threatening to bar those on the other side, my soul said, " what wilt thou do unto thy great name !" For now many eyes were on us; and should the people, gathered from places at many miles distance, have been so disappointed, I thought it would be interpreted Heaven's sentence against them and us. I was helped to submission, and to see and adore the holy becoming designs of Providence, if it should be so; and to be easy, believing God would do what is best. But he sent down, and delivered us from the reproach of men, gave us sweet days of the gospel, and not one shower all the time of the work, Sabbath or Monday; but for a great part of that time, spread his black clouds over us, with some intermixed sunshine. That threatening Sabbath morning kept the usual Sabbath day's multitude away from us; so that there was no great dif-

ference betwixt the Sabbath meeting and those of the other days.
The wind of divine assistance in the sermon blew upon me, fell, and
rose again. The Lord was with my brethren. I preached also on
the Monday with them ; so spoke none at dismissing of the congregation, which I am never wont to omit. I thought I saw in the conduct of Providence at this communion, as in an emblem, what is, and
is like to be, our case ; the multitude carried off from us ; the most
tender of the godly and Zion's mourners cleaving to us ; protection
allowed us as to the storm hanging over our heads from the church ;
with a blink now and then, and perhaps another communion allowed me here. I had a signal instance of the answer of prayer in my
wife's case ; who being in deep distress of a long time, it seemed to
come to a great height the week before, that I was put to cry,
that the Lord would at least heave up the cloud, so as it might not
deprive her of partaking at his table. In this I was heard ; and
she attained to much composure, that she was not only not barred
from it, but gave a very Christian account of the actings of her soul
in the case ; which was the doing of the Lord, and wondrous in my
eyes.

On the 10th of July, a motion was so made to me by my two
friends to write notes on the Marrow, that I was obliged seriously to
think of it. At length, having spent some time in prayer, purposely
for discovering the Lord's mind therein, I was determined to essay
it, on this consideration, that as matters now stand, the gospel-doctrine has got a root-stroke by the condemning of that book ; and
that whatever else be done for retrieving it, it will be but to little
purpose, while that book lies among the pots, people being stumbled
and frighted at it. And this day I began that work, being obliged
to lay aside thoughts of other business, viz., the preparing of the
Fourfold State for a second edition, and the publishing of some sermons ; both which I am engaged to do to Mr. Macewan ; and my
great work on the accentuation.

Having plied that work two weeks, on the Saturday's night of the
second, awaking out of sleep, I was taken extremely ill of a kind of
heart-swooning, a most vehement heat and sweat being felt by me,
my wife nevertheless testifying me to be cold as dead in the time.
While in my extremity death stared me in the face, the doctrine of
the Marrow concerning the gift and grant, and that scripture, 1 John
v. 11, " And this is the record, that God hath given to us eternal
life ; and this life is in his Son," accordingly understood, That God
hath given unto us mankind sinners, (and to me in particular) eternal life, &c., whereby it is lawful for me to take possession of it as
my own, was the sweet and comfortable prop of my soul, believing

it, and claiming accordingly. The effects of that illness hung about
me for some time ; so that I had much ado to preach the two Lord's
days after it, before the communion at Galashiels, Aug. 1. There I
was very ill on the Saturday, and had much ado to get through the
preaching. I was better on the Lord's day, and the Lord was with
my spirit, and signally owned the whole work. On the Monday
afternoon we went into the commission, Mr. Wilson and I having
been both brought within sight of death, threatening that we should
not have access to appear in that cause again ; and both about the
same time, he by a fall from his horse, I as aforesaid. Thus the
Lord dealt with us as with his own, and gave us a sight of death, to
take heed how we manage in his matters. The Lord's staying my
soul in the sight of death on that foundation of faith above said, con-
troverted at this time in our present struggle, was, and is, very confirming. We waited on three days; were never but once called before the committee, on the Wednesday, to tell us, that the committee
had prepared an overture about our affair, to be laid before the
commission ; and on the Thursday before the commission, to tell us,
that the commission had prepared an overture about it, to be transmitted to the assembly ; and we were appointed to wait on in November again. We were still deserted by all, not one offering to
join us. My courage for appearing before them, and reasoning, was
low at this time ; for there was little or nothing to do with it.

On the 22d of August I spent some time in prayer, for the case of
my own soul, and a multiplicity of business laid to my hand, while
in the mean time my strength was much decayed ; yet desiring to be
found so doing. That business then was, the writing notes on the
Marrow ; the preparing of the Fourfold State for a second edition,
which Mr. Macewan, the publisher, did demand ; the preparing some
sermons for the press, desired also by the same person, and which I
had some way yielded to ; and above all, the essay on the accentuation, the proceeding wherein my heart trembled to think of being
deprived of an opportunity for; all which require a great deal of
time, and strength too. I laid my soul over on my Lord Christ, and
desired to go on in my work as I was able, that if the Lord should
take me away in the midst of it, I might be found so doing. [But
now I thank my gracious God, that, however trying the prospect I
then had thereof was, in respect of the state of my health, I have
by this time (1730) got through all that business for the service of
my God, and more too, which hath cast up since that time.]

I was now led, for my ordinary, to treat of the two covenants,
which lasted a long time. I began on the covenant of works, Aug.
27, this year ; and handling it at large, from several texts, I insist-

ed thereon till May in the following year.* I studied it with considerable earnestness and application; being prompted thereto, as to the close consideration of the other covenant too afterwards, by the state of doctrine to which this church was then arrived.

My friend Mr. Wilson having been moderator of the April synod, at which I was run down, he, as in the chair, having little access to help, preached before them in October a faithful and excellent sermon; at which they took fire. And immediately they commenced a process against him, on the account of that sermon; which ended not till the general assembly 1723 put an end to it. The sermon is extant in print, entitled, *The Trust*, to be judged of by posterity; and was before four synods, as many committees of the synod, before the commission, and at length came before the general assembly; as one may see in the preface to it, done, I think, by Mr. Kid. It may easily be guessed, what a loss both these affairs meeting together at once would occasion. And indeed we were by this time become still more strangers to our brethren, and as aliens; and saw, that our mothers had born us men of contention. Besides what concerned the doctrine, there were in these days many occasions of difference in the matter of national fasts; the appointments for which sent from England, bare evident marks of little honour had for our church; such as the appointing of them to be observed on some of their superstitious days, and particularly on Fridays, contrary from all reason that could be drawn but from their superstition. These often occasioned us much uneasiness, and different practices from our brethren, most of them at least; but I am not ripe in the history of that affair, which hath been of a long course. However, for some time national fasts have been very rare. There was also introduced from England, into some of our civil courts, the corrupt custom of swearing on the book; which being laid before our synod, occasioned some debate before this time; but we could prevail nothing in this matter with them, towards moving for redress. But my friend Mr. Wilson exposed it, in his "New Mode of Swearing, *tactis et deosculatis evangeliis*," printed anno 1719.

In the month of November, we appeared again before the commission. There we were told, we were to answer certain queries to be given us in writing by them. And having gone away together to consult, what were best to be done in that matter, I was clear, that

* This valuable performance was published in 1772. Notwithstanding it labours under the common disadvantages of a posthumous publication, it contains a vein of solid thought, judicious reasoning, and enters deeper into the several branches of that important subject, than any treatise hitherto published. It is now printed along with the Covenant of Grace, in one volume 8vo.

whatever should be the consequences, we should receive and answer them. What determined me to this was, that I thought we were to lay our account with parting with our brethren, as being cast out by them; and, in that event, it would be safest, both for the cause of truth, and our own reputation. This was agreed to, and the queries were received with a protestation. And thus they turned the cannon directly against us.

While I was thus engaged in public trials, I met with a breaking disappointment in the case of my son John, whom I had designed for the holy ministry. Being, in that view, concerned to have given him a suitable education in every necessary branch of literature, I took care to have him taught at the College, Humanity, Greek, Hebrew, Mathematics, as well as Philosophy; and allowed him for that end a course of five years there. But that course being ended this year, he would not once enter on the study of Theology, which I had designed him for. But, after some struggle with him, I behoved to advance him money, for betaking himself to the employment of a sheep-master. This disappointment lay with a particular weight upon me, when my strength failing more, I greatly needed help; but all expectations of help from him was cut off; especially when I saw his comrade Mr. George Byres, son to Mr. George above mentioned, in case to help his father, still vigorous, and fit for his own business. But, O! the admirable conduct of Providence, challenging an entire resignation! The said George Byres elder is now removed by death; and I am yet spared, doing my work, though in much weakness.

In March 1722, we appeared again before the commission, and our answers to their queries were then given in. They are extant in print, with the protestation above mentioned prefixed to them. These answers were, as I remember, begun by Mr. Ebenezer Erskine; but much extended and perfected by my friend Mr. Wilson; where his vast compass of reading, with his great collection of books, were of singular use, and successfully employed.

In May we appeared before the General Assembly, where the affair was at length brought to an end, by their act May 21, 1722, which may be consulted; and we were admonished and rebuked. Easily foreseeing what would be the issue, in the assembly's determination of the affair, I drew a protestation while I was yet at home, and carried along with me. And the admonition and rebuke being received with all gravity, the said protestation, subscribed by us all, was given in by the hand of Mr. Kid; and instruments taken thereon in due form. But the assembly would not read it, but quickly closed the sederunt. The said protestation is also extant in print. I received the rebuke and admonition as an ornament put upon me, being for the cause of truth. This affair was brought to the issue aforesaid in the afternoon-session of that day; and their meeting for that black work appointed to be at three o'clock that day, there came on, a little before the hour, a most dreadful storm of thunder and hail, by means whereof their meeting was for a considerable time hindered. In the time thereof, I came down, with some others of our number, from the Westbow-head, to the chamber where we attended till called; and that almost running, the street being in a manner desolate. I well remember, with what serenity of mind, and comfort of heart, I heard the thunder of that day, the most terrible thunder-clap being just about three o'clock. It made impression on many, as Heaven's testimony against their deed they were then about to do; though in this it is not for me to determine.

Thus ended that weighty affair, by means whereof I received another sensible increase of light into the doctrine of grace; especially as to the gift and grant made of Christ unto sinners of mankind, and as to the nature of faith. In which last, my friend Mr. Wilson was the most clear and distinct; and my clearness and distinctness therein I owe to him, as the mean of conveying it unto me. He hath since that time travelled in that subject, with peculiar concern and industry, to great advantage; and is the man, of all I know, fittest to write upon it. Moreover, that struggle hath been, through the mercy of God, turned to the great advantage of truth in our church, both among some ministers and people; having obliged both, to think of these things, and inquire into them, more closely and nicely than before; insomuch that it has been owned, that few public differences have had such good effects. Meanwhile it is not to be doubted, but others have, on that occasion, been carried further to the side of legalism, than they were before; and that through the prevalence of their passions and prejudices; the gospel of Christ is by this time, with many, especially of the younger sort of divines, exchanged for rationalism. So that I believe the light and darkness are both come to a pitch, that they were before far from in this church; of which posterity may see a miserable and a glorious issue.

Having ended my sermons on the covenant of works, May 6, I did on July 1, enter on the covenant of grace, the which ordinary, meeting with occasional interruptions, and being pursued from several texts, lasted near about two years.

In the beginning of the month last mentioned, I finished the notes on the "Marrow of Modern Divinity;" which afterwards in the year 1726 were printed with the "Marrow" itself; in the which, out of regard to the authority of the church, that yet in that matter I durst not obey, I took to myself the name of PHILALETHES IRENÆUS, as bearing my real and sincere design therein, viz, truth and peace. In compiling of these notes, I had in view, what was advanced against the "Marrow," in the several prints extant at that time, and which had come to my hand; especially Principal Haddow's "Antinomianism of the Marrow of Modern Divinity Detected;" but naming no body. The unacquaintedness with these prints, may occasion posterity's judging several of the notes quite needless; but at that time many had been at much pains to find knots in a rush.

The sacrament of our Lord's supper was this year celebrated on the 19th of August. On the fast-day, being a presbyterial fast too, I had no help. But the Lord laid liberally to my hand, and I came easily by the several texts to be insisted on Sabbath before the fast-day, and the communion-day. After the fast-day I was seized with the toothache, which I was not acquainted with before. It broke my rest on the Friday's night; and from the Saturday all along there was a train of trying incidents and temptations came on me; so that I lost much of the Saturday's night's rest too. On the Lord's day my toothache was mercifully removed; and I was all along helped to trust in God in that matter.* As for my case, I was carried through, in heaviness, with some pleasant blinks and gales now and then; and the Lord was with my two helpers, for I had no more.

Sept. 9.—I assisted at the sacrament in Yarrow. The matter being laid before the Lord, the light calling me to go thither for the service of our common Master, made me put the knife to the throat of my old inclinations. Great was the uneasiness among many in this parish on that account; beyond what I really expected. As for the work itself, I endeavoured to eye the ordinance as the ordinance of God; and indeed in my personal duty of communicating, &c., and my public ministration there, (except serving the table), it was well with me. The Lord was with me; and what I met with there, both in public, private, and secret, leaves yet a savoury impression on me. Particularly, I had a plain answer of prayer, for assistance in the duty of public prayer.

On the Wednesday after I came from Yarrow, I spent some time in prayer, for direction as to what I should next take in hand. The notes on the "Marrow" were finished in the beginning of July last. My

---

* The author preached the action-sermon from Psalm cxlii. 5, which, with some more sermons on it afterwards, were published in 1773, in the volume intitled, "The Distinguishing Characters of True Believers."

doubt now was, whether to revise some notes concerning family and
personal fasting and humiliation, or to proceed in the essay on the
accentuation, which last was laid aside, by reason of the affair of the
" Marrow," some time in February 1721, excepting that a little was
done therein the April following. I could not get clearness to fall
on the former, and therefore necessarily fell in with the latter, as
what was already begun. So I put pen to paper again in that work,
September 12.

At the communion-table in Maxton, October 14, having upon my
spirit a particular concern for the salvation of my family, and the
case of my children; I think I was helped to believe, with particular
application, the great promise, "I will be thy God, and the God of thy
seed ;" and am verily persuaded it will be well with them at length.

It was with much fear and trembling that I entered at first on the
on the subject of the covenant of grace; and being, after some interruption, to return thereto, I did, from a sense of my great unacquaintedness with the mystery, on October 15, being the day before
my study-day, spend some time in prayer, for the Lord's manifest-
ing his covenant to me, and for some other causes. And soon after
that, I saw, the Lord had been graciously pleased to hear me; and
he gave me some sweet views of the mystery. And the truth is,
that, notwithstanding of what light into the doctrine of grace I had
by the divine favour reached, at several distant periods above marked, I was still all along dark and confused in my notions of that
covenant, until I entered on it at this time to preach it; and in the
progress therein, things were, by the good hand of God upon me,
gradually cleared unto me, endeavouring to study it, with the utmost
application, in dependence on the Lord for light thereunto.*

Feb. 10, 1723.—I entered on Psalm xv. and for a considerable
time dwelt on ver. 1 and 2, judging it meet to intersperse the doctrine of the covenant of grace with that kind of subjects; that I
might jointly teach the people the doctrine of grace and Christian
morality.†

The general assembly, in the month of May this year, put an end
to the process against Mr. Wilson, on the account of his synodical
sermon aforesaid. It came before them by a reference from our

* The author's sermons on this important subject, as transcribed and prepared for
the press by himself, were not published till 1734, two years after his death. The
book has passed through many editions, is justly considered as the best treatise on the
subject, and will, it is not doubted, be held in honour till the sounding of the last
trumpet.

† The sermons here mentioned are inserted in a volume, entitled, " The Distinguish
ing Characters of True Believers," published in 1773.

synod; who being bent to find error in the sermon, were in the school-house of Kelso, upon the very point of giving the stroke, but with great difficulty were got to stop. In the morning before the reference there was a meeting of a few, whether as a committee of the synod, or a private meeting for conference, which I rather suspect, I cannot be positive. There proposals were made for ending the affair; and I made them one, tending to peace, without prejudice to truth; which, though coldly received, yet all hopes of its taking were not cut off, till we came to the synod. But being read there, Mr. James Ramsay, minister of Kelso, fired upon it; and, as I remember, offered to dissent in case it should pass; and, on the contrary, he proposed a severe decision; against which I was resolved to dissent, in case of its being gone into. So the synod,* perceiving the affair would go before the general assembly, which way soever they would take, agreed to refer it to them, as it stood before them still entire. At the general assembly, where the proceeding was more wary, Mr. Wilson came off honourably; not one error being fixed on his sermon, notwithstanding all the clamour had been made against it. For this peculiar zeal and faithfulness, his brethren had shot at him particularly; but his bow abode in strength. And the truth is, he was never till that his trial known to them; but it set him in a clear light, and exceedingly raised his reputation. The publishing of his trial hath been much desired. I was comforted, in seeing the affair brought to such an issue. Howbeit, by my going in to Edinburgh to the assembly on that account, my proceeding in the essay on the accentuation was again interrupted.

On June 9, I administered the sacrament of the supper. I was much hurried by means of my necessary absence from the parish, in May, on account of Mr. Wilson's affair. My wife was in great distress, and I had no help on the fast-day; but kind Providence made my work easy: so that I got the fast-day's sermons on the Monday and the action-sermon on Thursday and Friday. On the Friday's night, by reason of the scurvy struck out on me, I slept little; on the Saturday's night none at all; which made me very heavy on Sabbath morning. But I remember my great concern was for the efficacy of the word. God mercifully helped me; so that I minded not my want of sleep during my work, till it was over. Thus my troubles and trials increased; but the hand that led them on helped. My wife with much difficulty got out to the table. It was at and after that communion the sermons were preached, which since that time have been published, under the title of "The Mystery of

---

* Mr. Wilson's speech delivered at this meeting is inserted in the Appendix, No. 4.

Christ in the Form of a Servant." The notion of Christ's state of
servitude, there advanced and improved, I had been led into by my
study on the covenant of grace.

On the 30th, I entered on the subject of the good fight of faith ;
being led thereto by my wife's case, and indeed much for her cause.
And this was not ended till October 20.*

July 14.—Mr. Henry Davidson and I were at the sacrament in
Penpont. It was the second time to him, and but the third to
me, though often desired. It was very much against my inclination
to go thither, ever since the first time in the year 1709 ; but I could
not evite it, though I left my wife in great distress. The conduct
of holy Providence hath been very strange and mysterious, with respect to my going to that place all along. All the three times the
Lord was with me remarkably in my work there, especially on the
Saturday the first time, and on the Sabbath afternoon the two last
times. Old notes have still been most blessed, in my case, in that
place. The first time I had but one sermon studied for it, and it
was not delivered at all there. The second time I had two sermons
studied, but one of them was new studied out of old notes ; and that
was it the Lord made most sweet both to them and me. This last
time we had kept a presbyterial fast on the Wednesday before we
went thither, on account of a drought altogether extraordinary ;
and the rain came on that Sabbath we were at Penpont. Several
other presbyteries kept it that same week, and the Lord heard
prayer. Foreseeing what I thus had to do, having two free days
the week before, I attempted to prepare for Penpont ; but by no
means could get any thing for it. Next week I had no time to prepare for it. I was brought to desire of God a message for that
place, old or new as he pleased ; and I was determined to use old
sermons, and fully satisfied and easy therein, as I use not to be in
such a case. My trials on all the three occasions of going thither
have been remarkable. The first time, the elder that went with me
died there, and I lost my horse, as above narrated. The second
time, I remember no notable thing that befel me there ; but out of
my being there at that time rose the business of Closeburn, which
was a very considerable trial to me. While I was busy about the
notes on the "Marrow," Mr. Davidson went in to my room ; and the
Lord was with him. But within a mile of Moffat, his horse was
some way wounded in the foot, that he went in to Moffat bleeding
all along ; and with difficulty enough he got to Penpont. He was

* The excellent sermons on this subject were printed, in 1756, in a volume with
other sermons.

so late a-returning next week, that I was in great pain about him, and thinking of going or sending to see what was the matter. This was occasioned by his horse's illness. At this time, just as we were got into Moffat water, I discerned my horse crooking. Alighting, I ript his feet, but could see nothing but a hurt on his heel, which seemed to be an old one, altogether unknown to me. Mr. Davidson fell ill of the gravel at Craigsbeck. But we made forward, lost our way in the hills beyond Moffat, going through mosses, &c., till in our greatest extremity, not knowing what hand to turn to, by kind Providence we saw a lad who set us on the way. Under night we lost the way again; but at length got to a house, where we were provided of a guide. My horse went crooking all along to Penpont. I industriously forbare to speak any thing of my horse that night, and on the morrow I spoke of him to a servant only; and the servant having taken him away some miles in the morning, told me he saw nothing ailed him. When we came off on Tuesday, my horse was perfectly right; but no sooner did Mr. Davidson begin to move with his, but two persons standing behind observed his horse to crook, and told him of it. Yet in a little the crook left him; and we arrived safe at Etterick that night, with much thankfulness to the Lord. On the morrow Mr. Davidson went home, and fell ill of the gravel; and I was indisposed always till the Thursday was eight days after, by which time I had completed my studies for the sacrament at Maxton, to which I went off on the morrow; notwithstanding of my toil, and a little of a sore throat I got there, I was very well after I came home. If there is any thing in this matter to be attributed to the agency of evil spirits, or not, I cannot say; but be it as it will, I know that nothing can fall out without the supreme management of my Father; and from his hand I take it, as a deep of holy Providence.

Sept. 5.—The writing of the essay on the accentuation of the Hebrew Bible, interrupted by my going to the assembly in May, being again entered to on the 6th of August, was ended this day, being Thursday, and laid before the Lord with thanksgiving.

Sept. 10. This day I spent some time in thanksgiving to the Lord, upon the account of the mercy of that book now ended; and prayer, for a blessing on it, and that the Lord may find out means whereby it may become of public use for advancing of Scripture knowledge, and for some other particulars in my circumstances, particularly with respect to my wife's affliction, &c. I had a heart-melting view of the conduct of holy Providence towards poor me, from my childhood even until now. O! how am I deeply indebted to a gracious God preventing me with kindness, and working about me for ends I knew nothing of in the time. I have had much sweetness in the original text, and it made me this day to think, how inconceivably sweet must the personal Original of the original text be! how sweet to see, by the light of glory, the glory of God in the face of Jesus! When I got Cross's Taghmical Art from Mr. Macghie, I knew nothing of the matter; but the Lord gave me some sweet discoveries by means of the accentuation, when he had so led me to notice it. Holy and wise was that Providence by which I in vain tried to understand and digest in order Mr. Cross's system, and that kept Wasmuth from me till I was begun to write; and that I had nothing of his character nor his books from anybody; and Pfeiffer I had not till the year 1720. By this means I was kept free of being preoccupied and impressed by anybody's authority, I was led to trust nothing but as I saw it with my own eyes, While I was making my collections of materials, which I did by reading attentively and observing the sacred text, they made me many errands to the throne of grace, finding myself travelling as in a pathless way, especially in making the observations, and being often as in a thicket, where, when I had set down one foot, I knew not where to set down another. But God the Father of lights, is in my experience the hearer of prayer. Oft times was I afraid that death should have prevented me; but glory to his name for life continued, for time and opportunity for study allowed, for strength to make use of that time, and for a blessing on my endeavours therewith made. It is the doing of the Lord, and it is wondrous in my eyes, that he has hid these things from many truly wise, and has revealed them to a babe; and I still find the sense of this humbles my soul within me before him, as being thereby made a great debtor, and it fills my heart with love to himself. I see there is one thing wanting in it, which I desire to wait on the Lord for, if so be he may be pleased to discover it to me, namely, the reason of double accentuation, which I have not yet been able to reach to my satisfaction. Whatever other wants there be in that essay towards the perfecting of the knowledge of that subject, this is a palpable one.

Having now of a long time had a great desire to translate the Hebrew text agreeable to the accentuation or sacred stigmatology, I spent some time in prayer, Oct. 30, for direction and assistance in that work, and on the morrow after I began it. Having dipt into that work, it proved at length quite another thing than I at first designed. Herein I was employed that winter and the spring following; wherein, having carried it to the 15th chapter of Genesis, translating, and writing notes on the translation, I left it in

April 1724; at which time my daughter Alison was taken ill of a

fever. That was but small progress made in so long a time, but afterwards it was much less. For my plan was by degrees brought
on still more difficult and laborious, and was but carried to its
height on the 18th and 19th chapters, and this, in the regress on it
made me much new work, towards the beginning of the book. One
will hardly have a just notion of the huge toil in tossing lexicons
and the Hebrew concordance, for finding out the formal significations
of the Hebrew words, set down in the literal translation, without
one make trial of it himself. But the more hard anything was to
reach, I had usually the greatest satisfaction and pleasure when discovered, and was in the whole abundantly rewarded.

On the seventh of June the sacrament was celebrated.* I had
had much weary work from the family of J. A., he having repeated
his abominations, and another of that family having fallen into fornication. Mrs. A. spouse to the said J. had much ado to bear my
proceedings in these odious cases, but her husband being a peaceable
man, things were kept in tolerable case betwixt them and me. But he
dying in February this year, she of a long time after came not to the
church. Having come at length some time before the sacrament, she
on the fast day, I think, desired of me a token to partake. Now a
woman had gone out of the family, and absconded, being famed to
be with child, and another had deposed that she told to Mrs. A. that
she thought the party foresaid was with child, the deponent and she
being fellow-servants and lying in one bed together. This relating
to the time before the absconding, I did, upon the occasion of de-
manding the token aforesaid, lay this matter before her; whereupon
she, taking it hainously, came not to the sacrament, and all along to
this day, hath turned her back on the public ordinances in the
church. I have dealt with her again and again, her children also
have dealt with her to return, but all in vain; she remains wilful
and goes nowhere on the Lord's day, but some few times has appeared at Mr. Macmillan's meetings, which now are very rare in the
country. To this she has added not to come into our house for so
many years, to visit my wife in her long distress; this is a piece of
malignity which one must lay his account with in following duty.

At this sacrament, having only my two helpers, and my wife's
case being at a great extremity, I have to notice to the praise of
free grace, that the Lord however made it a very comfortable
work, and orderly; yea, a special care of the divine providence was
about it. Mr. Wilson the week before had a fit of the ague, and not
coming on Friday's night, I had laid my account to preach on the
Saturday; and when he came up on the Saturday, I had given or-

* The action-sermon was on 1 John iv. 14, and published in a volume in 1753.

ders about sending for Mr. G., providentially at Cavers, but no more was done in that. I was helped to trust the Lord for carrying on his own work, and had not much uneasiness that way; hereto contributed my remembering that I myself fell indisposed on Wednesday, but was mercifully recovered, so as, on the morrow, I went about the whole fast-day's work alone, comfortably. Mr. Davidson that week was threatened with a fit of the gravel, but mercy stopt it. He was taken ill of a head-ache, about the latter end of the Sabbath work forenoon here, it left him when he went out to preach the afternoon sermon. In a word, nothing was lacking, neither strength of body, nor what was necessary for edifying the body of Christ, my wife being all the time in great distress, fixed to her bed, and a great throng in the house, yet things were managed with discretion and order. However, her case was evidently worsted by the weight of people's coming in to visit her. But to him I give thanks who has happily carried through this work; for my wife was not without thoughts that it might be the time of her departure, and on Tuesday, ere the ministers went away, she seemed indeed to be at the point of death, so that not only they, but a neighbour, were called to be witnesses to the issue. The frame of my spirit on the Saturday and Sabbath morning I found to be flat; but now for some time that my bodily strength is sensibly decayed, I have in some measure learned to trust in the Lord more, though my pains in secret duties are less than sometimes they have been, when my strength would bear more. And my trust was not in vain. At the table, even about the time of distributing the bread, my false heart was unseasonably carried off to a thought which was stunning and stumbling, but pressed with the sense of need, I was thereby stirred up to the exercise of faith on Christ, for the sanctification of my unholy nature. But O that hereby I might learn to watch.

This summer, 1724, has been the most trying time that ever my family had since we were a family. I had made some alterations in the house before the sacrament, turning the barn into a kitchen, the hall into a cellar, and so making two low bed-rooms which we had not before. The design we had in view was chiefly my wife's case in her heaviness requiring the little room, and then to have more room for strangers at the sacrament; for which cause a new bed was made, and set up in the low room. But providence had a design in it unknown to us, namely, that it might be a convenient sick-bed room; and for that use it was for more than two months.

On Lord's day, June 14, I closed my subject of the covenant of grace, my notes thereon being written so largely, that, in transcribing them since for the press, I needed rather, for the most part, to contract, than to add and enlarge.

On the following Sabbath, the 21st, having come in from the sermons, and sat down to dinner, I fell indisposed, endured the time of dinner, but while we were singing as usual, (I think the psalm was Psalm cvii. 23, and downwards) after it my trouble came to a height and I went off, with much ado, to my closet, where a prodigious vomiting and exquisite pain seized me, which afterwards I knew to be a fit of the gravel, which I had never been acquainted with before. It kept me till the Wednesday thereafter, though not always agonising. It was told me that one fit of the agony lasted about five hours, another about seven hours. In the meantime of my trouble, my wife, whom all had enough ado to wait on before, was helped to go up and down stairs, betwixt me and the children, then sick, and to be helpful to both. When all were recovered I was thinking on a day for a family thanksgiving, but was some way diverted from it; but that day or the morrow after the clouds returned after the rain; my son John fell sick, and at the same time our servant woman. His case was of all the most dangerous. The fever took no turn in the daughters till the eleventh day, in the sons till the thirteenth, but in the servant woman on the sixth. Thus was the summer spent, but no breach was made on us. They all came out of their fevers insensibly without a distinct crisis; but my eldest son was very long a-recovering, even till about the middle of August. Towards the end of that month we had a day of family thanksgiving, the whole family, except the manservant, having been under the rod.

I was sensibly helped to the exercise of faith in the time of our first distress, and had a sweet view of the Lord Jesus as administrator of the covenant, being a skilful pilot to carry us through the deep waters; which view was kept before me all along, after we were entered into them. My personal trouble was turned to my advantage. It was sore indeed; but kind Providence made it short, and timed it so happily, that my public work was not interrupted by it. I saw therein a palpable difference between groaning and grudging. For while in my agony I could not help groaning and crying, so that I was heard at a distance; yet my heart, sensible that I had had much health, was made by grace to say, Welcome, welcome; and kissed the rod, for the sake of him who groaned and died on the cross for me; and I was even made to weep for joy in his dying love to me. The foundation of faith, that " whosoever believeth, shall not perish, but have everlasting life," John iii. 16, was my anchor-ground. I had a satisfaction, in that while the rod was going about, my kind God had not forgotten me, but given me my share. But I had a greater difficulty to believe, upon the turning back of our broken ship into the deeps, after we were brought within

sight of land. But one day, as I was going into the pulpit, in the
time of our first distress, the congregation was singing Psalm cxxviii.
ver. 3, to the end, " Thy children like to olive-plants about thy table
round," &c. That came seasonably to me, and was of great use to
me all along thereafter. At length I got my wife and children so
planted about my table; and on the family-thanksgiving, I told
them how useful that psalm had been to me in the day of our distress; and so I sung it with them. And there is something more in
that psalm, that I have some expectation of still.

Meanwhile this shock by the gravel quite broke and shattered my
frame, and altered my constitution; so that thereafter I was no
more as I had been formerly.

PERIOD XII.

FROM THE NOTABLE BREACH IN MY HEALTH, TO THE TIME OF THE CLOSING
OF THIS ACCOUNT.

THIS notable alteration was the more remarkable, that it came on
when I was now going in the forty-ninth year of my age, the seventh
septenary; and here I reckon the groaning part of my life, more
plainly pointing to my dissolution, to have begun. And whatever
groanings I had, in the former part of my life, been witness to by
day or by night, it hath, in the depth of sovereign wisdom, for my
greater trial, been, from the preceding April 1724, unto this day,
my lot, to be solitary in my closet by night, as well as by day; but
good is the will of the Lord; he hath done all things well.

The summer thus spent as aforesaid, a weary season to me, at
best, as an idle time; being engaged in a course of drinking Moffat-
well water, at home, for the gravel; I did, on the last day of
August, put pen to paper again, in the beloved work aforesaid on the
Hebrew text; not knowing whether I would be able to sit close any
more at it or not. But it is but little I have had access to do in it
since; however, I desire to be thankful, that I have got the essay
on the accentuation done; how the Lord may dispose of me after, I
know not; but I desire to be resigned.

Now as the winter came on, my teeth began to be loosened, much
pain in them going before; and that season I lost three, whereof
two were fore-teeth; which marred my pronunciation in some measure. Nevertheless I was helped closely to ply the work aforesaid;
and my plan therein was carried to its height, with exceeding great
labour; and when at any time I happened to go to bed, with some
difficulty entered into, but not got through; the intenseness of the

mind upon it bereaved me of some sleep, which I think did harm.

In the time of our distress in the summer, watchful and kind Providence favoured me with a visit from Mr. J—— G——, a minister of the Church of Scotland, whom I had but little acquaintance of before; a man well seen in the doctrine of free grace, and to a pitch kind, and disposed to be useful, whereof I have since had signal proof. At that time I shewed him, that I could get no body to judge of the essay made on the Hebrew accentuation, the performance being upon such an-out-of-the-way subject; and that I had some view to Professor Simson for that end. And he having minded this, and taken occasion in his own country to inform himself, did afterwards write me a letter, giving me notice of Mr. George Gordon, professor of the Oriental languages in the King's College, Aberdeen, as the fittest in our island to judge in such matters. Mr. Wodrow was his informer, being a man of the most extensive correspondence. I had no acquaintance with Mr. Gordon, nor did I know his character, but by my correspondent's letter. I knew not till afterwards that I had it from himself, that he was that Gordon whom Mr. Cross mentions in his preface to the Taghmical Art. But without more ado, I quickly addressed myself to him, by a letter of the 14th December, committing the matter to the Lord.

Meanwhile, after closing my sermons on the Covenant of Grace, I had pursued my former subject of Christian morality, in the general, from John xv. 14, " Ye are my friends, if ye do whatsoever I command you ;" and Eccl. ix. 10, " Whatsoever thy hand findeth to do, do it," &c. Then I entered on some particulars, viz. against profane swearing, sinful anger, revenge; and pressed the love of our enemies; the which subjects were ended, December 27.*

On the 17th of January 1725, I received a letter from Mr. George Gordon aforesaid, large and friendly, quite beyond any thing I could have expected, shewing all readiness to peruse the essay, when it could conveniently be put in his hand. This step of Providence was great in my eyes, looking like a dawning of light, in a case right hopeless, even as to the getting any body's judgment upon it, that I could rely on, for which my attempts hitherto had been baffled. The date of the latter, being Jan. 1, was most sweet, when I called to mind, that that very day having spent some time in solemn prayer, (as usual on the occasion of the new year), my letter's finding favour with that man, had been much on my heart before

* All these sermons are published in the volume, intitled, " The Distinguishing Characters of true believers," printed in 1773, and are a most choice set of discourses.

the Lord. Whatever be the issue, it is a great mercy to me, to have hope of getting it put in one's hand capable to judge of it.

After carrying on the work aforesaid, through the first twenty chapters of Genesis, I found it necessary to stop; and that in consideration of my frailty, and that the notes were written in short-hand characters, and therefore useless to any but myself. And after seeking the Lord, I began, on the 9th of February, to write all over *in mundo*, in long hand, desiring to believe that he will give power to the faint, and to them that have no might, he will increase strength. The notes on the " Marrow" had now for some time been in a friend's hand at Edinburgh. And in the latter end of that month, there was a proposal made me, for publishing the " Marrow" with them. Mr. William Wardrobe apothecary there, above mentioned, was the chief undertaker in this. Hereupon I revised the notes again; and having spent some time in prayer for light in that matter, April 6, and again on the 13th, laid it before the Lord; I was cleared, and determined to give up the copy of the " Marrow," as corrected and new-modelled by me, together with the notes thereon, into his hand, to do therein as he should find himself conducted by Providence; and this in consideration that matters are still growing worse in this generation, and the declining is on the increase; for the sake of truth, and of the present and rising generation.

In this month of April, began my wife's entire barring from public ordinances, which lasteth unto this day.

About the middle of May, my son Thomas, who had got about two years' domestic teaching in the Latin tongue, especially by my own and my other son's means, was sent to the grammar-school at Hawick.

Now, after insisting for some time this year on the hiding of the Lord's face; Psalm xxx. 7, I entered on " the Son of man's coming to seek and to save the lost," Luke xix. 10, and dwelt thereon till the sermons preparatory for the sacrament of the supper. It was administered June 6, not without apprehensions, that it might be the last I should have occasion to administer. By that time I had carried on the work foresaid to Gen. iii. 22, MS. in folio, p. 44, I entered on it, and proceeded therein, with a view of death at my back; and was much eased in my mind, when I had brought it that length; judging that the church of God might thereby discern what it was I aimed at, in case I should never have had access to have had carried it on further.

Meanwhile great were my trials about this communion. My wife seemed to be in a dying condition for about two weeks before; on the Tuesday immediately before the communion, the surgeon told me, he thought she could not now last long. The want of my teeth made speaking difficult; and I had less strength to speak with, than some time before; and the remaining teeth were become blackish. But the Lord pitied, amidst these and other trying incidents.

Mr. Gordon aforesaid coming to Edinburgh to the summer-session, the essay on the accentuation was, according to our concert, put into his hand about this time.

I preached the action-sermon on the "bruising of the serpent's head," Gen. iii. 15. On the Monday I studied my sermons for the fast on the Wednesday, and that day preached twice in the fore-noon, though not much to my comfort. I began my studies of the action-sermon on Thursday afternoon, but they went not well with me. I began therefore over again on Friday; but being out of order, through want of sleep, I was forced to give it over, after I had done about the one half. So on Saturday morning I had the other half to study; and, for ought I remember, this was new; being always, one way or other, more timeously provided. I had resolved to preach but about an hour; but the watch for the time proved use-less to me; so I preached about an hour and a half in much weak-ness, and was at length exhausted. I quite forgot to pray after ser-mon; and never had the least thought of it, till returning into the tent after the first table, I reflected on it; and this did much con-found me. The most sensible breathings of the Spirit that I had that day, were in the prayer of consecration, and the giving of thanks after the action; in both which addresses to the throne, the Lord was so with my spirit, that bodily strength was afforded me too. My wife was carried through and preserved, but still in great distress. The weather was louring, yet we had very little disturbance by it. But on Monday, at the dismissing of the congregation, rain came on; and in a little after, there was a violent storm of wind and rain, falling on the Lord's people going to their own homes; of whom many having come from far, behoved to lodge all night somewhere by the way. It continued that afternoon, and most of the Tuesday. Mr. Wilson suggested to me, that the bruised serpent was raging, and we were in concern for the preservation of the Lord's people by the way. I saw it then, on his suggesting it; and was thereby pre-sently determined in my own mind to continue on that text; which accordingly I did insist on till Sept. 12. I know the serpent had more ends to serve by that disturbance in the air, than that one of molesting the Lord's people in their way home; it raised the afflic-tion also of a particular person to a height. On the Friday after, I was comforted by a letter I received, shewing, that from several it was understood to have been a time of the Lord's presence in a re-

z 2

markable manner; that it was no wonder the bruised serpent raged;
particularly as to one, that it was one of the best days they had ever
seen on earth. I have got a lesson to beware of fretting at long
prayers by others; it was for that I was checked, by my forgetting
to pray at all; and thereby also I have seen the need of dependence
on the Lord, in the most ordinary things wherein one would think
one can hardly mistake. The business of the journey to Penpont,
and this stormy weather aforesaid, with other incidents, incline me
to think, that I have but too little noticed Satan's activity in
such matters. But glory to Jehovah, who comforteth us in all our
tribulations; I have been perplexed, but not in despair.

Mr. Gordon returning to Edinburgh unto the winter-session, and
having read the essay on the accentuation, desired an interview.
Whereupon I made a stretch, and went thither on the 23d November. I was very apprehensive, that I would meet with discouragement from him. Tarrying there for eight days, I had in that time
several meetings with him; and we went through his remarks on
the essay. Not having given his judgment on the thing in gross,
nor like to do it at all, I, ere we should part, was obliged to put on
a brow, and downright to ask his judgment of the performance, as to
the main. To which he answered, That as to the main we were
agreed. I asked him again, Whether he could have freedom to give.
it his public approbation? and he replied, He not only had freedom
to do it, but thought it his duty to do it. Hereupon I was swallowed up with joy and comfort, that the Lord had so far pitied and
comforted me. But in that time, and after, I found the borrower to
be servant to the lender.

At the same time, my Lord Grange, of his own accord, offered me
encouragement in it; and told me, that Mr. Gordon said to him
about it, that it looked almost as if it had been done by inspiration.
But meeting all three together in his lodging, by appointment, they
both agreed, that the essay, or at least the abstract thereof, behoved
yet to be done in Latin; and offered nothing for publishing it in
English. Their reasons were, that it could not be done in Scotland,
nor yet in Holland, correctly, unless it was in Latin; that the thing
being so little known in this island, it could not be thought to find
buyers in it, being published in English. This new work laid upon
me, now when my strength was exhausted, was an occasion of heavy
thoughts to me; so after my lifting up, I was cast down again.
Thus the weight of apprehended discouragement from Mr. Gordon,
which I took from home with me, lay on me all the time I was in
town, till the day or so before I came away, that I interrogated him
as aforesaid, that it was lightened; and then the weight returned

again while I was thinking to return home, and the matter began to move slow again. Nighting at Cardrona, on my way home, on the morrow there was a great storm of snow driving; and I was importuned to stay. I went to the Lord as my father, for his pity; and had confidence in him, that he, who knew how unable I was to stand before the cold, and what need there was for me to be at home, would pity. So we came away, and still the snow drave on; but by the time we entered in among the hills, it ceased; so that I never in my life rode that way with greater ease. Howbeit, when we were come over all the hills, and were within two miles of home, it began to drive on again so vehemently, that we could hardly get looked up to discern our way. This was most acceptable and pleasant to me, as an emblem of my lot, viz. dificulties ventured on at the Lord's call, which I know not how to get through; carried through, meanwhile, in the greatest difficulties; and then the clouds returning again after the rain. When I came home, I found J. A's child, whom he had got baptized by a curate brought in by him to this parish, had died while I was from home, and was buried that same day, a little before my arrival.

Now for the remaining part of that year, to December 12, I did, for my ordinary, handle the subject of forsaking the fountain of living waters, and hewing out broken cisterns, &c. from Jer. ii. 13.

The parish of Selkirk having now for some time been vacant, through the death of Mr. Macghie; and my wife's case allowing my going abroad in the winter, rather than the summer; I went thither, and preached, Jan. 2, 1726. On the morrow after, I visited a sick person without the town; and from thence came to Faldhop in my way home, and visited another; but was taken ill there of a fit of the gravel. Mounting my horse, I rode from thence in great agony to Newhouse, in a cold frosty day; reaching which place with great difficulty, I just fell down; but getting a bed a while, I recovered some ease. Wherefore I mounted again; but by the way it seized me anew, and in great distress I came into Upper Delorain. There I staid all night, and turned easy again. On the morrow coming homeward, it again seized me, that I was obliged to go to Calcrabank; where recovering after a while, I came home, and it went off. This I reckon to have been owing to the unclearness of the drink I had got in my quarters at Selkirk; the which since that time has made me more cautious; drinking no ale while new, or very old, or muddy. A considerable time after this being at Midgehop, where was a little wench from Newhouse, who had said to them, that at such a time, viz. the foresaid, I came in there drunk; Jane Hope, a well disposed person, wounded me to the heart, telling me, most simply and imprudently, before not only the wench, as I remember, but another woman whom I was not yet well acquainted with, that the foresaid had said so. Thus was I most unjustly and cruelly wounded, in that place where I had often comforted, and been comforted ; but this happened not indeed in the family most comfortable to me. But O ! what need of that charity that " thinketh no evil ;" and of due caution as to the case and actions of others, not to judge rashly ! It is dangerous, as my experience in that matter hath taught me. I had, some years before that time, encounterd, in Newhouse, with a good man, whom I knew not ; him being paralytic in the tongue, and newly come home from a fair, I took to be drunk, so that I could not endure to converse with him, till Walter Bryden, then tenant there, cured me of my misapprehension about the honest man. So he is a jealous God with whom we have to do. But I cannot but admire the wisdom of that kind Providence, which, after I had complained in that house to the master of it, touching the misrepresentation that had been made of my illness in it, as above said, brought him to my house ; where being just to sit down to meat with him, I was seized with another fit of the gravel, and obliged to retire, and groan under it, leaving him and the table. I reckon myself debtor to my God for this beautifully-timed fit, which served to confirm, that I had been injured in the matter of the former.

On March 25, I finished the work on the first twenty chapters of Genesis ; that MS. consisting of 272 pages in folio, App. No 5. That winter my frailty was great, being quite unable to bear the cold, the blood and spirits deserting my fingers ; so that the parish was but once examined for that year, and that after the vernal equinox, save one diet only in the beginning of the winter, and I had several thoughts, that there would be a necessity of my demitting, as unable for the charge. Having read Dr. Cheyne's book on health, I had set myself to regulate my manner of living accordingly, for the cure of the scurvy ; so I ate very sparingly at dinner, and took do supper. This course I had used, I think, more than a year about this time ; going to bed withal about nine, and rising early about four or five ; making the time of dinner late in the afternoon, and thereafter doing nothing, until I went to bed again. Thus my work indeed went on, but my body was brought to that low pass. And whereas my head was now shaken, for several years, paralytically ; the first time I observed that shaking thereof, was on the Saturday's afternoons, when I shaved myself, in the time I was employed in writing the said manuscript. Afterwards I returned again to my ordinary way of living ; seldom succeeding in my projects for health by art, whether with or without the physician's advice.

About this time began my wife's constant confinement to her bed; for whereas formerly she was wont to have some respite in the winter, so as to rise out of her bed, in that season of the year; she hath, since the month of March 1726, lain constantly, all the year over, in winter as well as summer, unto this day.

Having carried on the work aforesaid with a most strictly literal version only, I did thereafter make a more smooth version of these chapters, consisting of twenty-two pages in folio; but which, upon a review, I do not judge smooth enough as yet. This I finished April 12, and, by the 21st had all read over, corrected, and laid up. Withal I had written the preface to the "Marrow" with notes, which was published about that time. It pleased the Lord, while I was engaged in the foresaid work, to let me in somewhat into the reason of double accentuation. And it is truly wondrous in my eyes, that I have been helped to finish that work which I had good reason some time to fear I might never see the end of.

April 25, Monday. From that 25th of March aforesaid, I have been endeavouring to know what I shall do next, and to lay that matter before the Lord, And this morning, being in Eskdalemoor, where I preached yesterday, in the laigh room in the manse there, having had the matter aforesaid much at heart before the Lord in secret, it fell in order, as being abroad, that I read Psalm lxxi. in the Hebrew original; and it pleased the Lord so to shine upon the latter part of it particularly, that from ver. 14, to the end, it was made most sweet to me, and encouraging, towards the matter of writing the essay on the accentuation in Latin, and the low circumstances I was then brought into in respect of bodily weakness. [*Nota*, I have now (Sept. 12, 1727,) got much of that scripture made out to me, I verily expect to get more; particularly that word of it, ver. 21, V'THISSOBH T'NAHH'MANI; "Thou shalt wheel round about," [and] "comfort me." has stuck much with me ever since that time.] So on the morrow, taking some time in secret at home, upon that matter, I came to this resolution, viz. That I could neither enter on revising and writing over my notes on the covenant of grace, which I would fain do; nor yet go on in the essay on Genesis; but venture on putting into Latin the essay on the accentuation; since it appears, that while this is not done, that want is a gravestone upon what I have done already both upon the accents and the text; and that this will be the most diffusively useful. From thence I gathered, that the Lord calls me to essay that now; and I am not without hopes of his pity, and his affording me strength for this new and unexpected work.

Accordingly on the Wednesday, April 27, I began to write the essay foresaid in Latin. And as I went on, I read something of Cicero, in my leisure hours, for the language, and noted in a book some terms and phrases, taken from him, and others; particularly out of Calepin's Dictionary, which Providence had in the year 1724 laid to my hand, when I knew not for what use it was designed. And to this collection I had frequent recourse, while I wrote that book; and found it to be of good use to me. I had formerly, upon occasion of appearing (in print, done the same as to the English tongue; by which means my style, that I had been careless of before, was now somewhat refined.

But, this year, the course of administering the sacrament of our Lord's supper was interrupted, through a disorder in the eldership, and my wife's heavy case meeting together. Meanwhile, after closing of the former subject, I entered on Christ's titles; Isa. ix. 6, " For unto us a child is born, unto us a Son is given, and the government shall be upon his shoulder; and his name shall be called, Wonderful, Counsellor, The mighty God, The everlasting Father, The Prince of peace," for my ordinary; the which I treated at large; and then added thereto several sermons on " believing the report" concerning him, on Isa. liii. 1, " Who hath believed our report? and to whom is the arm of the Lord revealed?" and concluded these subjects, August 12.

Having put the essay on the text of Genesis into Mr. Gordon's hand, I had, at his desire, another interview with him, in the end of November, at Edinburgh, where he gave me some remarks upon it. Both this and the former journey to Edinburgh, were undertaken purely on the head of meeting with him; by which I felt my bondage. At that time, I left with him the first part of the Latin essay on the accentuation, which I had completed by the 5th of September. And he promised me his testimony thereto, providing he should be satisfied therewith in the main, as he had been with the English essay; and afterwards he wrote me, that he was so satisfied. Nevertheless to this day I have not seen it, however I have tugged for it.

At the same time I waited of Mr. William Hamilton, Professor of Theology in the college of Edinburgh; who treated me very civilly. And having desired him to revise it, when Mr. Gordon should put it into his hand, he readily consented thereto; I allowing him, at his desire, to consult Dr. Crawford, Professor of Hebrew in that college thereupon.

I had, in the end of the preceding year, received a letter from my

Lord Grange, of the date Dec. 13, 1725, wherein, upon a perusal of the essay on the text, in the space of three or four hours, which had cost me near as many years, he shewed his dislike of my notion of the heavens; Gen. i. 1, but especially of the waters above the firmament, as collection of waters above the starry heavens; adding his remembrance of an old scholastic interpreter having said some such thing before. To this I made a return with all becoming respect, regretting his having so very little time for perusing that MS. and candidly pointing to the reason of my interpretation; withal giving him a good many valuable authorities in favour of my notion of the waters aforesaid, among whom were Pfeiffer, and Gregory of Oxon, a noted mathematician as well as a divine; and its being a common opinion among the Lutherans. But since that time I heard no more from him. And waiting on him again, at this time as I reckon, I found him quite strange and cold. Thus was I deserted by him, after putting me upon the new work of writing the work in Latin, as above narrated. Whether his disgust of the essay on the text, on [these few hours' reading, or my letter in return to his, or both, occasioned his casting me off, I know not; but thus was I taught, not to trust in princes.

All the remaining part of this year, I preached on resignation to the will of God in afflicting providences, from 1 Sam. iii. 18, "It is the Lord, let him do what seemeth him good;" and on acceptance with God from 2 Cor. viii. 12, "If there be first a willing mind, it is accepted," &c., and Eph. i. 6, "Having made us accepted in the beloved."*

That winter a copy of the essay on the text was taken at Edinburgh, half on Mr. William Hogg's charges, and half on mine, which I paid, leaving that copy to him. My body has kept up better this winter than the last. I am now almost a second time through the parish in examination; and since the middle of January 1727, have had a diet of examination of the younger sort, every fourteen days except one.

Having plied the writing of the Latin essay on the accentuation through the winter, I finished it on the 17th of March, 1727; consisting the first part of 182, the second of 322 pages in quarto. That day was to me, on this account, one joyful day among many heavy and sorrowful ones I have had; and it was my birth-day, upon which, not by any art of mine, but providentially, as I went on in my ordinary course, the finishing of that work of my life did fall. It

---

* The sermons on acceptance with God, from these two texts, are printed in the volume, entitled, " The Christian life Delineated."

being Friday, I had studied my sermons by eleven o'clock; and
having refreshed myself an hour, I finished that work about four
o'clock ; laid it before the Lord with thanksgiving, for life, strength,
and heart, graciously given me, for it; sang that latter part of the
71st psalm, given me for my launching out, as being now on the
shore; dined with my two daughters, with a kind of little solemnity;
and at night in the family sang again that part of the 71st psalm,
which I could not get conveniently done after dinner, in respect of
a stranger, a widow, being present in the house. She came in while I
was finishing my work; and in token of my thankfulness to God for
his bounty to me in this matter, I gave her a crown on the Monday
when she went away, and three shillings on Saturday to some others
in straits.   After some time spent on Saturday morning, in further
thanksgiving, being dissatisfied with some phrases in one or both of
the two last paragraphs, I wrote the last leaf over again ; and added
the Hebrew sentences, as the language of my heart and experience,
to the praise of a gracious God.

   In the spare time I had till March 28, I sought out and bound
up some papers which I incline not to leave behind me; read over
the MS. now finished; reformed my closet; took a list of borrowed
books with me; and made a catalogue of such of my own books, as I
desired to leave for prosecuting the study on the Hebrew Bible,
which I have begun, though I know not to whose hand they may
fall, but being desirous, that, if it shall please the sovereign Manager, they may be so disposed of and employed; and took some new
thoughts of the way of disposing my worldly goods to my children ;
but the then state of my affairs would not permit the putting them
as yet in execution.   These things were done, with design to have
no incumbrance from worldly affairs, when the Lord should be pleased to call me home.   Meanwhile my wife's furnace was heated.   In
the thought aforesaid of my demission, I had some view of carrying
her in to Edinburgh against the winter 1726, and going in thither
myself too, for the winter, and to make trial that way; but her indisposition increasing beyond what it had formerly in that season, barred
all moving that way ; meanwhile he helped us both through, and kept
me up better than the winter before. The Lord knows man's
thoughts to be vanity.   I was like to have little encouragement
from Professor Hamilton and Dr. Crawford.   But I adored the Providence that has led me to and through that work on the accentuation, and the essay on the text; the two things I had mainly at heart ;
and that has so far accomplished his word to me, Psalm lxvi. that I
was in a better case when I finished the essay in Latin, than when I
began it, in respect of my body.

For my ordinary, I had, on Feb. 19, entered on the subject of pro-
pagating religion to posterity, and discoursing it from Isa. xxxviii,
19. " The living, the living, he shall praise thee," &c., and insisted
thereon till May, 21, that I entered on sermons preparatory for the
sacrament. About which time, the weather proving exceeding rainy,
for about the space of a month, I was brought to a pitch of bodily
weakness, though my great task was now off my hand. In this case,
at the sacrament, June 11, my kind and gracious Master managed
me as ever a mother would have done a weak child; so that at that
time I got a lesson, just to be doing with the strength I have for the
time, without asking questions; the which hath been of good use to
me since. Now the bruised serpent began with a broadside; which
was heavy indeed, but made me the rather expect to see the goodness
of the Lord in this work an open door, since there were many adversaries. Some of the parish had a horse-race appointed to be just on
the Monday before, to which many were invited through the country.
I had no notice of it till the immediate preceding Sabbath betwixt
sermons ; and then told them the surprising indecency of it; got no
answer, but that they knew not if it could be diverted. Hereupon
I warned the congregation, that there was a snare laid for them;
and the distributing of the tokens, appointed to have been that Sabbath after sermon, was delayed till Thursday the fast-day. The issue was, that the manager of that matter seemed to be ashamed, declared he had done it inadvertently. None of the parish answered
their invitation but one ; a few came from other places ; the race
was dropped for the time, and they parted civilly. Thus, by the
Hearer of Prayer, Satan was outshot in his bow. He plied another
engine. I was wounded and vexed on the Thursday, with Mr. J.
M.'s two sermons, on Prov. xxviii. 13, " He that covereth his sins,
shall not prosper ; but whoso confesseth and forsaketh them, shall
have mercy." Wherein he explained repentance in three things, 1.
Confession, implying shame ; 2. Sorrow ; 3. Forsaking. Then he
endeavoured to confirm the necessity of repentance in order to remission ; held out the fear of hell as what all had reason to entertain,
to move them to repent ; and harangued against the delaying of repentance. The whole was shut up with that. We were not to do this
in our own strength, but in the strength of God, and in dependence
on Christ, from whom the grace must come. He had not one word of
confessing over the head of the great sacrifice, nor of the sin of our
nature, nor was faith in Jesus Christ, or remission by his blood, once
named, farther than that dependence on Christ above mentioned may
be thought to bear ; far less faith, as uniting the soul to Christ as
the fountain of holiness. I had reason to think it was designed

against the doctrine I preach. And thus was I rewarded for my preaching for him, April gone a year: employing him here on the fast before the last communion, which gave me dissatisfaction of the same kind; and employing him again this time, in hope of better things; all which I did, not from private inclination, but from a sincere desire to strengthen his hands in the Lord's work in his parish; being persuaded, that any reputation the Lord has given me, I was bound to lay it out for the furthering his own interest and kingdom. However, kind Providence ordered that I preached in the afternoon, contrary to what he seemed to expect at his coming; and that also was by the same hand kindly guided, some things falling in the way necessary on such an occasion, and on the other hand tenderness used for peace sake. Thus I have seen the strain prevailing among the young divines, whom I have had no other occasion to hear; and some of the people here have discovered their favour and discerning on this occasion; so that out of the eater hath come forth meat.

In respect of my bodily weakness, I thought I would provide timely for the sacrament, that I might rest and be refreshed the latter end of the week. So I prepared the fast-day's sermon the week before; but I was otherwise so taken up on Monday, that I could not get the action-sermon begun till Tuesday, nor perfected till Friday morning.* And then I had so much prepared, that I knew not how I would be able to deliver it. But then the Lord had given it so, that it was most easily impressed on my memory; and I had it mandated by two o'clock afternoon; a forwardness I do not remember to have been in before. Then I thought I would rest at length; but thereafter I was held so busy otherwise, that that afternoon I was exhausted; so was I on Saturday's night, (what time I was wont to mandate my sermon), that I was able to do nothing. So the first time I could again set myself to go over it again in my mind, was between seven and eight on Sabbath morning, which I did cursorily. And thus was I but just where I used to be formerly at that time. Mean while, being put off my ordinary time of going to bed, sleep departed from me in great measure, both Friday and Saturday nights. In this case was I, when to enter on the solemn work of the Sabbath, weaker than ever, toiled and exhausted more than ever. But, behold, strength was perfected in weakness; and I was in exercise, four hours together in the tent, and at the table. Only I rested a while in the midst of my sermon, the congregation sing-

---

* It was on Luke xix. 5, and is inserted in the volume containing, "The distinguishing characters of true believers." Some sermons preached after this sacrament are also in that volume.

to some sermons on Phil. ii. 7, "But made himself of no reputation, and took upon him the form of a servant, and was made in the likeness of men;" and they are now sent in to Mr. Macewan; and so I am relieved of a promise I made, namely, to give him some sermons for the press. When that promise was made several years ago, these sermons were not in being, and so could not be in my view. I hope never to make such a promise again, nor to print for printing's sake. And I bless God I am delivered from this by a plain providential call to publish these. Thereafter I began a short explication of the catechism; the occasion whereof was this, Some time ago, there was a motion for Messrs. Wilson, Davidson, and I, writing on the catechism, for the preservation of the doctrine. They took their parts assigned them; I declined any part, as having my hands otherwise filled; only they proposed to me the commands. What I perceived in my examinations of those of the younger sort, and in my own family, made me long for that work; but they not being likely to be hasty in it, I fell on this project to satisfy myself in the meantime; but could not get access to fix to it. After the sacrament at Galashiels, I inclined much to fall on that work; but by no means could I in my conscience evite the filling up of the passages of my life, at least as far as the account of the finishing the essay on the accentuation. So I filled it up from the beginning of Jan. 1716, to Nov. 9, 1727; and in doing of it was satisfied, and began to look on it as a sign of that matter of the essay moving to some point. That having been the most busy time of my life, in study and writing, there was but little of that nature recorded. What I have now in view, is that explication of the catechism, the notes on the covenant of grace, and the proceeding in the essay on the Hebrew text, which still as I read the Hebrew Bible, my heart is set upon.

As for the state of my body, all my upper teeth are now come out by the roots, except two in the end of each jaw, and two side-teeth. I have frequent pains of the toothache; can hardly continue close till two o'clock; am afterwards unfit for any thing, if it is not to read a little at night. I preach short now, but I think I pray longer than I was wont in public. I have found my weakness, this summer, subservient to my humiliation and self-denial in all my performances; and a kind of check on the lightness of the heart, that youth is ready to go out unto; yet have I found it withal insufficient of itself to that good purpose.

Sept. 25.—Having been this day eight days, after prayer, determined to that work on the catechism, as what would be of present use, I applied myself thereto; and for three days it went on com-

large paper, and close writ. I wrote to the Doctor, after I had heard it was put into his hands ; but he never made me any return. Only these his remarks were, after long onwaiting for the returning of my MS. sent out to me by Mr. Hogg, without any letter from the one or the other. The remarks discovered a great deal of rashness and ill-nature, but very little judgment or acquaintance with the subject. The Professor's letter was very civil and wary, and did much raise my esteem of him ; but withal it had no favourable aspect on the business. Afterwards I wrote him a large answer, dated June 16, 1727. His letter, and a copy of my answer, are both *in retentis*. See the Appendix.

July 16, 1727. The Lord was very signally present at the sacrament celebrated in Maxton this day. I got a lesson of living by faith, in my serving of tables, not knowing what to speak, but finding it given sweetly and liberally in the moments wherein it was needed. The issue of all unto me was, I found my faith much strengthened. Powerful were the prayers there put up for my wife, now in the eighth year of her distress, from May 1720. And for several of these years she hath been free among the dead, like the slain that lie in the grave, remembered no more, being overwhelmed with bodily maladies, her spirits drunk up with terror, by means of her imagination vitiated in a particular point, and harassed with Satan's temptations plied against her at that disadvantage. Meanwhile, in all things else, she remains clear in her judgment and pointed in her discourse, as before. As she has been all along supported to a wonder, so the Lord has at times given her remarkable visits in her prison, and manifested his love to her soul. And the reality of the grace of God in her, has, by means of her trial, been manifested to conviction. When I came home, she related to me how, that morning I went away, she had been reduced to the utmost extremity, and that which in the imagination thereof was the cause of her terror, really falling out that afternoon, which I very well knew in the time, but had no access to help her, but by lifting up my heart to the Lord on her account, yet she was strengthened to bear it, in such sort as she had particularly desired that day, and had not for several years before reached unto ; and how gracious the Lord had been to her on the Saturday, being the morrow after, and the Sabbath ; so that she was brought to say in her heart, who knows but the Lord may yet bring me again to the land of the living ! This surprising relation discovering that God had remarkably heard prayer on her behalf, I began to conceive more firm hopes of her deliverance. And they were strengthened when I considered that the foregoing year the Lord had led me to preach, at the same place, on the subject of deep humiliation going before the Lord's lifting up his people; and then this year to that of praying always and not fainting, from Luke xviii. 1, having at parting told her that I was going to tell yonder people from the Lord, that they who have business at the court of heaven, must hang on there and not faint, whatever entertainment they meet with; for that so doing they shall be heard at length. These texts were occasioned to me by her case. Now we were with our broken ship, within sight of the shore, and I was as one stretching forth his arms crying, help forward, help forward! But behold, in a little time after, the storm rose anew, and the ship was beat back into the main ocean, out of sight of land again.

July 31. Monday, I fell under a considerable illness, which I took to be the effect of Moffat-well water, having advanced to three chopins of it, being weary of the time the drinking of it took up. On the Thursday's night it came to an extremity, so that death stared me in the face, and the sending for help proposed was delayed, till it should be seen what the morrow would produce. This was a sharp-edged trial to me. I had been invited to the sacrament at E——r, to be administered Aug. 6, the very following Sabbath, but, for a testimony against the injury done by the minister of that place here to the truth of the gospel, refused. The copy of the paragraph of my answer to him, is to be found with that to Professor Hamilton. Now I feared I would be made the reproach of the foolish, being likely to preach none at all that Sabbath, nor at Galashiels sacrament the following Lord's day, Aug. 13, if ever to preach more. Thus I was obliged to review that refusal, and found, in the face of extremity, I had done no more in it but what was necessary for the sake of truth, and desired to lay my credit and my all at the Lord's feet. On the morrow my illness abated, but I was unable to study, and was satisfied in an old sermon I thought the Lord had use for. I was helped to deliver it on the Lord's day, and to go about my work as ordinary; which was a mercy exceeding great in my eyes, in that thereby I was not left to be the reproach of the foolish. On the Tuesday after I studied a little for Galashiels; but it was the Wednesday ere I was quite well; and that day and Thursday I was strengthened to do my work for that place.

Aug. 12. Saturday after sermons at Galashiels, I received a letter from Professor Gordon aforesaid, bearing a narrative of his conference with Professor Hamilton, Dr. Crawford and Mr. Matthew Crawford on that subject. It was comfortable, but withal shewed that those three still were of the mind it would not be for the interest of religion to publish anything on the subject till it were better un-

derstood in Britain. I preached this day on Luke xviii. 8, " I tell
you, he will avenge them speedily." I had, when at Maxton had
an eye to that text for this occasion, but afterwards laid aside
thoughts of it. Yet, when the time drew near I was driven back
to it. And this strengthened my hopes of my wife's deliverance, as
did also my late deliverance.

On the Sabbath morning minding to read Isa. liii. the 63d chapter turned up, and I was moved to read it, and the 4th verse thereof, " The day of vengeance is in mine heart, and the year of
my redeemed is come," so harmonizing with my text, sweetly
surprised me, and raised my hopes very full as to the deliverance aforesaid drawing near. At the table I had a view of
Christ himself as all to me, and going to view particular benefits, as pardon, &c., I was led back to behold himself as
containing all whatsoever. In concern for my children, that
word came, " I will be thy God, and the God of thy seed." Mr.
Wilson on the Saturday and at the tables insisted on believing the
gospel, and on Monday again to good purpose. But that day I had
wished in my heart he had handled some other subject. Mr. Hunter
preached after him on these words, " He is faithful that hath promised ;" whereby I was checked, and caused to say in my heart,
The foolishness of God is wiser than men, seeing how God did confirm what I did not so much approve. I was so refreshed with that
sermon of Mr. Hunter's, that I found my very body in good condition
when the work was over.

But after all this, coming home, I found my wife was extraordinary ill, and saw her not for some time. And when I saw her, she
told me that it had been extraordinary ill with her, and that she
had tasted of the bitterness of death, what she had not known before.
However this made me not to stagger, as to my hope of her deliverance. In prayer at parting with her it had been kept quite out of
my head to desire of the Lord a comfortable meeting with her. Ad-
verting to this ere I got out of the room I stood a little astonished,
and thought it not meet to tell her of it at that time. But now
from this my hopes were confirmed in that I thought the Lord's having kept me from seeking what he minded not to give was a ground
of hope that he would give the rest which he helped to seek of him.
When we went to family-worship, Josh. xxi, being the ordinary, was
read, and vers. ult., " There failed not ought of any good thing
which the Lord had spoken unto the house of Israel ; all came to
pass," was sweet, and pat to my present circumstances in that matter. And on the morrow, having been carried out in secret prayer
to plead with God in the same case I was anew surprised and comforted, reading in my ordinary in the Hebrew bible, Gen. xxv. 21

"And Isaac intreated the Lord for his wife, and the Lord was intreated of him."

Aug. 22. Tuesday. Saturday's night I was raised out of bed to see my wife in great extremity. Sabbath morning comforting her, and shewing that, notwithstanding of all this, the deliverance might not be a whit the farther off, she bid me speak to her as a dying person. Thereafter in secret being somewhat shaken, and expressing my fears before the Lord, that word given at Eskdalemoor, "Thou wilt comfort me on every side," was brought to me, and was staying. Monday she was better, but this morning I found she had been very ill all this night. Even thus in great measure hath it been for many years. Meanwhile I am called to wait on, and not to faint. This affliction has been very heavy to me, bowed me down, and contributed to the bringing me to the low case I am now reduced to; and by it I have been under a providential confinement at home for some years, which, however, in the wisdom of Providence, hath tended to the carrying on of my work in my closet. Three things I see clearly designed in it. 1. My correction; wherein God is just, very just, as I very well know. 2. My humiliation; this being as a weight hung at me, to balance the honour the Lord has put on me in the matter of the accentuation of the Hebrew bible. 3. The good of his people in clearing and comforting them by my public work, occasioned by the Lord's dealing thus with me, according to 2 Cor. iv. 15. and i. 6.

Aug. 24. I desired the Lord would clear up this day, being foul, that I might get to Mr. Robert Scott's burial, as a token he would hear in that foresaid. Singing at family worship Psalm cxxi, this view of the bible was given me, namely, that whatever were the particular occasions of the writing it, or any part thereof, I am to look upon it as written for me, as much as if there were not another person in the world, and so is everybody else to whose hand it comes. The day continued bad, but I thought, what, shall I not believe the promise of protection I have been singing? so I went away, hoping it might clear afterwards. But it did not, and it was very bad in our return; nevertheless, I was nothing worsted in the journey. Thus I got the main thing desired, getting to the burial, but not with the ease, and in the way, I would have had it. And perhaps it may even be so, in that weighty case I have so much at heart.

Aug. 26. My wife being under an impression that her dissolution was near, going to the Lord in the case, that word was seasonably given, me, "He is faithful that hath promised."

Aug. 27. Coming in from preaching on Rom. viii. 26, in secret prayer, I had an experience of the help of the Spirit in prayer, which I had been preaching on. And I got a view of the case of the children of God, and my wife's particularly, under melancholy, viz., that our Lord, minding to show the power of his grace in his children combating with Satan, he, by such a touch on their imagination in a particular point, gives Satan a palpable advantage against them, whereby his work may be more easy, than if they were to encounter on even ground; and then he lets the battle go to, and through a secret support and conveyance of strength from himself to his child, Satan is baffled, and that more shamefully, than if he had wanted that seen advantage of the ground.

Sept. 2. I had a letter from Mr. Wilson, whose daughter Marion had been prayed for at Galashiels, putting me in mind of the expression in prayer there used, viz., that the Lord would rebuke that fever; and bearing, that, as he understood, at that very hour the fever left her, and never recurred. This was a confirmation of the subject I was upon there. I remember I was straitened in that prayer, yet there were in that congregation who might be otherwise, and the Lord might help me as their mouth; and I question not but parts of prayer wherein there is straitening may be accepted.

Sept. 11. Being in hazard of fainting in my wife's case, it was seasonably suggested to me that it was surely by the Spirit I was led to carry that message, Luke xviii. 8, to the Lord's children; and she and I are the Lord's children too, having an interest in it as well as others. And that passage, Psalm lxxi. 20, 21, became fresh to me, that I was made confidently to plead it and expect from it, the Bible being God's word to me in particular, as before remarked.

Sept. 16. Some time ago I had another letter from Prof. Hamilton, bearing, that he would not discourage, and shewing a readiness to peruse the second part of the essay on the accentuation. Mr. Wilson had moved his writing to Jerviswood, or Mr. Bradbury a London minister, or to them both for encouraging that essay. But on the 5th instant, when I was resolved to go to the Presbytery to concert there with him the application to be made to them for that end, the day proved so exceeding stormy, that it was impracticable. But having many experiences of the wise conduct of Providence in such dispensations, I was not uneasy.

Since the finishing of that essay, I have revised the Fourfold State, which cost me much labour, through what was done to it by Mr. Wightman, and that the printers had destroyed most of the authentic copy. But, by kind Providence, Mr. Wardrobe had taken a copy of it, to the end of the third state, which, though not accurate, was useful to me in this case. I have also put the last hand to some sermons on Phil. ii. 7, "But made himself of no reputation, and took upon him the form of a servant, and was made in the likeness of men;" and they are now sent in to Mr. Macewan; and so I am relieved of a promise I made, namely, to give him some sermons for the press. When that promise was made several years ago, these sermons were not in being, and so could not be in my view. I hope never to make such a promise again, nor to print for printing's sake. And I bless God I am delivered from this by a plain providential call to publish these. Thereafter I began a short explication of the catechism; the occasion whereof was this, Some time ago, there was a motion for Messrs. Wilson, Davidson, and I, writing on the catechism, for the preservation of the doctrine. They took their parts assigned them; I declined any part, as having my hands otherwise filled; only they proposed to me the commands. What I perceived in my examinations of those of the younger sort, and in my own family, made me long for that work; but they not being likely to be hasty in it, I fell on this project to satisfy myself in the meantime; but could not get access to fix to it. After the sacrament at Galashiels, I inclined much to fall on that work; but by no means could I in my conscience evite the filling up of the passages of my life, at least as far as the account of the finishing the essay on the accentuation. So I filled it up from the beginning of Jan. 1716, to Nov. 9, 1727; and in doing of it was satisfied, and began to look on it as a sign of that matter of the essay moving to some point. That having been the most busy time of my life, in study and writing, there was but little of that nature recorded. What I have now in view, is that explication of the catechism, the notes on the covenant of grace, and the proceeding in the essay on the Hebrew text, which still as I read the Hebrew Bible, my heart is set upon.

As for the state of my body, all my upper teeth are now come out by the roots, except two in the end of each jaw, and two side-teeth. I have frequent pains of the toothache; can hardly continue close till two o'clock; am afterwards unfit for any thing, if it is not to read a little at night. I preach short now, but I think I pray longer than I was wont in public. I have found my weakness, this summer, subservient to my humiliation and self-denial in all my performances; and a kind of check on the lightness of the heart, that youth is ready to go out unto; yet have I found it withal insufficient of itself to that good purpose.

Sept. 25.—Having been this day eight days, after prayer, determined to that work on the catechism, as what would be of present use, I applied myself thereto; and for three days it went on com‑

fortably; so that I was too secure about it on the third night. But that night sleep fled from me, and on the morrow I was left to toil all the day to little purpose or satisfaction. Moreover, I was seized with a violent toothache, and was in great extremity, especially in the night; so that for two nights I could not lay down my head, but behoved to sit in my bed. Thus was I taught dependence on the Lord in this little work; and that both for the exercise of my gift, and for strength of body for it. The third night, being Saturday's, I got quiet sleep, with my head laid down; and on the morrow, access to my Master's work. And I am signally indebted to him; for that to this day, as far as I remember, I was never kept from preaching one Lord's day. The toothache has stormed my lower teeth so, that I think they are beginning to give way too. This day; Psalm xxix. ult., "The Lord will give strength unto his people, the Lord will bless his people with peace," was food for my faith in my wife's case; and I pleaded before the Lord for the accomplishment of it.

Oct. 2.—Monday. Last week the work on the catechism appeared a more solemn, serious, and weighty work, than at first I took it to be. I bless God that taught me that lesson. The toothache began on Tuesday to return in the other side of the head; which warned me again to seek of the Lord ability for the work; and he pitied. My wife rose out of her bed on Thursday at night, and sat by the fire about an hour and three quarters. It was the more comfortable, that it was the day wherein I spent some time in prayer for her case, which I have done once every week since the sacrament at Galashiels. This morning I accidentally cast my eye on Isa. xxx. 18, "And therefore will the Lord wait, that he may be gracious," &c.; and was thereby admonished, strengthened, and encouraged, to wait.

Oct. 4.—Having ordered to settle my younger son's quarters at Edinburgh for the ensuing winter, when he is to go in, I laid that matter over on the Lord; being encouraged therein from the conduct afforded Abraham's servant; Gen. xxiv. 27, "And he said, Blessed be the Lord God of my master Abraham, who hath not left destitute my master of his mercy, and his truth; I being in the way, the Lord led me to the house of my master's brethren." I found this day it was done according to my wish, and that without difficulty. And thereby I felt how experience strengthens faith. However, I clearly perceive a necessity of a blessing from the Lord on that settlement to make it comfortable.

Oct. 19.—This morning, a-bed, these words rolled in my mind, "And the angel that talked with me answered good and comfortable words." As soon as I rose, I looked my Bible, and found it was,

"And the Lord answered the angel that talked with me," &c. This was more sweet, while I considered Christ as my intercessor, having my suit in hand. Then I saw he had talked with me in that word, " I tell you he will avenge them speedily." Moreover I considered, that there he had interceded in a long trial of seventy years. All which encouraged to hang on, in my process before the throne, about the long trial.

Oct. 30.—Two days ago I had an account, that the sermons on Phil. ii. 7, "The mystery of Christ in the form of a servant," being printed, were going off well.

Nov. 6,—Monday. Last week was a heavy week to me, to the weakening of my very body, through an embargo from the Lord laid on me, in the study of the question concerning Christ's kingly office; the which lies yet untaken off. Tuesday's night we fell to sing Psalm xxv. 11—15, which being so close to my case, particularly ver. 14. I so laboured to gripe it, that being withal sore broken, I had begun ere I was aware, to sing over again the latter part of that verse a second time, "And he his holy covenant will manifest to them." On the morrow morning, reflecting on my past life, this thought heavily went through my heart, viz. That I had been neglected, and broken, and was now fallen down; presently after, I was surprisingly catched, and my case explained, and hope given, reading in my ordinary Psalm cvii. particularly ver. 11—13. Once, just as I was going to prayer, that was suggested to me, "They that wait on thee shall not be ashamed." See Isa. xlix. 23. And this passage, and that of Psalm xxv. are useful to help me to wait, though relief is not yet come. The conviction of my rashness in this undertaking is renewed; though still I cannot but think it is my duty to hold on; and thereto is added a conviction of my two little concern for the honour of Christ and his kingly office.

Nov. 9.—Being just on the point of settling my children's portions by assignation, I had yesterday an account of one of my debtors being broken, whereby my measures are quite disconcerted. This day having sent away my son, to use diligence on that head, and to arrest, I did some time after sit down to my studies, being several ways unfitted for them, and with little of success. But it pleased the sovereign Lord to loose the arrestment he had laid on my spirit, and kept on me about fourteen days. This sweet tryst made me very easy as to that secular affair. He has kept up the deliverance till the fittest time of giving it. O the nothingness of the creature, and of gifts, without the Spirit! God has accomplished his word that was my comfort in my affliction. He has manifested the covenant; I am not ashamed. I see now, this is a great work, and that I need to depend on the Lord for strength of body, and for light, for that effect, as in the former.

Nov. 14.—By letters from Edinburgh I find, that a third part of the Latin MS. on the accentuation is amissing; and nine sheets of the copy of the first part. My wife has been for some time worse than before. Considering those things, with the breach made on my substance, I saw myself beset, and upon the trial of my faith, hope, patience, resignation; and therefore aimed at exercising these graces, and I hope not in vain. I am now brought to look and cry to the Lord, for continuance of life, for bodily strength, and light, for the study of the catechism, as in my former of the Hebrew. On Sabbath night, Psalm xxxii. 7, to the end, sung in the family, was full of light and sweetness to me, "Thou art my hiding-place." &c.

Nov. 27.—On Wednesday last, having been in particular concern for my wife, that was seasonably brought me ; Psalm cxlvi. 7, 8, "The Lord looseth the prisoners,—raiseth them that are bowed down." At family-worship on Thursday's night, having observed, on David's leaving ten concubines of his to keep the house; 2 Sam. xv. compared with chap. xii. 11, how, without the Spirit's bringing to remembrance, a word may be quite forgot in the season thereof, I got a sad experience of it presently, after singing Psalm xxxvii. 8. On Saturday's night it was sweet to me to observe in singing ver. 26, ibid. that in the way of the covenant, the securing provision for our seed, lies not in getting in, but giving out; and it was comfortably brought to my remembrance, with what a good-will to do good to that man I put that sum of money in his hand.

Dec. 1.—Yesterday morning my son going away again to prosecute that business aforesaid, I was obliged to give him all the money I had, save a little; which money should have gone for family-use. I was helped to trust the Lord for provision; and that very night money was unexpectedly brought to my hand, wherewith I was furnished for sending to the market. In the conduct of Providence, at his going first away on that business, I saw how the Lord, who had seen that stroke necessary for me and my family, yet had managed me therein with fatherly pity and tenderness, which made me very easy about the matter.

Dec. 10.—Last week, I was informed, that the third part of the Latin MS. for which I had been in concern before the Lord, was recovered. Also the Lord dealt favourably in my domestic concerns.

Dec. 18.—Last week I had a fit of the gravel, owing to my suffering myself to be tossed with an old temptation, the fountain of much sorrow to me; whereby I perceived Providence was in earnest for subduing my spirit in that point. O, to be like a weaned child !

Jan. 8, 1728.—Matters appear more hopeless, with respect to my essay on the accentuation, and my wife's case. Only the nine sheets are also found again. I have this season had two experiences of the Lord's bearing me up, in going his errands in the parish, notwithstanding of the cold I am so unable to suffer. I find the consideration of electing love, and of affliction, as the common lot of God's children, helpful to me for patience under my trials.

Jan. 15.—Last week, being the only week for a good time that I did not catechise, having gone through the parish for the first time, I had two fits of the gravel. So I see I must be doing. I found I reaped some soul-advantage by them, especially the first, having given myself to solemn prayer on Wednesday.

Jan. 23.—On Friday last I had two fits of the gravel again. I received no relief in the case, but after sore vomiting. So recovering out of one of them, and going to family-worship, I was exceedingly comforted with the first word sung; Psalm lxviii. 13, " Though ye have lien among the pots." &c.

Jan. 29.—The gravel still hanging about me, my progress on the catechism is stopped. And now my soul is often saying, " Lord, shall I not have wherewith to feed thy lambs, to feed thy sheep !"

Feb. 12.—Still that illness hangs about me. Faith being strengthened, I had last week some comfortable view of the resurrection, being on that question.

March 5.—On the Lord's day, Feb. 18, I was to enter on the subject of the Lord's hearing of prayer, having been led thereto by my wife's case, and the exercise on my spirit about it; and insisted thereon from the first Sabbath of the preceding August. What I mainly insisted on, was, " the Spirit's help in prayer," from Rom. viii. 26, " The Spirit helpeth our infirmities," &c. I had fondly thought that perhaps the Lord might tryst the deliverance of my wife, with my being on that subject; but that morning I found she had all the night been, and still was, in a high fever; and thus was I met, at my entry on that subject. Yet it staggered me not, considering the usual method of Providence with me. The fever proceeded, with an inflammation that went over her face and head; and such were the turns in her case all that week, and part of the next, that I was made to reel and stagger like one drunk; often seeing the knife at the throat of all the tokens for hope I had. But readily in prayer, when hardest put to it, that came before me, " I will come and heal her ;" and my text; Psalm lxv. 2, " O thou that hearest prayer," had a kindly sweetness about it to me. On the Friday morning, when I should have entered on my studies, (that being my ordinary study day), and particularly on that head, That

God is the hearer of prayer, and will hear the prayers of his people,
I was called to wait on her, now brought to an extremity, and could
have no access to study all that day. This was a sharp trial. I
lay that night in the folding bed, in the room where she lay ; ordered away an express to Edinburgh, to call home my eldest son ; and
on the morrow got something scraped together on the head aforesaid.
On the Sabbath morning, being heavily affected with the case, I
went to 'prayer, and laid it before the Lord ; I desired he would
work a deliverance, and would please to allow us a breathing time
for a while, before our sun should set ; and I thought I saw, that
that prayer was made by the help of his Spirit, laid for acceptance
on the intercession of his Son ; and begged the outmaking of his
word to me. Thereafter taking the Bible, I thought with myself,
That is God's word to ME, wherein I am to hear from heaven, and
receive my answer ; so I read in my ordinary, and that was made
sweet to me ; Isa. lxiv. 4, and lxv. 8, but above all, ver. 10, " And
Sharon shall be a fold of flocks, and the valley of Achor a place for
the herds to lie down in, for my people that have sought me." I
have been thinking, I would tell her for her encouragement, how I
had purposely addressed the throne of grace for her case, once every
week since the time aforesaid, and was hopeful I would be heard ;
howbeit I did not tell her. But by that means that word, " And
the valley of Achor—that have sought me," through the divine
blessing, was as oil to my weary bones. As I sought, so I got an op-
tunity to preach the Lord's word, and particularly the head aforesaid. But never all the time did she, to me, look more like a dying
person, than just when I came from that sermon ; howbeit I was not
thereby staggered. On the Monday came Mr. Wilson, and my son
also ; and by that time the case appeared more hopeful. Yet such
turns were in it now and then, as made me reel and stagger again.
Next Friday morning, rising somewhat early for my studies of my
sermon ; hoping I would now get access thereto, I was called down
by the time I had got out of bed. And I having, the night before
expressed great confidence in her case, she desired me to let go some
of my confidence with respect to it, telling me what she felt as to the
case of her body. This brought me under a great damp, heightened
by my falling to study that day, as I could get access, how prayer
might be accepted, and yet not granted. By that means an embargo
was laid on my spirit, in private and secret, which continued till
Sabbath morning ; at which time there was a blowing on me. In
the time of this damp, I turned to the promise ; Rom. viii. 28, to
believe that with application whatever should come. She seems now,
by the good hand of God, to be returned to her ordinary.

During this additional trial in my wife's case, the Lord was very gracious to her. Before its coming on, she had a secret impression or intimation of a trial abiding her; and this word; Isa. xliii. 2, "When thou passest through the water, I will be with thee," &c., which was given her at her entering many years ago into the long dark valley, was made fresh on her spirit. About the beginning of the week, after falling into the fever, awaking out of sleep in the night, she found herself so very low, that she could hardly have spoke to awaken her daughter lying beside her, but still having the exercise of her judgment. She thought, that looked very like death, and therefore turned her thoughts towards the word; and the foundation of faith was cleared to her from John iii. 16, "God so loved the world," &c. She saw the promise as a boat on the water, free for any sinner to go into; and as a rope fixed on both sides of the water, free to them to take hold of, for their security, to be thereby wafted over; and she was helped to lay hold on it for her security, believing it. Then she thought with herself, O that I had comfort too! And considering, that when the promise comes not in, the sinner may go out unto it, and seek it, she set herself to seek accordingly; but then was brought into her, as without seeking, that word; Cant. iv. 8, "Come with me from Lebanon," &c., and that chap. ii. 11, "For lo, the winter is past," &c. That time appeared to her to be a gathering time; and accordingly she set herself to gather promises, and got them abundantly; and she sung in her heart, "To these long desolations, thy feet lift, do not tarry, for all the ills thy foes hath done within thy sanctuary." It was as it were said to her, What is thy petition? She found that all that time the body of death had not made its usual molestation; that she as it were looked about for it, saying What is become of the body of death now? And it was as it were answered, It was in the stocks. She looked about for her melancholy, to see what was become of it; and saw it as it had been a spark of fire under ashes; said within herself, Lord, if I shall be returned to life, and be set again on the gaping waters, I will fall a-doubting, and dishonouring thee again: and that bolted in on her, "My grace is sufficient for thee."

During the same time, the gravel hanging about me, I rode a little ordinarily every day, on that account. Twice I took horse with the fit on me, and the riding carried it off. I had resolved to settle my affairs anew by testament, and on the Monday after she fell ill I attempted it; but could do nothing to purpose; and hitherto I have had no access to effect it. On the last of February, my MS. on the accentuation was returned, being transcribed; and a letter by Mr. Wilson to Jerviswood was concerted.

On the 8th of March, the fever began to recur with the inflammation, but was mercifully carried by. That word has been much on her spirit, " Be still, and know that I am God;" sometime that, " Stand still, and see the salvation of the Lord." And the voice of God to her with respect to her melancholy seemed to be, That she should stand to her post. Whatever be the issue, the Lord has so kindly managed this additional trial, that neither she nor I have been put behind the hand.

March 14.—Since the first of this month, I have been sensibly easier as to my gravel, and in better health than before. Yesterday we kept a congregational fast for the season, and bodily strength was furnished me to my wonder.

March 25.—Howbeit, after it, the weather turned very bad; so the Lord has answered us by terrible things in righteousness. I am now near the end of my preaching on the hearing of prayer, but no appearance of my wife's deliverance, the trouble rather increasing; withal I am turned worse as to my own body. These things have shaken me sore; and now for some time it hath been my desire and aim, to be resigned, and to be content to sit still under my cloud the Lord has cast over me. Howbeit, the latter end of last week, the Lord renewed his comforts to my wife's soul, and made her to say, He hath well compensated all her seven years' trouble, her soul being carried out with full bent to Jesus Christ in the promise; she saw the Lord her dwelling-place, and tasted the sweetness of his relations, particularly that of a husband; in which case beginning to say, Might she not look for a deliverance; it was laid on her spirit, that she stood more in need of patience and resignation; and therewith a sweet calm went through her soul; particularly she gave me an account, which I have here set down in her name, as follows :—

" I have often aimed at embracing the everlasting covenant held forth in the gospel, and saw my welcome thereto; was willing also to betake myself to it, with my whole heart and often essayed it. My defect still lay in the want of that confidence of faith that the covenant should be made forthcoming to me, according to my needs, for time and eternity; fear still prevailing, and keeping me as it were standing on loose ground. But on March 21, betwixt two and four o'clock in the morning, on my bed of affliction, it pleased the Lord to stir me up, and help me to essay it again, and to get that gap in some measure filled up. Being deeply convinced of the sin of my nature, and judging it to be the source of my unfixedness, I did, in the first place, make confession of the sin of my nature, life, and practice, being as particular therein as I could reach; especially confessing my predominant sin, and laying my heart open to the omniscient God, to search and try it, in the most retired corners thereof; that if there was any lust or idol that I knew not of, I might be made sensible of the same; and I judged and condemned myself, as deserving nothing but the utmost of God's indignation. Then I looked to the way of salvation held forth in the word of the gospel; beheld Jesus Christ, a Saviour every way suited to my needs, my lost and undone condition. I saw an absolute need of him, in all his offices; and a glorious fitness in them, and each of them, for my case. So I did, with the whole bent of my soul, embrace the everlasting covenant held forth to me in the word of the gospel of grace; cast myself over on the Lord Jesus Christ, and receive him in all his offices; take God for my God in him; and, with my whole heart give up myself, soul and body, to be the Lord's for ever; my soul going out after Christ in his kingly office, as much as in the rest, for the sanctification of my nature, and subduing of my strong corruptions, without reserve; especially my predominant, which I saw head and shoulders above the rest; being sincerely desirous, in the sight of God, never to entertain peaceably, but, through his covenant-grace, to war against every lust whatsoever, though a right hand, or right eye. And I was in a good measure brought to a confident persuasion, that this foundation of the everlasting covenant, on which I had bottomed my soul for time and eternity, had all things in it needful for me; and that it should be made forthcoming to me, for my several needs for time and eternity, according to his faithful word of promise; pleading, that my failings should not make void this transaction, and that I be allowed to remember it, and renew it, as often as need requires. And having for my exercise a more than ordinary load on my spirit, I did, with all the solemn seriousness I was capable of, beg and request for the Lord's pity and help in that particular; and that if he saw it meet he might remove it, but if it must continue, that he would keep me near himself in it; that his grace may be sufficient for me, and I may be kept from sinking into despondency, still believing in the worst of times, that God is my God in Jesus Christ the Mediator, and will with the temptation give an outgate, or strength to bear it. And with the same solemn seriousness, I begged, that his Spirit, whom I was helped to look to for assistance in this my address, might all along direct, guide, and assist me in my addresses to him for the supply of my wants, and to aim at and seek my fruit, by sticking to the root Jesus Christ, and not from my sincerity, nor any thing else in myself; looking on the Lord Jesus as the head of influences, and as made of God unto me, wisdom, righteousness, sanctification, and redemption ; from whence I was led into a sweet view of my union and communion with him."

My work on the catechism still lying by without a return to it, I have been seeking of the Lord, that he will clear me as to what I am to do. I would fain be helped to be doing something for my Master while I am in life ; yet desiring to submit, if he will take no more in that kind off my hand, but that I might glorify him now by suffering. And now my way begins to clear somewhat towards revising the notes on the covenant of grace . and it is encouraging, that, whereas I found myself quite out of case for study on Friday and Saturday, yet was obliged to preach twice yesterday, the Lord helped thereto, allowing strength for his work.

April 2.—I have been still seeking to be cleared as aforesaid, three things being before me. 1. Going on in the work of the Hebrew text, which I can find no freedom to enter on at present, considering it as the chief, to make way for which other things are to be dispatched. 2. Going forward on the catechism; as to which I find I was providentially carried into it without design ; and having finished the first part of the catechism, I was stopped after the same manner ; and there appears a kind of justice in leaving the rest of it unto my two brethren ; it answers not my design for the parish, as to a form of examination, being after the first questions quite too large ; and for my children, as much is done in it, as will serve them a good time. I have nevertheless found it to be of valuable use to me since that time ; and I bless the Lord, who led me to it, in the manner above related. 3. Writing on the covenant of grace ; to which my light doth chiefly open; for, (1.) These sermons, most of them at least, were indeed studied with a design of more public usefulness. (2.) It seems fitter than new study, in respect of my bodily weakness. (3.) Great difficulty having appeared as to the modelling of the first part of these notes, some light for getting through the same begins to break, which does in a manner necessitate me to essay this work, ere that go out of my head. I have smarted, as usual in time of my being unfixed to some particular business.

April 8.—Yesterday I ended my sermons on the hearing of prayer ; but there is no appearance of my wife's deliverance. As to the frame of my spirit on that trying occasion, it was and is a resoluteness to wait on the Lord, with a contentment and pleasedness too, with what way he shall be pleased to take in it, as that which will be the best. Last week, as I had opportunity, I attempted the settling of my affairs ; and I did reach the way of disposing of the Latin essay on the accentuation, and the parcel of my books to be left for prosecuting my beloved study ; as to my other affairs I quite stuck, and could by no means reach the settling of them. Wherefore I cried to the Lord, that he would please either to teach me how to do it, or else carry me off from it, that it might not stand in the way of my proceeding to business. After which, the entanglement still remaining as to these other affairs, it came into my mind to settle the two things cleared; and as to the other, to let things stand much as formerly. And this I did on Saturday. When I consider how a year ago I was resolved to make a new settlement, my substance being increased, but was obliged to delay it; and being in November last just on the point of doing it, my affairs were suddenly perplexed; on February last being resolved on it, I was put then under a providential restraint; and now again was not able to reach it; I am satisfied not to proceed further, but let that of the date Jan. 1, 1725 stand; and that the design of this conduct of Providence will at length appear. So having spent some time in prayer, and thinking on my business of another nature, this day, I am determined to essay writing on the covenant of grace. What determined me was, that proceeding on the catechism seemed to me, as it were, an invading the province of others; and I can have no rational view of an end of my study on the Hebrew text, but what death will make; that this is a very necessary piece of work, clearing that grand subject much darkened; and I found I had been solicitous, that, in the event of my being prevented by death, Mr. Wilson might put these notes in order for the press. So, notwithstanding of the weakness of the performance as it stands, and inability to study, which are heavy to me, I am convinced I ought, and dare not slight this opportunity to essay it.

April 15.—Having on Tuesday spent some time in prayer for the Lord's presence with me in that work, spreading my notes before the Lord, and pleading for light from the Father of lights, through the Son by his Spirit, I did, on Wednesday April 10, begin that work; and found the effect of the application on my body; my head, which long since had begun to shake, being thereby made sensibly to shake more to a degree. Since that time I have not had time and strength both together, to do any more in it; but I desire to be found so doing as the Lord shall enable. My wife returned on Saturday to the little room; which is, in my view, the inner prison. The matter of the restraint on me, as to altering the settlement of my affairs, begins to open. I had little comfort in the gathering of that money; and Providence has now blown upon it being gathered. My great comfort now with respect to it is, I had no anxiety to gather it together. And I hope the Lord is teaching me to live by faith, with respect to my children's provision, and will provide for them another way than I meant.

April 22.—Last week the Lord was pleased to give strength to make a comfortable progress in my work. My wife also had an intermission of her melancholy, wherein it was removed for the space of one night. And this is the second time, or at most the third, that has fallen out in the course of so many years. This gives some hope. Meanwhile it becomes mighty, the floods lift up their voice.

May 7.—On Sabbath last, being very weak, and on a very weighty subject, I put up a request to the Lord, to get it delivered, and was graciously heard. I have had several experiences of this kind.

May 21.—Having been minded to go to Galashiels on the 7th, to concert about the sacrament here, I was the night before disabled by a bruise got by a fall from my horse; and last week being recovered, I went thither, and saw I had missed the one half of my errand if Providence had not given me that stop. About the end of April, I received a letter in Latin, from Mr. John Flint, above designed, concerning the essay on the accentuation, by him also revised; unto the which, tending to discourage, I made a return quickly in the same language. The sacrament was delayed till August, in regard of Mr. Davidson's weakness, and my wife's case. And I think it was of the Lord.

My next ordinary subject was, the slow procedure of Providence against the wicked, from Eccl. viii. 11, " Because sentence against an evil work is not speedily executed, therefore the heart of the children of men is fully set in them to do evil." This was occasioned by the case of the unhappy J—— A——, of whose guilt of adultery, he being now married, there were strong grounds of suspicion; but there was no bringing of the same to light, notwithstanding all endeavours made that way. Hereon I insisted till June 23; after which, by my own struggle in my wife's case, I was led, both abroad and at home, to that text; 2 Cor. v. 7, " For we walk by faith, not by sight." Then, with an eye to the administering of the sacrament, I entered on Luke vi. 46, " Why call ye me Lord, Lord, and do not the things which I say?" In this, I was led into the point of the possibility of getting all Christ's commands done acceptably; in the which I had a peculiar satisfaction; observing the usefulness thereof in point of practice to be very great, and reaching a clearer insight into it than I had ever had before.

June 16.—On the Thursday, that should have been our fast-day before the sacrament, was the most terrible inbreaking of our brook known in the memory of any alive. It laid much of the glebe under water, and seems to have ruined it; it came down by the end of the house also, and ran into the church-yard. The Sabbath also was a bad day. On the first of March there was an earthquake, but we felt it not in our house. This conduct of Providence was wonderfull in my eyes.

June 25.—I have for some time had much ado to keep up confidence in my wife's case, times wherein I looked for peace, no good coming. Last Saturday, being convinced of the necessity of living by faith in it, and of divine aid to recover and maintain my confidence, I was helped by a letter from my friend. But still matters held at an extremity. On Sabbath after, sitting by her bed-side, I saw the wonderful wisdom of Providence in the dispensation, darting its rays all around as it were to every point of the compass, and carrying on many different ends; and some of them contrary as east and west point, *e. g.*, humbling and lifting up; some things also having a far look back.

July 4.—Friday being to go to Maxton to the sacrament, before I rose in the morning, I found myself so feeble, that I knew not how to get thither. But the Lord gave me strength, I think, for this purpose; which held out by the way thither, all along while there, and to my return home, better perhaps than for several years before on that occasion. And I cheerfully bestowed it for the end it was given me. That morning ere I went away, I was surprised, in our family-ordinary, with the history of Æneas, that had kept his bed eight years; Acts ix. the present distressed case of my wife being now eight years complete in May last; and on Saturday morning with the return of Job's captivity, in their ordinary at Maxton; Job xlii. These things strengthened hope. On Saturday's night I lost my rest; but was really easy about it, finding the Lord just gives me strength for his work, as he sees meet; and indeed I did not miss that lost rest. The Lord was with me in my work; but the fear of man was a snare to me a little in preaching on Sabbath night, more in prayer, and worst of all at the presbytery dinner on Tuesday, letting a scripture-phrase unduly used by a brother pass without witnessing against it. This ruined my peace and comfort, to this day not fully recovered.

July 15.—A roll of about sixty persons being prayed for at the communion in Maxton, my brethren and I trysted to meet at the throne of grace on their account, and my wife's among the rest, every Wednesday betwixt seven and eight in the morning, each at his own home, till the week of the communion here. And being this day at that exercise, I was refreshed with that meeting me in my ordinary; Zech. viii. 19, "Thus saith the Lord of hosts, The fast of the fourth month, and the fast of the fifth, and the fast of the seventh, and the fast of the tenth, shall be to the house of Judah joy and gladness, and cheerful feasts."

Aug. 5.—Being now in a near view of the sacrament, my trials are many; Mr. Davidson's frailty continued; the life of my wife seeming to hang more in doubt than for some time before; and withal Satan has given a broadside in the parish. A couple of fornicators appear before the congregation next Lord's day, being the Sabbath immediately before the sacrament. Perceiving the awful design of Providence to humble me and the congregation thereby, I durst not shift their appearance till after; but put my neck under that yoke, precisely on the view I had of Providence's calling to take on that badge of our shame. I desire still to hope, to be doing, and to submit. If I am never more on earth to get up my back, this I aim at, with an eye to him for pity.

Aug. 22.—On the 18th the sacrament was celebrated here. The Lord has shewed me the necessity and usefulness of living by faith, being troubled on every side, yet not distressed. Satan hath laid at me, my God hath tried me with his own hand; but in neither case has he left me comfortless.

Since the latter end of June three fornications have broke out; the first, the man about fifty, who till that time had lived unmarried, with an unstained reputation; and a young woman of seeming singular modesty; the second, a stripling of seventeen, and a woman of thirty at least; the third, the woman a communicant, the man one of the catechumens that waited on the examination kept at the kirk for the younger sort, from January to about Whitsunday. On the other hand, of twenty examined for admission, nineteen were admitted; and I think I was never more satisfied, generally speaking, with those I so examined. All of them came to me orderly before the communion-week, except two, whereof one upon the fast-day, who was therefore examined before the session, resolving to examine no more privately in the communion-week.

The fast was kept on Wednesday; and I neither had nor sought help; but was helped every way, bodily strength bearing out quite beyond expectation. Seeing how Satan set himself to ruin the Lord's work in my hand, I judged it necessary to struggle the more resolutely; and upon that view, after sermons that day, called in the new communicants or competentees all together, and before the session put them explicitly to consent to the covenant, whereof they desired the seal, proposing to them the questions contained in the tenth paragraph of the paper of admission to the Lord's table above mentioned, (See Appendix), to which they consented by bowing their heads, as was expressly agreed upon. I used to take them engaged privately before, but was much satisfied with this. And this method I have since observed. But after this hopeful begin-

ning, that very night awaking uneasy, I found my wife was at an extremity ; and I rose, and went to her with a fit of the gravel on me;
which increasing, I was presently obliged to leave her, and put on
my clothes, and took my horse betwixt one and two o'clock in the
morning. I took several turns on horseback in great pain; but the
riding prevailed not to carry it off. So I behoved to take my bed
again, and wrestle under it till it went off.

By this means I was in no case on the morrow to pursue my study
of the action-sermon begun on Tuesday, having dispatched the fast-
day's on the Monday. But on the Friday, though of a long time I
have been unfit for study in the afternoons, I was enabled to pursue
that study in the afternoon as well as the forenoon, and finish it.

On Friday's night, missing my ordinary bed-time, I lost my sleep ;
but I rose in the morning, mandated my notes, and was by that
means so far set forward.

Saturday's night being set down to family-worship, and the Bible
opened, I was suddenly struck with indisposition ; and being in
hazard of fainting, left it and retired to my closet. In these trials
I was helped to trust in the Lord ; and at this nick of time particularly, was very peremptory that I would trust him come what
would. The indisposition went off, I got to the worship, and thereafter went timely to bed, being in no case to apply to business ; and
my circumstances could bear it.

Having slept well, I rose about five o'clock on Sabbath morning.
But a great coldness in my feet and legs seized me, and hung about
me that morning, threatening a fit of the gravel. I sat as I had
access with my legs over the fire, which I think was useful. But
going out to the public work before ten, I neither felt nor minded it
more ; and found myself very well, when, about three o'clock, I
came into the house after the first table. I divided my sermon in
two, but had forgot to take any thing in my pocket for refreshment ;
but was carried through without it.

Having refreshed myself a while, I went out and communicated,
and thereafter served another table with sufficient ease and vigour.
While I was in the house, I endeavoured to comfort my wife, the
Lord's prisoner, and was comforted by her in the Lord's goodness
to her at this time ; and at the communion-table I was helped to believe, that we should both stand on the shore yet, and sing, notwithstanding our swelling seas.

Mr. Wilson having in public put up a petition to the Lord, for
the MS. with much discretion ; when I came to my closet for bed,
I opened and read two letters; the one from Professor Hamilton,
wherein he says he hesitates to advise the publication ; the other

from Mr. Wardrobe, shewing Mr. Flint's taking the second part yet
to glance over, and mentioning Mr. Du Pont's speaking of sending
it to Geneva; and of him I had known nothing before. This some
way balanced the discouragement of the former.

On Saturday we had wind and rain, beginning and ending almost
with the work; on Monday, rain in the time of the work, and after;
but the Lord's day was fair and easy; only whereas the place of the
tent had been changed for the wind, from the east to the west side
for the Lord's day, I found, when I was begun, a wind began to
blow directly in my face, and once or twice I found it blow into my
mouth; but it was quickly laid.

I had never so much satisfaction in the household provision; for,
it being as I thought quite too much, it was eaten up in serving the
necessities of the Lord's people come from afar; so that one of my
brethren and I had but fragments to dine upon. The elements also
were near run to an end, though in part a greater provision than
ever. What occasioned this pleasure in the consumpt was, that the
sacrament being at Wilton and Peebles the same day, and the harvest in the low country begun, the provision appeared providential,
made by the hand of him who knew there would be need for it, that
we did not think.

The house was throng; but my wife bore up well, till on the Monday she was defeat; yet in measure. One of the servants being
laid by of a cholic a while, another came in her room. Some from
Edinburgh, losing their way, lodged in the fields on Friday's night;
whereof one, at parting, gratefully acknowledged the goodness of
God to her soul in bringing her to the place, notwithstanding the
difficulties met with. The horse of one from Fife ran away from
our house on that night, as if he had been driven. There was no
stopping him till he had gone six or seven miles; which occasioned
disturbance to the owner, and to our family; however, he was got
back. One of our servants having proved most uncomfortable, on
Monday we were secured of another.

Thus all along I was cast down with the one hand, and raised up
with the other. All things considered, the spite and rage of hell
appeared never more clearly engaged against me in my work.

Upon the uncomfortableness of that servant above mentioned, and
other occurrences, the world has, this season, appeared to me a most
loathsome world, seeing the best as a briar, and sharper than a
thorn-hedge. Considering how little we are able to endure one another, I have been made to wonder, how the Lord endures any of us,
being all of us so loathsome. I have thought, that as much of the
gratefulness of objects seen and heard by us, arises from this, that

our eye-sight and hearing are not more acute or sharp; even so, much of the comfort of society we have in the world, arises from our not being more fully acquainted. We have had several instances of persons freely taken in to our family, to lodge with us freely, some for shorter, some for longer time; but have met with a continued train of ingratitude, one of them after another. There remained only one exception in that case; and now that is gone with the rest. We have no satisfaction in these things now, but in reflecting on the principle which put us on these acts of kindness, and the service they did to the parties in the time. This has been a piece of trial, which, for most of the time I have had a family, sovereign pleasure has carved out for us.

Sept. 11.—I returned, on the 7th instant, to my work on the covenant of grace, interrupted by the sacramental work in the parish. That month I understood, that a letter from my friend Mr. Wilson, to Jerviswood at London, in favour of the essay on the accentuation, which had been sent in the spring unto him, together with the index of that essay, had come to his hand; and that he designed to do something in it. But unto this day there is nothing done effectually in it by him, so far as I know.

Sept. 23.—Having preached the action-sermon this year on John xiii. 8, " If I wash thee not, thou hast no part with me,"* and been led, in my subsequent sermons thereon, to shew how Christ washeth sinners, I have been much convinced, that the work of sanctification is a great mystery. Yesterday, the Lord's day, being under some uneasiness, that the doctrine would not be understood, I was made to cry for the Lord's help to make known the mystery; and I hope not without success.

Dec. 23.—On the 15th I ended my sermons on John xiii. 8, " Peter saith unto him, Thou shalt never wash my feet. Jesus answered him, If I wash thee not, thou hast no part with me." In the progress whereof, as I was unexpectedly led into the consideration of the way of Christ's cleansing sinners, or washing them; so I was in that point favoured with an unordinary assistance from the Father of lights, to my own conviction. And though no doubt my deceitful heart could not receive it, without making some undue motions; yet I know I was all along ashamed of my practical unacquaintedness with the mystery; and saw the discovery was quite beyond my gift

---

* This sermon, with several others on the same subject, in which the author says he was privileged with uncommon assistance, which must be apparent to every exercised Christian, was published in 1756, along with other sermons. These sermons require a deliberate perusal, with earnest prayer to the Father of light, for understanding the important mystery there handled.

2 B 2

with an ordinary assistance. I was helped by Owen on the Spirit,
and what I had writ last winter on the catechism, in the question of
sanctification. That book of Owen's was laid to my hand, for an
use I knew not till I had it. But last week, being to enter on a
new subject, and sitting down to my studies on Friday, the Lord
withdrew, and I stuck. The bands were kept on me Friday and
Saturday forenoon; and being satisfied to have recourse to old sermons, particularly those on Joel iii. 21, " I will cleanse the blood
that I have not cleansed," &c. and having prayed in order to mandate what I was to say therefrom, it came into my mind to look to
the text in the original; which done, I found the cleansing there to
be legal, that is, avenging the blood; and so that I had mistaken
that text when I studied these sermons on it upwards of twenty
years ago. So, not daring to give that for the meaning of the Lord's
word which I did not believe to be the meaning of it, I was forced
to quit it. And my bands were kept on to the end. So I behoved
at length to make a shift, and deliver something for sermon on
Ezek. xxxvi. 25, " Then will I sprinkle clean water upon you," &c.
and was not quite deserted in the pulpit. My God, I take it kindly
at thy hand! I acknowledge my holding is of thee; and that I am
nothing, and without thee can do nothing!

On the 29th, being the Sabbath after that foresaid, I entered on
the subject of this world lying in wickedness; the which, from
1 John v. 19,—" The whole world lieth in wickedness," and 2 Cor.
vi. 17, " Wherefore come out from among them," I insisted on till
the summer following.

Jan. 1, 1729.—Awaking in the morning, my heart was filled with
thankfulness, for that I had seen the year 1729; and I perceived
an honour the Lord puts upon me, in prolonging life. It was a good
morning to me; and from that time I was in a particular concern
to know more of the other world; of the which, I was convinced, I
had very little distinct knowledge. I look for it in the scripture
only. It is an awful thought, the case of the soul on its separation.
The carrying of it by angels into Abraham's bosom, is clear;
but —— ——. By this means I have seen my body to be something belonging to my soul; and that my soul in effect is I; that
therefore I, as it were, shall not die, but only drop this body to be
dissolved, I escaping.

A little before that, I had received a letter in Latin, from Professor Hamilton, bearing, that he found nothing in the essay on the
accentuation contrary to the doctrine of the reformed churches; and
that it was not unworthy of the notice of the learned, in case of
publication. These two things I had expressly desired of him, if he

could have freedom to testify the same; and according to my desire, he gave me the letter aforesaid. And now, towards the end of January, having been endeavouring, as it has often been my exercise, to compose myself to acquiesce in that essay its not seeing the light during the time of my life, by reason of my friendless circumstances in an ill-natured world, I received a letter from a friend at Edinburgh, giving a comfortable account of a very honourable testimony given to it, in conversation, by Mr. John Flint aforesaid. This filled me with thankfulness; but withal I was left to rejoice in this alone, which I found to be of good use. I prayed for a way of grave, calm, and serious delivery of the word to the people, which of late hath been much set by, with me, or valued; and I got it by divine favour.

Toward the end of February, I found myself so extremely weakened, that I could not see how I could be much longer able for my public work, without an assistant. But being immediately after closely engaged, in necessary work, above my ordinary, for the service of my God [drawing the presbytery's instructions to their commissioners about Mr. Simpson's affair]; as also before that in a congregational fast, at which I continued long; and withal lost my rest the night following; I was, from the beginning thereof, and for some time after, in better case than for a good time before: being thus taught still to be doing, without asking questions, or with the strength I have, till the Master shall say, Stop. Let the Lord do with me what seems him good.

This spring-season, especially in and about the month of April, was a time singularly heavy. Flocks were desolated, by an extraordinary drift, on the 24th day of March; there were scarcity of fodder, dearth of victual, general sickness, and frequent deaths; all come in upon the back of an impoverished state of the country. It made me often to reflect on what might be the design of Providence in leading to the text on the fast day, Feb. 26, aforementioned, Ezek. xii. 23, "Say unto them, the days are at hand, and the effect of every vision." That drifty day stopt a burial appointed to have been upon it, at Kirkhop; so that the corpse behoved to be kept another day. For about three weeks, as my study-day came about, I found myself unfitted for it, through bodily indisposition. All my children, except one, had some touch of illness; and the fever falling to my wife in the spring, came on in the first of that month of April, and continued long. On Tuesday's night, April 8, being abed, an express came, that Isabel Biggar, a worthy person, seemed to be just a-dying; whereupon I arose, and betook myself to prayer for her, that I might not have sorrow upon sorrow; and was comfort-

ed in her case with Psalm xli. 1—4. So I laid myself to rest again,
and in the morning was refreshed with the account of her being better, which I took as a sign for good in my wife's case. I have seen
of late much of my being a sign to this people, having drunk first
of the bitter cup. At that time there was a weighty conjuncture,
seeming to point towards the dissolution of my family. My own
body was in a weak condition; the Lord had distressed my family,
and blown on my worldly substance; withal the eastern gable of the
manse, which was built for me from the foundation twenty-one years
before, was in hazard of falling; and my glebe lay desolate, without a furrow drawn or to be drawn in it, through the ruins brought
upon it by the inbreaking of the brook aforementioned. This conjuncture occasioned thoughts of heart to me. But for some years
past I have observed, and to this day do observe, it to be a time,
wherein the Lord's hand is in a special manner stretched out against
his own, in their personal and domestic concerns, their bodies, relations, or substance, or all of them together, thereby filling up the
want of the trials, which his people formerly had, by persecution,
from the hands of men; and this while I looked at home within the
parish, and abroad through the land, so far as my acquaintance
goes. So that it is evident, that whatever be the issue of these
things, judgment is begun at the house of God.

Meanwhile the affair of the unhappy Professor Simson above
mentioned, touching his subverting the fundamental doctrines of the
necessary existence, independency, and supreme Deity of the Son of
God, &c. which had been before several preceding general assemblies,
was to be determined by the then ensuing general assembly; and I
was chosen to be a member thereof, as I had been in the years 1726
and 1727, which I could not attend, in respect of my domestic circumstances, which now are as bad, if not worse. In this pinching
strait, betwixt the public and my private case, I resolved to move
as the Lord should be pleased to point out my way.

April 15.—My wife's case continues at an extremity. Yesterday,
she having hardly as much life as to speak, I was called to Easter
Buccleugh to a sick man. With difficulty I got away; and the
Lord was with me there. Coming home, just at the end of the
manse, I met an express calling me to Etterick house. So having
just alighted, and seen her, I went thither; and found the man ago-
nizing, and he died a little after I came away. This conduct of
Providence appeared kind, though trying. On the Sabbath, I think,
with difficulty she got told me, that in her experience, none of the
good things the Lord had spoken had failed; yesterday, that she
was resolved never to part with Christ; at night, that she was like
a bird on the side of a wall, griping with its claws. I have pleaded
again, with submission, for a breathing before our sun go down.

Toward the end of that month of April, I received a long letter in Latin, from Mr. Peter Du Pont, minister of the French Church at Edinburgh, impugning the essay on the accentuation; which had been put into his hands by advice of Mr. John Flint aforesaid, who declared him the said Mr. Du Pont to be the person in that place most capable to judge in the matter. Thereto I quickly made a return in Latin also. Thus was I exercised, with cold entertainment met with in that matter, at the hands of all the men of note into which the essay fell; Professor Gordon only excepted. But it could make little impression on me to the disadvantage of the thing itself; finding, that none of them but he had studied the subject, nor believed the divine authority of the accentuation.

May 31.—My wife's fever being carried off, I got into the assembly, on Tuesday May 6, being the second week of their meeting; however I had much difficulty in it, both with respect to her case and my own. By the way I found Providence dealt favourably with me, in respect of my low circumstances, those with whom I lodged the Monday's night having, unknown to me, provided for my coming. I came just to the beginning of Mr. Simson's weighty affair; which extraordinary case could only have carried me thither in my circumstances. I waited on the assembly punctually, and on the private meeting of those against Simson at the Spread Eagle. Though the major part of the assembly were clear for deposing him, I found it necessary to propose one night to that meeting, what we should do in case it were carried against us! But they seemed not inclined to consult about that. They seemed to me to be inclined to oppose the committing of that affair to a committee, as what might tend to break us. But at length that was the issue in the assembly, to refer it to a committee to bring in an overture about it. This I opposed in the assembly; but was seconded by none but Colonel Erskine. The affair was in agitation whole eight days, managed with as great gravity as ever I was witness to in an assembly. The night before it was determined, being at the private meeting aforesaid, and observing how they were disposed, I stole away with a sorrowful heart, and left them. I went to my chamber, and there alone considered what course I was to take; and on the morning drew up a paper in short hand, to be used or not, as the case should appear to me to require. That morning I had an appointment with Professor Gordon at the Spread Eagle, at eight o'clock; and coming hither at that time, I was conveyed into that very room where the meeting aforesaid was always kept. While I waited there alone, I put the writing foresaid, being a dissent, *in mundo*, in long hand. And no body at all coming near me, by the time I was done it was

time for me to go to the assembly; and so I went off. Favourable
and kind was that Providence, that Mr. Gordon kept not the appointment; as it was remarkable, that I behoved to come to that
room for writing that dissent, where also I was left alone. In the
assembly, the committee's overture was produced; the putting it to
a vote was carefully guarded against, and the affair was brought to
a push, by the proposing to the assembly an acquiescing; and
though several had declared they were for deposition, yet all seemed,
for peace's sake, to acquiesce. Finding I durst not acquiesce, I
arose, and said, " I dissent in my own name, and in the name of all
that shall adhere to me ;" and finding no body at all to declare their
adherence, I added, " and for myself alone, if no body shall adhere."
Whereupon I was gravely accosted by the moderator to bring me off
from it, and when he had done speaking, I not being satisfied, had
the paper ready; and with an audible voice formally made my dissent, by reading it before them. The tenor thereof follows :—

" I dissent, as judging it, inasmuch as it doth not bear a deposition of Mr. Simson from the office of the ministry, of teaching and
preaching the gospel of the blessed God, to be no just testimony of
this church's indignation against the dishonour done by the said
Mr. Simson to our glorious Redeemer, the great God and our Saviour, and what hath been found both relevant and proved against
him by the two immediately preceding general assemblies ; and
judging the same also not to be agreeable to the rule of God's word
in such cases, nor to the form of process established in this church ;
to be saddening to the hearts of the generality of the ministers and
godly through the land, and not sufficient to dash the hopes of the
proud contemners of revealed religion, and the awful and incomprehensible mysteries of the same, both at home and abroad ; nor a fit
means to bring the said Mr. Simson himself to repentance, whereof
as yet he hath given no evidence. All which shall be fully manifested to the world, if need be."

Hereupon the moderator spoke to me very pathetically ; and I
stood, hearing all, gravely, without answering, until he said, " Will
you tear out the bowels of your mother ?" Whereunto I, being
sensibly touched, replied, That if I had the conviction of that's being
the tendency thereof, I would rather take it, (the paper I read), and
tear it in a thousand pieces. I had also before expressed my continued charity to those of my acquaintance who were for the overture. Then the marking of the dissent was proposed, and I was
urged not to insist in that. I said it might be marked, and that I
might afterward consider thereof, and there was still room to take
it up. This was by good providence over-ruled. At length, by

Professor Hamilton's means, I obtained, that the not insisting on
the marking of it for that time, should not preclude my access thereto in a subsequent diet. This was granted, and the matter ended
for that time. At that time Mr. Gabriel Wilson, though not a member, craved, and obtained leave to speak, and delivered himself
briefly, as follows :—

"Moderator, In regard I am persuaded this sentence does not
duly serve to glorify God our Saviour, nor to preserve this church
upon him as the foundation ; and in regard it is nowise agreeable to
the mind of the Church of Scotland, made known to this assembly;
and that it will, I am afraid, (or I am confident), hasten bringing
wrath upon this church,—I therefore declare my testimony against
it."

Culfargie also spoke something, shewing his dissatisfaction with
the assembly's decision ; but neither was he a member. As soon as
I could, I got to my chamber, to consider of my own difficult situation ; and in a little time after was sent for to meet with some ministers. When I came, I found Mr. Hog, and the two Erskines,
and, I suppose, some other. They began to speak of their adhering to my dissent. I thought this too precipitant, judging they
should first of all have considered what was expedient for me to do
in my present situation; and that the proper way for them, not
being members, was, in case of my insisting, to declare their adherence after, by a writing under their hand, to be tacked to it in case
of publication. So I was going away, that I might consider alone
what was proper for me ; but was kept ; and several other ministers
of the party against Mr. Simson came in, with Mr. Charles Erskine,
and the Colonel. They began to direct their discourse to me, and
some of them spoke with a keenness very uneasy to me. So I was
obliged to tell them, that the meeting was not called by me, but I
was sent for to it, and came, judging the design thereof to be a
friendly consultation of what was to be done by me in my present
circumstances ; that what I had done, I had not done rashly ; and
that I was content to overhear what they should discourse among
themselves on that point, and afterwards should consider of it, and
regulate my conduct as I should find freedom. And then I went
off to a side in the room, that they might not direct their discourse
to me. So they spoke upon it, and shewed they were against my
insisting.

Having come to my chamber, I considered my case alone, and on
the morrow morning drew up my resolution on another paper, which
I determined to read to the assembly. And having caused one intimate to the moderator aforehand the nature of my resolution, that

they might take no alarm at my offering to speak again, I did that day, after reading of the minutes, the house being full, crave leave to be heard, with reference to the advice given me yesterday from the chair. Which being granted, I did with an audible voice, say, reading as follows :—

"Moderator, I have, according to your desire, considered again my dissenting from the sentence and decision of this Venerable Assembly in the affair of Mr. Simson; and it was out of no design to break in upon the peace of this church, but for the necessary exoneration of my own conscience, that I did formally declare my dissent in that matter; so I can see no ground to retract it, and therefore am far from retracting the same. Yet, forasmuch as the marking of it in your records, which is the only thing that now remains in that matter, is judged by my Very Reverend Fathers and Brethren of this assembly, to be of dangerous consequence to the peace of this church, which I think myself obliged in conscience to be very tender of, I do not insist for the marking of it in your records; but having the dissent, as I declared it, by me in writ, from which I read it before this Venerable Assembly; and having also in writing what I have now delivered, I am resolved, through grace, to make such use of the same afterward, as pressing necessity, in any undesirable event, may be judged to require."

Which said, I immediately sat down; and the assembly seemed to be well satisfied.

The conduct of Providence in this matter is wonderful in my eyes I have seen so much of God in it, in guiding a poor fool, who in lesser matters uses, by being hurried and straitened as to time, to be put in confusion; and so much beyond what could be the produce of my talents; that I am, in my own eyes, a deep debtor to free grace for it; and am humbled to the dust, admiring sovereign condescension, doing things by me, because he will do them; and putting that honour on me, who for several years have looked on myself as a withered branch cast over the hedge, in respect of public management; and yet he hath made the withered branch to bud again. Upon reflection, I have full satisfaction as to the management of this matter, and find that word verified; Prov. iv. 12, "When thou runnest, thou shalt not stumble." Though it was an invidious appearance, in which I was left alone; yet being made out of conscience towards God, it was so ordered by providence, that it visibly tended to my reputation, both with the one party and the other; whereof several expressions were made me. And the party against Mr. Simson saw the usefulness of it, considering it as a warning of what they are to expect who afterwards may appear for him.

I was convinced, that the appearance in the matter of the act against the "Marrow," had an influence in this case, on worthy brethren, with respect to me; but, on the other hand, I see as plainly, that God hereby put an honour on that appearance. As I was the alone man of the twelve engaged in that affair, that was a member of this assembly; so I was left alone in this; yet in the end of it, the second day, others found themselves obliged publicly to declare to the assembly their going the same way with me; and so, upon the matter, to adhere.* What shall I say? The Lord hath both spoken it, and done it; I desire to go softly all my years.

This invidious appearance, which seemed to have an ill aspect on the affair of the essay on the accentuation, had a quite contrary effect; so that, before I came from Edinburgh, the printing of it there, and publishing proposals for that effect, were moved to me, by Mr. James Davidson, bookseller, and Robert Fleming, printer.

Another case was before the assembly, wherein Professor Gordon was deeply engaged; but I behoved to vote against his part of the question. I feared the effect of this also with respect to that book; but he afterward shewed more readiness to do for me in that matter, than he had done for a considerable time before. And favourable was that Providence that withheld him from keeping the tryst with me above mentioned.

I met with Mr. Du Pont, who was kind and respectful exceedingly, having before received my return to his letter. I applied to Mr. John Flint, for such a testimony to the essay as Professor Hamilton had given; and received from him a letter in Latin, dated May 14, 1729, bearing, that, under correction of the learned in the Eastern tongues, he judged the essay should be printed; and that he found nothing therein contrary to the fundamental doctrines of the Reformed religion. The innuendo in the word "fundamental," was in resentment of what was called the doctrine of the "Marrow;" with relation to which, I found some of the first jurors more equitable and easy, than some of the second; as in the case of Professor Hamilton's testimony, compared with this. I went thereafter to Mr. Flint's house, to have represented to him my observe of the word foresaid; but he was not within; so I saw him not. And some time after, that learned and worthy man departed this life.

Saturday the 17th, being the first free day to me, I had a conver-

---

* It is no secret, but very well known, that several very worthy ministers regretted to their dying-day, that they did not formally adhere to Mr. Boston's dissent; nay some of them expressed the greatest sorrow, that a formal protestation was not entered against the assembly's decision in Professor Simson's affair. It is remarkable, that, in this business Mr. Boston stood, as Athanasius of old, *contra totum orbem*.

sation with Professor Hamilton; who ingenuously declared to me
his satisfaction with what we called the deed of gift, and his conviction that the gospel could not be preached without it; and this
of his own accord. The same day the making and publishing of
proposals for printing the essay on the accentuation, was moved to me
What determined me to hearken to that motion was, that, after the
business of the dissent, a gentleman unknown to me, or I to him,
bid an acquaintance of mine tell me, that if I had any thing to publish, he might have notice, and would be an undertaker. Which
being so timed, served much to encourage me in that matter.

Finding Professor Gordon slow in performing his promise, viz. of
writing in favour of that essay, either by way of preface or simple
testimony to it, or epistle to me; I had, in consideration of my
own frailty, desired of him, that he would in the meantime give me
a testimony to it, in as few lines as he pleased; engaging myself to
return the same unto him, when he should have at his leisure written as aforesaid; but to my great mortification, I could not obtain
that of him. However, at this time, meeting with him, I desired
him now to set himself to perform his promise; the which also he
was pleased to shew himself ready to do, seeming inclined to write a
preface; the which I was most earnest for. And for that cause, at
his desire, he got the MS. along with him to Aberdeen, to be returned in the following November; he got also the essay on the text of
Genesis along with him at the same time.

I came home from Edinburgh on Wednesday, May 21; and found
my family, by the mercy of God, no worse than when I left them.
I found a cough, and a pain in my back, which had fallen to me in
the spring, both of them worse; and I was under great indisposition
for about ten days after. By that pain in my back, it was with
great difficulty that I could change my sitting posture into an erect
one. It had been carried to that height, by means of the extreme
long seats we had got at the assembly in Professor Simson's affair.
This was a new weight hung at me, under the aforementioned kind
appearances of Providence for me. I remember I had something
of that nature, after I came home from Edinburgh at the ending of
the affair of Closeburn. But having, as soon as I could, applied
myself to business, I ended the work on the covenant of grace, consisting of 485 pages in 4to, upon the 14th day of June. Going to
prayer I gave thanks, as I was able, for life and strength allowed
me for it; offered it to God through Jesus Christ; begged it might
be accepted of him, brought forth, and employed for the service of
my God; preserved and blessed while I live, and when I am dead

and gone; withal wondering at the divine condescension, in calling
me to preach the gospel, and write.

This summer the easter gable of the manse aforesaid was taken
down so far as was judged necessary, and rebuilt. And by this
means the course of administering the sacrament in the parish was
interrupted this year; the people being withal straitened for victual
to maintain their families, that I could not find in my heart to burden them with the strangers resorting to them on such occasions in
great numbers. When it was considered in the session, before the
summer came on, it was declared, that it would be hard to get as
much hay or straw in the parish as to make beds for strangers;
which touched me to the heart, on their account.

Having, on June 15, ended my sermons on this world lying in
wickedness, I was inclined to proceed to treat of the other world;
but finding the people crushed in their substance, I was desirous
also to handle something with relation to such circumstances. And,
by the good hand of God, I was led to Mark x. 30, " He shall receive
an hundred fold now in this time, houses, &c.—and in the world to
come eternal life." This answering both my intentions, I entered upon
June 22, and for three or four Sabbaths insisted on the first part of
the text, with a view to their worldly losses.

July 29.—Last week I was at the sacrament in Galashiels. Mr.
Davidson was loaded with bodily indisposition, having that work on
his hand. The trial was carried to a height, by rain falling,
while he, sore broken, preached the action-sermon. But from the
time the action began, it cleared, and continued a good day;
and he was furnished both with bodily strength and otherwise. I
clearly perceived, that God put an honour upon him by that trial!
O that I could perceive at that rate in my own case! On the Monday before, I reached the explication of my text. On the Tuesday
I stuck, and could do nothing. But on the Wednesday and Thursday I got forward, and had laid to my hand so much more than I
designed, that I cried to the Lord for strength to deliver it, since he
had given it; and accordingly I got it abundantly. At the table I
saw, that as soon as I should drop the tabernacle of my body, I
would be fully satisfied as to the conduct of Providence in the matter of my long trial in my wife's case.

While at Galashiels, I received from Edinburgh a printed specimen of the essay on the accentuation; which I found not well done
as to the Hebrew. However, looking on that essay as thus beginning to move into the world, though afterward it stopt; my courage
began to fail; wherefore I was fain to betake myself to the way of
trusting in the Lord, for support, under the view of its appearing

in the world. But the iron gate in its way was not as yet to be opened.

About the same time I entered on the subject of the other world, upon which I insisted for more than a year, from several texts.

After ending the work on the covenant of grace, I filled up more of the passages of my life. Turning my thoughts to what I should fix on next, and only two things of that kind now lying before me, viz. the notes on personal and family fasting, and proceeding in the essay on the Hebrew text, I gave myself to prayer on that head, on Monday morning, Aug. 4, remembering how I smarted for my rash advenventure on the explication of a part of the catechism; but I was not cleared. On the 5th, I renewed my addresses to God on that head; and was determined to the former, from a conviction of the necessity of a memorial on that subject to be presented to saints and sinners, and that I could not find myself easy to apply to the other work while that lay undone, and that some notice had been lately given me of people's desire that I would publish more of my sermons. I found the notes unsatisfying; but judged the revising of them might be of use to my own posterity, if no further use was to be made thereof. So I began it that 5th of August.

Toward the end of that month, I had two fits of the gravel; and in the beginning of September, much pain of the toothache. And about the middle of the month last mentioned, I observed, that not only my head shook; but my legs and whole body began to shake also. But death by that time was become somewhat familiar to me. However, at the writing hereof, near about a year after, all that shaking is very moderate.

Sept. 8. Often has it been my lot, but never more perhaps than yesterday, being the Lord's day, to cover the altar with tears, going to my work with a bowed down back; being like to sink in the pulpit, through heaviness occasioned by one of my domestics. Wounded by that hand some days before, on Saturday's night there was an addition that carried it much deeper. The pain of the toothache, whereof for some time I have had a touch every night, trysting with that vexation, I lost my rest that night. I see the folly of it now, and that I must be resigned, laying all down at the Lord's feet; that I must let one gripe go after another, and gripe unto God as my God for all. I have often thought of that holy Providence which made Heman, who was a man of great affliction, a singer in the temple-service; and have observed how the Lord hath made up to me the want of public persecution, by domestic trials.

Being minded to have gone to Leadhills, Aug. 19, with Mr. Wilson, to wait on Mr. Wightman, for concerting measures about the publishing of the essay on the accentuation, I inclined to have, for my health and refreshment, taken a tour through the country for about ten days; but this last I could not obtain with good-will, which proved a great temptation to me. The journey was providentially balked for altogether, though Mr. Wilson came hither. Meanwhile, that week, I was seized with two fits of the gravel; I returned on the Wednesday from convoying Mr. Wilson homeward again with a severe one of them upon me; took another of them on Saturday's night. The hand of the Lord was eminent in both; the one being owing to drink, the other to meat, unfit for my stomach. Thus both my wife and and I were reproved; I for my yielding to the temptation, and she having me at home with little comfort.

Last week, beginning to drive heavily in the work now on my hand, I again and again took my notes, laid them before the Lord, and prayed over them. And it was not in vain.

Sept. 15.—I have lately had a notable help in three things in my case, from three scriptures. One was Jer. 1. 7, rightly read according to the pointing;* whence I observed, that it is one of God's methods for his people's correction, that there shall be no convincing of those who wrong them, so as to own a fault. The other was a certain passage in Job xiii. and the last in Job xix. By the two last I had a great deal of ease last week; and to this day, Nov. 29, I find a thorn taken out of my foot by them, which has often been very uneasy.

For two nights past, the toothache has ceased; but the shaking of the head, legs, and, I think, my whole body, makes me somewhat apprehensive of a sudden downfalling in the palsy, which may either carry me off quickly, or make me a heavy time bed-fast. But I desire still to be doing till my God shall bid me cease; leaving these and all other events in his hand, whose are all my ways.

Oct. 1.—Wednesday. On Sabbath last was the sacrament at Maxton. From the time I heard of it, I had desired of the Lord a message for it; but remained unfixed until the time of setting to. I was under great heaviness, through various burdens lying upon me; so that I lost the night's rest, Friday and Saturday was eight days. Whence I was, on the Lord's day, but in ill case for my work; but was honourably carried through. On the Monday therefore I laid aside thoughts of study; only I fixed on my text, Rom. vi. 6, " Knowing that our old man is crucified with him," &c.; being, as usual now for some years, led thereto for my own case. On the

---

* See this text accurately translated, and illustrated, in the author's sermons on the " Crook in the Lot," and in his " Tractatus Stigmologious."

Tuesday I began to study, but presently stuck; cut out what I had written, and began a second time; but stuck again; it would not do. That was to me a most weary day, being deeply plunged, my burdens lying heavy on me, and God deserting me. So being exhausted, I had thoughts of using old notes. Awaking on the morrow, I found my strength gone. When I was ready, I just sat down, for clearing my conscience to use old notes, to make a third essay; and so cut out again, and began a third time, putting pen to paper with almost no hope at all of proceeding, or being able to reach it. But it pleased the Lord to loose my bands in some measure; so I went on; and was enabled also to do something at night, which now is not usual with me. That night sleep fled from me again. But necessity urging, I fell to my studies again on the morrow; but stuck again, and could not command, what the night before had occurred for explaining our old man's being crucified with Christ. It pleased the Lord to loose me again in some measure, so that I had done all before dinner. And the Lord having thus pitied, I grew easy under my burdens. At Maxton the Lord was very gracious to me. I slept well the two first nights. I cried to him that he would help me clearly and distinctly to utter the mystery, so as I myself might apprehend it, and the hearers also; for I saw myself in hazard of confusion in it. He graciously heard me, and to my own feeling gave me that request. After serving three tables on the Sabbath, I went away and refreshed myself; returned, and served another. But at the close of the communion-work, I found myself quite exhausted; no strength left, being to preach the afternoon-sermon. I was convinced it was neither meat nor drink that would strengthen me; so I went in to the barn at the end of the town, a few minutes, and there I desired of the Lord strength for his own work; and trusting in him for it, I got it in an uncommon measure, together with the clearness and distinctness above mentioned. It lasted with me that night after the work. But in bed I awaked out of sleep, pained with a fit of colic or gravel, and so spent much of the night drinking warm water and vomiting; but it was indeed gentler than such fits used to be at home.

That moment wherein I shall have dropt this tabernacle, has of a considerable time been much in my view, as that wherein the soul shall find either sin left in it without remedy, or totally abolished; therefore, at the table, I endeavoured, among other things, to get faith strengthened with respect to that moment, by the seal of the covenant.

While there, I had a comfortable account of the acceptance and usefulness of the " Fourfold State," in remote places, particularly in the highlands; which filled me with thankfulness. Also I found, that others of the Lord's ministers and people have sore trials as well as I; and several of them with sorer trials. I would therefore, if I could, sit down more quietly under mine.

I see God puts a great honour on me, and therefore razeth me off mine own bottom, and empties me, that I see, that what he does good with to others, by me, is not mine, but his own; and he will have me to acknowledge it, and on the bended knees of my soul!

When, upon my return from Maxton, I began to apply myself to my present business, what lay before me was the direction concerning personal covenanting. This particularly I entered on, and proceeded in, with much fear and trembling. Wherefore I did oft and again take my notes, and spread them before the Lord, and pray over them, for light into that matter; and it was not in vain.

About this time, having begun to suspect the business of the publishing of the essay on the accentuation was like to be at a stand, the printer who first moved it to me seeming to have lost his disposition for it; I was confirmed therein by a letter of October 15, and thereafter by my son, who had seen him. What has moved him I cannot yet learn. But I was very easy on that event, laying it at the Lord's feet, trusting on him, that he who brought it to me, will see to it in his own time. And upon this state of that affair, a second tryst with Mr. Wightman was given up by me.

Meanwhile, being in Buccleugh, October 29, at a diet of catechising, Mr. J. G. on his journey to London, came to me, and staying all night with me there, made very kind proposals of good offices in London, with respect to that and other performances of mine. This was the more comfortable to me, and bore the more of the signature of divine conduct in my eyes, that it fell out quite unexpectedly at such a nick of time; and that the Lord had made him the means of bringing that essay first of all out of its obscurity, by his bringing me acquainted with Mr. Gordon.

On Tuesday, November 11, I finished the memorial concerning personal and family fasting, begun August 5, and consisting of 149 pages; and laid it before the Lord for acceptance through Jesus Christ, and a blessing thereupon. Having had a severe cold these two days, and been in a sweat Tuesday's night, I was in doubt whether to keep the appointed diet of catechising at Calcrabank on the Wednesday, or not; but I was determined to go, through one's coming to me that morning from the parish of Yarrow, with a line, to get his child baptized there. So I went off, and my cold was no worse. But being come home again that night, I was seized with a severe fit of the gravel; in which vomiting up at length some

blackish matter, I was deeply impressed with a view of the loath-
someness of this body, bearing the image of the earthly first Adam,
and what it must come to by means of death, till it be reduced to
dust again; out of which it is to be reformed after the image
of the heavenly man, the second Adam, far removed for ever
from that corrupt constitution. The day had been very bad; and
this season I have not hitherto had one good day on that occasion;
but I have had a sort of pleasure and satisfaction in enduring these
little hardships, for my Master and his work's sake.

After I had finished the memorial aforesaid, considering that I
had now no more of that kind of work in view, I gave myself to set
matters in order for my departure out of this world; and for proceeding in the essay on the Hebrew text thereafter, while life should
be lengthened out. Accordingly on the 13th I transcribed a particular will concerning the Latin essay, and a parcel of my books,
dated April 6, 1728, and signed it, having made some addition to
the parcel of books. On the 14th, I signed an assignation of what
substance I had, that had been drawn at Edinburgh by Mr. Young
writer there. While I was at the assembly in May, I set that matter a-foot with him; and afterwards corresponded with him, till it
was done with due deliberation, and sent out; and that good man
bestowed that labour, as a labour of love, refusing payment afterward when offered him. On the 15th, I prepared the *errata* of the
second edition of the "Fourfold State," which was published about
that time; and that day eight days, letters for Edinburgh and
London, sending to Mr. G. then at London, a copy of the title and
index of the Latin essay. And on the 16th, being the Lord's day, I
finished my sermons on Mark x. 30, relating to the other world.
And that very night I received a letter for the burial of Mr. Robert
Lithgow, minister of Ashkirk, in whose ordination, *anno.* 1711, I
had been actor. He was a worthy brother; and though one of the
first jurors, yet now for many years kept his integrity in other
things. He was a faithful, serious, and moving preacher, having a
great insight into the doctrine of the gospel; a judicious, pious man,
endowed with an uncommon measure of ingenuity. Every day
thereafter, till Friday my study-day, I was obliged to ride, on occasion of my work in the parish On Saturday, I wrote the letters
already mentioned. I was resolved also to have sent Mr. G. as he
had desired, a copy of the "Everlasting Espousals," and of the mystery of Christ in the form of a servant; but calling for the former
in the house, found one copy was lent away, and another could not
be fallen on; which I embraced as a providential stop to the design
he had in view, which was to get some person of-note there to re-

commend them, and so to print them over again there ; thus to bring me acquainted in England. And having, on the Monday, prepared my sermon for the thanksgiving on Wednesday the 26th, I had no opportunity till this day, Nov. 25, to review matters since my return from Maxton. The Sabbath day was exceeding bad ; so that I could hardly be sure to get the notice of the thanksgiving through the parish timely. But the Lord heard prayer, and pitied, and gave a comfortable day and meeting on Wednesday.

Adam Linton in Brodgerhill, his wife, and son, being all together in great distress, and I being concerned for them both in public and private, I sent them word, that I would willingly visit them, if it might be accepted, they being followers of Mr. Macmillan. But word was returned me, that it could not be accepted on any intreaties. Now Adam himself is deceased. But these people will neither live nor die with us. O my soul, come not thou into their secret in the matter of church-communion! unto their assembly, mine honour, be not thou united, in point of separation !

In pursuit of my former design, I did, on November 27, prepare, and on the 28th draw up, a memorial for my wife, in case of her surviving me, concerning the assignation ; and some directions relative to my dead body. And that very night the reparations of the manse, which had been begun by the masons, and carried on by the slater, were completed by the wright. The meeting together of so many various events of a different aspect about this time, made a strange conjuncture, confirming, in that I was called to make ready for my removal, and yet still to be doing till my Lord bid me stop. As for the state of my body, my teeth remained in number as before, but less useful. For much of a year, I read my chapters in the morning with preserves ; but hitherto have not made ordinary use of them otherwise. However, I think I find my eyes begin to fail sensibly. Nevertheless I have ordinarily this season read something every night ; finding myself in better case for it than some years before. Particularly I am reading over the essay on the Hebrew text, to mark the texts of the Pentateuch therein occasionally expounded, if so be that I be allowed to return to that study. And this day, December 1, completed the filling up of the passages of my life to that date. Meanwhile, though I have ended my discourse on the text of the world to come, I am entered on another text relative to the same subject, viz. Psalm xxvi. 9, " Gather not my soul with sinners," intended for the use of the former doctrine.

Dec. 5.—Friday. On Tuesday the 2d instant I kept a secret fast, in order to my preparation for death. The night before, apprehending I would not be able to go through that work all at once, I re-

solved to pursue it, though on different days. And having begged
of God, that he would raise me up in the morning timely, even about
six o'clock, I did accordingly rise long before day. And after my
ordinary devotions, addressing myself to that work, in order to a
review of my sins, I read some scriptures, two written confessions,
one drawn thirty-three years ago, another thirty, both which I have
kept in short-hand characters, as also the larger catechism on what
is required and forbidden in the Ten Commands; then thought on
my ways in the several periods of my life, and in the order of the
Ten Commands; by all which means I got a humbling sight of myself.
Then bowing my knees before the Lord, I did silently read over the
two confessions before him; which done, I prayed, and made confession of my sins as fully and particularly as I could; and there I
got a view of my whole life as one heap of vanity, sin, and foolishness. It appeared a loathsome life in my eyes, so that my very
heart said, "I loath it; I would not live always;" and I loathed
myself on account of it. It cut to the heart to think of it, and
cut off desire of returning to it, if that had been possible. But such
as I was, I behoved to look again towards his temple. After confession made, minding to renew my acceptance of God's covenant of
grace, to write it also, and subscribe it with my hand, I viewed two
former ones, the one dated August 14, 1699, the other March 25,
1700, and drew up a new one. The former were drawn according
to the more dark views I then had of the covenant of grace; and
the substance and intent thereof I believe God did accept, and I adhere to, though I do not desire the form of them to be imitated.
The acceptance being written, I went through the whole of it, examining myself upon every point thereof; and finding a particular
difficulty in the point of submitting my lot, I had the testimony of my
conscience, afterwards to be mentioned, which coming clear before
my eyes, eased me. These things intermixed with prayer, being done,
I went, and kneeling at my bed-side, did, in prayer, then and there,
solemnly, and in express words, according to what I had written
with my hand, take hold of God's covenant of grace, for life and
salvation to me, with my whole heart, without known guile; and
rising up from prayer, I stood, and lifting up my eyes to the Lord,
I silently read before him the acceptance I had written, and subscribed it with my hand.

By this time I found myself so near exhausted, that I resolved
not to attempt to proceed to the remaining part of the work for the
time. But reflecting on what had passed, I desiderated satisfying
impressions of so solemn a work upon my heart; and therefore begged of God, that he would shew me a token for good, as to his ac-

cepting of it. In this case, two things were somewhat relieving to
me. One was, that God knew the acceptance of his covenant, as
above expressed, was the habitual bent of my heart and soul; and
apprehending, that the falling of the natural spirits had had some influence in the matter, I was hopeful, I might afterwards come to
judge better of that solemn transaction. Another was that scripture brought to my remembrance; Judg. xi. 11, "And Jephthah
uttered all his words before the Lord in Mizpeh." So I closed the
work betwixt three and four o'clock in the afternoon. And it was
matter of some wonder and thankfulness to God, that I had been
enabled to continue so long in that exercise, though in the time I
had taken a few pottage with small drink. But the uneasiness continued, and occasioned some bitterness of spirit; which my merciful
Father did afterwards pity, as a father doth his fretting child. That
night I burnt the bundle of papers laid by for that end, in March
1727, mentioned above, adding some others to them; but I had
taken out from among them two manuscripts, being yet in doubt
what to do with them. I continued to seek a token for good, and
on the morrow was abroad at a diet of catechising. I consulted
God as to the burning of these papers, and was so clear in it that I
had no freedom to let them survive that night.

On Thursday rising early in the morning, to pursue the work I
had begun, I spent that day in it. After my ordinary devotions,
addressing myself to that work, I spread the subscribed acceptance
of the covenant before the Lord, and (having resumed the confession
of my sins) I solemnly adhered to it, and renewed it. And in that
confession, I got such a view of each period of my life, by itself,
that every one of them singly was humbling in the dust; causing
admiration of the divine goodness and long-suffering, that I was not
cut off ere I had reached another; not excepting that of childhood,
remembering some early sproutings of corrupt nature in me in that
period, together with the vanity of the whole; though I was none of
those whom men call either vicious or roguish boys. Then proceeding
towards the covenant, I stated God's offer and exhibition of the covenant to me, in his own express words; such as, Isa. lv. 3, "I will
make an everlasting covenant with you, even the sure mercies of
David." Heb. viii. 10, "This is the covenant—I will put my laws
into their mind," &c.; Hos. iii. 19, "I will betroth thee unto me for
ever." John iii. 16, "God so loved the world, that he gave his
only begotten Son," &c. Rev. xxvii. 17, "Whosoever will, let him
take of the water of life freely." These, I pleaded, were his own
words, he could not deny; and thereupon I adhered, and solemnly
took hold of the same, as before. And then I saw so clearly the

matter concluded between God and my soul, that I could plead, and
see that, upon the separation of my soul from my body, my soul
should be carried up by angels unto Abraham's bosom, by virtue of
the covenant; and my dead body be carried down to the grave in
it, and lie there in it, and by virtue of it raised up at the last day,
reunited to my soul.   And tongue and heart jointly consented, that
this my vile body, bearing the image of the first Adam, should be
left lifeless, carried to the grave, and become more loathsome there,
till it be reduced to dust again; but so that, in virtue of the covenant, it be out of the same dust new framed and fashioned, after
the image of the second Adam, like unto his glorious body.   Rising
up from prayer, filled with joy in believing, I sang with an exulting
heart; Psalm xvi. 5, to the end, "God is of mine inheritance," &c.
Thereafter I set myself to gather some evidences for heaven.   And
these were as follows :—

1. I see that I believe the gospel, with application to myself ; and
find, that my expectations from it do ultimately resolve themselves
on the faithfulness of God in the word of the promise of the gospel.
The which is a good evidence, according to Isa. liii. 1 ; John iii. 33,
36 ; Heb. x. 23; 2 Tim. i. 12.

2. I find my soul acquiesceth in, being well pleased with, the covenant of grace, as God's plan of salvation in Christ ; and that I
have come into it with heart and good-will ; taking my offered place
in it in Christ the second Adam, putting down my little name within
the compass of his great and glorious name.   Whereby I, as a member of the mystical body of the second Adam, am as really intitled to
the promise of the covenant of grace, eternal life, made to him for
all his, as I was rendered liable to the penalty of the broken covenant of works, eternal death, in the first Adam ; 2 Sam. xxiii. 5 ;
Isa. lvi. 4, 5 ; 1 Cor. i. 24 ; Matth. xi. 6 ; Rom v. 19.

3. I find my heart so far at odds with sin, that if there were no
other hell, but just leaving one in his sin for ever, "He that is filthy,
let him be filthy still," my heart would, upon that sentence against
me, break in a thousand pieces.   And is not this the work of the
sanctifying Spirit of Christ in me ? Rom. vii. 23, 24, 25, and viii. 6;
Gal. v. 17.

4. I have a hope of heaven, through Jesus Christ; and the Lord
knows, it moves me to desire, long, and seek after being made meet
for it, in purification from sin ; 1 John iii. 3.

5. I love the purity of the divine image expressed in the holy
law, and every line of it, so far as I discern it ; and even there
where it strikes against the sin that most easily besets me; Heb.
viii. 10; Psalm cxix. 6; Rom. vii. 22.

6. I have a measure of confidence, that I will get complete life
and salvation; but that confidence is not in the flesh; for, God knows
I am heartily out with myself, with respect to all the periods of my
life, any one of which, I see, would undoubtedly ruin me, and that
most justly. So I am razed from off my own bottom, and have no
confidence of acceptance with God, but in Christ crucified, who loved
me, and gave himself for me; Matth. v. 3; Phil. iii. 3.

Lastly, As to that particular matter which it has pleased my God
to make the special continued trial of the most part of my life, which
has been the most exquisite one to me, and has often threatened to
baffle all my evidences for heaven, as being the one thing lacking;
I can say, 1. I sincerely desire to be as a weaned child in it, to get
above it, to quit it to the Lord, and to take Christ in its room and
stead; Matth. v. 6. 2. I have sometimes got above it, from spiritual
principles, motives, and ends; Mark ix. 47; Psalm xviii. 23. 3.
Whereas it has often got the mastery over me, and held me down,
like a giant on a little child, or a mountain on a worm, I am heartily
ashamed thereof before the Lord. And that is one of the main
things which have made the course of my past life so notably loathsome unto me, upon the review I have been making of it. And thus
it hath contributed to empty me, shake me out of myself, and to
drive me unto Christ; Ezek. xxxvi. 31. 4. Notwithstanding all my
unbecoming quarrelling with my Lord upon that head, I would lie
against my own soul, if I should deny, that I would rather have a
cross of his choosing for me, than a crown of my own choosing
for myself. The which now is, and was the testimony of my conscience, on Tuesday, when I was examining myself in the point of
submitting my lot to him; Psalm xlvii. 4. 5. And lastly, I love
God in Christ above it, being content to quit it for him, though I
cannot hinder the old man to reclaim; and could be satisfied in the
enjoyment of God without it, but by no means with it without him,
as sometimes I have clearly perceived, when the trial was like to be
removed. Wherefore, since that has been what of all worldly
things had most of my heart, and what I thought I could least brook
the want of, and yet my heart stands thus disposed towards it, I
conclude, that I love God in Christ above all; Matth. x. 37, with
Luke xiv. 26; Hab. iii. 17, 18; Psalm lxxiii. 25.

These things, intermixed with prayer, being dispatched, I then
set myself to prayers and supplications with reference particularly
to my removal out of this world. And in these, besides the main
thing touching the transportation of my soul, and the resurrection of
my body at the last day, I did particularly beg, that, having lived
so little to his glory, he would please to give me to die to his glory;

that in case of sudden death, which I neither durst nor inclined to deprecate, he, to whom all his works are known from the beginning, would secretly work in me actual preparation for it; and in case of longsome sickness, that he would arm me with patience; that if it were his will, he would continue with me the use of speech; but withal heartily submitting, that in case of losing the power of my tongue, which, from the paralytic state of my body, I am somewhat apprehensive of, my countenance might speak to his glory. In the event of my leaving my wife a widow, and my children fatherless, I left her, and them, each one by name, on my covenanted God, according to the promise; Jer. xlix. 11, requesting, that we might all meet together again in the happy part of the other world; and for her, that I might be allowed to see her deliverance; if not, that it may come speedily after my departure, if it be his will. The parish also, in that event, I left on him, to provide a minister for them. I was concerned also for a blessing on my servants, viz. John Bromfield and Christian Speedin, they having been a great comfort to me, and continuing to be so. Withal I begged grace for the Christian improvement of any time of my life that may be remaining; and the divine determination as to the disposal of the two manuscripts above mentioned. Being to close the work, and day-light failing, I lighted a candle, and sung the 23d Psalm, with some understanding of it, confidence and cheerfulness. But a particular concern for grace to bear my trial, carried me back to God again, in prayer for that purpose. I met with two scriptures that day, one in a light wherein I had not before observed it, viz. 2 Cor. v. 12, "Them which glory in appearance, (Gr. in the face), and not in heart;" denoting the skin-deep joy of ungodly men, who have none in the recesses of their heart; the other, exceeding strengthening food to faith, namely, the promise of God's making the worm " thresh the mountains, and beat them small," &c. Isa. xli. 14—16. Meanwhile the worm there acts only the part of the flail, but in the omnipotent hand it threshes them. O the wonders of grace, a spark of the holy fire drying up the sea of corruption, a worm threshing the mountains! I rejoice in that word, as one that hath found great spoil. The continuing of my strength for this exercise, as it has done, was what I did not expect, and is wondrous in my eyes; " I will bless the Lord, who hath given me counsel."

Dec. 8.—Monday. This night I had completed the filling up in the passages of my life the last week's progress. I have for a considerable time found the consideration of the goodness of the nature of God very strengthening. Last night my wife brought to mind again a remarkable passage in her case, which was this. Two

years ago, she having long wanted, sought, and at length got, a
clear view of her interest in Christ, was rejoicing in the goodness of
God. And the tempter suggested, that nevertheless her particular
trouble was not removed, nor were her bodily ailments taken away;
and therefore he should take a short cut for her own delivery, now
that she was secure for eternity. The which she replied, saying, She
would not do that, for that would be horrid ingratitude to God; but
all the days of her appointed time she would wait till her change
come; and moreover that the scripture saith, " No murderer hath
eternal life." Upon which the enemy slunk away as ashamed.

The spare time I had that week, was spent in reforming my closet,
and sorting of papers; at which time also I destroyed the assignation made under trust in the year 1712, together with some other
papers depending thereupon.

Having thus gone as far as I could reach, in matters of that nature, I gave myself to prayer, to seek of the Lord a right way, to
which I should next betake myself; for by this time another thing
had cast up, in competition with my beloved study, from which I
had now been so many years kept off, viz. from the year 1726; and
that was, to give a general account of my life. This competition
had cost me several thoughts of heart; and in end I was, contrary to
my expectation, and much contrary to my inclination, determined unto
this last. By which I was, in my own eyes, as one again beat back
from the desired harbour, when I was within sight of it, thinking that
now I had nothing more to keep me off from the beloved study of the
Hebrew text. On the morrow after that exercise, I was confirmed in
that determination. Wherefore, in compliance with what I judged to
be pointed out to me as my duty, I did without delay put pen to paper for that work, on the next day, being the 15th of December.

Sleep departing from me had for many years, now and then, been
my lot; and I was that day in some disorder, from that cause the
night before; so that my beginning of that work at that time, was
in a manner a resolute thrusting forward unto it, as it has often
fallen out with me in such cases. But I never had experienced the
departing of it at the rate I did about that time; wherein for fifteen
days then beginning, I could not reckon above five whole nights
rest got, whereof three only were sound as ordinary; howbeit I
always got some sleep, especially in the morning. By this means
the work went on slowly; but withal I read through a great part of
the two MSS. above mentioned, in my waking hours of the night,
and found reason to cease destroying them, for the time.

Dec. 29.—On Friday last studying my sermon, I had condescended
on some marks to distinguish betwixt the godly and ungodly; but,

being hurried in the time, I had no ease with respect to them when done, fearing they were not duly considered and balanced. Wherefore at night I just cut out that part of my notes, and began anew. I have always reckoned that to be one of the most difficult parts of preaching, how to steer an even course in these things, so as to guard duly on both sides.

Jan. 1, 1730.—Being Thursday, I spent some time in prayer with fasting, for the work aforesaid, that went on heavily, and for my wife's case. I adhered to the solemn transaction above mentioned, and with some confidence pleaded the witnesses taken thereto; and made supplication for bodily strength, as well as for light, finding the want of the former as well as the latter. And whereas I had before put my lost teeth in a box for conservation, I put another in that same day. I was for some days thereafter much tired with indisposition, and confusion; whereby an embargo was laid upon me with respect to the work aforesaid; but it pleased the Lord to take off that embargo on Friday the 9th; so that I then became capable to proceed in that work. So doth the Lord, in all things, shew me my own emptiness; and that without him I can do nothing.

Jan. 3.—I found myself fail mightily, in managing the diets of catechising this season; especially the two last diets. Considering the loss sustained by the people, through my inability to speak, and apply to it; it has been very heavy to me. But this day the Lord pitied, and helped me therein again; the which is the more welcome, that now I begin this work also, the catechising of those of the younger sort, which is carried on together with the public catechising of the parish; not daring as yet to ease myself of that accessory piece of my work.

It was but about this time that I had notice of the publication of the second edition of the Fourfold State; and on the morrow after a copy thereof came to my hand, I took and spread it before the Lord, praying for a blessing to be entailed on it, for the conviction and conversion of sinners, and edification of saints, for the time I am in life, and after I shall be in the dust.

Meanwhile there was no motion nor appearance in favour of the essay on the accentuation, from Edinburgh nor from Aberdeen; but that matter lay then dormant. But on the 7th of February came to my hand letters directed to Mr. W. H. merchant in Edinburgh, my correspondent there; one from Professor Gordon at Aberdeen, into whose hands I put the essay, in order to his prefacing it, to have been returned in November, as above said; advising, that, in respect of family or personal distress, since the end of August, he had thought very little on the matter; and that he could not tell when he might be able to read or consider any thing requiring close application; but the other, from Mr. G. at London, advising, that he had put the title and index of the essay sent him as afore-mentioned, into the hands of Dr. Ridgley, an Independent minister there, acting as a professor of theology, and Mr. Earns his colleague, training up dissenting students in the languages and liberal arts, and a fellow of the royal society; that they were much pleased with the design; and wished, that as there might be some-thing said by way of preface, for the divine authority of the accents, as to which point they themselves were entirely satisfied; so the rules concerning them might be illustrated and exemplified from particular passages of original scripture, to shew the usefulness of the essay, for understanding the mind of the Spirit in the original Hebrew; having observed, that Wasmuth and Ledheburius had mar-red the usefulness of their otherwise valuable works, by contenting themselves with a recital of a heap of rules, without a suitable illus-tration and exemplification; and further advising, that Mr. Brad-bury, a famous dissenting minister there, liked the account he had given him about it; and promised to go with him, on that score, to Dr. Knight and Dr. Waterland, both of the Church of England. It was comfortable to me to find the two dissenters aforesaid speak on the matter like men who had considered it, and the true state there-of as it stands in the world this day. Providence having thus awak-ened the affair again, yet keeping it still in a state of uncertainty, it was my exercise to be resigned to the Lord, and to be conducted of himself therein. I wrote to Professor Gordon again, allowing him to keep the MSS. for the end aforesaid, until the time of the meet-ing of the General Assembly in May this year. I had written also to the worthy Mr. David Anderson, professor of theology in the col-lege of Aberdeen, desiring his revising of both the MSS. viz. that on the accentuation, and that on the text; they being both there for the time.

It had been my manner of a long time, besides the catechising the parish already mentioned, to have diets of catechising those of the younger sort; and they met in the kirk, sometimes in my house. What time I began this course, I do not remember; but I think it has been early; for I learned it from Mr. Charles Gordon, minister of Ashkirk, whom I found so employed in his house when I went at a time to visit him; and he died, at furthest, in the year 1710. By this course I got several young people of both sexes, trained up to a good measure of knowledge; some of whom unto this day are solid and knowing Christians; but it suffered some interruptions. The time I found fittest for it, on their part, was from January to the beginning of May; and the whole youth of the parish, who were disposed, and had access to wait on, came together, and were welcome; as were others also, who inclined to hear. The intimation of their first diet was made from the pulpit; and then from time to time I set, and signified to them, their next diet; ordinarily they met once a-fortnight; sometimes once in twenty days only; sometimes once a-week, as occasion required. Several times these meetings were closed with a warm exhortation to practical religion; the which I sometime used also in the diets of catechising the parish. Thus this accessory work fell in the time when ordinarily I was weakest; and of late years, that my frailty notably increased, I wanted not inclination sometimes to give it over. But that I might the better comport with it, I did some years ago cause make a portable iron grate, in which I had a fire in the kirk to sit at, on these occasions. This year, after I had once and again found myself fail mightily in diets for the parish, through bodily inability, the time of beginning this course was returning; and the Lord pitied and helped again in another diet for the parish. So I was encouraged, and began that course again at the ordinary time, not daring as yet to give it over; and, through the mercy of God, it was yet carried on as usual.

This winter I did more at night than of a long time before, having ordinarily written something, for a while, after six o'clock at night. And on the 7th day of March, I had completed the catechising of the parish for the second time. This was a kind disposal of Providence; for about the same time began the breach of my health, which made me the heaviest spring I had ever felt. And preaching on Eccl. vii. 1, with the event foresaid trysted my entering on the latter part of that text, "The day of death is better than the day of one's birth." This was a comfortable subject; but whereas it could hardly miss to impress me with the thoughts, that this might be my last text; yet the experience I had formerly had in the like cases, left but little weight in them. On the Lord's day, the 22d, after the public worship was over, I betook myself to my bed; and at night, going about family-worship, which was a great pinch to me, we fell to sing Psalm lxviii. 13, and downwards, " Though ye have lain among the pots," &c. with which I was much comforted, as I had been on a former occasion. My ailments were many that season. I was pained in my breast-bone, in the fore and hinder shoulder, and under the arm-pit on the left side; and was under a very uneasy cough. Withal I had such a continued oppression and lowness of spirits, with difficulty of breathing, as never before; a continual stiffness and weakness in my knees, and weariness all over; so that with great difficulty I got up and down the stairs, mounted the pulpit, got the Sabbath's work managed, yea turned myself on my bed, where I had some touches of exquisite pain in the calf of my legs. And, by a particular dispensation of Providence, the springs of my comfort ran bitterness to me in my low condition; all created refuge failed, and I was solitary, and in great affliction. Withal my wife's fever returned on the 3d of April; but not so violent as formerly; and that month a pain of the mother kept her many days, which was quite new; and a cholic several days; besides her other ailments.

However, in this my low condition, I was determined, and ventured on Providence, to intimate the sacrament to be celebrated on the 31st of May; being led to that day, purely in compliance with our neighbours in Yarrow, that the administration of that ordinance in the two parishes might not be too close the one upon the other. And that time drawing near, I saw great weight hung upon the design; Mr. Davidson being extremely low; John Currie aforesaid, one of the elders, under the ague; Isabel Biggar in Midghop in a doubtful and dangerous case; her husband William Blaik in the meantime likely to fall in under the ague, to whose share a great weight of strangers on such occasions used to fall; moreover, my own wife continuing as formerly, and myself in a weak condition, going upon my staff; the pain in my back, which had fallen to me in the former spring, having returned; but not quite so ill as the former year, by means of my then attendance on the assembly. I desired of the Lord strength for the designed effect, to myself and others; and resolved, through grace, not to quarrel, nor think harshly of my Master, though he should quite lay me by on that occasion. But indeed in the event I found him very gracious in that matter. And it was remarkable to me, that my kind God and Father, most mercifully tempering the hardships of my lot that season, I had no fit of the gravel, no night-watchings, as some time before I fell ill; and whatever difficulty I had in delivering my sermons, I was never rendered incapable of study on my study-days, as several days before, till the Friday before the communion-week; and finally, whereas the visiting of the sick had often in that season of the year been a weighty burden on me, I had no occasion, from the time I fell ill, to visit one sick person without Etterick-house on the other side of the water, till after the sacrament.

Meanwhile there having come to my hand, about the 27th of March, a letter from Mr. G. desiring a specimen of the essay on the accentuation; I, after consulting God, and thinking thereupon, did, in the following week, make out a specimen thereof in about two sheets of paper, and wrote a return to him. On the Monday morning, after having no occasion from this place, I sent them away to Galashiels, from whence they went to Edinburgh on the morrow, and on the Wednesday were carried off towards London, by one going post thither. Withal the copy of the essay on the text, then at Aberdeen, being desired also, and this intimated there, there was a ship just going from thence to London, with which it was sent away. I could not but notice the conduct of Providence in the speedy dispatch, desiring to wait the issue.

The sacrament was administered on May 31, as had been appointed; and the Lord made it to me a time of hearing of prayer, and of rolling away one stone of difficulty after another.

The admission of my younger son to the Lord's table, was another piece of difficulty. Toward the end of the week preceding the communion-week, it became very heavy to me, while no help appeared in the case. I found myself pinched in a special manner, in that my own interest was mixed with the sacred interest; and would have been well content, to have sacrificed my own interest in it, if it had been in my power to have separated the two. For two days I was in particular concern, to see what I could safely do that way; and that the Lord would touch his heart. And in the end of the second day I received a letter from him, which gave me satisfaction. Thus was that stone rolled out of the way.

On the Friday that week, I having much of the Sabbath's sermon left of what had been prepared before, minded to have studied, with the Sabbath's sermons, the fast-day's too. But that morning, after beginning my studies, I became so indisposed, that I was obliged to betake myself to my bed again for a time. And this was the only study-day this season, since I fell ill, that I was unfit and indisposed for study. Howbeit I got something done that day, as also on the Saturday; and on the Monday I finished the fast-day's sermons.

Meanwhile, as my ordinary of the other world was nowise interrupted by this communion, I had been of a considerable time secure as to my text for the action-sermon, designing Isa. liv. 10, "For the mountains shall depart," &c., in view of handling thereof the general conflagration, and perpetuity of the covenant. But on that Sabbath night, consulting the Hebrew original, I found it was not understood of departing by the conflagration, but rather by an earthquake; and so I was deprived of my text, which was a new trial to me. But on the Monday's night I resolved to mandate the fast-day's sermons on the Tuesday, in the first place; the which I did accordingly, and no more; but that I had some thoughts in search for a new text.

Wednesday the fast day was kept; and as, in the family-fast in the preceding week, the Lord had pitied, howbeit the prayers lay on myself alone; so that day he was very gracious to me. Having much prepared, I delivered it in three sermons that day; and had great satisfaction in the Lord's helping me to spread out the net of the covenant, from Psalm l. 5, " Gather my saints together unto me; those that have made a covenant with me by sacrifice." But after the sermons, convening the new communicants before the session, to take their explicit consent to the covenant; I was damped and confounded, missing my own son among them. This was a heavy trial; but afterward I found, that it had proceeded of mistake, not of design. The new communicants at this time were far more than ordinary: I hope the word concerning the other world had some influence; but I apprehend, it was thought probable, this might be the last by my means, considering the low case I had been in for some time, and was in. And they had come to me before, for the private examination, very orderly, as that my low case required; the which I took first very kindly at the hand of my compassionate Father, and next at their hand.

Thursday, being determined to Luke xxiii. 42, " Lord, remember me when thou comest into thy kingdom," I entered on the study thereof, and perfected the explication thereof; on the Friday it came to me right easily, and I had finished the whole, much about my ordinary time, that is, before dinner. Meanwhile, Janet Scot, a good woman, who on the Sabbath had received a token from me for the Lord's table, (the tokens being usually distributed to the old communicants of the parish the Sabbath before the communion, she had brought forth twins before the due time, was fallen into a fever, and was in danger of her life. Isabel Biggar, a singular Christian, was in a dark, doubtful, and dangerous condition, not knowing when it might come to an extremity; her family at these times having a great weight of strangers; and at this communion they had about sixty. These women's husbands were in ill case too, as to bodily indisposition. John Currie above mentioned, having been seized with the ague in March last, still continued very ill; a flux for some time had been working in my wife's case; and Friday's night, when the strangers began to come, she had a touch of it, which occasioned her thoughts of heart; but there was no more of it from that time. Mr. Davidson came that night, in great weakness, having been obliged to lodge a night by the way: Mr. Wilson came then also; and Mr. Francis Craig, a probationer of singular worth, to take burden on him for Mr. Davidson. And these were my helpers.

On Saturday Messrs. Craig and Wilson preached. After distributing the tokens to strangers, at the tent, done as usual immediately after the public worship was over, I convened in the kirk the new communicants absent on the fast-day, and took their explicit consent, as aforesaid, before the session; and among these was my son. From what had happened on the fast-day, I had desired of the Lord, that he would make the people tractable, and cause that things might be done in order; and, I think, it was never so much so as at this communion. I got little sleep these nights; yet not from anxiety, but that I was put out of my ordinary course; for I was easy trusting in the Lord for all.

Sabbath morning, my soul was humbled within me; and I was in some concern to be, and really was in some measure, nothing in my own eyes. I divided my sermon in two; and the Lord was with me therein, and in the whole of my work; so that I lacked no strength for my work, no not so much as ordinarily when I was in a better state of body; for it failed not in any part thereof. Being sensible of what I was through my weakness liable to, I had desired of the Lord, that he would keep me from forgetting things, in the administration of that ordinance; and, to the praise of his grace, I think, I was never more pointed and distinct in these things. There were some very small drops of rain, in time, I think, of the first sermon; I did therefore, in the prayer before the second sermon, pray for pity in that matter; and rested in the Lord, closing the petition for it with this expression, " Our Father which art in heaven;" and the Lord graciously heard, so that we had no disturbance that way. This was a mercy the more remarkable to me, that the following Sabbath, which should have been the day for administering that ordinance, if the Lord himself had not determined otherwise, there was a continued rain with wind. The which made me admire the divine conduct, wish ever to be under it, and never to choose for myself; for it was purely in compliance with the desire of our neighbours in Yarrow, that we took that day, as above noticed. I had solemnly petitioned for strength to Mr. Davidson, for the effect of the Lord's work; he got it so far, that he served two tables, and preached on the Monday.

I had a special concern on my spirit in prayer all along, for the distressed persons above named. And Janet Scot, whose life I had begged, recovered; Isabel Biggar came to me on Monday morning, and told me she was very well. I understood after, that on the fast-day she was ill, but no more till the Wednesday after the sacrament. John Currie was at the Lord's table, and out on Monday too. I found all along a disposition to hang by the petitions for these persons, before the Lord. About the end of Mr. Craig's sermon on Monday, I was told, that Mr. Davidson, who was to preach the other sermon, had retired again into the house. Fearing he had fallen ill, it occasioned me some thoughts of heart; but in the case I was resigned, trusting in the Lord, only concerned that the Lord would discover his mind, as to what was to be done in the feared event, and looking to him for it. And my heart being brought to this temper, he came out again, and preached a sweet sermon.

I received at this communion a letter from Mr. Wightman before mentioned, moving me to hope in the case of my wife. And petitions were solemnly tabled again before the Lord, in her behalf, upon his word; Luke xviii. 8, " I tell you, he will avenge them speedily." Mr. Davidson praying on Monday, and pleading that she might be " comforted on every side ;" that word touched me, as being the word I got as aforesaid at Eskdalemoor, and am still pleading.

Thus the Lord carried on that great work, through many difficulties, and made it a time of hearing of prayer in a very particular manner; and out of weakness we were made strong. So that, considering the kind conduct of Providence in the whole, I was obliged, at the dismissing of the congregation on the Monday, publicly to give my testimony from my experience, to that truth, viz. That " it is better to trust in the Lord, than to put confidence in man."

On the Friday after, I got my text, Cant. ii. ult. " Until the day break, and the shadows flee away," &c. for the Sabbath, June 7, and entered upon it; and proceeded thereon on the Saturday. After which, being exhausted, I was not able to write some very necessary letters; yet towards night I was enabled thereto, and admired the kind management of Providence therein.

Withal on the Saturday before the communion I received letters from Mr. G. at London, directed to Mr. W. H. foresaid, together with a printed specimen of the essay on the accentuation, made on the MS. specimen I had sent as aforesaid; as also a specimen of new Hebrew types then casting at London. The first of these letters, dated May 2, bearing, Messrs. Ridgley and Eams their approving of the specimen I had sent; Dr. Bedford, of the Church of England, his approving the design of the work, on his hearing the title-page and index read to him; Dr. Ziegenhagen, a German divine, who, I think, had come over with the Princess, now Queen, his promising to send the specimen to Hall and Bremen; Rabbi Moses Marcus his taking in hand to write four copies thereof, to be sent to Hall, Bremen, Holland, and Leipsic; that the said Rabbi had a liberal education abroad to serve the Jewish interest; and did serve as a priest among them two years, but embraced Christianity about

VOL. XI.   2 D

eight years ago; for the which cause being disinherited by his rich
father, he is in prison for debt; and that he likes the specimen;
And further, that Sir Richard Ellys likes well the Fourfold State,
where of some copies, edit. 2, had been sent to London; and had thanks
from an Independent gentleman, who has bought six of them to give
in compliments to his friends; and that Mr. H. may venture to send
more of them to Mr. Oswald, stationer, there. A second, dated May 9,
bearing, That the Rabbi foresaid likes the work still more; that
Mr. Palmer, printer, proposes to print it in English, for that there
are in London five hundred who understand Hebrew, not understanding Latin; that Mr. G. expects, that after he has sent a specimen in print, he shall have some general plan sent him, how to com-
mune with Mr. Oswald about printing the work; that Sir Richard
Ellys is perhaps one of the greatest scholars in England, and is fond
of any thing tending to enlighten the purity of the gospel-scheme;*
and that he bought three of the Fourfold State, a few days before,
to give to gentlemen of his acquaintance. A third, May 12, bearing, the sending along a small specimen of the new types cast from
Athias's mould, received by me as aforesaid. A fourth, May 12,
bearing, that Sir Richard Ellys desired him to tell me, that his
purse shall not be spared, to encourage any work of mine. A fifth,
May 21, bearing, that the said Sir Richard having read the specimen, likes it, and the design of the work; and is disposed to encourage it; that he was to write to two friends in Holland along
with the specimen, and to send them withal a copy of the Fourfold
State; and that Mr. G. knows not if I can find such another patron
in the island, to dedicate the essay to: that Suicerus's "The-
saurus Ecclesiasticus," printed at Amsterdam 1728, is dedicated to
him, where is to be found a handsome character of him for his
learning; and that Mr. G. desires to be sent up to him the English
copy of the essay on the accentuation, as also the essay on the first
twenty chapters of Genesis, that he may put it in the hands of the
said Sir Richard and several others. In these letters also was expressed a desire of several to see the MS. on the Covenant of Grace.

* In an abstract of this letter in Mr. Boston's hand-writing, the following clauses
are to be found, which well merit a place, viz. " is fond of the Fourfold State, admires
the just views of gospel-truth in it, the spirit of it, the very style as in an uncommon
manner suited to the subject; is keen for printing the work on the Hebrew, longs to
see the treatise on the Covenant of Grace, has again and again expressed a concern to get
something handsome for Mr. Boston for the vast pains and labour, and that his friends
should concern themselves in it; that Messrs. Ridgley, Taylor, and Wilcox wish to
see the treatise on the Covenant of Grace; and that Mr. Grant thinks it will print,
and sell, to advantage in London."

These things, expressed more strongly in the letters foresaid, a more full abstract whereof is to be found among my papers, looked as if the Lord was in his way to fulfill a passage of the 71st psalm, which was given me as above mentioned. But for a balance hereto I heard on the Monday, that Professor Gordon was a-dying, I knowing of nothing done by him in the matter by him undertaken. Mr. Hogg being with us on the communion-occasion, I sent along with him the English copy of the essay on the accentuation; who soon after got an occasion of conveying it away to London.

In the second week of June, I had another letter from Mr. G. directed to Mr. Hogg, dated London, May 30, bearing the receiving of the essay on the text of Genesis from Aberdeen; the making out of a specimen thereof in print, the which I accordingly received; and that Drs. Knight and Bedford had read the specimen of the essay on the accentuation, esteemed the work as a work of great labour and curiosity, and were disposed for the work's being printed, though they are not entirely fixed in the belief of the divine authority of the accents.

That and the following week were spent in carrying on the account of my life, interrupted by the communion-work; and in preparing dispatches in consequence of the letters aforesaid. I wrote a letter to Sir Richard Ellys, and a memorial concerning the English copy of the essay on the accentuation, as also concerning the essay on the first twenty chapters of Genesis;* judging the same necessary for those into whose hands these MSS. might come. I considered the printed specimens; found that of the Latin essay intolerable in the Hebrew part of it, that of the essay on the text hopeful; and sent my remarks on both. Withal I wrote a long letter to Mr. G. upon the whole affair, as it seemed to me to require. The MS. on the covenant of grace I could not find; it being at Edinburgh when called for, and revised by none. But upon that occasion I called for it, and put it in the hands of my two friends, Messrs. Wilson and Davidson, to be by them revised.

About or a little after this time, I had a letter from Mr. G. dated London, June 8, before I wrote my foresaid to him; and therewith a letter† to him from Dr. Waterland, on his having read the specimen of the essay on the accentuation; the former bearing an account of Sir Richard Ellys's being turned from Arminianism; his making Sir John Philips purchase the Fourfold State; and that his

* A copy of this memorial, relative to the essay on the Hebrew text of Genesis, is in the Appendix, No. 5.

† A copy of this letter is to be found in the Appendix to this work.

letter to Mr. Loftus, minister of the English Church at Rotterdam,
and Mr. Gowin at Leyden, inclosing the title-page, index, and specimen, of the essay on the accentuation, to be shewn to the learned
there, was then in Mr. G.'s hands, to be sent over by next post, with
a copy of the Fourfold State; that he (Sir Richard) sends them;
that Mr. Ziegenhagen was by the (then) to-morrow's post to send
the title, syllabus, or index, and specimen foresaid, to his friend at
Bremen; and by the next post to send them to Mr. Franck at
Hall; and that Mr. G. gives copies of the Fourfold State, to be
sent along with them; and that he hopes to get a specimen sent to
Carpzovius at Leipsic; and thinks I should write to Sir Richard
Ellys.

On Thursday, July 30, having been abroad some four miles or
more, and coming home at night, I found there had been an express
for me to go to Dalgleish, to visit a dying woman, viz. Jane Hope
above mentioned, but night coming on, I found I could not go, desired of the Lord the woman's preservation in life; and was easy,
finding myself unable for that work. The Lord heard me; and
going thither on the morrow, I saw her, was helped to speak to her,
and was much satisfied in the divine conduct. This was the first
call of that nature I remembered myself ever to have sat, by day or
by night; and I thought, that the Lord was, by that occurrence,
training me to accommodate myself to my low circumstances of
body.

The said Jane recovered; Isabel Biggar's doubtful and dangerous case aforesaid cleared, and went off, and Janet Scott aforesaid
recovered. Whereupon I was much comforted in the Lord's dealing with me, as to the cases of these three persons; reckoning myself in his debt for the life and welfare of each of them.

Aug. 3.—No return being ever made by Mr. J. M. minister of
E———r, to my letter afore mentioned, the breach still continued
betwixt us, though kept very quiet on both sides. But, on Saturday, July 18, I received a letter from him, inviting me to preach
with them, on Monday after the sacrament, being the 27th; and
withal bearing, that the two sermons he preached here, were composed before he was licenced, especially the last; and that he could
not say they were altogether agreeable to his ordinary strain; and
that, however fond he had some time ago been of what some reckon
fashionable, yet he could now sincerely declare, he is fully persuaded, that those sermons which run in a gospel-strain, are only valuable. Herewith I was so satisfied, that I strongly inclined to answer his demand; the which too early readiness, caused that, going
to God with it, I found it not so bound on my conscience from him-

self as I could have wished. But having again and again considered and consulted the matter, I signified to him my resolution
to answer his demand, if I was able. But on the Monday, being
obliged to visit a sick person at Dalgleish, I found myself under an
unordinary indisposition after. Nevertheless I attempted to study
for the effect foresaid, on the Tuesday; but stuck that day, after
twice beginning it. I began it a third time on the Wednesday; but
stuck again, being quite unable to manage the text; Isa. xi. 10.
Whereupon I gave it over, and wrote to him that I could not be with
him; and thereupon was easy, considering both this dispensation,
and how it was quite above my strength to preach at home on the
Lord's day, and then to ride nine or ten miles, and preach on the
Monday again.

The sacrament was administered at Penpont the same day that it
was in Eskdalemoor; and thereat assisted my friend Mr. Wilson.
The strange conduct of Providence with respect to my two friends or
myself assisting at the sacrament in that place, from time to time,
is before observed. Never any of us went thither, on that occasion,
but we met with something of unordinary trial, about it. That time
wherein my journey to and from it was prosperous, the toss in the
affair of Closeburn arose out of it. The former time Mr. Wilson
was there, he was publicly contradicted by brethren, and obliged to
speak to the people, before dismissing of the congregation, in defence of his doctrine he had preached to them. This time he was
there, having had a prosperous journey, and comfortable being there,
upon his return hither we were comforted; and that strange course
of holy Providence seemed so far to be broken off.

In the last week of August I was obliged to visit one sick at Potburn, on the Monday; and on the Tuesday having thoughts of going to
Chapelhop, to visit the sick there, I was sent for express to Buccleugh,
to see Adam Linton, a-dying; and he died that day, while I was
with him. I had, on the Wednesday was eight days before, gone
to Buccleugh occasionally, knowing nothing of his illness, till I was
by the way: but so my God led me, by the way I knew not. On
the Wednesday I visited three sick persons at Chapelhop; and on
the Thursday went to Adam Linton's burial. This awful dispensation of Providence towards the poor parish, was the more weighty
to me, that I saw I was now toward the end of my ordinary subject,
viz. the doctrine of the other world; and perceived the voice of Providence thus join the voice of the word. I found myself worsted by
this unordinary loss; but I took it kindly at the hand of my gracious God and Father; admiring the divine condescension and goodness, that kept it off in the spring, when I myself was very ill, till

that time wherein I was in better condition; for by that time, I
think, I had laid aside my staff.

Having, from some time after writing the aforesaid to London in
June, been expecting time after time to hear from thence, but still
disappointed; which occasioned various thoughts of heart; I received a packet on the 4th of September. Before I opened it, I
went to God, to get my heart disposed for whatever might be found
the issue; but opening the same, I found there was a deep silence
still, both from Aberdeen and from London. Hereupon I went to
God again, and kissed the rod, accepting the trying dispensation, as
the way he deals with his own; bringing their matters through many
difficulties, and causing them to wait on. And being somewhat
afraid of unfair dealing, in the case of MSS. I found rest to my
heart in the Lord, as having the hearts of all in his hand. But
whereas, about the middle of March last, I had written to Mr.
Alexander Colden a letter of love and friendship, to testify my love
and regard to him, and to remove some dryness, that, by means of
our differences about the abjuration-oath, and the doctrine of the
" Marrow," had crept in betwixt that worthy man and me, specially
through a mighty jealousy in his temper; and withal had sent him a
copy of the second edition of the Fourfold State; but had never
heard from him since; in which case, nevertheless I rejoiced that I
had writ that letter, which I knew he soon received; I did on the
Lord's day after, being September 6, receive a kind return from him.
And this I desired to take as a pledge of a comfortable issue of the
other case, viz. the hearing from London; which, of a considerable
time, had been a matter of some exercise to me, considering the sudden stop of that affair, after such a notable run it appeared to
be on.

That same day I closed my ordinary of the other world; and on
the Sabbath after, being the 13th, entered on a new one, viz. " The
Crook in the Lot," from Eccl. vii. 13, " Consider the work of God:
for who can make that straight which he hath made crooked?" To
this I was led, by my own case, and the case of several in the parish;
and was confirmed in that's being the Lord's message to them, by
the providential occurrences of that day.

Having, on the 10th, advanced in the account of my life unto the
time when I began writing for it, I did thereafter carry on what remained, partly in it, and partly in the passages of my life. And
whereas, several years ago, thinking on the sacred name JEHOVAH,
I had fallen into a notion of its being a dittology, standing for
JEHOVAH ELOHIM; and had written in the essay on Genesis,
chap. xv. 2, let. f. that " Elohim" is never found before nor behind

it, as far as I had (then) observed : I had carried on the observing
of the texts where it occurs through the whole Hebrew Code ; and
found the observation foresaid to hold through the whole of it,
wheresoever the said sacred name occurs; I did this day, September
22, beyond which I have not as yet seen another, transcribe the list
I had taken of the texts wherein that sacred name JEHOVAH occurs, into the miscellany manuscript, for conservation. And there
it is to be found; an observation, which, I think, must determine
that point with equal judges, unless they can discover some oversight therein, or exception, that will overthrow it.*

On Friday September 25, I received a letter from Edinburgh,
bearing that as yet there was no word for me from London, but that
a letter was expected by the next post; and withal that Professor
Gordon at Aberdeen is dead some time ago. Both of these were
trying to me; but especially the latter; nothing, that I know of,
being done by him, in what he took in hand, in favour of the essay;
but I comforted myself, in that " the Lord liveth." In the following week, having an unexpected occasion to Edinburgh, I wrote to

---

* A list of all the passages observed throughout the Hebrew Code, wherein the sacred name JEHOVAH occurs ; but in none of them all is ELOHIM joined with it,
whether going before or coming behind.

Gen. xiv. 2, 8. Deut. ix. 26. Josh. vii. 7. Judg. vi. 22 ; xvi. 28. 2 Sam.
vii. 18, 19, twice, 20, 29. 1 Kings ii. 26 ; viii. 53. Isa. iii. 15 ; vii. 7 ; xxii. 5,
12, 14, 15 ; xxv. 8 ; xxviii. 16 ; xxx. 15 ; xl. 10 ; xlviii. 16 ; xlix. 22 ; l. 4, 5, 7,
9 ; lii. 4 ; lvi. 8 ; lxi. 1, 11 ; lxv. 13, 15. Occurs twenty-two times. Jer. v. 6 ;
ii. 19, 22 ; ix. 10 ; vii. 20 ; xiv. 13 ; xxxii. 17, 25 ; xliv. 26 ; xlvi. 10, twice ; xlix.
5 ; l. 25, 31 ; occurs fourteen times. Ezek. ii 4 ; iii. 11, 27 ; iv. 14 ; v. 5, 7, 8,
11 ; vi. 3, twice ; 11 ; vii. 1, 5 ; viii. 1 ; ix. 8 ; xi. 7, 8, 13, 16, 17, 21 ; xii. 10,
19, 23, 25, 28, twice ; xiii. 3, 8, twice, 13, 16, 18, 20 ; xiv. 4, 6, 11, 14, 16, 19,
20, 21, 22 ; xv. 6, 8 ; xvi. 3, 8, 14, 19, 23, 30, 35, 43, 48, 59, 63 ; xvii. 3, 9, 16,
22 ; xviii. 39, 23, 30, 32 ; xx. 2, twice, 5, 27, 30, 31, 33 ; xxii. 3, 12, 19, 28, 31.
xxiii. 22, 28, 32, 34, 35, 46, 49 ; xxiv. 3, 6, 9, 14, 21, 24 ; xxv. 3, 6, 8, 12, 13,
14, 15, 16 ; xxvi. 3, 5, 7, 14, 15, 19, 21 ; xxvii. 3 ; xxviii. 2, 6, 10, 12, 20, 24,
25 ; xxix. 3, 8, 13, 16, 19, 20 ; xxx. 2, 6, 10, 13, 22 ; xxxi. 2, 15, 18 ; xxxii. 3,
8, 11, 14, 16, 31, 32 ; xxxiii. 11, 25, 27 ; xxxiv. 2, 8, 10, 11, 15, 17, 20, 30, 31 ;
xxxv. 3, 6, 11, 14 ; xxxvi. 2, 3, 4, 5, 6, 7, 13, 14, 15, 22, 23, 32, 33, 37 ; xxxvii.
3, 5, 9, 12, 19, 21 ; xxxviii. 3, 10, 14, 17, 18, 21 ; xxxix. 1, 5, 8, 10, 13, 17, 20,
25, 29 ; xliii. 18, 19, 27 ; xliv. 6, 9, 12, 15, 27 ; xlv. 9, twice, 15, 18 ; xlvi. 1, 16 ;
xlvii. 13, 23 ; xlviii. 29. Occurs about 213 times. Amos i. 8 ; iii. 7, 8, 11, 13 ;
iv. 2, 5 ; v. 3, 16 ; vi. 8 ; vii. 1, 2, 4, twice, 5, 6 ; viii. 1, 3, 9, 11 ; ix. 5, 8. Occurs 22 times. Obad. i ; Michah i. 2 ; Hab. iii. 18 ; Zeph. i. 7 ; Zech. ix. 14 ;
Psalm lxviii. 21 ; lxix. 7 ; lxxi. 5, 16 ; lxxiii. 28 ; cxl. 8 ; cxli. 8. See JEHOVAH
ELOHIM, Gen. ii. 4. 5, 7, 8, *et passim*. ADONAI JEHOVAH HATZTZEBHAOTH, Amos
ix. 5. ADONAI JEHOVAH ELOHE HATZTZEBHAOTH, Amos iii. 13. JEHOVIH ADONAI,
Hab. iii. 19 ; Psalm lxviii. 21 ; cxl. 8 ; cxli. 8.

Professor Anderson, from whom I have as yet no return unto my first to him above mentioned ; that I might know how Professor Gordon left that affair. And expecting at length some account from London that week, I was again disappointed, Mr. Hogg not being in town. But I received from my eldest son, then occasionally at Edinburgh, a letter wherewith I was very much pleased, as satisfying me in a particular, which had occasioned me some uneasiness. And I took it also as providentially designed to teach me to wait with patience in the matter from London. The sacrament of the Lord's supper being administered at Maxton, October 11, I assisted there. The text I preached on was Isa. xli. 14, 15, " Worm Jacob,—thou shalt thresh the mountains," &c. which I had been led to by reading the passage of December last. I began my studies on it on Thursday October 1, having some thoughts of taking my journey that day eight days, that I might lodge a night by the way, not knowing if I would be able to accomplish the journey in one day. I dispatched the explication of it that day. But entering upon it on the Tuesday after, I could by no means strike the vein of it ; howbeit in the time I was helped to trust the Lord, that he would pity ; but in the afternoon, when I had given it over, I was under great perplexity through unbelief, notwithstanding of former experience, and the last year's particularly on the same occasion. On the Wednesday having cut out, as usual on such occasions, I was helped to proceed in it satisfyingly ; and had bodily strength sufficient for the work, though ordinarily I am that day of the week unable to study, for which cause I usually go abroad on it. On the Thursday I completed my studies. Thus Providence barred my making haste to go away, as I had designed. That night Mr. Murray came from Penpont, to assist also at Maxton. On the Friday we took our journey. But Mr. Murray being seized with the gravel, having with great difficulty made our way to Newburgh, I was obliged to leave him there, and my daughter to attend him. So I went thence all alone, and the wind and rain blowing in my face ; in bearing of which, for my work's sake, I had a satisfaction. Getting safe, though weary, to Maxton that night, I found Mr. Davidson, being also taken ill that day, was not come up. So there was none for the work, but Mr. Wilson himself and I. But the Lord having thus tried us, pitied, and sent up both on the morrow. And that day Mr. Murray and I preached. On the Sabbath I served three tables, and preached in the afternoon, and was at no time in want of strength. In myself and fellows my text was accomplished. While at the table I saw and heard the elements distributed, I was thereby helped to a firm faith of my union with Jesus Christ. Monday morning I was greatly comforted by a good woman, whose husband having been seized with a fit of distraction, had, on that account, been remembered in the public prayers at the communion in Galashiels the preceding year. She had then and there spoke to me on that case; and now she told me, that having advised her to roll the case over on the Lord, she was helped so to do; and when she went home, found him restored to his sound mind; which deliverance has continued all along since. The good woman was concerned to be advised how to improve such a mercy. On Wednesday we came to Galashiels, where awaking out of sleep that night, I found myself at the gates of death, by a sickness that had suddenly seized me. Providence seasonably awoke Mr. Murray, to whom I could hardly speak at all, to call for help; which I received by vomiting; being still in hazard of fainting away, especially when sitting up, and more especially when on my knees, as in my younger years; inasmuch that at secret prayer on the Thursday morning I durst not kneel, but sit. Thus the same God who tried my brethren before the solemn work, took trial of me after it was over. It seems to have been owing to my eating of a pear and a half at supper, which by their coldness had oppressed me. We came safe home at night; and on the morrow, convoying Mr. Murray the length of Potburn, I proposed to him to take that part of the catechism to explain which fell, as above said, to Mr. Davidson, now reduced to a pitch of weakness, if so be that work, as above proposed, might not yet be marred; and he has taken it into his consideration, being resolved to seek counsel of the Lord concerning it.

At Maxton I thought I would get the long-expected word at length; but there was none for me; only I heard, that Mr. G. is somewhat embarrassed in his private affairs at London. Meanwhile, on the Monday, there arose in my heart an inclination to publish the treatise on the covenant of grace; the which, I believe, was partly owing to the interest I found I had, beyond what I could have expected, with ministers; and would fain improve to edification, and advancing of the interest of the truth of the gospel. I had this summer put the copy in the hand of my friend Mr. Wilson; who having revised a part of it, and put it in the hand of Mr. Davidson, it was by a mistake returned to me about the middle of August. Wherefore at this time I carried it back to Maxton, to be revised throughout. On the Sabbath after I came home, being the 18th, I received a letter, bearing, that as yet there was no word to me from London. Thus I find myself obliged to shut up this account of my life, without being capable to shew the issue and present state of that affair, either at Aberdeen or London. But I do believe, that my God and Father, who of his great mercy brought it to me, will at length cause the iron gates in the way thereof to fly open; and will bring it forth, to his own glory, and the benefit of the church, even though I should never see it, but be laid in the dust ere it come to pass.

This day, October 22, 1730, having laid the matter of the two MSS. above mentioned before the Lord, and considered the same, I was, upon the one hand, made to adore that gracious and kind divine conduct, whereby I was kept from destroying them, December 2, 1729, as narrated above, of the which I now see the then secret cause; and on the other hand, I was cleared to destroy them, now that the preceding account of my life was written; and accordingly I have committed them to the flames. At the end of the first of the two, I found some scriptures comfortably superscribed; the tenor whereof follows :—

"Mine. Blessed are they that hunger and thirst after righteousness; for they shall be filled," Matth. v. 6, "Blessed are the poor in spirit; for theirs is the kingdom of heaven," Matth. v. 3. I dwell in the high and holy place, with him also that is of a contrite and humble spirit, to revive the spirit of the humble, and to revive the heart of the contrite ones," Isa. lvii. 15. "Let your soul delight itself in fatness—hear, and your soul shall live," Isa. lv. 2, 3. "Whoso confesseth and forsaketh, shall find mercy," Prov. xxviii. 13. See 1 John i. 9, "And we know that all things work together for good to them that love God," Rom, viii. 28. "Delight thyself also in the Lord, and he shall give thee the desires of thine heart," Psalm xxxvii. 4, "When I sent you forth, lacked ye any thing ?" "Thou hast ravished my heart—with one of thine eyes," Cant. iv. 9. "Who is this that cometh up from the wilderness, leaning upon her beloved ?" Cant. viii. 5. "Cast thy burden on the Lord; he will sustain thee," Psalm lv. 22. "Not by might, nor by power, but by the Spirit of the Lord," Zech iv. 6. "Yea, I have loved thee with an everlasting love; therefore with loving-kindness have I drawn thee," Jer. xxxi. 3, "Seek ye first the kingdom of God, and his righteousness, and these things shall be added to you," Matth. vi. 33. "Go thy way; thy faith hath made thee whole," Mark x. 52. "Though I walk in the midst of troubles, thou wilt revive me; thou shalt stretch forth thy hand against the wrath of mine enemies, and thy right hand shall save me. The Lord will perfect that which concerneth me," Psalm cxxxviii. 7, 8. "I will instruct thee, and teach thee in the way that thou shalt go," Psalm xxxii. 8. "He hath determined the times before appointed, and the bounds of their habitation," Acts xvii. 26.—That MS. ended Feb. 16, 1699.

[Thus far the author had proceeded both in the general account of his life, and in the passages thereof, on the 22d of October 1730; and on the 25th of that month, he shut up the account with seven paragraphs more, of a general nature. But as he afterwards continued that account till Nov. 13, 1731, we shall first add that continuation, and then close with the seven paragraphs.]

Having, on the 24th of October, ended the above account, I laid it before the Lord, for acceptance of him through Christ; begging he would preserve and bless it, and giving thanks for that he had inclined my heart to do it. And that same night I ended also the reading over of it, and the passages of my life; the which I had some time before begun and carried on.

There had come to my house on Saturday's night, Oct. 3, three dissenters of the party adhering to Mr. John Hepburn while he lived, with a letter directed to me and my two friends Mr. Wilson and Mr. Davidson, from their correspondence, desiring a meeting with us. The which being, at the communion in Maxton, appointed to be at the manse of Etterick on Tuesday the 27th, there came early that day five of them to me; but, to our great disappointment, Mr. Wilson came not; and Mr. Davidson was not expected, in regard of the broken state of his health. Their design mainly was, to establish a correspondence with such as they considered as the purer part of the corrupt church; and that some way might be fallen on, towards their enjoying the benefit of public ordinances, for they had us occasionally at communions. I found them to be men having a sense of religion on their own spirits, much affected with their circumstances as destitute of a minister, endowed with a good measure of Christian charity and love, and of a very different temper from that of Mr. Macmillan's followers. I perceived their separation ultimately to resolve into that unwarrantable principle, viz. That joining in communion with the church, in the ordinances of God, is an approbation of the corruptions in her; the very same from which all the rest of the separations do spring; some carrying that principle farther than others, in different degrees. I understood, that the abjuration-oath straitened them, as to addressing the general assemblies any more. I shewed a readiness to administer ordinances to them, on testimonials from their ministers; but found, they scrupled to seek them; and I had no freedom to do it on testimonials from their meeting; since I could not in conscience approve of their separation, and had seen and felt so much of the mischief of separating. So we parted on the morrow after; but with great affection, and much heaviness on both sides.

The preface to the above account now being also written, and the examination of the parish interrupted on the occasion foresaid, I did, on Thursday the 29th, spend some time in prayer, laying the two MSS. viz. this and the passages, before the Lord, with thanksgiving, and supplication for preserving and blessing them, and for a right way to betake myself to next.

At the monthly meeting of the session on Monday, Nov. 2, I had a dismal view of the case of the generation, finding, by a scandal broke out, how the children of religious parents are degenerated, as a token of approaching judgment. On the morrow I spent some time in prayer, particularly for two causes: 1. Direction as to what I should take in hand; 2. The preservation of my children from snares in this dangerous time of apostasy. Having reviewed myself, made confession, and renewed my acceptance of the covenant, I laid these, and other things before the Lord, committing my children, and other members of my family, to the protection of the great Shepherd of the sheep. And having considered the matter of my studies, I found that the work on the Hebrew text was begun already; that God had allowed an occasion of returning to it, of the which there was some time little hope; that nothing did now cast up in competition therewith, even when I looked about to observe; that this has been what I much desired; and that, being an immediate study of the holy scripture, it is a business in which I may becomingly spend my remaining time, as the Lord shall please to give access; and therefore I concluded, that I was called to address myself thereto though my strength is small, and these things are now much out of my head. Wherefore, that I might just begin, I did that same night put pen to paper; but did nothing to purpose.

It pleased the Lord, for my trial, to make the entry on that work difficult; and the progress has, through several interruptions, been small to the writing hereof; whatever he minds to do about it. On the morrow I catechised at Buccleugh. I continued about three hours in that exercise without my spirits or strength failing; which is the more sweet, and filled my heart with thankfulness, that in the morning I had, in consideration of my weakness, prayed for pity. I was minded next day to have spent some time in prayer for assistance in the aforesaid work; but being called out of my bed that night, to visit a sick person supposed to be a-dying, I found in the morning that I was not in case for it. So I applied myself to writing of letters, which at length I was obliged also to give over. Being seized with a colic, I behoved to take my bed that night and rising on the Friday, I was obliged to take bed again, where I was fixed till the Saturday morning. Then the pain was removed; but I was unfit for business, save writing of letters. But though

the Lord's day was so bad that few came to church, it was a good
day to me, in delivering the Lord's word, weak and crazy as I was.
I admired the indulgence of my gracious master, in timing the trial
so as not to mar my public work ; and in that I had as much studied
the preceding week, as fully served that Sabbath; so that as I was
not able, so I did not need to study. He is a good Master to me ;
and I kissed that rod. In the prayers of Monday, November 9, I
spread the Hebrew Bible before him, and cried to the Father, that,
for the sake of his Son, he would by his Spirit shine on it, unto me,
give light into, and discover his mind in, the word ; that he would
give me life, health, strength, time, and inclination, to the study ;
and a blessing thereon ; that he would teach me how to manage
that work, and would pity me as to sleep, having been somewhat
bereaved of sleep since I was determined to that work. And that
week I made an entrance upon it, meeting in the threshold with a
particular difficulty like to break down my hopes of proceeding ;
and falling under indisposition, by means of a misty night, in coming over the hills from Chapelhop ; and being hampered as to time.
But I was encouraged again, surmounting the difficulty, and the indisposition going off.

Nov. 16.—Monday, I understand, that two sick persons I had
been concerned for before the Lord, were relieved from their distress ;
and was thankful, and concerned for grace to them to improve the
deliverance. And I had a view of the merciful nature of God, from
his requiring a merciful disposition in men one towards another ;
Psalm xli. ; encouraging to be concerned for others in such cases.
I am now going to visit other two, for whom I have hope of pity.
[*Nota,* It pleased the Lord to pity them accordingly.]

On the morrow I went from Upper Dalgleish, where I was catechising, to Eskdalemoor, and visited the minister there, out of conscience towards God, to cherish the disposition he appeared to be in,
as above recorded ; and that out of regard to the welfare of the interest of the gospel in the country. And this journey, as I was
helped to depend on the Lord with respect to it, so it was made a
comfortable journey to me, going thither and returning ; and that
by a vicissitude of smiles of Providence, and trials. At this time
I plainly saw the necessity and design of the above-mentioned conduct of Providence, in my entering on that work on the Hebrew
text ; for exciting me to a continued dependence on the Lord, for
life, strength, light, and time for it ; and I thankfully took the lesson. Meanwhile, as to the remaining part of that month, I had
thereof but what I could spend of three days for the said work ; my
hope in the matter being only in God, who is the same as before ;

though I am so altered, that I am not able to apply as in those days.

On the 29th I entered on Prov. xvi. 19, " Better it is to be of an humble spirit with the lowly, than to divide the spoil with the proud."

Nov. 30.—Monday. On Wednesday last I spent some time with John Currie, above mentioned, at his desire, in giving thanks for his recovery of the long illness under the ague. And the Lord's hearing of prayer for him, and others last summer, was sweet in reflecting thereon. Hitherto I have been strengthened in the diets of cate-chising. That week a member of the family having unmercifully treated a beast, to the disturbing of the whole family, was season-ably rebuked for it, by the Lord's own word falling to be read in the family-ordinary; Prov. xii. 10, " A righteous man regardeth the life of his beast," &c.

On Tuesday, December 1, I spent some time in prayer, with fast-ing, chiefly for two causes : 1. The work on the Hebrew text; and therein I found a pinching sense of need carrying me to that exer-cise, my hope of success being in the Lord alone ; 2. For my younger son, who the day before had gone towards Edinburgh, to at-tend the school of divinity only. I reviewed my whole life, made confession, and renewed my acceptance of the covenant, as that time twelve months before; and then I made my supplications on these accounts and some other, particularly the affair at London as to the MSS. concerning which there was still a deep silence; and came away with hope, rolling them on the Lord, on the morrow I cate-chised at Calcrabank. I had a singular satisfaction in that little journey, while I observed how Providence taught me, trying me and delivering me. It being a very hard frost, it was dangerous riding ; and my horses being both away to Edinburgh with my son, I was mounted on a beast that would hardly stir under me. At the se-cond ford above Hopehouse, I was quite stopped, the ford being frozen, and the horse not able to make the brae where the water was open. Alighting therefore to take the hill-side, the bridle slipped off, and my horse got away homeward, and I pursued. But kind Providence had a well-inclined lad coming down on the other side of the water, who coming through to my help, catched my horse, led him on, and I walked on foot once and again. Coming home, I was cast under night; but the lad staid, and came along with me, and led my horse again, while I walked with some uneasiness, by means of my boots, and otherwise. Meanwhile it was some moonlight; and I had a pleasure in that trial, beholding how my God took notice of me, even in my little matters, and how he balanced them for me ! " Lord, what is man that thou takest knowledge of him! or the son

of man, that thou makest account of him !''   After all, having only
got two falls, perfectly harmless, while walking, I came home safe ;
and found not the least ill effect of this adventure, save some weariness in my legs on the morrow after. And I got what I could spend
of the next day, on the beloved study ; but still Providence kept
me on trial, as to time for it.

But now the Lord remembered me, as to the affair in London,
which for my trial had been so long buried in absolute silence as
to me, even for the space of five months and upwards. And on the
following day, December 4, came to my hand a letter from Mr. G.
to Mr. Hogg, of the date Nov. 20, 1730, London, bearing, that my
letter was delivered to Sir Richard Ellys; that he received the letter obligingly; could not then give an answer, being immediately
going out of town; had been little in town that season, partly by
his being building a house on a new purchase he had made, partly
being abroad with his lady for her health ; so that he had seen him
but once these three months ; that at that time he regretted to him,
it had not been in his power, with the hurry he had been in that
season, to give me a return; but shewed a disposition to send me a
compliment as a token of his regard for me ; that he had not yet
got accounts from Holland, nor Dr. Ziegenhagen from Bremen and
Hall, about the specimen received in all those parts; as also, that
Dr. Waterland has been still in the country ; and Mr. Abraham
Taylor so much in it, that he had not seen him ; that he is a great
man, and owns the divine authority of the accents ; and further,
that Dr. Hay, our countryman, a clergyman of the church of England, though he is for the novelty of the points, yet values the
work, and owns he has been instructed by reading both the one and
the other MS.; that he has sometimes engaged to lay out himself to
get some of the ablest of their church to write a preface to it,
recommending it ; that the author has made him a present of
the Fourfold State ; that he has urged the author to wait on the
Archbishop of Canterbury, and the Bishops of Durham and London,
in order to their encouraging of it; and had it not been for their
titles they must have, he had ere now been introduced to them for
that effect; and, finally, desiring that I would send him a title for
the translation, with a view of printing a new specimen of both,
with proposals, if possibly he can find encouragement ; promising to
write me, how soon he should get Sir Richard's answer.

On the first reading of that letter, all I could do, was to lift my
eyes to the Lord, that he would mould my heart into such a frame
and disposition as might be agreeable to it. But upon further considering of it, I was thankful for it; yet still seeing the necessity

of dependence on the Lord to be continued, with respect to that matter; and I could not but observe, that, on the Monday after, being the 7th, having begun a narration of that letter, and abstract of the same, before I could have access so finish the same, we sang in our ordinary at family-worship the last part of the psalm which I have a particular expectation from, as above hinted, to wit, Psalm lxxi. 20, to the end, "Thou, Lord, who great adversaries," &c.; the which I did with heart and good will, having now had time to think more of the matter, and see further into the import and aspect of that letter.

To that letter I made a large return. I prepared also, and sent therewith, a title-page for the essay on the text.

But before the said return had reached him, there came to my hand on the 27th, being the Lord's day, a letter from him dated London, Dec. 10, bearing that Sir Richard Ellys having sent for him, communicated Mr. Gowan above said, his return to the above-mentioned letter concerning the specimen; of the which, taken down in writing by Mr. G. from Sir Richard's mouth dictating the same, the tenor follows:—" The specimen of the Hebrew accentua-tion has been carefully read and examined, by the ablest judges of that sort of learning that I know; I mean, by Mr. Schultens and Mr. Gronovius; both of them think, the author has given surprising instances of the usefulness of the accents to settle the meaning of the text; and on supposition that the rest of the work is equal to this sketch, it will upon the whole be the best book that has been written on the subject, and deserves to be made public." The said letter further bare, that Sir Richard talked several things very warm, as to his concern for me and that work, and was for its being handsomely printed, having had both the MSS. by him for some time: that he gave him ten guineas to be transmitted to me, as an acknowledgment of his sincere regard and esteem for me, and as a pledge of doing all in his power to encourage any work of mine; with salutations, and an excuse for his not writing as yet; and that he longs to see the MS. on the covenant of grace; and has as warm a way of taking of the gospel, and of the absolute need of divine saving teaching, to see its glory, and comply with its noble design, as any that ever the author was in company with; that Mr. Laraque, a French minister, an acquaintance of Sir Richard's, coming in, and hearing the story talked over to him, promised to procure twenty-five subscriptions from his relations and acquaintance abroad; that the Earl of Ilay had promised to be a subscriber; and that it would be difficult to keep the charges, &c. of the two parts of the work distinct, as I had proposed; but that the printer might make the exactest calculation as to both, still keeping in view the printing both together, and one subscription for all.

Upon the reading of that letter, I was somewhat as before in the case of the preceding one; the slowness of my natural temper having had a very discernible effect, on these occasions. But in the morning of the next day, I had a good time of it; seeing then, how my God was a faithful promise-keeping God to me; had begun to fulfil more of the latter part of the 71st psalm to me; and given me at length what he had long delayed, but by providential notices and pledges had bid me wait on for; and giving thanks for his faithfulness and bounty; withal perceiving, I as really needed his hand, to suit my heart to what the thing done required of me, as I needed it to do it for me. I remembered, that on the Friday's morning before (as I think) the petitions with reference to that affair, arose in my heart like water from a spring, which even then upon reflection made me to hope. And that morning above mentioned, being Dec. 28, I had something of the same nature in prayer for Sir Richard Ellys, that word being brought me, Prov xi. 25, "He that watereth, shall be watered also himself." The signature of a divine hand, on the raising up of him to befriend me, and in such a manner as he has done in various respects, did indeed appear with a glaring evidence. Janet Scot above mentioned being much in the like case as before the communion; considering I had the same God to go to, and the same Mediator still; I renewed the petitions in her behalf; and ere long after, I heard the Lord had pitied her. And Providence now appearing to be in motion, according to the words contained in Psalm lxxi. I was hopeful, my wife's turn expected therein, would come about at length. That afternoon I received the ten guineas above mentioned, by the hand of the bearer who the day before had brought me the letter.

Together with the said letter I received another, from my Lord Grange, directed to Mr. Hogg, desiring him to acquaint me, concerning a book, intitled, "Biblia Hebraica accentuata; sive, Codicis Hebræi, accentuum radiis collustrati, ultra bis mille specimina, &c.: opera et curis M. Georgii Christoph, Pashsellii, Lipsiæ, 1729 ;" where and how I might get it, if I desired it; and shewing, that if, after seeing of it, I desired to communicate thoughts with the author, perhaps a way might be fallen on for that effect. Hereby it seemed to me, that Providence was at this time at work to diffuse that light, making it to arise from very distant quarters; the more to be regarded, that there were never perhaps so formidable attacks made against revealed religion in Christian countries, as at this day.

What spare time I had that week, was entirely spent on letters.

What part of Tuesday I was able so to employ, was spent in scrolling a letter to Sir Richard Ellys; and yet I was not able so to effect it; my God thus humbling me, and teaching me my dependence, and what a mere nothing I am without him. Howbeit, taking a diet of catechising on the morrow, I wrote my letter to Sir Richard on the Thursday, Dec. 31, a copy whereof is *in retentis* (see the appendix); and also begun a very long letter to Mr. G.

On Friday, Jan. 1, 1731, I entered, in pursuance of my former subject, on a new text; 1 Pet. v. 6, "Humble yourselves therefore under the mighty hand of God, that he may exalt you in due time." And I was led into the meaning of being " under the mighty hand of God," new to me; namely, that it mainly points at that inferiority to, and dependence on others, which God hath appointed for men's trial, now in this world; the which is to be wholly taken away at the end of time. When I had almost ended my studies, there arrived from Selkirk an express with letters from Edinburgh and London. One of these was from Sir Richard Ellys, dated Dec. 16, 1730.—See the appendix.

These letters did, leisurely, as before, fill me with comfort and thankfulness. The friendliness, openness, and savouriness of Sir Richard's were really surprising, notwithstanding all the favour he had shewn me before; and I could not miss to admire and adore that hand of God, which had given his heart such a touch, upon that design; and which also had first set, again excited, and still keeps, Mr. G. in motion therein. That night, thinking to proceed in my begun answer to Mr. G. my strength would not serve; so I was obliged to lay it aside. Nevertheless I behoved to write two short letters, to go off on the morrow early; in one of which I desired my friend Mr. Wilson forthwith to transmit the MS. on the covenant of grace, then with him, to Mr. Hogg at Edinburgh, to be by him sent off to London, to be shewn to Sir Richard; as to which I know not, at writing hereof, what is done by him; but I have committed it to the Lord.

On Saturday's morning, being the 2d, perceiving myself overcharged with necessary business, I prayed for strength for it, trusted I would get it; and accordingly I did get it. And with that strength afforded me *in hunc effectum*, I dispatched all I had to do that day, both as to my public and private work, though it kept me late that night. I wrote that day another letter to Sir Richard, (see appendix); and a letter to Mrs. Balderstone; and several others. I had a good time of it, on the Lord's day morning, in prayer, particularly in praying for Sir Richard Ellys. But for all the sweet morning I thus had, that I might know what a poor de-

pending thing I was, I had no gust nor feeling in the public ordinances, lecture or preaching, that day; but I comforted myself,
in that my Lord Christ is to the fore, and he changes not.

On the morrow our session met, and I had access to the Lord in
prayer, and felt the power of "his hand put in by the hole of the
door." And that night I saw it necessary, solemnly to address the
throne of grace, for carrying on that work now again set in motion.
Accordingly, on Tuesday the 5th, I spent some time in prayer on
that account, as also for assistance in the work on the Hebrew text,
again entered on some time ago, and for the divine pity with respect
to my case in the ensuing spring.

Becoming faint, I took a refreshment; but withal it pleased the
Lord all along to withdraw, so that I had no sense nor feeling in
that work, which was carried on heavily, in my usual method. At
length, thinking I was like to lose that day's work, I resolved to
believe over the belly of sense; and resolutely laid my petitions on
these heads, for Mr. G. my wife, and Mr. Henry Davidson, before
the Lord, in the name of Jesus Christ; professing that I did
not at all look for the acceptance of my person, performances, or
petitions, upon the account of any thing about me, which was but
variable; but for the sake of Christ only, who, whatever I was, remained still the same; and therefore had confidence, they should be
accepted, for his sake, over the belly of my want of sense. And I
found much benefit in this course.

Thus, as has been narrated, did the Lord bring my five months'
trial to a comfortable issue; which helped to trust him for what
remains at the writing hereof. I observed, that this turn came not,
until I was engaged again in the work on the Hebrew text, in which
the Lord has pitied me as to sleep, according to my desire; and
this timing of that favourable turn, was so agreeable to the Lord's
ordinary way of dealing with me, that I had some expectation before I returned to that work, that I behoved to be yoked to it
again, ere that dark piece of Providence relating thereto would
open. Moreover, I observed, that it came at a time wherein I had
attained, through grace, to more weanedness and quieting of myself under a particular in my case, than I had of a long time before.
And I cannot but further remark, to the praise of glorious free
grace, and the covenant-order in dispensing the benefits thereof,
that on the Wednesday before the first of the letters directed to
myself came, being Dec. 23, 1730, we had been led to keep a congregational thanksgiving, for the removal of the late touch of dearth,
and the good harvest. This had been in my view since my conversing with the five dissenters above mentioned, who, from their per-

sonal knowledge, informed me of more dismal effects of that dearth than I had been aware of, though I knew it to be very grievous; but it was put off so long, waiting if perhaps we might be called thereto by a superior authority. However, the people were sensible of the call of Providence, and we had a very full meeting that day.

Now the sense of the above-mentioned signal appearance of Providence for my comfort, in that work which has long been at heart with me moved me, to begin, and thus far to carry on the account of my life, before I should return to my work broke off by these letters. And that filled my hand till this Saturday's night the 9th of January. As for the diets of catechising, whereof one only now remains, viz. for the first time, I have been comfortably carried through them all, except that at Calcrabank above-mentioned.

On the morrow there came to my hand a letter, shewing that Mr. Du-Pont, who had urged me to write to M. Maurice, professor of theology at Geneva, impatiently expected a letter for him. The accentuation, so far as I could understand, being of little reputation in those parts, I was not fond of the toil of that writing, whence I could have so little expectation. But upon that repeated call thereto, I addressed myself to it; and on the Monday and Tuesday, the Lord helping me, I made out a specimen, of two sheets, for him. Being on the morrow to catechise at Kirkhop, I, thus exhausted, fearing I should be confused in that work, prayed that the Lord would make me clear and distinct in it; and my God heard me, to my own conviction. On the Thursday with some difficulty I carried the scrolling of my letter some length; but at night applying thereto again, I was so worsted thereby, that on the morrow, my study-day, I was quite out of case, though I got through with difficulty. In the matter of this letter I had much ado to believe and wrestle against anxiety, which on the Friday's night being like to rob me of my rest, I turned to my knees on my bed, made supplication for sleep, and got it. On the Saturday I dispatched that letter, which being in Latin is *in retentis*; as also several others. And on the Monday morning they were conveyed away. According to my faith, so it was with me; I had much ado to believe and trust the Lord in that matter; and I had much ado to get it accomplished.

Moreover, in the following days, I found my indisposition much increased, so that my studies on the Friday were in part marred, and behoved to be pursued on the Saturday. And in the time thereof, before I had taken meat or drink, I was seized with a vomiting, and threw up a great quantity of crudities; the which turned to my benefit. But perceiving this to arise from not getting my meat chewed, for lack of teeth, I set myself to use more caution in that matter.

On the last of January came to my hand a letter from G. G. whereby I understood his brother Mr. John was to return home, in the latter end of February, or beginning of March; while as yet I knew nothing done effectual in my affair. But therewith came Led-hebhurius's book on the accents; by the preface whereof I under-stood the disappointments he had been exercised with, as to the publishing of it. Upon this and other incidents, I was made to be-take myself anew to my God, and in the name of Christ to lay my se-veral requests very particularly before him; the which I was helped to do with confidence. And thus was I set anew to hang on about the Lord's own hand.

But having unhappily suffered the monthly meeting of the session, which should have been kept the first Monday of February, to drop, that I might have more time for my beloved study, which I had al-most all along that far been hampered in, I found myself disap-pointed. Acknowledging my sin, and resolving to keep that meet-ing on the second Monday, I got that week both strength and time for that study, in a measure, I think, I had not till then obtained. And on the Saturday, after much weariness, came to my hand se-veral letters, whereof one from Hall in Saxony, directed to M. Ziegenhagen above mentioned; the tenor whereof follows:—

" Vir plurimum Reverende ac Doctissime, amice in Christo pie colende. Tandem post quatuor mensium intervallum, his ipsis die-bus redditæ mihi sunt literæ, quas 18 superioris Augusti, una cum specimine novi operis de accentibus sive interstinctionibus sacri Ebræi textus, ad me dedisti. Grato omnino animo agnosco tui in me benevoli adfectus constantiam, nec minus etiam clarissmo atque eruditissimo Bostono, pro testificatione amoris obstrictum me agno-sco. Non putaveram inter Transmarinos esse, qui ob qualemcunque notitiam sacrarum literarum me diligeret; quum præter binas, eas-que primas meas disputationes academicas, jam ultra triginta et sex annos conscriptas, nihil de accentibus Ebraicis, Latina lingua edi-derim. Memini tamen in adnotationibus Biblicis sæpius ad eorum usum et subsidium, in dignoscenda vera dictorum sententia, me pro-vocare. Impense gratulor rei sacræ literariæ, quod etiam inter di-visos ab orbe nostro Britannos, divinæ illius cynosuræ jubar clarius incipiat fulgere; atque ex animo precor, ut nisi jam factum illud sit, opus egregium felicibus auspiciis propediem in lucem mittatur; quantum enim ex transmissis ejus speciminibus constat, adeo soler-ter et exquisite, circumspecte, ac solide, ex sedulo observatis na-turalibus hujus doctrinæ principiis, plurimum Reverendus author hoc argumentum pertractavit, ut cæteros, qui a me visi aut lecti fuerunt, longe, post se relinquat. Quod judicium meum etsi præmaturum videri queat, quod non totum opus, sed pauciores tantum illius particulas, inspicere mihi licuerit, ideo tamen non fallet, quod illarum partium exquisito venustas, de totius operis præstantia, luculentum indicium faciat. Nec obesse poterit præclaro instituto, si quid forte in allatis exemplis adhuc dubium occurrat, aut monendum quid restet; si quidem regulis bene ac solide constructis sua nihilominus certitudo constabit. Sic, exempli causa, in capite 8 partis 1. Exod. xxv. 12, non quatuor sed octo ut putat, interstinctione. Ea tamen in sententia vix alios habebit consentientes, quia et verbis et interstinctionibus posterioris hemistichii, ut sæpius fieri oportet, explicative accipiatur, h. m. Duos nimirum annulos adfiges, non in parte anteriori vel posteriori ad angulos, sed in latere arcæ uno, et sic duos in latere ejus altero. De quo tamen pluribus nunc disputare nec vacat, nec per tempus licet, tantum ad præcautionem Reverendi authoris id moneo, et aliud potius exemplum urgeat, quod exceptionibus minus sit obnoxium. Id quod cum plurima et officiosissima salute viro pio et erudito ut meo nomine renuncies te etiam atque etiam rogo. Quod reliquum ad finem decurrit annus quem agimus per Dei gratiam, et, novus instet, ut ille tibi et sacro tuo muneri sit auspicatissimus, ex auimo voveo. Fale itaque in Domino Jesu, in longos annos omni ex parte salvus atque incolumis; et quod facis porro ama Plur. Reveren. nominis tui studiosissimum. (Sic subscribitur) D. Jo. HENR. MICHAELIS. Dabam raptim, die 24, Decemb. 1730, Halæ."

The sight hereof with the rest, sent me to the Lord, that he might manage my heart as the matter might require. And afterward reading it, I was almost made to break out in tears of joy at the goodness of God towards poor me. I had therewith a letter from Mr. G. of the date Jan. 17, 1731, in which was no word of his returning, but recommending to me to write both to Dr. Ziegenhagen and Dr. Michaelis, and bearing his having as yet got no account of the reception of my papers from Sir John Philips and the prelates, Sir Richard being out of town, and (the author) not having seen Sir John. The morrow after, finding that the treatise of the covenant, which I had committed to the Lord, was arrived safe at London, I found myself moved solemnly to return him thanks for that, committing it again to him, and praying he would honour himself by it; and herein the Lord was with me in a special manner.

Having on the Monday, Feb. 8, held the session, as resolved, I applied myself that week, as I had access, to prepare a letter for Dr. Michaelis, wishing to have the same over that week. But I was

so straitened therein, that having finished the scrolling of it not till
Saturday at eleven o'clock, I had laid my account not to have that
business dispatched till the beginning of the following week. But
going down stairs at the time aforesaid, I was surprised to hear of
an occasion to Edinburgh on the Monday. Whereupon finding myself sore pressed, and already outwearied, I made my supplication
unto God; then dispatched in the first place my work for the Sabbath, and immediately thereafter applied myself to writing that
letter. After dinner I took my horse, and spent some time in riding for my health, and for strength; at half six went to my closet
again; and a friend having gifted me some bottles of white wine, I
took a glass of it, some time after, for the same causes aforesaid;
and by eleven o'clock at night had all dispatched, viz. a letter to
Dr. Michaelis, another to Dr. Hagen, both in Latin, a third to Mr.
G. and other two to other persons. Through this closeness of application I lost much of the night's rest, not being able to command
sleep, as usual with me in such cases. But on the morrow, being
the Lord's day, I had full strength for my work; only, heaven was
made more sweet to me, as a rest from toil and labour. On the
Monday I was obliged to visit a sick person at Buccleugh. This
conduct of Providence was admirably sweet. The Lord tried me,
and brought to me my purpose, in his way, though not in mine.
Had I known sooner of the occasion to Edinburgh, I could have
done no more than I was doing; but it would have rendered me
more uneasy; so it was kindly kept up from me till the due time,
though human inadvertency was the means Providence made use of
for that end. And as I desired, so I got, strength *in hunc effectum*,
when I saw what lay upon me. And O what kindness I saw in the
necessity laid on me to ride seven miles on the Monday. I was
heartily pleased to see how my God ordered my labour, my rests,
and my motions, wishing ever to be under no other conduct. But
upon the neck of this, Satan laid a train for me; and I was catched,
and defiled; but was washed again in the Redeemer's blood.

Thereafter the presbyterial exercise and addition lying on me, I
set myself, as I had access, to study the same. And being helped
through grace to trust the Lord, I was most comfortably carried
through the study thereof. So that on Tuesday, Feb. 23, I had access with much thankfulness, to my kind Father, to return to my
beloved study, which I had been broke off from by the arrival of
the letters foresaid.

On March 1, I went to Selkirk, where on the morrow I delivered
the discourse aforesaid to an unexpectedly frequent auditory. Looking on this as probably the last of the kind I might have occasion

to deliver, I had been concerned, that the Lord would give it me
with a relish; and the relish that I sought, I got, according to his
great mercy, even to the filling of my heart with satisfaction, as in
the study of it. And, with thankfulness to my gracious Father, I
returned in the Thursday's night, with a humbling view of my un-
profitableness in conversation, and a conviction, as usual, that my
obscure and retired life is really best for me. Being through weariness unfit for study on the morrow, I had no need, having enough
provided beforehand. But while abroad, one of the remaining comforts of my life endured a shock, that had some time before been
a-working; the which was very affecting, seeing how the Lord was
drawing one comfort from me after another.

On the Monday and Tuesday after, I was obliged to ride to the
utmost corners of the parish to visit sick persons; and on the two
following days applied myself, as I was able, to my private business; but recovered not till Friday, my study day. And hereby I
perceived, how little I had to expect from riding in the way of cure.
Meanwhile, on the 17th, I had perfected the versions and notes on
Gen. xxi. and on the 20th began to write it over *in mundo*. But
that day last named I was extremely indisposed and oppressed, so
that I was obliged to betake myself to my bed. Howbeit that extremity continued not; neither did my trouble this March arrive at
the height it went to in the March preceding. On the 28th I closed
my ordinary, of humiliation, having been comfortably assisted.*
About this time, in several instances of mothers and children, moved to pray for them, I was graciously heard, and my soul filled
with praise on that score. Moreover having, on occasion of the late
occurrences relating to the MSS. observed from time to time a certain run of temper prevailing, I was let into the view of human nature, not much adverted to before, viz. That whereas there are two
parts of sympathy, namely, weeping with them that weep, and re-

---

* The author took next for his ordinary, Matth. vii. 13, 14, concerning the way to
life, and the way to destruction, which he began April 4, and continued therein till
Dec. 26, 1731; and the following Lord's day, being Jan. 2, 1732, he began to discourse of the end of time, and the mystery of God finished with it, from Rev. x. 6, 7,
on which subject he continued till March 26, that year. All these sermons were
printed in a volume in 1753. On the second of April following he took for a new
ordinary, the necessity of self-examination, from 2 Cor. xiii. 5, which he preached on
that day and the following Sabbath, from a window in the manse, to the people standing without; but his growing frailty hindered him from further work, till his divine
Master called him home to receive the reward of his labours on the 20th of May.
What he had wrote on the last-mentioned subject is published in his " Body of Divinity," vol. III. p. 396, *et seq.*

joicing with them that rejoice, human nature is far more ready to go into the former than into the latter, from a certain undue care for one's self, and a jealousy of others, which in the former there is not so much place or occasion for. Meanwhile all had enough ado to keep my head above the water, having had no account of these MSS. since the time above noted; but having taken God for my friend, prayed he would, and trusted he will do the part of a friend to me in the matter, I endeavoured not to be uneasy, as under the former disappointment.

Having for a considerable time in the spring taken thought about administering the sacrament, finding myself straitened with Mr. Davidson's growing indisposition, whereby he was laid aside from preaching, I often laid the matter before the Lord. And, after many thoughts, I was so far resolved to call Mr. Macgarroch to my assistance on that occasion, that on April 13, being catechising at Etterick house, I told my resolution to one there. The reason moving me thereto, was indeed to consult the good of the country, after I should be gone, if so be that man might be pliable. But coming home, just as I alighted, one of his parish, who had been at my house, was drawing his horse to go away. Him I asked concerning that brother; and he told me he was just the day before gone for Ireland. Herewith I was struck, perceiving the divine hand so eminent in my encounter with the man, which a minute or two's delay would have prevented. This made me cast about again in my thoughts; and on the morrow I gave myself to prayer, on that head particularly; and at length soon resolved to hold on as before, without moving another way, judging providence to point me thereto; and leaving it to the Lord to provide for the country in his own way, after my removal. So I wrote to Mr. Wilson and Mr. Davidson on the 14th, and to Mr. Craig on the 17th.

By the 15th of April I had transcribed the versions and notes on Gen. xxi. and thereafter, as I had opportunity, went on in that beloved study. But there still continuing a deep silence from London about my MSS. the case of which was still laid before the Lord, I was on May 19, brought to that, that the Lord would glorify himself, either by the burying of them, or the publishing of them. And having now the administration of the sacrament in view, there was an addition to the infirmities hanging about my crazy body, by a new pain in my right knee, which seized me on the night of the 24th; but through grace it was welcome. The time of the sacrament being fixed to the second Sabbath of June, from the third day of that month I laid aside my beloved study for the time; and on the 4th came to my hand a letter from Sir Richard Ellys, of the date

April 13, 1731, insisting, that I should send the MS. on the covenant of grace to the press, assuring, that nothing should be wanting on his part to set it forward.

And therewith came a letter, directed to Sir Richard, from Mr. Loftus, concerning the specimen on the accentuation, dated Rotterdam, April 20, 1731, wherein he insinuates, that some great men in the sacred literature at Leyden had modestly refused to give their thoughts of it; but gives his own judgment thereon as follows:—

"I have persued the MS. and take it for a certainty, or great probability, that the other parts and pages of the MS. are done with equal care and judgment; and then I think it is a very good undertaking, which shews the diligence, industry, and accuracy of the author. He is clear, orderly, and methodical, and has some observations in the specimen, that I take to be most judicious and useful, which I never met with in my small reading, though I have compared and still am comparing authors. And I should be glad to see this *criticus criticorum*, &c., encouraged, not only to excite the languishing taste of our nation to put such critics as Le Clerk out of countenance, who make so little account of the Hebrew accents, as if they were superflous niceties, but also to give some occasion for the revival of the controversy, which many think was sufficiently wrought into a decision by Capel and Buxtorff." [Signed BARTHO-LOMEW LOFTUS.]

Meanwhile there was no account thereof from London, as to the state of the matter there.

On Monday June 7, having kept the house two weeks, to attend the new communicants coming to me in order to their admission, I rode out a mile, but with great pain in my knee. Being come back the length of the glebe, much moved herewith, in respect of what might happen in being called to visit the sick, I tried hanging my leg out of the stirrup; and riding so with pretty much ease, I was encouraged again with respect to the event foresaid. I rode out again in the same posture on the morrow; and continued that way for some time after, as I had occasion.

Thus I was become lame, the scurvy having fallen down into my knee, at the time above mentioned. And I was put from kneeling; at prayer either standing upright, or prostrating myself on a bed. But now the pain I formerly had in my back, which came to me in the spring, and towards the autumnal equinox, went off, and came no more. But this seemed to have taken its place, the humour now landing in my knee, which formerly had annoyed my back.

There had been a hay-stack burnt, and about £4 sterling stolen from the owner of the stack, in Deephop, in the spring; but no find-

ing out of the actor or actors of these wickednesses; only there was
one vehemently suspected. Therefore on the fast-day before the
sacrament, in my preface, I read to the congregation, Deut. xxi. concerning the expiation of uncertain murder; and accordingly, in the
prayer immediately following, begged the Lord would not impute it
to the congregation.

The sacrament was administered, June 13, quite beyond my expectation, having laid my account with the first Sabbath of that
month. But from that event, together with the former of April 13,
I thought God had something comfortable to bring out in that matter; and I rejoiced that the Lord himself led, and left me to follow.
He carried on the work with much of his countenance to his servants, and refreshment to his people; and that in the way that by
his providence he himself had determined. The distributing of the
tokens was most orderly; and as external decency in management,
with favour in the weather, were sought of the Lord, we got the
same to a pitch. My children were kept up in health for the time.
Isabel Biggar was healed on the fast-day at night; but Rachel
Grieve's daughter continued ill; only in the time she was easier
than after. It happened that there was but one single person at the
last table. Mr. Wilson was gone away, and Mr. Davidson declined
serving it. Whereupon I addressed myself to the work. I shewed
the people that our Lord Christ received every one that came to
him; that the action was one continued action, and not then closed;
and so proceeding as usual without any variation. The tokens distributed to communicants were about 777; the collection on the
three days, £71 : 13 : 4d, Scots. There were about nine score strangers in Midgehope; fourscore of them William Blaik, husband of
Isabel Biggar, aforesaid, entertained, having before baken for them
half a boll of meal for bread, brought 4s. 10d, Sterling worth of
wheat bread, and killed three lambs, &c. made thirty beds. And I
believe their neighbour, Robert Biggar, Isabel's brother, would be
much the same. This I record once for all, for a swatch of the hos-
pitality of the parish; for God hath given his people a largeness of
heart, to communicate of their substance, on these, and other occasions also. And my heart has long been on that occasion particularly concerned for a blessing on their substance; with such a natural emotion, as if they had been begotten of my body. Those
within a mile of the church still had the far greater weight on solemn occasions.

Being just settled to business in my closet, on Tuesday, June 22,
I was called to see Rachel Grieve's child aforesaid in Ramsaycleugh,
a-dying; and before I could get away, I was called to see a woman,

a communicant, a-dying too. The child was just expired when I got to the place. From thence I went to Glenkirry to the woman, whom I found in a most dangerous condition, all means proving ineffectual. Thus the Lord seemed to refuse to be intreated : and I thought that woman was gone too. Wherefore I went back on the Thursday, judging she could not last at that rate ; but when I came hither, I found her sitting at the fire, pretty well recovered ; and they thought themselves out, that they had not prevented my trouble of this new visit. But I rejoiced and gave thanks ; and when I came home, I saw that God had hindered them ; to check me for my so soon giving over hopes of his hearing of prayer. I took the rebuke kindly ; and it was useful to me in another case. For whereas I had put up petitions, for the prospering of the affairs of the people, who on the late occasion had honoured him with their substance ; but understood that since that time some of them had got but a sorry market ; I hereby saw more into the method of Providence, and believed that God would notwithstanding make out his word, and they should not lose their reward. The first four days of that week, lame as I was, I was obliged to be on horseback, thankful to God that I was able, and was not laid by from that piece of service. But supping ordinarily at that time on a glass of mum, and a piece of white-bread, it was humbling to me ; and a point of submission to the will of God, who had made it necessary for me to be at such pains about the body, and that I could not put it off with as little choice as sometimes before. On the Monday morning after, having had some comfortable account and view of the fruits of the Lord's work in my hand ; and being withal led into some admiration of the glorious mystery of the incarnation of the Son of God ; I had a comfortable while in my bed, while I could not sleep ; and it came to my remembrance, that before I came to Etterick, one concerned for me had had that view of it, that if I went, it should be for the good of a young generation ; now the then young generation is the old now, in several of whom I have comfort.

About the 7th of July, my knee became worse than ever, the pain having in the night gone to extremity ; with the which trysted a letter, inviting me to the communion at Galashiels, to be on the 1st of August. In the morning I took the letter, and spread it before the Lord, crying for pity. And thereafter my knee returned to its ordinary, the great pain having abated by degrees. About that time I was let into a strengthening view of the fulness of a God in Christ, whereby I perceived, that whatever were the communications of divine love, to others more than to me, there was still the same

room for me as if there were not another object of it in all the
world. And this continued to be of great use to me.

The work at Galashiels lying wholly on my two friends and me,
and Mr. Craig, probationer, I was led for my subject to 2 Cor. xii.
9, "For my strength is made perfect in weakness." I made my
way thither on the Friday, but with much difficulty; not from pain
or sickness, but mere weariness to sit the horse. Howbeit I had
abundant strength given me for my work there, preached Saturday
and Sabbath afternoon, and served five tables; and the Lord was
with me in my public, and private work in my chamber; and at the
table helped me to believe in him as my God. On the Saturday,
there was, I think, some thunder before we went out; but between
two and three o'clock, when I had begun my sermon, it returned,
and went to a great pitch. Upon the back of the second or third
clap, I said to the people, "The God of glory thundereth; he will
give his people strength, and bless them with peace." So I went on
undisturbed, the fire every now and then flashing in my eyes. The
people sat gravely and decently, without any disturbance discerned
by me, perceiving nothing of that nature among them, more than the
drawing of their cloaks about them, as in the case of rain. In time of
the prayer after sermon, the thunder went to a prodigious height,
that I could not miss the imagination of being struck down in a moment; but through grace was kept undisturbed in my work. In
time of singing psalms, while I looked for Mr. Davidson to come
up, to speak to the people, as usual, I was told he could not come;
so I addressed myself to officiate for him. But whereas there had
been but little rain before, there came such a mighty pouring out of
rain, that I was obliged to dispatch quickly. Then we distributed
the tokens, the papers meanwhile being damnified with the rain,
while they were produced and read. Having done the work without, when I came into the house, Mr. Davidson was lying groveling
and groaning on his chamber-floor, under a most exquisite fit of the
gravel; and after sitting some time with him, who in his extremity
declared himself under his Father's hand, I left him as I found him.
The pain going off, he was sick through the night, and rose not
soon. So I had laid my account to officiate for him before the action;
but said nothing, waiting to see how Providence would move. But,
after all, he went out betwixt nine and ten, preached a sweet sermon, and did his other work, without the least vestige of his illness
about him, in it; speaking with as much vigour as ever, I think, I
heard him at any time when at his best; so that the multitude seemed in no uneasiness at all to hear. This was a wonderful stroke of
Providence, carrying matters to such an extremity, and then bring-

ing to such a comfortable issue. But that was the full-sea-mark as to him, since which time the day of the writing hereof, more than a quarter of a year after, so far as I know, he has not had a return of his usual pains, but a turn to the better, and seems to be in a way of recovery. On the Sabbath morning we heard of two persons, in the neighbouring parish of Stow, slain by the thunder; and afterwards of a third; the which made it the more signal mercy, that there was no breach on the multitude, either in the place, or going to their places of abode. Long was the roll of the sick and distressed which was read. In prayer I found sensible help of the Lord, to go through the several kinds, and petitions for them laid to my hand. This was the prayer after the afternoon sermon, on the Lord's day.

I saw at Galashiels a letter from Sir Richard Ellys to Mr. Hogg, approving and encouraging the design of printing the MS, on the covenant; and a postscrip by Mr. G. bearing, that it should be returned as soon as might be; but no word of the other MSS. There also I had a letter from a younger minister, shewing some difficulty in conceiving about the covenant of grace, and desiring my thoughts on that subject. I took it for a providential hint, towards publishing of the said MS. And afterwards I wrote him my thoughts at large, willingly embracing that occasion of serving the interest of truth, whatever use should be made of it.

Having been of a considerable, time again and again urged with a project in favour of a certain person, in the which I had no clearness to be active, but only to yield and give way to it; the case some time in August became heavy to a degree, so that I set myself to seek of the Lord a right way in it; and after frequent addresses to the throne of grace on that head, I was at length fully cleared to be active in the matter, considering it as it stood circumstanced. But upon my declaring and offering to be active in carrying it on, the party to my surprise declined it; so it behoved to be dropt.

Some time after, standing without, and seeing a tree tossed with a violent wind, which caused the withering leaves to fall off, that otherwise in a little would have dropt off of themselves; I received instruction as to heavy trials trysting with a declining state.

From some time after my return from Galashiels, till towards the latter end of September, I was on the study, Gen. xxiii. the two former being transcribed. That study proved so difficult and slow, that it seemed to me, I was not in case for such work, by reason of the state of my body; and I often thought Providence would oblige me to give it over, and so take away that remaining comfort of my life. But in that time I was twice remarkably pitied, after serious application to God by prayer, on that head.

On the 3d September, I had, by a letter, an account of an apparent beginning of Mr. Davidson's deliverance and recovery. And being on the 5th to begin lecturing on the Song of Solomon, considering the growing infidelity and profaneness of the day, I was moved to preach on the first verse thereof, to vindicate the divine authority and spirituality of it, &c. before I should enter on my explaining it. I was much satisfied in the divine conduct in that matter, several persons of some distinction falling to hear that day, beyond what was ordinary with us, it being the first Sabbath after Tushilaw's return from his travels.

Having had some expectation, that as in some former years, I would become somewhat better in health about the autumnal equinox: instead thereof, I became sensibly worse; the knee particularly swelled more, and the leg became weaker; so that I was fain to betake myself to my staff again, as in the beginning of that trouble. This turn as to my body, gave me a rational view of what might be expected from the spring shock added thereto, in case of my seeing the spring; and I had some comfortable prospect of the weary's getting to rest.

William Blaik's family, who had a train of trials since the sacrament, was tossed in a sea of trouble for a long time from the beginning of August, he, his wife, and three children, all fixed to sick-beds together. They were attended by a neighbour, a weak woman, who declared she had not of a long time had so much health as was afforded her during the time of her attendance. After a long trial of several turns, the hearer of prayer brought all safe through; and at length, at their desire, thanks were returned in the congregation for their recovery, as prayers had been put up there for them.

Concerning the continued silence as to the MSS. relating to the Hebrew, and thence perceiving that they do not take at London, this did sometimes put me almost out of conceit with them myself; but yet the value for them revived again with me, when I cast my eyes on the discoveries made by that study. However, I came to be in good measure weaned in the matter, only had some difficulty, as to the calling them home peremptorily, being afraid of not allowing Providence full scope in the business; and wanting only to be cleared as to my duty in that point. But the MS. on the covenant was again written for.

The sacrament of the Lord's supper was administered at Maxton, Oct. 3. Looking on it as possibly the last such occasion I might have there, I was determined to John i. 29, "Behold the Lamb of God," &c. that I might make another offer of Christ to sinners; my sermons of that nature abroad having for some time been fitted to

the case of serious persons exercised.   Being to go off on Thursday,
that by reason of my weakness I might take two days for the journey, I began my study of that text on the Monday.   But on the
Tuesday I quite stuck therein, and could not proceed; which made
it a heavy day.   Having earnestly begged of the Lord, that he
would give me a message, whether old or new, as he saw meet;
laying a-bed at night, that word came to me; Prov. ix. 12, " If
thou be wise, thou shalt be wise for thyself," &c. an old text.   Finding the agreeableness hereof to the public circumstances of the land,
and to my own private circumstances, as a concluding word, I was
that night much eased, and on the morrow fully determined thereto;
as I was also to Gen. vi. 9, " Noah was—perfect in his generations;"
recommending integrity in a declining generation unto all, and
particularly to the younger sort.   I was earnest for the blowings of
the Spirit; and the Lord was with me in delivering these two
words,* which in my own eyes, and in the eyes, I believe, of some
others too, looked like farewell sermons, whatever be the issue.   But
day-light failing on the Lord's day at night, and not being able to
command the lines of the psalm I was minding to have given out,
there was no psalm sung; the which I heartily was sorry for afterward.   During that time I was pitied also in my private work.

As we were coming away homeward from Maxton, Mr. Wilson
put into my hand a printed paper of the Commission of the General
Assembly, 1650, intitled, " The great sin and chief guiltiness of Scotland, in the contempt of the gospel," designed to be reprinted; desiring me to write a preface to it.   This I utterly refused, and that
in earnest; knowing nothing particularly about the matter, and
judging him more fit to manage things of that nature.   However, he
obliged me to keep it, to read it at my leisure, and shew what I observed in it.   Getting home on Wednesday, as I lay a-bed that
night, I read the paper above mentioned; and I was thereby,
through the blessing of God on it, convinced, instructed, directed,
comforted, and recovered; and particularly helped towards a right
use-making of sacraments received.   And the impression it made
was, through grace, lasting.   On the morrow, finding I had several
occasional things laid to my hand to do, and knowing myself liable
to an unfitness for action after travel, I chose to transcribe in mundo
something of what was written on Gen. xxiii. that being the thing
which the bent of my spirit lying mainly toward, I judged best to
bring me in case for applying to work in my closet.

* These two discourses are both printed; the former in the author's " Body of Divinity," vol. III., the latter in the second volume of a collection of his sermons, published in 1753.

But holy Providence had designed a piece of new trial for me, that I was not aware of. When I came home from Maxton, I was told, that one had advised blistering, and putting a pea in my leg, for my sore knee, and had left me a blistering-plaister for that end. The plaister was applied on the Friday's night. On the Sabbath night the pea was put in; and through pain I slept none that night. The pain continuing, the pea was taken out again on the Tuesday; and on the morrow after, I had my first diet of catechising at Chapel-hope. After taking away the pea, the hole quickly closed; but there grew upon it a hard callous substance, and withal the leg was inflamed. This created thoughts of heart, and the sore knee was forgotten. On the Monday after I wrote for a surgeon; who returned me answer, that he apprehended no danger, and sent me an ointment to apply. Expecting some benefit by the ointment, I wrote him on the morrow, that he needed not come till again called. But finding the ointment quite ineffectual as to the substance aforesaid, I was sorry I had prevented his coming up. In these heavy circumstances that week, the Lord comforted me more ways than one.

On the Monday there had come to my door a begging cripple, who seeing me without, begged of me a book of my own composing. I told him I had none but single copies, except of the Fourfold State, value 4s. sterling; and he insisted not for one of them. I gave him something out of my pocket; but he told me, he would rather have had a book. Surprised with this unusual request from such a sort of person, after he was gone away I called him back, and told him, I would think of a book for him, bidding him call some other time. Thinking on this matter, and taking it for a call from the Lord himself, I resolved to give him a copy of the Fourfold State, not knowing but God might have something to do with it, by that means, among the vagrant poor. So on Monday, October 18, while I was sitting with my sore leg in my closet, he came back; and calling him up to me, I gave him the book, taking him engaged not to shew from whom he had it, but read it occasionally among his fellows, and was concerned for a blessing on it. This afforded me a satisfaction far beyond what money could have done; and before that, on occasion of giving of them away, I had a satisfying view of that as the very best I could make of them, having got two dozen of them, and sold one half-dozen of them, few being then left.

From the time I read the aforementioned paper, I was so taken with it, that I cried earnestly again and again unto the Lord, that he would vouchsafe to put the honour on me to be instrumental, in the way desired, towards its public usefulness; and on the Wednesday and Thursday, while I sat in my bed, by reason of my leg, the Lord gave something by way of recommendation of it. Herein my soul rejoiced. And by the time that I was near the close of it, on the Thursday, the surgeon came. And I was the more comforted, in that I saw the Lord had sent him, having got the contrary word, as above said. He opened the side of the callous substance with the point of his scissors; then pulled it up with pincers, which I was helped to bear: and what was raised of it, he clipped away; but near a third part of it remained, which he apprehended was not then ripe. And thus I was more comforted.

The hand of God was eminent in bringing this trial on me. I was not seeking cure of my knee by medicine, or any such way, having, from a continued tract of experience, little or no hope at all that way; but I was put upon it by those concerned for my welfare. Providence, by a repeated incident, frowned on it from the beginning; which I saw, and created me thoughts of heart. There was hardly a step of the management of the pea, wherein there was not an error committed, afterward discerned by the effects. This not being fairly acknowledged, and duly regretted, while my leg appeared to be in danger, ruffled my spirit; but it was calmed, ere Providence set on the way of help by a surgeon; who, when he came, discovered one false step more, viz. that the pea had been put in the belly of the muscle, not between two muscles.

About that time I observed, on a particular emergent, what I had often observed before, the necessity and advantage of a principle of justice and reason, and acting therein, in cases where softer principles have no ground left them to stand on.

Meanwhile the catechising of the parish was interrupted; and I sat in the pulpit when I preached. But my soul rejoiced to observe, how my gracious God and Master still timed the hardest of my trouble, so as it had been designed, that it should be over before the Sabbath should return. But with this trouble of my leg there was joined sore eyes, occasioned by my sitting in the bed writing, in the sun-light, on the Tuesday before the surgeon came; so that, for some nights, leg and eyes were to be buckled up with their respective applications at once; and one night a dint of the toothache joined them. The callous substance was got away by degrees; and on Nov. 7, at night, what day I had intimated from the pulpit a diet of catechising again, the sore appeared closed.

That week the transcribing what I had written on Gen. xxiii. being ended; that I might afterward proceed as I should have access, I set myself to fill up the passages and account of my life from where I had left off, Jan. 9. While I was going on in that, there came to my hand on Saturday, Nov. 13, a letter from Mr. Hogg,

bearing, his writing once more to Mr. G. and intreating his friends
at London to get the MS. on the covenant from him; and proposing
to me to review the notes on the "Crook in the Lot," for publication,* and advising of a motion to call me to Jedburgh, which he
had heard; and withal obscurely hinting something of carrying me
to a more healthy air, out of Etterick. As for the proposal of new
work for me, I found myself content to be employed whatever way
the Lord himself should point out. As to that relating to Jedburgh,
I neither hoped nor feared it, considering my circumstances. But
the last did touch me very near, being ignorant of the particular,
or what might be of it; I considered how matters were, in all outward appearance, making towards my transportation to the grave;
and having a terror of making a stumble near the end of my journey, I cried from the bottom of my heart, "Wilt not thou who hast
saved me from death, keep my feet from falling?" I could not but
observe the mercy, that I was not quite forgotten and overlooked
in the world; but I found the weight of the thought of parting with
the parish of Etterick, otherways than by death, or civil violence,
unless I saw them comfortably provided.

I observed the diet of catechising aforesaid; but the day was so
very bad that few came to it, being at Kirkhope. The week following I had another at Buccleugh. Considering my frailty, the
season, and how Providence had, by the above-mentioned trial, carried me by the time I thought fittest for the utmost corners of the
parish, I laid the matter before the Lord. And rising early in the
morning, I got a good seasonable day, visited a sick man by the way,
had a full allowance of strength for my work of catechising, without
failing of my spirits, and got home again with day-light. This merciful conduct of Providence was big in my eyes.

That week I finished filling up thus far; my eyes being now somewhat better, and the sore in the leg almost whole; but the knee
always swelled, and the leg swelling somewhat in the day, and falling again in the night, the lameness continuing, and the staff still
needed, and used. On the foregoing Sabbath I stood lecturing;
but delivered the sermon sitting. But from the time I fell under
the sore leg, I was freed from an oppression of my spirits in the
morning, as to such a degree thereof as I laboured under before
that time. "He doth all things well."

---

* Mr. Boston in compliance with this proposal, did, some time before his death, begin to transcribe, and prepare for the press, his sermons on this subject; but was prevented by his growing frailty from finishing the transcript. What remained, was
transcribed from the original MS. by another hand; and they were published in 1737,
with an excellent preface by his dear friends, Messrs. Colden, Wilson, and Davidson.

[Thus far the author proceeded in his narrative in November, 1731, without resuming the subject; owing, no doubt, to his growing frailty. We now for a conclusion, add the several paragraphs formerly omitted, and reserved till now.]

And now, as for the state of my body, it was never very strong; yet, considering my manner of life, there seems to have been something in my constitution, *bona stamina vitæ*, that has worn pretty well. A sharp cold, if withal I was dry, was agreeable to me, making me more vigorous than at other times. I had a very strong voice, till the notable breach in my health. I cannot say that ever I took very well with riding; but I could have supped better, after sitting all day in my closet, than after coming home from the presbytery at Selkirk. I remember not to have had, all my life, any formed sickness but twice; once when I had the small pox; and none at all since I was a boy. However, I have often been, since that time, in apparent danger of death, and under languishing indisposition; and could hardly have thought to have seen so many years, as I have now by the mercy of God passed; but was never to this day, that I remember, kept from preaching through indisposition; which, with my utmost thankfulness, I desire to record, to the praise of free grace. I took very little care of my diet, ate whatsoever was laid to my hand; only for many years very little salmon, being frighted from it by the effects it had on me in my youth, having unwarily mixed milk with it in my stomach; and this, as to my diet, till of late years, that I began notably to decline. I do not remember myself ever to have been sensibly the better of medicine, except the wormwood, aforementioned. I have now much given over the use of it; and do not bind up myself so strait, even in point of diet, as for some time after the notable breach in my health. My eyes do yet serve me pretty well; only I have, about a year or two, read my chapters in the morning with preserves; for many years I have used to wash my eyes, opening them in the water, which I conceive may have been profitable. But it is now long since I had teeth, wherewith duly to get my meat chewed; and there are at this time fifteen of them, and a piece of one, laid up in a box, for conservation till the due time of disposing of them otherwise. Many years ago, I found the spring-season weakening to me, even when I was in Simprin.

But the last spring [1730] was the heaviest that ever I saw. As the summer went on, I became more easy; but still a lowness of spirits seized me, and I ran out like a watch, after six o'clock at night whereby it came to pass, that I had much ado, oft-times, to be in case for the evening worship in the family. Since the autumnal equinox, [1730], I think I have been better, even in that point. I had also a great difficulty in passing urine; but that also of late seemed to become more easy. I have slept well since the time I fell ill in March last [1730]. In October I was brought to the gates of death, in Galashiels, by a sudden illness seizing me there in the night, as narrated above. At present, I am, by the mercy of God, pretty well; having some hope, I may yet, through his favour, have some access to return to my beloved study of the sacred Hebrew text.

That cast of temper, whereby I was naturally slow, timorous, and diffident, but eager in pursuit when once engaged; as it early discovered itself, so, I think, it hath spread itself along, through the whole of my course. It hath been a spring of much uneasiness to me, in the course of my life; in that I was thereby naturally fond, where I loved. Yet I cannot but observe, that my God hath made a valuable use of it; especially in my studies, combating special difficulties therein, till surmounted by his favour. Agreeable unto it, I was not of a quick apprehension; but had a gift of application; and things being once discovered, I was no more wavering in them. I was addicted to silence, rather than to talking. I was no good spokesman, but very unready even in common conversation; and in disputes especially at a loss, when engaged with persons of great assurance; the disadvantage of which last I often found in Etterick, where an uncommon assurance reigned. The touching of my spirit, so as to set me above fear, the moving of my affections, and being once well dipped into the matter, were necessary to give me an easy exercise of my faculties, in these and other extempore performances. My talent lay in doing things by a close application, with pains and labour. I had a tolerable faculty at drawing of papers; yet no faculty at dictating, but behoved to have the pen in my own hand; and even in that case it would often have been a while ere I could enter on. Accordingly, as for my sermons, it was often hard for me to fix on a text; the which hath ofttimes been more wasting and weakening to me, than the study of my sermon thereon. I studied my sermons with the pen in my hand, my matter coming to me as I wrote, and the bread increasing in the breaking of it; if at any time I walked, it was occasioned by my sticking. Meanwhile, it would frequently have been long ere I got the vein of my subject struck; but then I could not be easy, unless I thought I had hit it. Thence it was, I often tore out what I had written, and began anew again; but ordinarily I found, this turned to my greatest comfort and satisfaction, in the end falling upon the vein. Hence it was not my manner, to shift from text to text; but to insist long on an ordinary; the closing of which at length I readily found to relish as much, with myself, and the serious godly, as the other parts preceding.

Thus also I was much addicted to peace, and averse to controversy; though once engaged therein, I was set to go through with it. I had no great difficulty to retain a due honour and charity for my brethren differing from me in opinion and practice; but then I was in no great hazard neither, of being swayed by them, to depart from what I judged truth or duty. Withal it was easy to me, to yield to them in things wherein I found not myself in conscience bound up. Whatever precipitant steps I have made in the course of my life, which I desire to be humbled for, rashness in conduct was not my weak side. But since the Lord, by his grace, brought me to consider things, it was much my exercise to discern sin and duty in particular cases; being afraid to venture on things, until I should see myself called thereto; but when the matter was cleared to me, I generally stuck fast by it, being as much afraid to desert the way which I took to be pointed out to me. And this I sincerely judge to have been the spring of that course of conduct upon which Mr. James Ramsay above mentioned did, before the commission *anno* 1717, in my hearing, give me the following character, viz. That if I thought myself right, there would be no diverting of me by any means.

I never had the art of making rich; nor could I ever heartily apply myself to the managing of secular affairs. Even the secular way of managing the discipline of the church, was so unacceptable to me, that I had no heart to dip in the public church management. What appearances I made at any time in these matters, were not readily in that way. I had a certain averseness to the being laid under any notable obligation to others, and so was not fond of gifts, especially in the case of any whom I had to deal with as a minister. And Providence so ordered, that I had little trial of that kind. I easily perceived, that in that case, " the borrower is servant to the lender."

As to the parish, there are few now alive that subscribed my call; nor are there, that I know, above two of the congregation of my hearers, paying rent this day, that were so doing, when I came among them, twenty-three years ago, [viz. from May 1, 1707, to Oct 24, 1730]. They are by far more polished in their manners, than at that time; and much more tractable, and easy to me; and fewer scandals fall out among them. The old dissenters continue immoveable; but their increasing is ceased. There is still a handful of serious Christians among them, as there hath been all along; and I have often observed, that as some such, from time to time, have been one way or other carried away, there came others in their stead; and whatever the Lord laid to my hand to preach on unto them, I used not to be straitened on their account; judging I would be understood, on any subject I was led to treat of. The late sickness is now, by the mercy of God, abated.

And thus have I given some account of the days of my vanity, being this 24th of October, 1730, 54 years, 7 months, and one week old.* Upon the whole, I bless my God in Jesus Christ, that ever he made me a Christian, and took an early dealing with my soul; that ever he made me a minister of the gospel, and gave me some insight into the doctrine of his grace; and that ever he gave me the blessed Bible, and brought me acquainted with the originals, and especially with the Hebrew text. The world hath all along been a stepdame to me; and wheresoever I would have attempted to nestle in it, there was a thorn of uneasiness laid for me. Man is born crying, lives complaining, and dies disappointed from that quarter. "All is vanity and vexation of spirit.—I have waited for thy salvation, O Lord."†

T. BOSTON.

POSTSCRIPT.

Thus far did the author bring down the history and account of his own life and times. His disorder (which was of the scorbutic kind) resisting the power of medicine, increased in its violence until May 20, 1732, when he entered into the joy of his Lord. His public services in the church of Christ, were not much interrupted by his indisposition; and when he was so dibilited by it as to be unable to

---

* The continuation of this account, before inserted, was written after this time, as has been already observed.

† From his Diary it will be seen, that he was a very hard student; a close and humble walker with God; a most accurate observer of providences; a careful keeper of his heart; a peaceable but faithful ruler of the church,—most careful in admitting persons to the seals of God's covenant. He allowed none to be baptized but visible believers and their infants. Nor of the admission of any to the Lord's table, but such whose knowledge and practice, in the judgment of charity, manifested their true faith in Christ, and obedience to him; and required, that all new communicants should be admitted by an examination of them before the session, and a solemn renewal of their baptismal engagements.

go out to the church, he preached from a window in the manse, the auditory standing without. His fortitude in the immediate prospect of dissolution never forsook him. His patience under the chastisement of a Father's hand was uninterrupted. Inured to afflictions, as well personal as domestic, he bore them with that quiet submission, and unreluctant resignation, which a filial spirit can only inspire. Viewing them as originating from his heavenly Father, the habitual language of his heart was, " Shall I receive all good at the hand of God, and shall I not receive evil."

It will be obvious to the intelligent reader, that the radical principle upon which the narrative in these memoirs is founded, is, " That God hath foreordained whatsoever comes to pass." This principle the author believed with his whole heart; it was often an anchor to his soul; and every minister of the Church of Scotland is bound, by his subscription, and ordination-vows to maintain it. This kept in view, will account for the author's ascribing to an over ruling providence many incidents, which some may think might be resolved into natural causes.

During his last illness he received the following affectionate and consolatory letter from his endeared friend, Mr. Gabriel Wilson.

" Rev. Dearest Brother,
         " It has been a most real pain to me, after I was fully purposed to be with you sometime this day, to think of sending any. But the ordering seems to be of the Lord. I design to assay it again without delay, according as I hear from you.

" I hear the trial is become still more fiery; but hope you will be kept from thinking it strange, as though some strange thing had happened you. O it is difficult; but you are allowed, and even called to rejoice, in as much as you are thus made a partaker of Christ's sufferings.

" The Lord has in great favour led you forth into his truth, and is now in his fatherly wisdom giving you use for it all; calling you to shew forth the supporting and comforting power of it. Our season (if need be) of being in heaviness through manifold temptations, is made up of hours and minutes, and will soon run out; 2 Cor. iv. 17, 18.

" The Son of God, your Lord and Master, is with you in the furnace, though not always visible, and will never leave you nor forsake you. May the God of hope, of patience, and consolation, the God and Father of our LORD JESUS CHRIST, the Father of mercies, and the God of all comfort, comfort you in all your tribulation with comforts of his covenant, and with the same comforts he has enabled you to comfort others in any trouble. You mind, Psalm xxxi. ult. that it is in the way of our labouring to be of good courage, that he promises to strengthen our hearts. I will yet still hope and seek, he may turn the shadow of death into morning, and spare to recover strength.

"Our session being met this day, in token of their love and sympathy, have sent the bearer, one of their number, to visit you, and bring them word.—Dearest brother, I desire to remember your bonds, as bound with you. Great grace be upon you. I am, with love to all yours, Dearest Sir, yours,

GAB. WILSON."

Maxton, April 8, 1732.

A few weeks before his death, he likewise wrote the following letter to a correspondent in Edinburgh; which, as it terminated a correspondence of twelve years' standing, and is perhaps the last letter the author ever wrote, we shall conclude this postscript with a copy of it.

"My very dear Sir,

"I am obliged downright to acquaint you, that I have been of a considerable time, and am still, in an apparently dying condition. All business is quite given over; and I can no more, as matters stand, correspond with any about the MSS. or any thing else, but must leave them to the Lord, and the management of my friends, as he shall direct them. I do not doubt but your God, who has seen meet to row you into deep waters, will in due time bring you out; but there is need of patience.

"I cannot insist.—The eternal God be your refuge, and underneath the everlasting arms, and plentifully reward your twelve years' most substantial friendship.—I am, very dear Sir, yours, most affectionately, &c.

SKETCH OF THE AUTHOR'S CHARACTER.

MR. Boston's character is drawn by three of his most intimate friends,* in the following words :—

"He was of a stature above the middle size ; of a venerable, amiable aspect; of a strong and fruitful genius ; of a lively imagination, such as affords what is called a ready wit, which instead of

* Messrs. Calder, Wilson, and Davidson.

cultivating, he laid under a severe restraint; of tender affections; a clear and solid judgment; his temper candid, modest, cautious, benevolent, obliging and courteous; had a natural aversion to any thing rude or uncivil in words or behaviour, and a delicate feeling, in case of meeting with ought of that sort; could be heavy and severe in his words, when there was just occasion, or he judged the same necessary. He was early called by divine grace; all along afterwards, exercised unto godliness; walked indeed with God, in all his ways daily acknowledging him, frequent in solemn, extraordinary applications to Heaven, (viz. upon every new emergent of duty, difficulty or trial), followed with evident, comfortable, and confirming testimonies of divine acceptance and audience; a judicious observer, recorder, and improver of the dispensations of divine providence, in connection with the Word, his own frame and walk, and consequently of great experience in religion. He was accurately and extensively regardful of the divine law, in all manner of life and conversation, (even in things that escape the notice of the most part of Christians); of a tender conscience, carefully watching against, and avoiding the appearance of evil; compassionate, and sympathising with the distressed; charitable to the needy; a dutiful husband; an indulgent father; a sincere, a faithful, and an affectionate friend; to which he had a particular cast in his temper, which proved a rich blessing to those who were favoured with his friendship. He was a considerable scholar in all the parts of theological learning, and excelled in some of them. What he was for a humanist, (even towards the latter end of his days), his translation of his own work on the Hebrew accentuation, into good Roman Latin, will abundantly testify. Was well seen in the Greek; and for the skill he attained in the Hebrew, he will, we are satisfied, in ages to come, be admired, and had in honour by the learned world; especially when it is understood, under what disadvantages, in what obscurity and seclusion from learned assistances the work was composed; and when it is considered, how far, notwithstanding, he has outstripped all that went before him, in that study, viz. of the Hebrew accentuation. He understood the French, and for the sake of comparing translations, could read the Dutch Bible. There were few pieces of learning, that he had not some good taste of. But all his knowledge behoved to be otherwise discovered, than by professing of it. He was a hard student, of indefatigable application, so that whatever he was once heartily engaged in, he knew not to quit, till by help from heaven, and incessant labour, he got through it. Had a great knowledge and understanding of human nature, of the most proper methods of addressing it, and the most likely handles for

catching hold of it. He had an admirable talent at drawing a paper, which made a statesman,* a very able judge say, (when Mr.
Boston was clerk of the synod of Merse and Teviotdale), that he was
the best clerk he had ever known, in any court civil or ecclesiatical.
An admirer of other men's gifts and parts, liberally giving them
their due praise, even though in some things they differed from him ;
far from censorious, assuming or detracting.

As a minister, he had on his spirit a deep and high sense of divine things ; was mighty in the scriptures, in his acquaintance with
the letter, with the spirit and sense of them, in happily applying
and accommodating them, for explaining and illustrating the subject. His knowledge and insight in the mystery of Christ was
great ; though a humbling sense of his want of it, was like to have
quite sunk and laid him by, after he began to preach. He had a
peculiar talent for going deep into the mysteries of the gospel, and
at the same time for making them plain ; making intelligible their
connection with, and influence upon gospel holiness ; notable instances of which may be seen in his most valuable " Treatise of the
Covenant," and in his " Sermons of Christ in the form of a Servant."
His invention was rich, but judiciously bounded ; his thoughts were
always just, and often new ; his expressions proper and pure, his
illustrations and similies often surprising ; his method natural and
clear ; his delivery grave and graceful, with an air of earnestness,
meekness, assurance, and authority, tempered together. No wonder
his ministrations in holy things, were all of them dear and precious
to the saints. He was fixed and established upon solid and rational
grounds, in the reformation principles, in opposition to popery, prelacy, superstition, and persecution ; was pleasant and lively in conversation, but always with a decorum to his character ; quite free of
that sourness of temper or ascetical rigidity, that generally pos-
seses men of a retired life. He fed and watched with diligence, the
flock over which the Holy Ghost made him overseer ; and notwithstanding his eager pursuit of that study which was his delight, he
abated nothing of his preparation for the Sabbath, nor his work
abroad in the parish : nor did he so much as use the short hand,
whereof he was master, but always wrote out his sermons fair, and
generally as full as he preached them ; far from serving the Lord
with that which cost him nothing, it was his delight to spend, and
be spent in the service of the gospel ; was a faithful, and at the
same time, a prudent reprover of sin ; was endued with a rich measure of Christian wisdom and prudence, without craft or guile, where-

* Mr. Baillie, of Jerviswood.

by he was exceedingly serviceable in judicatories, and excellent
fitted for counsel in intricate cases; zeal and knowledge were in him
united, to a pitch rarely to be met with. Had a joint concern for
purity and peace in the church; no man more zealous for the former
and at the same time more studious of the latter; having observed
and felt so much of the mischief of division and separation, was exceedingly cautious and scrupulous of any thing new or unprecedented, until he was thoroughly satisfied of its necessity and ground. It
was his settled mind, that solidly and strongly to establish the
truth, was in many cases, the best, the shortest, and most effectual
way to confute error, without irritating and inflaming the passions
of men, to their own, and to the truth's prejudice; on all which
accounts, he was much respected and regarded, by not only his brethren that differed from him, but generally by all sorts of men. To
conclude, he was a scribe singularly instructed into the kingdom.—
Happy in finding out acceptable words, a workman that needed not
to be ashamed, rightly dividing the word of truth, a burning and a
shining light. The righteous shall be had in everlasting remembrance." His friends add; "Though a skilful hand might, in fewer
words, have drawn his character, to much better purpose, there is
no partiality, by overdoing in what is said, if intimate friendship for
many years, and the account of his own life done by himself, are
allowed for competent evidence."

The late worthy Rev. Thomas Davidson, late minister of Burntee,
adds:

"The acquaintance I had with him, and the frequent opportunities I had of hearing him preach, I look upon as one of the
greatest privileges wherewith I was favoured in my early days, and
which I still reflect on with great pleasure. He was indeed one of
the most powerful preachers I ever heard open a mouth. It is true,
he was no Boanerges, as to his voice, his delivery being grave and
deliberate, yet there was a majestic energy in it which, together
with his venerable and comely aspect, made no small impression to
his advantage, on the minds of those who had the pleasure of hearing him. There were but few men, (if any), in his day, who courted
popularity less than he did; nay, he rather shunned it; but, like
his shadow, it followed him wherever he went; for his ministrations
were savoury and acceptable to all who had a relish for the truth as
it is in Jesus, and a love to that holiness of heart and life, which
the belief of it never fails to influence in the minds of all the chidren
of God. He had a talent peculiar to himself in pointing out the
propriety of the proofs of the doctrines he was handling. His more
than ordinary critical knowledge of the original languages in which

the scriptures were written, enabled him in a brief but comprehen-
sive way, to glance at the meaning of the Spirit of God in them,
that was both surprising and edifying to the hearers; these enlargements were not written, but left to the time of delivery."

COPY OF HIS PERSONAL COVENANT.

O LORD, the God and Father of our Lord Jesus Christ, I confess
from my heart, that I am by nature a lost and undone sinner, wholly
corrupted, and laid under the curse, in Adam, through the breach
of the covenant of works; and have ruined myself more and more
by my innumerable actual transgressions, whereby my whole life
appears in mine eyes this day a heap of vanity, sin, and foolishness.
I am fully convinced, and do from my heart acknowledge, that I am
utterly unable to help myself, in whole or in part, out of this gulf of
sin and misery, into which I am plunged; and that it is beyond the
reach of the whole creation to help me out of it; so that I must in-
evitably perish for ever, if thine own strong hand do not make help
to me. But forasmuch as there is a covenant of grace, for life and
salvation to lost sinners, established between THEE and thine own
SON, the Lord Jesus Christ, as second Adam; wherein, upon condition of his fulfilling all righteousness, which is now performed, in
his having been born perfectly holy, lived altogether righteously, and
made perfect satisfaction to justice by his death and sufferings,
thou hast promised that thou wilt be their God, and they shall be
thy people, to the making of them holy and happy for ever; and
that this covenant is, in Christ the head thereof, offered and exhibited to me in thy gospel, and thou callest me into the fellowship thereof, in him; therefore, (adhering to my former acceptings and taking
hold of it, declared whether by word or writ before thee, without
wilful mistaking of it, or known guile), upon the warrant of, and in
obedience to, thy command and call, I in myself a poor perishing
sinner, and worthy to perish, do now again TAKE HOLD of that co-
VENANT, for life and salvation to ME; believing on the name of
Christ crucified, the head thereof, offered and exhibited to me, as
the great High Priest, who, by the sacrifice of himself, hath made
atonement, paid the ransom, and brought in everlasting righteousness for poor sinners. I CREDIT his word of grace to me, and accordingly TRUST on him, that he with his righteousness will be mine,
and that, in and through him, God will be my God, and I shall be
one of his people, to the making of me holy and happy for ever. O
my God, I do by thy grace acquiesce in that covenant, as all my sal-

vation, and all my desire, with my whole heart and soul. The SON incarnate is my only PRIEST, my surety, my intercessor, and my Redeemer; and, in him, the FATHER my FATHER; the HOLY GHOST my SANCTIFIER; GOD in CHRIST my GOD. I resign myself, soul and body, to him, to be saved by his blood alone; renouncing all confidence in mine own righteousness, doings, and sufferings. With my whole heart and soul, he is my HEAD and HUSBAND; and I am his only, wholly, and for ever; to live by him, to him, and for him. I take him for my alone PROPHET, Oracle, and Guide; give up myself wholly to him, to be taught, guided, and directed, in all things, by his word and Spirit; and renounce mine own wisdom, and the wisdom of this world. He is, with my heart's consent, my alone KING and LORD. And I resign myself wholly, soul and body, unto him, to be rescued, by the strength of his mighty hand, from sin, death, the devil, and this present evil world, for to serve him for ever, and to be ruled by the will of his command, as to my duty, and the will of his providence as to my lot. I am with my whole heart content (Lord, thou knowest) to part with, and do renounce every known sin, lust, or idol, and particularly that sin which most easily besets me; together with my own foolish will, and all other lords besides him; without reservation, and without exception againt his cross. *Protesting* in thy sight, O Lord, that I am, through grace, willing to have discovered unto me, and upon discovery to part with, every sin in me that I know not; and that the doubtings and averseness of heart, mixed with this my accepting of thy covenant, are what I allow not; and that notwithstanding thereof, I look to be accepted of thee herein, in the Beloved thine only Son and my Saviour, purging away these, with all my other sins, by his precious blood. Let it be recorded in heaven, O Lord, and let the bed on which I leaned, the timber, and the stones, and all other things about me here, in my closet, bear witness, that I, though most unworthy, have this second day of December, One thousand seven hundred and twenty-nine years, here taken hold of, and come into thy covenant of grace, offered and exhibited to me in thy gospel, for time and eternity; and that thou art my God in the tenor of that covenant, and I am one of thy people, from henceforth and for ever.

T. BOSTON.

SUBSTANCE OF THE GOSPEL TRUTHS, FOR WHICH MR. BOSTON MADE HIS NOBLE STAND, IN THE CASE OF THE MARROW OF MODERN DIVINITY.

1. IT is the duty of all that hear the gospel, upon the revelation of Christ therein, without looking for any previous qualification in

themselves, instantly to believe in him for salvation, both from sin and wrath, that only by so doing, will persons be enabled in a gospel manner to forsake sin—that it is inconsistent with the method of gospel grace, and absolutely impossible, for a man to forsake his sins, in a way of gospel repentance, (which kind of forsaking only can please God), till the Spirit determine him to come to Christ as a Prince and Saviour exalted to give repentance and remission of sins.

2. That though there is no universal atonement, yet in the word there is a warrant given to offer Christ to all mankind, whether elect or reprobate, and a warrant to all freely to receive him, however great sinners they are, or have been.

3. That in justifying faith, there is a real persuasion in the heart of the sinner, that Christ is his; and that he shall have life and salvation by him, and that whatever Christ did for the redemption of mankind, he did it for him in particular; which persuasion is founded (not upon the uptaking of one's real regeneration, as the reflex assurance is, but) upon the promise of Christ in the gospel, made to sinners of Adam's family as such; and so there is resting upon him alone, for the whole of salvation.

4. That the gospel strictly taken, is only a declaration and promise, containing glad tidings of a Saviour, and all grace, mercy and salvation in him to sinners—that all precepts, particularly those enjoining faith and repentance, belong to the law—that as believers, holiness has no causual influence upon his everlasting happiness as a federal and conditional means thereof; but the perfect righteousness of Christ as a surety, is the believer's plea both with respect to law and justice, and that whether as to the purchase, or actual obtaining the possession of everlasting happiness.

5. That believers being heirs of heaven, though they ought to be powerfully minded to obedience to the law as a rule, by a view of the excellency of their inheritance of God in Christ, by their having the begun possession of this inheritance, and by the sure hope of the perfect possession thereof, being secured by free grace, through the blood of Christ; yet they ought not be influenced to obedience, by hopes of obtaining the possession of that inheritance, by any good works done by them; and that though believers are to entertain an holy dread of the majesty of God, and his power to cast into hell, and of the awfulness of his threatenings and judgments against sin and sinners, and to consider from these, the due desert of their sins; and though they ought to be influenced by the feeling or fear of afflictions in this life, temporal and spiritual, considered as the discipline of the covenant, sent by a kind Father on a kind design, to the study of habitual improvement of the blood and Spirit of Christ, for

the mortifying of remaining corruption, and exercising gospel holiness; yet they ought not to be excited to obedience by any fear, that God shall for their sins actually cast them into hell; but ought always to believe their full security against falling into the pit, in order to influence them to a more cheerful obedience.

6. That believers are, through Christ, altogether delivered from the law as a covenant of works; the asserting of which, doth no way infer their being loosed from the law as a rule of life; and that though all unbelievers are under the law as a covenant of works, yet it doth not follow that they are obliged to seek justification by their own righteousness; nay, all of them are obliged to seek justification by the blood of Christ alone, without the works of the law.

7. That there is a wide difference between the law as a rule of life, and as a covenant of works—that believers are not under the law as a covenant of works, but are under it, as it is the law of Christ, or a rule in the hand of a Mediator; that therefore a believer cannot sin against the law as a covenant of works, but only against it as a rule of life—that God cannot see sin in a believer, as committed against the law as a covenant, but only as committed against the law as a rule of life; that therefore God can have no vindictive or legal anger at them for their sins, but only a fatherly anger and displeasure; that therefore, believers ought not to mourn over, or confess their iniquities, in a legal manner, viewing them as committed by persons under the covenant of works; but ought to confess and mourn over them, as sins done against a reconciled father, and breaches of his law as a rule of life.

8. That the grace of the gospel is so far from loosing men from the obligation of the law as a rule of life, that it superadds more weighty and powerful incitements to obedience, than any thing which the law itself can afford.

APPENDIX.

No. I.

THE situation of the people of Etterick at this time, with regard to their entertainment of the gospel, their divisive temper, and the author's vexation and disquiet thereby occasioned, may be learned from the following extracts of sermons preached this year, 1710.

On the 25th of June he had begun an ordinary preparatory to the sacrament, viz. Jer. l. 4, 5. On the fast day, July 13, he preached from that clause, " Going and weeping." The doctrine observed from which was, " that the frame and exercise suitable to a covenanting time is " going and weeping." Having shewed that such a time should be a going time; he proceeded also to shew, that it should be a weeping-time. Here he exhorted the people to drop a tear for the case of the land, branching it out into several particulars of great importance, which want of room obliges us to omit. He then added as follows :—

" Go, weeping over the case of the congregation. Weep over,

1. Our barrenness under the means of grace. Ah! how many sermons are lost, for any benefit the most part get of them ! Generally, he that was filthy is filthy still. It is an observation of some on Luke xiii. 7, that if a minister do any good in a place, it is ordinarily in the first three years of his ministry. God forbid it hold true in our case! If the gospel meet with no better entertainment after, than for these three years past, it would be telling many of you, that ye had never seen my face, nor I yours. I had some experience that way elsewhere, and it was not so in my case.

2. The slight and contempt of gospel ordinances among us. Our parish is not great, but our congregation is less by reason of the principles, passions, and prejudices, of not a few. But yet smallest of all is the company of ordinary hearers; when those are taken off that come once in twenty days, a month or six weeks; who are taken up with their beasts all the summer in the fields, and sleep at home with them all the winter; yet some whose faces I seldom or never discern, but when I surprise them at their houses, though I tell publicly in the congregation that I am to be that way. Weep over the slighting of the preaching of the word among us. Some that have not far to come, will loiter away Lord's days at home; though if they would come little further than half-way from their own houses, they might possibly sometimes hear the sound of my voice. When I come into the church, and the worship is begun, I will see some of you sitting or standing in the church-yard in pairs, as close at your discourse, that sometimes I think we would not have seen your faces that day, if you had

not had business with some body ye would see at the church; in which I am the more confirmed, when I will see they have staid all the time between sermons, and when the congregation is assembling again, they will go away home.   Some will spend a good part of sermons about the dykes; ay and go out of the church in the very time thereof, and lie about the dykes and crack. I cannot get you pleased with short enough preaching; though some of you make it short enough, what with your sleeping, what with your leaving it, even when there is no milking; and some will sit at the door all the afternoon, that they may get away when they think they have got enough of it.

3. Weep over the slighting of sacraments.   That of baptism is dolefully slighted.   If the child be like to die, then, without any regard to the congregation, or the strugglings of this church against private baptism, the minister must come and give the child a name, without any more.   But if not, Sabbath shall go over after Sabbath, one opportunity after another: and they never trouble themselves about the baptising of their children, even when neither weakness nor the weather hinders.   As to the sacrament of the supper, go weeping, Sirs, that there are so few in this congregation to go with you.   They need Christ as well as you; the blood they slight, is the blood they must be saved by, if ever; the covenant they prepare not to seal, is that they must enter into, if they would enter into heaven.   It is long since Christ made such a visit to Etterick.   O weep that they are so few to receive him, so few fit to be admitted, and so few going out to meet the bridegroom.   This slighting of ordinances, as it is something more than ordinary, is a very sad sign.

4. Weep over the loose lives of many of us; the abounding sin of swearing, that devil-like sin, by which there is neither profit nor pleasure; lying and backbiting, supplanting of one another, the lack of common honesty in many, to the disgrace of the society they live in, and the reproach of those that entertain them; the brutish ignorance of many, even of those who pretend to be high-flown professors; the contentious spirit of those who live like fire-brands in the place.   Let none such presume to approach the Lord's table in that their wickedness.

5. Weep over the woful divisions among us, that have prevailed to the breaking of us so far, that we are among the most broken and shattered congregations in the country.   Weep over that rent that was so early made amongst us, in which Satan hotly pursued me, ere I knew well where I was. Ye are but too little affected with it.   It has been an engine of Satan against the kingdom of Christ in people's hearts, under a pretence of zeal for his kingdom in the land; and a notable hinderance of the success of the gospel among us.   For, 1. Some are thereby turned aside from the ordinary means of grace and knowledge, that know not the right hand by the left in religion, being specially ignorant of God in Christ. 2. Many that remain are thereby made to hear with prejudices; and are so fickle and loosed at the root, that they cannot take on growth by the preached word.   And I know not what influence it may have on the slighting of the ordinance before us; I am apprehensive that it has had some influence.   If it have, I

desire to lament the case of such ; and for the confirmation of you that are
to join, I promise you, in my Maker's name, that if you honestly consent
to the marriage-covenant, and come with longing desires after him, he will
not refuse to keep communion with you, Rev. iii. 20. Your own defections
lie nearer you than the defections of the land do ; but if ye be mourning
over them, they shall not mar your communion with him. I think they may
look with bashful faces before the Lord, that are so scared at their mother's
deformities, that they will not come into her house, when yet her Husband
is there feeding his children whom she has brought forth to him.

6. *Lastly*, Forget not when ye are going, to weep over the frequent sin
of uncleanness that has fallen out among us within these few years. If
ever the devil raged in a parish at the coming of the gospel among them,
he has done it here one way and another. What with fornications, what
with adulteries, the place of repentance has been seldom empty since the
planting of this parish. I may say to you as the apostle said to the church
at Corinth, " I speak not this to shame you." But well may I say with
him, I have reason to bewail those who have sinned already, and have not
repented of the uncleanness, and fornication, and lasciviousness which they
have committed, 2 Cor. xii. 21, seeing we so much resemble that church
in her three grand evils, self-conceit, a divisive temper, and sins of uncleanness."

The author had also, in a sermon from 2 Cor. vi. 1, preached at Etterick,
on the national fast day, March 29, in the same year, 1710, censured with
some freedom the people's itch for public things, their contempt of the gospel, their unsettled and giddy humour, &c. This sermon is printed in the
" Body of Divinity," and deserves a serious perusal.

Notwithstanding these repeated warnings, many of the people were so
giddy and inconstant, that, Sept. 3, the very Lord's day that the author
began his ordinary on Mark x. 21, 22, they deserted his ministry, and went
off to hear Mr. Macmillan preaching, in the neighbourhood ; which gave
occasion to the following reflection and awful rebuke, publicly given from
the pupit on the 10th.

" An unstable mind and judgment is very prejudicial. No wonder the
tree withers that is never fast at the root, Eph. iv. 14. This was the one
thing that ruined the Galatians ; for though they had received the Spirit
by the hearing of faith, yet when Satan broke in on them with that, they
quickly lost all the savoury impressions they had of the hearing of faith.
The wavering temper among us, I am confident, is no small hinderance in
the way of the success of the gospel. And as I bless God for what stability
any of you have attained to, so as for you that deserted the message I had
from the Lord to you this day eight days, whether there were many of you
or few, and joined yourselves to those whose work it is to break down what
we build up, and that after that solemn reproof of and lamentation over
that practice, and of other heart-breaking pieces of your contempt of the
gospel, which was given on the fast day, and after what ye heard and saw
on the sacrament day, I do, as the messenger of the Lord, in his name,
rebuke you here as obstinate contemners of the message sent by God unto

you, and protest, as the messenger of God to you, that this rebuke stand before the Lord that sent me, till it be wiped out by repentance, and fleeing to the blood of Christ for pardon ; and so I leave it before him, who confirms the word of his servants."

No. II.

This doctrine reproves those who at this time are secure, careless, and unconcerned spectators of the present confusions, which is the prevailing plague among us at this day. Ah ! Sirs, " Shall a trumpet be blown in the day, and the people not be afraid ?" Amos iii. 6. Yes, we see there are such people. " The lion hath roared, who will not fear ? the Lord God hath spoken, who can but prophesy?" ver. 8. Why, some will sleep full sound amidst all the roarings of the Lord in his anger this day. Ah ! Sirs, our sleeping so sound in the ship of his church and nation, while the storm is blowing, and the waves are like to sink it, if there were no more, is enough to prove the deep hand we have, like another Jonah, in raising the storm.

I know some still say, to cloak their loathsome indifferency, that it is not religion, but crowns and kingdoms they are fighting for. If it were so, is there not a right and a wrong even in that ? and why do not ye take part with the right, according to the fifth commandment ? Is not even that enough to make the land a field of blood ? and may not yours go among the rest ? But pray you, Sirs, is religion nowise concerned, whether a Protestant king or a Papist be on the throne ? whether an army of malignants, avowed enemies to the Church of Scotland, carry the day, or an army employed to break them ? Do the rebels so much as pretend any favour to this church ? Are congregations laid desolate, mass said, and the English service set up, where they come, and yet religion not concerned in the matter ? It were telling religion that such people pretended not to it, for the way of God is ill spoken of through their unreasonableness. If ye believe what ye say, I think ye lie pretty fair for embracing Popery if it were come, seeing ye can already believe things over the belly of sense and reason.

I tell you, that your security and unconcernedness at this time is more dangerous than ye are aware of; Psalm xxviii. 5, " Because they regard not the works of the Lord, nor the operation of his hands, he shall destroy them, and not build them up." They do not lie most safe that lie most secure, when the cause of God is at stake. I mind what word Mordecai sent to Esther, chap. iv. 14, " If thou altogether holdest thy peace at this time, then shall their enlargement and deliverance arise to the Jews from another quarter : but thou and thy father's house shall be destroyed." I remember that he was burnt in his own house, that said he could not burn for Christ ; Matth. xvi. 25, " For whosoever will save his life, shall lose it : and whosoever will lose his life for my sake, shall find it." We have made ourselves singular in our backwardness and unconcernedness in the cause of God at this time, beyond all our neighbours ; take heed God make not our stroke as remarkable, as our backwardness and unconcernedness has been, ere all be done.

No. III.

As these overtures, " of admission to the Lord's table, and debarring from it," are excellent in themselves, were crowned with success in the author's own practice, and seem to be peculiarly seasonable at this day, it has been judged proper to give the following exact copy of them, taken from the author's original:—

" 1. Admission to the Lord's table, and debarring from it, being acts of church discipline and government in a particular congregation, belong to the session of the congregation, and are not to be exercised by any minister or elder by themselves, nor any society of ministers and elders in an extra-judicial capacity.

2. Besides the ordinary examination in parishes, it is meet there be diets of examination particularly for non-communicants, and specially for those of the younger sort. And for this end, that once every year at least, especially before the celebration of the Lord's supper in the congregation, ministers, from the pulpit, exhort and stir up non-conformists to serious godliness, and the use of the means of knowledge : and intimate to all such as desire to be prepared to partake of that ordinance, that they give in their names to him, and wait on the diets of catechising to be appointed for such.

3. The names of such as offer themselves to be instructed, in order to their being admitted to the Lord's table, are to be kept in a roll separate from that of the whole congregation, and to be brought into the session, and read before them ; that it may be recommended to all the brethren, to have a particular eye on the enrolled, each especially on those of his own district : to excite, admonish, and exhort them, to a walk becoming the gospel, and the high privilege they are aspiring to.

4. When a non-communicant removes out of one parish into another, it were fit that he produce sufficient testimonials from the place of his former abode, before he be inrolled amongst those who have offered themselves to be instructed as above said, in the congregation to which he comes.

5. When one desires to be admitted to the Lord's table, he is in due time to intimate his desire to the session, that they may maturely consider of it. But it were fit, that the party should in the first place acquaint the minister with his purpose ; who, if he finds he has not made a competent proficiency by the pains taken on him, in the examinations of non-communicants, or otherwise, may advise him yet to forbear for a time.

6. The session entering on this affair, a strict inquiry is to be made among the members, particularly at the elder or elders of the district which the party belongs to, concerning his life and conversation ; whether he be guilty of any scandal ; owns, submits to, and ordinarily attends, the ordinances of Christ, the public and private worship of God ; if he be of a pious and sober deportment, and reputed to be a worshipper of God in secret ; and if he be the head of a family, whether he worships God in his family.

7. If nothing be found on that part to hinder his admission to the Lord's table, the session convening on a set day, in the place of public worship, and the doors being open, that all the communicants, and those who have

offered themselves to be instructed as above said, may have access, if they please ; he is, in the face of session; to give proof of his knowledge of the principles of the Christian religion, and particularly of the nature, use, and ends, of the ordinance of the supper, by making a confession of his faith, either in the way of a continued discourse, or by answering questions thereupon proposed by the minister.

8. And here special consideration is to be had of some who are known to be serious, and willing to learn, yet are weak ; namely, that the questions be proposed to them, so as they may be answered by Yes, or No ; or that the truth and error be both laid before them, and they asked, which of them they believe.

9. The trial being ended, the session is to judge, whether the party be endowed with competent knowledge of the principles of the Christian religion or not.

10. And if they be satisfied in this also, the party is to be put explicitly to consent to the covenant, (whereof he desires the seal), to be the Lord's, live unto him, and serve him all the days of his life, by answering expressly the following (or the like) questions. 1. Do you believe the doctrine of the Shorter Catechism of this church, so far as you understand the same, to be the true doctrine agreeable to the holy scriptures and resolve through grace, to live and die in the profession of the same? 2. Do you consent to take God in Christ to be your God, the Father to be your Father, the Son to be your Saviour, and the Holy Ghost to be your Sanctifier ; and that, renouncing the devil, the world, and the flesh, you be the Lord's for ever? 3. Do you consent to receive Christ as he is offered in the gospel, for your prophet, priest, and king ; giving up yourself to him, to be led and guided by his word and Spirit ; looking for salvation only through the obedience and death of Jesus Christ, who was crucified without the gates of Jerusalem ; promising, in his strength, to endeavour to lead a holy life, to forsake every known sin, and to comply with every known duty? 4. Lastly, Do you promise to subject yourself to exhortation, admonition, and rebuke, and the discipline of the church, in case (which God forbid) you fall into any scandalous sin?

11. The party having professed, consented, and promised, as above said, is to be admitted to the table of the Lord, by a sentence of the session which is to be recorded in their register, and an extract thereof allowed to be given him, when called for.

12. It were fit, that the names of all those who, from time to time, are admitted to the Lord's table, be inrolled in a bound book belonging to the session.

13. And how often soever that ordinance be administered in a congregation, the aforesaid roll of those who have at any time been admitted, is always to be read over distinctly, in presence of the session, some competent time before, and the members required to declare, if they know any thing against the life and conversation of any of them.

14. If any thing be objected, the session is to order private exhortation or admonition, or sist the accused before them, as they shall see ground,

and find the matter to require. And this is to be so managed, as that the accused be sisted, as aforesaid, on report concerning the private exhortation or admonition made, before the time of the administration of the sacrament. But those who have been once orderly admitted, are at no time after to be denied the privilege they were admitted to, except in the case of scandal; for which they are to be debarred by the session, till they have removed the scandal according to the discipline of the church; which done, they are restored to their former church-state."

No. IV.

Mr. Gabriel Wilson's speech before the Synod of Merse and Teviotdale, in defence of his sermon preached before that synod, Oct. 1721.

MODERATOR.—How many soever may be otherwise minded, this day I take to be a day of the Lord's jealousy and indignation on all ranks and conditions of men, and on all societies and assemblies. The anger of the Lord has set us on fire round about, yet we know it not; and though it consumes us, we lay it not to heart. Of all which this present occasion, being such an one as I know not if the like, in all its circumstances, has happened in any Reformed church since Calvin's days, is an instance none of the least notable and discernible.

Moderator, according to the measure of the gift bestowed on me, I delivered before this Reverend Synod, what I took to be the Lord's mind and message by me. In which message, I, according as I conceived the state of religion in these lands required, and as my subject led me, endeavoured to witness for truth, and against sin. Among others, I offered my poor and mean testimony to that glorious gospel-truth, the justification and salvation of the lost and undone sinners by free grace, without works, through faith in a crucified Saviour; where, at the same time, the unalterable obligation of the law of God upon believers, and the necessity of holiness in the redeemed, was in the strongest and plainest terms asserted. I likewise bore witness, not immodestly, as I thought, though somewhat plainly, against sin, the defections of former and present times, for which I did, and do still, apprehend the Lord's anger is not turned away, but his hand is stretched out still. Upon some words, Moderator, and occasional passages, in my enlargement on these two heads, am I this day called in question before this court.

Moderator—It is known all the world over, and will be while the world lasts, that where a man's discourse is generally solid, sound, and to the purpose, little notice is taken, or severity used, as to some words or phrases, though not so well chosen, or fitly set; because men for most part remember themselves to be but men, who cannot promise on every occasion to write or speak infallibly; else process of this sort had not unto this day been such a rarity in the churches of Christ, and particularly in the Church of Scotland. Now, since it is undeniable, so might it have been expected, if the main of what I delivered on these subjects had been agreeable, and acceptable, the want of some of that accuracy and exactness of words, or prudence, which others knew themselves could have managed these subjects with, would have been overlooked or pardoned? But the measures which have been taken, will, I am afraid, occasion suspicions, which I heartily wish may be groundless.

There are, Moderator, many things to persuade a shyness and wariness in judging and condemning what is delivered as a message from the Lord, which it might be reckoned impertinent for me to insist upon before such a reverend judicatory: and therefore I shall not do it. Far be it for me to mean hereby, that it should be any screen to a man's delivering error or heresy, that he does it from the pulpit; or that this Reverend Synod should not shew a due zeal for the purity of gospel-doctrine; but I must say, it was a sore matter, if so many learned men, having their spiritual senses exercised to discern betwixt good and evil, could not judge of the doctrine of a sermon they heard, without so much ado, and such a procedure, so very extraordinary; having for its native tendency (however the mercy and wisdom of Divine Providence may turn it) the utter and irretrievable ruin of a man's reputation and usefulness in the world; things that no judicatory of Jesus Christ should be very fond or rash of attempting. This, I say, being the native tendency of such measures, every failing or imperfection, the wit and invention of men set on work, and doing their utmost, may find out in a man's papers, forced from him, will be so far from justifying such pomp and solemnity before the Lord, the world, or their own consciences, acting a faithful part, that, without they have some very considerable matter for their foundation, they must be a persecution less merciful, and more bloody, than carrying one to a scaffold would be.

Moderator—It is given out of me, propagated among the people, and through the church, as far as it will go, that I deny the Father in the glorious Godhead, the necessity of holiness in believers, that the law of God is binding upon them, or that there is any need of a preparatory work of the Holy Spirit on the souls of men, &c. and what not? and now, when the sermon is delivered, that I have altered it, and kept back all the gross things that were in my papers, and which I delivered before the Synod; whereas the brethren appointed to receive the copy knew, and the brethren of the committee know, they have a faithful copy of my notes; and not only so, but of all things delivered by me, though they were not in my notes, so far as I can remember them. Whatever measure I have got, or may further get, never did one give his judges fairer play against himself, than I have done. What shall I say, Moderator? I am made a gazing-stock, a reproach, and a world's wonder, throughout Scotland, and may be further too, for any thing I know. Reproach sometimes breaks my heart; and were it not in some measure I believe the promises, and the special providence of God, I behoved to sink, and be broken effectually

Moderator—It is not in the power of this Synod, were they ever so willing, to make reparation of the injuries done me by means of their procedure; for infamy will stick better.

As to the point of prudence and expedience, under which consideration some of the quarrelled passages will fall, I will not pretend so much as a tolerable skill of that sort; but I desire to depend on him on whom the spirit of wisdom and understanding rests, and in whom dwell all the treasures of wisdom and knowledge. The expediency of speaking and acting in particular instances, is a point we will never all be agreed in; but good folks, as they will be differing among themselves, so they may happen to be of a different judgment from our Lord Jesus Christ himself in cases. The gospel furnishes us with instances enow of this, particularly of the woman who was not only accepted and approved of our Lord, but has an everlasting badge of honour put upon her for a deed which was the object of the disciples' indignation. Moderator—I adduce this, not as if I took mine for an exact parallel case, but only as a document of what may be, where even good folk are very confident, and reckon themselves pretty sure; and it is not very choiceable, nor what any of us would wish, to be of a different judgment from Christ, especially in such matters as concern his own glory.

Moderator—As ministers should shew an example of impartiality one towards another, in case of error or vice, so ought they to set people a pattern of charity, tenderness and brotherly love, in not wresting, stretching, or straining one another's words or actions, to such meanings as they neither fairly bear, nor were ever intended to express, or so as to discover the prevalence of such works of the flesh in themselves, as we condemn and preach against in others. This hath been, and will be the way of the world; the way of enemies towards the saints, especially towards the ministers of Christ; and it is both pity and shame that it should ever be their way one towards another. Charity rejoiceth not in iniquity, but rejoiceth in the truth. If there had dropped from one's pen, on a paper which on his account the world was never to see, expressions not so well chosen, or guarded; would not the love of God, the love of truth, and the love of our neighbour, which the gospel so much teacheth and recommends, make all men in whom it dwells, rejoice to see those things elsewhere in the same paper, more plainly and fully expressed to satisfaction? And will not that humility, modesty, and compassion, which a sense of human weakness and frailty, with a sense of our own imperfections, and liableness to mistake, begets, persuade the same thing? Even the wisest of societies happen at times to express themselves, for removing such misapprehensions as their words have given occasion to.

The straining or wresting of words, or occasional passages in this case, in order to the fathering inferences or consequence not owned, or to the fixing of odious notions, that the words neither express, nor, candidly interpreted, give any countenance to, cannot miss to be held as a clear evidence, that something is aimed at, either with respect to the person or doctrine, that is not fairly or honestly owned, and spoken out.

Moderator.—Though I shall readily own, that any who hear the word at the Lord's mouth, and bear his message, may be able to express the truth in more fit and acceptable words than I have done in these papers; yet, considering my unskilfulness, and my profound security from all fears of such unprecedented measures, I conceive I have much reason to bless the name of the Lord, who instructs the simple, and guides the blind in the way they know not; and accordingly here I desire, with all my soul, to bless him, that my escapes were not both more and greater than they are; else, alas! where had I been? I had been swallowed and eaten up as bread; the truth had suffered by my means, and the friends of truth had been ashamed for my sake. Which brings to mind another thing, namely, whatever imperfections or alleged offensive things may be found in that sermon, you are not, Moderator, so much as in thought, to impute them to any but me. My reason for saying so is, that I know it has been strongly, though most invidiously suggested, that there was concert and advice in this affair; but never was any thing less true, Moderator. No advice, no consultation, about word or thing in these papers; yea, so far from it, that I sincerely declare, no one in the world knew so much as the text I was to preach from, till I read it in this place. Moderator, we have not so learned Christ as to consult with man in such cases.

I own, Moderator, I have cause, more than for all the committee's remarks to be humbled, that I had not more of the Lord's presence in the delivery of that sermon, (yet I desire to bless him for carrying me through); and that so little of the Lord's power accompanied the word from my mouth; for it is but too evident, it has been an unblessed sermon to many; woes me for it! However, it might have been expected, some regard might have been had to conscience, honesty, and sincerity, in declaring one's mind as to what he reckoned amiss or in danger, on an occasion the most solemn and public he ever had before, or was like to have again. Whereas, or at the same time, it may be easily seen, these measures tend to discourage all faithfulness and plain dealing for the time to come, be the evidence or aspect of affairs in the church what it will; which, therefore, some will perhaps think might have fallen less unseasonably out in some other juncture than this.

Moderator—However contemptible I may be in the eyes of many, this piece of conduct being so very extraordinary, and of such a conspicuous judicatory in the Church of Scotland, will be under the observation and examination of, not only both friends and enemies at home among ourselves, but of strangers (I doubt not) also; for all people are at this day wrestling for liberty, and many will be curious to look into a case reckoned to have so unfavourable an aspect upon it.

To conclude—Moderator, I can say it in truth, though my brethren and mother's children have been very angry with me, and have dealt roughly with me, my Lord and master has not yet, to my discerning, discovered himself displeased with me on account of that sermon, or of any one thing in it. No doubt, he saw many more faults, and other sort of ones, than you can find; yea, the whole performance, I know, was full of blemishes, and would not at all abide a trial at the bar of his holy law; yet I believe he has graciously pardoned all, and will never article me on that head; which, though it may be of no consideration with others, nor do I desire it should be of any, yet it is of great importance to me. And as for the little remarks some people make on it, I believe I may venture to say, he laughs at them; nay, I will say more, Moderator, I believe he will deliver me out of all this trouble I am meeting with on account of it, when such as seek my hurt have done their worst and utmost against me ; yea though I should be tossed like a broken vessel to assemblies and commissions, I am not afraid of the issue. But though in such an event I may be delivered, allow me to say it, Moderator, though it may seem bold, it shall not, I hope, be found irrelevant ; and was their soul in my soul's stead, none here present would think much of any thing I have yet said, or am going to say ? whoever shall send me there, I regard their doing so, can import no less than that they reckon me worthy of death, or of bonds, neither of which I deserve at the hand of man ; they shall be held guilty of my blood before the Lord.

To the above is subjoined another speech.

MODERATOR—I own the copy by me delivered to the brethren appointed by the synod to receive the same, to be a true copy of the notes or papers from which I preached the sermon before the last synod ; and that the said copy contains nothing but what is my sentiments ; and being favourably constructed, will be found, I hope, to bear no ground of offence. The additions, being mostly of words deficient, transitions, or enlargements upon heads barely named in the papers, together with the filling up of some pieces of the method proposed, but left blank, are all distinctly marked, and do not touch the sense of what is in the notes ; nor do I crave any benefit of them. But for as much as it ought to be presumed, that the Reverend Synod did peremptorily require the copy aforesaid, only in order to satisfy themselves as to some particular points touched in the sermon, and not out of it to form a libel, or draw articles against me, upon which I may be judged in order to censure ; and since I neither did, nor could exactly repeat these notes or papers in the pulpit, and likewise since many things in them were not at all delivered, and other things were delivered that were not in the said notes, which nevertheless are now added in their proper places, so far as I could remember them, and several things were delivered purposely in other and smoother words than were written ; I do protest the said copy cannot be improved to the forming of a libel or articles against me, as said is ; and that the using it to such a purpose, would be in effect to make me mine own accuser, contrary to the word of God, the form of process, and the natural rights of mankind ; and also that the said copy can never be used, and sustained as probative, in any process against me, on the account of the sermon above mentioned. And finally, that which I reckon myself concerned to say here on this affair, for satisfying the committee as to my sentiments on the heads they may be pleased to bring into question, shall not militate against me in any process upon the account of these heads, or that sermon aforesaid. Upon all which I take instruments in the clerk's hands.

No. V.

Concerning this Essay on the Hebrew text of Genesis, the author wrote the following memorial, when a copy of it was sent to Mr. Grant at London.

1. " The design of it is, to explain the text immediately from the Hebrew phraseology. For that effect, the sacred Hebrew pointing, or stigmatology, is religiously stuck to, and expressed in the versions by equivalent stops ; and in the rigidly literal version, the words are generally ranged according to their order in the Hebrew ; but where that could not be obtained, the Hebrew order is notified by a figure above the word ; as, Gen. i. 1,

I
" God he created ;" the figure " I" notes, that word to be the first of the two in the Hebrew ; and more than that, the original words are, wheresoever they occur, rendered in that version, in their one formal signification, according to their use of them in the Bible ; the which signification is established in the notes, being discovered by comparing of other places where the words occur. For which effect, the Bible itself, with Buxtorf's Hebrew Concordance, is, I humbly conceive, the best Lexicon. Upon this subject I cannot but mention with honour, " Guesset's Comment. ling. Ebr." Meanwhile this cannot miss of making that version uncouth, and even shocking to some. Nevertheless, by means thereof, the English reader hath a kind of original (if I may so express it) in his own language, by which he may the better judge of smooth versions ; and the Hebrew reader may discover the true sense of a text, together with the reason thereof, from the language itself, and the phraseology of the Holy Ghost. But however shocking it may be to any, I am apt to think, that a version of any Roman author, on such a plan, and under such strict rules, would be far more so.

2. The notes are formed on the rigidly-literal version ; and in compiling of them, the philological part was first studied and written, and from thence was the theological sense of the text inferred and written. Howbeit, transcribing the whole *in mundo*, I judged it expedient, especially for the sake of the unlearned reader, to invert that order ; so that the philological part comes last, that they who have no gust for it may pass it. Meanwhile it contains the reason of the versions, and sense of the text, which are given.

3. The more smooth version will, I apprehend be judged by far too harsh and literal ; and therefore it may yet again be licked over ; and I am resolved to expunge, in many places therein, the word " even," very frequently occurring, satisfying myself with its standing in the other version. But I must own, I am much addicted to the letter of the sacred text ; and to depart from it, but upon evident necessity. For I am fully convinced, that a cloud hath been cast over the true sense of several texts, by interpreters allowing themselves a great liberty in departing from it ; instance Gen. iii. 1 ; and humbly conceive there is a becoming reason for the sacred Hebrew phraseology. Withal I am of opinion with a famed author, that the Hebrew manners of speech kindly mix and incorporate with the English language ; and, if I mistake not, we may in several instances express them more happily in our native language than in the Latin.

4. The authentic copy written with my own hand, from which it must be printed, if deemed worthy to see the light, is in my closet. I do not remember that I have so much as seen, far less revised, the whole of the other, now at London, it being kept partly at Edinburgh, and partly at Aberdeen, till it was sent thither."

No. VI.

The copy of the paragraph here mentioned is as follows:—" I sincerely desired to have been useful to you, to my power, since you were settled in the neighbourhood; and that was the spring of some parts of my conduct. But we having now twice encountered, you treating of faith, and I of repentance, and again you of repentance, and I of faith, I perceive our strain is so very different, that there seems to me to be a danger in our encountering before a multitude from several places in the country wherein our lot is cast. However venturous others may be, I, who have had about twenty years' experience of the temper of the people in these parts, would be very inexcusable if I should not be wary."

No. VII.

The following is a copy of the memorial here mentioned:

" 1. The English copy of the Essay on the Hebrew accentuation, being written several years before the Latin copy, there are some things in the former altered in the latter; particularly, one whole section is dropped, being, I suppose the third of the 5th chapter; another chapter or section is transposed; and there are some few alterations and amendments of another kind made in the writing it over in Latin. Being sent off in a time when I was otherwise busy, I had no access to take a note of these things. However, it will give a view of the nature of the whole essay; but it is not fit for the press.

2. No body needs to be amused at the sight of the chapters and sections of the second part, intitled, " Observations," &c. as if they contained so many rules for the understanding the art itself. That is taught in the chapters or sections preceding respectively; and these are but so many helps offered, for the practical use of the art, in order to reach the true sense of the sacred text by means thereof; and therefore none of the books teaching the art, which have as yet come into my hands, had any thing in them of that kind. Besides one who embraceth the notion of the fixed value of the accents, and withal understands and observes the five heads of rhetorical accentuation mentioned in the specimen, will hardly find a new labour, I hope, in these observations; but in reading attentively his Bible, will observe the sense of texts accordingly, keeping these two things in his view.

3. If it shall please the sovereign disposer of all things to make way for the printing of the Essay, it must be done from the Latin copy with me. But the printer must view the English copy, and take particular notice of the schemes and tables, which I conceive must be done in copperplate; as also of the several stops, and marks of continuation, used in the Essay, that proper types may be got for them. These characters are to be found gathered together, and explained in the English copy, after the title page."

There is among Mr. Boston's manuscripts an English copy of the Essay on the accentuation, written with his own hand in folio; but it is so very different from the printed Latin copy, that it is supposed to be his first draught; and that he afterwards wrote a more full and perfect copy, the one mentioned in the above memorial, which probably was never returned from London, or perhaps was sent to Amsterdam, where the Latin copy was printed in 1738, and never got back.

No. VIII.

Letter from Dr. Waterland to Mr. G.

DEAR SIR.—I return you my hearty thanks for favouring me with these papers. I have read them over, and find them too deep for me to give a judgment of; for I have never yet entered into the heart of that subject. But I shall be mighty glad to read and consider a set treatise upon it, that I may learn from it. It will be curious, useful, instructive; and may strike new light into several obscure texts, though it should not entirely answer in all points. I must own, I am at present a little prejudiced against the supposed antiquity of the Hebrew accents; but I shall be always glad to see the utmost that can be pleaded for it. Their use in clearing up texts must, I believe, at last be their best commendation, and strongest proof of their antiquity. I know, that some tolerable answers may be given to the arguments brought for their novelty; and I know again, that tolerable answers may be made to the arguments urged for their antiquity. Both sides are better at weakening each other's proofs, than at maintaining their own. But whatever becomes of the dispute about their antiquity or authority, if the use of them for understanding scripture can be clearly and uniformly made out, that will be sufficient, and will be also a strong presumption for their being ancient.

I have seen what Buxtorf, Pfeiffer, Michael, and some others, have pleaded in their favour. But of all the writers I have met with, none has expressed himself with greater assurance of their divine authority, and inestimable use and value, than Gottfrid Icohlreiffius, in his "Chronologia Sacra," published at Hamburgh, 1724; an octavo volume it is, pages 481. That gentleman has run very wide from the common chronology, and sets the year of Christ, A.M. 4509. He builds his new chronology mostly upon the discoveries made by the Hebrew accents, according to his rules of interpreting them. I should be mighty glad to know what this other curious gentleman would think of Icohlreiffius's rules and method, and how far their observations agree. I confess I am no master at all of the science; but heartily wish, that the subject may be reduced to certain rules, that we learners may be able to judge when a person argues justly from the accents, and when not. In the perfect darkness I am under, I cannot do it.

It is now about six years since Peter Guarin, a Benedictine, published the first tome of his Hebrew grammar, in 4to. The other tome, as I am informed by a letter from Paris, is just now published, or publishing. In this second tome, as I learn from the preface to the first, will be a particular dissertation upon the accents, with a large account of their use in the synagogue-music. What other uses he will take notice of, is not said. I suppose your friend will be willing to see what M. Guarin has said upon the subject. The book will be sent me over hither as soon as it can be had.

I shall just say a word or two upon what this gentleman has relating to Gen. iii. 8, in p. 6. I was of the same opinion with Junius and Tremellius before, not upon account of the accents, which I understand not, but because that construction appeared to me more natural than the other, and more reasonable. This gentleman further gives us a new interpretation of " Kol," which, I must own, I cannot readily come into. And I wonder a little why he should think, that " Mithhallech" may not be metaphorically applied to a voice or sound, when himself gives instances of such metaphorical application in other cases : or why he should think it must be understood of a person here, (though there are instances where it is not so understood), and yet interpret " Kol" of a person, contrary to its common acceptation. I am afraid our adversaries will think we strain hard to fetch in the λόγος. And unless it can be strongly backed, and substantially made out, I should rather we did not. But perhaps this gentleman may have more to plead for such construction than I may be aware of; and therefore I suspend my judgment of it. But it is time I should ease you. I shall only add, that I am hugely pleased with the piety, gravity, and dignity, of your general assembly's answer to his Majesty's letter. It is the more seasonable while our convocations are mute ; and I hope will be of good use for keeping religion alive in these kingdoms, at a time when it appears much declining.—I am, good Sir, your obliged humble servant,

DAN. WATERLAND.

LETTERS TO AND FROM THE AUTHOR.
No. IX.

Letters from the Rev. Mr. Henry Davidson, late minister of the gospel at Galashiels, to the author.

March, 25, 1728.

(1) VERY DEAR SIR,—Your two letters of the last month's date, breathing so much of a kindly concern, and bearing so many seasonable advices, and relieving grounds of comfort, could not miss to be most acceptable to me, when plunged in the deep ; and this should have been acknowledged to you before this, but my indisposition of body being considered, will, I know, sufficiently plead the excuse of my delay.

Dear Sir, when there is a keeping in any measure from a despising of the Lord's chastening, yet I find no small difficulty to bear off from the other rock, a fainting under his rebukes. Faith's views, that it is the Lord, will prove quieting. A right of his sovereignty, wisdom, righteousness, and faithfulness, works up the soul into a holy acquiescence in, and composure under, the eternal decree, now revealed by the event. But O! how hard to believe a father's love it is with us under trials, especially those of a complicated nature, or that have some entangling especially in them, as it was with the disciples when the Lord came upon the water in a tempestuous night to their relief. They thought he was a spirit ! so we look upon God as our enemy, when he comes to sanctify and save. The promise reconciles the roughest of a father's hand with the sweetness of his voice, and love of his heart. He calls to his children, in the darkest night, "It is I, be not afraid." Our disquietments do enter at the door of unbelief; for in every case, however trying, joy and peace accompany believing, and keep measures with it. That heroic grace performs surprising achievements under sharpest trials, as they stand registered in Heb. xi.; and whatever our trials are, the strength of the conduct lies betwixt faith and unbelief; and as the balance sways towards the one or the other, so is the situation in other regards. All goes backward, and towards ruin, as unbelief prevails; for it carries its train alongst; and did not our gracious God stem the current from time to time, and be the lifter up of the head, we would infallibly sink beneath the stream; nevertheless, upon the begun recovery of faith, matters are accordingly set at rights. It is in this way that, in the Lord's strength, we are to look out for his kind scattering the clouds, and making us to hear, and to give in to the voice of his rod. It is by faith the soul must be moulded into a serene composure of mind, and a kindly compliance with the Lord's heart-weaning methods of providence. It is in this way of believing, that we must take up with God alone for our portion and great all; and seek to have all our losses and wants made up and supplied in him who has proclaimed himself God all-sufficient.—Dear Sir, yours very affectionately,

H. DAVIDSON.

May 11, 1720.

(2) VERY DEAR SIR,—Yours bearing the resolve about the sacrament came to hand some weeks ago. Difficulties taking rise in holy wise providence from your own circumstances, and likewise from those of your own ordinary assistants, I make no doubt, have caused various thoughts not a little perplexing to every one of us; I would fain hope, the Lord on our head, as the breaker-up going before, will make the way clear. When we are saying among ourselves, and within ourselves, who shall roll us away the stone? he will possibly shew us the stone, though very great, rolled away. The account of your weakness, and your wife's distress, gave me no little pain; infinite wisdom and love make all things work together for good; his ways and thoughts are above ours; in due time, the perplexing riddles shall be fully expounded, and it shall then be seen, what we are now to believe, that our God and guide hath not taken one wrong step; and that unquestionably he had a very good reason for whatever he did. We must account that our Lord hath even gone the best way that could have been done, in all that is past, and we should have no doubting thoughts about what he will do afterwards.

Dear Sir, I give you no trouble at present with any account of my circumstances; may I be helped to wait on and not weary; and may his rich blessing make the afflicting rod fruitful.—I remain, Very Dear Sir, yours affectionately,

H. DAVIDSON.

GALASHIELS, *Dec.* 30, 1730.

(3) VERY DEAR SIR,—To have owned my receipt of your kind letters, three of them with Mr. Glass's pamphlet, has been often resolved. The delay has been much owing to bodily disorder, by no means to a want of due respect and gratitude. My long silence after your writing once and again made it appear necessary to me to say so much by way of apology. The whole of our time is divided between summer and winter, heat and cold, night and day, a constant revolution there is of storms and a calm. There is a shining beauty in the conduct of Providence, that we are not always fed with honey, nor yet is our cup always filled with gall and wormwood. There is a wise mixture in our lot of light and shade, as there is in ourselves of flesh and spirit ; there is the mixture of anger and love in the trials of the Lord's children, not the anger of an enemy intending ruin and hurt, as flowing from hatred and revenge ; but the anger of a father, which is guided by wisdom, and tempered by love, intending the good of his offending child. It is a piece of prerogative-royal, to have the power of life and death, which God reserves to himself. He only knows when the appointed work is finished ; he alone is fit to give the sailing orders, and assign the time when the sore tossed and shattered vessel shall be laid up in a safe harbour.—Very dear Sir, yours very affectionately,

H. DAVIDSON.

GALASHIELS, *Feb.* 25, 1732.

(4) VERY DEAR SIR,—Your several letters came safe to hand, and were very acceptable. This comes to inform you, that the good old woman my mother went home to her own, the better country, this morning betwixt three and four o'clock. She took her bed upon the Lord's day evening ; had a fever pretty high, but retained all her senses to her dying hour. How cruel is her love ! how blind and inconsiderate is our affection ! we would prefer the small advantages or greater gains we reap from their abode with us, to their entire satisfaction and complete happiness ; a very great but common solecism in true friendship we are often guilty of. However frightful and ill-favoured death appear to the eye of sense, it is viewed by faith as the messenger of our heavenly Father ; and when the Christian opens its hard cold hands, and looks into them, there are to be found gracious letters full of love, bearing an invitation to come home, a call from the new Jerusalem to come up and see. When death with the one hand covers our eyes, and deprives of the light of the stars, with the other it rends in pieces the vail, and so makes way for our being set immediately under the refreshing beams of the Sun of righteousness, without the least appearance of a cloud through the long days of eternity. Now that his way is in the sea, and his path in the deep waters, and his footsteps are not known, we must believe loving-kindness in all the mysterious passages of Providence ; we shall in due time see a wheel in the wheel, and be taught how to decipher the dark characters ; we shall, with an agreeable surprise, perceive an all-wise Providence in all its intricate, oblique, and seemingly-contrary

motions, to have been a faithful servant to the divine promise ; so that we must say amen to Heaven's disposals, and cry out in the dark and gloomy night, Hallelujah. I should certainly make an apology for giving you so much trouble, but allow it to be written to the Lord's prisoner of hope with you, as I design it, though the direction bears your name. The fault of its length, will, I hope, appear less when taken in that view. My affectionate respects to Mrs. Boston, with yourself, are offered, by him who is, Very dear Sir, yours very affectionately, in the straitest bonds,

H. Davidson.

No. X.

A Letter from Professor Hamilton to the Author.

Vir Reverende, Frater dilectissime,—Tuas Aug. 13, datas accepi, et cum delectatione perlegi ; nam multa continent attentione digna ; et quod ad levandos scrupulos meos, circa certitudinem et utilitatem stigmatologiæ Hebraicæ, prosunt, quamvis non possum dicere illos penitus sublatos esse ; utinam possem. Scio autum te optare ut sincere tecum agam, nec cupere assentationes blandientes, quas nec mihi cordi est dare, nec tibi, ut puto, accipere. Verum, ut antea, in meis, sine fuco, id quod vere mihi animi suit de opere tuo lubens testatum feci, ita nunc rursus idem repetam ; nempe, illud insigne documentum præbere indefessæ tuæ diligentiæ, et improbi laboris, in eo concinnando ; nec non quod, ex bono et laoudando animi affectu erga divina eloquia, molimen illud arduum et onerosum suscepisti, et prosequutus es, in duobus illis voluminibus de stigmatologia sacra ; quæ ut voluisti, perlegi ; et tibi ago gratias, qui id agendi facultatem mihi dederis. Nunc autum insuper addam, exceptionibus meis in præmissis epistolis de hoc opere non obstantibus, nihil a me observatum fuisse, dum opus illud perlegerem, quod, quatenus judicare potui, contrarium erat doctrinæ puræ theologiæ in nostra vel aliis ecclesiis reformatis receptæ ; et, si contigerit illud opus publicum fieri, opinor minime indignum esse eruditorum seria attentione, quo origo et autoritas accentuationis Hebraicæ penitus considerentur et examinentur, ut aliquid reperiatur cui ut certo fidendum in tanta tamque gravi quœstione, de qua docti hucusque adeo disputarunt. Hæc sunt quæ tuis supra memoratis respondere lubuit ; quæ spero te benevolenter accepturum, ut quæ proveniunt ex animo optime erga te disposito. Quod restat, omina fausta tibi precatur, et sincere optat,—Vir Reverende, Frater dilectissime,—tui observantissimus, tibique deditissimus,

Gul. Hamilton.

Datum Edinæ, *Nov.* 20, 1728.

No. XI.

Extract of a letter from Mr. Grant to the Author, dated June 8, 1730.

—————— My former letters to our worthy and dear friend Mr. Hogg, will give you a tolerable account of that rare gentlemen Sir Richard Ellys, and of your obligations to him ; though I own it is much above me to give either his character, or express how much you are obliged to him. But I cannot help saying that I do sincerely think, that there is ground of many thanks-givings to sovereign grace, that we have in our island a gentleman of his rank, (being one of the first for birth and estate in England), and one of the ablest scholars in it, who, I hope and am persuaded, is such a pleasant scholar in Christ's school, and is let into the wonders and glories of free grace, and whose soul thirsts after further and further discoveries of the purity and beauty of the gospel. He has many a time warmed my heart, to hear him speak of that subject. He speaks indeed of grace like one that has seen its glory, felt its power, and tasted its sweetness. There is one amongst many lovely accounts he was pleased to communicate to me, which I am satisfied will be pleasing to you, viz. that when he was a bigotted Ar-minian, God was pleased to give an old gentlewoman, of an understanding entirely weak as to every thing but free grace and the mystery of Christ, an uncommon concern about him, at whose notions of Christ and grace he was wont to laugh. However, a sovereign and gracious God made this weak woman conquer this Goliah, and teach this Rabbi. O! with what respect he talks of her memory! and O! what a glorious demonstration does he reckon such a one of the reality of divine teaching, who knows no-thing of the world, has weak understanding of all the concerns of human life, but knows more of the mysteries of the kingdom of heaven than thousands of scholars, nay, and thousands of divines! She died full of the faith and hopes that God would take care of him, and keep him by his power through faith to salvation. Your " Fourfold State" has engaged his heart to you ; he has made presents of it to several of his friends, and made another great man, Sir John Philips, purchase it, who says, free grace is his Bible, and admires your book, reads it daily himself, and makes all his family read it. This gentleman, Sir Richard assures me, is a man of great worth, and has a great concern about the declining of religion, and has a noble public spirit for doing good.

No. XII.

A letter from the Author to Sir Richard Ellys, Bt.

ETTRICK-MANSE, *June* 13, 1730.

HONOURED SIR,—It was no small encouragement to me, to find by my good friend Mr. John Grant's letters, that you had been pleased to read the specimen of the Essay on the Hebrew accentuation, lately sent from this place ; that you relished the design of that essay, and shewed a favourable inclination in the matter. This was unto me ground of thankfulness to the Sovereign Disposer of all, and natively issued in determining to do myself the satisfaction of expressing, by a line, the warm sense I have of your fa-vour, though I cannot pretend to the honour of your acquaintance.

It is very natural to think, that such a work falling " just because so it seemed good in the sight of the Father," to the share of an obscure person, living in a desert, exercised with a variety of personal and domestic trials, and under some uncommon disadvantages beside, must needs with him re-main in obscurity, unless it obtain the countenance of one of your Honour's character in the learned world; and that especially at this time of day, when, in the depth of sovereign wisdom, so many learned men of all denominations reckon any such work a mere laborious trifling; because they believe not the divine original and authority of the points themselves, on which the essay is made.

That I was led to the study of the Hebrew accentuation, was owing purely to the conduct of Providence, bringing Cross's Taghmical Art into my hand; and through the divine favour falling on the scent, I was carried into the belief of the divine original and authority of that accentuation as stigmatological; seeing glaring evidence of the same, in my reading of the sacred Hebrew text, shining by means thereof with its own intrinsic light. And therefore I am inclined to think, that, after all that has been said, on both sides of the question, by the learned, the most habile method of conviction therein, is to " come and see;" and that a happy explication, or genuine representation of the nature of the accentuation of the Hebrew Bible, in its natural and artless contrivance, is the only thing wanting to procure it the same awful regard with the other parts of the sacred text. This is what is aimed at in the essay, though I am not so weak as to think I have fully reached it; but I have the fondness to imagine, that, being brought forth to the public view, it might possibly minister occasion unto some learned men to enter into a further consideration of that matter; and so set it at length in a due light, to the increase of scripture-knowledge in the churches of Christ.

I have now sent off the English copy of the essay, hoping that, through the favourable conduct of Providence, it may come safe to London. It is what I wrote at first, while I was not dreaming of putting it in Latin; the which I was afterwards engaged in, by the advice of some, for whose judgment I had a great deference. And in case of its coming safe to my friend's hand, I humbly entreat, that, if your affairs will permit, you will be pleased to take the trouble of glancing it over; to the end you may have a more clear view of the nature of the work, and may be fully satisfied in the point of your affording or denying it your countenance; for, bating some alterations which I found ground for making, when the Latin copy was written, the former is the same with the latter.

If, upon perusal of the English copy, your favourable inclination shall continue, I will presume to beg your advice to Mr. Grant, as to his management of the affair.

The weight and importance of the matter, and the justice of allowing one to express a due gratitude, will, I hope, plead excuse for offering you the trouble of this from a stranger; who craves leave to subscribe himself,—Honoured Sir,—your Honour's very obedient, most humble servant,

T. BOSTON.

No. XIII.

Sir Richard Elly's Answer.

Dec. 16, 1730.

SIR,—I received yours with great pleasure; and can assure you, it is not for any want of respect that I have been so long in returning you my thanks for it. Believe me, from what I have read of yours, and the character I have from others concerning you, I have the highest regard for you. The " Fourfold State," which I went through with much satisfaction, has given me no small idea of your piety; and I have reason to think your " Essay on the Hebrew accentuation" may in time give the learned world as great a value and esteem for your knowledge in that abstruse part of literature. I cannot pretend to much depth in any part of learning; in this I must own myself entirely ignorant; but this I know, if it succeeds, it is a glorious work, as it must necessarily be subservient in the highest degree towards settling our minds, and composing our differences, in these sad distracted times. Has Providence directed you to rules for the ascertaining the sense of scripture, or at least for reducing it in some good measure to a greater certainty than heretofore? For my own part, I had rather be author of such a book, than master of the Indies.

After I have said this, Sir, I hope I need not add much to assure you, I will do whatever lies in my power to serve you in this noble design. The very failing in an attempt of this nature has its merit:

——Magnis tamen excidit ausis,

you know, is given as no mean character.

The specimen has been shewed to Messrs. Schultens and Abraham Gronovious, the two best judges of that sort of learning at Leyden, or perhaps in all Holland. I shall not trouble you with their answer, our common friend Mr. Grant having undertaken to send it you *verbatim;* but this I must say, it pleased me. The specimen is, I suppose, before this time, in the hands of Mr. Loftus at Rotterdam, who has promised me to examine it himself, put it into the hands of others, and then give me his and their impartial sentiments.

And now, Sir, I have a favour to beg of you, or rather I insist upon it, that you think of me sometimes in your most retired hours. It is what I desire with some earnestness; and reckon I have a sort of right to it, as being your hearty well-wisher and friend, though unknown to you, as well as, dear Sir, your very humble servant,

R. ELLYS.

No. XIV.

A second letter from the Author to Sir Richard Ellys.

ETTRICK-MANSE, *Dec.* 31, 1730.

HONOURED SIR,—Often have I been made to adore that sovereign gracious hand, which pointed into the much-neglected path travelled in, in the MSS. some time ago sent from hence; and which, in dependence upon him, opened a passage through several thickets there, in which I found myself entangled; having frequently been in such a situation therein, that when I had set down one foot, I knew not where to set down another. But when, by the divine favour, I had got through it in some measure, such as was comfortable to myself, and might, I apprehend, be of some use to the church of God, my friendless circumstances were perplexing. These have for several years been matter of exercise to me; and, I am not ashamed to own, have often made me to cry unto my God, who doth all things for me, that he would raise up instruments for the work. And now, Sir, that, after disappointments and discouragements from several hands, whence I looked for encouragement, it hath pleased the Lord, there where I could have no expectation, to raise me up a friend, by inclining your heart to take notice of and comfort me, and to bestir yourself to act in favour of that and me.

May not I be allowed to say unto you, though I have never with mine eyes seen your face, and it is likely never will in this world, " I have seen thy face as if I had seen the face of God ?" A person of honour, learning, and piety, stirred up to befriend me. The acceptableness of the " Fourfold State" to you, notwithstanding of its homely dress, gave me an inexpressible pleasure. Your transmitting the specimen, title, and index, and friendly writing along therewith, to Mr. Gowan and Mr. Loftus, in Holland, was a most charitable action ; and the sending therewith the " Fourfold State," was such an encouraging token of your regard for it as I could not have expected, more than I could have dreamed of what else you did in favour of it. Mr. Gowan's return, concerning the specimen, which you was pleased to dictate to my worthy friend Mr. Grant, coming into my hand, was, " as cold waters to a thirsty soul." And your generosity, preventing the remotest thought in me, is quite surprising ; having received at your hand ten guineas, a gift in that kind, of such value in itself, that it was new to me, and therefore received with proportionable thankfulness ; the which value is yet but a very small thing, in comparison of the value I put upon it, as a token of the regard you are pleased to have for me, and pledge of your readiness to lay out yourself to encourage any work of mine. What remains on my part is, on your account to bless the Lord, who hath given you wealth and honour, and, which is more rare, a heart and wisdom to improve them to the honour of his name ; and to pray, that he so multiply his blessings on you and your consort, as you may plainly perceive, that what you have done, and are disposed to do, in this matter, is a good work, acceptable unto God, through our Lord Jesus Christ. And I am not without confidence in the Lord, upon the ground of his own word ; Prov. xi. 25, " He that watereth, shall be watered also himself," that it shall be even so unto you in due time ; the view being carried, but without limiting of sovereignty, towards the particular trial it hath pleased God to exercise you and my lady Ellys with ; the which, since it came to my knowledge some several months ago, hath been much on my heart, continuing in a disposition to wait on the Lord's hand in that matter ; having also recommended it to the prayers of two godly ministers, my intimate friends. Herein I am the more encouraged, that as we learn from the word, I have learned also by forty years' experience, and upwards, that the more signal and eminent mercies designed for one in the way of the covenant, are usually brought through iron gates ; which for a time making their access apparently hopeless, for the exercise and trial of faith, hope, and patience, do yet, in the Lord's own time, open of their own accord. However, other kinds of mercies may fall into the lap of the receiver sitting at ease.

The MS. on the covenant of grace is not as yet returned to me, but expected shortly. I will greedily embrace an opportunity of putting it into your hand, how soon I can ; being exceedingly refreshed with the accounts of your savour and relish of the doctrine of the free grace of God in Christ Jesus, the foundation of all our hopes.

I own the great civility of your honour's noticing your not writing me ; though I think the circumstantiate case leaves not an apology to be necessary. If at any time I shall have the honour of a few lines at your hand, it will be very acceptable ; but while you shew such a warm concern otherwise, I can be in no pain about it. If you have had any leisure to glance the MSS. your judgment and remarks thereon would be an additional favour.

I hope you will pardon the prolixness of this, since it is occasioned by the multiplicity of your favours, and the warm sense of them had by,—Honoured Sir,—your Honour's most obliged, and most obedient humble servant,

T. Boston.

No. XV.

A third letter from the Author to Sir Richard Ellys.

ETTRICK-MANSE, *Jan.* 2, 1731.

Honoured Sir,—Yesterday I had the honour of yours, which added exceedingly to the satisfaction I had before in your favours. I sincerely declare, that the friendliness and openness of it outdid any thing I had been able to expect, notwithstanding of the signal proofs you had been pleased to give me of your kindness, and which were then fresh in my view. The regard you are pleased to have for me, I accept with all humility and gratitude, imputing it to the Lord's touching of your heart on a particular design. As to what concerns literature, I have a secret pleasure and glorying in infirmities, that the power of Christ may rest upon me, and more satisfaction in the character of a little child leading, than if I were capable of speaking and writing on all the parts of learning. Your judgment of the valuableness of the design or end aimed at in the MSS. which judgment speaks a becoming regard to the very words of the Holy Ghost, I am much strengthened with ; and I need no more, Sir, than what I have, to assure me of your readiness to favour me in that matter which I have so much at heart. I have long travelled as in pain about it, not without fears sometimes, that both it and I should be hissed off the stage, though I dare not say I ever altogether lost hopes in its behalf ; how then could the judgment of Schultens and Gronovius upon the specimen miss of affording me a very

singular comfort ? And if what is expected from Mr. Loftus should prove
to be a balance to it, I will, through grace, fall down, and kiss the high
hand that sends it. I wrote at large to your honour the other day, before
yours came to my hand, in the which dispensation I saw a beauty ; and I
shall not enlarge here. As to what ye require of me, I shall only add, that
I think it will henceforth be natural to me to rejoice and weep with Sir
Richard Ellys, in all his concerns ; being—Honoured Sir,—your Honour's
most obliged, and most obedient humble servant,

T. Boston.

No. XVI.

Letters from the Author to his correspondent in Edinburgh.

October 8, 1720.

(1) Dear Sir,—Last time I wrote to you, I was in a mind to have written
you anent the matter I have now in hand ; but that I was hurried, and
time would not allow. The prospect of engaging in it, which is awful,
whether I consider myself or the matter, and the proof I have had of your
Christian friendship, natively led me to impart it you, as I have done to a
very few others.

The subject is the accentuation of the Hebrew Bible, which in the depth
of sovereign wisdom has been less cultivated by the learned than any thing
else I know of relating to the sacred volume. My acquaintance with books
is very narrow ; but I know no translations of the Bible in which the trans-
lators have not thought themselves very much at liberty in pointing of the
text. I am of their opinion who think the Hebrew text is most accurately
pointed ; and from my own observation, as well as from books, I am convinced the sacred stigmatology bears the signature of a divine hand. The
difficulty has been, and is, to assign the proper value to the several stops
therein used. Now, if that divine pointing can be cleared, it is easy to see
what influence it must have on translations, and commentaries too, fixing
the grammatical sense of the words. There have been but very few books
written purposely for that effect. I have but two of them, viz. " Cross's
Taghnical Art," and " Wasmuth's Institutiones Accent." If either of
them could have satisfied me, they had saved me a considerable labour. I
have employed some to get me other two ; but they have not found them.
I hope I have, through the blessing of our gracious God, attained to some
insight into this matter. I will no longer say, if it be a delusion ; but several
difficulties there are, which I see, that I know not how to get through ;
besides others, which (it is like) I see not. But, in dependence on the same
Father of lights, who, in other points of the same kind, has been pleased to
guide me through thickets, where I could discern no outgate when I entered
them, I design to press forward in the study ; and if any essay of mine on
that subject might prevail to awaken the learned to the further study of that
point, it might be reckoned good service. I have some materials prepared,
though I see I want some others. I cannot obtain it of myself, to fall at
this season in quest of them ; but in regard my health and strength are not

so firm as before, and that I know not what may befall me, I desire (if the Lord will) this winter to begin to put in form what I have, that it may not be useless to others, in case Providence do not allow me to finish it. As for printing expenses, there is no occasion to speak of that; he only knows whether ever I shall have any thing of that nature prepared for the press, or not.

Sir, I have imparted this matter to you out of an earnest desire that you would be concerned in prayer for me with respect to that business of so great importance, that, if it be his holy will, I may have life and health, and the light of his Spirit, to lead me into all truth; that he will make darkness light before me, and crooked things straight, in this matter particularly. I do not desire it to be propaled, nor would it be prudent for me to do it, the matter not being ripe, and it remain·ng doubtful if ever it shall be so. But I am content you impart it to the Honourable person you speak of, if you judge it proper. As for " Buxtorf De punctis," I shall be obliged to any who will get me a loan of it; but I would rather have it of my own; and I suppose you have correspondents both in London and Holland; and if you could help me that way, I would desire the favour of you to do it; not only to that book, but to the other two I spoke of before,— I hope to hear from you by the bearer; and continue, dear Sir, yours, &c.

Sept. 25, 1721.

(2) Dear Sir,—I received yours with the inclosed letter and paper; the which last, when I had considered, I found my heart disposed to bless the Lord, who had given you counsel wisely to manage this important affair. I had got the contrary paper before, which had come also from your hand; by the reading of which I was much confirmed in what we have done; but withal perceiving so little regard to truth, (I mean not only gospel truths, but truth and ingenuity in conversation), I am made to think they can have little hope from that airth, whose lot it is to fall into such hands. But I should account myself happy to get garments kept clean, whatever the Lord may see meet otherwise to do; and I hope that through the supply of the Spirit, and the prayers of the godly, whose eyes are opened in this matter, it may be our mercy to find pity in the eyes of the Lord, to be carried cleanly through, which the Lord knows is that which I mainly desire. I heard nothing of the meeting you speak of, till I read it in yours; but I think I cannot be at it, nor do I think Mr. Wilson will, and perhaps not Mr. D. neither, who is now in Nithsdale. As matters appear to me now, (whatever I might by conference be brought to), I do not think it proper, that any thing which is not to be publicly owned as the common deed of the whole, should undergo so solemn a trial; and if it was mine own case, I would expect more of a half, if not of a fourth part, their perusing the same privately in their closets, than of the whole men together. As for myself, I hope our Dr. B., to whom the Lord has given a quick wit, and a clear apprehension, needs not be very solicitous about the matter of getting our thoughts of it. I long to see it, but in such a manner as will be common to all; and heartily wish that no time may be lost that can be gained. You are still remembered

by me in my most solemn addresses ; and the true reason why I have not
written to you for some time is, that my strength I find to be much abated ;
but work is laid to my hand, upon which all I have is laid out. So that
when an occasion of conveying letters does offer, I am much out of case for
writing ; that time being to me the Saturday's night readily, because of our
occasions on the Monday. I must now have some breathing-time wherein
to do nothing, otherwise I must be quite laid aside ; and any little thing I
have to do costs me much application ; but I bless the Lord for any thing
he gives me upon dilligence and application, and desire to be thankful to
my bountiful God, who gives me for digging what others would find as it
were lying above the ground. The best way that I know for keeping up religion in a hurry of business, is to look on the business as a duty of the eighth
command of our Sovereign Lord, Creator, and Redeemer ; and so going
about it in compliance with his will, who has alloted to every man their
station, and determined the duties of it ; to make application to him ordinarily in your stated addresses to the throne of grace, for wisdom to guide
your affairs with discretion, and for the success of them according to his
promises thereanent ; and actually to go about them in dependence on the
Lord. Thus, while you served your lawful purposes in the world, you
would serve the Lord Christ ; the which I put you in remembrance of,
albeit you know, and I doubt not aim at the same. From the little experience that I have had of the management of worldly affairs, I can say there
is communion with God to be had in the way of that management. Sweet
lessons of dependence, experience of the accomplishment of promises, and
even kind rebukes for heart-sins, sweeter than the world's smiles. Esau's
face with no traits of malice and revenge in it, was but a worldly good
thing ; yet Jacob saw it as though he had seen the face of God ; for Jacob
read the answer of his prayers, and the success of his dependence on the
Lord, upon the face of that little-worth man. My wife kindly remembers
you, and desires to be remembered by you, as doth, very dear Sir, yours, &c.

Dec. 28, 1721.

(3) VERY DEAR SIR,—If that project wherein my good friend would have
had me concerned, (for my advantage I'm sure), do miscarry, it is but of a
piece with other tokens of the Lord's anger against us ; and I know that
when he was in greatest concern for advancing that and other projects, he
still shewed himself uuder apprehensions of impending public judgments ;
and we are already under a signally heavy one, in respect of the present
state of our church affairs, which hath a very terrible aspect. That burning mountain cast into the sea ; Rev. viii. 8, makes sometimes awful impressions on my heart ; but I hope still God will arise, and have mercy on
our Zion yet though he may cause us, in the first place, to pass under the
rod. I know some would reckon themselves not obliged to believe me in
what I have said of the burning mountain, alleging I have contributed to
the setting of it on fire ; the truth is, Scotland's sins, and mine among the
rest, have done it ; especially the sin of not improving the glorious gospel
we have so many years enjoyed ; and I doubt not if the Lord were returned

to us as in former days, he will write shame on the faces of us altogether; and my heart cries, Why tarry the wheels of his chariot? But I reckon it in the meantime the safest course to endeavour to hold at a distance from causes of farther declining. Grace be with you, and with your yoke-fellow, whom my wife kindly remembers. May you be helped to live as heirs of the grace of life, and as followers of those who through faith and patience inherit the promises. I am, with the greatest respect, dear Sir, yours, &c.

August 8, 1724.

(4) DEAR SIR,—There is no appearance of the dissolution of the cloud that for several years now has been over my wife. We have made a new essay this season in the use of means for her help; but all hitherto serves for nothing, but to discover that vain is the help of man in the case. She has not wanted seasonable supports from a higher hand; and when several coals were by wise and holy Providence cast in together into our furnace, she who behoved to be waited on and served before, was even helped to wait on, and be very helpful to others in distress; and then the clouds returned after the rain, and now she comes little out of the bed at all. But all is necessary, and he is infinitely wise who has the management of all in his hand. It is a very sweet view of affliction, to view it as the discipline of the covenant; and so it is indeed; and nothing else to the children of our Father's family. In that respect it is medicinal; it shines with many gracious purposes about it; and end as it will, one may have the confidence of faith, that it shall end well. And O how happy would we be if we could always maintain the confidence of faith! The soul in that case would be like that babe in the shipwrecked woman's arms on the plank, smiling amidst the waves, unconcerned with the hazard. I desire to remember, and be remembered by you. I am, with cordial respects to   yours, &c.

(5) DEAR SIR,—You will excuse me when I have told you, that since I saw you, I have been in the furnace of affliction through the rod of a kind and gracious God on myself and family. My eldest daughter had a fever when you was here last; and on the morrow after you went off, my other daughter took her bed also by a fever; after her my youngest son; another boy of the family being in the meantime indisposed. While thus several were together in sickness, but my eldest daughter beginning to recover, I myself was, on a Lord's day after sermons, suddenly seized with a violent illness, which afterwards I knew to be a fit of the gravel, before that time unknown to me. It was sharp; but the time was kindly shortened, for I got up again on the Wednesday; neither did I agonize all that time, but was favoured with intermissions; but I had one fit of six or seven hours' continuance. Meanwhile my distressed wife was helped to get from her bed, and to go between me and the children, and to be useful to both. Our ship seemed to be hard at the shore, in mine and the children's recovery, when behold a wave came, and drove back the shattered vessel again. My eldest son and our servant-woman being taken ill on one day, and his fever the most dangerous of all, the woman's fever abated on the 6th, my son's

not till the 13th, my second daughter's on the 11th. My eldest son is now recovering, though slowly, and all are well again ; except my distressed wife, whose chastisements are new every morning. I have given you this particular account, as making no doubt of your sympathy, and that you will join with us in the deliverance wrought for us, and in seeking pity and help in the continued affliction and grace rightly to improve both the one and the other. The Lord was very gracious according to his word, and I felt him to be the lifter up of mine head, while carried through the deep waters ; and my soul blesseth his holy name for this dispensation in this trial, in which he made me inwardly to rejoice when nothing of that kind appeared about me. O that I could praise and trust him ! he is a skilful pilot, and one might be very easy in doubtful events, trusting and relying on him, be-lieving that what is good he will give. I am, &c.

Dec. 14, 1724.

(6) DEAR SIR,—I rejoice to hear of the success of your affairs ; which you take as you ought from him who keeps the balance of trade, as well as of crowns and of kingdoms, in his own hand. O but the management of the kingdom of grace must be a great thing ! and our Mediator must be well furnished for the managing of it ! since the vast and extensive kingdom of Providence is put in his hand as a subordinate, there to be administered in a subserviency to the kingdom of grace, and to carry on the glorious pur-poses thereof. He sits enthroned in Zion ; and as Zion's King, his power reaches through the whole earth, the seas, heaven, and hell ! All power is given him every where. His subjects in Zion are but few, but the whole world is rolled hither and thither for that little kingdom. For their sakes he sent to Babylon, and brought down the Chaldeans, whose cry is in the ships ; for it the Babylonian, Persian, Grecian, and Roman monarchies, were brought down. O, Sir, continue to follow your business in the actual faith of this ; and as, when there is a prosperous turn in it, you willingly give it under your hand, you are the Mediator's debtor for it ; so when there comes about an awkward-like turn at any time, labour to believe the same hand does it for the best ; for this reason, that he never does any thing but what is best done ; which will one day be demonstrated beyond contradiction. As for the discourses on the covenant of grace, I have long ago ended that subject ; but 1 am so engaged otherwise, that I cannot take it in hand for some time to be counted by years, for ought I yet see ; and my years now appear to me in a manner more than formerly uncertain ; and I would fain do, as the Lord is pleased to enable, what I conceive might be of greatest usefulness, as long as life is continued with strength. I am, dear Sir, &c.

April 25, 1726.

(7) DEAR SIR,—I understood by yours, that your wife continues in her ordinary tender condition ; may it be sanctified by grace to her and to you! The different states of persons, in respect of health and infirmity, is a piece of sovereign disposal, which the afflicted are to reverence and adore. Our

Lord himself was a man of sorrows, and acquainted with griefs; and if we suffer with him, we shall also reign with him. The heaviest burden of affliction is but light in respect of the weight of glory we have in hope; and the affliction that is of such continuance as the party has forgot prosperity, is but for a moment, being compared with the eternity of that weight which faith has the view of.

My wife has now kept her bed these five weeks; and, together with her ordinary distress, she has had a fever, with a great inflammation, which began in her face, and went up over her head; but he who delivered in six troubles, has delivered in that seventh also, and it is gone off; but she is very weak. My youngest daughter was frequently ill this winter, but since the return of the spring, and warmer weather, she is better. The rest are as ordinary. From about the time of the equinox, when the weather became warmer, the blood and spirits deserting my fingers, has not been so uneasy and frequent as before. I have now for some time stirred about on my work in the parish, which I could not manage in the winter as formerly; and still, as I have time, I am furnished with so much strength as to go about my closet-work. But my weakness is nevertheless so felt as occasions thoughts of heart. This is an account of our hospital; but sometimes the voice of melody, of joy, and praise, is heard among us. We are cast down, but not destroyed; perplexed, but not in despair; and are aiming at resignation. This morning the latter part of the 71st psalm was very sweet to me. I was abroad in our neighbour parish on the south hand, at ten miles distance from this, preaching yesterday. I have not been so far abroad since I was at Selkirk in the winter; and I had not gone to that place neither at this time, had it not been to shew good-will to the strengthening of the hands of the minister of the place, which is a parish that has been sore broken with division; but to do any thing to purpose in such a case, sad experience teacheth me is very difficult. It may be wished for; but how shall it be effected, till another spirit be poured upon both ministers and people? I am, &c.

May 21, 1726.

(8) DEAR SIR,—I had yours, with the much-affecting account of your loss of a dear child. I travelled that gloomy road six times, and learned, that God has other use for children than our comfort; a use far more honourable and happy for them; and the parents often come to see it afterwards, that it is peculiar kindness to the dear babes they were so early carried off. It likewise serves to let into the sweetness of that word in particular, " I will be thy God, and the God of thy seed." While parents are taken up for the eternal salvation of their dying little ones, and look about to see what the word says with relation to the case, O do not grudge the freedom the Lord has used with you, in pitching upon a precious thing of yours for himself, and accordingly taking it away. Both of you have offered your all to the Lord; and though, when it comes to the pinch, the heart is ready to misgive; yet in calm blood I am persuaded you will stand to the bargain, and check yourselves for any semblance of rueing. The next time

you see your child, you will see him shining white in glory, having been washed "in the blood of the Lamb," who was an infant, a child, a boy, a youth, as well as a grown man, because he came a Saviour of infants, little children, &c. as well as of persons come at age. Perhaps his cries are not yet out of your and his mother's ears; but then you will see him capable of managing his harp as well as the saint that died an hundred years ago. Ah! ah! why are we thus not fully satisfied and acquiescing in the wise management of the great Counsellor, who puts clouds and darkness round him, bidding us follow at his back through the cloud, promising an eternal uninterrupted sunshine on the other side, "Lord, increase our faith," is a petition we need to be oft putting up. But I hope the Lord has taught you and your spouse resignation to the will of him who does all things well. But I find it is a difficult lesson to learn; the flesh still spurns and rises against the rod. And O how difficult it is to get our "how's" and "why's" crucified, and to resolve all into, and rest satisfied in infinite wisdom tempered with covenant-love! Our affliction is returned to an extremity, and the storm has blown hard now for some time; but the Lord sits on the flood; and though it seems to be without all order, yet certainly there is an order in it, though imperceptible to our eyes, and several drops keep their ranks according to the word of command. I am, with the most endeared respects, &c.

August, 6, 1726.

(9) DEAR SIR,—As to the matter of the sacrament not celebrated here this season, some things falling out in our session did put me off from aiming at it in our usual time; which I was otherwise of thoughts of as ordinary; but when it was so determined to pass the diet, the extreme distress of my wife did perfectly confirm me in it. We have had a heavy summer of it in that respect; which yet continues. We exceedingly need the prayers of our friends; and know that several do carry our afflicted case before the Lord; and hope, that he will at length incline his ear to hear, though the afflicted cries, "Why are his chariot-wheels so long in coming?" It seems we are not yet sufficiently humbled, and ripe for deliverance. May the Lord himself send forth humbling influences, and so prepare our hearts, and cause his ear to hear! For my own part, I am much as when you saw me; the Lord still affording me strength to go on in the work I was then engaged in; and am not without hopes, that he will carry me through it.

It would be comfortable to hear of a favourable turn in your wife's afflicted case; but whatever be in that, the time will come, when the Lord's children, prisoners of affliction and iron, as the words of the Holy Ghost are, Psalm cvii. 10, will be as light, free, and easy, as if never an iron had been on their legs, and afflictions on their spirits, nor a prison-door closed on them, if the sun, that is making post-haste, had made a few rounds more. I am, &c.

June 5, 1727.

(10) VERY DEAR SIR,—The bearer comes for the wine, and will take the same quantity as usual; though I apprehend our throng here will not be so

great as sometime heretofore, the same ordinance being to be celebrated the same day in two places in the neighbourhood, from whence people used to come hither. The bruised serpent, who ordinarily is not idle among us at such a time, has given us a broadside at this time; but I hope our Lord will see to his own honour. I remember the word, "A great door, and effectual is opened; and there are many enemies."

Our letters shew us to be companions in tribulation; and I hope we shall be companions in victory, everlasting victory. Let us leave it to our Lord how to carry it through the world; his own glory is at stake, seeing by his grace we have committed ourselves to him. He is a skilful pilot; and his skill appears best in guiding the ship among the rocks and shelves. The natural effect of affliction on a sinner is, to drive him away from God; but we must consider affliction as an ordinance of God, and the discipline of the covenant, having a promise annexed to it; and believe the promise; and so the bitter pill, taken by faith in the vehicle of the promise, will lose its natural efficacy, and have its instituted one. If your affairs are in confusion, it is not your riotous living, nor carelessness about them, that has brought them to that pass, but that over-ruling providence of God; and so it is not your sin, but your affliction; and you have many a time laid your substance, and your all, at the Lord's feet, never to break with him on any such head, nor any whatsoever. And now word is sent to you about some of it from heaven, as was sent to the owner of the ass, saying, "the Lord hath need of him;" i. e. he has use for it for his own glorious purposes. And he can make you an ornament to the gospel in the confused state of your affairs, as well as when they went on more prosperously. My heart is feelingly touched with your dear wife's case; but ere all be done, she shall be nothing behind the hand with her Lord, for all she suffers at his will and pleasure.—The broad blessing of the covenant be on you and her, and your seed. Pray for us. I am, &c.

P. S. O! what think ye? will he not come to the feast!

July 22, 1727.

(11) VERY DEAR SIR,—I had yours of the 11th instant, and was concerned to understand by it, the increasing of your wife's distress, and the additional trial of the seizing of the ship at Cadiz. Here's work for faith, to see and believe that he into whose hands the Father hath committed all judgment, doth in a consistency with his love to our souls, make deep call unto deep, and manages all to work together for our good. This is too fine a thread to be perceived by the eye of sense; but by the help of the glass of the Word, it may be seen satisfyingly, and believed. Jacob and Job are two very plain instances of saints meeting with a train of crosses, one upon the neck of another, as if providence had designed to run them aground, and break them in pieces; and yet we see also the end of the Lord in these cases, that it was quite otherwise. I have had use for consulting these instances often; and the first particularly hath been very staying to me. I cannot but with tender affection observe your care of my affairs, in midst of your plunges; and it is with some difficulty, in that re-

spect, that I can lay them to your hand. However, you may consider, that what of that nature is done, it is for a companion in tribulation, &c. I am, with tender respects, very dear Sir, yours most affectionately.

My wife continues as formerly; but the prayers at M———n I found she had remarkably reaped the benefit of; for which we desire to praise, and thereby be encouraged to hope.

August 26, 1727.

(12) VERY DEAR SIR,—Yesterday I had yours, together with news-papers, and a letter from P. Hamilton; some account of which you will meet with in the inclosed to Mr. Gordon; which I commit to your care, for the forwarding of it to him. You will perhaps think strange of my writing in the inclosed, that passage anent prayers with respect to that affair. I considered ere I did it; and judging him that acknowledgeth the Lord in his ways, as well as I, and that it might be of use for exciting and encouraging him for his part of the work he has undertaken, and that it may abide the censure of the learned, being Christians, I gave that general account of the thing. As for Professor Gordon's differing from me in the matter of expressing the dignity of accents, by marks of our own stigma-tology; he does not refuse it simply, but only that always, and every where, they are to be expressed by the same marks; and this depends upon the question, Whether the value of the accents is ambulatory, or fixed? in which there is a main difference betwixt Wasmuth and the MS.; the former holding it to be ambulatory; so that e. g. ATHNACH may be expressed by a colon in one verse, but in another only by a comma, the latter holding it to be fixed. This I have no doubt of, and I hope it will make its way through prejudices by the divine blessing. I find Mrs. G. has had a trial by the way home. I rejoice that she was pitied of our gracious God, and that her son recovered. That is the discipline of our father's family, by which they are conformed to the image of Christ, that he may appear the first-born among many brethren. It sincerely touches me to hear, that your wife's affliction is continued, and for the time growing worse, so that you fear the issue. I understand that very well, through long experience of such fears, not only of late years, but even formerly. That is a vanity that attends all our earthly enjoyments; the more dear they are to us, the more piercing fears and sorrows arise to us from fear of losing them; but I hope your Father will stay his rough wind in the day of his east wind; and your Lord, Head, and Husband, who is at the helm, will carry you safe even where two seas meet. Our broken ship has been long in a storm, and yet we are not within eye-sight of land; but we hope to get through, and stand upon the shore yet, and sing and say, He has done all things well; and would say to you our fellow-voyagers, Fear not; we will all get safe ashore at length. When I came home from Galashiels, I found matters had been, and were extraordinary ill; yet the Lord kept me, that I was not staggered; but that I was still to pray, and not to faint, on the credit of the word he tells us, and it was not in vain; and since that time we have been down and up. Dear

Sir, let us, by all means, endeavour to believe, and hang on, and beware of
surmises of ill designs of Heaven against us, to appear in end, as we
would beware of coals of hell flung into our breasts. God is love. Amen.
I am as formerly.

January 27, 1728.

(13) VERY DEAR SIR,—The last letter I had from you gave a very affecting account of the increase of your wife's indisposition, of the trial of
your affairs continuing without any prospect as yet of an issue. When the
storm is hard where two seas meet, great is the hazard of fainting ; but patience must have her perfect work. These things are designed, I believe,
by a holy wise God, not against you, but against the unrenewed part in you,
called in scripture " the flesh," which is not to be amended, but to be mortified gradually till it die out in the close of the spiritual warfare ; at which
time the new creature will be perfected, and the image of God, that is never
on the whole soul, will wholly occupy every part of the soul, through full
and perfecting supplies of grace from Christ the Head, not communicated
during the course of this life. Then will be fully seen the beauty of these
perplexing dispensations, the necessity of them, and every one of them,
which is now to be believed, but not to be clearly seen, by reason of the remains of darkness that is to be found together with the light of grace in
the mind. Be we so happy as to take part with the Spirit against the flesh
in this war ; and though this last complaint under great hardships put upon
it, let us secretly rejoice, that the Lord is at such pains to advance mortification in us, that we may be still aiming to be as weaned children, and look
upon your afflictions as what the Lord is laying on, to conform you to the
image of his Son, whereof suffering and holiness are joint parts. If we suffer
with him, we shall also reign with him. These things I aim at to stay my
own heart with them in the afflicted lot he has pleased to carve out for
me, and have found some advantage thereby in my case, wherein the waters
break in at several hands at once too. My wife's case has made notable
advances this season, in point of growing weakness ; and the gravel has come
heavily on me, in so much that the two last weeks I had two sore fits of it
each week, and still it hangs about me. I am, dear Sir, yours, &c.

April 13, 1728.

(14) VERY DEAR SIR,—It is long now since we had an occasion to the
town. We have had a very threatening season, and the effects of the Lord's
anger are found in the country, both on the sown ground, and on the flocks.
And I see the Lord's own children, in common calamity, miss not their
leal share ; so that all falls alike to all in respect of the matter. But O the
difference that there is in the manner of conveyance ! The two covenants
are very different channels of conveyance ; and it is the work of faith to perceive the coming of trials in the way of the covenant of grace, wherein the
heaviest things bring down blessings with them. It has been something relieving to me of late, in consideration of the Lord's hand, gone out against
me, and many of my dear friends in Christ, that whereas it is now a time

of the church's peace ; and others that went before us in the way of the Lord
to the kingdom, through much tribulation, some suffering the spoiling of their
goods, some long and tedious imprisonments, some the loss of their relations, lives, &c., and all these were needful to purify and make them white
in giving evidence of their love to the Lord ; the Lord is making up that
want to us another way, bringing about to us, by his own immediate hand,
or by the hands of naughty men, the same things on the matter as he did
formerly by the hand of persecutors. Now it is his to make choice of the
manner of our trial ; it is our part to take it as they did ; and our work
shall be rewarded, even our suffering work. My wife is brought through
the additional storm ; and it pleased the great manager not to carry her
back again into the main sea at the time I last wrote to you. She is now
returned to her ordinary, which is great and continued trial ; but of late
the Lord has been pleased to make his refreshing visits to her soul somewhat more frequent than formerly. I long to hear how it is with your wife,
the prisoner of Jesus Christ with you ; they will both hear at length, " Woman, thou art loosed from thine infirmity." And I am, very dear Sir, yours
affectionately.

October, 5, 1728.

(15) VERY DEAR SIR,—I am in health, through the goodness of God ;
enabled to pursue my public work, and to do some little thing in my closet.
I should be glad to hear of some relaxation continuing in your wife's case,
and of some outgate in your affairs. Afflictions are appointed means of
sanctification, which, I am persuaded, is as great a mystery, as our justification is the work of the Spirit carrying it on by several means, all of them
concurring to the effect, is a great depth. We see, the forming and nourishing of the natural body is a thing we perceive very little as to the way
how it is brought about ; what wonder that we can so little comprehend
the forming and nourishing of the new creature ? which should move us to
endeavour to live by faith, believing what we see not, and to yield ourselves
willingly, without disputing, unto the Spirit's method with us, though some
of the means may be in their own nature pinching. The promoting the
growth of the new creature, requires the bearing down and subduing the
old man ; and to this effect, even sharp and long trials, all have enough
ado. May we be aiming at this temper of spirit ! I am, very dear Sir,
yours, &c.

April 19, 1729.

(16) VERY DEAR SIR,—I see by yours, that your wife continues sickly,
and that your affair with that man is not like to have any comfortable issue.
But in the meantime, Providence supports. I have of a considerable time,
observed, that Providence has been directing particular strokes against the
most serious godly of my acquaintance ; but it has here of late made such
steps of that kind on the bodies and substance of those in whom I had most
comfort, whereof some removed by death, that I think judgment is begun
at the house of God, as a sign of more to follow. For my own part, I am
kept close in the furnace ; and the receipt of your letters last week, came

very seasonably for some refreshment to me in the course of Providence. My wife has had a fever again, since the beginning of this month, and an unusual sinking of the spirit is brought in by it. I was comforted this day, reading, in my ordinary, the Queen of Sheba's admiring particularly Solomon's ascent by which he went up to the house of the Lord; he was a type of Christ. We hear, while here, the report of the ascent by which Christ brings his people to the temple above; when we see it in the word indeed by faith, we say, it becomes his wisdom; but when we look into it with our eyes, there are so many turnings and windings in it, so many black steps, we know not what to make of it many times. But O! to think of the view will be got of it in Immanuel's own land. We will be rapt into admiration of that ascent, and see the beauty of every step thereof, &c. I am, with great regard for you and yours, very dear Sir, &c.

Nov. 22, 1729.

(17) DEAR SIR,—My daughter gives but a sorry account of your wife's health. These bodies of ours, that bear the image of the first Adam, are pieces of wretched matter; and must be more so, till they be reduced to dust, of which they were originally framed. But we must comfort ourselves in the believing expectation of the new fashioning of them, after the image of the second Adam, the Lord from heaven; in which fashion they will be incorruptible, glorious, powerful, and spiritual bodies. It is observed, that bodies the higher they are lifted up towards heaven, they become less ponderous, the lighter; this may help to some notion of the spiritualness of our raised bodies, when all relation betwixt them and this cursed earth is dissolved, and we are in heaven. I am, dear Sir, yours affectionately, &c.

October 31, 1730.

(18) DEAR SIR,—I had yours of the 14th, and was much concerned with the account of your wife's low condition. You and she have my sympathy and concern before the Lord. I am persuaded he minds better things for you both, than the ease and comforts of this life; and by these ingredients in your lot here, is preparing you for the better life; and though you do not sensibly perceive much success at the time, yet afterwards the fruit will appear. I am convinced there are acts of faith, resignation, lustings against the flesh, and old man, approbation of the divine procedure in trials, &c. which, in a Christian's struggle, are excited, and which we little notice, for that apparent *raræ nantes in gurgite vasto*, that will yet at length be found recorded of God, as so many good works to be rewarded by him, and to our surprise. Therefore be stedfast, unmoveable, always abounding in the work of the Lord, knowing that your labour shall not be in vain in the Lord. If you have any desire to see the notes on " The Worm threshing the Mountains," delivered at Maxton, call for them from Mrs. S. who got them from me. That scripture came seasonably to me for my own private case, Dec. 4, 1729; and O but the faith of it is animating to a poor creature in a struggle in itself hopeless! I notice your friendliness, not only in forwarding my letters to Professor Anderson, but also writ-

ing him. I wish to hear of your son's welfare, who, I understand, has
been under some illness. Pray, fail not to let me hear, though in never
so few words, concerning your wife, if in life. The God of all consolation comfort you in all your distresses, and after the storm send a calm.
I am, dear Sir, yours, &c.

Nov. 21, 1730.

(19) VERY DEAR SIR,—I had yours, with the melancholy news I was fearing, and wish I could bear a part of your burden, which, I doubt not,
presseth sore. It will be your wisdom to consider it as the work of God,
your God in Christ; being persuaded that according to the measure of that
persuasion, so will the Christian carriage under the rod be. O what kind
of hearts do they imagine themselves to have, that can think to employ them
for one moment of the creature, farther than they can fill them farther
with a God in Christ, as their God, in its room and stead! By any experience I have had, I judge the heart of man to be such a hungry, craving,
and griping thing, that it will part with nothing, but for what it takes to be
as good, or better than what it gives up with; so that the gospel-offer, by
faith embraced, and the benefit thereof claimed, must, of necessity, be the
most sovereign remedy against the heart's hankering after the withdrawn
comforts of the creature. I was sensibly gladdened with your Christian
conduct, in going out on the Saturday and Sabbath; and bless the Lord
who gave you counsel. It is a desirable thing to see Christians walking by
the rules of Christianity in their greatest trials. Mr. Davidson has had no
access yet to communicate your letter to me; but what you shew me, sufficiently seals the character she bore in mine eyes; and will, I hope, alleviate
your affliction; since, without controversy, that mourning that is only for
ourselves, must, with considering persons, be the most supportable. My
wife was much affected with your trial. Grace be with you and the child.
I am, &c.

Dec. 8, 1731.

(20) VERY DEAR SIR,—I have yours of October 26, together with Sir
Richard Ellys's letter to you, the copy of the letter from Keydan, together
with my notice on three texts, therewith transmitted. The first I return;
the second I keep, as your letter allows. I never saw that letter of yours,
nor knew any thing about it, or what it inclosed, till Saturday's night last,
that my daughter came home; the which happened by inadvertency of my
servant. But divine providence manages inadvertencies of men to carry on
his purposes; and I doubt not but there was a becoming design in this,
though I know not what it was; and by some lessons I have got of that
kind, I am engaged to think it was a kind one; and so, taking it out of
the hand of God, will not grudge it, but hope for the best of it.—I had been
long waiting for a providential signal to move anent the MSS.; and
now I have got it fair and clear by your last, and am on the road pointed
out to me, disposed to march on, or halt, as I can take up my orders.

I am much satisfied that I can gather from yours, that your affair is in
a hopeful situation; and I hope, that by the hand into which it is com-

mitted, it will be carried on. Only believe that God will do the best ; and being conscious to yourself of your desire not to manage, but to be managed by the Great Leader, pray hold off, and refuse to admit fears of being left to your own management ; for however rational, well-grounded, and but just in a sort, these may appear to you from your sins, assure yourself they are the fruit of unbelief, and measuring God's ways by our own, and if you yield to them, you are in a fair way to bring on you that which you feared. To believe over the belly of felt foolishness, that God will be as good as his word, is most acceptable to him, and most for our interest ; though the difficulty thereof, in practice, is great ; whereby it appears the more to be of God, and a trial and proof of faith. I speak the more confidently of this, that sometimes I have seen in such circumstances I could not have known where to have fixed my feet, had not the doctrine of free grace pointed out to me a sure ground ; and I would pity them from my heart that would look on this as a dangerous course, and tending to make one careless and untender.—I have your further account of the affair of transporting Gronovius to Edinburgh, which is a favour to me. I wish it may succeed, whether he be of my mind with respect to the points or not. Were the Hebrew language itself brought amongst us into greater reputation, people would perhaps hear the points before they would condemn them. If he has vented any thing to the prejudice of their divine authority, it is likely it will be improven to lessen the credit of my essay industriously. It is an ill-natured world.—I forgot to tell you in the due place, that I do not forget, but have a hearty concern in the matter of your obtaining a partner in trade ; that you might be delivered from that overwhelming engagement in business you have so long been immersed in ; and yet, after all, it must be owned, that one is well employed in the work the Sovereign Manager shapes out for him, be the kind and measure of it what it will, and therefore dare not but advise to protest, that it be not taken off, till he who laid it on take it off with his own hand. Happy are they who are impressed with a terror of choosing for themselves, and hold it for a principle, that he shall choose out the lot of our inheritance for us. We are here as ordinary ; and, remembering your son, I am, in straitest bonds, very dear Sir, yours affectionately, &c.

Dec. 30, 1731.

(21) Very Dear Sir,—Yours of the 16th I received ; which refreshed my bowels, and opened my mouth to return thanks unto God, who had condescended to make my last of use to you, and kept you in a way with respect to your affair, which cannot miss of a happy issue, go as it will. 'I think I never saw more than about this time, how absolutely nothing the creature is in point of action and usefulness to us in itself, and how God is all ; the former nothing, but just as he touches it for motion, and resting moveless like a stone when he moves it not ; and therefore would fain learn to overlook all, and look to him as my party in all things, finding this view of matters mightily staying and quieting to the heart, and a promoter of faith and hope. Wherefore let us aim at this, rolling ourselves securely

and confidently over on him, whether we see or see not whither he is like to carry us; " For he careth for us." Let us exercise patience to wait the end of the Lord; and as sure as the Bible is the word of God, we will see there is nothing in the conduct of Providence, about us and our matters, should have been out, and nothing out that should have been in. O! he doth all things well; no hazard of singing this triumph before the victory.—I find myself obliged to essay what you moved to me, whatever the Lord minds to do with me in it; and whether I am to see the end of it or not, I desire to be found so doing. I know there is solid comfort in that, " Thou didst well that it was in thine heart." You will know somewhat of the disposition of my heart by the premises, with respect to the situation of my affair at London, I think I may, if the Lord will, need so requiring, write Sir Richard Ellys, in February, or before, if I find my letter to Mr. G. successless. Take kindly your concern about my son. We continue here much as ordinary. My love to your son. I am, in the straitest bonds, very dear Sir, yours, &c.

March 9, 1732.

(22) MY VERY DEAR SIR,—It was on Friday the 3d instant that yours of the 1st came to my hand. That of the 18th and 24th of February coming on the Sabbath thereafter, being the 5th, I had withal, on the Tuesday before, got an uncertain word of the ill situation of your affairs, which, by reason of what you had shewn me before, did seem very probable. But while I was altogether uncertain of the state of your affairs in my concern for you before the Lord, you still appeared to me smiling; so that getting the letter of the 1st instant, it did so answer the continuing idea of you, that I declare, though the situation of your affairs was very affecting, I behoved to lay that letter before the Lord, and solemnly give him thanks for it; and afterwards receiving that of the 18th February, wherein you was under the damp, I could not but observe that kind and wise Providence, that kept it up till I had got the former of that date; and reckon it up among the many happy well-ordered disappointments I have met with. It is ordinary with the Lord's people falling into trouble, as it is with a person wading a deep and cold water; who is, upon his first entering it, struck to the heart; but the first gliff, as we call it, is the worst. In this point the world's frowns and smiles do readily agree: appearing at some distance, or in the first encounter, they shew ordinarily greater than afterward they are found really to be. Hence our fears of the one, as well as hopes from the other, are readily carried beyond the just bounds; and Satan presently falls a-fishing in the drumly waters, stirs them assiduously, to make them more drumly and awful like. Many a time have I thought a great point gained, when one gets a view of His naked cross and trial; for it is hard to get a sight of it without a ponderous cover on it, partly of our own, and partly of Satan's making: and therefore I am convinced there is great need of making use of Christ as a prophet under our troubles, that by his light shining into our souls, we may see what that cross or trouble is precisely which he has laid before us, to take up and bear,

that we may set ourselves to bear that and no more. And I am very sure that at this rate crosses and trials lose a great deal of their weight. What but the art of hell used in a disturbed mind, would bring in the wounding of the interests of religion, by the pass your affairs were brought to, the opening of the mouths of the wicked shaming the faces of the godly, &c.? Every body knew you to be a sober man, a man of unordinary application to your business. The occasion of the confusion of your affairs, arising from others at a distance from you, would not be hid. And no body is so ignorant of the state of human affairs, but they know the wealthiest, fairest, and most diligent traders, may be broken to pieces by providential incidents, or the treachery of false men with whom they may have dealings. However, glad am I it has pleased the Lord to confound that temptation, and to satisfy you perfectly on that head. But, my dear Sir, take heed, and be on your guard against other devices of that kind; lest, if you suffer your feet to be entangled therewith, it may not be so easy to be extricated therefrom: and therefore I cannot cease to put you in remembrance, that as you employ Jesus Christ in his priestly office, for the removal of guilt, and address him as your king for strength to bear your trial, so you are still to be eying him in his prophetical office for light to give you just views of it. I see our Lord, the great prophet, has come to you already in your darkness. I perceive the Interpreter, one among a thousand, was with you in a particular manner on Monday, Feb. 20. He was in these two hours exercising his prophetical office in you. He was letting you see your trial in its just colours, not putting colours on it; for he is the Amen, the faithful and true Witness; and therefore, though it do not always appear in these colours to you, that is the native hue of it, and the fault is in your eyes when it appears otherwise. He was taking you by the arms, and teaching you to go; and that you will employ him for his light, as well as his strength, in time to come; that if he comes not to you, you will go to him; and if a promise be not laid to your hand, you will go out and fetch in one: and welcome. The blessed Bible is a richly-loaden tree of that kind of fruit. Sometimes his people has no more ado, but to take of the fruit falling into their lap; but that is only a piece of indulgence that they sometimes meet with; the ordinary way is to look up to the tree, and reach out the hand of faith, perhaps, with no little difficulty, and pluck the fruit; and O but a sharp trial makes the promise sweet! Witness your experience of the two last verses of Psalm cxxxiii. Sir, you are in a plunge; but I make no question, he that sits at the Father's right hand, having all judgment committed to him, will bring you out of it; and the day will come, when you will say from leisurely observation, " He hath done all things well." Yea, Sir, look for seeing God's wonders in the deeps, and he will not disappoint you. However, if you were through this trial, you will not be at the end of trials, lesser or greater, till you be in the better country; only this is a deep step, a deep water; but "the Lord Jesus is the lifter up of mine head," you must say with David, Psalm iii. That psalm has appeared of late to me, to bear an instance of as strong a faith as readily appears in the whole book of Psalms, considering its firmness, and the circumstances there described;

only it must be owned, the terror of God on his soul, with which nothing is to be laid in the balance, was indeed wanting in it. But O how piercing was that, that the common saying on that melancholy occasion was, " There is no help in God for him," (say the Jews) who stole the ewe and killed the shepherd (Bathsheba and Uriah)! the very thing God was pursuing him for. I was so affected with your friend's manner of entertaining your trial, that I was obliged to give God thanks for it; and since that time, my heart blesses that person as acting like a Christian; and doubt not, but if that mind continue, as I hope it will, it will have a plentiful reward of free grace; but will own myself quite mistaken, if ever the change on that head prove a gainful one at balancing accounts. The news of Mr. Archibald Stewart's death and burial was stunning. It is an awful dispensation of a wrathful aspect to this generation. Oh! what does it speak, that such a promising instrument is laid aside at this time a-day. But the Lord's ways are not ours, nor his thoughts as our thoughts. We must be silent to him.

That the state of your own affairs did not keep you from proceeding in mine, is a rare token of a rare kind of friendship. It will not be unacceptable to me to hear of the matter's being determined, with the joint advice of Mr. W. and yourself, without hearing further from me. My infirmity increases apace. The leg, still painful, is now almost useless; so that I know not if I get down stairs again, without being carried, till I be provided with two stilts. My wife, I hear, is somewhat feverish to-day. The presence of him who dwelt in the bush while it burned, be with you! I am, in the straitest bonds, my very dear Sir, yours affectionately, &c.

March 23, 1732.

(23) My Very Dear Sir,—The use of the providential distress in your affairs, and its influence relative to your other business, I doubt not, you will see in due time to be an event, both in the kind of it, and the timing of it, becoming the divine wisdom and goodness, and that God acts like himself. Esau and his posterity, who had their lot by common Providence, were soon and easily settled in the land of Edom; but Jacob and his, whose lot was to be brought about in the way of accomplishing of a promise of the covenant, met with many rubs in their way, and some of them such as seemed to render it quite hopeless. Your present circumstances put you in much need of direction from the Lord, as you remark. But, dear Sir, is it not a great privilege to be allowed to come to the great Counsellor in all our straits? and you may go to him with your greater and your smaller matters; for all is comprehended in the word, Prov. iii. 6; both the precept and promise takes in all. You are neither to look for impressions, nor any thing else of that kind, whatever indulgence the Lord makes to some of his people in some circumstances; but lay you the matter before the Lord, and yourself open to the divine determination, and believe the promise of direction, with application to your own case, firmly trusting that he will be as good as his word, Prov. iii. 6, Psalm xxv. 9, and xxxii. 8, to you; and then, depending on the promise of Heaven's directions, set yourself as a Christian man to perceive what in the circumstances appears reasonable to be done;

to the clearing whereof, observation of concurring dispensations of Providence notably contributes, that being in many cases the finger of God pointing out our way. In this way of management, there is a real communion with God to be had in providences as in ordinances, Psalm cvii. ult.

You have here my whole day's work. I am at my *ne plus ultra*, my distress being considerable, whereof there is some account in the enclosed. The eternal God be your refuge: and underneath the everlasting arms, may he be eyes, and all to you in the wilderness! Kindly remembering your son, I am, in the straitest bonds, very dear Sir, yours most affectionately &c.

P.S.—I have got Mr. Du Pont's letter. I am sorry Professor Mauritius had not vouchsafed a few lines to me for the many sheets I sent him. The Lord has for my trial restrained him, and I take it kindly off that hand ; but I keep foot in the main under the several pieces of that treatment ; *Quam si dura silex aut stet cautes.*

No. XVII.
Letter from the Author to the Reverend Mr. James Hogg, minister of the gospel at Carnock.

Nov. 24, 1727

REVEREND AND VERY DEAR SIR,—Yours on the 22d September came to my hand October 28, and I have taken this very first occasion to make you a return, that I may show the cordial sympathy I have with you in your afflicted lot, and may not put you to a tiresome waiting for any thing that can come from me to you, from whom I would rather hear, than speak to in such matters. I could not but think, that the very writing of your letter to me, behoved, through the divine blessing accompanying it, to be of use to you in your affliction for your comfort. Sure I am it was an apt mean ; though the most fit means can of themselves effect nothing, but only as they are blown upon by the Spirit, and so rendered effectual to their ends. The account you give of the situation of matters with you with respect to the way, as it has a comfortable distinctness in it, without any thing of the confusion you speak of discernible to me ; so it carries such an agreeableness to the way marks set up by the Spirit, the leader in the way, to be seen standing for the direction of travellers in the scripture of truth, that you have ground from the word to take the comfort of your being in the way in spite of hell, and consequently of your coming assuredly to the end of the journey in a happy sort, since the great leader drops none by the way, but perfects what he has begun, and never leaves nor forsakes the work of his own hands, nor those in whom it is wrought. I think I need not insist to add to what you have advanced from the scripture on that head. What pincheth you, seems to be the blowing of the wind in your face, particularly the rising of storms and tempests upon you, so that sometimes you lose sight, are blown aside, yea, blown down and foundered. But, dear Sir, if you were beyond these, you would not be a traveller, but one got home from your travels ; you would not be in, or by the way, but come to the end of it. It is the glory of the man who

is the Father's fellow, to be " an hiding-place from the wind, and a covert
from the tempest," Isa. xxxii. 2, to be a strength to the needy in his distress, a refuge from the storm, when the blast of the terrible ones is a storm
against the wall.   When should that glory of his be, if these tempests and
storms did not rise, if the terrible ones did not get leave to blow sometimes
furiously, like a storm against the wall ?   If then our Lord Jesus, whose
strength is made perfect in weakness, sees meet to take away your ease for
a time, to make of it a stepping-stone to his own glory, where you hear
the Lord hath need of it, you will straightway send it.   I verily think,
that when a poor believer is engaged in a combat with the powers of darkness, our Lord Jesus has an occasion of signalizing his victory over the
bruised serpent next to that which he had on the cross.   It is true, that
staggering, even on that place, is to be lamented as a sinful weakness ;
but, I think, all the travellers and combatants will be found to have been
staggerers through stress, though that gives them not their denomination
from their believing.   Ye have heard of the patience of Job, yet we hear
very much of his impatience too.   Peter remained with an unfailing faith
when he was sifted, yet he was shamefully foundered.   Even Abraham,
though in that instance, Rom. iv., he staggered not ; yet in another case he
did, Gen. xii. 11, and downwards, and in that same instance Sarah, who
was a type of the church, as Abraham was of Christ, staggered ; and fell
foully, but recovered, Gen. xviii.   In this last, faith had but one single
word, " My lord," and unbelief had all the rest of the speech ; and yet the
Spirit of God makes honourable mention of that one word in the New Testament, 1 Pet. iii. 6 ; drawing a veil over the rest.   I own that temptations
within, and troubles from without, trysting together, make a very heavy
case ; yet it is scriptural too, that without be fightings, and within be fears.
You have been particularly honoured of God to contend for the faith ; and
it is no wonder Satan's malice prompt him to dispute it with you immediately ; and the wisdom of the God of truth appears in permitting it to be
so, to teach dependence on himself in managing the contending otherwise.
The strong champion of truth, Luther, found himself hardly bestead in the
several conflicts within his own breast.   I desire to maintain a cordial sympathy with you in all your trials ; being yours very affectionately.

No. XVIII.

*A letter from an eminent Dissenting Minister in Essex, to the Author's
grandson.*

[As this letter contains a minute and circumstantial narrative of Mr. Boston's appearance before the General Assembly in Professor Simson's process, and records some circumstances omitted in the Memoirs, it justly deserves a place here.]

March 26, 1776.

MY VERY DEAR SIR,—Since the receipt of your last, I have been thinking of what I hinted to you relating to the appearance your worthy grand-

father made at the Assembly, 1729, when Professor Simson's affair was concluded. I could have wished, indeed, that the account I wrote of it to Mr. Davidson had been preserved; for I wrote it immediately after it happened, when it was fresh in my memory, and had made great impression on me; for it was the most solemn and affecting scene I ever was witness to before any judicatory. It is not to be supposed, that now, at the distance of near forty-seven years, I can remember every particular; but, to the best of my remembrance, when the act was read, and the Moderator asked if the Assembly acquiesced in it; there was profound silence all over the house for the space of a minute or so, and then your grandfather rose, and spoke to this effect: " Moderator, I find myself laid under a necessity of declaring my dissent from this decision of the Assembly, as I think the censure inflicted by it on Professor Simson, is not adequate to the offence he has given, as to the points of doctrine that have been proved he taught the students under his care, and have been found relevant to infer censure. I cannot help thinking, Sir, that the cause of Jesus Christ, as to the great and essential point of his supreme deity, has been at the bar of this Assembly requiring justice; and, as I am shortly to answer at his bar for all I do or say, I dare not give my assent to the decision of this act; on the contrary, I find myself obliged on this occasion to offer a protest against it; and therefore, in my own name, and in the name of all that shall adhere to me, and if none here will, (and when he pronounced these words, he looked round the house with an air of majesty and importance that I shall never forget), for myself alone, I crave leave to enter my protest against the decision of this act."

The Moderator, who was himself a very solemn, grave man, seemed to be much moved, and addressed him thus:—" Brother, I hope, in this matter, where you see such an appearance of unanimity, you will not do any thing that may have a tendency to rent and divide this church, and tear out the bowels of your mother?" Answer:—" Rather, Sir, than what I am now offering should have that effect, I would wish that I and my protest should be buried under a mountain. There are many in this Assembly whom I never saw in the face before, nor know; but such of them as I know, and differ from me in this matter, I not only have the utmost charity for them notwithstanding, but I could willingly sit at their feet and learn Christ. However, I cannot see there should be any danger of a breach in this church on this occasion, to permit one member who is grieved and gravelled by this decision, to enter his protest against it." Reply:—" Second thoughts, Sir, are always best; may not Mr. Boston, before he insists on this, lay the matter before the throne of grace, and consult praying ministers and Christians, and attend to their counsel and advice, before you come to a positive determination as to this your protest?" Had the Moderator thought ever so long on something that would weigh with Mr. Boston in such a case, he could not have fallen on any thing that would sooner have done it than this; for he immediately, in a submissive manner, said he would take it under further consideration, providing the matter was left open to him to enter his protest at any subsequent meeting of the Assembly;

and so the matter ended at that sederunt.   I was present that same evening,
where there were several ministers and elders, members of the Assembly,
who met with Mr. Boston, who all advised his not insisting of his protest
at that time, providing it was left open for him to do it at any future occasion, if this decision of the Assembly was attended with such consequences
as he was afraid of.   And when the minutes of the Assembly were read
next sederunt, this was declared, and acquiesced in; and so the matter ended.

This, I can well remember, was reckoned at that time one of the strongest
bars in the way of Mr. Simson's ever being restored to the privilege of
teaching and preaching any more; and even his warmest friends never attempted it, because he was hereby secured in his salary, which the sentence
of deposition would have deprived him of.   Thus, what was then called
mercy to the man, mixed perhaps with a little worldly policy, put an end to
the most important point, in respect of doctrine and discipline, that ever
came before any judicatory of the Church of Scotland, or, I hope, ever
will come again.

I am, very dear Sir, your affectionate friend and brother in the work and
bonds of the gospel, &c.

The Reverend Mr. Thomas Boston's Letter to the Presbytery of Selkirk.

                                             ETTRICK MANSE, *Feb.* 22, 1732.

REV. DEAR BRETHREN,—I had the favour of yours, acquainting me of the
meeting of the Presbytery of Selkirk, on the last Tuesday of this month;
from which meeting my growing indisposition and frailty bar me.   Meanwhile, apprehending that the Presbytery will then have under their consideration the act by way of overture, transmitted to Presbyteries, as to the
planting of congregations, 1731; of the which I have by me a just double,
I crave leave to declare my mind thereanent.

I do believe, as I have all along from my youth, that the Christian people
have, of divine right, the power of choosing their own pastors; and therefore, I judge that it is altogether to be avoided, that any man be thrust violently upon the congregation, or intruded in any of the offices of the kirk,
contrary to the will of the congregation, as the Books of Discipline and policy
of this church do express it.   And this being the known principle of this
church, I dare not be so unjust as, by offering the reasons thereof, to in-
sinuate that you, my brethren, are of a contrary mind.   But I am fully convinced that, by the transmitted act aforesaid, the body of the Christian people
is robbed of that their sacred right; inasmuch, as thereby the power of electing
and calling of ministers is appropriated to heritors, being protestants, and to
elders; and in royal burghs, to the magistrates, town-council, and kirk-
session, and is cut off from the rest of the Christian people, who are not so
dignified; no comparative judgment of candidates, or choice of such, being
left to these last, who are, in case they disapprove of the choice made, allowed only to offer their reasons to the Presbytery, to be judged of by them;
by which means they are staked down to the choice made for them, unless
they can advance something against the life or doctrine of the called; the
which strangers, as well as they of the congregation, have access to.   I own

there has all along been too much of this, in the way of settling ministers in this church ; but judge, there is a wide difference betwixt labouring under hardships imposed through iniquity of times, making the best of bad, and men's wreathing a yoke about their own necks, binding themselves to an iniquitous way.

This church hath now groaned long under the yoke of patronages ; but who can, without breaking sorrow of heart, stand and see the poor remains, in that point, left her by the laws, disposed of in the house of her friends, in manner proposed by the said act, to the utter enslaving of the body of the Christian people, in that their spiritual concern of calling their ministers ?   How naked is that quality of heritors being protestants !   'Tis obvious, that under it, the people may have men brought in to choose their ministers for them, who are known enemies to the government both in church and state ; are none of our communion, yea, excommunicate for their notorious wickedness, are Arians, Socinians, Deists, and what not, except papists.   So that I cannot help thinking, but the method proposed in the foresaid overture for planting of congregations, hath a native tendency to sap our constitution, break this church in pieces, fill their pulpits with naughty ministers, and to mar the success of the glorious gospel, and ruin the interests of true religion among us.   For which causes, I declare myself altogether against passing of the said act or overture into a standing act, and durst not, in Presbytery or Assembly, vote in favour of it, for a thousand worlds.

I desire and hope the Reverend Presbytery will do me, their afflicted brother, not having access to meet with them, the justice to record their receiving of this my letter, and its bearing my not consenting to, but being altogether against, the passing of the said transmitted act or overture, into a standing act.

May the Lord himself countenance your meeting with his own presence, guide you by his spirit into all truth, and preserve you from every evil thing.

I am, Rev. Dear Brethren, your affectionate brother, and humble servant,   T. Boston.

Part of the Latter Will of Mr. Boston.

In the name of the three that bear record in heaven, the Father, the Word, and the Holy Ghost, one undivided, self-existent and eternal Jehovah, Amen.   I, Thomas Boston, of Ettrick, being, through rich mercy and free grace, enabled to sit at the feet of Jesus Christ, clothed with his righteousness, in my right mind and memory, and of sound judgment respecting my eternal state, and those truths which are essential to salvation ; considering the mortality of this life, knowing it is appointed for men once to die, and not knowing how soon it may be my heavenly Father's will to remove me out of this time-state, and rank my immortal spirit among the spirits of just men made perfect, do hereby make this my last will and testament, in manner and in form following.   That is to say, first, I commit my immortal soul to him, (with humility and reverence be it spoken), to him who is my everlasting light, my God, and my glory; to him who is my head, guardian, and has promised to be my guide even unto death; to him who ordained me to eternal life, from before the foundation of the world; to him who has shined into my heart, and has given me the light of the knowledge of the glory of himself in the face of Jesus Christ; to him who hath caused me to pass from death to life, and promised I shall never more come into condemnation; to him who has promised never more to leave me nor forsake me, and to this end has implanted his fear in my heart, and will not let me depart from him; to him who hath loved me with an everlasting love, and with loving-kindness hath drawn me; to him who passed by me when I lay in the open field, (a state of nature), exposed to the just vengeance of a broken law, polluted in my sins, and in my blood; who, when he saw me in this ruined state and condition, said unto me, live! Yea, he said unto me, live; to him who hath promised my bread shall be given me and my water made sure; and that, as my day is my strength shall be; to him who will not suffer me to be tempted above what I am able to bear; but, blessed be his holy name, has promised, with every temptation, to make a way for my escape, and that all things shall work together for my good, and has given me a full persuasion, that neither life nor death, principalities nor powers, things present nor things to come, shall ever separate me from his eternal love in Christ Jesus; this is my God, my strength, my rock, my fortress, my deliverer, my buckler, the horn of my salvation, and my high tower, and this is the God whom I adore.   And secondly, I commit my body to him who is the resurrection and the life, knowing, that at the last day he will raise it up and fashion it like unto his own most glorious body, and re-unite it to my glorified soul, and will condescend to take me into a more close union with himself, than I have ever yet experienced, where I shall behold him as he is, and see him face to face; for the arrival of which most glorious time, my soul often pants, as do the harts for the water brooks, and am ready to say, come, Lord Jesus, come quickly.   To this glorious personage, I desire to ascribe equal honour, power, and praise, with him who ordained me to eternal life before the foundation of the world; for, blessed be his glorious name, he has paid my ransom price, and become my surety of the better covenant, and fulfilled the law, which I, through sin, had broken.   He has magnified the law and made it honourable, and brought in an everlasting righteousness to me, and taken all my iniquities upon himself, by which means, I stand as complete, before the throne of his glory, as if I had never sinned; for which I humbly pray I may be kept humble, while in this time-state; knowing that a man's pride shall bring him low, but honour shall uphold the humble in spirit, &c. &c.

EPITAPHS.

Epitaph drawn up by the Rev. Ralph Erskine.

Thomam Bostonum, nuper pastorem Atricensim.
Dotibus illustris nitiut Bostonus opimis,
Haud perperere virum, tempora nostra parem;
Ornarunt nec e radiis, tot eum pulcherrima juretis,
Ut caluere, omnes ejus, amore pii.

On the Death of the Rev. Thomas Boston.

The great, the grave, judicious, Boston's gone,
Who once,* like Athanasius bold, stood firm alone ;
Whose golden pen, to future times, will bear
His fame, till in the clouds his Lord appear.

RALPH ERSKINE.

The following is a copy of the Inscription on Mr. Boston's Monument :—

AS A TESTIMONY OF ESTEEM,

FOR THE

REV. THOMAS BOSTON, SEN,

WHOSE PUBLIC CHARACTER WAS HIGHLY RESPECTABLE,

WHOSE PUBLIC LABOURS WERE BLESSED TO MANY,

AND WHOSE VALUABLE WRITINGS

HAVE CONTRIBUTED MUCH TO THE ADVANCEMENT OF VITAL CHRISTIANITY,

This Monument,

(BY THE PERMISSION OF RELATIVES),

WAS ERECTED BY A RELIGIOUS AND GRATEFUL PUBLIC,

A. D. 1806.

HE WAS BORN AT DUNSE, MARCH 17, 1676,

ORDAINED TO THE PASTORAL CHARGE OF SIMPRIN, MAY 19TH 1699,

REMOVED FROM THENCE TO ETTRICK, SEPT. 1, 1707,

AND DIED, SEPTEMBER 20TH, 1732, AGED FIFTY-SIX YEARS,

LEAVING A WIDOW AND FOUR CHILDREN.

---

* Referring to the appearance made by him in the General Assembly, 1729, in the affair of Professor Simson.

ABERDEEN:
PRINTED BY GEORGE AND ROBERT KING,
ST. NICHOLAS STREET.

www.ingramcontent.com/pod-product-compliance
Lightning Source LLC
Chambersburg PA
CBHW070942150426
42812CB00063B/2716